SHORTER
LEXICON
OF THE
GREEK
NEW TESTAMENT

SHORTER
LEXICON
OF THE
GREEK
NEW TESTAMENT

F. Wilbur Gingrich

SECOND EDITION

Revised by

Frederick W. Danker

THE UNIVERSITY OF CHICAGO PRESS

CHICAGO AND LONDON

This book is an abridgment, with some revision, of *A Greek-English Lexicon of the New Testament and Other Early Christian Literature*, second edition, 1979, revised by F. Wilbur Gingrich and Frederick W. Danker. The first edition, by William F. Arndt and F. Wilbur Gingrich, was published in 1957 by the University of Chicago Press as a translation and adaptation of Walter Bauer's *Griechisch-deutsches Wörterbuch zu den Schriften des Neuen Testaments und der übrigen urchristlichen Literatur.*

F. WILBUR GINGRICH is professor emeritus of Greek and religion at Albright College in Reading, Pennsylvania.

FREDERICK W. DANKER is a professor in the Department of Exegetical Theology, New Testament, at Christ Seminary–Seminex and Lutheran School of Theology at Chicago.

The University of Chicago Press, Chicago 60637
The University of Chicago Press, Ltd., London

13 12 11 10 09 08 07   9 10 11 12

Library of Congress Cataloging-in-Publication Data

Gingrich, F. Wilbur (Felix Wilbur), 1901–
   Shorter lexicon of the Greek New Testament.
   Abridgment, with some revisions, of: A Greek-English lexicon of the New Testament and other early Christian literature / Walter Bauer. 2d ed. / rev. and augm. by F. Wilbur Gingrich and Frederick W. Danker.
   1. Greek language, Biblical—Dictionaries—English.
I. Danker, Frederick W. II. Bauer, Walter, 1877–1960. Griechisch-deutsches Wörterbuch zu den Schriften des Neuen Testaments und der übrigen urchristlichen Literatur. English. III. Title.
PA881.G5   1983   487'.4   82-10933
ISBN 0-226-13613-2

♾ The paper used in this publication meets the minimum requirements of the American National Standard for Information Sciences—Permanence of Paper for Printed Library Materials, ANSI Z39.48-1992.

Preface to the Second Edition

This book is an abridgment, with some revision, of *A Greek-English Lexicon of the New Testament and Other Early Christian Literature* (first edition, by W. F. Arndt and F. Wilbur Gingrich, 1957 = BAG; second edition, by F. Wilbur Gingrich and Frederick W. Danker, 1979 = BAGD). The latter work is in turn a translation and adaptation of Walter Bauer's *Griechisch-deutsches Wörterbuch zu den Schriften des Neuen Testaments und der übrigen urchristlichen Literatur* (1958).

Professor Gingrich, of Albright College, produced the first edition of this *Shorter Lexicon* (1965). The publication of BAGD and the revision of the Greek text of the New Testament, as found in the twenty-sixth edition of *Novum Testamentum Graece* (Nestle-Aland, 1979) and in the corresponding third edition of *The Greek New Testament*, published in 1975 by the United Bible Societies (= UBS), necessitated a revision of Gingrich's earlier work.

The scope of the book is limited to the words of the New Testament itself, to the exclusion of the Apostolic Fathers and other pieces of early Christian literature recognized in the larger lexicon. Numerous variant readings of Nestle-Aland[26] and the UBS edition are included.

Emphasis is placed on the bare meanings of words; for more information the user must consult BAGD or other works. However, scholars' challenges and the flood of data from papyri and inscriptions do not abate, and the student will find here fresh information or modification of conclusions reached in the larger lexicon.

The greatly increased number of inflectional forms that are parsed in this revision should make it unnecessary for a beginner in the study of New Testament Greek to search for other analytical aids.

Another new feature of this revision is the inclusion of a number of English-language derivatives. These should prove valuable in two ways. First, students will more easily remember the meanings of Greek words if they associate them with familiar or even not-so-familiar English terms. (The reverse is also true: "difficult" English words become clear if one knows their Greek roots.) Second, the derivatives quickly demonstrate the massive impact of Greek culture on the popular and specialized vocabularies of the English-speaking world.

The student should note that when derivatives are part of the definition itself (as, for example, in the entry καθολικός, ή, όν, *catholic*), they are not repeated, within brackets, at the end of the entry. The abbreviation "Cf." is ordinarily used to introduce a derivative which, though its association with the entry word may not be perfectly obvious (for example, *thyme,* from θύω) or whose form is mediated through another language (for example, *permanent,* via Latin), is nevertheless related to the entry word in whole or in part. Complicated etymological data, of interest primarily to specialists, are avoided.

An asterisk (*) at the end of an entry means that all occurrences of the word in the New Testament are cited. When this is not the case, a representative sample of usages is provided.

To my friend and coworker, Dr. F. Wilbur Gingrich, I herewith express appreciation for the opportunity to share in enterprises that began with his and Professor Arndt's work on Bauer's classic.

FREDERICK W. DANKER

Foreword to the First Edition

This book is a condensed version of the translation and adaptation of the late Walter Bauer's *Griechisch-deutsches Wörterbuch zu den Schriften des Neuen Testaments und der übrigen urchristlichen Literatur* by the late William F. Arndt and me, published in 1957 under the title *A Greek-English Lexicon of the New Testament and Other Early Christian Literature.*

The scope of this smaller book is limited to the words of the New Testament itself, to the exclusion of the Apostolic Fathers and other pieces of early Christian literature included in the larger lexicon. The variant readings of the Nestle (now Nestle-Aland) text of the New Testament are included in this work, together with a few others.

The emphasis is here placed upon the bare meaning of the words; for more information the user must consult the unabridged lexicon or other works. A large number of more or less difficult inflectional forms have been included.

An asterisk (*) at the end of an entry means that all the occurrences of the word in the New Testament have been noted. Where this is not the case, it will be found that a more or less representative list of occurrences is given.

The writer wishes to acknowledge gratefully the assistance of the following students in his advanced Greek classes at Albright College in checking references and various other matters: James W. Adam, Guy W. Camp III, Michael L. Ervin, James F. Getz, Fred A. Grater, Paul F. Jacobs, Faith King, John King, Robert W. Martin, Gene M. Miller, Joanne E. O'Dell, Eugene H. Stecher, Richard E. Stetler, David N. Treaster, and Dennis L. Trout.

F. WILBUR GINGRICH

READING, PENNSYLVANIA

Abbreviations

BOOKS OF THE NEW TESTAMENT

Ac	Acts of the Apostles	2 J	2 John	1 Pt	1 Peter
		3 J	3 John	2 Pt	2 Peter
Col	Colossians	Jd	Jude	Ro	Romans
1 Cor	1 Corinthians	Js	James	Rv	Revelation
2 Cor	2 Corinthians	Lk	Luke	1 Th	1 Thessalonians
Eph	Ephesians	Mk	Mark	2 Th	2 Thessalonians
Gal	Galatians	Mt	Matthew	1 Ti	1 Timothy
Hb	Hebrews	Phil	Philippians	2 Ti	2 Timothy
J	John	Phlm	Philemon	Tit	Titus
1 J	1 John				

The few abbreviations used for books of the Old Testament are easily understood without explanation.

GENERAL

acc.	accusative	fut.	future	neut.	neuter
act.	active	gen.	genitive	nom.	nominative
adv.	adverb	gener.	generally	oft.	often
alt.	alternate	Gk.	Greek	opt.	optative
aor.	aorist	H.	Hellenistic	pass.	passive
c.	circa, about	Heb.	Hebrew	passim	here and there
ch.	chapter	i.e.	id est, that is	pf.	perfect
cf.	compare	impf.	imperfect	perh.	perhaps
dat.	dative	impv.	imperative	pl.	plural
e.g.	exempli gratia, for example	ind.	indicative	plupf.	pluperfect
		indecl.	indeclinable	prep.	preposition
esp.	especially	inf.	infinitive	pres.	present
exclus.	exclusively	inscr.	inscription, title	priv.	privative
expl.	explanation	intrans.	intransitive	prob.	probably
f	following	km.	kilometer	pron.	pronoun
ff	following, of more than one	lit.	literal(ly)	ptc.	participle
		mid.	middle	q.v.	quod vide, which see
fig.	figurative(ly)	mng.	meaning	ref.	reference

s.	see	subst.	substantive	voc.	vocative
sing.	singular	s.v.	sub verbo,	vs.	verse
specif.	specifically		under the word	w.	with
subj.	subjunctive	trans.	transitive		
subscr.	subscription,	t.t.	technical term		
	short statement	v.l.	varia lectio,		
	at end of a book		variant reading		

SHORTER
LEXICON
OF THE
GREEK
NEW TESTAMENT

A

A, α *alpha*, first letter of the Greek alphabet. α' as numeral = *one* or *first*, in titles of 1 Cor, etc. See also ἄλφα.

Ἀαρών, ὁ indecl. *Aaron*, brother of Moses (Ex 4:14) Lk 1:5; Ac 7:40; Hb 5:4; 7:11; 9:4.*

Ἀβαδδών, ὁ indecl. (Heb. = 'destruction') *Abaddon*, Gk. Ἀπολλύων *Destroyer*, the ruling angel in hell Rv 9:11.*

ἀβαρής, ές, gen. **οὖς** *not burdensome* ἀβαρῆ ἐμαυτὸν ὑμῖν ἐτήρησα *I kept myself from being a burden to you* 2 Cor 11:9.*

ἀββά (Aram.) voc. case *abba = (O) father,* a specially intimate term Mk 14:36; Ro 8:15; Gal 4:6.*

Ἄβελ, ὁ indecl. (Heb.) *Abel* (Gen 4) Mt 23:35; Hb 12:24.

Ἀβιά, ὁ indecl. (Heb.) *Abijah*—**1.** Son of Rehoboam (1 Ch 3:10) Mt 1:7a, b.—**2.** Founder of the class of priests to which Zechariah belonged (1 Ch 24:10) Lk 1:5.*

Ἀβιαθάρ, ὁ indecl. (Heb.) *Abiathar,* priest at Nob (1 Sam 22:20ff) Mk 2:26.*

Ἀβιληνή, ῆς, ἡ *Abilene,* the territory around the city of Abila, northwest of Damascus Lk 3:1.*

Ἀβιούδ, ὁ indecl. (Heb.) *Abiud* Mt 1:13a, b.

Ἀβραάμ, ὁ indecl. (Heb.) *Abraham,* ancestor of the Hebrew people (Gen 12:1–3) and in a transferred sense of the Christians Ro 4:1ff.

ἄβυσσος, ου, ἡ *unfathomable depth, abyss, underworld* abode of the dead Ro 10:7; of demons Lk 8:31; of the beast Rv 11:7. [*abyss*]

Ἄγαβος, ου, ὁ *Agabus,* a Christian prophet Ac 11:28; 21:10.*

ἀγαγεῖν, ἀγάγετε, ἀγαγών 2 aor. act. inf., impv., and ptc. of ἄγω.

ἀγαθοεργέω (contracted form ἀγαθουργέω) *do good, confer benefits* Ac 14:17; 1 Ti 6:18.*

ἀγαθοεργός, όν *doing good;* used as a noun Ro 13:3 v.l.*

ἀγαθοποιέω—**1.** *do good, be helpful* Lk 6:9; τινά *to someone* 6:33.—**2.** *do what is right* 1 Pt 2:15, 20.

ἀγαθοποιΐα, ας, ἡ *doing what is good* or *right* 1 Pt 4:19.*

ἀγαθοποιός, όν *doing good;* used as a noun *one who does good* or *is a good citizen* 1 Pt 2:14.*

ἀγαθός, ή, όν *good, beneficial*—**1.** of persons: of God *perfect, complete* Mk 10:18. Morally *good, upright, exceptional* of Christ J 7:12; of people Mt 12:35; Ac 11:24. *Kind, benevolent, beneficent* Ac 9:36; 1 Pt 2:18.—**2.** of things: *fertile* Lk 8:8; *sound* Mt 7:17f; *beneficial, wholesome* 7:11; *helpful* Eph 4:29; *prosperous, happy* 1 Pt 3:10; *clear* 1 Ti 1:5; *firm* Tit 2:10; *dependable* 2 Th 2:16. *Better* Lk 10:42.—**3.** neut., used as a noun *what is good* in a moral sense Ro 2:10. *Good deeds* J 5:29. *Advantage* Ro 8:28. *Goods, property* Lk 12:18. [*Agatha*]

ἀγαθουργέω see ἀγαθοεργέω.

1

ἀγαθωσύνη, ης, ἡ goodness, uprightness Ro 15:14; Eph 5:9; 2 Th 1:11. Generosity Gal 5:22.*

ἀγαλλίασις, εως, ἡ rejoicing, exultation. ἔλαιον -εως = oil used for anointing on festive occasions Hb 1:9.

ἀγαλλιάω usually mid. rejoice, be overjoyed, exult w. dat. rejoice in or because of Lk 10:21, with 1 Pt 1:8.

ἄγαμος, ου, ὁ and ἡ an unmarried man or woman 1 Cor 7:8, 11, 32, 34.*

ἀγανακτέω be aroused, be indignant or angry; perh. = express displeasure Mk 14:4; Lk 13:14.

ἀγανάκτησις, εως, ἡ indignation 2 Cor 7:11.*

ἀγαπάω to love, have affection for—1. of persons: God J 3:16, Jesus Mk 10: 21, and people 2 Cor 12:15 love, cherish, show the greatest solicitude for, of the finest and most typical Christian virtue (more frequent and typically Christian than φιλέω but prob. equivalent to it in J 21:15–17). Prove or show love (for) J 13:1; 1 J 3:18.—2. of the love for things love, long for, value, hold in high esteem Lk 11:43; J 12:43; 2 Ti 4:8.

ἀγάπη, ης, ἡ—I. love, affection the highest Christian virtue 1 Cor 13:13; Gal 5:22.—1. of God and Christ to each other J 15:10; 17:26, and to people Ro 5:8. The essence of God 1 J 4:8, 16.—2. of people, to God or Christ J 5:42, or to other people 2 Cor 8:7.—3. as an abstract quality Ro 13:10; 1 Cor 8:1; 13:1–3.—II. a love feast, a common meal of the Christian church Jd 12; 2 Pt 2:13 v.l.

ἀγαπητός, ή, όν beloved, dear: of children, friends, fellow Christians 1 Cor 4:17; Col 4:14; 3 J 2, 5, 11. Of the Messiah, with connotation of special choice by God Mt 3:17.

Ἁγάρ, ἡ indecl. Hagar (Gen 16), symbol of the Mosaic law Gal 4:24, 25.*

ἀγγαρεύω requisition, press into service (originally for the Persian royal post; in Rom. times for any military or civil service), then force, compel Mt 5:41; 27:32; Mk 15:21.*

ἀγγεῖον, ου, τό vessel, flask, container Mt 25:4; 13:48 v.l.*

ἀγγελία, ας, ἡ message concerning God 1 J 1:5; command 3:11.*

ἀγγέλλω announce, report J 20:18; 4:51 v.l.*

ἄγγελος, ου, ὁ—1. messenger, envoy Lk 7:24.—2. angel, a supernatural being who acts as messenger Mt 1:20, guardian Ac 12:15, mediator Gal 3:19, and generally as the servant of God. Also of servants of Satan Mt 25:41. [Angelus; angelology, ἄγγελος + λόγος]

ἄγγος, ους, τό vessel, basket for fish Mt 13:48.* [hydrangea, ὕδωρ + ἄγγος]

ἄγε (pres. impv. of ἄγω, used as interjection) come Js 4:13; 5:1.*

ἀγέλη, ης, ἡ herd of swine Mt 8:30–32.

ἀγενεαλόγητος, ον without genealogy Hb 7:3.*

ἀγενής, ές, gen. οῦς base, low, insignificant, lit. not of noble birth 1 Cor 1:28.* [-γενής, genetic]

ἁγιάζω make holy, sanctify, consecrate, dedicate, purify: of things Mt 23:17, 19; of persons J 10:36; 1 Cor 7:14; Hb 9:13. οἱ ἡγιασμένοι = the Christians as sanctified, purified Ac 20:32. Treat as holy, hold in reverence Mt 6:9; 1 Pt 3:15.

ἁγιασμός, οῦ, ὁ holiness, consecration, sanctification Ro 6:19, 22; 1 Ti 2:15. Mediated by God through Christ 1 Cor 1:30.

ἅγιος, ία, ον set apart for or by God, morally or ceremonially holy.—1. of things sacred, consecrated 1 Cor 3:17. The superlative ἁγιωτάτη πίστις most holy commitment Jd 20. Neut. as noun τὸ ἅγιον perh. holy food Mt 7:6. τὰ ἅγια sanctuary, temple Hb 9:12.—2. of persons: of God cultically set apart, morally perfect J 17:11. Of Christ Mk 1:24. Of Christians, οἱ ἅγιοι God's people, saints Ro 1:7. Of pers. gener. pure, upright, worthy of God Eph 1:4. [hagiography, hagiology]

ἁγιότης, ητος, ἡ holiness, moral purity 2 Cor 1:12 v.l.; Hb 12:10.*

ἁγιωσύνη, ης, ἡ holiness, uprightness Ro 1:4; 2 Cor 7:1; 1 Th 3:13.*

ἀγκάλη, ης, ἡ arm, bent as to receive something Lk 2:28.*

ἄγκιστρον, ου, τό *fishhook* Mt 17:27.*

ἄγκυρα, ας, ἡ *anchor* lit. Ac 27:29, 30, 40; fig. Hb 6:19.* [*anchor*]

ἄγναφος, ον *unshrunken* of cloth not yet treated by the fuller (γναφεύς, q.v.) Mt 9:16; Mk 2:21.*

ἁγνεία, ας, ἡ, ἡ *purity,* esp. *chastity* 1 Ti 4:12; 5:2.*

ἁγνίζω *cleanse, purify* ceremonially Ac 21:24, 26; morally Js 4:8.

ἡγνίσθητι 1 aor. pass. impv. of ἁγνίζω.

ἁγνισμός, οῦ, ὁ *purification,* ceremonial Ac 21:26.*

ἀγνοέω *not to know, be ignorant* Ro 2:4. W. neg. *know (quite well), be sure* Ro 1:13; 2 Cor 2:11. *Not to understand* Mk 9:32. *Sin in ignorance* Hb 5:2. *Disregard* 1 Cor 14:38.

ἀγνόημα, ατος, τό *sin committed in ignorance* Hb 9:7.*

ἄγνοια, ας, ἡ *ignorance,* excusable Ac 3:17; 17:30; willful Eph 4:18; 1 Pt 1:14; 2:15 v.l.; 2 Pt 2:13 v.l.*

ἁγνός, ή, όν *holy, pure* (first ceremonially, then ethically) Phil 4:8; Js 3:17. *Chaste* Tit 2:5. *Innocent* 2 Cor 7:11.

ἁγνότης, ητος, ἡ *purity, sincerity* 2 Cor 6:6; 11:3.*

ἁγνῶς *purely, sincerely* Phil 1:17.*

ἀγνωσία, ας, ἡ *ignorance, lack of spiritual discernment* 1 Cor 15:34; 1 Pt 2:15.* [*agnosia*]

ἄγνωστος, ον *unknown* Ac 17:23.* [*agnostic,* α priv. + γνῶσις]

ἀγορά, ᾶς, ἡ *marketplace,* the center of civic life. 'When they come' is to be understood w. ἀπ' ἀγορᾶς Mk 7:4. The Agora at Athens Ac 17:17.

ἀγοράζω *buy, purchase,* lit. Mt 13:44; fig. 1 Cor 6:20.

ἀγοραῖος, ον *pertaining to a market,* used only as a noun. οἱ ἀ. *idlers, rabble* Ac 17:5. ἀ. (supply 'days' or 'sessions') ἄγονται *the courts are in session* 19:38.*

ἄγρα, ας, ἡ *catching, a catch* of fish Lk 5:4, 9.*

ἀγράμματος, ον *illiterate* in the sense *uneducated* Ac 4:13.*

ἀγραυλέω *live out of doors* Lk 2:8.*

ἀγρεύω *to catch* fig. Mk 12:13.*

ἀγριέλαιος, ου, ἡ *wild olive tree* Ro 11:24; perh. as adj., with 'branch' to be supplied 11:17.*

ἄγριος, ία, ιον *wild* Mt 3:4; Mk 1:6; Jd 13.*

Ἀγρίππας, α, ὁ *Agrippa,* i.e. Herod Agrippa II, brother of Bernice Ac 25 and 26 passim. His father, Herod Agrippa I, is called simply Herod in Ac 12:1ff.

ἀγρός, οῦ, ὁ *field* Mt 6:28; Lk 17:7; *country* as opposed to city or village Mk 15:21. Pl. *farms, hamlets* Lk 9:12. [*acre, agriculture, agronomy*]

ἀγρυπνέω *keep oneself awake,* fig. *be on the alert* Mk 13:33. *Keep watch (over), guard, care for* Eph 6:18; Hb 13:17. [Cf. ὕπνος.]

ἀγρυπνία, ας, ἡ *sleeplessness* 2 Cor 6:5; 11:27.*

ἄγω—1. *lead, bring, take* or *bring along* Mt 21:7; Ac 17:15; 20:12; to trial or punishment Ac 6:12; 9:2. Fig. *lead, guide* Ro 2:4; Gal 5:18. Of time *spend* Lk 24:21 (supply 'Jesus' as subj.); of court sessions *hold* Ac 19:38.—2. *go,* always hortatory subjunctive *let us go* Mk 1:38; J 11:7, 15f.

ἀγωγή, ῆς, ἡ *way of life, conduct* 2 Ti 3:10.*

ἀγών, ἀγῶνος, ὁ athletic *contest, race* fig. Hb 12:1; *struggle, fight* Phil 1:30. ἐν πολλῷ ἀγῶνι *under a great strain* 1 Th 2:2. *Care, anxiety, concern* Col 2:1. [*agonistic*]

ἀγωνία, ας, ἡ *agony, anxiety* Lk 22:44.* [*agony*]

ἀγωνίζομαι *engage in an (athletic) contest* 1 Cor 9:25; *fight, struggle, strive* J 18:36; Col 4:12; 1 Ti 4:10; *strain every nerve* Lk 13:24. [*agonize*]

Ἀδάμ, ὁ indecl. (Heb.) *Adam* (Gen 1:27ff) Ro 5:14. ὁ ἔσχατος Ἀδάμ *the last Adam* = Christ 1 Cor 15:45.

ἀδάπανος, ον *free of charge* 1 Cor 9:18.*

Ἀδδί, ὁ indecl. (Heb.) *Addi* Lk 3:28.*

ἀδελφή, ῆς, ἡ *sister:* lit. Lk 10: 39f; fig. Ro 16:1; 2 J 13.

ἀδελφός, οῦ, ὁ *brother:* lit. J 1:41; fig. Mk 3:35; Phil 1:14. *Fellow countryman*

4   ἀδελφότης–ἄθεσμος

or *national* Ro 9:3; *neighbor* Mt 5:22ff. Pl. *brothers and sisters* Lk 21:16; Eph 6:23. *[Philadelphia]*

ἀδελφότης, ητος, ἡ *brother-and-sisterhood, fellowship* (group of believers) 1 Pt 2:17; 5:9.*

ἄδηλος, ον *unseen* Lk 11:44; *indistinct* 1 Cor 14:8.*

ἀδηλότης, ητος, ἡ *uncertainty* 1 Ti 6:17.*

ἀδήλως adv. *uncertainly, without a definite goal* 1 Cor 9:26.*

ἀδημονέω *be anxious, be distressed* Mt 26:37; Mk 14:33; Phil 2:26.*

ᾅδης, ου, ὁ *Hades* (Heb. Sheol), *the underworld* as the place of the dead Lk 16:23; personified Rv 20:13f.

ἀδιάκριτος, ον *unwavering, impartial* Js 3:17.*

ἀδιάλειπτος, ον *unceasing, constant* Ro 9:2; 2 Ti 1:3.*

ἀδιαλείπτως adv. *unceasingly, constantly* Ro 1:9; 1 Th 1:2; 2:13; 5:17.*

ἀδιαφθορία, ας, ἡ *sincerity, integrity* Tit 2:7 v.l.*

ἀδικέω *do wrong* Col 3:25; ὁ ἀδικῶν *the evildoer* Rv 22:11. *Be in the wrong* Ac 25:11. *Do wrong to* someone, *cheat* someone Mt 20:13; Ac 7:26; Gal 4:12; 2 Pt 2:13. *Injure, harm, damage, spoil* Rv 9:4, 10, 19; *if he has caused you any loss* Phlm 18.

ἀδίκημα, ατος, τό *misdeed, crime, wrong* Ac 18:14; 24:20; Rv 18:5.*

ἀδικία, ας, ἡ *injustice* Ro 9:14; *wrong* (ironic) 2 Cor 12:13; *wickedness, wrongdoing, unrighteousness* Ro 6:13; 1 Cor 13:6; 1 J 5:17. The gen. ἀδικίας = *unjust* Lk 16:8, 9 (cf. 11); 18:6.

ἀδικοκρίτης, ου, ὁ *unjust judge* Tit 1:9 v.l.*

ἄδικος, ον *unjust, unrighteous* Mt 5:45; 1 Cor 6:1; 1 Pt 3:18; *dishonest, untrustworthy* Lk 16:10.

ἀδίκως adv. *unjustly, undeservedly* 1 Pt 2:19; 2:23 v.l.*

Ἀδμίν, ὁ indecl. (Heb.) *Admin* Lk 3:33.*

ἀδόκιμος, ον *failing to stand the test, unqualified, worthless* 2 Cor 13:5–7; *disqualified* 1 Cor 9:27; *unworthy* Ro 1:28; *useless* Hb 6:8.

ἄδολος, ον *unadulterated, pure* 1 Pt 2:2.*

Ἀδραμυττηνός, ή, όν *belonging to Adramyttium,* a seaport in northwest Asia Minor, on the Aegean Sea Ac 27:2.*

Ἀδρίας, ου, ὁ *the Adriatic Sea* (the sea between Crete and Sicily is included in it) Ac 27:27.*

ἀδρότης, ητος, ἡ *abundance, lavishness* 2 Cor 8:20.*

ἀδυνατέω *be powerless,* only impersonal *it is impossible* Mt 17:20; Lk 1:37.* *[adynamic]*

ἀδύνατος, ον *powerless, weak* of persons Ac 14:8; Ro 15:1. *Impossible* of things Ro 8:3; Hb 6:4, 18.

ᾄδω *sing* Eph 5:9; Col 3:16; Rv 5:9; 14:3; 15:3.* *[ode]*

ἀεί adv. *always* 2 Cor 6:10; 1 Pt 3:15; *continually, constantly* Ac 7:51; 2 Cor 4:11; *from time to time* 2 Pt 1:12.

ἀετός, οῦ, ὁ *eagle* Rv 12:14; *vulture* Lk 17:37.

ἄζυμος, ον *free from yeast* or *leaven* fig. 1 Cor 5:7. As a noun, pl. *unleavened bread* Lk 22:1; fig. 1 Cor 5:8. *The festival of unleavened bread* Mk 14:1, immediately following the Passover and often identified with it Lk 22:1, 7.

Ἀζώρ, ὁ indecl. *Azor* Mt 1:13f; Lk 3:23–31 v.l.

Ἄζωτος, ου, ἡ *Azotus,* the O.T. Ashdod (Is 20:1), a Philistine city on the coast of S. Palestine Ac 8:40.*

ἀηδία, ας, ἡ *enmity,* lit. 'unpleasantness' Lk 23:12 v.l.*

ἀήρ, ἀέρος, ὁ *air, upper regions* Ac 22:23; 1 Cor 9:26; Eph 2:2. *[aerial]*

ἀθᾶ see μαράνα θά.

ἀθανασία, ας, ἡ *immortality* 1 Cor 15:53f; 1 Ti 6:16.* *[athanasia]*

ἀθάνατος, ον *immortal* 1 Ti 1:17 v.l.* *[ἀ* priv. + *θάνατος,* death]

ἀθέμιτος, ον *unlawful* Ac 10:28; *illicit, wanton* 1 Pt 4:3.*

ἄθεος, ον *without God,* i.e. not having a share in the God of Israel Eph 2:12.* *[atheism]*

ἄθεσμος, ον *lawless, unprincipled* 2 Pt 2:7; 3:17.*

ἀθετέω—**1.** declare invalid, nullify, set aside Mk 7:9; Gal 2:21; thwart, confound 1 Cor 1:19.—**2.** reject, ignore of persons Lk 10:16; break faith with Mk 6:26. [athetize, reject a passage as spurious]

ἀθέτησις, εως, ἡ annulment technical legal term Hb 7:18; removal 9:26.*

Ἀθῆναι, ὧν, αἱ Athens, the intellectual capital of the Greek world Ac 17:15f.

Ἀθηναῖος, α, ον Athenian Ac 17:21f.*

ἀθλέω compete in a contest 2 Ti 2:5.* [athletic]

ἄθλησις, εως, ἡ contest, struggle fig. Hb 10:32.* [athlete]

ἀθροίζω collect, gather Lk 24:33.*

ἀθυμέω be discouraged, lose heart Col 3:21.*

ἀθῷος, ον innocent Mt 27:4, 24.*

αἴγειος, εία, ειον of a goat Hb 11:37.*

αἰγιαλός, οῦ, ὁ shore, beach Mt 13:2; Ac 27:39.

Αἰγύπτιος, ία, ιον Egyptian Ac 7:24.

Αἴγυπτος, ου, ἡ Egypt Mt 2:13–15; = Jerusalem Rv 11:8.

ἀΐδιος, ον eternal, everlasting Ro 1:20; Jd 6.*

αἰδώς, οῦς, ἡ unpretentiousness, modesty 1 Ti 2:9; reverence, respect Hb 12:28 v.l.*

Αἰθίοψ, οπος, ὁ Ethiopian Ac 8:27.*

αἷμα, ατος, τό blood. σὰρξ καὶ αἷμα a (mere) human being Gal 1:16; human nature Hb 2:14. Pl., of physical descent J 1:13. Murder Rv 6:10; bloody deed Mt 27:6. As a means of purification, of animals Hb 10:4, or of Christ Col 1:20; 1 Pt 1:19. [hemophilia]

αἱματεκχυσία, ας, ἡ the pouring of blood Hb 9:22.*

αἱμορροέω suffer from a flow of blood or hemorrhage Mt 9:20.* [hemorrhea]

Αἰνέας, ου, ὁ Aeneas Ac 9:33f.*

αἴνεσις, εως, ἡ praise Hb 13:15.*

αἰνέω praise, extol Rv 19:5.

αἴνιγμα, ατος, τό lit. riddle, then indirect image; ἐν αἰ. by reflection, indirectly as opposed to personal encounter 1 Cor 13:12.* [enigma]

αἶνος, ου, ὁ praise Mt 21:16; Lk 18:43.*

Αἰνών, ἡ indecl. Aenon, a place probably in the upper Jordan valley J 3:23.*

αἴξ, αἰγός, ὁ, ἡ goat Lk 15:29 v.l.*

αἱρέομαι choose 2 Th 2:13; prefer Phil 1:22; Hb 11:25.*

αἵρεσις, εως, ἡ religious sect Ac 5:17; 26:5; perh. schismatic sect Ac 24:5, 14; 28:22. Dissension, division 1 Cor 11:19; Gal 5:20. Opinion, dogma 2 Pt 2:1. [heresy]

αἱρετίζω choose, select Mt 12:18.*

αἱρετικός, ή, όν factious, causing divisions, schismatic Tit 3:10.* [heretic]

αἱρέω exclus. mid. in N.T.; s. αἱρέομαι.

αἴρω—**1.** raise, lift, take up, pick up Mt 16:24; Lk 17:13; J 8:59; keep in suspense J 10:24; weigh (anchors) Ac 27:13; take or carry along Mt 16:24; 27:32; w. φωνή cry out loudly Lk 17:13. The transition to mng. 2 may be seen in J 1:29, where αἴ. means both take up and remove.—**2.** take or carry away, remove Lk 6:29; J 2:16; 19:38. Do away with, kill J 19:15 (s. ἆρον); sweep away Mt 24:39; conquer, take over J 11: 48; expel 1 Cor 5:2; cut off J 15:2. Supply τι something Mt 9:16. [arsis]

αἰσθάνομαι understand Lk 9:45.*

αἴσθησις, εως, ἡ insight, experience Phil 1:9.* [aesthetic]

αἰσθητήριον, ου, τό sense, faculty Hb 5:14.*

αἴσθωμαι 2 aor. subj. of αἰσθάνομαι.

αἰσχροκερδής, ές fond of dishonest gain, greedy for money 1 Ti 3:8, 3 v.l.; Tit 1:7.*

αἰσχροκερδῶς adv. greedily 1 Pt 5:2.*

αἰσχρολογία, ας, ἡ evil speech, in the sense of obscene or abusive speech Col 3:8.*

αἰσχρός, ά, όν shameful, disgraceful 1 Cor 11:6; 14:35; Eph 5:12. Dishonest Tit 1:11.*

αἰσχρότης, ητος, ἡ indecency Eph 5:4.*

αἰσχύνη, ης, ἡ modesty, shame 2 Cor 4:2; shame, disgrace, ignominy Phil 3:19; Hb 12:2; Rv 3:18; disgrace Lk 14:9. Shameful deed Jd 13.*

αἰσχύνομαι exclus. mid. and pass. in N.T. *be ashamed* Lk 16:3; 1 Pt 4:16. *Be put to shame, be disgraced* 1 J 2:28; *be embarrassed* 2 Cor 10:8; Phil 1:20.*

αἰτέω *ask, ask for, request* Mt 27:20; Ac 16:29; *make a request of* someone 13:28. W. double acc. *ask someone for something* Mt 7:9. The classical meaning *demand* may fit some passages, e.g. 1 Cor 1:22.

αἴτημα, τος, τό *request* Phil 4:6; 1 J 5:15. *Demand* Lk 23:24.*

αἰτία, ας, ἡ—**1.** *cause, reason* Mt 19:3; Ac 10:21; *relationship* Mt 19:10.— **2.** legal term *charge, ground for complaint, accusation* J 18:38; Ac 25:18, 27. [*aetiology* or *etiology, αἰτία + λόγος*]

αἰτίαμα, τος, τό (see *αἰτίωμα*) Ac 25:7 v.l.*

αἰτιάομαι *to charge* Ro 3:9 v.l.*

αἴτιος, ία, ον *responsible, guilty* only as noun: masc. *cause, source* Hb 5:9. Neut. *cause* Ac 19:40; *guilt, complaint* Lk 23:4, 14; *αἰ. θανάτου reason for capital punishment* vs. 22.*

αἰτίωμα, τος, τό *charge, complaint* Ac 25:7.*

αἰφνίδιος, ον *sudden* Lk 21:34; 1 Th 5:3. S. also *εὐθέως*.*

αἰχμαλωσία, ας, ἡ *captivity* Rv 13:10. Abstract for concrete, (many) *captives, prisoners of war* Eph 4:8; Hb 7:1 v.l.*

αἰχμαλωτεύω *take captive* Eph 4:8; 2 Ti 3:6 v.l.*

αἰχμαλωτίζω *capture* in war: lit. *be scattered as captives* Lk 21:24. Fig. *take captive, subdue* Ro 7:23; 2 Cor 10:5; *mislead* 2 Ti 3:6.*

αἰχμάλωτος, ώτου, ὁ *captive* Lk 4:18.* [*αἰχμή*, spear + *ἁλωτός*, caught, seized]

αἰών, αἰῶνος, ὁ—**1.** *very long time, eternity:* in the past, *earliest times, ages long past* Lk 1:70; *ἐκ τοῦ αἰῶνος since the world began* J 9:32. In the future *εἰς τὸν αἰῶνα to eternity, in perpetuity* J 6:51, 58. *εἰς τοὺς αἰ. τῶν αἰώνων forevermore* Ro 16:27; Hb 13:21.—**2.** *age, era: ὁ αἰὼν οὗτος*, etc. *this present* (evil) *age*, before the *παρουσία* Mt 12:32;

13:22; Lk 16:8 (the people of *the world*); 2 Cor 4:4; Gal 1:4. *ὁ αἰὼν ὁ ἐρχόμενος*, etc. *the* (happy) *age to come,* after the *παρουσία* Mk 10:30; Eph 1:21.—**3.** *world, material universe* 1 Ti 1:17; Hb 1:2.—**4.** the *Aeon,* a powerful evil spirit Eph 2:2; perh. Col 1:26. [*aeon*]

αἰώνιος, ία, ον *eternal, everlasting: without beginning* Ro 16:25; *without beginning or end* 16:26; *without end* Mt 25:46; Lk 10:25; Hb 13:20.

ἀκαθαρσία, ας, ἡ *impurity, refuse:* lit. Mt 23:27. *Immorality, viciousness* Ro 1:24; Gal 5:19. [Cf. *καθαίρω*.]

ἀκάθαρτος, ον *impure, unclean:* ceremonially Ac 10:14, vs. 28; 1 Cor 7:14. Morally Eph 5:5; of demons Mk 1:23.

ἀκαιρέομαι *have no time, no opportunity* Phil 4:10.*

ἀκαίρως adv. *out of season, inopportunely* 2 Ti 4:2.*

ἄκακος, ον *innocent, blameless* Hb 7:26; *unsuspecting* Ro 16:18.*

ἄκανθα, ης, ἡ *thorn plant* Mt 13:7; 27:29.

ἀκάνθινος, η, ον *made of thorns* Mk 15:17; J 19:5.* [*acanthous,* spinous]

ἄκαρπος, ον *unfruitful, useless, unproductive* lit. Jd 12; fig. Mk 4:19; 1 Cor 14:14; Eph 5:11. [*acarpous,* sterile]

ἀκατάγνωστος, ον *above reproach* Tit 2:8.*

ἀκατακάλυπτος, ον *uncovered, unveiled* 1 Cor 11:5, 13.*

ἀκατάκριτος, ον *without a proper trial* Ac 16:37; 22:25.*

ἀκατάλυτος, ον *indestructible, indissoluble,* hence *endless* Hb 7:16.* [-*κατάλυτος,* catalytic]

ἀκατάπαστος, ον *of uncertain mng.,* perh. *insatiable* 2 Pt 2:14 v.l.*

ἀκατάπαυστος, ον *unceasing, restless,* w. gen. *unable to cease from* 2 Pt 2:14.*

ἀκαταστασία, ας, ἡ *disturbance* 2 Cor 6:5; *disorder, unruliness, unrest* 1 Cor 14:33; 2 Cor 12:20; Js 3:16; *insurrection* Lk 21:9.*

ἀκατάστατος, ον *restless* Js 3:8; *unstable* 1:8.*

ἀκατάσχετος, ον *uncontrollable* Js 3:8
v.l.*

'Ακελδαμάχ (Aram. = field of blood;
s. expl. in Mt 27:8) *Akeldama* Ac 1:19.*

ἀκέραιος, ον *pure, innocent* lit. 'unmixed' Mt 10:16; Ro 16:19; Phil 2:15.*

ἀκηδεμονέω, *found nowhere else than*
Mk 14:33 v.l., for ἀδημονέω, q.v.*

ἀκήκοα pf. act. ind. 1 sing. of ἀκούω.

ἀκλινής, ές *unwavering* τ. ὁμολογίαν ἀ.
κατέχειν *hold fast the confession without wavering* Hb 10:23.*

ἀκμάζω *become ripe* Rv 14:18.*

ἀκμήν adverbial acc. (of ἀκμή 'present
moment') *even yet, still* Mt 15:16; Hb
5:13 v.l.* [acme]

ἀκοή, ῆς, ἡ—1. the faculty of *hearing* 1
Cor 12:17. The act of *hearing, listening*
2 Pt 2:8; ἀκοῇ ἀκούσετε *you will indeed hear* Mt 13:14. The organ of hearing, the *ear* Mk 7:35; Ac 17:20.—2. that
which is heard: *fame, report, rumor* Mt
4:24; 14:1; 24:6. *Account, report,
preaching* J 12:38; Gal 3:2, 5; Hb 4:2;
1 Th 2:13.

ἀκολουθέω *follow* Mt 21:9; *accompany*
J 6:2; *follow* as disciple Mk 1:18; 2:14.
[Cf. acolyte, anacolouthon.]

ἀκουσθεῖσι dat. pl., 1 aor. pass. ptc. of
ἀκούω.

ἀκουστός, ή, όν *audible*, hence *known*
Ac 11:1 v.l.* [acoustical; cf. ἀκούω.]

ἀκούω *hear*, lit. Mt 11:5. *Heed, listen to*
18:15, *understand* 1 Cor 14:2; Gal 4:21.
Learn of Ro 10:18; pass. *be reported*
1 Cor 5:1; *learn* (a body of teaching) 1
J 1:5; 2:7, 24. Legal term *give* (someone) *a hearing* J 7:51; Ac 25:22.

ἀκρασία, ας, ἡ *lack of self-control* 1
Cor 7:5; *self-indulgence* Mt 23:25.*

ἀκρατής, ές *without self-control, dis-
solute* 2 Ti 3:3.*

ἄκρατος, ον *unmixed, in full strength* Rv
14:10.* [A κρατήρ was a bowl in which
wine and water were *mixed*. Cf. κεράννυμι.]

ἀκρίβεια, ας, ἡ *exactness* κατὰ ἀ.
strictly Ac 22:3.*

ἀκριβέστερον see ἀκριβῶς.

ἀκριβής, ές *strict* Ac 26:5.*

ἀκριβόω *ascertain (exactly)* Mt 2:7, 16.*

ἀκριβῶς adv. *accurately, carefully, well*
Lk 1:3; Eph 5:15. Comparative ἀκριβέστερον *more exactly, more accurately* Ac 18:26; 24:22.

ἀκρίς, ίδος, ἡ *locust, grasshopper* Mt
3:4; Mk 1:6; Rv 9:3, 7.*

ἀκροατήριον, ου, τό *audience room* or
chamber, hall Ac 25:23.*

ἀκροατής, οῦ, ὁ *a hearer, one who hears*
or *listens to* Ro 2:13; Js 1:22, 23, 25.*

ἀκροβυστία, ας, ἡ *foreskin, uncircum-
cision* Ac 11:3; Ro 2:25ff; of precon-
version conduct Col 2:13. Those who
do not practice traditional Jewish cult,
the Gentiles Ro 4:9; Col 3:11.

ἀκρογωνιαῖος, α, ον *lying at the extreme corner.* ἀ. λίθος *cornerstone* or
capstone Eph 2:20; 1 Pt 2:6.*

ἀκροθίνιον, ου, τό *spoils, booty* Hb 7:4.*

ἄκρον, ου, τό *top* Hb 11:21; *tip* Lk 16:24;
extreme limit, end Mt 24:31; Mk 13:27.*
[acrobat, ἄκρος + βαίνω]

'Ακύλας, acc. αν, ὁ *Aquila* (accent on
first syllable), a friend of Paul, husband
of Priscilla Ac 18:2, 18, 22 v.l., 26; Ro
16:3; 1 Cor 16:19; 2 Ti 4:19.*

ἀκυρόω *make invalid, cancel, repeal* Mt
15:6; Mk 7:13; legal term Gal 3:17.*

ἀκωλύτως adv. *without hindrance* Ac
28:31.*

ἄκων, ἄκουσα, ἄκον *unwilling;* to be
translated as an adv. *unwillingly* 1 Cor
9:17.*

ἄλα see ἅλας.

ἀλάβαστρος, ου, ὁ and ἡ, also ἀλά-
βαστρον, ου, τό *alabaster flask* Mt
26:7; Mk 14:3; Lk 7:37.*

ἀλαζονεία, ας, ἡ *pretension, arrogance*
Js 4:16; *pride* 1 J 2:16.*

ἀλαζών, όνος, ὁ *boaster* Ro 1:30; 2 Ti
3:2.*

ἀλαλάζω *wail loudly* Mk 5:38; *clash,
clang* 1 Cor 13:1.*

ἀλάλητος, ον *unexpressed, inexpressible* στεναγμοὶ ἀ. *sighs too deep for
words* Ro 8:26.*

ἄλαλος, ον *unable to speak* or *articulate*
Mk 7:37; 9:17, 25.*

ἄλας, ατος, τό (v.l. ἄλα Mt 5:13 and elsewhere. The classical ἅλς is represented only by the v.l. ἁλί Mk 9:49) salt lit. Lk 14:34; fig. Mt 5:13a; Col 4:6.

ἁλεεῖς, οἱ see ἁλιεύς.

ἀλείφω anoint Mk 16:1; Lk 7:38, 46; Js 5:14.

ἀλεῖψαι 1 aor. mid. impv. 2 sing. of ἀλείφω.

ἀλεκτοροφωνία, ας, ἡ cockcrow; in genitive of time = the period from midnight to 3 a.m. Mk 13:35.*

ἀλέκτωρ, ορος, ὁ cock, rooster Mk 14:30; J 18:27. [Cf. alectryomancy, divination involving the use of a cock.]

Ἀλεξανδρεύς, έως, ὁ an Alexandrian Ac 6:9; 18:24.*

Ἀλεξανδρῖνος, η, ον Alexandrian Ac 6:9 v.l.; 27:6; 28:11.*

Ἀλέξανδρος, ου, ὁ Alexander: (1) Mk 15:21. (2) Ac 4:6. (3) 19:33. (4) 1 Ti 1:20; 2 Ti 4:14.*

ἄλευρον, ου, τό wheat flour Mt 13:33; Lk 13:21.*

ἀλήθεια, ας, ἡ truth: truthfulness, dependability, uprightness Ro 15:8; 2 Cor 7:14; truth as opposed to untruth Mk 5:33; Eph 4:25. Truth as characteristic of divine or human action J 1:17; 3:21; 1 Cor 13:6; Eph 4:24. Reality Phil 1:18; 2 J 1. With ἐν, ἐπί, κατά in reality, truly, certainly Mt 22:16; Mk 12:14; Lk 22:59; Ro 2:2.

ἀληθεύω be truthful, tell the truth Gal 4:16; Eph 4:15.*

ἀληθής, ές true J 19:35; Phil 4:8; 2 Pt 2:22; dependable J 5:31f; Tit 1:13. Truthful, righteous, honest Mt 22:16; J 3:33; 2 Cor 6:8. Real, genuine Ac 12:9; 1 Pt 5:12. [Cf. λανθάνω.]

ἀληθινός, ή, όν true, dependable Hb 10:22; Rv 6:10; true, in accordance with truth J 4:37; 19:35; Rv 19:9; genuine, real Lk 16:11; J 4:23; 17:3; 1 Th 1:9; Hb 8:2.

ἀλήθω grind Mt 24:41; Lk 17:35.*

ἀληθῶς adv. truly, really, actually Mt 14:33; Lk 9:27; 1 J 2:5. With adjectival function = real J 1:47; 8:31.

ἁλιεύς, έως, ὁ fisher lit. Mk 1:16. Fig. ποιήσω ὑμᾶς ἀ. ἀνθρώπων I will make you fish for people Mt 4:19.

ἁλιεύω to fish J 21:3.*

ἁλίζω to salt, make salty, season Mt 5:13; Mk 9:49.*

ἁλίσγημα, ατος, τό pollution (ceremonial) Ac 15:20.*

ἀλλά adversative particle but (stronger than δέ): most frequently after a negative, as Mt 5:17; Mk 9:37; Eph 1:21. Followed by οὐ, in strong contrast to a preceding positive statement 1 Cor 10:23. Yet, and yet J 1:31; 8:26; 12:27; rather Lk 1:60; instead of that 1 Cor 6:6; nevertheless Ro 5:14; except Mk 4:22; 2 Cor 1:13; certainly, at least Mk 14:29; Ro 6:5. Strengthening an imperative now, so Mt 9:18; Mk 9:22. Alone, or with καί, γε καί, or οὐδέ, emphatically introducing what follows indeed, why!, and not only this, but also 2 Cor 7:11 (6 times); J 16:2; 1 Cor 3:2. Elliptical ἀλλά (τοῦτο γέγονεν, e.g.) ἵνα but (this has happened, e.g.) in order that Mk 14:49; J 1:8.

ἀλλάσσω change, alter Ac 6:14; Gal 4:20; exchange Ro 1:23. [Cf. ἄλλος.]

ἀλλαχόθεν adv. at (lit. 'from') another place J 10:1.*

ἀλλαχοῦ adv. elsewhere, in another direction Mk 1:38.*

ἀλληγορέω speak symbolically or allegorically Gal 4:24.* [allegory]

ἀλληλουϊά (Heb.) praise the Lord (Yahweh), transliterated 'hallelujah' Rv 19:1, 3, 4, 6.*

ἀλλήλων reciprocal pron., genitive pl. each other, one another J 13:34; Js 4:11. [parallel, παρά + ἀλλήλων]

ἀλλογενής, ές foreign; used as noun foreigner Lk 17:18.*

ἀλλοιόω change Lk 9:29 v.l.*

ἄλλομαι leap up Ac 3:8; 14:10; of water well up J 4:14.*

ἄλλος, η, ο other, another, different Mt 13:5, 24; 1 Cor 9:27; 15:41; more, additional Mt 4:21; 25:20. οἱ ἄλλοι the rest 1 Cor 14:29. Joined with other of its own cases, as in the formulation ἄλλοι ἄλλο λέγουσιν some say one *thing, others another* Ac 19:32 (w. κράζω); 21:34 (w. ἐπιφωνέω). Contrary to the best classical usage, ἄ. invades the domain of ἕτερος (q.v.) and means *other* of two Mt 5:39; 12:13; it is used interchangeably with ἕτερος 2 Cor 11:4, and prob. also Gal 1:7, for which see ἕτερος. [Lat. alius; *alias, alien*]

ἀλλοτριεπίσκοπος, ου, ὁ a rare word of uncertain meaning; among those suggested are *busybody, informer, infringer on the rights of others* 1 Pt 4:15.*

ἀλλότριος, ία, ιον *belonging to another, strange, foreign* Lk 16:12; Ac 7:6; 2 Cor 10:15; Hb 11:9. ἀλλοτρίοις ἐπίσκοπος *meddling in other people's affairs* 1 Pt 4:15 v.l. *Hostile, enemy* Hb 11:34.

ἀλλόφυλος, ον *foreign,* as noun *Gentile* Ac 10:28; 13:19 v.l.*

ἄλλως adv. *otherwise;* τὰ ἄ. ἔχοντα the *opposite* 1 Ti 5:25.*

ἀλοάω *thresh* 1 Cor 9:9, 10; 1 Ti 5:18.*

ἄλογος, ον *without reason* of animals 2 Pt 2:12; Jd 10. *Contrary to reason, absurd* Ac 25:27.* [*illogical*]

ἀλόη, ης, ἡ *aloes* J 19:39.*

ἅλς, ἁλός, ὁ see ἅλας.

ἁλυκός, ή, όν *salty; a salt spring* Js 3:12.*

ἄλυπος, ον *free from grief* or *anxiety* Phil 2:28.*

ἅλυσις, εως, ἡ *chain,* also *handcuffs* Mk 5:3; Ac 28:20; generally *captivity, imprisonment* Eph 6:20; 2 Ti 1:16.

ἀλυσιτελής, ές *unprofitable, of no help,* perhaps *harmful* Hb 13:17.*

ἄλφα, τό indecl. *alpha,* first letter of the Greek alphabet; = *beginning* or *first* Rv 1:8, 11 v.l.; 21:6; 22:13.*

Ἀλφαῖος, ου, ὁ *Alphaeus*—**1.** The father of Levi the tax-collector Mk 2:14; Lk 5:27 v.l.—**2.** The father of James, one of the twelve Mt 10:3; Mk 3:18; Lk 6:15; Ac 1:13.*

ἄλων, ωνος, ἡ *threshing floor* and the threshed grain upon it Mt 3:12; Lk 3:17.*

ἀλώπηξ, εκος, ἡ *fox* lit. Mt 8:20; Lk 9:58; fig. 13:32.*

ἅλωσις, εως, ἡ *capture, catching* 2 Pt 2:12.*

ἅμα adv. *at the same time, together* Ac 24:26; Ro 3:12; Phlm 22. Prep. w. dat. *together with* Mt 13:29; 1 Th 5:10, ἅ. πρωῒ *early in the morning* Mt 20:1.

ἀμαθής, ές *ignorant* 2 Pt 3:16.*

ἀμαράντινος, η, ον *unfading,* perhaps *made of amaranth* 1 Pt 5:4.*

ἀμάραντος, ον *fadeless* 1 Pt 1:4.*

ἁμαρτάνω *do wrong, sin* 1 Cor 7:28: *against God* Lk 15:18; Christ and the brethren 1 Cor 8:12; oneself 6:18; the law Ac 25:8. ἁ. ἁμαρτίαν *commit a sin* 1 J 5:16.

ἁμάρτημα, τος, τό *sin* (lit. 'the result of sinning') Mk 3:28f.

ἁμαρτία, ας, ἡ *sin:* a sinful *deed* Mt 26:28; Ac 3:19; 1 Cor 15:17; 1 Th 2:16; Js 2:9; *sinfulness* J 1:29; 9:41; 1 J 1:7; at times viewed by Paul as an invading power Ro 5:12; 6:12–14, 23. σῶμα τῆς ἁ. a *body ruled by sin* 6:6. προσφορὰ περὶ ἁ. = *sin offering* Hb 10:18. [*hamartiology,* theological study of sin]

ἀμάρτυρος, ον *without witness* Ac 14:17.*

ἁμάρτω 2 aor. subj. act. of ἁμαρτάνω.

ἁμαρτωλός, όν *sinful* Mk 8:38; Ro 7:13. ὁ ἁ. *sinner:* of one not free from sin Hb 7:26; of one not careful in the observance of ceremonial duties *unobservant* or *irreligious person* Mt 9:10f; Lk 15:1f; of one especially sinful 7:37, 39; = *unbelievers* Lk 6:32–34 (cf. Mt 5:47); Gal 2:15.

Ἀμασίας, ου, ὁ (Heb.) *Amaziah* Mt 1:8 v.l.; Lk 3:23ff v.l.*

ἄμαχος, ον *peaceable, not quarrelsome* 1 Ti 3:3; Tit 3:2.*

ἀμάω *reap, mow* Js 5:4.*

ἀμέθυστος, ου, ἡ or ὁ *amethyst,* a precious stone of violet color Rv 21:20.*

ἀμείνων, ον comp. of ἀγαθός, q.v.

ἀμελέω *neglect* w. gen. 1 Ti 4:14; Hb 2:3; w. inf. 2 Pt 1:12 v.l. *Disregard* w. gen. Hb 8:9. *Pay no attention* Mt 22:5.*

ἄμεμπτος, ον *blameless, faultless* Lk 1:6; Phil 2:15; 3:6; 1 Th 3:13; Hb 8:7.*

ἀμέμπτως adv. *blamelessly* 1 Th 2:10; 5:23.*

10   ἀμέριμνος–ἄν

ἀμέριμνος, ον *free from care* 1 Cor 7:32; ἀ. ποιεῖν τινα *keep someone out of trouble* Mt 28:14.*

ἀμετάθετος, ον *unchangeable* Hb 6:18; τὸ ἀ. *unchangeableness* 6:17.* [-μετάθετος, *metathesis*]

ἀμετακίνητος, ον *immovable* 1 Cor 15:58.* [-κίνητος, *kinetic*]

ἀμεταμέλητος, ον *not to be regretted* 2 Cor 7:10; *not to be taken back, irrevocable* Ro 11:29.*

ἀμετανόητος, ον *unrepentant* Ro 2:5.*

ἄμετρος, ον *immeasurable*; εἰς τὰ ἄ. *beyond limits* 2 Cor 10:13, 15.*

ἀμήν (Heb.) asseverative particle *truly,* only with words of Jesus Mt 5:18; Mk 3:28; Lk 4:24; J 1:51. Liturgical formula *amen* = *so let it be* 1 Cor 14:16; 2 Cor 1:20; Gal 6:18; 1 Pt 4:11. ὁ ἀ. of Jesus, explained by the following clause Rv 3:14.

ἀμήτωρ, ορος *without a mother* Hb 7:3.*

ἀμίαντος, ον *undefiled, pure, unsullied* Hb 7:26; 13:4; Js 1:27; 1 Pt 1:4.*

Ἀμιναδάβ, ὁ (Heb.) indecl. *Amminadab* Mt 1:4; Lk 3:33.*

ἄμμον, ου, τό *sand* Ro 4:18 v.l.*

ἄμμος, ου, ἡ *sand* Mt 7:26; Ro 9:27; Hb 11:12; Rv 12:18; 20:8.*

ἀμνός, οῦ, ὁ *lamb* used only in reference to Jesus J 1:29, 36; Ac 8:32; 1 Pt 1:19.*

ἀμοιβή, ῆς, ἡ *(adequate) return, recompense* 1 Ti 5:4.*

ἄμορφος, ον *misshapen, ugly* 1 Cor 12:2 v.l.* [*amorphous*]

ἄμπελος, ου, ἡ *vine, grapevine* Mk 14:25; fig. J 15:1, 4, 5.

ἀμπελουργός, οῦ, ὁ *vinedresser, gardener* Lk 13:7.*

ἀμπελών, ῶνος, ὁ *vineyard* Mk 12:1f; 1 Cor 9:7; perh. *orchard* Lk 13:6.

Ἀμπλιᾶτος, ου, ὁ (v.l. Ἀμπλιᾶς) *Ampliatus,* common as a slave name Ro 16:8.*

ἀμύνομαι *retaliate;* another possibility is *help, come to the aid of* Ac 7:24.*

ἀμφιάζω variant form of ἀμφιέζω.

ἀμφιβάλλω *cast a net* Mk 1:16.*

ἀμφίβληστρον, ου, τό *a circular casting net* Mt 4:18; Mk 1:16 v.l.*

ἀμφιέζω *dress, clothe* Lk 12:28.*

ἀμφιέννυμι *dress, clothe* Mt 6:30; 11:8; Lk 7:25.*

Ἀμφίπολις, εως, ἡ *Amphipolis,* capital city of southeast Macedonia Ac 17:1.*

ἄμφοδον, ου, τό *street* (lit. 'quarter of a city') Mk 11:4; Ac 19:28 v.l.*

ἀμφότεροι, αι, α *both* Lk 6:39; Eph 2:16. *All* (even when more than two are involved) Ac 19:16; 23:8.

ἀμώμητος, ον *blameless, unblemished* 2 Pt 3:14; Phil 2:15 v.l.*

ἄμωμον, ου, τό *amomum* an Indian spice plant Rv 18:13.*

ἄμωμος, ον *unblemished* Hb 9:14; 1 Pt 1:19; *blameless* Eph 1:4; Phil 2:15; Rv 14:5.

Ἀμών, ὁ indecl. (Heb.) *Amon* Mt 1:10 v.l.*

Ἀμώς, ὁ indecl. (Heb.) *Amos*—1. Lk 3:25.—2. Mt 1:10; Lk 3:23ff v.l.*

ἄν an adverb incapable of translation by a single English word, denoting that the action of the verb is dependent on some circumstance or condition; its effect upon the meaning of its clause varies with the construction.—1. With the indicative—a. impf. or aor. to indicate repeated action in past time, in relative and temporal clauses: ὅσοι ἂν ἥψαντο αὐτοῦ, ἐσῴζοντο *whoever touched him was cured* Mk 6:56; cf. Ac 2:45; 4:35.—b. In the apodosis of contrary-to-fact (assumed as unreal) conditions, with impf. tense for present time, aor. or plupf. for past time: εἰ ἦν προφήτης, ἐγίνωσκεν ἄν *if he were a prophet, would (now) know* Lk 7:39. εἰ ἔγνωσαν, οὐκ ἂν ἐσταύρωσαν *if they had known him, they would not have crucified him* 1 Cor 2:8. Plupf. 1 J 2:19. ἐλθών Lk 19:23 and ἐπεί Hb 10:2 are equivalents of a protasis.—2. With the subjunctive—a. in the protasis of conditional relative clauses of the future more vivid type ὃς ἂν ἐσθίῃ . . . ἔνοχος ἔσται *whoever eats will be guilty* 1 Cor 11:27, or the present general type ἃ ἂν ἐκεῖνος ποιῇ, ταῦτα καὶ ὁ υἱὸς ὁμοίως ποιεῖ *whatever he does, the Son does also* J 5:19. Similarly with temporal clauses ὅταν = ὅτε + ἄν *whenever* Mt 15:2. ἡνίκα ἂν *as often as* 2 Cor 3:15.

ὡς ἄν as soon as 1 Cor 11:34. ἔως ἄν until Mt 10:11.—b. in purpose clauses with ὅπως, with no appreciable change in meaning Lk 2:35.—3. With the optative: rare and literary in the N.T. In a main clause εὐξαίμην ἄν I might wish Ac 26:29 (potential optative); in a rhetorical question πῶς γὰρ ἄν δυναίμην how could I? Ac 8:31; in an indirect question τί ἄν ποιήσαιεν τῷ Ἰησοῦ what they might do with Jesus Lk 6:11.—4. ἄν for ἐάν = if J 5:19a; 13:20; 20:23.

ἀνά prep. with acc., originally 'up, along' etc.—1. Alone, in distributive sense ἀνὰ δύο two by two Lk 10:1; ἀνὰ πεντήκοντα by fifties 9:14; ἀνὰ δηνάριον a denarius each Mt 20:9f. Fixed as an adverb ἀνὰ εἷς ἔκαστος each one singly Rv 21:21.—2. In combinations ἀνὰ μέσον w. gen. among Mt 13:25; ἀ. μ. τῶν ὁρίων into the (midst of the) district Mk 7:31; between 1 Cor 6:5, w. omission of the second member; in the center of Rv 7:17. ἀνὰ μέρος in turn 1 Cor 14:27. [ana, a pharmaceutical term, meaning 'an equal quantity of each,' and prefix in numerous words of Greek derivation]

ἀνάβα 2 aor. act. impv. 2 sing. of ἀναβαίνω.

ἀναβαθμός, οῦ, ὁ step; pl. flight of stairs (from the temple to the tower Antonia) Ac 21:35, 40.*

ἀναβαίνω go up Ac 1:13, esp. to Jerusalem or the temple Mt 20:17f; J 7:14. Climb up Lk 19:4. Come up Mt 3:16; Mk 4:7; Ac 21:31. Ascend Ac 2:34; 10:4. ἀ. ἐπὶ τὴν καρδίαν enter the mind 1 Cor 2:9. ἀ. ἐν τῇ καρδίᾳ arise in the heart Lk 24:38. [anabasis]

ἀναβάλλω defer, postpone. ἀ. αὐτούς he put them off, he adjourned their trial legal term Ac 24:22.*

ἀναβέβηκα perf. act. of ἀναβαίνω.

ἀναβήσομαι fut. mid. (dep.) of ἀναβαίνω.

ἀναβιβάζω bring up, pull up Mt 13:48.*

ἀναβλέπω—1. look up Mt 14:19; Mk 8:24; Ac 22:13.—2. regain one's sight Mt 11:5; Mk 10:51; Ac 9:12, 17f. Receive sight, become able to see J 9:11, 15, 18.

ἀνάβλεψις, εως, ἡ recovery of sight Lk 4:18.*

ἀναβοάω cry out Mt 27:46; Mk 15:8 v.l.

ἀναβολή, ῆς, ἡ delay, postponement Ac 25:17.* [anabolism, constructive metabolism]

ἀνάγαιον, ου, τό a room upstairs Mk 14:15; Lk 22:12.*

ἀναγγέλλω report Ac 14:27; 2 Cor 7:7. Make known Ac 19:18; proclaim J 16:13; 1 Pt 1:12; preach Ac 20:20.

ἀναγεννάω cause to be born again 1 Pt 1:3, 23.*

ἀναγινώσκω read Mk 12:26; J 19:20; Ac 8:28, 30 (the eunuch was reading aloud to himself); read (aloud) in public Lk 4:16; Col 4:16; Rv 1:3.

ἀναγκάζω force, compel Ac 26:11; Gal 2:3, 14; invite, urge strongly Mt 14:22.

ἀναγκαῖος, α, ον—1. necessary, urgent 1 Cor 12:22 Tit 3:14.—2. intimate, close Ac 10:24.

ἀναγκαστῶς adv. by compulsion 1 Pt 5:2.*

ἀνάγκη, ης, ἡ—1. necessity Hb 7:12; compulsion, pressure 2 Cor 9:7. ἀ. ἔχω I must Lk 14:18. ἀ. with ἐστίν understood = it is necessary, one must Hb 9:16, 23.—2. distress, calamity Lk 21:23; 1 Cor 7:26.

ἀναγνούς, ἀναγνῶναι, ἀναγνωσθῆναι 2 aor. act. ptc. and inf. and 1 aor. pass. inf. of ἀναγινώσκω.

ἀναγνωρίζω make known again Ac 7:13.*

ἀνάγνωσις, εως, ἡ public reading in synagogue Ac 13:15; 2 Cor 3:14 or church 1 Ti 4:13.*

ἀνάγω—1. lead or bring up Mt 4:1; Ac 9:39; Ro 10:7. Bring before Ac 12:4. ἀ. θυσίαν bring an offering 7:41.—2. mid. or pass. put out to sea, set sail Ac 13:13; 18:21. [anagogic]

ἀναδείκνυμι show clearly Ac 1:24; appoint Lk 10:1.*

ἀνάδειξις, εως, ἡ commissioning, installation Lk 1:80.*

ἀναδέχομαι accept, receive Hb 11:17; welcome Ac 28:7.*

ἀναδίδωμι hand over, deliver Ac 23:33.*

ἀναζάω come to life again Ro 14:9 v.l.; fig. Lk 15:24, 32 v.l. *Spring into life* Ro 7:9.*

ἀναζητέω *look for, search for* Lk 2:44f; Ac 11:25.*

ἀναζώννυμι *bind up, gird up* the long robes to facilitate work or walking, fig. 1 Pt 1:13.*

ἀναζωπυρέω *rekindle* 2 Ti 1:6.*

ἀναζωσάμενος 1 aor. mid. ptc. of ἀναζώννυμι.

ἀναθάλλω *grow again* or *cause to grow again, revive* Phil 4:10.*

ἀνάθεμα, ατος, τό—1. *something dedicated to the deity, a votive gift* Lk 21:5 v.l.—2. What is dedicated to a divinity may be either blessed or cursed (cf. Joshua 6:17; 7:12 LXX as an example of the latter sense, which came to predominate). So in the N.T. *cursed, a curse, anathema* Ac 23:14; Ro 9:3; 1 Cor 12:3; 16:22; Gal 1:8f.*

ἀναθεματίζω *bind with an oath* or *under a curse* Ac 23:12, 14, 21; intransitive *invoke a curse* Mk 14:71.*

ἀναθεωρέω *look at* or *examine carefully* Ac 17:23; *consider* Hb 13:7.*

ἀνάθημα, ατος, τό *a votive gift* Lk 21:5.*

ἀναίδεια, ας, ἡ *persistence*, lit. 'shamelessness' Lk 11:8.*

ἀναίρεσις, εως, ἡ *murder, killing* Ac 8:1; 13:28 v.l.; 22:20 v.l.*

ἀναιρέω—1. *take away, abolish* Hb 10:9. *Do away with, kill, murder* Mt 2:16; Ac 16:27; 2 Th 2:8. Pass. *be condemned to death* Ac 26:10.—2. mid. *take up (for oneself), adopt* Ac 7:21.

ἀναίτιος, ον *innocent* Mt 12:5, 7; Ac 16:37 v.l.*

ἀνακαθίζω *sit up* Lk 7:15; Ac 9:40.*

ἀνακαινίζω *renew, restore* Hb 6:6.*

ἀνακαινόω *renew* 2 Cor 4:16; Col 3:10.*

ἀνακαίνωσις, εως, ἡ *renewal* Ro 12:2; Tit 3:5.*

ἀνακαλύπτω *uncover, unveil* 2 Cor 3:14, 18 (see Exodus 34:34).*

ἀνακάμπτω *return* Mt 2:12; Lk 10:6; Ac 18:21; Hb 11:15. *Turn back again* 2 Pt 2:21 v.l.*

ἀνάκειμαι *lie down, recline* Mk 5:40 v.l.; *at table as a dinner guest* Mt 9:10; J 12:2. ὁ ἀνακείμενος *guest* Lk 22:27.

ἀνακεφαλαιόω *sum up, recapitulate* Ro 13:9; *gather up, unite* Eph 1:10.* [Cf. κεφάλαιον.]

ἀνακλίνω act. *cause to lie down* or *recline* Lk 12:37; *put to bed* 2:7. Mid. and pass. *lie down, recline* at a meal Mt 8:11; Mk 6:39.

ἀνακόπτω *hinder, restrain* Gal 5:7 v.l.*

ἀνακράζω *cry out* Mk 1:23; 6:49; Lk 4:33; 8:28; 23:18.*

ἀνακραυγάζω *cry out* Lk 4:35 v.l.*

ἀνακρίνω—1. *question, examine* Ac 11:12 v.l.; 17:11; 1 Cor 10:25, 27.—2. *judge, call to account* 1 Cor 2:14f; 14:24.—3. legal term *examine, investigate* Ac 12:19; 28:18; *conduct an examination* Lk 23:14.

ἀνάκρισις, εως, ἡ *preliminary investigation, hearing* Act 25:26.*

ἀνακυλίω *roll away* Mk 16:4 v.l.*

ἀνακύπτω *stand erect, straighten oneself* lit. Lk 13:11; J 8:7, 10; fig. Lk 21:28.*

ἀναλαμβάνω *take up* Ac 1:11; *take* Eph 6:13, 16; *take along* Ac 7:43; 2 Ti 4:11; *take on board* Ac 20:13f.

ἀναλημφθείς 1 aor. pass. ptc. of ἀναλαμβάνω.

ἀνάλημψις, εως, ἡ *ascension*; perhaps *death, departure*; lit. *taking up* Lk 9:51.*

ἀναλίσκω or ἀναλόω *consume* Lk 9:54; Gal 5:15; 2 Th 2:8 v.l.*

ἀνάλλομαι *jump up* Ac 14:10 v.l.*

ἀναλογία, ας, ἡ *right relationship, proportion* κατὰ τὴν ἀ. *in agreement with* or *in proportion to* Ro 12:6.* [analogy]

ἀναλογίζομαι *consider, think of* Hb 12:3.*

ἀναλοῖ aor. opt. 3 sing. of ἀναλίσκω.

ἄναλος, ον *without salt, tasteless* Mk 9:50.*

ἀναλόω see ἀναλίσκω.

ἀνάλυσις, εως, ἡ *departure* i.e. *death*, lit. 'dissolution' 2 Ti 4:6.* [analysis] ἀναλύω *loose, untie* Ac 16:26 v.l. *Return, depart* Lk 12:36; *depart = die* Phil 1:23.*

ἀναλῶσαι, ἀναλώσει 1 aor. act. inf. and fut. act. ind. 3 sing. of ἀναλίσκω (ἀναλόω).

ἀναμάρτητος, ον *without sin* J 8:7.*

ἀναμένω *wait for* 1 Th 1:10.*

ἀναμιμνῄσκω *remind* τινά τι *someone of something* 1 Cor 4:17; cf. 2 Ti 1:6. Mid. and pass. *remember* Mk 11:21; 14:72; Ac 16:35 v.l.; 2 Cor 7:15; Hb 10:32.*

ἀνάμνησις, εως, ἡ *reminder* Hb 10:3; *remembrance, memory* Lk 22:19; 1 Cor 11:24f.* [*anamnesis*]

ἀναμνήσω fut. ind. 1 sing. of ἀναμιμνῄσκω.

ἀνανεόομαι *be renewed* Eph 4:23.*

ἀνανήφω *come to one's senses*, lit. 'become sober again' 2 Ti 2:26.*

Ἀνανίας, ου, ὁ (Heb. Hananiah)—1. A member of the Jerusalem church, husband of Sapphira Ac 5:1.—2. A Christian of Damascus who helped Paul 9:10; 22:12.—3. A Jewish high priest (c. 47–59 A.D.) 23:2; 24:1.

ἀναντίρρητος, ον *not to be contradicted, undeniable* Ac 19:36.*

ἀναντιρρήτως adv. *without raising any objection* Ac 10:29.*

ἀνάξιος, ον *incompetent, unfit*, lit. 'unworthy' 1 Cor 6:2.* [Cf. axiom.]

ἀναξίως adv. *in a careless or unworthy manner* 1 Cor 11:27, 29 v.l.*

ἀναπαήσομαι 2 fut. pass. ind. of ἀναπαύω.

ἀνάπαυσις, εως, ἡ—1. *stopping, ceasing* ἀνάπαυσιν οὐκ ἔχουσιν λέγοντες *they say without ceasing* Rv 4:8; cf. 14:11. *Rest* Mt 11:29.—2. *a resting-place* Mt 12:43; Lk 11:24.*

ἀναπαύω act. *cause to rest, give someone rest, refresh* w. acc. Mt 11:28; 1 Cor 16:18; Phlm 20. Pass. *be set at rest, be refreshed* 2 Cor 7:13; Phlm 7. Mid. *rest, take one's rest or one's ease, relax* Mt 26:45; Mk 6:31; Lk 12:19; *remain quiet* Rv 6:11; *rest upon* 1 Pt 4:14.

ἀναπείθω *induce, incite*, lit. 'persuade wrongly' Ac 18:13.*

ἀνάπειρος, ον Hellenistic Gk. for ἀνάπηρος, q.v.

ἀναπέμπω *send (up) to one in a higher position* Lk 23:7; Ac 25:21; 27:1 v.l. *Send back* Lk 23:11, 15; Phlm 12.*

ἀνάπεσε, ἀναπεσεῖν 2 aor. act. impv. and inf. of ἀναπίπτω.

ἀναπηδάω *jump up, stand up* Mk 10:50.*

ἀνάπηρος, ον *crippled*, as noun *a cripple* Lk 14:13, 21.*

ἀναπίπτω *lie down, recline* esp. at a meal, *take one's place to eat* Mk 6:40; Lk 11:37; J 13:12. *Lean (back)* J 13:25.

ἀναπληρόω *make complete, fill up the measure of* 1 Th 2:16. *Make up for* 1 Cor 16:17; Phil 2:30. *Take or fill a place* 1 Cor 14:16. *Fulfill, carry out* Mt 13:14; Gal 6:2.*

ἀναπολόγητος, ον *without excuse* Ro 1:20; 2:1.*

ἀναπράσσω *demand, exact a payment* Lk 19:23 v.l.*

ἀναπτύσσω *unroll of a book in scroll form* Lk 4:17.*

ἀνάπτω *kindle* Lk 12:49; Js 3:5; Ac 28:2 v.l.*

ἀναρίθμητος, ον *innumerable* Hb 11:12.* [-αρίθμητος, *arithmetic*]

ἀνασείω *stir up, incite* Mk 15:11; Lk 23:5.*

ἀνασκευάζω *upset, unsettle* Ac 15:24.*

ἀνασπάω *pull up* Ac 11:10; *pull out* Lk 14:5.*

ἀνάστα, ἀναστάς 2 aor. act. impv. and ptc. of ἀνίστημι.

ἀνάστασις, εως, ἡ *rise, rising* Lk 2:34. *Resurrection* of the dead Mt 22:31; Lk 20:35; J 11:24f; Ac 1:22; Ro 6:5; 1 Cor 15:12f; Rv 20:5f. [*Anastasia*]

ἀναστατόω *disturb, upset, trouble* Ac 17:6; 21:38; Gal 5:12.*

ἀνασταυρόω *crucify again* Hb 6:6.*

ἀναστενάζω *sigh deeply* Mk 8:12.*

ἀνάστηθι, ἀναστῆναι, ἀναστήσας, ἀναστήσω 2 aor. act. impv., 2 aor. act. inf., 1 aor. act. ptc., and fut. act. ind. 1 sing. of ἀνίστημι.

ἀναστρέφω—1. *overturn, upset* J 2:15 v.l.—2. *return, come back* Ac 5:22; 15:16.—3. mid. and pass. *turn here and there, stay, live* in a place Mt 17:22 v.l. Thus *conduct* or *behave oneself, live, act,* always with moral or religious coloring 2 Cor 1:12; 1 Ti 3:15; Hb 13:18; 2 Pt 2:18.

ἀναστροφή, ῆς, ἡ *way of life, conduct, behavior* Gal 1:13; Js 3:13; 1 Pt 2:12. [*anastrophe*]

ἀναστῶ 2 aor. act. subj. 1 sing. of ἀνίστημι.

ἀνασῴζω *save* Hb 10:14 v.l.*

ἀνατάσσομαι *draw up, compile,* lit. 'arrange in proper order' Lk 1:1.*

ἀνατεθραμμένος pf. pass. ptc. of ἀνατρέφω.

ἀνατείλας 1 aor. act. ptc. of ἀνατέλλω.

ἀνατέλλω—1. *cause to rise* Mt 5:45.— **2.** intrans. *spring up, rise* Mt 13:6; Mk 16:2; 2 Pt 1:19; *dawn* Mt 4:16. *Come up* Lk 12:54. *Be descended* Hb 7:14. [Cf. ἀνατολή.]

ἀνατέταλκα perf. act. ind. of ἀνατέλλω.

ἀνατίθημι mid. *lay a matter before* someone for consideration Ac 25:14; Gal 2:2.*

ἀνατολή, ῆς, ἡ—1. *rising* of a star: ἐν τῇ ἀνατολῇ *in its rising, when it rose* Mt 2:2.—**2.** *rising* of the sun, *East, Orient* Mt 2:1; 8:11; Rv 7:2; 21:13. Fig. ἀ. ἐξ ὕψους *the dawn from heaven,* i.e. the Messiah Lk 1:78. [*Anatolia.* Cf. ἀνατέλλω.]

ἀνατολικός, ή, όν *eastern* Ac 19:1 v.l.*

ἀνατρέπω *overturn* lit. J 2:15; fig. *upset, ruin* 2 Ti 2:18; Tit 1:11.*

ἀνατρέφω *bring up, care for, rear* Lk 4:16 v.l.; Ac 7:20, 21; 22:3.*

ἀναφαίνω *cause to appear;* ἀναφάναντες τὴν Κύπρον *we came within sight of Cyprus,* i.e. we sighted it Ac 21:3. Pass. *appear* Lk 19:11.*

ἀναφάναντες 1 aor. act. ptc. of ἀναφαίνω.

ἀναφέρω—1. *take* or *lead up* Mk 9:2.— **2.** *offer up* (as) a sacrifice Hb 7:27; 1 Pt 2:5.—**3.** *bear, assume* (as of one who incurs danger) sins Hb 9:28 (cf. Is 53:12). [*anaphora*]

ἀναφωνέω *cry out* Lk 1:42.*

ἀναχθείς 1 aor. pass. ptc. of ἀνάγω.

ἀνάχυσις, εως, ἡ *stream, flood,* lit. 'pouring out' 1 Pt 4:4.*

ἀναχωρέω *go away* Mt 2:13. *Withdraw, retire, take refuge* 2:14; J 6:15; Ac 23:19. *Return* Mt 2:12. [*anchorite*]

ἀνάψας 1 aor. act. ptc. of ἀνάπτω.

ἀνάψυξις, εως, ἡ *refreshing, relief, rest* Ac 3:20.*

ἀναψύχω *revive, refresh* 2 Ti 1:16; intr. *be refreshed* Ro 15:32 v.l.*

ἀνδραποδιστής, οῦ, ὁ *kidnapper, slavedealer* 1 Ti 1:10.*

Ἀνδρέας, ου, ὁ *Andrew,* one of the twelve Mk 3:18; 13:3; J 1:40, 44.

ἀνδρίζομαι *act in a valiant* or *courageous way* 1 Cor 16:13.*

Ἀνδρόνικος, ου, ὁ *Andronicus* Ro 16:7.*

ἀνδροφόνος, ου, ὁ *murderer* 1 Ti 1:9.*

ἀνεβαλόμην 2 aor. mid. ind. 1 sing. of ἀναβάλλω.

ἀνέβην 2 aor. act. ind. of ἀναβαίνω.

ἀνεγκλησία, ας, ἡ *blamelessness* ἀ. τοῦ θεοῦ *blamelessness before God* Phil 3:14 v.l.*

ἀνέγκλητος, ον *blameless, irreproachable* 1 Cor 1:8; Col 1:22; 1 Ti 3:10; Tit 1:6f.*

ἀνέγνων 2 aor. act. ind. of ἀναγινώσκω.

ἀνέδειξα 1 aor. act. ind. of ἀναδείκνυμι.

ἀνεζωσάμην 1 aor. mid. ind. of ἀναζώννυμι.

ἀνέθαλον 2 aor. act. ind. of ἀναθάλλω.

ἀνεθέμην 2 aor. mid. ind. of ἀνατίθημι.

ἀνέθην 1 aor. pass. ind. of ἀνίημι.

ἀνεθρεψάμην 1 aor. mid. ind. of ἀνατρέφω.

ἀνεῖλα, ἀνεῖλον 2 aor. act. ind. of ἀναιρέω.

ἀνείς 2 aor. act. ptc. of ἀνίημι.

ἀνειχόμην impf. mid. of ἀνέχω.

ἀνεκδιήγητος, ον *indescribable* 2 Cor 9:15.*

ἀνεκλάλητος, ον *inexpressible* 1 Pt 1:8.*

ἀνέκλειπτος, ον *unfailing, inexhaustible* Lk 12:33.*

ἀνεκρίθην 1 aor. pass. ind. 1 sing. of ἀνακρίνω.

ἀνεκτός, όν bearable, tolerable; comp. ἀνεκτότερος more tolerable Mt 10:15; 11:22, 24; Lk 10:12, 14.*

ἀνέλαβον 2 aor. act. ind. 1 sing. of ἀναλαμβάνω.

ἀνελεήμων, ον unmerciful Ro 1:31; Tit 1:9 v.l.*

ἀνελεῖν, ἀνέλω, ἀνέλοι 2 aor. act. inf., subj. 1 sing., and opt. 3 sing. of ἀναιρέω.

ἀνέλεος, ον merciless Js 2:13.*

ἀνελήμφθην 1 aor. pass. ind. 1 sing. of ἀναλαμβάνω.

ἀνεμίζω pass. be moved by the wind Js 1:6.*

ἀνεμνήσθην 1 aor. pass. ind. 1 sing. of ἀναμιμνῄσκω.

ἄνεμος, ου, ὁ wind Mt 11:7; 14:30; Ac 27:14; the four directions or cardinal points Mk 13:27; fig. Eph 4:14. [anemometer, ἄνεμος + μετρέω]

ἀνένδεκτος, ον impossible Lk 17:1.*

ἀνενέγκαι, ἀνενεγκεῖν 1 aor. act. inf. and 2 aor. act. inf. of ἀναφέρω.

ἀνέντες 2 aor. act. ptc. of ἀνίημι.

ἀνεξεραύνητος, ον unfathomable, inscrutable Ro 11:33.*

ἀνεξίκακος, ον bearing evil without resentment, patient 2 Ti 2:24.*

ἀνεξιχνίαστος, ον inscrutable, mysterious Ro 11:33. Fathomless, inexhaustible Eph 3:8; lit. 'not to be tracked out.'*

ἀνέξομαι fut. mid. ind. of ἀνέχομαι.

ἀνεπαίσχυντος, ον who does not need to be ashamed 2 Ti 2:15.*

ἀνέπεσα, ἀνέπεσον 1 aor. act. ind. and 2 aor. act. ind. of ἀναπίπτω.

ἀνεπίλημπτος, ον beyond reproach 1 Ti 3:2; 5:7; 6:14.*

ἀνέπτυξα 1 aor. act. ind. of ἀναπτύσσω.

ἀνέρχομαι go up J 6:3; Gal 1:17, 18.*

ἀνέσεισα 1 aor. act. ind. of ἀνασείω.

ἄνεσις, εως, ἡ rest, relaxation 2 Cor 2:13; 7:5; 8:13; 2 Th 1:7. Freedom, relief Ac 24:23.*

ἀνέστην 2 aor. act. ind. of ἀνίστημι.

ἀνεσχόμην 2 aor. mid. ind. of ἀνέχομαι.

ἀνέστησα 1 aor. act. ind. of ἀνίστημι.

ἀνετάζω examine someone, give someone a hearing Ac 22:24, 29.*

ἀνέτειλα 1 aor. act. ind. of ἀνατέλλω.

ἄνευ prep. w. gen. without Mk 13:2 v.l.; 1 Pt 3:1; 4:9. Without the knowledge and consent of Mt 10:29.*

ἀνεύθετος, ον unfavorably situated, poor Ac 27:12.*

ἀνευρίσκω find after searching Lk 2:16; Ac 21:4.*

ἀνέχομαι put up with, bear with, endure Mt 17:17; 1 Cor 4:12; 2 Cor 11:1. Hear or listen to willingly Hb 13:22. Accept a complaint Ac 18:14.

ἀνεψιός, οῦ, ὁ cousin Col 4:10.* [Cf. Lat. nepos, nephew.]

ἀνέῳγα, ἀνέῳγμαι, ἀνέῳξα, ἀνεῴχθην 2 pf. act. ind., 2 pf. pass. ind., 1 aor. act. ind., and 1 aor. pass. ind. of ἀνοίγω.

ἀνήγαγον 2 aor. act. ind. of ἀνάγω.

ἀνήγγειλα, ἀνηγγέλην 1 aor. act. ind. and 2 aor. pass. ind. of ἀναγγέλλω.

ἄνηθον, ου, τό dill Mt 23:23; Lk 11:42 v.l.*

ἀνῆκα 1 aor. act. ind. of ἀνίημι.

ἀνήκω be proper or fitting impersonal Eph 5:4; Col 3:18. τὸ ἀνῆκον what is proper, one's duty Phlm 8.*

ἀνῆλθον 2 aor. act. ind. of ἀνέρχομαι.

ἀνηλώθην, ἀνήλωσα 1 aor. pass. ind. and 1 aor. act. ind. 1 sing. of ἀναλίσκω.

ἀνήμερος, ον savage, brutal, lit. 'untamed' 2 Ti 3:3.*

ἀνήνεγκον 2 aor. act. ind. of ἀναφέρω.

ἀνήρ, ἀνδρός, ὁ man, normally an adult (1 Cor 13:11) male (Ac 8:3, 12). Specialized senses: husband Mk 10:2, 12; bridegroom Rv 21:2; in address, pl. gentlemen Ac 27:10, 21, 25; ἄνδρες ἀδελφοί brethren 15:7, 13. Pleonastic ἀνὴρ ἁμαρτωλός = simply a sinner Lk 5:8. Rarely person = ἄνθρωπος, see Lk 11:31; Js 1:12; cf. Ac 17:34. [Cf. Andrew; androgynous, ἀνὴρ + γυνή.]

ἀνῃρέθην 1 aor. pass. ind. of ἀναιρέω.

ἀνήφθην 1 aor. pass. ind. of ἀνάπτω.

ἀνήχθην 1 aor. pass. ind. of ἀνάγω.

ἀνθέξομαι fut. mid. ind. of ἀντέχομαι.

ἀνθέστηκα pf. act. ind. of ἀνθίστημι.

ἀνθίστημι set oneself against, oppose, resist, withstand Lk 21:15; Ro 13:2; Gal 2:11; Js 4:7; stand one's ground Eph 6:13. [antithetic, antithesis]

ἀνθομολογέομαι praise, thank Lk 2:38.*

ἄνθος, ους, τό flower; ἀ. χόρτου wild flower Js 1:10, cf. 11; 1 Pt 1:24.* [anthology, ἄνθος + λέγειν]

ἀνθρακιά, ᾶς, ἡ a charcoal fire J 18:18; 21:9.* [anthracite]

ἄνθραξ, ακος, ὁ charcoal; ἄνθρακες πυρός burning embers Ro 12:20 (cf. Proverbs 25:22).*

ἀνθρωπάρεσκος, ον as subst., one who tries to please people by sacrificing principle Eph 6:6; Col 3:22.*

ἀνθρώπινος, η, ον human Ac 17:25; 1 Cor 2:13; Js 3:7. A temptation common to people, i.e. bearable 1 Cor 10:13. Speak in human terms Ro 6:19. Commonly accepted 1 Ti 1:15 v.l.; 3:1 v.l.

ἀνθρωποκτόνος, ου, ὁ murderer J 8:44; 1 J 3:15.*

ἄνθρωπος, ου, ὁ human being, person; pl. people Mt 5:13, 16; Mk 10:27; J 10:33 (a mere mortal); 1 Cor 1:25; 2 Cor 3:2; Phil 2:7; humanity in general Mk 2:27. In address, w. a connotation of familiarity, friend Lk 5:20; of impatience 22:58, 60; of contempt, fellow Mk 14:71; J 5:12. Indefinite = τίς someone J 4:29; 1 Cor 4:1; w. negative nobody J 5:7; 7:46. Anyone Ro 14:20. Restricted to adult males man, husband Mt 19:5, 10; 1 Cor 7:1. Son Mt 10:35. May be omitted in translating such combinations as ἄ. φάγος = simply a glutton Lk 7:34; cf. Mt 13:52; 18:23; Ac 21:39. κατὰ ἄ. in a human way 1 Cor 9:8; (formulated) merely to please people Gal 1:11. [anthropology]

ἀνθυπατεύω be proconsul Ac 18:12 v.l.*

ἀνθύπατος, ου, ὁ proconsul governor of a senatorial province in the Roman Empire Ac 13:7; 18:12.

ἀνιείς, ἀνιέντες pres. act. ptc. masc. sing. and pl. of ἀνίημι.

ἀνίημι—1. unfasten, untie Ac 16:26; 27:40.—2. abandon, desert Hb 13:5.—3. give up, stop Eph 6:9.*

ἀνίλεως, neut. ων, gen. ω merciless Js 2:13 v.l. for ἀνέλεος.*

ἄνιπτος, ον unwashed, i.e. ceremonially unclean Mt 15:20; Mk 7:2, 5 v.l.*

ἀνίστημι—1. trans. raise, erect, raise up Ac 9:41. Of the dead raise (up), bring to life J 6:39f; Ac 2:24; 13:34. In the sense cause to appear or to be born Mt 22:24; Ac 3:22.—2. intr. (2 aor. and all mid. forms) rise, stand up, get up Mt 26:62; Lk 11:7f; rise from the dead Mk 9:10, 31; 1 Th 4:16. Short for stand up and go Mk 14:60; Lk 4:38. In the sense appear, come Mt 12:41; Hb 7:11, 15. Weakened to set out, get ready Mk 2:14; Lk 1:39; Ac 8:26; 10:20. [Cf. anastatic, printed from plates in relief.]

Ἅννα, ας, ἡ Anna Lk 2:36.*

Ἅννας, α, ὁ Annas, high priest 6–15 A.D., father-in-law of Caiaphas Lk 3:2; J 18:13, 24; Ac 4:6.*

ἀνόητος, ον foolish, senseless Lk 24:25; Gal 3:1; 1 Ti 6:9. [-νόητος, noetic]

ἄνοια, ας, ἡ foolishness 2 Ti 3:9; fury Lk 6:11.*

ἀνοίγω—1. trans. open Mt 3:16; J 9:10; Ac 5:19; 14:27; Rv 5:9.—2. intr. (2 pf. ἀνέῳγα; cf. the 2 aor. pass. ἀνοίγην Ac 12:10) open (itself), be open J 1:51; 1 Cor 16:9. στόμα ἡμῶν ἀνέῳγεν our mouth is open, i.e. we have spoken freely 2 Cor 6:11.

ἀνοικοδομέω build up again Ac 15:16; Jd 20 v.l.*

ἄνοιξις, εως, ἡ the act of opening ἐν ἀ. τοῦ στόματός μου when I open my mouth Eph 6:19.*

ἀνοίσω fut. of ἀναφέρω.

ἀνοιχθήσομαι fut. pass. of ἀνοίγω.

ἀνομία, ας, ἡ lawlessness, sin as a frame of mind Ro 6:19a; 1 J 3:4. A lawless deed Mt 13:41; Ro 6:19b; Hb 10:17.

ἄνομος, ον simply without law 1 Cor 9:21a, b; lawless, godless, criminal Lk 22:37; Ac 2:23; 1 Ti 1:9. ἀ. θεοῦ rejecting God's law 1 Cor 9:21c. ὁ ἄ. = the Antichrist 2 Th 2:8.

ἀνόμως without the law Ro 2:12.*

ἀνόνητος, ον useless 1 Ti 6:9 v.l.*

ἀνορθόω rebuild, restore lit. make erect again Ac 15:16. Of a crippled woman Lk 13:13; strengthen Hb 12:12.*

ἀνόσιος, ον unholy, wicked 1 Ti 1:9; 2 Ti 3:2.*

ἀνοχή, ῆς, ἡ forbearance, clemency Ro 2:4; 3:26.*

ἀνταγωνίζομαι struggle Hb 12:4.*

ἀντάλλαγμα, ατος, τό that which is given in exchange, an equivalent Mt 16:26; Mk 8:37.* [ἀντί + ἀλλάσσω]

ἀνταναπληρόω fill up, complete Col 1:24.*

ἀνταποδίδωμι give back, repay, return Lk 14:14; Ro 12:19; 1 Th 3:9.

ἀνταποδοθήσομαι fut. pass. ind. of ἀνταποδίδωμι.

ἀνταπόδομα, ατος, τό repayment Lk 14; 12; retribution Ro 11:9.* [Cf. ἀποδίδωμι.]

ἀνταπόδοσις, εως, ἡ repaying, reward Col 3:24.*

ἀνταποδοῦναι, ἀνταποδώσω 2 aor. act. inf. and fut. act. ind. 1 sing. of ἀνταποδίδωμι.

ἀνταποκρίνομαι answer in turn, make reply Lk 14:6; answer back Ro 9:20.*

ἀντεῖπον 2 aor. only speak against, contradict Lk 21:15; say in reply Ac 4:14.*

ἀντέχω in N.T. only in mid. cling to, be devoted to Mt 6:24; Lk 16:13. Take an interest in, pay attention to Tit 1:9; help 1 Th 5:14.*

ἀντί prep. w. gen., orig. mng. local, opposite—1. instead of, in place of Mt 2:22; Lk 11:11; Js 4:15.—2. for, as, in place of Mt 5:38; Ro 12:17; 1 Cor 11:15; after or upon J 1:16.—3. for, in behalf of Mt 17:27; 20:28. ἀνθ' ὧν because Lk 1:20; 2 Th 2:10; therefore Lk 12:3; cf. Eph 5:31. (In exchange) for Hb 12:16. [anti-, combining form in numerous words]

ἀντιβάλλω put or place against, exchange ἀ. λόγους discuss Lk 24:17.*

ἀντιδιατίθημι mid. oppose oneself, be opposed 2 Ti 2:25.*

ἀντίδικος, ου, ὁ enemy, opponent in a lawsuit or generally Mt 5:25; Lk 12:58; 18:3; 1 Pt 5:8.*

ἀντίθεσις, εως, ἡ opposition, objection, contradiction 1 Ti 6:20.* [antithesis, antithetical]

ἀντικαθίστημι intr. oppose, resist Hb 12:4.*

ἀντικαλέω invite in return Lk 14:12.*

ἀντίκειμαι be opposed Gal 5:17; 1 Ti 1:10. ὁ ἀντικείμενος the opponent Phil 1:28; cf. Lk 13:17; 21:15; 1 Cor 16:9; 2 Th 2:4; 1 Ti 5:14.*

ἄντικρυς adv., functions as prep. w. gen. opposite, off Ac 20:15.*

ἀντιλαμβάνω mid. come to the aid of, help Lk 1:54; Ac 20:35. Take part in, devote oneself to or perh. enjoy, benefit by 1 Ti 6:2.*

ἀντιλέγω speak against, contradict Ac 13:45; 28:19, 22; Tit 1:9; 2:9; deny Lk 20:27. Oppose, be obstinate Lk 2:34; J 19:12; Ro 10:21.*

ἀντίλημψις, εως, ἡ help pl. helpful deeds 1 Cor 12:28.*

ἀντιλογία, ας, ἡ contradiction, dispute Hb 6:16; 7:7. Hostility, rebellion 12:3; Jd 11.* [antilogy, a contradiction in terms or ideas]

ἀντιλοιδορέω revile in return 1 Pt 2:23.*

ἀντίλυτρον, ου, τό ransom 1 Ti 2:6.*

ἀντιμετρέω measure in return Lk 6:38.* [-μετρέω, metric]

ἀντιμισθία, ας, ἡ exchange τὴν αὐτὴν ἀ. πλατύνθητε widen your hearts in the same way in exchange 2 Cor 6:13. Penalty Ro 1:27.*

Ἀντιόχεια, ας, ἡ—1. Antioch in Syria, on the Orontes River Ac 11:19–26; 13:1; Gal 2:11.—2. Antioch in Pisidia in Asia Minor Ac 13:14; 2 Ti 3:11.

Ἀντιοχεύς, έως, ὁ a man from Antioch in Syria Ac 6:5.*

ἀντιπαρέρχομαι pass by on the opposite side Lk 10:31f.*

Ἀντιπᾶς, ᾶ, ὁ Antipas Rv 2:13.*

Ἀντιπατρίς, ίδος, ἡ Antipatris, a city in Judaea Ac 23:31.*

ἀντιπέρα adv., functions as prep. w. gen. *opposite* Lk 8:26.*

ἀντιπίπτω *resist, oppose* Ac 7:51.*

ἀντιστῆναι 2 aor. act. inf. of ἀνθίστημι.

ἀντιστρατεύομαι *be at war with* Ro 7:23.*

ἀντιτάσσω mid. *oppose, offer resistance* Ac 18:6; Ro 13:2; Js 4:6; 5:6; 1 Pt 5:5.*

ἀντίτυπος, ον *serving as a counterpart to, corresponding to* 1 Pt 3:21. As a noun *copy, antitype, representation* Hb 9:24.*

ἀντίχριστος, ου, ὁ *the Antichrist* 1 J 2:18, 22; 4:3; 2 J 7; pl. 1 J 2:18.*

ἀντλέω *draw* water J 2:8, 9; 4:7, 15.*

ἄντλημα, ατος, τό *bucket* for drawing water J 4:11.*

ἀντοφθαλμέω *look directly at, face* Ac 27:15; 6:10 (11) v.l.* [-οφθαλμέω, *ophthalmologist*]

ἄνυδρος, ον *waterless* Mt 12:43; Lk 11:24; 2 Pt 2:17; νεφέλαι ἄ. *clouds that yield no rain* Jd 12.* [*anhydrous*]

ἀνυπόκριτος, ον *genuine, sincere*, lit. *without hypocrisy* or *insincerity* Ro 12:9; 1 Ti 1:5; Js 3:17.

ἀνυπότακτος, ον *not made subject, independent* Hb 2:8. *Undisciplined, disobedient, rebellious* 1 Ti 1:9; Tit 1:6, 10.* [-υπότακτος, *hypotactic*]

ἄνω adv. *above* J 8:23; Ac 2:19; Gal 4:26; Col 3:1f; ἕως ἄνω *to the brim* J 2:7. *Upward* J 11:41; Phil 3:14; Hb 12:15.*

ἀνῶ 2 aor. subj. act. of ἀνίημι.

ἄνωθεν adv.—**1.** *from above*, esp. heaven Mk 15:38; J 19:23; Js 3:15.—**2.** *from the beginning* Lk 1:3; *for a long time* Ac 26:5.—**3.** *again, anew* Gal 4:9. In J 3:3, 7 ἄ. is purposely given a double meaning *again* and *from above*.

ἀνωτερικός, ή, όν *upper, inland, interior* Ac 19:1.*

ἀνώτερος, ερα, ον neut., as adv. *higher*, i.e. to a better place Lk 14:10; *above, earlier* Hb 10:8.*

ἀνωφελής, ές *useless* τὸ ἀ. *uselessness* Hb 7:18; *harmful* Tit 3:9.*

ἀξίνη, ης, ἡ *ax* Mt 3:10; Lk 3:9; 13:7 v.l.*

ἄξιος, ία, ον *worthy* Mt 10:37f; 1 Ti 1:15; 4:9; Hb 11:38; *worthy to be compared* Ro 8:18; *in keeping with* Lk 3:8; *deserving* Lk 12:48; 23:15; Ac 25:11, 25; Ro 1:32; *fit* Lk 15:19; *good enough* J 1:27. Impers. ἄξιόν ἐστι *it is worth while, proper* 1 Cor 16:4. [*axiom*]

ἀξιόω *consider worthy* Lk 7:7; Hb 10:29; *make worthy* 2 Th 1:11. *Consider fitting*, hence *ask, desire, request* Ac 15:38; 28:22.

ἀξίως adv. *worthily, in a manner worthy of* Ro 16:2; Phil 1:27; Col 1:10.

ἀόρατος, ον *unseen, invisible* Ro 1:20; Col 1:15f; Hb 11:27.

Ἀουλία alt. form of Ἰουλία *Julia* Ro 16:15.

ἀπαγγείλοι 1 aor. act. opt. 3 sing. of ἀπαγγέλλω.

ἀπαγγέλλω *report, announce, tell* Mt 11:4; Mk 6:30; Lk 7:18; Ac 12:14; *proclaim* Mt 12:18; *confess* 1 Cor 14:25.

ἀπαγγελῶ, fut. act. ind. 1 sing. of ἀπαγγέλλω.

ἀπάγχω mid. *hang oneself* Mt 27:5.*

ἀπάγω—**1.** trans. *lead away* Lk 13:15. As legal term *bring before, arraign* Mt 26:57; Mk 14:53 Ac 23:17. *Lead away* to trial, prison, or execution Mk 14:44; Lk 23:26; Ac 12:19.—Pass. *be misled* 1 Cor 12:2.—**2.** intr. of a road *lead* Mt 7:13f.

ἀπαίδευτος, ον *stupid* lit. 'uneducated' 2 Ti 2:23.*

ἀπαίρω pass. *be taken away* Mk 2:20 (= Mt 9:15; Lk 5:35).*

ἀπαιτέω *ask for* or *demand* something back, dun Lk 6:30. Of life regarded as a loan 12:20.*

ἀπαλγέω *become callous* Eph 4:19.* [-αλγέω, *(an)algesic*]

ἀπαλλάσσω act. *free, release* Hb 2:15. Pass. *be released, be cured* Ac 5:15 v.l.; *come to a settlement* with someone Lk 12:58; intr. *leave, depart* Ac 19:12.*

ἀπαλλοτριόω pass. *be estranged, alienated* Eph 2:12; 4:18; Col 1:21.*

ἀπαλός, ή, όν *tender* Mt 24:32; Mk 13:28.*

ἀπαντάω *meet* Mk 14:13; Lk 17:12.*

ἀπάντησις, εως, ἡ the act of *meeting someone*; εἰς ἀπάντησιν *to meet* Mt 25:6; 27:32 v.l.; Ac 28:15; 1 Th 4:17.*

ἅπαξ adv. *once* 2 Cor 11:25; Hb 9:27. ἔτι ἅ. *once more* = *for the last time* 12:26f. ἅ. καὶ δίς *more than once, repeatedly* Phil 4:16; 1 Th 2:18. *Once for all* Hb 10:2; 1 Pt 3:18; Jd 3, 5.

ἀπαράβατος, ον *permanent, unchangeable* Hb 7:24.*

ἀπαρασκεύαστος, ον *unprepared* 2 Cor 9:4.*

ἀπαρθῇ, ἀπαρθῶ 1 aor. pass. subj. forms of ἀπαίρω.

ἀπαρνέομαι *deny, disown, repudiate* Mk 14:30f, 72; Lk 12:9.

ἀπαρτί adv. *exactly, certainly* conjectural emendation for ἀπ᾽ ἄρτι Rv 14:13.*

ἀπάρτι see ἀπ᾽ ἄρτι s.v. ἄρτι.

ἀπαρτισμός, οῦ, ὁ *completion* Lk 14:28.*

ἀπαρχή, ῆς, ἡ *firstfruits*, the first of any crop or offspring of livestock, consecrated before the rest could be used Ro 11:16 (cf. Num 15:18–21). Fig. Ro 16:5; 1 Cor 15:20; Rv 14:4; *foretaste* Ro 8:23 (the meaning *birth certificate* or 'identification card' also suits the context).

ἅπας, ασα, αν used in Attic Gk. for πᾶς after consonants; this distinction is not always maintained in the N.T. *all, whole, every* Mt 24:39; Mk 8:25; Lk 8:37; 23:1; Ac 4:31; 16:3, 28; Js 3:2.

ἀπασπάζομαι *take leave of, say farewell to* Ac 21:6; 20:1 v.l.*

ἀπατάω *deceive, cheat, mislead* Eph 5:6; 1 Ti 2:14; Js 1:26.*

ἀπάτη, ης, ἡ—1. *deception, deceitfulness* Col 2:8; 2 Th 2:10; Hb 3:13; ἐπιθυμία τ. ἀπάτης *deceptive desire* Eph 4:22. In Mt 13:22; Mk 4:19 ἡ ἀ. τοῦ πλούτου may mean *the seduction which comes from wealth* or (see 2 below) *pleasure.*—2. *pleasure, pleasantness* 2 Pt 2:13; perhaps Mt 13:22; Mk 4:19 (see

1 above) and possibly Hb 3:13.* [*apatite*, a mineral]

ἀπάτωρ, gen. ορος *without father* Hb 7:3.* [-πάτωρ, s. πατήρ]

ἀπαύγασμα, ατος, τό act. *radiance, effulgence*, pass. *reflection*; the act. is prob. preferable in Hb 1:3.*

ἀπαφρίζω *cast off like foam* Jd 13 v.l.*

ἀπαχθῆναι 1 aor. pass. inf. of ἀπάγω.

ἀπέβαλον 2 aor. act. ind. of ἀποβάλλω.

ἀπέβην 2 aor. act. ind. of ἀποβαίνω.

ἀπέδειξα 1 aor. act. ind. of ἀποδείκνυμι.

ἀπέδετο Hellenistic form for ἀπέδοτο, 2 aor. mid. ind. 3 sing. of ἀποδίδωμι.

ἀπεδίδουν impf. act. ind. of ἀποδίδωμι.

ἀπεδόμην 2 aor. mid. ind. of ἀποδίδωμι.

ἀπέθανον 2 aor. act. ind. of ἀποθνῄσκω.

ἀπεθέμην 2 aor. mid. ind. of ἀποτίθημι.

ἀπεῖδον 2 aor. act. ind. of ἀφοράω.

ἀπείθεια, ας, ἡ *disobedience, disbelief* Ro 11:30, 32; Hb 4:6, 11. υἱοὶ ἀ. *disobedient sons*, i.e. *people* Eph 2:2; 5:6; Col 3:6 v.l.*

ἀπειθέω *disobey, be disobedient* or *disloyal* Ro 10:21; 11:30f; Hb 3:18; 11:31. The mng. *disbelieve* (in the Christian gospel), *be an unbeliever* is probable for such passages as J 3:36; Ac 14:2; Ro 15:31.

ἀπειθής, ές *disobedient* Ac 26:19; Ro 1:30; Tit 1:16.

ἀπειλέω *threaten, warn* Ac 4:17; 1 Pt 2:23.*

ἀπειλή, ῆς, ἡ *threat* Ac 4:17 v.l., 29; 9:1; Eph 6:9.*

I. ἄπειμι (εἰμί) *be absent* or *away* 1 Cor 5:3; 2 Cor 13:2, 10; Phil 1:27.

II. ἄπειμι (εἶμι) *go, come* lit. 'go away' Act 17:10.*

ἀπειπάμην mid. of ἀπεῖπον.

ἀπεῖπον *disown, renounce* 2 Cor 4:2.*

ἀπείραστος, ον *incapable of being tempted* κακῶν *by evil* Js 1:13.*

ἄπειρος, ον *unacquainted with* Hb 5:13.*

ἀπεκαλύφθην 1 aor. pass. ind. of ἀποκαλύπτω.

ἀπεκατεστάθην, ἀπεκατέστην 1 aor.
pass. ind. and 1 aor. act. ind. of ἀποκαθίστημι.

ἀπεκδέχομαι await eagerly Ro 8:19, 23,
25; Phil 3:20; Hb 9:28.

ἀπεκδύομαι take off, strip off fig. Col
3:9. Disarm 2:15.* [-εκδύομαι, ec-
dysis]

ἀπέκδυσις, εως, ἡ removal, stripping
off fig. Col 2:11.*

ἀπεκρίθην 1 aor. pass. ind. of ἀποκρίνομαι.

ἀπεκτάνθην 1 aor. pass. ind. of ἀποκτείνω.

ἀπέλαβον 2 aor. act. ind. of ἀπολαμβάνω.

ἀπελαύνω drive away Ac 18:16.*

ἀπελεγμός, οῦ, ὁ refutation, discredit,
disrepute Ac 19:27.*

ἀπελεύθερος, ου, ὁ freedman fig. 1 Cor
7:22.*

ἀπελεύσομαι, ἀπεληλύθειν, ἀπελ-
θών fut. mid. ind., plupf. act. ind., and
2 aor. act. ptc. of ἀπέρχομαι.

ἀπέλιπον 2 aor. act. ind. of ἀπολείπω.

Ἀπελλῆς, οῦ, ὁ Apelles Ro 16:10.*

ἀπελπίζω give up hope, despair Eph 4:19
v.l. In Lk 6:35 μηδὲν ἀπελπίζοντες =
expecting nothing in return; cf. vs. 34.*

ἀπέναντι functions as prep. w. gen. opposite Mt 27:61; Mk 12:41 v.l.; before
Mt 27:24; Ac 3:16; Ro 3:18; against,
contrary to Ac 17:7.*

ἀπενεγκεῖν, ἀπενεχθῆναι 2 aor. act.
inf. and 1 aor. pass. inf. of ἀποφέρω.

ἀπέπεσα 2 aor. act. ind. of ἀποπίπτω.

ἀπέπλευσα 1 aor. act. ind. of ἀποπλέω.

ἀπεπνίγην 2 aor. pass. ind. of ἀποπνίγω.

ἀπέραντος, ον endless 1 Ti 1:4.*

ἀπερισπάστως adv. without distrac-
tion 1 Cor 7:35.*

ἀπερίτμητος, ον uncircumcised,
fig. = obdurate Ac 7:51.*

ἀπέρχομαι go away, go Mt 8:21, 33;
19:22; Mk 1:35; 5:17; Ro 15:28; leave
Mk 1:42; pass away Rv 21:1, 4; go out
and spread Mt 4:24. ἀ. ὀπίσω follow
Mk 1:20; go in search of Jd 7; ἀ. εἰς
τὰ ὀπίσω draw back J 6:66; 18:6.

ἀπεστάλην, ἀπέσταλκα, ἀπέστειλα
2 aor. pass. ind., 1 pf. act. ind., and 1
aor. act. ind. of ἀποστέλλω.

ἀπέστην, ἀπέστησα 2 aor. act. ind.
and 1 aor. act. ind. of ἀφίστημι.

ἀπεστράφην 2 aor. pass. ind. of ἀποστρέφω.

ἀπέχω—1. act., trans. receive a sum in
full and give a receipt for it (commercial term) Mt 6:2, 5, 16; Lk 6:24; Phil
4:18. Keep Phlm 15. Among the possibilities for ἀπέχει in the difficult passage Mk 14:41 are it is enough and,
taking 'Judas' as the subj. and 'his
money' as the obj., he has received.—
2. act., intrans. be distant lit. Mt 14:24;
Lk 7:6; 15:20; 24:13; fig. Mt 15:8.—3.
mid. keep away, abstain Ac 15:20, 29;
1 Th 4:3; 1 Ti 4:3; 1 Pt 2:11.

ἀπηγγέλην, ἀπήγγειλα 2 aor. pass.
ind. and 1 aor. act. ind. of ἀπαγγέλλω.

ἀπήγαγον 2 aor. act. ind. of ἀπάγω.

ἀπήγξατο 1 aor. mid. ind. of ἀπάγχο-
μαι.

ἀπῄεσαν impf. act. ind. of ἄπειμι (εἶμι).

ἀπήλασα 1 aor. act. ind. of ἀπελαύνω.

ἀπήλγηκα pf. act. ind. of ἀπαλγέω.

ἀπῆλθα, ἀπῆλθον 2 aor. act. ind. of
ἀπέρχομαι.

ἀπηλλάχθαι pf. pass. inf. of ἀπαλλάσσω.

ἀπήνεγκα 1 aor. act. ind. of ἀποφέρω.

ἀπήρθη 1 aor. pass. ind. of ἀπαίρω.

ἀπίδω 2 aor. act. subj. of ἀφοράω.

ἀπιστέω—1. disbelieve, refuse to believe Lk 24:11, 41; Ac 28:24; 1 Pt 2:7.—
2. be unfaithful Ro 3:3; 2 Ti 2:13.

ἀπιστία, ας, ἡ—1. unfaithfulness Ro
3:3.—2. lack of faith, unbelief Mk 6:6;
9:24; Ro 11:20; 1 Ti 1:13. καρδία ἀ-
πιστίας an unbelieving heart Hb 3:12.

ἄπιστος, ον—1. unbelievable, incredi-
ble Ac 26:8.—2. faithless, unbelieving
Mk 9:19; J 20:27; 1 Cor 6:6; 7:12–15;
14:23f; Rv 21:8.

ἁπλότης, ητος, ἡ simplicity, sincerity,
frankness Eph 6:5; Col 3:22; 2 Cor 1:12
ἀ. εἰς Χριστόν sincere devotion to
Christ 2 Cor 11:3. Sincere concern of
people who give ungrudgingly, i.e.

without reservation, with no strings attached Ro 12:8; 2 Cor 8:2; 9:11, 13.*

ἁπλοῦς, ῆ, οῦν lit. 'single, sincere,' then open and aboveboard, honest, with no 'hidden agendas' Mt 6:22; Lk 11:34.— Superl. ἁπλούστατος quite innocent, guileless Mt 10:16 v.l.*

ἁπλῶς adv. without reserve, generously Js 1:5.*

ἀπό prep. w. gen from, away from, out of (separation, departure, origin) Mt 17:25f; Mk 5:17; 8:11; Lk 1:52; 16:18; 22:71; Ac 2:5; 1 Th 1:8. Because of, from, with (cause, manner) Lk 21:26; 22:45; J 21:6; Ac 11:19. With (means) Lk 15:16 v.l.; by (agent), direct Ac 2:22, indirect Js 1:13. As substitute for the partitive genitive of, some of Mt 27:21; Mk 7:28; J 21:10; for the genitive of material Mt 3:4.—ἀ. τῶν καρπῶν by the fruit Mt 7:16, 20. ἀφ' ἧς or οὖ since, when Lk 7:45; 13:25; 24:21. ἀ. ἐτῶν δώδεκα for twelve years Lk 8:43. ἀ. μιᾶς alike, unanimously Lk 14:18. ἀ. σταδίων δεκαπέντε (by) fifteen stades J 11:18. ἀνάθεμα ἀ. Χριστοῦ separated from Christ by a curse Ro 9:3. ἀ. μέρους in part Ro 11:25. The extraordinary expression ἀπὸ ὁ ὤν κ.τ.λ. Rv 1:4 may be due to the writer's reverence for the divine name, which he leaves undeclined; it is one of the many grammatical peculiarities of this book.

ἀποβαίνω get out, lit. 'go away' Lk 5:2; J 21:9. Turn out, lead (to) Lk 21:13; Phil 1:19.*

ἀποβάλλω throw off Mk 10:50; lose, throw away Hb 10:35.*

ἀποβήσομαι fut. mid. ind. of ἀποβαίνω.

ἀποβλέπω look, pay attention Hb 11:26.*

ἀπόβλητος, ον rejected (as unclean) 1 Ti 4:4.*

ἀποβολή, ῆς, ἡ rejection Ro 11:15; loss Ac 27:22.* [Cf. βάλλω.]

ἀπογενόμενος 2 aor. mid. pct. of ἀπογίνομαι.

ἀπογίνομαι die fig. 1 Pt 2:24.*

ἀπογραφή, ῆς, ἡ census, registration Lk 2:2; Ac 5:37.*

ἀπογράφω register, record Lk 2:1, 3, 5; Hb 12:23.*

ἀποδεδειγμένος pf. pass. ptc. of ἀποδείκνυμι.

ἀποδείκνυμι, exhibit, display 1 Cor 4:9; prove Ac 25:7; proclaim 2 Th 2:4; recommend, attest Ac 2:22.* [apodictic]

ἀπόδειξις, εως, ἡ proof. ἀ. πνεύματος proof consisting in possession of the Spirit 1 Cor 2:4.*

ἀποδεκατεύω tithe, give one-tenth of Lk 18:12 v.l.*

ἀποδεκατόω—1. tithe, give one-tenth of Mt 23:23; Lk 11:42.—2. Collect a tithe (one-tenth) from Hb 7:5.*

ἀπόδεκτος, ον pleasing, pleasant 1 Ti 2:3; 5:4.*

ἀποδέχομαι—1. welcome, receive favorably Lk 8:40; 9:11; Ac 18:27; 21:17; 28:30. Accept Ac 2:41.—2. acknowledge, praise 24:3.*

ἀποδημέω go on a journey Mt 25:14f; Lk 20:9; be away, absent 2 Cor 5:6 v.l.*

ἀπόδημος, ον away on a journey Mk 13:34.*

ἀποδιδοῦν pres. act. neuter ptc. of ἀποδίδωμι Rv 22:2.

ἀποδίδωμι—1. give away, give (up) or (out) Mt 27:58; Lk 16:2; Ac 4:33; pay (out) Mt 20:8; Mk 12:17; fulfill 1 Cor 7:3; keep Mt 5:33; yield Rv 22:2.—2. give or pay back, return Lk 9:42; 12:59; 19:8. Render, recompense Mt 6:4, 6, 18; Ro 2:6; 12:17; Rv 18:6.—3. mid. sell Ac 5:8; 7:9; Hb 12:16. [apodosis]

ἀποδιορίζω divide, separate οἱ ἀποδιορίζοντες those who cause a division Jd 19.*

ἀποδοθῆναι 1 aor. pass. inf. of ἀποδίδωμι.

ἀποδοκιμάζω reject (after scrutiny), declare useless Mt 21:42; Lk 9:22; Hb 12:17.

ἀπόδος, ἀποδοῦναι, ἀποδούς 2 aor. act. impv., inf., and ptc. of ἀποδίδωμι.

ἀποδοχή, ῆς, ἡ acceptance, approval 1 Ti 1:15; 4:9.* [Cf. δέχομαι.]

ἀποδώῃ, ἀποδώς 2 aor. act. opt. 3 sing. and 2 aor. act. subj. 2 sing. of ἀποδίδωμι.

ἀποθανεῖσθε, ἀποθάνῃ, ἀποθανεῖν from ἀποθνῄσκω: fut. mid. ind. 2 pl., 2 aor. act. subj. 3 sing., and 2 aor. act. inf.

ἀποθέμενος, ἀποθέσθαι, ἀπόθεσθε 2 aor. mid. ptc., mid. inf., and mid. impv. 2 pl. of ἀποτίθημι.

ἀπόθεσις, εως, ἡ removal, getting rid of fig. 1 Pt 3:21; 2 Pt 1:14 (euphemistic for death).* [Cf. τίθημι.]

ἀποθήκη, ης, ἡ storehouse, barn Mt 3:12; Lk 12:18. [Cf. τίθημι.]

ἀποθησαυρίζω store up, lay (up) 1 Ti 6:19.*

ἀποθλίβω press upon, crowd Lk 8:45.*

ἀποθνῄσκω die—1. lit., of physical death Mt 8:32; 9:24; Ro 14:8; Hb 10:28; Rv 14:13. Decay 1 Cor 15:36.—2. fig. be freed from Ro 6:2; Gal 2:19; Col 2:20. Of mystical death with Christ Ro 6:8. Of losing the true, eternal life Ro 7:10; Rv 3:2; oft. in J: 6:50, 58; 8:21, 24; 11:26.—3. be about to die, face death, be mortal 1 Cor 15:31; 2 Cor 6:9; Hb 7:8.

ἀποθῶμαι 2 aor. mid. subj. of ἀποτίθημι.

ἀποίσω fut. act. ind. of ἀποφέρω.

ἀποκαθιστάνω and ἀποκαθίστημι restore, reestablish Mk 9:12; Ac 1:6. Cure Mk 3:5; intr. 2 aor. act. be cured 8:25; bring back, restore Hb 13:19. [Cf. ἀποκατάστασις.]

ἀποκαλύπτω reveal, disclose Mt 10:26; Lk 17:30; Ro 1:17; 1 Cor 3:13; Gal 1:16; 1 Pt 5:1.

ἀποκάλυψις, εως, ἡ revelation, disclosure Lk 2:32; Ro 8:19; Gal 1:12; 2:2; Eph 3:3; 1 Pt 1:7, 13. [apocalypse]

ἀποκαραδοκία, ας, ἡ eager expectation Ro 8:19; Phil 1:20.*

ἀποκαταλλάσσω reconcile Eph 2:16; Col 1:20, 22.*

ἀποκατάστασις, εως, ἡ restoration Ac 3:21.* [apocatastasis. Cf. ἀποκαθιστάνω.]

ἀποκαταστήσω fut. act. ind. of ἀποκαθίστημι.

ἀποκατηλλάγην 2 aor. pass. ind. of ἀποκαταλλάσσω.

ἀπόκειμαι be stored up, put away lit. Lk 19:20. Fig. Col 1:5; be reserved 2 Ti 4:8. Impers. ἀπόκειταί τινι it is reserved or certain for someone, one is destined to w. inf. Hb 9:27.*

ἀποκεφαλίζω behead Mk 6:16, 27.

ἀποκλείω close, shut Lk 13:25.*

ἀποκόπτω cut off, cut loose Mk 9:43, 45; J 18:10, 26; Ac 27:32. Make a eunuch of, castrate Gal 5:12.* [apocope]

ἀπόκριμα, ατος, τό official report, decision, sentence 2 Cor 1:9.*

ἀποκρίνομαι answer, reply Mt 3:15; 8:8; Mk 7:28; 9:6; Lk 4:4; 23:9; J 1:21; 3:5. Hebraistically with εἰπεῖν and λέγειν = continue Mt 22:1; 26:25 or begin, speak up Mk 9:5; J 5:19; Ac 5:8 or left untranslated Mt 16:16; Mk 7:28; Lk 23:3.

ἀπόκρισις, εως, ἡ answer Lk 2:47; 20:26; J 1:22; 19:9.*

ἀποκρύπτω hide, conceal Lk 10:21; 1 Cor 2:7; Eph 3:9; Col 1:26.*

ἀπόκρυφος, ον hidden, secret Mk 4:22; Lk 8:17; Col 2:3.* [Apocrypha]

ἀποκτείνω or ἀποκτέννω kill Mt 14:5; Lk 11:47; J 8:22; 16:2; deprive of spiritual life Mt 10:28; 2 Cor 3:6. Fig. Eph 2:16.

ἀποκυέω give birth to, bring into being fig. Js 1:15, 18.*

ἀποκυλίω roll away Mt 28:2; Mk 16:3, 4; Lk 24:2.*

ἀπολαλέω speak out freely Ac 18:25 v.l.*

ἀπολαμβάνω receive Gal 4:5. As 'commercial' term Lk 16:25; 23:41; Ro 1:27. Receive in return, get back Lk 6:34; 15:27. Take aside Mk 7:33. Welcome 3 J 8 v.l.

ἀπόλαυσις, εως, ἡ enjoyment 1 Ti 6:17; Hb 11:25.* [apolaustic, self-indulgent]

ἀπολείπω leave behind 2 Ti 4:13, 20; Tit 1:5; desert Jd 6. Remain Hb 4:9; 10:26; impers. it is certain 4:6.*

ἀπολεῖται, ἀπολέσαι, ἀπολέσῃ fut. mid. ind. and 1 aor. act. inf. and subj. of ἀπόλλυμι.

ἀπολείχω lick, lick off Lk 16:21 v.l.*

ἀπολήμψομαι fut. mid. ind. of ἀπολαμβάνω.

ἀπολιμπάνω An Aeolic and Hellenistic Gk. by-form of ἀπολείπω 1 Pt 2:21 v.l. for ὑπολιμπάνω, q.v.

ἀπολιπών 2 aor. act. ptc. of ἀπολείπω.

ἀπόλλυμι—1. act. destroy, ruin, kill Mt 2:13; Ro 14:15; 1 Cor 1:19. Lose Mt 10:39, 42; 2 J 8.—2. mid. and pass. be lost, perish, die, be ruined Mt 8:25; 9:17; 26:52; Lk 15:24; J 11:50; Js 1:11; pass away Hb 1:11. [Apollyon] Ἀπολλύων, ονος, ὁ Apollyon, the Destroyer (see Ἀβαδδών) Rv 9:11.*

Ἀπολλωνία, ας, ἡ Apollonia, a city in Macedonia Ac 17:1.*

Ἀπολλῶς, ῶ, ὁ (short for Ἀπολλώνιος, which is a v.l. in Ac 18:24) Apollos Ac 18:24; 19:1; 1 Cor 1:12; 3:4–6, 22; 4:6; 16:12; Tit 3:13.*

ἀπολογέομαι speak in one's own defense, defend oneself Lk 21:14; Ac 19:33; 24:10; Ro 2:15; 2 Cor 12:19. περί τινος against something Ac 26:2. [apologetic]

ἀπολογία, ας, ἡ defense Ac 25:16; Phil 1:7, 16; 2 Ti 4:16; 1 Pt 3:15; answer, reply 1 Cor 9:3. [apology]

ἀπολούμαι fut. mid. ind. of ἀπόλλυμι.

ἀπολούω mid. wash oneself 1 Cor 6:11; wash away Ac 22:16.*

ἀπολύτρωσις, εως, ἡ release Hb 11:35. Fig. redemption (lit. 'buying back'), deliverance, acquittal, ransoming Lk 21:28; Ro 3:24; 8:23; Eph 1:7; Hb 9:15. Redeemer 1 Cor 1:30.

ἀπολύω—1. release, set free, pardon Mt 18:27; 27:15–26; Lk 6:37; 13:12.—2. let go, send away, dismiss Mt 15:23, 32, 39; Mk 8:9; Ac 4:23. Euphemistic for let die, discharge Lk 2:29. Divorce Mk 10:2, 4, 11f.—3. mid. go away Ac 28:25. In Hb 13:23 Timothy has been set free or sent away or has gone away.

ἀπολῶ, ἀπολωλός fut. ind. act. and 2 pf. act. ptc. of ἀπόλλυμι.

ἀπομάσσω mid. wipe off in protest Lk 10:11.*

ἀπομένω remain behind Lk 2:43 v.l.*

ἀπονέμω assign, show, pay 1 Pt 3:7.*

ἀπονίπτω wash off mid. (for) oneself Mt 27:24.*

ἀποπέμπω send out J 17:3 v.l.*

ἀποπίπτω fall, drop (from) Ac 9:18.*

ἀποπλανάω mislead Mk 13:22; pass. wander away 1 Ti 6:10.*

ἀποπλέω sail away Ac 13:4; 14:26; 20:15; 27:1.*

ἀποπλύνω wash off or out Lk 5:2 v.l.*

ἀποπνίγω choke trans. Mt 13:7 v.l.; Lk 8:7. Pass. drown 8:33.*

ἀπορέω be at a loss, in doubt, uncertain Lk 24:4; J 13:22; Ac 25:20; 2 Cor 4:8. πολλὰ ἠπόρει he was very much disturbed Mk 6:20. ἐν ὑμῖν because of you Gal 4:20.*

ἀπορία, ας, ἡ perplexity, anxiety Lk 21:25.*

ἀπο(ρ)ρίπτω intr. throw oneself down Ac 27:43.*

ἀπορφανίζω make an orphan of fig. 1 Th 2:17.*

ἀποσκευάζω pack up Ac 21:15 v.l.*

ἀποσκίασμα, ατος, τό shadow Js 1:17.*

ἀποσπάω—1. lit. draw Mt 26:51.—2. fig. draw away, attract Ac 20:30. Pass. be parted 21:1; withdraw Lk 22:41.*

ἀποσταλῶ, ἀποσταλείς 2 aor. pass. subj. and ptc. of ἀποστέλλω.

ἀποστάς 2 aor. act. ptc. of ἀφίστημι.

ἀποστασία, ας, ἡ rebellion, abandonment, apostasy Ac 21:21; 2 Th 2:3.* [apostate]

ἀποστάσιον, ου, τό divorce Mt 5:31; 19:7; Mk 10:4.*

ἀποστάτης, ου, ὁ deserter, apostate Js 2:11 v.l.*

ἀποστεγάζω unroof ἀ. τ. στέγην remove the roof Mk 2:4.*

ἀποστεῖλαι, ἀποστείλω, ἀπόστειλον 1 aor. act. inf., subj., and impv. of ἀποστέλλω.

ἀποστέλλω send, send away or out Mt 13:41; 14:35; Mk 8:26; 12:2, 13; Lk 1:19, 26; J 3:28; Ac 5:21; 1 Cor 1:17; esp. on a divine mission Mt 10:5; Mk 9:37; J 3:17, 34; Ac 3:20. Put in Mk 4:29. ἀποστείλας ἀνεῖλεν he had the boys killed Mt 2:16; similarly Mk 6:17; J 11:3; Ac 7:14; Rv 1:1. [Cf. ἀπόστολος.]

ἀποστελῶ fut. act. ind. of ἀποστέλλω.

ἀποστερέω *steal, rob, defraud* Mk 10:19; 1 Cor 6:7f; Js 5:4. *Deprive* 1 Cor 7:5; 1 Ti 6:5.*

ἀποστῇ, ἀποστῆναι, ἀποστητε 2 aor. act. subj. 3 sing., 2 aor. act. inf., and aor. impv. 2 pl of ἀφίστημι.

ἀποστήσομαι fut. mid. ind. of ἀφίστημι.

ἀποστολή, ῆς, ἡ *apostleship, office of an apostle* Ac 1:25; Ro 1:5; 1 Cor 9:2; Gal 2:8.* [Cf. ἀποστέλλω.]

ἀπόστολος, ου, ὁ—1. *delegate, envoy, messenger* Lk 11:49; J 13:16; 2 Cor 8:23; Eph 3:5; Phil 2:25; Hb 3:1; Rv 2:2; 18:20.—2. *apostle,* one holding the most responsible position of service in the Christian communities (1 Cor 12:28f), esp. of Jesus' original 12 disciples (Mt 10:2; Ac 1:26; Rv 21:14), but also of other prominent leaders outside their number Ac 14:14; Ro 1:1; 16:7; Gal 1:19.

ἀποστοματίζω *question closely, interrogate, 'grill'* Lk 11:53.*

ἀποστρέφω—1. trans. *turn away* 2 Ti 4:4; *remove* Ro 11:26; *mislead* Lk 23:14; *return, put back* Mt 26:52. In Ac 3:26 the usage may be trans. or intrans.—2. mid. and pass. *turn away from, reject, repudiate* Mt 5:42; Tit 1:14; Hb 12:25; *desert* 2 Ti 1:15.* [*apostrophe*]

ἀποστυγέω *hate, abhor* Ro 12:9.*

ἀποσυνάγωγος, ον *expelled from the synagogue* ἀ. ποιεῖν *excommunicate* J 16:2. ἀ. γενέσθαι *be excommunicated* 9:22; 12:42.*

ἀποτάσσω mid. *say farewell (to), take leave (of)* Mk 6:46; Lk 9:61; 2 Cor 2:13. Fig. *renounce, give up* Lk 14:33.

ἀποτελέω *bring to completion, perform* Lk 13:32. Fig. pass. *come to completion, be fully formed* or *matured* Js 1:15.*

ἀποτίθημι mid. *take off* lit. *take off and lay down* Ac 7:58; fig. *lay aside, rid oneself of* Ro 13:12; Hb 12:1. *Put in prison* Mt 14:3. [Cf. *apothecary.*]

ἀποτινάσσω *shake off* Lk 9:5; Ac 28:5.*

ἀποτίνω *pay the damages, make compensation* Phlm 19.*

ἀποτολμάω *be bold, come out boldly* Ro 10:20.*

ἀποτομία, ας, ἡ *severity* Ro 11:22.*

ἀποτόμως adv. *severely, rigorously* 2 Cor 13:10; Tit 1:13.*

ἀποτρέπω mid. *turn away from, avoid* 2 Ti 3:5.*

ἀπουσία, ας, ἡ *absence* Phil 2:12.*

ἀποφέρω *take, bring* or *carry (away)* Lk 16:22; Ac 19:12; 1 Cor 16:3; Rv 17:3; 21:10; *lead away* Mk 15:1.*

ἀποφεύγω *escape, escape from* 2 Pt 1:4; 2:18, 20.*

ἀποφθέγγομαι *speak out, declare* Ac 26:25; with reference to inspiration 2:4, 14.* [*apothegm*]

ἀποφορτίζομαι *unload* Ac 21:3.*

ἀπόχρησις, εως, ἡ *consuming, using up* Col 2:22.*

ἀποχωρέω *go away* with ἀπό *leave, desert* Ac 13:13; *depart* Mt 7:23; Lk 20:20 v.l.; *withdraw* 9:39.*

ἀποχωρίζω *separate* Mt 19:6 v.l. Pass. *be separated* Ac 15:39; *be split* Rv 6:14.*

ἀποψύχω *breathe out, stop breathing,* hence either *faint* or *die* Lk 21:26.*

Ἀππίου φόρον *Appii Forum, the Forum of Appius,* a market town on the Appian Way, 43 Roman miles from Rome Ac 28:15.*

ἀπρόσιτος, ον *unapproachable* 1 Ti 6:16.*

ἀπρόσκοπος, ον *blameless* Phil 1:10; *clear* Ac 24:16; *giving no offense* 1 Cor 10:32.*

ἀπροσωπολήμπτως adv. *impartially* 1 Pt 1:17.*

ἄπταιστος, ον *without stumbling* Jd 24.*

ἅπτω—1. *light, kindle* Lk 8:16; Ac 28:2.—2. mid. *touch, take hold of, hold* w. gen. as obj. 2 Cor 6:17; Col 2:21 (perh. = *eat*); *cling to* J 20:17; of sex relations 1 Cor 7:1. *Touch* for blessing or healing Mt 9:21, 29; 17:7; Mk 10:13 (here perh. *hold*); Lk 7:14; 22:51. *Harm, injure* is probable for 1 J 5:18.

Ἀπφία, ας, ἡ *Apphia,* a Christian woman, prob. the wife of Philemon, at Colossae Phlm 2.*

ἀπωθέω mid. *push aside* lit. Ac 7:27. Fig. *reject, repudiate* 7:39; 13:46; Ro 11:1f; 1 Ti 1:19.*

ἀπώλεια, ας, ἡ *destruction, ruin, annihilation* Ac 8:20; esp of the eternal destruction of the wicked Mt 7:13; Phil 1:28; Hb 10:39; 2 Pt 3:7; Rv 17:8, 11. *Waste* Mk 14:4.

ἀπώλεσε, ἀπώλετο 1 aor. act. and 2 aor. mid. ind. of ἀπόλλυμι.

ἀπωσάμην 1 aor. mid. ind. of ἀπωθέω.

Ἄρ see Ἁρμαγεδδών.

ἀρά, ᾶς, ἡ *curse* Ro 3:14.*

ἄρα inferential particle, sometimes with γε and οὖν: *so, then, consequently, you see, as a result* Mt 7:20; 18:1; Lk 1:66; Ro 5:18; 7:21; 8:1; 1 Cor 15:14; Gal 6:10; Hb 12:8. After ἐπεί *for otherwise* 1 Cor 5:10; after εἰ *if, on the other hand* 15:15. In indirect questions εἰ ἄ. *whether (perhaps)* Mk 11:13; Ac 8:22. In a question τίς ἄ. *who would you say?* Mk 4:41; Mt 24:45.

ἆρα interrogative particle indicating anxiety or impatience, introducing direct questions only, usually incapable of direct translation, as Lk 18:8; Ac 8:30; cf. ἄ. Χριστὸς ἁμαρτίας διάκονος; *is Christ, then, a servant of sin?* Gal 2:17.*

Ἀραβία, ας, ἡ *Arabia:* in Gal 1:17 prob. the Nabataean kingdom south of Damascus; in 4:25 the Sinai peninsula.*

Ἄραβοι in Ac 2:11 v.l. could have been wrongly formed from the gen. pl. Ἀράβων.*

ἆραι, ἄρας, ἄρατε 1 aor. act. inf., ptc., and impv. of αἴρω.

Ἀράμ, ὁ indecl. *Aram* Mt 1:3f; Lk 3:33 v.l.*

ἄραφος, ον *seamless* J 19:23.*

Ἄραψ, βος, ὁ an *Arab* Ac 2:11.*

ἀργέω *be idle, grow weary, delay* 2 Pt 2:3.*

ἀργός, ή, όν *idle, unemployed* Mt 20:3, 6; *idle, lazy* 1 Ti 5:13; Tit 1:12; *useless* Js 2:20; 2 Pt 1:8; *careless* Mt 12:36.*

ἀργύριον, ου, τό *silver,* always of money except 1 Cor 3:12 v.l. Of silver money generally Ac 3:6; 7:16. Of particular silver coins *silver shekel* (worth about 4 drachmas) Mt 26:15; *silver drachmas*

Ac 19:19. Of *money* in general Mt 25:18, 27; Lk 9:3. Of a *bribe* Mt 28:15.

ἀργυροκόπος, ου, ὁ *silversmith* Ac 19:24.*

ἄργυρος, ου, ὁ *silver* as a material in general Ac 17:29; 1 Cor 3:12; Js 5:3; Rv 18:12. As money Mt 10:9.* [Cf. *argentine,* like silver.]

ἀργυροῦς, ᾶ, οῦν *(made of) silver* Ac 19:24; 2 Ti 2:20; Rv 9:20.*

ἀρεῖ fut act. ind. 3 sing. of αἴρω.

Ἄρειος πάγος, ὁ *the Areopagus* or *Hill of Ares* (Ares, the Greek god of war = the Roman Mars, hence the older 'Mars' Hill'), northwest of the Acropolis in Athens Ac 17:19, 22. The council which met there from early times was also known as the Areopagus; in Roman times it supervised education and visiting lecturers, and it is not improbable that Paul was brought up it for this reason.*

Ἀρεοπαγίτης, ου, ὁ *Areopagite,* member of the council of the Areopagus Ac 17:34.*

ἀρέσαι, ἀρέσει 1 aor. act. inf. and fut. ind. of ἀρέσκω.

ἀρεσκεία, ας, ἡ (also accented ἀρέσκεια) *desire to please* Col 1:10.*

ἀρέσκω—1. *strive to please, accommodate,* almost = *serve* w. dat. Ro 15:2; 1 Cor 10:33; Gal 1:10.—2. *please, be pleasing* Mk 6:22; Ac 6:5; Ro 8:8; 1 Cor 7:32f.

ἀρεστός, ή, όν *pleasing, desirable* J 8:29; Ac 6:2; 12:3; 1 J 3:22.*

Ἀρέτας, α, ὁ *Aretas;* the one mentioned in 2 Cor 11:32 is Aretas IV, king of Nabataean Arabia c. 9 B.C. to 40 A.D.*

ἀρετή, ῆς, ἡ *moral excellence, virtue* Phil 4:8; 2 Pt 1:5; for 1 Pt 2:9 *praise* or *manifestation of divine power* are both poss.; the latter is preferable for 2 Pt 1:3.*

ἄρῃ 1 aor. act. subj. of αἴρω.

Ἀρηί alt. form of Ἀρνί.

ἀρήν, ἀρνός, ὁ *lamb* Lk 10:3.*

ἀρθῆναι, ἀρθῇ, ἄρθητι 1 aor. pass. inf., subj., and impv., and ἀρθήσομαι, fut. pass. ind., of αἴρω.

ἀριθμέω count Mt 10:30; Lk 12:7; Rv 7:9.* [arithmetic]

ἀριθμός, οῦ, ὁ number, total Lk 22:3; Ac 4:4; 16:5; Rv 13:17f.

Ἀριμαθαία, ας, ἡ Arimathaea, a city in Judaea Mt 27:57; Mk 15:43; Lk 23:51; J 19:38.*

Ἀρίσταρχος, ου, ὁ Aristarchus of Thessalonica Ac 19:29; 20:4; 27:2; Col 4:10; Phlm 24.*

ἀριστάω eat breakfast J 21:12, 15; eat a meal, dine Lk 11:37; 15:29 v.l.*

ἀριστερός, ά, όν left (opposite to right) Mt 6:3. ἐξ ἀ. on the left Mk 10:37; Lk 23:33. ὅπλα ἀ. weapons used by the left hand, i.e. for defense 2 Cor 6:7.*

Ἀριστόβουλος, ου, ὁ Aristobulus οἱ ἐκ τῶν Ἀριστοβούλου those who belong to (the household of) A. Ro 16:10.*

ἄριστον, ου, τό breakfast Lk 14:12; noon meal Mt 22:4; meal generally Lk 11:38; 14:15 v.l.*

ἀρκετός, ή, όν enough, sufficient Mt 6:34; 10:25; 1 Pt 4:3.*

ἀρκέω act. be enough, sufficient Mt 25:9; J 6:7; 14:8; 2 Cor 12:9. Pass. w. dat. be satisfied or content with Lk 3:14; 1 Ti 6:8; Hb 13:5; 3 J 10.*

ἄρκος, ου, ὁ, ἡ a bear Rv 13:2.* [Cf. Arctic.]

ἅρμα, ατος, τό chariot for traveling Ac 8:28f, 38; for military use Rv 9:9.*

Ἁρμαγεδ(δ)ών indecl. Armageddon, a symbolic place name, sometimes identified with Megiddo and Jerusalem Rv 16:16.*

Ἁρμίν alt. form of Ἀδμίν.

ἁρμόζω join or give in marriage, betroth mid. for act. 2 Cor 11:2.* [Cf. harmony.]

ἁρμός, οῦ, ὁ joint Hb 4:12.*

ἄρνας acc. pl. of ἀρήν.

ἀρνέομαι—1. deny Lk 8:45; J 1:20; 2 Ti 3:5; 1 J 2:22. ἀ. ἑαυτόν disregard oneself Lk 9:23, but be untrue to oneself 2 Ti 2:13.—2. repudiate, disown Mt 10:33; 1 Ti 5:8; 2 Ti 2:12; Tit 1:16.—3. refuse Hb 11:24.

Ἀρνί, ὁ indecl. Arni Lk 3:33.*

ἀρνίον, ου, τό lamb, sheep fig. J 21:15; Rv 5:6, 8, 12f.

ἀρνῶν gen. pl. of ἀρήν.

ἆρον 1 aor. act impv. of αἴρω. ἆρον, ἆρον, away, away (with him) J 19:15.

ἀροτριάω to plow Lk 17:7; 1 Cor 9:10.*

ἄροτρον, ου, τό a plow Lk 9:62.*

ἁρπαγείς 2 aor. pass. ptc. of ἁρπάζω.

ἁρπαγή, ῆς, ἡ robbery, plunder Hb 10:34; greediness Lk 11:39. In Mt 23:25 either greediness or plunder (what has been stolen) is possible.* [Harpy]

ἁρπαγμός, οῦ, ὁ prob. = ἅρπαγμα a thing to be seized or greatly desired, a prize, a piece of good fortune, something to hold on to Phil 2:6; robbery is rather improbable.*

ἁρπάζω steal, carry off, drag away, take or snatch away Mt 12:29; J 10:12, 28f; Jd 23; tear out Mt 13:19. Of the Holy Spirit or other divine agency catch up, carry away Ac 8:39; 2 Cor 12: 2, 4; Rv 12:5. Perh. seize or claim for oneself Mt 11:12.

ἅρπαξ, αγος adj. rapacious, ravenous Mt 7:15. As noun robber, swindler Lk 18:11; 1 Cor 5:10f; 6:10; Tit 1:9 v.l.*

ἀρραβών, ῶνος, ὁ (Semitic loanword) first installment, deposit, down payment, pledge fig. 2 Cor 1:22; 5:5; Eph 1:14.*

ἄρραφος see ἄραφος.

ἄρρην see ἄρσην.

ἄρρητος, ον too sacred to tell 2 Cor 12:4.*

ἀρρωστέω be ill, sick Mt 14:14 v.l.*

ἄρρωστος, ον sick, ill Mt 14:14; 1 Cor 11:30.

ἀρσενοκοίτης, ου, ὁ one who engages in same-sex activity, sodomite, pederast 1 Cor 6:9; 1 Ti 1:10.*

ἄρσην, εν gen. ενος male Mt 19:4; Mk 10:6; Lk 2:23; Ro 1:27; Gal 3:28; Rv 12:5, 13.*

Ἀρτεμᾶς, ᾶ, ὁ Artemas Tit 3:12.*

Ἄρτεμις, ιδος, ἡ Artemis, a Greek goddess (Diana is her Roman name) Ac 19:24, 27f, 34f.*

ἀρτέμων, ωνος, ὁ sail, prob. foresail Ac 27:40.*

ἄρτι adv. *now, just.* Of the immediate past *just* Mt 9:18; Rv 12:10, or the immediate present *at once, immediately, now* Mt 26:53; J 13:37. In H. Gk. it is extended to refer to the present in general *now, at the present time* J 9:19, 25; 1 Cor 13:12; 1 Pt 1:6, 8; as adj. 1 Cor 4:11. ἀπ᾽ ἄρτι *from now on* J 13:19; Rv 14:13 (see ἀπαρτί). ἕως ἄρτι *up to the present time, until now* Mt 11:12; J 2:10; 1 Cor 4:13.

ἀρτιγέννητος, ον *newborn* 1 Pt 2:2.*

ἄρτιος, ία, ον *complete, capable, proficient* 2 Ti 3:17.*

ἄρτος, ου, ὁ *bread, loaf (of bread)* Mt 26:26; Mk 6:38, 44, 52; Lk 9:3; Hb 9:2. *Food* in general Mk 3:20; Lk 15:17; 2 Th 3:8, 12. In a transferred sense J 6 passim.

ἀρτύω *season, salt* lit. Mk 9:50; Lk 14:34; fig. Col 4:6.*

Ἀρφαξάδ, ὁ indecl. *Arphaxad* Lk 3:36.*

ἀρχάγγελος, ου, ὁ *archangel* 1 Th 4:16; Jd 9.*

ἀρχαῖος, αία, αῖον *ancient, old, former* Lk 9:8, 19; Ac 15:7, 21; 2 Pt 2:5; Rv 12:9; 20:2; *of long standing* Ac 21:16. οἱ ἀ. *the people of ancient times* Mt 5:21, 27 v.l., 33. τὰ ἀ. *what is old* 2 Cor 5:17.* [*archaic*]

Ἀρχέλαος, ου, ὁ *Archelaus,* son of Herod I, ethnarch of Judaea, Samaria, and Idumaea from his father's death in 4 B.C. to 6 A.D., when he was deposed by the emperor Augustus Mt 2:22.*

ἀρχή, ῆς, ἡ—1. *beginning, origin* Mt 19:4; 24:8; Mk 1:1; 13:8; Lk 1:2; J 1:1; 15:27; Ac 11:15. ἀρχὴν λαμβάνειν *begin* Hb 2:3. στοιχεῖα τῆς ἀ. *elementary principles* 5:12. ὁ τῆς ἀ. τοῦ Χ. λόγος *elementary Christian teaching* 6:1. ἀ τῆς ὑποστάσεως *original conviction* 3:14. ἀ. τῶν σημείων *first of the signs* J 2:11. τὴν ἀρχήν = ὅλως *at all* 8:25. Fig. Col 1:18. *First cause* Rv 3:14. Concrete = *corner* Ac 10:11.—2. *ruler, authority, official* Lk 12:11; 20:20; Tit 3:1. Of angels and demons Ro 8:38; 1 Cor 15:24; Col 2:10, 15.—3. *Rule, domain, sphere of influence* Jd 6. [The derivative *arch-* serves as a prefix, and *-archy* as a suffix, in numerous words.]

ἀρχηγός, οῦ, ὁ either *leader, ruler, prince* or *originator, founder;* the former is more likely for Ac 5:31; for 3:15 either is poss. The latter is more likely for Hb 2:10; 12:2, but the author may have something like *exemplar* in mind.*

ἀρχιερατικός, όν *highpriestly.* ἐκ γένους ἀ. *of the high priest's family* Ac 4:6.*

ἀρχιερεύς, έως, ὁ *high priest* head of the Jewish religion and president of the Sanhedrin Mk 14:60f, 63; J 18:19, 22, 24. The pl. denotes members of the Sanhedrin who belonged to highpriestly families Mt 2:4; Lk 23:13; Ac 4:23. Fig. of Christ Hb 2:17; 4:14.

ἀρχιλῃστής, οῦ, ὁ *robber chieftain* J 18:40 v.l.*

ἀρχιποίμην, ενος, ὁ *chief shepherd* 1 Pt 5:4.*

Ἄρχιππος, ου, ὁ *Archippus* Col 4:17; Phlm 2.*

ἀρχισυνάγωγος, ου, ὁ *leader* or *president of a synagogue* a lay person whose duty it was to take care of the physical arrangements for the worship services Mk 5:22; Lk 13:14; Ac 13:15.

ἀρχιτέκτων, ονος, ὁ *master builder* 1 Cor 3:10.* [*architect*]

ἀρχιτελώνης, ου, ὁ *chief tax collector* Lk 19:2.*

ἀρχιτρίκλινος, ου, ὁ *head waiter, butler;* in the context of J 2:8f prob. *toastmaster, master of the feast.**

ἀρχοστασία, τά = ἀρχαιρεσία *election of magistrates.* The term in 1 Cor 3:3 v.l. appears to be the result of a gloss on the political term ἔρις.

ἄρχω—1. act. *rule* w. gen. Mk 10:42; Ro 15:12.—2. mid. *begin* Mt 4:17; Lk 15:14; 24:27; Ac 8:35; 10:37; and perh. 1:1. At times ἄ. is used with an inf. and functions as a periphrasis for the imperfect of the accompanying verb, as in Mt 26:37; Lk 7:15, 24, 38.

ἄρχων, οντος, ὁ *ruler, lord, prince* Mt 20:25; Ac 4:26; Rv 1:5. Of *authorities, officials* gener., both Jewish Mt 9:18; Lk 8:41; 14:1; 18:18; J 3:1; Ac 3:17 and Gentile Ac 16:19. Of evil spirits Mt 9:34; 12:24; Lk 11:15; J 12:31; 14:30; Eph 2:2. The ἄρχοντες of 1 Cor 2:6, 8 may be demonic powers or earthly rulers. Of a judge Lk 12:58. [archon]

ἄρωμα, ατος, τό pl. spices, aromatic oils or salves Mk 16:1; Lk 23:56; 24:1; J 19:40.*

Ἀσά alt. form of Ἀσάφ.

ἀσάλευτος, ον immovable Ac 27:41; unshaken Hb 12:28.*

Ἀσάφ, ὁ indecl. Asaph or Asa Mt 1:7f; Lk 3:23ff v.l.*

ἄσβεστος, ον inextinguishable Mt 3:12; Mk 9:43, 45 v.l.; Lk 3:17.* [asbestos]

ἀσέβεια, ας, ἡ impiety, godlessness Ro 1:18; 11:26; 2 Ti 2:16; Tit 2:12; Jd 15, 18.*

ἀσεβέω act impiously 2 Pt 2:6; Jd 15.*

ἀσεβής, ές impious, godless 2 Pt 3:7; Jd 15. Mostly as a noun ὁ ἀ. the godless (person) Ro 5:6; 1 Ti 1:9; 1 Pt 4:18.

ἀσέλγεια, ας, ἡ licentiousness, debauchery, sensuality Mk 7:22; Ro 13:13; 2 Pt 2:2, 7, 18. Insolence Jd 4.

ἄσημος, ον obscure, insignificant Ac 21:39.*

Ἀσήρ, ὁ indecl. Asher Lk 2:36; Rv 7:6 (see Gen 30:13).*

ἀσθένεια, ας, ἡ weakness 1 Cor 15:43; 2 Cor 11:30; Hb 5:2; 11:34. Sickness, disease Mt 8:17; Lk 5:15; J 5:5; Ac 28:9; Gal 4:13. Fig. timidity Ro 6:19; 1 Cor 2:3. [asthenia, α priv. + σθένος, strength]

ἀσθενέω be weak. Bodily be sick Mt 10:8; 25:39; J 11:1ff; Ac 9:37; Phil 2:26f. Gener. Ro 8:3; 2 Cor 12:10; 13:3. Fig. Ro 4:19; 14:1f; 2 Cor 11:29. Economically be in need Ac 20:35.

ἀσθένημα, ατος, τό weakness Ro 15:1.*

ἀσθενής, ές weak. Bodily sick, ill Lk 10:9; Ac 4:9; 1 Cor 11:30. Gener. weak Mk 14:38; 1 Pt 3:7; = unimpressive 2 Cor 10:10. Fig. Ro 5:6; 1 Cor 1:25, 27; 4:10; 9:22; Hb 7:18.

Ἀσία, ας, ἡ Asia, a Roman province in western Asia Minor Ac 2:9; 19:10, 22, 26f; Ro 16:5; 2 Cor 1:8.

Ἀσιανός, οῦ, ὁ a man from the Roman province of Asia Ac 20:4.*

Ἀσιάρχης, ου, ὁ Asiarch a wealthy and influential man, prob. connected with the imperial cult Ac 19:31.*

ἀσιτία, ας, ἡ lack of appetite; πολλῆς ἀ. ὑπαρχούσης since almost nobody wanted to eat Ac 27:21.*

ἄσιτος, ον without eating Ac 27:33.*

ἀσκέω do one's best, lit. practice Ac 24:16.* [ascetic]

ἀσκός, οῦ, ὁ wineskin Mk 2:22. [ascidium, botanical term for pitcher-shaped plants or leaves]

ἀσμένως adv. gladly Ac 2:41 v.l.; 21:17.*

ἄσοφος, ον unwise, foolish Eph 5:15.*

ἀσπάζομαι greet, welcome Mk 9:15; Lk 1:40; take leave of Ac 20:1; hail, acclaim Mk 15:18; pay one's respects to Ac 25:13; like, be fond of, cherish Mt 5:47. Imperative, w. acc. greetings to someone, remember me to someone Ro 16:3, 5ff; Phlm 23; Hb 13:24; 3 J 15.

ἀσπασμός, οῦ, ὁ greeting Mt 23:7; Lk 1:29; 11:43; 1 Cor 16:21.

ἄσπιλος, ον spotless, without blemish lit. 1 Pt 1:19; fig. 1 Ti 6:14; Js 1:27; 2 Pt 3:14.*

ἀσπίς, ίδος, ἡ asp, Egyptian cobra Ro 3:13.*

ἄσπονδος, ον irreconcilable 2 Ti 3:3; Ro 1:31 v.l.*

Ἀσσά alt. form of Ἀσά.

ἀσσάριον, ου, τό assarion a Roman copper coin, worth about one-sixteenth of a denarius Mt 10:29; Lk 12:6.*

Ἀσσάρων, ωνος a variant form of Σαρών Ac 9:35 v.l.*

ἆσσον adv. (comparative of ἄγχι) nearer Ac 27:13.*

Ἄσσος, ου, ἡ Assos, a seaport in northwest Asia Minor Ac 20:13f.*

ἀστατέω be unsettled, homeless, a vagabond 1 Cor 4:11.* [astatic]

ἀστεῖος, α, ον beautiful, well-formed Hb 11:23. In Ac 7:20 ἀ. may mean acceptable, well-pleasing. However, if τῷ θεῷ is to be taken as a superlative, the meaning would be a wonderfully beautiful child.*

ἀστήρ, έρος, ὁ star Mt 2:2; Rv 1:16; 9:1. Perh. meteor Jd 13. [aster, asterisk, astral]

ἀστήρικτος, ον unstable, weak 2 Pt 2:14; 3:16.*

ἄστοργος, ον unloving, without affection Ro 1:31; 2 Ti 3:3.*

ἀστοχέω miss the mark περὶ τὴν πίστιν with regard to the faith 1 Ti 6:21; cf. 2 Ti 2:18. Deviate, depart w. gen. from something 1 Ti 1:6.*

ἀστραπή, ῆς, ἡ lightning Mt 24:27; Rv 4:5; light, ray Lk 11:36.

ἀστράπτω flash, gleam Lk 17:24; 24:4.*

ἄστρον, ου, τό star, constellation Ac 7:43; 27:20; Hb 11:12; Lk 21:25.* [astro-, combining form in numerous words]

Ἀσύγκριτος, ου, ὁ Asyncritus Ro 16:14.*

ἀσύμφωνος, ον not harmonious, fig. in disagreement Ac 28:25.*

ἀσύνετος, ον senseless, foolish Mk 7:18; Ro 1:21, 31.

ἀσύνθετος, ον faithless, untrustworthy, perh. undutiful Ro 1:31.*

Ἀσύνκριτος see Ἀσύγκριτος.

ἀσφάλεια, ας, ἡ security, safety Ac 5:23; 1 Th 5:3. Fig. certainty, truth Lk 1:4.*

ἀσφαλής, ές certain, safe, secure, firm Phil 3:1; Hb 6:19; definite Ac 25:26. τὸ ἀ. the certainty, the truth 21:34; 22:30.*

ἀσφαλίζω mid. fasten Ac 16:24. Make secure Mt 27:64–66. Guard Ac 16:30 v.l.*

ἀσφαλῶς adv. securely Ac 16:23; under guard Mk 14:44; beyond a doubt Ac 2:36.*

ἀσχημονέω behave disgracefully, dishonorably, indecently 1 Cor 7:36; 13:5. For the latter passage feel that one ought to be ashamed is probable.*

ἀσχημοσύνη, ης, ἡ shameless deed, indecent act Ro 1:27; shame = private parts Rv 16:15.*

ἀσχήμων, ον shameful, unpresentable. τὰ ἀ. the private parts 1 Cor 12:23.*

ἀσωτία, ας, ἡ debauchery, dissipation Eph 5:18; Tit 1:6; 1 Pt 4:4.*

ἀσώτως adv. dissolutely, loosely Lk 15:13.*

ἀτακτέω be idle, lazy lit. 'be out of order' 2 Th 3:7.*

ἄτακτος, ον idle, lazy lit. 'disorderly' 1 Th 5:14.*

ἀτάκτως adv. idly, in idleness, irresponsibly 2 Th 3:6, 11.*

ἄτεκνος, ον childless Lk 20:28f.*

ἀτενίζω look intently, fix one's eyes Lk 4:20; Ac 7:55; 13:9; 2 Cor 3:7, 13.

ἄτερ prep. w. gen. without, apart from Lk 22:6, 35.*

ἀτιμάζω dishonor, treat shamefully, insult Mk 12:4; Lk 20:11; J 8:49; Ac 5:41; Ro 2:23; Js 2:6; degrade Ro 1:24.*

ἀτιμάω means the same as ἀτιμάζω Mk 12:4 v.l.*

ἀτιμία, ας, ἡ dishonor, disgrace, shame 1 Cor 11:14; 15:43; 2 Cor 6:8. πάθη ἀτιμίας shameful passions Ro 1:26. εἰς ἀ. for (a) dishonor(able use) Ro 9:21; 2 Ti 2:20. κατὰ ἀ. λέγω to my shame I must confess 2 Cor 11:21.*

ἄτιμος, ον unhonored, dishonored, despised 1 Cor 4:10; 12:23. οὐκ ἄ. εἰ μή honored everywhere, except Mt 13:57; Mk 6:4.*

ἀτιμόω means the same as ἀτιμάζω. Pass. be disgraced Mk 12:4 v.l.*

ἀτμίς, ίδος, ἡ mist, vapor Ac 2:19; Js 4:14.*

ἄτομος, ον lit. indivisible. ἐν ἀ. in a moment 1 Cor 15:52.* [atomic]

ἄτοπος, ον out of place. Improper, wrong, evil Lk 23:41; Ac 25:5; 2 Th 3:2. Unusual, surprising Ac 28:6.*

Ἀττάλεια, ας, ἡ Attalia, the seaport of Perga in Pamphylia Ac 14:25.*

αὐγάζω see 2 Cor 4:4; less likely shine forth.*

αὐγή, ῆς, ἡ dawn lit. 'light' Ac 20:11.* [augite, a mineral]

Αὔγουστος, ου, ὁ Augustus (Lat. = revered) a title given Octavian, the first Roman emperor (31 B.C.–14 A.D.) in 27 B.C.; Lk 2:1.* [august]

αὐθάδης, ες self-willed, stubborn, arrogant Tit 1:7; 2 Pt 2:10.*

αὐθαίρετος, ον of one's own accord 2 Cor 8:3, 17.*

αὐθεντέω have total authority, domineer over w. gen. 1 Ti 2:12.* [authentic] αὐλέω *play the flute* Mt 11:17; Lk 7:32; 1 Cor 14:7.*

αὐλή, ῆς, ἡ *courtyard* Mk 14:54; J 18:15; *fold* for sheep J 10:1, 16; *house* or *farm* Lk 11:21; *(outer) court* Rv 11:2; *palace* Mt 26:3. [*aulic,* courtly]

αὐλητής, οῦ, ὁ *flute player* Mt 9:23; Rv 18:22.*

αὐλίζομαι *spend the night, find lodging* Mt 21:17; Lk 21:37; *spend some time* is also possible for the Lk passage.*

αὐλός, οῦ, ὁ *flute* 1 Cor 14:7.*

αὐξάνω and αὔξω—1. trans. *grow, cause to grow* or *increase* 1 Cor 3:6f; 2 Cor 9:10.—2. intrans., act. and pass. *grow, increase* Mk 4:8; Lk 13:19; J 3:30; Ac 6:7; 2 Cor 10:15; Col 1:6, 10. [Cf. *auxiliary, augment.*]

αὔξησις, εως, ἡ *growth, increase* Eph 4:16; Col 2:19.*

αὐξήσω fut. act. ind. of αὐξάνω.

αὔξω see αὐξάνω.

αὔριον adv. *tomorrow* Ac 23:20; Js 4:13. With the article and ἡμέρα to be supplied ἡ αὔ. *the next day* Mt 6:34 b; Lk 10:35. In the sense *in a short time, soon* Lk 12:28; 1 Cor 15:32.

αὐστηρός, ά, όν *severe, strict, exacting, austere* in both favorable and unfavorable senses Lk 19:21f.*

αὐτάρκεια, ας, ἡ *sufficiency* 2 Cor 9:8; *contentment, self-sufficiency* 1 Ti 6:6.* [*autarky,* self-sufficiency]

αὐτάρκης, ες *content, self-sufficient,* either meaning is possible for Phil 4:11.*

αὐτοκατάκριτος, ον *self-condemned* Tit 3:11.*

αὐτόματος, η, ον *by itself* of something that happens without visible cause Mk 4:28; Ac 12:10.* [*automatic*]

αὐτόπτης, ου, ὁ *eyewitness* Lk 1:2.* [*autopsy*]

αὐτός, αὐτή, αὐτό—1. *self* intensive, setting the word it modifies from everything else, emphasizing and contrasting. αὐτὸς Ἰησοῦς *Jesus himself* Lk 24:15. Cf. Mk 12:36f; Lk 24:36; Ac 24:15; 1 Cor 11:13; Hb 13:5. αὐ. ἐγώ *I alone* 2 Cor 12:13. *Of oneself, of one's own accord* J 2:25; 16:27; *thrown on one's own resources* Ro 7:25. καὶ αὐ-

τός *even* Ro 8:21; Hb 11:11. αὐ. τὰ ἔργα *the very deeds* J 5:36; cf. Mt 3:4; Lk 13:1. αὐτὸ τοῦτο *just this, the very same thing* 2 Cor 7:11. Adverbial accusative τοῦτο αὐ. *for this very reason* 2 Cor 2:3; cf. 2 Pt 1:5. As an emphatic personal pronoun Mt 5:4ff.—2. In the oblique cases, as a third pers. personal pronoun, esp. in the gen., used as a possessive pronoun *him, her, it* Mt 4:23; 8:1; Mk 1:10; Lk 2:22; J 15:2; 1 Cor 8:12; Rv 2:7, 17. Used, as it seems to speakers of English, superfluously (pleonastically) with relative pronouns ἥν οὐδεὶς δύναται κλεῖσαι αὐτήν *which no one can close (it)* Rv 3:8; cf. Mk 1:7; J 6:39; Ac 15:17.—3. Preceded by the article ὁ αὐτός, ἡ αὐτή, τὸ αὐτό *the same* Mt 5:46; 26:44; Lk 6:33; Ro 2:1; Eph 6:9. τὸ αὐ. λέγειν *agree* 1 Cor 1:10. τὸ αὐτό as adv. *in the same way* Mt 27:44. ἐπὶ τὸ αὐτό *at the same place, together* Mt 22:34; 1 Cor 11:20; *to the total* Ac 2:47. κατὰ τὸ αὐτό *together* of place and time 14:1. [*autocrat,* αὐτός + κράτος]

αὐτοῦ adv. *here* Mt 26:36. *There* Ac 18:19.

αὐτόφωρος, ον *(caught) in the act* in the expression ἐπ᾽ αὐτοφώρῳ J 8:4.*

αὐτόχειρ, ρος *with one's own hand* Ac 27:19.*

αὐχέω *boast* Js 3:5.*

αὐχμηρός, ά, όν *dark* 2 Pt 1:19.*

ἀφαιρέω *take away, remove, rob* Lk 1:25; 10:42; Ro 11:27; Hb 10:4; Rv 22:19; *cut off* Mk 14:47. [*aphaeresis,* the dropping of a letter or syllable from the beginning of a word]

ἀφανής, ές *invisible, hidden* Hb 4:13.* [*aphanite,* a close-textured dark rock]

ἀφανίζω *cause to disappear, destroy* Mt 6:19f; *render invisible* or *unrecognizable* or *disfigure* 6:16. Pass. *disappear* Js 4:14; *perish* Ac 13:41.*

ἀφανισμός, οῦ, ὁ *disappearance, destruction* Hb 8:13.*

ἄφαντος, ον *invisible* Lk 24:31.*

ἀφεδρών, ῶνος, ὁ *latrine* Mt 15:17; Mk 7:19.*

ἀφέθην, ἀφεθήσομαι 1 aor. pass. ind. and fut. pass. ind. of ἀφίημι.

ἀφειδία, ας, ἡ severe (lit. unsparing) treatment Col 2:23.*

ἀφεῖλον, ἀφελεῖν 2 aor. act. ind. and inf. of ἀφαιρέω.

ἀφεῖναι, ἀφείς 2 aor. inf. and ptc. of ἀφίημι.

ἀφελότης, ητος, ἡ simplicity Ac 2:46.*

ἀφελπίζω see ἀπελπίζω.

ἀφελῶ, ἀφέλωμαι 2 fut. act. ind. and 2 aor. mid. subj. of ἀφαιρέω.

ἄφες 2 aor. act. impv. of ἀφίημι.

ἄφεσις, έσεως, ἡ release Lk 4:18. Pardon, cancellation of an obligation, a punishment, or guilt, hence forgiveness of sins Mk 1:4; 3:29; Lk 3:3; Ac 10:43; Eph 1:7. [aphesis, ἀφίημι]

ἀφέωνται pf. pass. ind. of ἀφίημι.

ἀφή, ῆς, ἡ ligament Eph 4:16; Col 2:19.*

ἀφῆκα, ἀφήσω 1 aor. act. ind. and fut. act. ind. of ἀφίημι.

ἀφθαρσία, ας, ἡ incorruptibility, immortality Ro 2:7; 1 Cor 15:42, 50, 53f; 2 Ti 1:10. ἐν ἀ. in immortality or forever Eph 6:24.

ἄφθαρτος, ον imperishable, incorruptible, immortal Ro 1:23; 1 Cor 9:25; 15:52; 1 Pt 1:4; imperishable quality 1 Pt 3:4.

ἀφθονία, ας, ἡ freedom from envy, hence willingness Tit 2:7 v.l.*

ἀφθορία, ας, ἡ soundness, purity Tit 2:7.*

ἀφίδω 2 aor. act. subj. of ἀφοράω.

ἀφιέναι pres. act. inf. of ἀφίημι.

ἀφίημι—1. let go, send away Mk 4:36; give up Mt 27:50; utter Mk 15:37; divorce 1 Cor 7:11ff. Cancel, pardon Mt 18:27, 32; remit, forgive sins, etc. Mt 6:12, 14f; Mk 3:28; Lk 12:10; Ro 4:7; 1 J 1:9; 2:12.—2. leave lit. Mt 4:11; 19:27; Mk 13:34; Lk 10:30; abandon Mk 14:50. Let someone have something Mt 5:40; give peace J 14:27. Fig. give up, abandon Ro 1:27; Hb 6:1; Rv 2:4; neglect Mt 23:23.—3. let, let go, permit, tolerate Mk 5:19; Ac 5:38; Rv 2:20; 11:9. Let someone go on J 11:48. The imperatives ἄφες, ἄφετε are used with the subjunctive, esp. in the first person ἄφες ἐκβάλω τὸ κάρφος let me take out the speck Mt 7:4; ἄφες ἴδωμεν

let us see 27:49; also with ἵνα and the third person ἄφες αὐτήν, ἵνα τηρήσῃ αὐτό let her keep it J 12:7.

ἀφικνέομαι reach = become known to Ro 16:19.*

ἀφιλάγαθος, ον not loving the good 2 Ti 3:3.*

ἀφιλάργυρος, ον not loving money, not greedy 1 Ti 3:3; Hb 13:5.*

ἄφιξις, εως, ἡ departure Ac 20:29.*

ἀφίστημι—1. trans. (1 aor. act.) cause to revolt, mislead Ac 5:37.—2. intrans. (middle, and 2 aor., pf., and plupf. act.) go away, withdraw Lk 2:37; 13:27; Ac 12:10; ἀπό τινος desert someone Ac 15:38. Fall away, become apostate Lk 8:13; Hb 3:12. Keep away Lk 4:13; 2 Cor 12:8; abstain 2 Ti 2:19. [apostate]

ἄφνω adv. suddenly Ac 2:2; 16:26; immediately, at once 28:6.*

ἀφόβως adv. fearlessly Lk 1:74; Phil 1:14; without cause to be afraid or perh. without causing fear 1 Cor 16:10; boldly or shamelessly Jd 12.*

ἀφομοιόω make like or similar Hb 7:3.*

ἀφοράω look away, fix one's eyes trustingly Hb 12:2; see Phil 2:23.*

ἀφορίζω set apart, take away, separate, exclude Mt 13:49; 25:32; Lk 6:22; Ac 19:9; 2 Cor 6:17; Gal 2:12. Set apart, appoint Ac 13:2; Ro 1:1; Gal 1:15.* [aphorize]

ἀφοριῶ Attic fut. of ἀφορίζω.

ἀφορμή, ῆς, ἡ occasion, pretext, opportunity Ro 7:8, 11; 2 Cor 11:12; 1 Ti 5:14.

ἀφρίζω foam at the mouth Mk 9:18, 20.*

ἀφρός, οῦ, ὁ foam Lk 9:39.*

ἀφροσύνη, ης, ἡ foolishness, lack of sense Mk 7:22; 2 Cor 11:1, 17, 21.*

ἄφρων, ον, gen. ονος foolish, ignorant Lk 11:40; 2 Cor 11:16, 19; 1 Pt 2:15.

ἀφυπνόω fall asleep Lk 8:23.*

ἀφυστερέω withhold, keep back Js 5:4 v.l.*

ἀφῶμεν 2 aor. subj. act. of ἀφίημι.

ἄφωνος, ον silent Ac 8:32. Incapable of speech 1 Cor 12:2; 2 Pt 2:16; incapable of conveying meaning 1 Cor 14:10.*

Ἀχάζ, ὁ indecl. *Ahaz* Mt 1:9; see 2 Kings 16:1ff.*

Ἀχαΐα, ας, ἡ *Achaia*, a Roman province created 146 B.C., including the most important parts of Greece, i.e. Boeotia, Attica, and the Peloponnesus Ac 18:12, 27; Ro 15:26; 2 Cor 1:1.

Ἀχαϊκός, οῦ, ὁ *Achaicus* 1 Cor 16:17, 15 v.l.*

ἀχάριστος, ον *ungrateful* Lk 6:35; 2 Ti 3:2.*

Ἀχάς v.l. for Ἀχάζ.

ἀχειροποίητος, ον *not made by* (human) *hand, not of (mere) human origin* Mk 14:58; 2 Cor 5:1; Col 2:11.*

Ἀχελδαμάχ see Ἀκελδαμάχ.

ἀχθῆναι, ἀχθήσεσθαι 1 aor. pass. inf. and 1 fut. pass. inf. of ἄγω.

Ἀχίμ, ὁ indecl. *Achim* Mt 1:14.*

ἀχλύς ύος, ἡ *mistiness, dimness of sight* Ac 13:11.*

ἀχρεῖος, ον *useless, worthless* Mt 25:30; *unworthy, miserable* Lk 17:10.*

ἀχρειόω pass., fig. *become depraved, worthless* Ro 3:12.*

ἄχρηστος, ον *useless, worthless* Phlm 11.*

ἄχρι, ἄχρις—**1.** adv. functioning as prep. w. gen. *until* Mt 24:38; Lk 4:13; Ro 1:13; Gal 4:2; *to* Hb 6:11; *within* Ac 20:6; *before* Ro 5:13; *as far as* Ac 22:22; Hb 4:12; *to, unto* Ac 22:4; Rv 2:10.— **2.** as conj. *until (the time when)* with or without οὗ Ac 7:18; Ro 11:25; Gal 3:19; *as long as* Hb 3:13.

ἄχυρον, ου, τό *chaff* Mt 3:12; Lk 3:17.*

ἄψας 1 aor. act. ptc. of ἅπτω.

ἀψευδής, ές *free from all deceit, trustworthy* Tit 1:2.*

ἀψίνθιον, ου, τό and ἄψινθος, ου, ἡ *wormwood* Rv 8:11b; as name of a star and masc. Rv 8:11a.* [*absinthe*]

ἄψυχος, ον *inanimate, lifeless* 1 Cor 14:7.*

B

β' as numeral = *two, second* superscriptions of 2 Cor, etc.

Βάαλ, ὁ indecl. *Baal*, Hebrew for 'lord' Ro 11:4.*

Βαβυλών, ῶνος, ἡ *Babylon* lit. Mt 1:11f; fig., of worldly power Rv 14:8; 18:10, 21. In 1 Pt 5:13 B may be a code word for God's people in dispersion.

βαθέως genitive of βαθύς.

βαθμός, οῦ, ὁ *step;* fig. *rank, standing* 1 Ti 3:13.*

βάθος, ους, τό *depth* lit. Mt 13:5; Lk 5:4; fig. Ro 8:39; 11:33; κατὰ βάθους *reaching down into the depths* = *extreme, abysmal* 2 Cor 8:2. [*bathos*]

βαθύνω *make deep* and intrans. *go down deep;* the latter is preferable in Lk 6:48.*

βαθύς, εῖα, ύ *deep* lit. J 4:11; fig. Ac 20:9; Rv 2:24. ὄρθρου βαθέως *early in the morning* Lk 24:1.* [*bathetic, bathy-*, a combining form, as in *bathysphere*]

βάϊον, ου, τό *palm branch* (Coptic loanword) J 12:13.*

Βαλαάμ, ὁ indecl. *Balaam* 2 Pt 2:15; Jd 11; Rv 2:14; see Num 22–24.*

Βαλάκ, ὁ indecl. *Balak* Rv 2:14; see Num 22:2ff. Βαλααμ Jd 11 v.l.*

βαλλάντιον, ου, τό *money-bag, purse* Lk 10:4; 12:33; 22:35f.*

βάλλω—**1.** *throw* Mt 3:10; 5:29f; 13:48; Rv 2:10; 6:13; *sow, scatter* Mk 4:26; *cast* 15:24. Fig. *drive* 1 J 4:18. Pass. *lie* Mt 9:2; Lk 16:20.—**2.** *put, place, lay, bring* Mt 10:34; Mk 7:33; Lk 13:8; J

13:2; Rv 2:14; *pour* Mt 9:17; J 13:5; Rv 12:15f; *swing* Rv 14:19; *deposit* Mt 25:27.—3. intrans. *rush down, break loose* Ac 27:14. [*ballistics*]

βαλώ fut. act. ind. of *βάλλω*.

βαπτίζω *dip, immerse—*1. of Jewish ritual washings, mid. and pass. *wash one's hands* Mk 7:4; Lk 11:38.—2. *baptize*, of ritual immersion by John the Baptist and Christians Mt 3:11, 13f, 16; 28:19; Mk 6:14, 24; J 4:1f; Ac 2:38, 41; 8:12f, 36, 38; 1 Cor 1:14–17; 15:29.—3. fig. Mt 3:11; 1 Cor 10:2; 12:13. Of martyrdom Mk 10:38f.

βάπτισμα, ατος, τό *baptism* Mt 3:7; Mk 1:4; Ac 18:25; Ro 6:4; Eph 4:5; 1 Pt 3:21. *βαπτίζεσθαι βάπτισμα undergo a baptism* Lk 7:29. Fig., of martyrdom Mk 10:38f.

βαπτισμός, οῦ, ὁ *dipping, ceremonial washing* Mk 7:4, 8 v.l.; Hb 6:2; 9:10; *baptism* Col 2:12.*

βαπτιστής, οῦ, ὁ *Baptist*, always as a surname of John Mt 3:1; 11:11f; Mk 6:25; Lk 9:19. [*baptistery*]

βάπτω *dip, dip in* Lk 16:24; J 13:26; Rv 19:13; for the latter passage *dye* is also possible.*

βαρ Aramaic = *son* Mt 16:17 v.l.*

Βαραββᾶς, ᾶ, ὁ *Barabbas* Mt 27:16f; Lk 23:18; J 18:40.

Βαράκ, ὁ indecl. *Barak* Hb 11:32; see Judg 4f.*

Βαραχίας, ου, ὁ *Barachiah* Mt 23:35.

βάρβαρος, ον *speaking a foreign, unintelligible language* adj. or noun 1 Cor 14:11. As noun *a person who is not Greek, a foreigner* Ac 28:2, 4; Ro 1:14; Col 3:11.* [*barbarian*]

βαρέω *weigh down, burden,* pass., fig. *be burdened, be overcome, become heavy* Lk 9:32; 21:34; 2 Cor 1:8; 1 Ti 5:16.

βαρέως adv. of *βαρύς; with difficulty ἀκούειν be hard of hearing* Mt 13:15; Ac 28:27.*

Βαρθολομαῖος, ου, ὁ *Bartholomew*, one of the 12 apostles Mt 10:3; Mk 3:18; Lk 6:14; Ac 1:13. Often identified w. Nathanael.*

Βαριησοῦς, οῦ, ὁ *Bar-Jesus*, a false prophet Ac 13:6.*

Βαριωνᾶ or **Βαριωνᾶς, ᾶ, ὁ** *Bar-Jona* Mt 16:17.*

Βαρναβᾶς, ᾶ, ὁ *Barnabas*, apostle and for a time companion of Paul Ac 4:36; 9:27; 11:22, 30; 12:25; chapters 13–15 passim; 1 Cor 9:6; Gal 2:1, 9, 13; Col 4:10.*

βάρος, ους, τό *weight, burden* fig. Mt 20:12; Ac 15:28; Gal 6:2; Rv 2:24; *fullness* 2 Cor 4:17; *importance ἐν β. εἶναι insist on one's importance* 1 Th 2:7.* [*barometer, βάρος + μέτρον*]

Βαρσαββᾶς, ᾶ, ὁ *Barsabbas*, a patronymic of two different men Ac 1:23; 15:22.*

Βαρτιμαῖος, ου, ὁ *Bartimaeus* Mk 10:46.*

βαρύνω *burden, grieve* Ac 3:14 v.l.; 28:27 v.l.; 2 Cor 5:4 v.l.*

βαρύς, εῖα, ύ *heavy, weighty* fig. Mt 23:4; *burdensome, difficult* 1 J 5:3; *severe* 2 Cor 10:10; *weighty, important* Mt 23:23; Ac 25:7; *fierce, savage* Ac 20:29.* [*baritone, βαρύς + τόνος*]

βαρύτιμος, ον *very expensive, very precious* Mt 26:7.*

βασανίζω *torture, torment* Mt 8:6, 29; 2 Pt 2:8; Rv 12:2; 14:10; *press hard* Mt 14:24.

βασανισμός, οῦ, ὁ *torture, torment* Rv 9:5; 14:11; 18:7, 10, 15.*

βασανιστής, οῦ, ὁ *torturer, jailer* Mt 18:34.*

βάσανος, ου, ἡ *torture, torment* Lk 16:23, 28; *great pain* Mt 4:24.*

βασιλεία, ας, ἡ—1. *kingship, royal power* or *rule, kingdom* Lk 19:12, 15; 1 Cor 15:24; Hb 1:8; Rv 1:6; 17:12.— 2. *kingdom*, territory ruled over by a king Mt 4:8; Mk 6:23; Lk 21:10.—3. *the royal reign* or *kingdom* of God or the heavens (the expressions are equivalent) Mt 3:2; 5:3, 10, 19f; Mk 4:11; Lk 8:1; J 3:3, 5; Ac 28:23, 31; Ro 14:17; 1 Cor 4:20; Gal 5:21. It is thought of as present Mt 12:28; Lk 11:20 or future Mt 3:2; Lk 21:31.

βασίλειος, ον *royal* 1 Pt 2:9. τὰ *β*. *the (royal) palace(s)* Lk 7:25.*

34   βασιλεύς–Βηθανία

βασιλεύς, έως, ό king lit. Mt 2:1; 17:25;
Mk 6:14; J 6:15; Ac 12:1; 2 Cor 11:32;
Hb 7:1f; Rv 1:5. Of the Roman emperor 1 Ti 2:2; 1 Pt 2:13, 17. Fig. of
God and Christ Mt 2:2; J 1:49; 1 Ti
1:17; Rv 17:14. [Basil]
βασιλεύω be king, rule w. gen. over or
of something Mt 2:22; also w. ἐπί and
gen. or acc. Lk 19:14, 27; Rv 5:10. Fig.
Ro 5:14. Of God and Christ Rv 11:15.
In aor. (ingressive) become king Rv
11:17; 19:6.
βασιλικός, ή, όν royal Ac 12:20f; Js 2:8;
royal official J 4:46, 49.* [basilica]
βασιλίσκος, ου, ό petty king v.l. in J
4:46 and 49.* [basilisk]
βασίλισσα, ης, ή queen Mt 12:42; Lk
11:31; Ac 8:27; Rv 18:7.*
βάσις, εως, ή that with which one steps
(βαίνω), the (human) foot Ac 3:7.*
βασκαίνω bewitch with the evil eye Gal
3:1.*
βαστάζω—1. pick up J 10:31.—2. carry,
bear lit. Lk 11:27; 22:10; J 19:17; fig.
Mt 20:12; J 16:12; Gal 6:2; bear patiently, put up with Ro 15:1; Rv 2:3. β.
κρίμα bear one's judgment, pay the
penalty Gal 5:10.—3. carry away, remove Mt 3:11; 8:17; J 20:15; steal J
12:6.
βάτος, ου, ό and ή thornbush Lk 6:44;
Ac 7:30, 35. ἐπὶ τ. β. in the passage
about the thornbush Mk 12:26; Lk
20:37.*
βάτος, ου, ό bath a Hebrew liquid measure = between 30 and 34 liters Lk
16:6.*
βάτραχος, ου, ό frog Rv 16:13.* [batra-
chian]
βατταλογέω babble Mt 6:7; Lk 11:2 v.l.*
βδέλυγμα, ατος, τό abomination, detestable thing esp. of idolatry Lk 16:15;
Rv 17:4f; 21:27. β. τῆς ἐρημώσεως the
detestable thing causing desolation Mt
24:15; Mk 13:14.*
βδελυκτός, ή, όν abominable, detestable Tit 1:16.*
βδελύσσομαι abhor, detest Ro 2:22; pf.
pass. ptc. ἐβδελυγμένος abominable
Rv 21:8.*

βέβαιος, α, ον firm, strong, secure lit.
Hb 6:19. Fig. firm, reliable, dependable, certain Ro 4:16; 2 Cor 1:7; Hb
2:2; 3:14; 2 Pt 1:10, 19; valid Hb 9:17.*
βεβαιόω confirm, establish 1 Cor 1:6, 8;
Col 2:7; fulfill Ro 15:8; strengthen 2
Cor 1:21; guarantee Hb 2:3.
βεβαίωσις, εως, ή confirmation Phil 1:7;
confirmation, guarantee Hb 6:16.*
βεβαμμένος pf. pass. ptc. of βάπτω.
βέβηλος, ον profane, worldly, godless
1 Ti 1:9; 4:7; 6:20; 2 Ti 2:16; irreligious
Hb 12:16.*
βεβηλόω desecrate, profane Mt 12:5; Ac
24:6.*
βέβληκα, βέβλημαι pf. act. ind. and
pf. pass. ind. of βάλλω.
βέβρωκα pf. act. ind. of βιβρώσκω.
Βεελζεβούλ, ό indecl., with variant
readings Βεελζεβούβ and Βεεζεβούλ
Beelzebub, i.e. Satan Mt 10:25; 12:24,
27; Mk 3:22; Lk 11:15, 18f.*
Βελιάρ, ό indecl., with v.l. Βελιάλ Be-
lial, i.e. Satan or the Antichrist 2 Cor
6:15.*
βελόνη, ης, ή needle Lk 18:25.*
βέλος, ους, τό arrow Eph 6:16.*
βελτίων, ον better; neut. as adv. very
well 2 Ti 1:18; Ac 10:28 v.l.*
Βενιαμ(ε)ίν, ό indecl. Benjamin Ac
13:21; Ro 11:1; Phil 3:5; Rv 7:8.*
Βερνίκη, ης, ή Bernice, sister and companion of Herod Agrippa II Ac 25:13,
23; 26:30.*
Βέροια, ας, ή Beroea, a city in Macedonia Ac 17:10, 13.*
Βεροιαῖος, α, ον from Beroea, as noun
the Beroean Ac 20:4.*
Βέρος, ου, ό Beros Ac 20:4 v.l.
Βεωορσόρ alt. form of Βεώρ 2 Pt 2:15
v.l.
Βεώρ, ό indecl. Beor for Βοσόρ 2 Pt 2:15
v.l.*
Βηθαβαρά, ή Bethabara v.l. for Βηθα-
νία in J 1:28.*
Βηθανία, ας, ή Bethany—1. a village on
the Mount of Olives, nearly 3 km. from
Jerusalem Mt 21:17; 26:6; Mk 11:11f;
Lk 24:50; J 12:1.—2. place on the east

side of the Jordan where John baptized J 1:28.

Βηθαραβά error for Βηθαβαρά.

Βηθεσδά, ἡ indecl. *Bethesda*, a pool in Jerusalem J 5:2 v.l.*

Βηθζαθά, ἡ indecl. *Bethzatha* J 5:2.*

Βηθλέεμ, ἡ indecl. *Bethlehem*, a town in Judaea, about 7 km. south of Jerusalem Mt 2:1, 5f, 8, 16; Lk 2:4, 15; J 7:42.*

Βηθσαϊδά(ν), ἡ indecl. *Bethsaida*, the name of a city (perh. two cities) near the Sea of Galilee Mt 11:21; Mk 6:45; 8:22; Lk 9:10; 10:13; J 1:44; 12:21. Also as v.l. for Βηθζαθά J 5:2.*

Βηθφαγή, ἡ indecl. *Bethphage*, a place on the Mount of Olives Mt 21:1; Mk 11:1; Lk 19:29.*

βῆμα, ατος, τό—1. *step, stride* οὐδὲ β. ποδός *not even a foot of ground* Ac 7:5.—**2.** *tribunal, judicial bench* Mt 27:19; J 19:13; Ac 18:12, 16f; 25:6, 10, 17; Ro 14:10; 2 Cor 5:10; *speaker's platform* Ac 12:21, 23 v.l.* [*bema*]

Βηρεύς, εως, ὁ *Bereus* Ro 16:15 v.l.

βήρυλλος, ου, ὁ, ἡ *beryl* a semiprecious stone of sea-green color Rv 21:20.*

βία, ας, ἡ *force, violence* Ac 21:35; 27:41; *use of force* 5:26; cf. 24:7 v.l.* [Cf. Lat. *vis.*]

βιάζω mid. *force one's way, enter forcibly* Lk 16:16; pass., prob. *be forcibly entered, suffer violence* (w. other possibilities) Mt 11:12.*

βίαιος, α, ον *violent, strong* Ac 2:2.*

βιαστής, οῦ, ὁ a *violent, impetuous man* Mt 11:12.*

βιβλαρίδιον, ου, τό *little book* Rv 10:2, 9f, vs. 8 v.l.*

βιβλιδάριον, ου, τό v.l. for βιβλαρίδιον in the Rv passages above.

βιβλίον, ου, τό *book, scroll* Lk 4:17; J 20:30; Gal 3:10; 2 Ti 4:13; Rv 5:1ff; 6:14; 13:8. β. ἀποστασίου a *certificate of divorce* Mk 10:4. [*biblio-*, combining form in numerous words]

βίβλος, ου, ἡ *book, scroll* esp. *sacred book* Mt 1:1; Mk 12:26; Lk 3:4; Ac 7:42; 19:19; Phil 4:3; Rv 3:5. [*Bible*]

βιβρώσκω *eat* J 6:13.*

Βιθυνία, ας, ἡ *Bithynia*, a Roman province in northern Asia Minor Ac 16:7; 1 Pt 1:1.*

βίος, ου, ὁ—1. *life, everyday life* Lk 8:14; 1 Ti 2:2; 2 Ti 2:4; 1 Pt 4:3 v.l.—**2.** *livelihood, property* Mk 12:44; Lk 8:43; 15:12, 30; 21:4. β. τοῦ κόσμου *worldly goods* 1 J 3:17. ἀλαζονεία τοῦ β. *pride in one's possessions* 2:16.* [*biology*]

βιόω *live* 1 Pt 4:2.*

βίωσις, εως, ἡ *manner of life* Ac 26:4.*

βιωτικός, ή, όν *belonging to (daily) life, ordinary* Lk 21:34; 1 Cor 6:3, 4.*

βλαβερός, ά, όν *harmful* 1 Ti 6:9.*

βλάπτω *harm, injure* Mk 16:18; Lk 4:35.*

βλαστάνω, βλαστάω *sprout, put forth* trans. *produce* Js 5:18. Intrans. *bud, sprout* Mt 13:26; Mk 4:27; Hb 9:4.*

Βλάστος, ου, ὁ *Blastus* Ac 12:20.*

βλασφημέω in relation to people *revile, defame, slander* Ro 3:8; 1 Cor 10:30; Tit 3:2. In relation to a divine being *speak irreverently of, blaspheme* Mt 9:3; 27:39; Mk 3:29; Ac 19:37; Ro 2:24; 14:16; 2 Pt 2:10.

βλασφημία, ας, ἡ *slander, abusive speech, blasphemy* Mt 12:31; 26:65; J 10:33; Eph 4:31; Rv 13:5f; a *reviling judgment* Jd 9.

βλάσφημος, ον *slanderous, scurrilous, blasphemous* Ac 6:11; 2 Ti 3:2 β. κρίσιν φέρειν *pronounce a defaming judgment* 2 Pt 2:11. As noun *slanderer* 1 Ti 1:13.

βλέμμα, ατος, τό *glance, look* βλέμματι *by what he saw* 2 Pt 2:8.*

βλέπω *see, look (at)—1.* *be able to see* J 9:7, 15, 25; Ac 9:9; Ro 11:8; Rv 3:18.—**2.** *see, look at* Mt 5:28; 7:3; Mk 5:31; Lk 9:62; 10:23f; Ac 9:8f; Ro 8:24f; Rv 1:11f; *look on* Ac 1:9. βλέπων βλέπω *see with open eyes* Mt 13:14. βλέπων οὐ βλέπει *though he looks he does not see* Lk 8:10.—**3.** *watch, beware of* Mk 13:9; Phil 3:2; *see to it, take care* Mt 24:4; Gal 5:15; *perceive* Mt 14:30; *discover, find* Ro 7:23; Hb 3:19. [Cf. *blepharitis*, inflammation of the eyelids.]

βληθήσομαι fut. pass. ind. of βάλλω.

βλητέος, α, ον verbal adj. from βάλλω must be put Lk 5:38; Mk 2:22 v.l.*

Βοανηργές Boanerges Mk 3:17.*

βοάω call, shout, cry out Mt 3:3; Mk 15:34; Lk 18:7; J 1:23; Ac 8:7.

Βόες, ὁ indecl. Boaz Mt 1:5; cf. Ruth 4:21.*

βοή, ῆς, ἡ cry, shout Js 5:4.*

βοήθεια, ας, ἡ help Hb 4:16; nautical term support, perh, in the form of cables Ac 27:17.*

βοηθέω come to the aid of, help w. dat. Mt 15:25; Mk 9:22, 24; Ac 16:9; 21:28; 2 Cor 6:2; Hb 2:18; Rv 12:16.*

βοηθός, όν helpful, as noun helper Hb 13:6.*

βόησον 1 aor. act. impv. of βοάω.

βόθρος, ου, ὁ pit, cistern Mt 15:14 v.l.*

βόθυνος, ου, ὁ pit Mt 12:11; 15:14; Lk 6:39.*

βολή, ῆς, ἡ a throw λίθου β. a stone's throw Lk 22:41.* [Cf. βάλλω.]

βολίζω take soundings Ac 27:28.*

βολίς, ίδος, ἡ missile, arrow, javelin Hb 12:20 v.l.*

Βόος, ὁ indecl. Boaz Lk 3:32.*

βόρβορος, ου, ὁ mud, filth 2 Pt 2:22.*

βορρᾶς, ᾶ, ὁ the north ἀπὸ β. on the north Rv 21:13 but from (the) north Lk 13:29.*

βόσκω act. feed, tend Mk 5:14; J 21:15, 17. Pass. graze, feed Mk 5:11.

Βοσόρ, ὁ indecl. Bosor 2 Pt 2:15.*

βοτάνη, ης, ἡ vegetation Hb 6:7.* [botany]

βότρυς, υος, ὁ bunch of grapes Rv 14:18.*

βουλευτής, οῦ, ὁ member of a council in this case the Sanhedrin Mk 15:43; Lk 23:50.*

βουλεύω mid. deliberate, consider Lk 14:31. Decide, plan Ac 27:39; 15:37 v.l.; 2 Cor 1:17; plot J 11:53; 12:10; Ac 5:33 v.l.*

βουλή, ῆς, ἡ plan, purpose Lk 7:30; Eph 1:11; resolution, decision Ac 2:23; 5:38; 20:27; 27:12, 42; Hb 6:17; motive 1 Cor 4:5.

βούλημα, ατος, τό intention, will Ac 27:43; Ro 9:19; 1 Pt 4:3.* [Cf. volition.]

βούλομαι wish, be willing, want, desire Mt 1:19; 11:27; Lk 22:42; Ac 5:28; 25:20, 22; 1 Cor 12:11; 1 Ti 6:9; Phlm 13. βουληθείς according to his will Js 1:18. βούλεσθε ἀπολύσω; shall I release? J 18:39.

βουνός, οῦ, ὁ hill Lk 3:5; 23:30.*

βοῦς, βοός, ὁ ox Lk 14:5, 19; J 2:14f; 1 Cor 9:9. [Cf. bucolic.]

βραβεῖον, ου, τό prize in a footrace 1 Cor 9:24; of the resurrection-life Phil 3:14.*

βραβεύω rule Col 3:15, lit. 'award prizes, judge, control.'*

βραδύνω intr. hesitate, delay 1 Ti 3:15; hold back in hesitation 2 Pt 3:9.*

βραδυπλοέω sail slowly Ac 27:7.*

βραδύς, εῖα, ύ slow Lk 24:25; Js 1:19.*

βραδύτης, ητος, ἡ slowness 2 Pt 3:9.*

βραχίων, ονος, ὁ arm fig. Lk 1:51; J 12:38; Ac 13:17.*

βραχύς, εῖα, ύ short, little: of distance Ac 27:28; of time Lk 22:58; Ac 5:34; Hb 2:7, 9; of quantity J 6:7. διὰ β. in a few words Hb 13:22; 1 Pt 5:12 v.l.* [brachy-, combining form, as in brachylogy]

βρέφος, ους, τό baby, infant Lk 1:41, 44; 2:12, 16; 18:15; Ac 7:19; 2 Ti 3:15; fig. 1 Pt 2:2.*

βρέχω wet Lk 7:38, 44. Of rain fall Rv 11:6. Send rain, cause to rain Mt 5:45; Lk 17:29. Impersonal βρέχει it rains Js 5:17.*

βριμάομαι be indignant J 11:33 v.l. S. ἐμβριμάομαι.

βροντή, ῆς, ἡ thunder Mk 3:17 (part of a nickname); J 12:29; Rv 6:1; 10:3f. [brontosaurus, βροντή + σαῦρος]

βροχή, ῆς, ἡ rain Mt 7:25, 27.*

βρόχος, ου, ὁ noose fig. restraint 1 Cor 7:35.*

βρυγμός, οῦ, ὁ grinding, gnashing Mt 8:12; 25:30; Lk 13:28.

βρύχω grind, gnash Ac 7:54.*

βρύω pour forth Js 3:11.*

βρῶμα, ατος, τό food, solid food lit. Lk 3:11; Ro 14:15; 1 Cor 6:13; Hb 9:10; 13:9; fig. J 4:34; 1 Cor 3:2.

βρώσιμος, ον eatable Lk 24:41.*

βρῶσις, εως, ἡ—1. eating Ro 14:17; 1 Cor 8:4. As a general term for consuming, β. may mean corrosion or a destructive insect or worm Mt 6:19f.—**2.** food lit. Hb 12:16; fig. J 6:27, 55.

βυθίζω sink Lk 5:7; plunge 1 Ti 6:9.*

βυθός, οῦ, ὁ the deep, open sea 2 Cor 11:25.*

βυρσεύς, έως, ὁ tanner Ac 9:43; 10:6, 32.*

βύσσινος, η, ον made of fine linen as noun fine linen garment Rv 18:12, 16; 19:8, 14.*

βύσσος, ου, ἡ fine linen Lk 16:19; Rv 18:12 v.l.*

βωμός, οῦ, ὁ altar Ac 17:23.*

Γ

γ′ as numeral = three, third in the superscription of 3 J.

Γαββαθᾶ indecl. Gabbatha J 19:13.*

Γαβριήλ, ὁ indecl. Gabriel Lk 1:19, 26.*

γάγγραινα, ης, ἡ gangrene, cancer fig. 2 Ti 2:17.*

Γάδ, ὁ indecl. Gad Rv 7:5 (Gen 30:11).*

Γαδαρηνός, ή, όν from Gadara, a city in Transjordania; ὁ Γ. the Gadarene Mt 8:28; Mk 5:1 v.l.; Lk 8:26 v.l., 37 v.l.*

Γάζα, ης, ἡ Gaza a city in southwest Palestine Ac 8:26.*

γάζα, ης, ἡ (Persian loanword) the (royal) treasury Ac 8:27.*

γαζοφυλακεῖον or **γαζοφυλάκιον, ου, τό** treasury J 8:20; contribution box or receptacle Mk 12:41, 43; Lk 21:1.*

Γάϊος, ου, ὁ Gaius—**1.** Ro 16:23; 1 Cor 1:14.—**2.** Ac 19:29.—**3.** Ac 20:4.—**4.** 3 J 1.*

γάλα, γάλακτος, τό milk lit. 1 Cor 9:7. Fig. 3:2; Hb 5:12f; 1 Pt 2:2.* [galaxy. Cf. the Milky Way.]

Γαλάτης, ου, ὁ a Galatian Gal 3:1.*

Γαλατία, ας, ἡ Galatia, a district in Asia Minor settled by the Celtic Galatians 1 Cor 16:1; Gal 1:2; 2 Ti 4:10 (where Gaul may be meant); 1 Pt 1:1.*

Γαλατικός, ή, όν Galatian Ac 16:6; 18:23.*

γαλήνη, ης, ἡ a calm on the lake Mt 8:26; Mk 4:39; Lk 8:24.*

Γαλιλαία, ας, ἡ Galilee, the northern third of Palestine Mt 4:18; Mk 1:9, 14, 28; Lk 5:17; J 2:1, 11; Ac 9:31.

Γαλιλαῖος, α, ον Galilean Mt 26:69; Mk 14:70; Lk 13:1f; J 4:45; Ac 5:37.

Γαλλία, ας, ἡ Gaul v.l. in 2 Ti 4:10 for Γαλατία.*

Γαλλίων, ωνος, ὁ Gallio, proconsul of Achaia (A.D. 51–52) Ac 18:12, 14, 17.*

Γαμαλιήλ, ὁ indecl. Gamaliel, i.e. Rabban Gamaliel the Elder, a renowned teacher of the law Ac 5:34; 22:3.*

γαμέω marry, enter matrimony of both men and women Mt 5:32; 19:10; Mk 10:12; 12:25; Lk 16:18; 1 Cor 7:9f, 28, 34. Pass. get married, be married 7:39. [gamete, gamic, biological terms relating to sexuality]

γαμίζω give in marriage Mt 24:38; Mk 12:25. This may be the sense in 1 Cor 7:38, but it is even more likely that γ. here = γαμέω and means simply marry. Pass. be given in marriage, be married Mt 22:30; Mk 12:25; Lk 17:27; 20:35.*

γαμίσκω give in marriage Mt 24:38 v.l. Pass. be given in marriage Mk 12:25 v.l., Lk 20:34 in text, 35 v.l.*

γάμος, ου, ὁ wedding celebration γ. ποιεῖν give a wedding celebration Mt 22:2; cf. verses 3, 4, 9; J 2:1f. ἔνδυμα γ. wedding garment Mt 22:11f. Wedding banquet Rv 19:7, 9; banquet Lk 12:36. Wedding hall Mt 22:10. Marriage Hb 13:4. [Cf. bigamy, digamy.]

γάρ conjunction used to express cause, inference, or continuation or to explain; never comes first in its clause.—1. cause or reason: for Mt 2:2; 3:2f; Mk 1:22; J 2:25; Ac 2:25; 1 Cor 11:5. καὶ γάρ simply for Mk 10:45; J 4:23; 1 Cor 5:7 but for also, for even Mt 8:9; Lk 6:32f; 2 Cor 2:10. γὰρ καί for also, for precisely 2 Cor 2:9. In questions γάρ can be left untranslated as in 1 Pt 2:20 or prefixed by what! as in 1 Cor 11:22 or why! in Mt 27:23.—2. explanatory for, you see Mt 12:40, 50; Mk 7:3; Ro 7:2; Hb 3:4.—3. inferential certainly, by all means, so, then Hb 12:3; Js 1:7; 1 Pt 4:15. οὐ γάρ no, indeed! Ac 16:37.—4. continuation or connection indeed, to be sure, but Ro 2:25; 5:7; 1 Cor 10:1; Gal 1:11.

γαστήρ, τρός, ἡ belly—1. fig. glutton Tit 1:12.—2. womb Lk 1:31. ἐν γαστρὶ ἔχειν be pregnant Mt 1:18, 23; 1 Th 5:3; Rv 12:2. [gastritis]

Γαύδη alt. form of Καῦδα (Κλαῦδα).

γέ emphatic particle, enclitic yet, at least Lk 11:8; 18:5. Even, as a matter of fact Ro 8:32. εἴ γε if indeed, inasmuch as 2 Cor 5:3; Gal 3:4; Eph 3:2. εἰ δὲ μή γε otherwise Mt 6:1; 9:17; 2 Cor 11:16. μενοῦνγε rather Ro 9:20. μήτι γε not to mention, let alone 1 Cor 6:3. Often γε is left untranslated.

γεγένημαι pf. mid. ind. of γίνομαι.

γέγονα, γεγόνει pf. act. ind. forms of γίνομαι.

γέγραπται, γέγραφα pf. pass. ind. 3 sing. and pf. act. ind. 1 sing. of γράφω.

Γεδεών, ὁ indecl. Gideon Hb 11:32 (Judg 6–8).*

γέεννα, ης, ἡ Gehenna, Valley of Hinnom, a ravine south of Jerusalem. Fig. a place of fire for the punishment of

the wicked, hell Mt 5:22, 29f; 23:15; Mk 9:45, 47; Js 3:6.

Γεθσημανί indecl. Gethsemane, an olive orchard on the Mount of Olives Mt 26:36; Mk 14:32.*

γείτων, ονος, ὁ and ἡ neighbor Lk 14:12; 15:6, 9; J 9:8.*

γελάω laugh Lk 6:21, 25.*

γέλως, ωτος, ὁ laughter Js 4:9.*

γεμίζω fill Mk 4:37; 15:36; J 2:7; Rv 8:5.

γέμω be full w. gen. or acc. Mt 23:25, 27; Lk 11:39; Ro 3:14; Rv 15:7; 17:3, 4.

γενεά, ᾶς, ἡ clan, race, kind Lk 16:8. Generation, contemporaries Mt 12:41f; 17:17; Mk 9:19; 13:30; Lk 21:32; Hb 3:10. Age, period of time Mt 1:17; Lk 1:48, 50; Col 1:26. Perh. family or origin Ac 8:33.

γενεαλογέω derive descent pass. Hb 7:6.*

γενεαλογία, ας, ἡ genealogy, pedigree 1 Ti 1:4; Tit 3:9.*

γενέθλια, ίων, τά birthday or birthday celebration Mk 6:21 v.l.*

γενέσθαι 2 aor. mid. inf. of γίνομαι.

γενέσια, ίων, τά birthday celebration Mt 14:6; Mk 6:21.*

γένεσις, εως, ἡ birth Mt 1:18; Lk 1:14. In Mt 1:1 γ. may mean origin or descent, and the expression βίβλος γενέσεως may mean genealogy as Gen 5:1. πρόσωπον γ. natural face Js 1:23. τροχὸς τῆς γ. course of life 3:6.* [Genesis]

γενετή, ῆς, ἡ birth J 9:1.* [genetics]

γενηθήτω 1 aor. pass. impv. 3 sing. of γίνομαι.

γέννημα, ατος, τό product, fruit, yield of plants lit. Mt 26:29; Mk 14:25; Lk 12:18 v.l.; 22:18; fig. 2 Cor 9:10.*

γενήσομαι fut. mid. ind. of γίνομαι.

γεννάω—1. be or become the father of, beget lit. Mt 1:2ff, 20; J 8:41; 9:34; Ac 7:8, 29. Fig. J 1:13; 1 Cor 4:15; Phlm 10; 1 J 2:29.—2. of women: bear Lk 1:13, 35, 57; Ac 2:8; 22:28.—3. fig. cause, produce 2 Ti 2:23.

γέννημα, ατος, τό that which is produced or born of living creatures, offspring, brood Mt 3:7; 12:34; 23:33; Lk 3:7.*

Γεννησαρέτ, ἡ indecl. Gennesaret, the plain south of Capernaum Mt 14:34; Mk 6:53; also the lake adjacent to this plain Lk 5:1 (called Sea of Galilee in Mk 1:16).*

γέννησις, εως, ἡ birth v.l. in Mt 1:18, Lk 1:14, and 1 J 5:18.*

γεννητός, ή, όν born γ. γυναικῶν all humanity Mt 11:11; Lk 7:28.*

γένοιτο 2 aor. mid. opt. 3 sing. of γίνομαι.

γένος, ους, τό race, stock—1. descendants Ac 4:6. τοῦ γὰρ καὶ γένος ἐσμέν we, too, are descended from him 17:28. Family 7:13.—2. nation, people Mk 7:26; Ac 7:19; Gal 1:14; 1 Pt 2:9.—3. class, kind Mt 13:47; 1 Cor 12:10.

Γερασηνός, ή, όν from Gerasa, a city in Peraea, east of the Jordan, about 55 km. S.E. of Lake Gennesaret. ὁ Γ. the Gerasene Mt 8:28 v.l.; Mk 5:1; Lk 8:26, 37.*

Γεργεσηνός, ή, όν from Gergesa, a town on the eastern shore of the Sea of Galilee. ὁ Γ. the Gergesene v.l. in Mt 8:28, Mk 5:1, and Lk 8:26, 37.*

γερουσία, ας, ἡ council of elders in Ac 5:21 the Sanhedrin in Jerusalem.*

γέρων, οντος, ὁ old man J 3:4.* [geriatrics]

γεύομαι w. gen. or acc. taste, partake of, enjoy Lk 14:24; J 2:9; Ac 20:11; Col 2:21; eat Ac 10:10. Fig. come to know, experience Mk 9:1; J 8:52; Hb 2:9; 1 Pt 2:3; obtain Hb 6:4. [Cf. gusto, disgust.]

γεωργέω cultivate Hb 6:7.*

γεώργιον, ου, τό cultivated land, field fig. 1 Cor 3:9.* [georgic; cf. the Georgics of Vergil.]

γεωργός, οῦ, ὁ farmer 2 Ti 2:6; Js 5:7. Tenant farmer, vinedresser Mt 21:33ff, 38, 40f; J 15:1.

γῆ, γῆς, ἡ soil, earth, ground Mt 5:18; 10:29; 13:5, 8, 23; Mk 8:6; Lk 6:49; 13:7; J 12:24; Col 1:16; Hb 6:7; 2 Pt 3:13. (Dry) land Mk 4:1; 6:47; J 6:21; Ac 27:39, 43f; land, region, country Mt 2:6; Mk 15:33; Ac 7:3f, 6, 36. The in-

habited earth Lk 21:35; Ac 1:8; as the locale of people, humanity Mt 5:13; Lk 18:8; Ro 9:28; Rv 14:3. [geo-, as prefix in numerous words]

γήμας, γήμω 1 aor. act. ptc. and subj. of γαμέω.

γῆρας, ως or ους, dat. γήρει or γήρᾳ, τό old age Lk 1:36.*

γηράσκω grow old J 21:18; Hb 8:13.*

γίνομαι capable of many translations in various contexts, of which these are typical:—1. be born or produced Mt 21:19; J 8:58; Ro 1:3; 1 Cor 15:37; with emphasis on the fragility of human life Gal 4:4. Arise, come about, occur, come Mt 8:26; Mk 4:37; Lk 4:42; 23:19, 44; J 6:17; Ac 6:1; 11:19; 27:27; 1 Ti 6:4; Rv 8:5, 7.—2. be made or created, be done Mt 6:10; 11:20f; Lk 14:22; J 1:3; Ac 19:26; 1 Cor 9:15; Hb 11:3; be established Mk 2:27.—3. happen, take place Mt 1:22; 18:31; Lk 1:38; 8:34; J 10:22; Ac 7:40; 28:9. Expressions like γέγονε ἐμοί τι something has come to me = I have or have received something Mt 18:12; Mk 4:11; Lk 14:12; 1 Cor 4:5. μὴ γένοιτο by no means, far from it, God forbid lit. 'may it not be' Lk 20:16; Ro 3:4, 6, 31; Gal 2:17. καὶ ἐγένετο and ἐγένετο δέ, with or without καί following, is usually felt to be superfluous and is left untranslated; older versions rendered it it came to pass Mt 7:28; 9:10; Lk 2:1, 6, 46; 8:1, 22.—4. become Mt 5:45; 24:32; Mk 1:17; 6:14; Lk 6:16; J 1:12, 14; 1 Cor 13:11; Gal 3:13; Col 1:23; Hb 5:5. Come, go Mk 1:11; Lk 1:44; Ac 13:32; 20:16; 21:35; Gal 3:14.—5. be largely = εἰμί Mt 10:16; Mk 4:19; Lk 6:36; 17:26, 28; J 15:8; Ac 22:17; Gal 4:4; 1 Th 2:8; Hb 11:6. With dat. of a person belong Ro 7:3f. Appear Mk 1:4; J 1:6. [genesis]

γινώσκω—1. know, come to know Mt 13:11; Lk 12:47f; J 8:32; 14:7; Ac 1:7; 19:35; 1 Cor 3:20; 13:9, 12; 2 Cor 5:16; 1 J 4:2, 6; it struck me Mt 25:24. Imperative γινώσκετε you may be quite sure Mt 24:33, 43; J 15:18.—2. learn (of), ascertain, find out Mt 9:30; Mk 6:38; 15:45; Lk 24:18; J 4:1; Ac 17:20; 21:34.—3. understand, comprehend Mk 4:13; J 8:43; 10:6; Ac 8:30; 21:37; 1 Cor

40   γλεῦκος–γράμμα

2:8, 11, 14; *have the law at one's fin-gertips* Ro 7:1.—**4.** *perceive, notice, realize* Mk 5:29; 7:24; Lk 8:46; J 6:15; Ac 23:6.—**5.** *acknowledge, recognize* Mt 7:23; J 1:10; *choose* 1 Cor 8:3; Gal 4:9.—**6.** euphemistically, of sex relations *know* Mt 1:25; Lk 1:34.

γλεῦκος, ους, τό *sweet new wine* Ac 2:13.* [*glucose*]

γλυκύς, εῖα, ύ *sweet* Js 3:11f; Rv 10:9f.*

γλῶσσα, ης, ἡ *tongue*—**1.** lit as an organ of speech Mk 7:33, 35; Lk 16:24; 1 Cor 14:9; Js 1:26; Rv 16:10.—**2.** *language* Ac 2:11; Phil 2:11; Rv 5:9. The expressions γλῶσσαι, γένη γλωσσῶν, ἐν γ. λαλεῖν etc. refer to the ecstatic speech of those overcome by strong emotion in a cultic context. The latter expression is usually rendered *speak in tongues*. Ac 19:6; 1 Cor 12:10; 13:1, 8; 14 passim. [*glosso-*, as prefix in numerous words]

γλωσσόκομον, ου, τό *money box* J 12:6; 13:29.*

γναφεύς, έως, ὁ *bleacher, fuller* one who cleans woolen cloth Mk 9:3.*

γνήσιος, ία, ον *true* lit. 'legitimate' Phil 4:3; 1 Ti 1:2; Tit 1:4. τὸ γ. *genuineness, sincerity* 2 Cor 8:8.*

γνησίως adv. *sincerely, genuinely* Phil 2:20.*

γνοῖ 2 aor. act. subj. of γινώσκω, Hellenistic form.

γνούς, γνόντος 2 aor. act. ptc. of γινώσκω.

γνόφος, ου, ὁ *darkness* Hb 12:18.*

γνῶ 2 aor. act. subj. of γινώσκω.

γνῶθι, γνῶναι, 2 aor. act. impv. and inf. of γινώσκω.

γνώμη, ης, ἡ—**1.** *purpose, intention, mind* 1 Cor 1:10; Rv 17:13; *decision, resolve* Ac 20:3; Rv 17:17.—**2.** *opinion, judgment* 1 Cor 7:25, 40; 2 Cor 8:10; Ac 4:18 v.l.—**3.** *previous knowledge, consent* Phlm 14.* [*gnomic*]

γνωρίζω *make known, reveal* Lk 2:15; J 15:15; Ac 7:13 v.l.; Ro 9:22f; Eph 6:19, 21; Phil 4:6; *know* Phil 1:22.

γνώριμος, ον *acquainted (with), known (to)* J 18:16 v.l.*

γνωσθήσομαι fut. pass. ind. of γινώσκω.

γνῶσις, εως, ἡ *knowledge* Lk 1:77; 11:52; Ro 11:33; 1 Cor 8:1, 7, 11; 12:8; 2 Cor 6:6; 10:5; 2 Pt 1:5f; 3:18; *personal acquaintance with* w. gen. Phil 3:8. Heretical *knowledge* of sectarians 1 Ti 6:20. [*gnostic*]

γνώσομαι fut. mid. (deponent) of γινώσκω.

γνώστης, ου, ὁ *one acquainted (with), expert (in)* w. gen. Ac 26:3.*

γνωστός, ή, όν *known* Ac 2:14; 4:10; 9:42; 19:17. As noun *acquaintance, friend, intimate* J 18:15f; Lk 2:44. τὸ γ. *what can be known* Ro 1:19.

γογγύζω *grumble, mutter, complain* Mt 20:11; Lk 5:30; J 6:41, 43, 61; 1 Cor 10:10; *speak secretly, whisper* J 7:32.*

γογγυσμός, οῦ, ὁ *grumbling, complaint, displeasure* Ac 6:1; Phil 2:14; 1 Pt 4:9; *secret talk, whispering* J 7:12.*

γογγυστής, οῦ, ὁ *grumbler* Jd 16.*

γόης, ητος, ὁ *swindler, impostor* lit. 'sorcerer' 2 Ti 3:13.*

Γολγοθᾶ, ἡ acc. Γολγοθᾶν *Golgotha* Aram., translated 'place of a skull' Mt 27:33; Mk 15:22; J 19:17.*

Γόμορρα, ων, τά and **ας, ἡ** *Gomorrah* (Gen 19:24ff) Mt 10:15; Mk 6:11 v.l.; Ro 9:29; 2 Pt 2:6; Jd 7.*

γόμος, ου, ὁ *cargo* Ac 21:3; Rv 18:11f.*

γονεύς, έως, ὁ only pl. in N.T. οἱ γονεῖς, έων *parents* Mk 13:12; J 9:2f; 2 Cor 12:14. [Cf. *gonad*.]

γόνυ, γόνατος, τό *knee* Lk 5:8; Eph 3:14; Hb 12:12. τιθέναι τὰ γ. *bow the knees* Mk 15:19; Lk 22:41; Ac 9:40. [Cf. *genuflect*, via Latin.]

γονυπετέω *kneel down (before)* Mt 17:14; 27:29; Mk 1:40; 10:17.*

γράμμα, ατος, τό—**1.** *letter* of the alphabet 2 Cor 3:7; Gal 6:11. γράμματα οἶδεν *he knows the Scriptures* J 7:15. τὰ γράμματα. *(higher) learning* Ac 26:24.—**2.** *document, piece of writing* in the form of a *letter, epistle* Ac 28:21; a promissory *note* Lk 16:6f. *Book* J 5:47. ἱερὰ γ. *sacred Scriptures* of the O.T. 2 Ti 3:15. *Letter* of the literally correct form of the Mosaic law Ro 2:27, 29; 7:6; 2 Cor 3:6.* [*grammar*]

γραμματεύς, έως, ό—**1.** *secretary, clerk* a high official in Ephesus Ac 19:35.— **2.** *an expert in the law, a scholar versed in the law, scribe* Jewish Mt 2:4; 23:2, 13ff; Mk 2:16; Lk 9:22; Ac 6:12; 1 Cor 1:20. *Of their Christian counterparts* Mt 13:52; 23:34.

γραπτός, ή, όν *written* Ro 2:15.*

γραφή, ῆς, ἡ *writing.* In the N.T. always *Holy Scripture,* i.e. the O.T. Mt 21:42; Mk 14:49; Lk 24:27; J 20:9; Ac 8:32; 1 Cor 15:3f; Gal 3:8, but including Paul's letters 2 Pt 3:16. *Individual passage of Scripture* Lk 4:21; Ac 8:35; Js 2:8. [*graph*]

γράφω *write* Mt 4:4, 6f, 10; J 19:22; Ac 1:20; Ro 15:15; 1 Cor 7:1; 3 J 13. *Write down, record* J 20:30; Rv 1:11, 19. *Compose, write* Mk 10:4; J 21:25b; 2 Pt 3:1. *Cover with writing* Rv 5:1. *Write about* J 1:45. [*graphite*]

γραώδης, ες *characteristic of elderly women* γ. μῦθοι *tales such as elderly women tell* 1 Ti 4:7.*

γρηγορέω *be* or *keep awake* lit. Mt 24:43; Mk 13:34; 14:37; Lk 12:37. Fig. *be on the alert, be watchful* Mt 26:41; Mk 14:38; Ac 20:31; 1 Cor 16:13; Rv 16:15; *be alive* 1 Th 5:10. [*Gregory*]

γυμνάζω *exercise, train* fig. 1 Ti 4:7; Hb 5:14; 12:11; 2 Pt 2:14.*

γυμνασία, ας, ἡ *training* 1 Ti 4:8.* [*gymnasium*]

γυμνητεύω v.l. for γυμνιτεύω.

γυμνιτεύω *be poorly dressed* 1 Cor 4:11.*

γυμνός, ή, όν—**1.** *naked, stripped, bare* Mk 14:52; Ac 19:16; Rv 16:15. τὸ γ. *the naked body* Mk 14:51.—**2.** *without an outer garment* J 21:7.—**3.** *poorly dressed* Mt 25:36; Js 2:15.—**4.** *bare, uncovered* 1 Cor 15:37; 2 Cor 5:3; Hb 4:13. [*gymn-,* a combining form, as in *gymnosperm*]

γυμνότης, ητος, ἡ *nakedness* Rv 3:18. *Destitution, lack of sufficient clothing* Ro 8:35; 2 Cor 11:27.*

γυναικάριον, ου, τό *weak, vulnerable woman* lit. 'little woman' 2 Ti 3:6.*

γυναικεῖος, α, ον *feminine* σκεῦος γ. *wife* 1 Pt 3:7.* [*gynecology*]

γυνή, αικός, ἡ *woman*—**1.** *of any adult female* Mt 9:20; Lk 1:42; Ac 5:14; 1 Cor 11 passim; 14:34f. The voc. γύναι Mt 15:28; Lk 22:57; J 2:4 is by no means disrespectful, but there is no generally accepted English equivalent for it, and it is best to omit the word in translation.—**2.** *wife* Mt 5:28, 31f; Lk 1:5, 13, 18, 24; 1 Cor 7:2ff; Col 3:18f. [*gynics*]

Γώγ, ὁ indecl. *Gog* Rv 20:8 (Ezk 38 and 39).*

γωνία, ας, ἡ *corner* Mt 6:5; Rv 7:1. κε-φαλὴ γωνίας *cornerstone* or *keystone* Mk 12:10; Ac 4:11; 1 Pt 2:7. [*gonion; diagonal,* διά + γωνία]

Δ

Δαβίδ see Δαυίδ.

δαιμονίζομαι *be possessed by a demon* κακῶς δαιμονίζεται *is cruelly tor-* *mented by a demon* Mt 15:22. The ptc. ὁ δαιμονιζόμενος *the demoniac* 9:32; Mk 1:32; J 10:21. [*demonize*]

δαιμόνιον, ου, τό—1. *a deity, divinity* Ac 17:18.—2. *demon, evil spirit* Mt 11:18; Mk 1:34, 39; Lk 9:49; J 7:20; 1 Cor 10:20f; 1 Ti 4:1; Js 2:19; Rv 16:14; 18:2.

δαιμονιώδης, ες *demonic* Js 3:15.*

δαίμων, ονος, ὁ *demon, evil spirit* Mt 8:31; Mk 5:12 v.l.; Rv 18:2 v.l.

δάκνω *bite* fig. Gal 5:15.*

δάκρυον, ου, τό *tear* Lk 7:38, 44; Ac 20:19; 2 Cor 2:4; 2 Ti 1:4; Hb 5:7; Rv 21:4. [Cf. *lachrymal*.]

δακρύω *weep* J 11:35.*

δακτύλιος, ου, ὁ a *ring* Lk 15:22.*

δάκτυλος, ου, ὁ *finger* Mt 23:4; Mk 7:33; Lk 11:20; 16:24; J 20:25. [*dactylic; pterodactyl*]

Δαλμανουθά, ἡ indecl. *Dalmanutha* a place of uncertain location near the Sea of Galilee Mk 8:10.*

Δαλματία, ας, ἡ *Dalmatia*, a Roman province across the Adriatic from S. Italy 2 Ti 4:10.*

δαμάζω *subdue* lit. Mk 5:4; *tame* Js 3:7. Fig. *tame, control* 3:8.*

δάμαλις, εως, ἡ *heifer, young cow* Hb 9:13.*

Δάμαρις, ιδος, ἡ *Damaris* Ac 17:34.*

Δαμασκηνός, ή, όν *from Damascus* οἱ Δ. *the Damascenes* 2 Cor 11:32.*

Δαμασκός, οῦ, ἡ *Damascus*, capital city of Coelesyria Ac 9:2f; 22:5f; 2 Cor 11:32; Gal 1:17.

Δάν, ὁ indecl. *Dan* Rv 7:5 v.l. (Gen 30:6).*

δαν(ε)ίζω act. *lend (money)* Lk 6:34f. Mid. *borrow (money)* Mt 5:42.*

δάν(ε)ιον, ου, τό *loan* Mt 18:27.*

δαν(ε)ιστής, οῦ, ὁ *moneylender, creditor* Lk 7:41.*

Δανιήλ, ὁ indecl. *Daniel* Mt 24:15; Mk 13:14 v.l. (Dan 1:6f).*

δαπανάω *spend freely* Mk 5:26; Ac 21:24; 2 Cor 12:15; *spend wastefully* Lk 15:14; Js 4:3.*

δαπάνη, ης, ἡ *cost, expense* Lk 14:28.*

δαρήσομαι 2 fut. pass. of δέρω.

Δαυίδ, ὁ indecl. *David* Mt 1:6; 9:27; Mk 2:25; Lk 20:42, 44; Ac 2:29; Ro 1:3; Rv 3:7.

δέ adversative particle, never first in its clause *and* Mt 1:2ff; *but* Mt 6:1; 1 Cor 2:15. Simply indicating a transition *now, then* Mk 5:11; Lk 3:21; 1 Cor 16:12; *that is* Ro 3:22; 1 Cor 10:11; Phil 2:8. After a neg. *rather* Lk 10:20; Ac 12:9, 14; Eph 4:15; Hb 4:13, 15. δὲ καί *but also, but even* Mt 18:17; Mk 14:31; J 2:2; Ac 22:28; 1 Cor 15:15. καὶ . . . δέ *and also, but also* Mt 16:18; J 6:51; Ac 22:29; 2 Ti 3:12. For μέν . . . δέ see μέν. δέ may often be omitted in translation.

δέδεκται pf. mid. ind. of δέχομαι.

δέδεμαι, δεδεκώς pf. pass. ind. and pf. act. ptc. of δέω.

δέδομαι, δεδώκει pf. pass. ind. and plupf. act. ind. of δίδωμι, without augment.

δέῃ pres. act. subj. 3 sing. of δεῖ.

δεηθείς, δεήθητι 1 aor. pass. ptc. and impv. of δέομαι.

δέησις, εως, ἡ *entreaty, supplication, prayer* Lk 1:13; Ro 10:1; Eph 6:18; 1 Ti 2:1; 1 Pt 3:12.

δεθῆναι 1 aor. pass. inf. of δέω.

δεῖ impersonal verb *it is necessary, one must* or *has to* Mt 17:10; Mk 14:31; Lk 2:49; Ac 9:6; 1 Cor 11:19; *one ought* or *should* Mt 18:33; Lk 18:1; Ac 5:29; 2 Ti 2:6, 24. δέον neut. ptc. *what one should* δέον ἐστίν = δεῖ Ac 19:36; εἰ δέον *if it must be* 1 Pt 1:6. The impf. ἔδει *had to* Lk 15:32; J 4:4; *should have, ought to have* Mt 18:33; Ac 27:21; 2 Cor 2:3. [Cf. *deontology*, the science of duty.]

δεῖγμα, ατος, τό *example* Jd 7.*

δειγματίζω *expose, disgrace* Mt 1:19; *mock, expose* Col 2:15.*

δείκνυμι, δεικνύω *show, point out, make known* Mt 8:4; Lk 22:12; J 14:8f; 1 Cor 12:31; Hb 8:5; Rv 1:1. *Explain, prove* Mt 16:21; Ac 10:28; Js 2:18. [*deictic, indicate*]

δειλία, ας, ἡ *cowardice* 2 Ti 1:7.*

δειλιάω *be cowardly, timid* J 14:27.*

δειλινός, ή, όν in the afternoon τὸ δειλινόν toward evening Ac 3:1 v.l.*

δειλός, ή, όν cowardly, timid Mt 8:26; Mk 4:40; Rv 21:8.*

δεῖνα, ὁ, ἡ, τό so-and-so of a person or thing one cannot or does not wish to name a certain man, somebody Mt 26:18.*

δεινός, ή, όν fearful, terrible as noun affliction at end of Mk in the Freer ms. 8.*

δεινῶς adv. fearfully, terribly Mt 8:6. δ. ἐνέχειν act in a very hostile manner Lk 11:53.*

δεῖξον, δείξω 1 aor. act. impv. and fut. act. ind. of δείκνυμι.

δειπνέω eat, dine Mt 20:28 v.l.; Lk 17:8; 22:20; 1 Cor 11:25; Rv 3:20.*

δειπνοκλήτωρ, ορος, ὁ host at a banquet Mt 20:28 v.l.*

δεῖπνον, ου, τό dinner, supper the main meal of the day, eaten toward evening Lk 14:12; J 21:20; 1 Cor 11:20f; (formal) dinner, banquet Mt 23:6; Lk 14:17, 24; J 12:2; 13:2; Rv 19:9, 17. [deipnosophist]

δεῖπνος, ου, ὁ as v.l. for δεῖπνον Lk 14:16; Rv 19:9, 17.*

δείρας 1 aor. act. ptc. of δέρω.

δεισιδαιμονία, ας, ἡ religion Ac 25:19.*

δεισιδαίμων, ον, gen. ονος religious comparative degree δεισιδαιμονεστέρους ὑμᾶς θεωρῶ I perceive that you are very religious people Ac 17:22.*

δειχθείς 1 aor. pass. ptc. of δείκνυμι.

δέκα indecl. ten Mt 20:24; Mk 10:41; Lk 17:12; Rv 12:3. [deca-, a prefix in numerous words]

δεκαδύο indecl. twelve Ac 19:7 v.l.; 24:11 v.l.

δεκαέξ indecl. sixteen Rv 13:18 v.l.*

δεκαοκτώ indecl. eighteen Lk 13:4, 11.

δεκαπέντε indecl. fifteen J 11:18; Ac 27:5 v.l., 28; Gal 1:18 (ἡμ. δεκ. means two weeks).*

Δεκάπολις, εως, ἡ Decapolis, a league originally consisting of ten Greek cities nearly all of which were southeast of the Sea of Galilee Mt 4:25; Mk 5:20; 7:31.*

δεκατέσσαρες, ων fourteen Mt 1:17; 2 Cor 12:2; Gal 2:1.*

δέκατος, η, ον tenth J 1:39; Rv 11:13; 21:20; tithe Hb 7:2, 4, 8f.*

δεκατόω collect or receive tithes from w. acc. Hb 7:6; pass. pay tithes 7:9.*

δεκτός, ή, όν acceptable Phil 4:18; welcome Lk 4:24; Ac 10:35; favorable Lk 4:19; 2 Cor 6:2.*

δελεάζω lure, entice Js 1:14; 2 Pt 2:14, 18.*

δένδρον, ου, τό tree Mt 7:17ff; Mk 8:24; Lk 13:19; Rv 7:1, 3. [dendrology]

δεξιοβόλος a word of uncertain meaning, found only as a v.l. for δεξιολάβος in Ac 23:23 and nowhere else.*

δεξιολάβος, ου, ὁ an extremely rare word of uncertain meaning; bowman, slinger, bodyguard are among the meanings suggested Ac 23:23.*

δεξιός, ά, όν right as opposed to left Mt 5:30; Ac 3:7; Rv 10:2. τὰ δ. the right side Mk 16:5. ἡ δ. the right hand Mt 6:3; Rv 1:17, 20; δ. διδόναι give the right hand as a pledge of mutual trust Gal 2:9. ἐκ δ. on the right side Mt 20:21, 23. ὅπλα δ. weapons for offense (e.g. swords) 2 Cor 6:7. [dexterous]

δέομαι ask, pray, beg Mt 9:38; Lk 8:38; Ac 8:24; 10:2; 2 Cor 8:4; 10:2. δέομαί σου I beg of you, as in Gal 4:12, can sometimes = please Lk 8:28; Ac 21:39.

δέον see δεῖ.

δέος, ους, τό fear, awe Hb 12:28.*

Δερβαῖος, α, ον from Derbe Ac 20:4.*

Δέρβη, ης, ἡ Derbe, a city in Lycaonia, in the Roman province of Galatia Ac 14:6, 20; 16:1.*

δέρμα, ατος, τό skin Hb 11:37.* [dermatology]

δερμάτινος, η, ον (made of) leather Mt 3:4; Mk 1:6.*

δέρρις, εως, ἡ skin Mk 1:6 v.l.*

δέρω beat, strike Mk 12:3, 5; Lk 22:63; J 18:23; Ac 22:19; 1 Cor 9:26; 2 Cor 11:20. δαρήσεται πολλάς he will receive many blows Lk 12:47, cf. vs. 48.

δεσμεύω bind Lk 8:29; Ac 22:4; tie up Mt 23:4.*

δεσμέω v.l. for δεσμεύω, with the same meaning Lk 8:29.*

δέσμη, ης, ἡ bundle Mt 13:30.*

δέσμιος, ου, ὁ prisoner Mk 15:6; Ac 16:25, 27; Phlm 1, 9; Eph 4:1.

δεσμός, οῦ, ὁ bond, fetter of a physical defect Mk 7:35; Lk 13:16. Lit., pl. Lk 8:29; Ac 26:29, 31; Hb 11:36. Imprisonment, prison Phil 1:7, 13f; 2 Ti 2:9; Phlm 10, 13. [desmoid, as noun a dense connective-tissue tumor]

δεσμοφύλαξ, ακος, ὁ warden, keeper of the prison Ac 16:23, 27, 36.*

δεσμωτήριον, ου, τό prison, jail Mt 11:2; Ac 5:21, 23; 16:26.*

δεσμώτης, ου, ὁ prisoner Ac 27:1, 42.*

δεσπότης, ου, ὁ vocative δέσποτα lord, master, owner 1 Ti 6:1f; 2 Ti 2:21; 1 Pt 2:18. Of God Lk 2:29; Rv 6:10; of Christ Jd 4. [despot]

δεῦρο adv. of place come, come here Mk 10:21; J 11:43; Ac 7:3, 34; Rv 17:1. Of time until now ἄχρι τοῦ δ. thus far Ro 1:13.

δεῦτε adv. (serves as pl. of δεῦρο) come! come on! Mt 11:28; 25:34; 28:6; Mk 1:17; 6:31; J 21:12.

δευτεραῖος, αία, ον on the second day Ac 28:13.*

δευτερόπρωτος, ον a word of doubtful meaning (lit. 'second-first') and genuineness, found only as v.l. in Lk 6:1.*

δεύτερος, α, ον second Mt 22:26; Lk 12:38; 19:18; J 4:54; Ac 12:10; 1 Cor 15:47; 2 Cor 1:15; Hb 8:7; Rv 2:11. Neut. as adv. (for) the second time Mt 26:42; J 3:4; 21:16; 2 Cor 13:2; Jd 5; secondly 1 Cor 12:28. [a combining form, as in deuterocanonical]

δέχομαι take, receive Mt 18:5; Lk 16:4, 6f; 22:17; Ac 7:59; 22:5; 2 Cor 7:15; 11:4; Phil 4:18. Welcome Mk 6:11; J 4:45; Col 4:10. Accept, approve Mt 11:14; Mk 10:15; Lk 8:13; 2 Cor 6:1; 8:17. Put up with, tolerate 2 Cor 11:16.

δέω bind, tie lit. Mt 13:30; J 19:40; of arrest and imprisonment Mk 6:17; Ac 9:2, 14, 21; 21:11; Col 4:3. Fig. Lk 13:16; Ac 20:22; Ro 7:2; 1 Cor 7:27. Forbid Mt 16:19; 18:18. [Cf. diadem, διά + δέω.]

δή emphatic particle; never comes first in its clause indeed Mt 13:23; now, then, therefore Lk 2:15; Ac 6:3 v.l.; 13:2; 15:36; 1 Cor 6:20.*

δηλαυγῶς very clearly Mk 8:25 v.l.*

δῆλος, η, ον clear, plain, evident ἡ λαλιά σου δῆλόν σε ποιεῖ your speech gives you away Mt 26:73. With ἐστίν understood 1 Cor 15:27; Gal 3:11; 1 Ti 6:7 v.l.*

δηλόω make clear, reveal, show 1 Cor 3:13; Hb 9:8; 2 Pt 1:14; give information 1 Cor 1:11; indicate Hb 12:27.

Δημᾶς, ᾶ, ὁ Demas Col 4:14; 2 Ti 4:10; Phlm 24.*

δημηγορέω deliver a public address Ac 12:21.*

Δημήτριος, ου, ὁ Demetrius—1. a Christian 3 J 12.—2. a silversmith at Ephesus Ac 19:24, 38.*

δημιουργός, οῦ, ὁ artisan, maker, Creator Hb 11:10.* [demiurge]

δῆμος, ου, ὁ people, populace, crowd Ac 12:22; 17:5; perh. popular assembly 19:30, 33.* [demotic, demography]

δημόσιος, ία, ιον public Ac 5:18. δημοσίᾳ publicly Ac 16:37; 18: 28; 20:20.*

δηνάριον, ου, τό (Latin) denarius a Roman silver coin; it was a worker's average daily wage Mt 20:2, 9f, 13; Mk 6:37; Lk 10:35; J 12:5; Rv 6:6.

δήποτε adv. with relative οἵῳ whatever J 5:4 v.l.*

δηποτοῦν see οἷος.

δήπου adv. of course, surely Hb 2:16.*

δήσω 1 aor. act. subj. of δέω.

Δία, Διός acc. and gen. of Ζεύς.

διά prep. w. gen. and acc. through—**A.** w. gen.—**I.** of place through Mt 12:43; Lk 5:19; 6:1; J 10:1f; Ac 9:25; 20:3; Ro 15:28; 1 Cor 3:15; throughout 2 Cor 8:18; out of Mt 4:4.—**II.** of time—**1.** to denote extent through, during, throughout Lk 5:5; Ac 23:31; Hb 2:15. διὰ παντός always, continually, constantly Mk 5:5; Ac 10:2; 2 Th 3:16; Hb 9:6. During Ac 5:19.—**2.** to denote an interval after Mk 2:1; Ac 24:17; Gal 2:1.—**III.** of means, instrument, agency by means of, through, with—**1.** of means, instrument, manner Ac 1:16; 15:27; 20:28; 1 Cor 16:3; 1 Pt 1:7; 2 J 12; *in* Lk 8:4.—**2.** of attendant circumstance *with* Ro 2:27; 8:25; 14:20; 2 Cor 2:4; *in a state of* Ro 4:11.—**3.** of cause *through, because of, by means of* Ro 3:20; 7:5; 1 Cor 1:21; 4:15; Gal 2:16; 5:6.—**4.** of persons *through (the agency of), by* Mt 2:15; Ac 11:28; Ro 1:5; 1 Cor 1:9; Gal 1:1; 3:19; Hb 2:2; *in the presence of* 2: Ti 2:2; *represented by* Ro 2:16.—**B.** w. acc.—**I.** of place *through* Lk 17:11.—**II.** to indicate the reason *because of, for the sake of* Mt 10:22; Mk 2:27; Lk 23:25; Ac 21:34. *Out of* Mt 27:18; J 7:13; Phil 1:15. διὰ τί; *why?* Mk 2:18; Lk 5:30; J 7:45; 1 Cor 6:7. [*dia-*, a combining form in numerous words]

διαβαίνω *go through, cross, come over* Lk 16:26; Ac 16:9; Hb 11:29.* [Cf. *diabase, diabetes.*]

διαβάλλω *bring charges* Lk 16:1.*

διαβάς 2 aor. act. ptc. of διαβαίνω.

διαβεβαιόομαι *speak confidently, insist* 1 Ti 1:7; Tit 3:8.*

διαβλέπω *look intently* or *open one's eyes (wide)* Mk 8:25; *see clearly* Mt 7:5; Lk 6:42.*

διάβολος, ον *slanderous* 1 Ti 3:11; 2 Ti 3:3; Tit 2:3. As noun ὁ δ. *the slanderer,* specifically *the Devil* Mt 4:1, 5, 8, 11; J 13:2; Ac 13:10; Eph 4:27; 1 Ti 3:7; 1 Pt 5:8. [*diabolic*]

διαγγέλλω *proclaim far and wide* Lk 9:60; Ro 9:17; Mk 5:19 v.l. *Give notice of* Ac 21:26.*

διαγγελῶ 2 aor. pass. subj. of διαγγέλλω.

διαγίνομαι *pass, elapse* of time Mk 16:1; Ac 25:13; 27:9.*

διαγινώσκω *decide, determine* Ac 24:22. ἀκριβέστερον δ. *determine by thorough investigation* 23:15.*

διαγνωρίζω *give an exact report* Lk 2:17 v.l.*

διάγνωσις, εως, ἡ *decision* legal t.t. Ac 25:21.* [*diagnosis*]

διαγογγύζω *complain, grumble* (aloud) Lk 15:2; 19:7.*

διαγρηγορέω *awake fully,* perh. *keep awake* Lk 9:32.*

διάγω *live, spend (one's life)* 1 Ti 2:2; Tit 3:3; Lk 7:25 v.l.*

διαδέχομαι *receive in turn* Ac 7:45.*

διάδημα, ατος, τό *diadem, crown* ordinarily *worn by rulers* Rv 12:3; 13:1; 19:12.*

διαδίδωμι *distribute, give* Lk 11:22; 18:22; J 6:11; Ac 4:35; Rv 17:13 v.l.*

διάδος 2 aor. act. impv. of διαδίδωμι.

διάδοχος, ου, ὁ *successor* Ac 24:27.* [the *Diadochi,* specif. the successors of Alexander the Great]

διαζώννυμι *tie around* δ. ἑαυτόν *tie* (a towel) *around oneself* J 13:4, cf. 5; *put on* 21:7.*

διαθήκη, ης, ἡ—**1.** *last will and testament* Gal 3:15; Hb 9:16f. Gal 3:17 shades into sense 2.—**2.** in a transferred sense, with emphasis on binding character, *covenant* only in the sense of a *declaration of (God's) will* or *decree* in which God alone sets the conditions, not an agreement between equals. *Covenant* Lk 22:20; 1 Cor 11:25; 2 Cor 3:6, 14; Gal 4:24; Hb 8:8; 9:4, 15; *declaration of will* Lk 1:72; Ac 3:25; Ro 11:27; *ordinance* Ac 7:8; *decree, assurance* Ro 9:4; Eph 2:12.

διαθήσομαι fut. mid. ind. of διατίθημι.

διαίρεσις, εως, ἡ *apportionment, allotment* or *variety, difference* 1 Cor 12:4, 5, 6.* [*diaeresis*]

διαιρέω *divide, distribute, apportion* Lk 15:12; 1 Cor 12:11.*

διακαθαίρω *clean out,* διακαθᾶραι 1 aor. act. inf. Lk 3:17.*

διακαθαρίζω *clean out* only in the fut. act. ind. form διακαθαριεῖ Mt 3:12; Lk 3:17 v.l.*

διακατελέγχομαι *refute (completely)* w. dat. Ac 18:28.*

διακελεύω *order* w. dat. J 8:5 v.l.*

διακονέω w. dat. of pers.—**1.** *wait on* someone *at table* Lk 12:37; 22:26f; J 12:2.—**2.** *serve* generally, lit. and fig. Mt 4:11; Mk 10:45; Ac 19:22; 2 Ti 1:18; 1 Pt 1:12; *wait on* Mt 27:55. *Take care of* Ac 6:2; 2 Cor 3:3. *Help, support* Mt

25:44; Lk 8:3; Hb 6:10.—3. *serve as deacon* 1 Ti 3:10, 13.

διακονία, ας, ἡ *service* Ac 6:4; 2 Cor 11:8; Eph 4:12; Hb 1:14; Rv 2:19; specif. *domestic* Lk 10:40. *Service, office, ministry* Ac 1:17; 20:24; Ro 12:7; 1 Cor 12:5; 2 Cor 5:18. *Aid, support, distribution* Ac 6:1; 11:29; δ. τῆς λειτουργίας *kind contribution* 2 Cor 9:12.

διάκονος, ου, ὁ, ἡ—1. *servant* Mt 20:26; 22:13; Mk 9:35; specifically *waiter* J 2:5, 9. *Agent* Ro 13:4; Gal 2:17.—2. *helper* of people who render service as Christians—**a.** in the general service of God, Christ, or other Christians 2 Cor 6:4; 11:23; Eph 6:21; Col 1:23, 25; 1 Ti 4:6.—**b.** in official or semiofficial capacity Ro 16:1; Phil 1:1; 1 Ti 3:8, 12. The later t.t.'s 'deacon' and 'deaconess' derive from this usage. [*diaconate*]

διακόσιοι, αι, α *two hundred* Mk 6:37; J 6:7; 21:8; Ac 23:23f.*

διακούω as legal t.t. w. gen. *give someone a hearing* Ac 23:35.*

διακρίνω—1. act.—**a.** *make a distinction, differentiate* Ac 11:12; 15:9; *single out, concede superiority* 1 Cor 4:7.—**b.** *pass judgment* 14:29; *judge correctly* Mt 16:3; *recognize* 1 Cor 11:29; *render a decision* 6:5.—**2.** mid. and aor. pass.—**a.** *take issue, dispute* Ac 11:2; Jd 9.—**b.** *doubt, waver* Mt 21:21; Ro 4:20; Js 1:6; Jd 22; *hesitate* Ac 10:20.

διάκρισις, εως, ἡ—1. *distinguishing, differentiation* 1 Cor 12:10; Hb 5:14.—**2.** *quarrel* Ro 14:1; Ac 4:32 v.l.* [*diacritical*]

διακωλύω *prevent* impf. *he tried to prevent* Mt 3:14.*

διαλαλέω *discuss* Lk 1:65; 6:11.*

διαλέγομαι—1. *discuss, conduct a discussion* Mk 9:34; Ac 19:8f; 20:7; 24:12.—**2.** *speak, preach* 18:4; Hb 12:5.

διαλείπω *stop, cease* Lk 7:45.*

διάλεκτος, ου, ἡ *language* Ac 2:6, 8; 21:40; 26:14. [*dialect*]

διαλιμπάνω by-form of διαλείπω *stop, cease* Ac 8:24 v.l. and 17:13 v.l.*

διαλλάγηθι 2 aor. pass. impv. of διαλλάσσομαι.

διαλλάσσομαι *become reconciled* Mt 5:24.*

διαλογίζομαι *consider, ponder, reason, discuss, argue* Mt 16:7f; Mk 2:6, 8; 8:16f; 11:31; Lk 1:29; 20:14.

διαλογισμός, οῦ, ὁ—1. *thought, opinion, reasoning, design* Mk 7:21; Lk 2:35; 6:8; Ro 1:21; 14:1. κριταὶ δ. *judges who hand down corrupt decisions* Js 2:4.—**2.** *doubt, dispute, argument* Lk 9:46; 24:38; Phil 2:14. [*dialogism, dialogue*]

διαλύω *break up, disperse* Ac 5:36; 27:41 v.l.* [*dialysis*]

διαμαρτύρομαι—1. *charge, warn, adjure* w. dat. of the person Lk 16:28; 1 Ti 5:21; 2 Ti 2:14; 4:1.—**2.** *testify (of), bear witness (to)* solemnly Ac 8:25; 20:21, 24; 28:23; 1 Th 4:6; Hb 2:6.

διαμάχομαι *contend sharply* Ac 23:9.*

διαμένω *remain (continually)* Lk 1:22; Gal 2:5; 2 Pt 3:4; *continue* Hb 1:11. δ. μετά *stand by* Lk 22:28.*

διαμερίζω *divide, distribute* Mk 15:24; Lk 11:17f; 22:17; Ac 2:3, 45.

διαμερισμός, οῦ, ὁ *dissension, disunity* Lk 12:51.*

διανέμω only in pass. *be spread,* of a report; lit. 'be distributed' Ac 4:17.*

διανεύω *nod, beckon* Lk 1:22.*

διανόημα, ατος, τό *thought* Lk 11:17; 3:16 v.l.*

διάνοια, ας, ἡ *mind, understanding, intelligence* Mt 22:30; Eph 4:18; Hb 8:10; *insight* 1 J 5:20; *disposition, thought* Lk 1:51; 2 Pt 3:1; *attitude* Col 1:21; *sense, impulse* Eph 2:3. [*dianoetic,* of reasoning process]

διανοίγω *open* Mk 7:34; Lk 2:23; 24:31, 45; Ac 7:56; 16:14. *Explain, interpret* Lk 24:32; Ac 17:3.*

διανυκτερεύω *spend the whole night* Lk 6:12.*

διανύω *complete* Ac 21:7.*

διαπαντός = διὰ παντός; see διά. [*diapason*]

διαπαρατριβή, ῆς, ἡ *mutual* or *constant irritation* 1 Ti 6:5.*

διαπεράω *cross (over)* Mt 9:1; 14:34; Mk 5:21; 6:53; Lk 16:26; Ac 21:2.*

διαπλέω *sail through* Ac 27:5.*

διαπονέομαι *be (greatly) disturbed, annoyed* Ac 4:2; 16:18; Mk 14:4 v.l.*

διαπορεύομαι *go, walk* or *pass through* Mk 2:23 v.l.; Lk 6:1; 13:22; Ac 16:4; Ro 15:24; *go by* Lk 18:36.*

διαπορέω *be greatly perplexed, be at a loss* Lk 9:7; Ac 2:12; 5:24; 10:17; Lk 24:4 v.l.*

διαπραγματεύομαι *gain by trading, earn* Lk 19:15.*

διαπρίω lit. 'saw through'; fig. pass. *be cut to the quick, be infuriated* Ac 5:33; 7:54.*

διαρθρόω *render capable of articulate speech* Lk 1:64 v.l.*

διαρπάζω *plunder thoroughly* Mt 12:29; Mk 3:27.*

δια(ρ)ρήγνυμι and διαρήσσω *tear* Mt 26:65; Mk 14:63; Lk 5:6; Ac 14:14; *break* Lk 8:29.*

διασαφέω *explain* Mt 13:36; *tell in detail, report* 18:31; Ac 10:25 v.l.*

διασείω *extort money by violence (from)* lit. 'shake violently' Lk 3:14.*

διασκορπίζω *scatter, disperse* Mk 14:27; J 11:52; Ac 5:37; *waste, squander* Lk 15:13.

διασπαρείς 2 aor. pass. ptc. of διασπείρω.

διασπάω *tear apart* Mk 5:4; Ac 23:10.*

διασπείρω *scatter* Ac 8:1, 4; 11:19.*

διασπορά, ᾶς, ἡ *dispersion, diaspora* of Jews J 7:35; of Christians Js 1:1; 1 Pt 1:1.*

διαστάς 2 aor. act. ptc. of διΐστημι.

διαστέλλω mid. *order, give orders* Mk 5:43; 7:36; Ac 15:24; pass. τὸ διασταλλόμενον *the command* Hb 12:20.

διάστημα, ατος, τό *interval* Ac 5:7.*

διαστήσας 1 aor. act. ptc. of διΐστημι.

διαστολή, ῆς, ἡ *difference, distinction* Ro 3:22; 10:12; 1 Cor 14:7.* [*diastole*, relating to heart movement]

διαστρέφω *make crooked* fig. Ac 13:10. διεστραμμένος *perverted, depraved* Mt 17:17; Lk 9:41; Ac 20:30; Phil 2:15. *Mislead* Lk 23:2; *turn away* Ac 13:8.* [*diastrophism*, of deformation undergone by the earth's crust]

διασῴζω *bring safely (through)* Ac 23:24; 27:44; 1 Pt 3:20; *rescue, save* Ac 27:43; 28:1, 4; *cure* Mt 14:36; Lk 7:3.*

διαταγείς 2 aor. pass. pct. of διατάσσω.

διαταγή, ῆς, ἡ *ordinance, direction* Ro 13:2. εἰς (= ἐν) διαταγὰς ἀγγέλων *by directions of angels*, i.e. God directed angels to transmit the Law) Ac 7:53.*

διάταγμα, ατος, τό *edict, command* Hb 11:23.*

διαταράσσω *confuse, perplex (greatly)* Lk 1:29.*

διατάσσω *order, direct, command* in act. and mid. Mt. 11:1; Lk 3:13; Ac 18:2; 24:23; 1 Cor 7:17; 9:14; 11:34; *arrange* Ac 20:13. διαταγεὶς δι' ἀγγέλων *ordered through angels* Gal 3:19.

διαταχθείς 1 aor. pass. ptc. of διατάσσω.

διατελέω *continue, remain* Ac 27:33.*

διατέταγμαι, διατετάχέναι pf. pass. ind. and pf. act. inf. of διατάσσω.

διατηρέω *keep, preserve* Ac 15:29; *treasure* Lk 2:51.*

διατί = διὰ τί; see διά.

διατίθημι only mid. διατίθεμαι *decree, ordain* Ac 3:25; Hb 10:16; διαθήκην δ. *issue a decree* 8:10. *Assign, confer* Lk 22:29. *Make a will* ὁ διαθέμενος *the testator* Hb 9:16f.* [*diathesis*, of predisposition to a disease]

διατρίβω *spend* (lit. 'rub away') time, etc. Ac 14:3, 28; 16:12; 20:6; 25:6, 14. *Stay, remain* J 3:22; Ac 12:19; 15:35.* [*diatribe*, an abrasive speech]

διατροφή, ῆς, ἡ pl. *food, sustenance* 1 Ti 6:8.*

διαυγάζω *shine through* 2 Cor 4:4 v.l. *Dawn, break* 2 Pt 1:19.*

διαυγής, ές *transparent* Rv 21:21.*

διαφανής, ές *transparent* Rv 21:21 v.l.* [*diaphanous*]

διαφέρω—1. trans. *carry through* (perh. on a shortcut) Mk 11:16; *spread* Ac 13:49; pass. *drift* of a ship 27:27.—2. intrans. *differ, be different from* w. gen. 1 Cor 15:41; Gal 4:1. *Be worth more than, be superior to* w. gen. Mt 6:26; 10:31; 12:12; Lk 12:7, 24. τὰ διαφέροντα *the things that really matter* Ro

2:18; Phil 1:10. Impers. *it makes a difference* Gal 2:6.* [*diaphoretic*, sudorific]

διαφεύγω *escape* Ac 27:42.*

διαφημίζω *make known by word of mouth, spread the news about* someone Mt 9:31. *Spread widely, disseminate* Mk 1:45; Mt 28:15.*

διαφθείρω *spoil, destroy* Lk 12:33; 2 Cor 4:16; Rv 8:9; 11:18a. *Ruin morally* 1 Ti 6:5; Rv 11:18b; 19:2 v.l.*

διαφθορά, ᾶς, ἡ *destruction, corruption* Ac 2:27, 31; 13:34ff.*

διάφορος, ον *different* Ro 12:6; Hb 9:10; *outstanding, excellent* 1:4; 8:6.*

διαφυλάσσω *guard, protect* Lk 4:10.*

διαχειρίζω mid. *lay violent hands on, kill, murder* Ac 5:30; 26:21.*

διαχλευάζω *mock, deride* Ac 2:13.*

διαχωρίζω separate pass. *be separated, part, go away* Lk 9:33.*

διγαμία, ας, ἡ *second marriage* Tit 1:9 v.l.*

δίγαμος, ον *married for the second time* Tit 1:9 v.l.* [*digamy*]

διδακτικός, ἡ, όν *skillful in teaching* 1 Ti 3:2; 2 Ti 2:24.* [*didactic*]

διδακτός, ἡ, όν *taught, instructed* δ. θεοῦ *taught by God* J 6:45; *taught, imparted* 1 Cor 2:13.*

διδασκαλία, ας, ἡ *the act of teaching, instruction* Ro 12:7; 15:4; 2 Ti 3:16. In a pass. sense = *that which is taught, instruction* Mk 7:7; Col 2:22; 1 Ti 1:10; 4:6; 2 Ti 3:10; Tit 1:9.

διδάσκαλος, ου, ὁ *teacher* Ro 2:20; Hb 5:12. As a term of honor and respect Mt 8:19; Mk 10:17; Lk 9:38; J 3:10. Of teachers in the Christian church Ac 13:1; 1 Cor 12:28f; Js 3:1.

διδάσκω *teach* Mk 1:21; Ac 15:35; 1 Cor 11:14; Col 3:16; Rv 2:14. ὑμᾶς διδάξει πάντα *he will instruct you in everything* J 14:26.

διδαχή, ῆς, ἡ *teaching* as an activity, *instruction* Mk 4:2; 1 Cor 14:6; 2 Ti 4:2. In a pass. sense = *what is taught, instruction* Mt 16:12; Mk 1:27; J 7:16f; Ro 16:17; Rv 2:14f, 24. Both act. and pass. aspects may be connoted in Mt 7:28; Mk 11:18; Lk 4:32.

διδόασιν, διδόναι, δίδου, διδούς pres. act. ind. 3 pl., pres. act. inf., pres. act. impv. 2 sing., and pres. act. ptc. of **δίδωμι.**

δίδραχμον, ου, τό *a double drachma, two-drachma piece* a Greek silver coin about equal to a half-shekel Mt 17:24.*

Δίδυμος, ου, ὁ *Didymus;* the name means 'twin.' J 11:16; 20:24; 21:2.*

διδῶ by-form of **δίδωμι** *I give* Rv 3:9.*

δίδωμι *give* Mt 4:9; 7:6, 11; Lk 17:18; J 9:24; Ac 20:35; Rv 4:9. The context often permits variations in translation, e.g. *bring* Lk 2:24; *grant* Mt 13:11; *cause* Ac 2:19; 1 Cor 9:12; *put* Lk 15:22; 2 Cor 6:3; Rv 17:17; *inflict* 2 Th 1:8; *permit* Ac 2:27; Mk 10:37; *yield* Js 5:18; *produce* 1 Cor 14:7f; *entrust* Mt 25:15; J 6:37, 39; *pay* Mk 12:14; *appoint* Ac 13:20; Eph 1:22; *give up, sacrifice* Mk 10:45; Lk 22:19. λόγον δ. *render account* Ro 14:12. δὸς ἐργασίαν *take pains, make an effort* Lk 12:58. ἔδωκαν κλήρους *draw* or *cast lots* Ac 1:26. [Cf. *dose.*]

διέβην 2 aor. act. ind. of **διαβαίνω.**

διεγείρω *wake up, arouse* lit. Mk 4:39; Lk 8:24; fig. J 6:18; 2 Pt 1:13.

διεγερθείς 1 aor. pass. ptc. of **διεγείρω.**

διεδίδετο, διέδωκα impf. pass. 3 sing. and 1 aor. act. ind. of **διαδίδωμι.**

διέζωσα, διεζωσάμην, διεζωσμένος 1 aor. act. ind., 1 aor. mid. ind., and pf. pass. ptc. of **διαζώννυμι.**

διεῖλον 2 aor. act. ind. of **διαιρέω.**

διεκρίθην 1 aor. pass. ind. of **διακρίνω.**

διελεύσομαι, διεληλυθώς, διελθεῖν fut. mid. ind., pf. act. ptc., and 2 aor. act. inf. of **διέρχομαι.**

διελέχθην 1 aor. pass. ind. of **διαλέγομαι.**

διέλιπον 2 aor. act. ind. of **διαλείπω.**

διενέγκω aor. act. subj. of **διαφέρω.**

διενεμήθην 1 aor. pass. ind. of **διανέμω.**

διενθυμέομαι *ponder, reflect* Ac 10:19.*

διεξέρχομαι *come out* Ac 28:3 v.l.*

διέξοδος, ου, ἡ lit. 'a way out through'; δ. τῶν ὁδῶν *the place where a highway leaves the city*, perhaps *street-crossing* Mt 22:9.*

διέπλευσα 1 aor. act. ind. of διαπλέω.

διερμηνεία, ας, ἡ explanation, interpretation, translation 1 Cor 12:10 v.l.*

διερμηνευτής, οῦ, ὁ interpreter, translator 1 Cor 14:28.*

διερμηνεύω translate Ac 9:36. Explain, interpret Lk 24:27; Ac 18:6 v.l. Explain, interpret, or translate 1 Cor 12:30; 14:5, 13, 27.*

διέ(ρ)ρηξα 1 aor. act. ind. of δια-(ρ)ρήγνυμι.

διέρχομαι—1. go through Mt 12:43; Mk 10:25; Ac 13:6; 1 Cor 10:1; Hb 4:14; pierce Lk 2:35. Go about Ac 20:25; go from place to place 8:4; spread Lk 5:15. Pass Ac 12:10.—2. simply come, go Lk 2:15; J 4:15; Ac 9:38; Ro 5:12.

διερωτάω find by inquiry Ac 10:17.*

διεσπάρην 2 aor. pass. ind. of διασπείρω.

διεστείλατο 1 aor. mid. ind. of διαστέλλω.

διέστη 2 aor. act. ind. of διΐστημι.

διεστραμμένος pf. pass. ptc. of διαστρέφω.

διεσώθην 1 aor. pass. ind. of διασώζω.

διεταράχθην 1 aor. pass. ind. of διαταράσσω.

διετής, ές two years old Mt 2:16.*

διετία, ας, ἡ a period of two years Ac 24:27; 28:30. Cf. Mt 2:16 v.l.*

διεφθάρη, διέφθαρμαι 2 aor. pass. ind. and pf. pass. ind. of διαφθείρω.

διήγειρα 1 aor. act. ind. of διεγείρω.

διηγέομαι tell, relate, describe Mk 9:9; Lk 9:10; Ac 8:33; 12:17; Hb 11:32.

διήγησις, εως, ἡ narrative, account Lk 1:1.*

διηγοῦ pres. mid. impv. of διηγέομαι.

διῆλθον 2 aor. act. ind. of διέρχομαι.

διηνεκής, ές continuous εἰς τὸ δ. forever Hb 7:3; 10:14; for all time 10:12; continually 10:1.*

διηνοίχθην 1 aor. pass. ind. of διανοίγω.

διθάλασσος, ον surrounded on both sides by the sea; the τόπος δ. Ac 27:41 may be a sandbank or reef or headland or crosscurrent.*

διϊκνέομαι pierce, penetrate Hb 4:12.*

διΐστημι—1. intr. (2 aor.) go away, part Lk 24:51; pass 22:59.—2. trans. (1 aor.) drive on with τὴν ναῦν supplied βραχὺ διαστήσαντες after they had sailed a short distance farther Ac 27:28.* [Cf. diastase, an enzyme that converts starch into sugar.]

διϊστορέω examine carefully Ac 17:23 v.l.*

διϊσχυρίζομαι insist, maintain firmly Lk 22:59; Ac 12:15; 15:2 v.l.*

δικάζω judge, condemn Lk 6:37 v.l.*

δικαιοκρισία, ας, ἡ fair or righteous judgment Ro 2:5; 2 Th 1:5 v.l.*

δίκαιος, αία, ον applied to model citizens in the Graeco-Roman world. Upright, just, righteous Mt 10:41; 13:43; Mk 6:20; Ro 1:17; 5:7; Hb 12:23; 1 J 3:7; law-abiding 1 Ti 1:9; honest, good, just Mt 1:19. Of God and Christ just, righteous, upright, fair J 17:25; Ac 7:52; 2 Ti 4:8; of Jesus upright, innocent Lk 23:47, cf. Mt 23:35 and 27:24 v.l. τὸ δίκαιον (what is) right or fair Mt 20:4; Lk 12:57; Ac 4:19; Col 4:1; δίκαιον ἡγοῦμαι consider it a duty 2 Pt 1:13.

δικαιοσύνη, ης, ἡ righteousness, uprightness Mt 5:6; Ac 24:25; Ro 9:30; Phil 3:6; Tit 3:5; religious requirement Mt 3:15. Mercy, charitableness Mt 6:1; 2 Cor 9:9f. Justice, equity Ac 17:31; Hb 11:33. In Paul the phrase δ. θεοῦ and its variations refer to God's equitable way of dealing with humanity in grace Ro 1:17; 3:21f, 26; 5:17 and the meaning approximates salvation. δ. approaches the sense Christianity Mt 5:10; Hb 5:13; 1 Pt 2:24; 3:14. ποιεῖν δ. do what is right 1 J 2:29; Rv 22:11.

δικαιόω—1. justify, vindicate, treat as just Mt 11:19; Lk 10:29; 16:15. δ. τὸν θεόν acknowledge God's justice 7:29. God is proved to be right Ro 3:4; also Christ 1 Ti 3:16.—2. pass., with reference to people be acquitted, be pronounced and treated as righteous, in theological language be justified = receive the divine gift of δικαιοσύνη Mt 12:37; Ac 13:39; Ro 2:13; 5:1, 9; Gal 2:16f; Tit 3:7; Js 2:21, 24f. Act., of God's activity Ro 3:26, 30; Gal 3:8; for this and other passages make upright is

possible. *Make free* or *pure* act. and
pass. Ac 13:38f; Ro 6:7; 1 Cor 6:11.

δικαίωμα, ατος, τό—1. *regulation, requirement, commandment* Lk 1:6; Ro
1:32; 2:26; 8:4; Hb 9:1, 10.—**2.** *righteous deed* Ro 5:18; Rv 15:4; 19:8. In
Ro 5:16 δ. = δικαίωσις *acquittal.**

δικαίως adv. *justly, uprightly, rightly* Lk
23:41; 1 Th 2:10; Tit 2:12; 1 Pt 2:23; *as
one ought* 1 Cor 15:34.*

δικαίωσις, εως, ή *justification, vindication, acquittal* Ro 4:25. δ. ζωής *acquittal that brings life* 5:18.*

δικαστής, οὗ, ὁ *judge* Ac 7:27, 35; Lk
12:14 v.l.* [*dicast*]

δίκη, ης, ή *penalty, punishment* 2 Th
1:9; Jd 7; Ac 25:15 v.l. *Justice* personified as a goddess Ac 28:4.* [*theodicy,*
θεός + δίκη]

δίκτυον, ου, τό *net* Mk 1:18f; J 21:6, 8,
11.

δίλογος, ον *double-tongued, insincere* 1
Ti 3:8.*

διό inferential conjunction (= δι' ὅ)
therefore, for this reason Mt 27:8; Lk
7:7; Ac 27:25, 34; Ro 15:22; 2 Cor 5:9.

διοδεύω *go* or *travel through* Ac 17:1.
Go about Lk 8:1.*

Διονύσιος, ου, ὁ *Dionysius* Ac 17:34.*

διόπερ inferential conjunction (= δι'
ὅπερ) *therefore, for this very reason* 1
Cor 8:13; 10:14; 14:13 v.l.*

διοπετής, ές *fallen from heaven* τὸ δ.
the image (of Artemis = Diana) *fallen
from heaven* Ac 19:35.*

διόρθωμα, ατος, τό *reform* Ac 24:2.*

διόρθωσις, εως, ή *improvement, reformation, new order* Hb 9:10.*

διορύσσω *dig through, break in* Mt 6:19f;
24:43; Lk 12:39.*

Διός gen. of Ζεύς.

Διόσκουροι, ων, οἱ (= Διὸς κοῦροι,
'sons of Zeus') *the Dioscuri,* Castor
and Pollux, twin sons of Zeus and Leda,
patron deities of sailors, used as identification symbols for ships Ac 28:11.*

διότι (= δι' ὅτι) conjunction *because* Lk
2:7; 1 Cor 15:9; Hb 11:5. *Therefore* Ac
13:35; 20:26. *For* Lk 1:13; Ro 1:19, 21;
1 Pt 1:16, 24. *That* = ὅτι perh. Ro 8:21
v.l.

Διοτρέφης, ους, ὁ *Diotrephes* 3 J 9.*

διπλοῦς, ῆ, οὖν *double, twofold* 1 Ti
5:17; Rv 18:6. Comp. διπλότερος, neut.
as adv. *twice as much* Mt 23:15.*

διπλόω *to double* δ. τὰ διπλᾶ *pay back
double* Rv 18:6.* [*diploma*]

δίς adv. *twice* Mk 14:30, 72; Lk 18:12;
Jd 12. ἅπαξ καὶ δ. *once and again* =
several times Phil 4:16; 1 Th 2:18.*

δισμυριάς, άδος, ή *a double myriad* =
20,000 Rv 9:16.*

διστάζω *doubt* Mt 14:31; 28:17.*

δίστομος, ον *double-edged* Hb 4:12; Rv
1:16; 2:12; 19:15 v.l.*

δισχίλιοι, αι, α *two thousand* Mk 5:13.*

διϋλίζω *filter out, strain out* Mt 23:24.*

διχάζω *cause a separation* δ. ἄνθρωπον
κατὰ τ. πατρός *turn a man against his
father* Mt 10:35.* [*dichasium,* botanical term referring to production of two
main axes]

διχοστασία, ας, ή *dissension* Ro 16:17;
Gal 5:20; 1 Cor 3:3 v.l.*

διχοτομέω *cut in two,* though in the context of Mt 24:51 and Lk 12:46 *punish
with utmost severity* is a likely meaning.* [*dichotomy*]

διψάω *thirst—1.* lit. *be thirsty, suffer from
thirst* Mt 25:35, 37; J 4:13, 15; 1 Cor
4:11.—**2.** fig. *thirst for the water of life*
J 4:14; 7:37; *thirst* or *long for* something Mt 5:6. [*dipsomania*]

δίψος, ους, τό *thirst* 2 Cor 11:27.*

δίψυχος, ον *irresolute, doubting, hesitating* lit. *double-minded* Js 1:8; 4:8.*

διωγμός, οῦ, ὁ *persecution* (for religious
reasons only) Mk 4:27; Ac 8:1; 13:50;
Ro 8:35; 2 Ti 3:11.

διώκτης, ου, ὁ *persecutor* 1 Ti 1:13.*

διώκω—1. *persecute* Mt 5:11f, 44; Lk
21:12; J 5:16; 1 Cor 4:12; Gal 5:11; 2
Ti 3:12.—**2.** *run after, pursue* lit. Lk
17:23. Fig. *pursue, strive for, seek after*
Ro 9:30f; 14:19; 1 Cor 14:1; 2 Ti 2:22.
Hasten, run, press on Phil 3:12, 14.—
3. *drive away, drive out* Mt 23:34.

δόγμα, ατος, τό *decree, commandment*
Lk 2:1; Ac 16:4; 17:7; *ordinance* Eph
2:15; *requirement* Col 2:14.* [Formed
on δοκεῖν; cf. *doctor.*]

δογματίζω decree pass. submit to rules and regulations Col 2:20.* [dogmatism]

δοθείς, δοθήσομαι, δοῖ, 1 aor. pass. ptc., fut. pass. ind., and 2 aor. act. subj. 3 sing. of δίδωμι.

δοκέω—1. trans. think, believe, suppose, consider Mt 3:9; Lk 24:37; 1 Cor 3:18; Hb 10:29; Js 4:5; be disposed 1 Cor 11:16.—2. intrans. seem Lk 10:36; Ac 17:18; 1 Cor 12:22; Hb 12:11. ἔδοξα ἐμαυτῷ I was convinced Ac 26:9. Be influential, have a reputation, be recognized Mk 10:42; Gal 2:2, 6, 9.—3. impers., w. dat. it seems (to me, etc.), hence I think or believe (etc.) Mt 17:25; J 11:56. κατὰ τὸ δοκοῦν αὐτοῖς at their discretion Hb 12:10. Of individual decisions it seems best to me, I resolve or decide Lk 1:3; as t.t. in collective formal proceedings and frequent in Hellenistic decrees resolve Ac 15:22, 25, 28. [docetism]

δοκιμάζω—1. put to the test, examine Lk 14:19; 1 Cor 11:28; Gal 6:4; 1 Th 5:21; 1 Ti 3:10; try to learn Eph 5:10; discover Ro 12:2.—2. prove by testing 1 Pt 1:7. Accept as proved, approve 1 Cor 16:3; 2 Cor 8:8, 22; see fit Ro 1:28. For Ro 2:18 and Phil 1:10 discover and approve are both possible.

δοκιμασία, ας, ἡ testing, examination πειράζειν ἐν δ. put to the test Hb 3:9.*

δοκιμή, ῆς, ἡ lit. 'the quality of being approved,' hence character Ro 5:4; 2 Cor 2:9; 9:13; Phil 2:22; test, ordeal 2 Cor 8:2; proof 13:3.*

δοκίμιον, ου, τό testing Js 1:3; genuineness, unalloyed quality 1 Pt 1:7.*

δόκιμος, ον approved, genuine 2 Cor 10:18; 13:7; 2 Ti 2:15; Js 1:12; tried and true Ro 16:10; 1 Cor 11:19; respected, esteemed Ro 14:18.*

δοκός, οῦ, ἡ beam of wood Mt 7:3ff; Lk 6:41f.*

δόλιος, ία, ον deceitful, treacherous, dishonest 2 Cor 11:13.*

δολιόω deceive Ro 3:13.*

δόλος, ου, ὁ deceit, cunning, treachery Mk 7:22; 14:1; J 1:47; 2 Cor 12:16.

δολόω falsify, adulterate 2 Cor 4:2; 1 Cor 5:6 v.l.*

δόμα, ατος, τό gift Mt 7:11; Lk 11:13; Eph 4:8; Phil 4:17.*

δόξα, ης, ἡ—1. brightness, radiance, splendor Lk 9:31f; Ac 22:11; 1 Cor 15:40f. Glory, majesty as ascribed to God and heavenly beings Ac 7:2; Ro 1:23; 1 Cor 2:8; Phil 3:21; Col 1:11; Hb 1:3; Js 2:1; Rv 15:8; with connotation of power Ro 6:4. Reflection 1 Cor 11:7. Magnificence, splendor of kings, etc. Mt 4:8; 6:29; Rv 21:24, 26.—2. fame, renown, honor, prestige J 5:41, 44; 8:54; 12:43; Ro 3:23; 1 Th 2:6, 20. Praise as enhancement of reputation Lk 2:14; Ac 12:23; Ro 11:36; 1 Cor 10:31; Phil 2:11; Rv 19:7.—3. glorious angelic beings Jd 8; 2 Pt 2:10; majesties, illustrious persons is also possible in these passages. [doxology]

δοξάζω—1. praise, honor, magnify Mt 5:16; 6:2; Lk 5:25f; Ac 11:18; Ro 11:13; 1 Cor 12:26; 1 Pt 4:16.—2. clothe in splendor, glorify J 8:54; 13:31f; 17:1, 4; 21:19; 2 Cor 3:10; 1 Pt 1:8; of life after death J 12:16, 23; Ac 3:13; Ro 8:30.

Δορκάς, άδος, ἡ Dorcas woman's name meaning gazelle Ac 9:36, 39.*

δός 2 aor. act. impv. of δίδωμι.

δόσις, εως, ἡ gift Js 1:17. The act of giving Mt 6:1 v.l. δ. καὶ λήμψις giving and receiving, debit and credit Phil 4:15.*

δότης, ου, ὁ giver 2 Cor 9:7.*

Δουβέριος Ac 20:4 v.l., see s.v. Δερβαῖος.

δουλαγωγέω enslave, bring into subjection fig. 1 Cor 9:27.*

δουλεία, ας, ἡ slavery fig. Ro 8:15, 21; Gal 4:24; 5:1; Hb 2:15.*

δουλεύω be a slave, be subjected lit. J 8:33; Ac 7:7; Gal 4:25; fig. Ro 7:6. W. dat. serve someone as a slave, serve Mt 6:24; Lk 15:29; 16:13; Ro 14:18; Gal 5:13; Eph 6:7; be a slave fig. Ro 6:6; 7:25.

δούλη, ης, ἡ female slave, bondmaid Lk 1:38; 48; Ac 2:18.*

δοῦλος, η, ον slavish, servile Ro 6:19.*

δοῦλος, ου, ὁ slave lit. Lk 7:2f; J 8:35; 1 Cor 7:21ff; Gal 4:1, 7; Phil 2:7; Col

3:11, 22. Fig. Mt 20:27; Ro 6:16f, 20; 2 Cor 4:5. To God or Christ with emphasis on their unique claim Lk 2:29; Ac 4:29; Ro 1:1; Gal 1:10; Js 1:1; Rv 2:20. Of a king's officials *minister* Mt 18:23, 26ff.

δουλόω *make someone a slave, enslave, subject* lit. Ac 7:6; 2 Pt 2:19. Fig. Ro 6:18, 22; 1 Cor 7:15; 9:19; Gal 4:3; Tit 2:3.*

δοῦναι, δούς 2 aor. act. inf. and ptc. of δίδωμι.

δοχή, ῆς, ἡ *reception, banquet* Lk 5:29; 14:13.*

δράκων, οντος, ὁ *dragon, serpent* as a term for the Devil Rv 12:3f, 7, 9; 20:2.

δραμεῖν, δραμών 2 aor. act. inf. and ptc. of τρέχω. [*syndrome,* σύν + δραμεῖν]

δράσσομαι *catch, seize* 1 Cor 3:19.*

δραχμή, ῆς, ἡ *drachma* a Greek silver coin Lk 15:8f.*

δρέπανον, ου, τό *sickle* Mk 4:29; Rv 14:14–19.*

δρόμος, ου, ὁ *course, race* fig. 2 Ti 4:7; *course, career* Ac 13:25; 20:24.* [*hippodrome,* ἵππος + δρόμος]

Δρούσιλλα, ης, ἡ *Drusilla,* daughter of Herod Agrippa I, wife of Felix the procurator Ac 24:24, 27 v.l.*

δυναίμην pres. mid. opt. of δύναμαι.

δύναμαι *I can, am able* Mt 6:24; Mk 3:23; Lk 9:40; Ac 4:20; 26:32. δ. approaches the meaning *like* in J 6:60. *Be able to do* something Mk 9:22; Lk 12:26; 2 Cor 13:8.

δύναμις, εως, ἡ *power, might, strength, force* Mt 14:2; 22:29; Ac 1:8; Ro 1:4; Col 1:11; 2 Ti 3:5; Hb 7:16; 2 Pt 1:3. δ. = *God* Mk 14:62. *Ability, capability* Mt 25:15; 2 Cor 1:8; *meaning* 1 Cor 14:11. Specialized senses *deed of power, miracle* Mt 11:20f; Mk 6:5; 2 Cor 12:12; Hb 2:4. *Force* in a military sense Mk 13:25; Lk 21:26. *Power* as a divine being or angel Ac 8:10; Ro 8:38; 1 Cor 15:24. [*dynamite*]

δυναμόω *strengthen* Col 1:11; Hb 11:34; Eph 6:10 v.l.*

δυνάστης, ου, ὁ *ruler, sovereign* Lk 1:52; 1 Ti 6:15. *Court official* Ac 8:27.* [*dynasty*]

δυνατέω *be strong* 2 Cor 13:3; *be strong enough, be able* Ro 14:4; 2 Cor 9:8.*

δυνατός, ή, όν *powerful, strong, mighty, able* Lk 1:49; Ac 25:5; Ro 4:21; 2 Cor 10:4; 13:9; Js 3:2. Neuter δυνατόν *possible* Mt 19:26; 26:39; Gal 4:15. τὸ δ. = ἡ δύναμις Ro 9:22.

δύνῃ pres. mid. ind. 2 sing. of δύναμαι.

δύνω *go down, set* of the sun Mk 1:32; Lk 4:40.*

δύο gen. and acc. δύο, dat. δυσί *two;* εἰς δύο *in two* Mk 15:38. ἀνὰ δ. *two apiece* Lk 9:3; J 2:6; *two by two* Lk 10:1. κατὰ δ. *two at a time* 1 Cor 14:27. δύο δύο *two by two* Mk 6:7.

δυσβάστακτος, ον *hard to bear* Lk 11:46; Mt 23:4 v.l.*

δυσεντέριον, ου, τό *dysentery* Ac 28:8.*

δυσερμήνευτος, ον *hard to explain* Hb 5:11.*

δυσί see δύο.

δύσις, εως, ἡ *west* lit. 'setting' (of the sun) short ending of Mark.*

δύσκολος, ον *hard, difficult* Mk 10:24.*

δυσκόλως adv. *hardly, with difficulty* Mt 19:23; Mk 10:23; Lk 18:24.*

δυσμή, ῆς, ἡ *west* lit. 'setting' (of the sun) Mt 8:11; Lk 13:29. ἀπὸ δ. *in the west* Rv 21:13. ἐπὶ δυσμῶν *in the west* Lk 12:54. ἕως δ. *to the west* Mt 24:27.*

δυσνόητος, ον *hard to understand* 2 Pt 3:16.*

δυσφημέω *slander, defame* 1 Cor 4:13.*

δυσφημία, ας, ἡ *slander, ill repute* 2 Cor 6:8.*

δύω 2 aor. act. subj. of δύνω.

δῷ, δώσῃ 2 aor. act. subj. 3 sing. and 1 aor. act. subj. 3 sing. of δίδωμι.

δώδεκα indecl. *twelve* Mt 10:1f, 5; Mk 5:25, 42; Lk 2:42; 1 Cor 15:5. [*dodecagon,* δώδεκα + γωνία]

δωδέκατος, η, ον *twelfth* Rv 21:20.*

δωδεκάφυλον, ου, τό *the twelve tribes* Ac 26:7.*

δῴη 2 aor. act. opt. 3 sing. of δίδωμι.

δώη 2 aor. act. subj. 3 sing. of δίδωμι.

δῶμα, ατος, τό roof, housetop Mt 10:27; Mk 13:15; Lk 5:19; 17:31; Ac 10:9.

δωρεά, ᾶς, ἡ gift, bounty J 4:10; Ac 8:20; Ro 5:15, 17; Hb 6:4.

δωρεάν acc. of δωρεά used as adv.—1. as a gift, without payment, gratis Mt 10:8; Ro 3:24; 2 Cor 11:7; 2 Th 3:8; Rv 21:6; 22:17.—2. undeservedly, without reason J 15:25.—3. in vain, to no purpose Gal 2:21.*

δωρέομαι give, bestow Mk 15:45; 2 Pt 1:3f.*

δώρημα, ατος, τό gift Ro 5:16; Js 1:17.*

δῶρον, ου, τό gift Mt 2:11; Eph 2:8; Rv 11:10. Sacrificial gift, offering Mt 5:23f; Mk 7:11; Hb 5:1; 11:4. τὰ δῶρα offering chest Lk 21:4. [Dorothea or Dorothy, δῶρον + θεός; cf. Theodore.]

δωροφορία, ας, ἡ the bringing of a gift Ro 15:31 v.l.*

δώσω fut. act. ind. of δίδωμι.

E

ε′ as numeral = five, fifth Ac 19:9 v.l.*

ἔα exclamation denoting surprise or displeasure ah!, ha! Mk 1:24 v.l.; Lk 4:34; some connection with ἔα, imperative of ἐάω, let alone! seems possible in both passages.*

ἐάν conjunction if: in a present general condition, w. pres. or aor. subj., and present in apodosis (main clause) Mt 8:2; Mk 3:24; Lk 6:33; J 5:31; 1 Cor 8:8. In a future more vivid condition, w. pres. or aor. subj. and future in apodosis Mt 6:14; 9:21; Mk 8:3; Lk 4:7; J 15:10. With the indicative: fut. Lk 19:40; Ac 8:31; pres. 1 Th 3:8. At times ἐάν closely approaches ὅταν whenever, when J 12:32; 1 J 2:28. ἐὰν καί even if Gal 6:1. ἐὰν δὲ καί but if 1 Cor 7:11. ἐὰν μή if not, unless Mt 10:13; Mk 3:27; J 4:48; Ro 10:15. ἐάν is frequently used in place of ἄν with relative words Mt 5:19, 32; 8:19; 1 Cor 16:6; Rv 11:6.

ἐάνπερ conj. if indeed Hb 6:3.

ἐάσω, ἐᾶτε fut. act. ind. and pres. act. impv. 2 pl. of ἐῶ (ἐάω).

ἑαυτοῦ, ῆς, οῦ pl. ἑαυτῶν—1. reflexive pronoun: of the third person himself, herself, itself, themselves Mt 18:4; 27:42; Mk 5:5; J 19:24. γίνεσθαι ἐν ἑ.

or εἰς ἑ. ἔρχεσθαι come to one's senses Lk 15:17; Ac 12:11. ἀφ' ἑαυτοῦ by itself J 15:4.—Of the first and second persons plural ourselves, yourselves Mt 23:31; 1 Cor 11:31; perh. also for second pers. sing. J 18:34 v.l.—2. reciprocal pronoun = ἀλλήλων each other, one another Mk 10:26; J 12:19; Eph 4:32; Col 3:13, 16; 1 Th 5:13.—3. possessive pronoun = αὐτοῦ, etc. his, her, their Mt 8:22; 21:8; Lk 9:60; 11:21; 12:36.

ἐάω let, permit Mt 24:43; Ac 14:16; 23:32; 1 Cor 10:13. Let go, leave alone Ac 5:38 v.l.; Rv 2:20 v.l.; leave Ac 27:40. Stop! Lk 22:51.

ἔβαλον 2 aor. act. ind. of βάλλω.

ἐβδομήκοντα indecl. seventy Lk 10:1, 17; Ac 7:14 w. πέντε; 23:23.*

ἐβδομηκοντάκις indecl. seventy times ἑβ. ἑπτά may be short for ἑβ. ἑπτάκις seventy times seven times, but it is more likely seventy-seven times (as Gen 4:24) Mt 18:22.*

ἕβδομος, η, ον seventh J 4:52; Hb 4:4; Jd 14; Rv 8:1. [hebdomadal, weekly]

ἐβεβλήκει, ἐβέβλητο plupf. act. and pass. of βάλλω.

Ἔβερ, ὁ indecl. Eber Lk 3:35.*

ἐβλάστησα, ἐβλήθην 1 aor. act. ind. and 1 aor. pass. ind. of βάλλω.

'Εβραϊκός, ή, όν Hebrew Lk 23:38 v.1.*

'Εβραῖος, ου, ὁ a Hebrew 2 Cor 11:22; Phil 3:5; one speaking Aramaic Ac 6:1.*

'Εβραΐς, ίδος, ή Hebrew language, i.e. the Aramaic spoken at that time in Palestine Ac 21:40; 22:2; 26:14.*

'Εβραϊστί adv. in Hebrew or Aramaic J 5:2; 19:13, 17, 20; 20:16; Rv 9:11; 16:16.*

ἐγγέγραμμαι pf. pass. ind. of ἐγγράφω.

ἐγγίζω come near, approach Mt 21:1; 26:45; Mk 1:15; Lk 7:12; 10:9, 11; 18:35; Ac 9:3; Ro 13:12; draw near Hb 7:19; come close Phil 2:30.

ἐγγράφω write (in), record lit. Lk 10:20; fig. 2 Cor 3:2f.*

ἔγγυος, ον as noun ὁ ἔ. guarantee Hb 7:22.*

ἐγγύς adv. followed by gen. or dat. near, close to Mt 26:18; Lk 19:11; J 3:23; 19:42; Ac 9:38; Ro 10:8; Eph 2:13, 17; Phil 4:5.

ἐγγύτερον comparative degree of ἐγγύς.

ἐγεγόνει plupf. act. ind. of γίνομαι.

ἐγείρω—1. trans. wake, rouse Mt·8:25. Raise, help to rise Mt 12:11; Mk 1:31; Ac 3:7. Raise the dead Mt 10:8; J 12:1, 9, 17; 1 Cor 15:15ff; Gal 1:1. Raise up, bring into being Mt 3:9; Ac 13:22; cause Phil 1:17. Passive: awaken Mt 1:24; Ro 13:11. Be raised, rise Lk 9:7; 11:8; J 2:22; 1 Cor 15:12. Appear Mt 11:11; Mk 13:22; J 7:52.—2. intr., only in imperative get up!, come! Mk 2:9, 11; 14:42; Lk 5:23f; J 5:8; Eph 5:14; Rv 11:1.

ἐγενήθην, ἐγενόμην 1 aor. pass. ind. and 2 aor. mid. ind. of γίνομαι.

ἐγερθήσομαι fut. pass. ind. of ἐγείρω.

ἔγερσις, εως, ή resurrection Mt 27:53.*

ἐγερῶ, ἐγήγερμαι fut. act. ind. and pf. pass. ind. of ἐγείρω.

ἔγημα 1 aor. act. ind. of γαμέω.

ἐγκάθετος, ον lying in wait, as noun spy Lk 20:20.*

ἐγκαίνια, ίων, τά the festival of Rededication J 10:22, known also as Hanukkah and the Feast of Lights, beginning the 25th of Kislev (roughly = November–December) to commemorate the rededication of the temple by Judas Maccabaeus on that date in 165 B.C.*

ἐγκαινίζω lit. 'renew'; inaugurate, dedicate Hb 9:18; open 10:20.*

ἐγκακέω become weary, tired, lose heart, despair Lk 18:1; 2 Cor 4:1, 16; Gal 6:9; Eph 3:13; 2 Th 3:13.*

ἐγκαλέω accuse, bring charges against sometimes w. dat. Ac 19:38; 23:28; Ro 8:33.

ἐγκαταλείπω—1. leave behind Ro 9:29; leave, allow to remain Ac 2:27, 31.—2. forsake, abandon, desert Mt 27:46; Mk 15:34; 2 Cor 4:9; 2 Ti 4:10, 16; Hb 10:25; 13:5.*

ἐγκατέλειπας, ἐγκατέλιπας alternate forms of aor. ind. 2 sing. (Mk 15:34) and ἐγκατέλιπον 2 aor. act. ind. of ἐγκαταλείπω.

ἐγκατοικέω live, dwell (among) 2 Pt 2:8.*

ἐγκαυχάομαι boast, be proud 2 Th 1:4.*

ἐγκεντρίζω graft (in) Ro 11:17, 19, 23f.*

ἐγκλείω lock up Lk 3:20 v.l.* [Cf. enclave.]

ἔγκλημα, ατος, τό charge, accusation Ac 23:29; 25:16; 23:24 v.l.*

ἐγκομβόομαι clothe oneself with, put on fig. 1 Pt 5:5.*

ἐγκοπή, ῆς, ή hindrance 1 Cor 9:12.*

ἐγκόπτω hinder, thwart Gal 5:7; 1 Th 2:18; 1 Pt 3:7; prevent Ro 15:22; weary or detain Ac 24:4.*

ἐγκράτεια, ας, ή self-control Ac 24:25; Gal 5:23; 2 Pt 1:6.*

ἐγκρατεύομαι control oneself, exercise self-control 1 Cor 7:9; 9:25.*

ἐγκρατής, ές in full control of oneself, disciplined Tit 1:8.*

ἐγκρίνω class someone in a certain group 2 Cor 10:12.*

ἐγκρύπτω put, lit. hide Mt 13:33; Lk 13:21 v.l.*

ἔγκυος, ον pregnant Lk 2:5.*

ἔγνωκα, ἔγνων, ἐγνώσθην, ἔγνωσμαι pf. act., 2 aor. act., 1 aor. pass. ind., and pf. mid. and pass. ind. of γινώσκω.

ἐγχρίω rub or put on Rv 3:18.*

ἐγώ gen. ἐμοῦ (μου), dat. ἐμοί (μοι), acc. ἐμέ (με); pl. ἡμεῖς, ἡμῶν, ἡμῖν, ἡμᾶς. I; its use often serves to emphasize the first pers. of a verb Mt 5:22, 28; Lk 21:8; J 10:7–14; sometimes no emphasis appears to be conveyed Mk 12:26; J 10:34. Sing. and pl. sometimes used without distinction 1 Cor 1:23; 4:10. ἐγώ alone = I (will) or yes Mt 21:29 v.l. The expression τί ἐμοὶ καὶ σοί; may be rendered what have I to do with you? what have we in common? leave me alone! never mind! this is no affair of yours! Mk 5:7; Lk 8:28; J 2:4; cf. Mt 8:29; Mk 1:24; Lk 4:34. [egotism]

ἐδάρην 2 aor. pass. ind. of δέρω.

ἐδαφίζω dash to the ground, raze to the ground only in the fut. act. ind. 3 pl. ἐδαφιοῦσιν Lk 19:44.*

ἔδαφος, ους, τό ground Ac 22:7.*

ἐδεδώκειν, ἐδίδοσαν, ἐδίδου plupf. act. ind., impf. act. 3 pl., and impf. act. 3 sing. of δίδωμι.

ἐδεήθην 1 aor. pass. ind. of δέομαι.

ἔδειξα 1 aor. act. ind. of δείκνυμι.

ἔδειρα 1 aor. act. ind. of δέρω.

ἔδησα 1 aor. act. ind. of δέω.

ἐδιδάχθην 1 aor. pass. ind. of διδάσκω.

ἐδόθην 1 aor. pass. ind. of δίδωμι.

ἐδολιοῦσαν impf. 3 pl. of δολιόω.

ἔδοξα 1 aor. act. ind. of δοκέω.

ἑδραῖος, (αία), αῖον firm, steadfast 1 Cor 7:37; 15:58; Col 1:23.*

ἑδραίωμα, ατος, τό foundation, perh. mainstay 1 Ti 3:15.*

ἔδραμον 2 aor. act. ind. of τρέχω.

ἔδυν 2 aor. act. ind. of δύνω.

ἐδυνάμην impf. mid. of δύναμαι.

ἔδωκα 1 aor. act. ind. of δίδωμι.

Ἐζεκίας, ου, ὁ Hezekiah Mt 1:9f; Lk 3:23ff v.l.*

ἔζην impf. act. of ζάω.

ἐθελοθρησκία, ας, ἡ self-made religion, perh. would-be religion Col 2:23.*

ἐθέλω classical form for θέλω; not in N.T.

ἐθέμην, ἔθηκα 2 aor. mid. ind. and 1 aor. act. ind. of τίθημι.

ἐθίζω accustom τὸ εἰθισμένον the custom Lk 2:27.*

ἐθνάρχης, ου, ὁ deputy, ethnarch, i.e. head of an ethnic group or minority 2 Cor 11:32.*

ἐθνικός, ή, όν Gentile, non-Jew; in the N.T. only as noun ὁ ἐθνικός the Gentile in contrast to the Jew Mt 5:47; 6:7; 18:17; 3 J 7.* [ethnic]

ἐθνικῶς adv. like a non-Jew, like the rest of the world Gal 2:14.*

ἔθνος, ους, τό—1. nation, people Mt 24:14; Lk 12:30; Ac 8:9; 10:22; 13:19.—2. τὰ ἔθνη Gentiles, non-Jews as contrasted with Jews Mt 6:32; 10:18; Ac 11:1, 18; 14:5; Ro 3:29. Gentiles who are Christian Ro 16:4; Gal 2:12; Eph 3:1. [ethnology]

ἔθος, ους, τό habit, usage Lk 22:39; J 19:40; Ac 25:16; Hb 10:25. Custon, law Lk 1:9; Ac 6:14; 21:21; 28:17. [ethics]

ἔθου 2 aor. mid. ind. 2 sing. of τίθημι.

ἔθρεψα 1 aor. act. ind. of τρέφω.

ἔθω obsolete pres. from which εἴωθα is formed.

εἰ—1. conditional particle if: with indicative in general conditions Mt 4:3; 26:33, 42; Lk 16:11f; Ro 2:17 or in contrary-to-fact conditions (see ἄν) Mt 11:21; Lk 7:39; J 9:33. With subjunctive Rv 11:5. With optative in a future less vivid (should–would) condition Ac 24:19; 1 Pt 3:14, 17; εἰ τύχοι it may be, for example, perhaps 1 Cor 14:10; 15:37. If = since Mt 6:30; J 7:23; Ro 6:8. After verbs of emotion that Mk 15:44a; Ac 26:23; 1 J 3:13. In strong assertions, with the apodosis omitted εἰ has a negative effect (Hebraistic) εἰ δοθήσεται . . . σημεῖον if a sign shall be given (something fearful will result), hence a sign will certainly not be given Mk 8:12; cf. Hb 4:3, 5.—2. interrogative particle: with direct questions, εἰ is left untranslated Mt 12:10; Lk 13:23; Ac 1:6. With indirect questions whether, if Mt 26:63; Mk 3:2; Ac 17:11.—3. with other particles εἰ δὲ μή if not, otherwise Mk 2:21f; J 14:2; Rv

2:5, 16. εἰ καί *even if, even though* Lk 11:8; 1 Cor 7:21. εἰ μή *except, if not* Mt 5:13; 11:27; Ro 7:7; Gal 1:19 or *but* Mt 12:4; Gal 1:7. εἴ πως *if perhaps, if somehow* Ac 27:12; Ro 1:10.

εἰ μήν, *more correctly* εἶ μήν *surely, certainly* Hb 6:14.*

εἴα, εἴασα *impf. act. 3 sing. and 1 aor. act. ind. 1 sing. of* ἐάω.

εἰδέα, ας, ἡ *appearance, perh. face* Mt 28:3. S. ἰδέα.* [idea]

εἰδέναι *pf. act. inf. of* οἶδα.

εἰδήσω *fut. act. ind. of* οἶδα Hb 8:11.

εἶδον *used as 2 aor. of* ὁράω; *the Hellenistic forms* εἶδα, *etc., are often found in the N.T. see.*—**1.** lit. *see, perceive* Mt 2:2, 9f; 3:7; Mk 5:14; J 1:46; Ac 10:17; Gal 6:11; *look at* Mk 8:33; Lk 14:18. ἰδὼν εἶδον *I have surely seen* Ac 7:34.—**2.** non-lit. and fig. *feel, become aware of* Mt 27:54. *Notice, note* Mt 9:2; Ro 11:22. *Consider, deliberate* Ac 15:6; 1 J 3:1. *See = experience* Lk 2:26; J 3:3; 1 Pt 3:10. *Visit* 1 Cor 16:7; *learn to know* Lk 9:9; Ro 1:11.

εἶδος, ους, τό *form, outward appearance* Lk 3:22; 9:29; J 5:37. *Kind* 1 Th 5:22. *Seeing, sight* 2 Cor 5:7.*

εἰδυῖα, εἰδῶ *pf. ptc. fem. and pf. act. subj. of* οἶδα.

εἰδωλεῖον, ου, τό *an idol's temple* 1 Cor 8:10.*

εἰδωλόθυτος, ον *only as noun* τὸ εἰδωλόθυτον *meat offered to an idol* Ac 15:29; 21:25; 1 Cor 8:1, 4, 7, 10; 10:19, 28 v.l.; Rv 2:14, 20.*

εἰδωλολάτρης, ου, ὁ *idolater* 1 Cor 5:10f; 6:9; 10:7; Eph 5:5; Rv 21:8; 22:15.*

εἰδωλολατρία, ας, ἡ *idolatry* 1 Cor 10:14; Gal 5:20; Col 3:5; 1 Pt 4:3.*

εἴδωλον, ου, τό *idol as an image* Ac 7:41; 1 Cor 12:2; Rv 9:20. *Idol as a false god* Ac 15:20; Ro 2:22; 1 Cor 8:4, 7; 10:19; 2 Cor 6:16; 1 Th 1:9; 1 J 5:21.*

εἰδώς, υἶα, ός *pf. act. ptc. of* οἶδα.

εἰθισμένος *pf. pass. ptc. of* ἐθίζω.

εἰκῇ *adv. without cause* Col 2:18; Mt 5:22 v.l. *In vain, to no avail* Gal 3:4; 4:11. *To no purpose* Ro 13:4; 1 Cor 15:2.*

εἴκοσι *twenty* Lk 14:31; Ac 27:28. [icosahedron]

εἴκω *yield* Gal 2:5.*

εἰκών, όνος, ἡ *image, likeness* Mk 12:16; 1 Cor 11:7; 15:49; Rv 13:14f. *Form, appearance* Ro 1:23; 8:29; Col 3:10; Hb 10:1. [icon]

εἴλατο *2 aor. mid. ind. 3 sing. of* αἱρέομαι.

εἴληφα, εἴλημμαι *pf. act. and pass. ind. of* λαμβάνω.

εἰλικρίνεια, ας, ἡ *sincerity, purity of motive* 1 Cor 5:8; 2 Cor 1:12; 2:17.*

εἰλικρινής, ές, gen. οὖς *pure, unsullied, sincere* Phil 1:10; 2 Pt 3:1.*

εἶλκον, εἵλκυσα *impf. and 1 aor. act. ind. of* ἕλκω.

εἱλκωμένος *pf. pass. ptc. of* ἑλκόω.

εἱλόμην *2 aor. mid. ind. of* αἱρέω.

εἰμί *ptc.* ὤν, οὖσα, ὄν; *inf.* εἶναι *be* Mt 11:29; 12:11; Mk 3:11; Lk 16:1, 19; J 3:1. *Exist* Ro 4:17; Hb 11:6. *Be present* Mk 8:1. *Live* Mt 23:30; *stay, reside* 2:13. *Take place* 24:3. *Mean* 9:13; 13:38; 27:46; 1 Cor 3:7; 10:19. *Belong w. gen.* 1:12; 3:4; w. ἐκ or ἐξ Lk 22:3; Col 4:9. *There is, there was,* etc. Lk 16:1, 19; 1 Cor 8:5; 12:4ff. Impers. *it is possible* 1 Cor 11:20; Hb 9:5. In explanations or interrogations, esp. with τοῦτο or τί *means* Mt 26:26; 27:46; Lk 18:36. W. dat. *have* Lk 1:7. With a participle as periphrasis for a single verb form Mk 1:22; 2:18; 4:38; Lk 1:20; 5:10, 17; 2 Cor 9:12. ὁ ἦν, *where* ἦν *is a substitute for a past ptc. the one who was* Rv 1:4, 8. ἡ οὖσα ἐκκλησία *the church there* Ac 13:1. *Followed by* εἰς *become* Mk 10:8; Ac 8:23; 2 Cor 6:18; *serve (as something)* 1 Cor 14:22; Js 5:3. There are obviously many other possible translations of εἰμί in various contexts.

εἶμι *in Attic used as fut. of* ἔρχομαι = *I shall go* J 7:34 v.l.

εἵνεκεν *prep. w. gen. (see* ἕνεκα) *on account of* Lk 4:18; 2 Cor 3:10.*

εἶξα *1 aor. act. ind. of* εἴκω.

εἶπα *a form of* εἶπον *with endings of the 1 aor.*

εἴπερ *if indeed, granted* Ro 3:30; 8:9, 17.

εἶπον used as 2 aor. of λέγω: *say, speak* Mt 2:8; 28:7; Mk 12:12; Lk 8:4; 19:11; J 1:15; 12:27. *Order* Mk 5:43; *tell* 8:7; *call* J 10:35; *foretell* Mt 28:6; J 14:28. Also see s.v. εἴρω.

εἴπως see εἰ.

εἰργασάμην, εἰργασμένος 1 aor. mid. ind., and pf. mid. and pass. ptc. of ἐργάζομαι.

εἴρηκα, εἴρημαι pf. act. and pass. ind. of εἴρω, q.v.

εἰρηνεύω *live in peace, keep the peace* Mk 9:50; Ro 12:18; 2 Cor 13:11; 1 Th 5:13.*

εἰρήνη, ης, ἡ *peace*—1. *peace, harmony, tranquillity* Mt 10:34; Lk 11:21; Ac 9:31; 24:2; Ro 3:17; 14:19; 1 Cor 14:33; Js 3:18.—2. *peace* esp. in the Hebrew sense = *welfare, health*, ordinarily in the context of one's relation to God Mk 5:34; Ro 1:7; 1 Cor 1:3; 16:11; 1 Th 1:1; Js 2:16.—3. *peace* in a specif. Christian sense, connoting *messianic salvation* Lk 2:14; J 16:33; Ro 5:1; Eph 6:15; Phil 4:7. [*Irene*]

εἰρηνικός, ή, όν *peaceable, peaceful* Hb 12:11; Js 3:17.* [*irenic*]

εἰρηνοποιέω *make peace* Col 1:20.*

εἰρηνοποιός, όν *making peace* as noun ὁ εἰ. *the peacemaker* Mt 5:9.*

εἴρω *say, speak*. The pres. of this verb is served by λέγω and φημί, the aor. by εἶπον. Fut. ἐρῶ Mt 7:4; 21:3; Mk 11:29; Lk 12:10; 17:21; Ro 4:1 (*conclude*); 1 Cor 15:35; Phil 4:4; Rv 17:7. Aor. ἐρρέθη Mt 5:38; Ro 9:26; Rv 6:11. Pf. εἴρηκα, εἴρημαι Lk 4:12; J 6:65; Ac 13:40; Hb 1:13; Rv 19:3; *call* J 15:15. [Cf. *oratory, verbal.*]

εἰς prep. w. acc.—1. of place *into* Mt 26:18; Lk 2:15; J 1:9; Ac 17:10; 2 Th 2:4; *to* Mk 7:31; 13:14; J 8:26; *toward* Lk 9:16. *On, in* Mt 5:39; Lk 14:10. *Among* Mk 4:7; Lk 10:36. εἰς is frequently used where ἐν would be expected *in* Mk 10:10; 13:9; Lk 11:7; J 1:18; Ac 8:40; 21:13; Hb 11:9.—2. of time *to, up to, until* Mk 13:13; 2 Ti 1:12. *For, at, on, in* Mt 6:34; Lk 1:20; 12:19; Ac 13:42; Phil 2:16; Hb 7:3.—3. gen-

erally *to, into, toward* Mt 6:13; J 13:1; Ro 1:26; 5:8; 2 Cor 11:13f; Hb 2:10. *With reference to* Ac 2:25. *In response to* Mt 12:41. *In* 18:6. *Against* Lk 15:18, 21. *For* Mt 5:13; Lk 5:4b; 9:13; 1 Cor 16:1; Rv 22:2. *As* Ac 10:4; *serving as* Lk 2:32. *Of* 1 Pt 1:11. *By* after a verb of swearing Mt 5:35; *by* or *with* in the instrumental sense Ac 7:53. εἰς τριάκοντα *thirty-fold* Mk 4:8. εἰς τοῦτο *for this reason* or *purpose* J 18:37; Ac 9:21. εἰς τό with inf. *so that* (result) Ro 1:20; 2 Th 2:10f but *in order to* (purpose) Mt 20:19; Mk 14:55. To be omitted in translation ἐγένετο εἰς δένδρον Lk 13:19.

εἰς, μία, ἕν gen. ἑνός, μιᾶς, ἑνός numeral *one* Mt 5:41; 19:5; Mk 8:14; Ac 21:7; Ro 5:12; 12:5. For emphasis *one and the same* Lk 12:52; Ro 3:30; 1 Cor 12:11; *only, one, (a) single* Mt 23:15; Mk 12:6; 10:21; Ro 3:10; 1 Ti 3:2 of one who is married only once; *alone* Mk 2:7. Equivalent to the indefinite τις *someone, anyone* Mt 18:24; Lk 24:18; with τις *a certain (òne)* Mk 14:47; J 11:49; equivalent to the indefinite article *a, an* Mt 8:19; Mk 12:42; Rv 8:13. Equivalent to πρῶτος *first* Mt 28:1; 1 Cor 16:2; Tit 3:10. (ὁ) εἰς . . . (ὁ) εἰς *(the) one . . . the other* Mt 20:21; J 20:12; Gal 4:22. εἰς τὸν ἕνα *one another* 1 Th 5:11. καθ᾽ ἕνα *one by one* 1 Cor 14:31. εἰς κατὰ εἰς *(the second* εἰς *is an undeclined nominative) one after the other* Mk 14:19; J 8:9. [*heno-*, combining form, as in *henotheism*]

εἰσάγω *bring* or *lead in, into* Lk 2:27; 14:21; J 18:16; Ac 9:8; 21:28f, 37; Hb 1:6.

εἰσακούω *hear, listen to*—1. of people *heed, obey* 1 Cor 14:21.—2. of God's attention to prayer Mt 6:7; Lk 1:13; Ac 10:31; Hb 5:7.*

εἰσδέχομαι *take in, receive, welcome* 2 Cor 6:17.*

εἰσδραμοῦσα 2 aor. act. ptc. fem. of εἰστρέχω.

εἴσειμι *go (in, into)* Ac 3:3; 21:18, 26; Hb 9:6.*

εἰσελεύσομαι, εἰσελήλυθα fut. mid. ind. and pf. act. ind. of εἰσέρχομαι.

εἰσενέγκειν 2 aor. act. inf. of εἰσφέρω.

εἰσέρχομαι come (in, into), go (in, into), enter Mt 19:24; Mk 1:21; 5:12f; 11;11; 15:43; Lk 17:7; J 18:1; Ro 5:12; reach into Hb 6:19. Fig. come (into) = share (in), come to enjoy Mt 5:20; 18:8f; 26:41; J 4:38; Hb 3:11, 18.

εἰσήγαγον 2 aor. act. ind. of εἰσάγω.

εἰσῄει impf. act. 3 sing. of εἴσειμι.

εἰσήνεγκον 2 aor. act. ind. of εἰσφέρω.

εἰσίασι pres. act. ind. 3 pl. of εἴσειμι.

εἰσκαλέομαι invite in Ac 10:23.*

εἴσοδος, ου, ἡ entering, entrance, access 1 Th 1:9 with connotation of welcome; 2:1; Hb 10:19; 2 Pt 1:11; coming Ac 13:24.*

εἰσπηδάω leap or rush in Ac 16:29; 14:14 v.l.*

εἰσπορεύομαι go (in), come (in), enter Mt 15:17; Mk 1:21; 4:19; 5:40; Lk 19:30; Ac 8:3.

εἰστήκει plupf. act. 3 sing. of ἵστημι.

εἰστρέχω run in Ac 12:14.*

εἰσφέρω bring or lead (in) Mt 6:13; Lk 5:18f; 11:4; Ac 17:20; 1 Ti 6:7; Hb 13:11; drag in Lk 12:11.*

εἶτα adv. then, next Mk 4:17; J 13:5; 1 Cor 15:7, 24; 1 Ti 2:13; furthermore Hb 12:9.

εἴτε = εἰ + τε; εἴτε . . . εἴτε if . . . if, whether . . . or Ro 12:6–8; 1 Cor 3:22; 12:26; 2 Cor 1:6; 1 Th 5:10.

εἶτεν Ionic-Hellenistic form of εἶτα Mk 4:28 v.l.*

εἶχαν, εἶχον, εἴχοσαν three forms of the impf. act. 3 pl. of ἔχω.

εἴωθα pf. of an obsolete pres. ἔθω be accustomed Mt 27:15; Mk 10:1. τὸ εἰωθός custom Lk 4:16; Ac 17:2.*

εἴων impf. act. 3 pl. of ἐάω.

ἐκ; before vowels ἐξ prep. w. gen. from, out of, away from—1. to denote separation Mt 2:15; 26:27; Mk 16:3; J 12:27; 17:15; Ac 17:33; Gal 3:13; Rv 14:13; from among Lk 20:35; Ac 3:23.—2. to denote the direction from which something comes from, out from Mt 17:9; Mk 11:20; Lk 5:3; in answer to the question where? at, on Mt 20:21, 23; Ac 2:25, 34.—3. to denote origin, cause, motive reason from, of, by Mt 1:3, 5, 18; J 1:13, 46; 1 Cor 7:7; 2 Cor 5:1; Gal

2:15; 4:4; Phil 3:5. Because of, by Mk 7:11; 2 Cor 2:2; Rv 8:11. By reason of, as a result of, because of Lk 12:15; Ac 19:25; Ro 4:2; with Lk 16:9. Of, from of source or material Mt 12:34; J 19:2; 1 Cor 9:13; Rv 18:12. According to, in accordance with Mt 12:37; 2 Cor 8:11, 13. ἐκ τούτου for this reason, therefore J 6:66. οἱ ἐκ νόμου partisans of the law Ro 4:14.—4. in periphrasis for the partitive gen. Mt 10:29; 25:2; Lk 11:15, which may even function as subject of a sentence ἐκ τ. μαθητῶν some of the disciples J 16:17; used with εἶναι = belong to someone or something Mt 26:73; Ac 21:8; 1 Cor 12:15f. After verbs of filling with Lk 15:16; J 12:3; Rv 8:5. For the gen. of price or value for Mt 20:2; 27:7; Ac 1:18.—5. of time from, from this or that time on Mt 19:12; Mk 10:20; J 9:1, 32; for Lk 23:8; after 2 Pt 2:8.

ἕκαστος, η, ον each, every J 19:23; Hb 3:13; Rv 22:2; perh. both kinds Lk 6:44. As noun each one, every one Mt 16:27; Lk 13:15; 1 Cor 15:38. εἰς ἕκαστος every single one Mt 26:22; Lk 4:40; 1 Cor 12:18. For ἀνὰ εἷς ἕκαστος Rv 21:21 see ἀνά 1.

ἑκάστοτε adv. at any time, always 2 Pt 1:15.*

ἑκατόν indecl. one hundred Mt 13:8, 23; Lk 15:4; J 19:39; Ac 23:23 v.l.; Rv 7:4. [hectare]

ἑκατονταετής, ἑς a hundred years old Ro 4:19.*

ἑκατονταπλασίων, ον a hundredfold Mk 10:30; Lk 8:8; Mt 19:29; Lk 18:30 v.l.*

ἑκατοντάρχης, ου or ἑκατόνταρχος, ου, ὁ centurion, captain Mt 8:13; Ac 27:1, 6, 11, 31, 43 (all -ης), and Mt 8:5, 8; Ac 22:25 (all -ος).

ἐκβαίνω go out, come (from) Hb 11:15.*

ἐκβάλλω—1. drive out, expel lit. throw out more or less forcibly Mt 9:25, 34; 21:12, 39; 25:30; Lk 9:40; 11:20; J 2:15; Ac 9:40. Disdain, spurn Lk 6:22; repudiate Gal 4:30; 3 J 10.—2. without the connotation of force: send out Lk 10:2; of assignment to a task Mk 1:12; release Ac 16:37.—3. take out, remove Mt 7:4f; Mk 9:47; Lk 10:35; bring out

Mt 13:52; J 10:4; *evacuate* 15:17. *Leave out* of consideration Rv 11:2. *Lead on* Mt 12:20.

ἔκβασις, εως, ἡ *a way out* 1 Cor 10:13; *end*, perh. *outcome, result* Hb 13:7.*

ἐκβεβλήκει plupf. act. ind. 3 sing. of **ἐκβάλλω** Mk 16:9.

ἐκβλαστάνω *sprout up* Mk 4:5 v.l.*

ἐκβολή, ῆς, ἡ *jettisoning*, lit. 'throwing out' of a ship's cargo Ac 27:18.*

ἐκγαμίζω *marry, give in marriage* as v.l. for γαμίζω in the following passages: Mt 22:30; 24:38; Lk 17:27; 20:35; 1 Cor 7:38.*

ἔκγονος, ον as noun ὁ, ἡ ἔκγονος *descendant* specifically *grandchild* 1 Ti 5:4.*

ἐκδαπανάω *spend completely, exhaust* fig. 2 Cor 12:15.*

ἐκδέχομαι *wait for, expect* J 5:3 v.l.; Ac 17:16; 1 Cor 11:33; 16:11; Js 5:7; *look forward to* Hb 11:10; followed by ἕως *wait until* 10:13.*

ἔκδηλος, ον *quite evident, plain* 2 Ti 3:9.*

ἐκδημέω *leave one's home* or *country*, fig. *leave, get away from* 2 Cor 5:8. *Be in a strange land*, fig. *be away, be absent* 5:6, 9.*

ἐκδίδωμι mid. *let out for hire, lease* Mt 21:33, 41; Mk 12:1; Lk 20:9.*

ἐκδιηγέομαι *tell (in detail)* Ac 13:41; 15:3.*

ἐκδικέω—**1.** *take vengeance for, punish* 2 Cor 10:6; Rv 6:10; 19:2.—**2.** *avenge* someone, *procure justice for* someone Lk 18:5. ἐ. με *see to it that I get justice* 18:3. ἐ. ἑαυτόν *take one's revenge* Ro 12:19.*

ἐκδίκησις, εως, ἡ *vengeance, punishment* Lk 21:22; 2 Cor 7:11; 2 Th 1:8; 1 Pt 2:14. ἐμοὶ ἐ. *vengeance belongs to me* Ro 12:19; Hb 10:30. ἐ. ποιεῖν *see to it that justice is done* Lk 18:7f; Ac 7:24.*

ἔκδικος, ον *avenging* as noun *the avenger, the one who punishes* Ro 13:4; 1 Th 4:6.*

ἐκδιώκω *persecute severely* 1 Th 2:15; Lk 11:49 v.l.*

ἔκδοτος, ον *given up, delivered up* Ac 2:23.*

ἐκδοχή, ῆς, ἡ *expectation* Hb 10:27.*

ἐκδύω *strip, take off* Mt 27:28, 31; Mk 15:20; Lk 10:30; fig. 2 Cor 5:3f.* [*ecdysis*, zoological term for shedding outer cuticular layer]

ἐκεῖ adv.—**1.** *there, in that place* Mt 2:13, 15; Mk 5:11; Lk 12:34. οἱ ἐκεῖ *those who were there* Mt 26:71. Pleonastic, to be omitted in translation Rv 12:6, 14.—**2.** *there, to that place*, 'thither' Mt 2:22; Lk 21:2; J 11:8; Ro 15:24.

ἐκεῖθεν adv. *from there* Mt 4:21; Mk 6:1; Lk 9:4; J 4:43.

ἐκεῖνος, η, ο demonstrative adj. or pron. *that person* or *thing, that* Mk 4:11; Hb 12:25; Js 4:15. Equivalent to *he, she, it* Mk 16:10; J 5:37; 14:21, 26. Emphatic Mt 17:27; Tit 3:7. As adj. Mt 7:25, 27; 10:15; Mk 1:9; 2 Th 1:10; Rv 11:13. Adverbial gen. ἐκείνης *there* Lk 19:4.

ἐκεῖσε adv., in N.T. = ἐκεῖ 1 *there, at that place* Ac 21:3; 22:5.*

ἐκέκραξα 1 aor. act. ind. of κράζω Ac 24:21.

ἐκέρασε 1 aor. act. ind. of κεράννυμι.

ἐκέρδησα 1 aor. act. ind. of κερδαίνω.

ἐκζητέω *seek out, search for* Ac 15:17; Ro 3:11; Hb 11:6; 12:17; 1 Pt 1:10. *Charge with, require of* Lk 11:50f.*

ἐκζήτησις, εως, ἡ *useless speculation* 1 Ti 1:4.*

ἐκθαμβέω pass. *be amazed* Mk 9:15; *be distressed* 14:33; *be alarmed* 16:5f.*

ἔκθαμβος, ον *utterly astonished* Ac 3:11.*

ἐκθαυμάζω *wonder greatly* Mk 12:17.*

ἔκθετος, ον *exposed, abandoned* Ac 7:19.*

ἐκκαθαίρω *clean out, cleanse* 1 Cor 5:7; 2 Ti 2:21.*

ἐκκαθάρατε 1 aor. act. impv. 2 pl. of ἐκκαθαίρω.

ἐκκαίω pass. *be inflamed* Ro 1:27.*

ἐκκακέω *lose heart* as v.l. for ἐγκακέω in all these passages: Lk 18:1; 2 Cor 4:1, 16; Gal 6:9; Eph 3:13; 2 Th 3:13.*

ἐκκεντέω *pierce* J 19:37; Rv 1:7.*

ἐκκέχυται pf. pass. ind. of ἐκχέω.

ἐκκλάω *break off* pass. *be broken off* Ro 11:17, 19, 20.*

ἐκκλείω shut out, exclude Gal 4:17; eliminate Ro 3:27.*

ἐκκλησία, ας, ἡ—1. assembly regularly convened for political purposes Ac 19:39; meeting generally 19:32, 40.— 2. congregation, assembly of the Israelites Ac 7:38; Hb 2:12.—3. the Christian church or congregation: as a church meeting 1 Cor 11:18; 14:4f; 3 J 6; as a group of Christians living in one place Mt 18:17; Ac 5:11; Ro 16:1, 5; 1 Cor 1:2; Gal 1:22; 1 Th 1:1; Phlm 2; as the church universal, to which all believers belong Mt 16:18; Ac 9:31; 1 Cor 12:28; Eph 1:22; 3:10. Church of God or Christ 1 Cor 10:32; 1 Th 2:14; Ro 16:16. [ecclesiastical]

ἐκκλίνω turn away Ro 16:17; 1 Pt 3:11; turn aside Ro 3:12.*

ἐκκολυμβάω (dive overboard) and swim away Ac 27:42.*

ἐκκομίζω carry out Lk 7:12.*

ἐκκοπή, ῆς, ἡ lit. cutting out v.l. for ἐγκοπή hindrance 1 Cor 9:12.*

ἐκκοπήσῃ fut. pass. ind. 2 sing. of ἐκκόπτω.

ἐκκόπτω cut off or down Mt 3:10; 5:30; 7:19; 18:8; Lk 3:9; 13:7, 9; Ro 11:24; fig. 11:22. Remove 2 Cor 11:12.*

ἐκκρεμάννυμι mid. hang on fig. Lk 19:48.*

ἐκλαλέω tell Ac 23:22.*

ἐκλάμπω shine (out) Mt 13:43.*

ἐκλανθάνομαι forget (altogether) w. gen. Hb 12:5.*

ἔκλαυσα 1 aor. act. ind. of κλαίω.

ἐκλέγομαι choose, select Mk 13:20; Lk 9:35; 10:42; J 15:16; Ac 15:22, 25; Eph 1:4; Js 2:5. In Lk 6:44 ἐκλ. is v.l. for συλλέγω. [eclectic]

ἐκλείπω fail, die out Lk 22:32; give out of money 16:9 (the v.l. ὅταν ἐκλίπητε here means when you die); grow dark, perh. be eclipsed 23:45; come to an end Hb 1:12.* [eclipse]

ἐκλεκτός, ή, όν chosen, select Mt 22:14; 24:22, 24, 31; Lk 18:7; 23:35; Col 3:12; 1 Ti 5:21; 2 Ti 2:10; 1 Pt 2:9; 2 J 1, 13. Choice 1 Pt 2:4, 6; ὁ ἐ. ἐν κυρίῳ the outstanding Christian Ro 16:13.

ἐκλελεγμένος pf. pass. ptc. of ἐκλέγομαι.

ἐκλέλησμαι pf. pass. ind. of ἐκλανθάνομαι.

ἐκλήθην 1 aor. pass. ind. of καλέω.

ἐκλογή, ῆς, ἡ selection, choosing, election Ro 9:11; 11:5, 28; 1 Th 1:4; 2 Pt 1:10. σκεῦος ἐκλογῆς a chosen instrument Ac 9:15. In passive sense those selected Ro 11:7.* [eclogue]

ἐκλύω pass. become weary or slack, give out Mt 15:32; Mk 8:3; Gal 6:9. Lose courage Hb 12:3, 5.*

ἐκμάσσω wipe Lk 7:38, 44; J 11:2; 12:3; dry 13:5.*

ἐκμυκτηρίζω sneer at, ridicule Lk 16:14; 23:35.*

ἐκνεύω turn aside, withdraw J 5:13.*

ἐκνήφω become sober fig. come to one's senses 1 Cor 15:34.*

ἑκούσιος, ία, ιον voluntary, as a volunteer κατὰ ἑκούσιον of one's own free will as opposed to legal compulsion Phlm 14.*

ἑκουσίως adv. willingly 1 Pt 5:2. Without compulsion, i.e. deliberately, intentionally Hb 10:26.*

ἔκπαλαι adv. for a long time, long ago 2 Pt 2:3; 3:5.*

ἐκπειράζω put to the test, try, tempt Mt 4:7; Lk 4:12; 10:25; 1 Cor 10:9.*

ἐκπέμπω send out or away Ac 13:4; 17:10.*

ἐκπέπτωκα pf. act. ind. of ἐκπίπτω.

ἐκπερισσῶς adv. excessively ἐ. λαλεῖν say with great emphasis Mk 14:31.*

ἐκπεσεῖν 2 aor. act. inf. of ἐκπίπτω.

ἐκπετάννυμι spread or hold out Ro 10:21.*

ἐκπηδάω rush out Ac 14:14; start up, get up quickly 10:25 v.l.*

ἐκπίπτω—1. fall off or from Ac 12:7; Js 1:11; 1 Pt 1:24; perh. Ac 27:32, but see 2 below.—2. drift off course, run aground Ac 27:17, 26, 29, perh. 32 (see 1 above).—3. fig lose w. gen. Gal 5:4; 2 Pt 3:17. Fail, weaken Ro 9:6; 1 Cor 13:8 v.l.*

ἐκπλεῦσαι 1 aor. act. inf. of ἐκπλέω.

ἐκπλέω sail away Ac 15:39; 18:18; 20:6.*

ἐκπληρόω *fulfill (completely)* Ac 13:33.*

ἐκπλήρωσις, εως, ἡ *completion* Ac 21:26.*

ἐκπλήσσω pass. *be amazed, overwhelmed* Mt 19:25; 22:33; Mk 6:2; Lk 2:48; Ac 13:12.

ἐκπνέω *breathe one's last, expire* Mk 15:37, 39; Lk 23:46.*

ἐκπορεύομαι *come* or *go out, proceed* Mt 17:21; Mk 7:15, 20; Lk 3:7; J 15:26; Rv 4:5. *Spread* Lk 4:37; *project* Rv 1:16; *flow out* 22:1.

ἐκπορνεύω *indulge in immorality* Jd 7.*

ἐκπτύω *despise, disdain* lit. 'spit out' Gal 4:14.*

ἐκπυρόω *set on fire, destroy by fire* conjectural emendation for εὑρεθήσεται 2 Pt 3:10.*

ἐκριζόω *uproot, pull out by the roots* Mt 13:29; 15:13; Lk 17:6 Jd 12.*

ἐκρίθην 1 aor. pass. ind. of κρίνω.

ἐκρύβην 2 aor. pass. ind. of κρύπτω.

ἔκστασις, εως, ἡ—1. *astonishment, bewilderment, terror* Mk 5:42; 16:8; Lk 5:26; Ac 3:10.—2. *trance, ecstasy* Ac 10:10; 11:5; 22:17.*

ἐκστρέφω pass. *be turned aside, be perverted* Tit 3:11.*

ἐκσῴζω 1 aor. act. inf. ἐκσῶσαι *bring safely* v.l. for ἐξωθέω Ac 27:39.*

ἐκταράσσω *agitate, throw into confusion* Ac 16:20; 15:24 v.l.*

ἐκτεθείς 2 aor. pass. ptc. of ἐκτίθημι.

ἐκτείνω *stretch out, hold out, extend* Mt 8:3; 26:51; Mk 3:5; Lk 22:53; J 21:18; Ac 4:30; 26:1. Of an anchor *run out* 27:30. [Cf. *extension.*]

ἐκτελέω *finish, bring to completion* Lk 14:29f.*

ἐκτένεια, ας, ἡ *perseverance, earnestness* Ac 26:7; 12:5 v.l.*

ἐκτενής, ές *eager, earnest* Ac 12:5 v.l.; *constant* 1 Pt 4:8.*

ἐκτενῶ fut. act. ind. of ἐκτείνω.

ἐκτενῶς adv. *eagerly, fervently, constantly* Ac 12:5; 1 Pt 1:22. Comparative ἐκτενέστερον prob. *very fervently* Lk 22:44.*

ἐκτίθημι *expose, abandon* Ac 7:21. Fig. *explain, set forth* 11:4; 18:26; 28:23.*

ἐκτινάσσω *shake off* Mt 10:14; Mk 6:11; Ac 13:51; Lk 9:5 v.l.; *shake out* Ac 18:6.*

ἕκτος, η, ον *sixth* Mt 20:5; Mk 15:33; Lk 1:26, 36; J 4:6; Rv 6:12.

ἐκτός adv. *outside*—1. ἐκτὸς εἰ μή *unless, except* 1 Cor 14:5; 15:2; 1 Ti 5:19. As noun τὸ ἐ. *the outside* Mt 23:26.— 2. functions as prep. w. gen. *outside* 1 Cor 6:18; 2 Cor 12:2; *except* Ac 26:22; 1 Cor 15:27.* [*ecto-*, combining form, as in *ectoplasm*]

ἐκτρέπω mid. and pass. *turn, turn away* 1 Ti 1:6; 5:15; 2 Ti 4:4; *avoid* 1 Ti 6:20. For Hb 12:13 *turn away* is possible, but *be dislocated* is perh. better.*

ἐκτρέφω *feed, nourish* Eph 5:29; *bring up* 6:4.*

ἔκτρομος, ον *trembling* Hb 12:21 v.l.*

ἔκτρωμα, ατος, τό *untimely birth, miscarriage* 1 Cor 15:8.*

ἐκφέρω *carry* or *bring out* Lk 15:22; Ac 5:6, 9f, 15; 1 Ti 6:7; *lead out* Mk 8:23. *Produce* Hb 6:8.*

ἐκφεύγω *run away, seek safety in flight* Ac 19:16. *Escape* Lk 21:36; Ac 16:27 ('were clean gone'); Ro 2:3; Hb 12:25.

ἐκφοβέω *frighten, terrify* 2 Cor 10:9.*

ἔκφοβος, ον *terrified* Mk 9:6; Hb 12:21.*

ἐκφυγεῖν 2 aor. act. inf. of ἐκφεύγω.

ἐκφύω *put forth*, lit. 'cause to grow' Mt 24:32; Mk 13:28.*

ἐκφωνέω *cry out* Lk 16:24 v.l.*

ἐκχέαι 1 aor. act. inf. of ἐκχέω.

ἐκχέω or ἐκχύννομαι *pour out, shed, spill* Mt 9:17; 23:35; Mk 14:24; J 2:15; Ac 1:18; Rv 16:6; fig. *pour out* Ac 2:17f, 33; Ro 5:5; Tit 3:6. Pass. *give oneself up, abandon oneself* Jd 11.

ἐκχωρέω *go out, go away* Lk 21:21.*

ἐκψύχω *breathe one's last, die* Ac 5:5, 10; 12:23.*

ἑκών, οῦσα, όν *willing(ly), of one's own free will* Ro 8:20; 1 Cor 9:17.*

ἔλαθον 2 aor. act. ind. of λανθάνω.

ἐλαία, ας, ἡ *olive tree* Mt 21:1; Ro 11:17, 24; Rv 11:4; *olive, the fruit* Js 3:12. τὸ ὄρος τῶν ἐλαιῶν *the Mount of Olives* Mt 21:1.

ἔλαιον, ου, τό *(olive) oil* Mt 25:3f, 8; Mk 6:13; Lk 10:34; Hb 1:9; *olive orchard* Rv 6:6. [Cf. *oleo-*, a combining form, and *oil*.]

ἐλαιών, ῶνος, ὁ *olive grove, olive orchard* Lk 19:29; 21:37; Ac 1:12.*

ἐλάκησα 1 aor. act. ind. of λακάω.

Ἐλαμίτης, ου, ὁ *an Elamite,* from the region east of the lower Tigris valley Ac 2:9.*

ἐλάσσων, ἔλασσον (the Attic ἐλάττων is found 1 Ti 5:9; Hb 7:7) used as comparative of μικρός: *smaller* = *younger* Ro 9:12; *inferior* J 2:10; Hb 7:7; Mt 20:28 v.l. Adv. ἔλαττον *less* 1 Ti 5:9.*

ἐλαττονέω *have less* or *too little* 2 Cor 8:15.*

ἐλαττόω *make inferior* Hb 2:7, 9. Pass. *diminish* J 3:30; *be worse off* or *in need* 2 Cor 12:13 v.l.*

ἐλάττων see ἐλάσσον.

ἐλαύνω *drive* Lk 8:29; Js 3:4; 2 Pt 2:17; *row* Mk 6:48; J 6:19.*

ἐλαφρία, ας, ἡ *vacillation, levity* τῇ ἐ. χρᾶσθαι *be vacillating, fickle* 2 Cor 1:17.*

ἐλαφρός, ά, όν *light* in weight Mt 11:30. τὸ ἐ. *insignificance, triviality* 2 Cor 4:17.*

ἔλαχε 2 aor. act. ind. of λαγχάνω.

ἐλάχιστος, ίστη, ον used as superlative of μικρός: *smallest, least* 1 Cor 15:9. Usually reduced in degree *very small, quite unimportant, insignificant* Mt 2:6; Js 3:4; *trivial* 1 Cor 6:2; *least important, of little importance* Mt 25:40, 45; 1 Cor 4:3. With comparative ending added *very least* Eph 3:8.

Ἐλεάζαρ, ὁ indecl. *Eleazar* Mt 1:15.*

ἐλεάω an alternate form for ἐλεέω *have mercy on,* found in Ro 9:16; Jd 22, 23.*

ἐλεγμός, οῦ, ὁ *reproof, conviction* or *punishment* 2 Ti 3:16.*

ἔλεγξις, εως, ἡ *rebuke, reproof* 2 Pt 2:16.*

ἔλεγχος, ου, ὁ *proof, proving* perh. *inner conviction* Hb 11:1; *reproof, correction* 2 Ti 3:16 v.l.* [*elenchus*]

ἐλέγχω—1. *bring to light, expose, set forth* J 3:20; Eph 5:11, 13; Tit 2:15.— 2. *convict, convince, point out* J 8:46;

Js 2:9; Tit 1:9, 13; Jd 15.—3. *reprove, correct* Mt 18:15; Lk 3:19; 1 Ti 5:20; *discipline, punish* Hb 12:5; Rv 3:19.

ἐλεεινός, ή, όν *miserable, pitiable* 1 Cor 15:19; Rv 3:17.*

ἐλεέω *have mercy* or *pity on* someone, *show mercy to* someone Mt 5:7; 18:33; Mk 5:19; Lk 16:24; 1 Cor 7:25; Phil 2:27; *do acts of mercy* Ro 12:8.

ἐλεημοσύνη, ης, ἡ *kind deed,* then *alms, charitable giving* Mt 6:2ff; Lk 11:41; Ac 9:36; 10:2, 4, 31. [*eleemosynary*]

ἐλεήμων, ον, gen. ονος *merciful, sympathetic* Mt 5:7; Hb 2:17.*

ἐλέησον 1 aor. act. impv. of ἐλεέω.

ἔλεος, ους, τό *mercy, clemency, compassion, pity* Mt 23:23; Lk 1:72; Ro 15:9; Gal 6:16; Eph 2:4; Hb 4:16. [Cf. *alms.*]

ἐλευθερία, ας, ἡ *freedom, liberty* Ro 8:21; 1 Cor 10:29; 2 Cor 3:17; Gal 2:4; 5:1, 13; Js 1:25; 2:12; 1 Pt 2:16; 2 Pt 2:19.*

ἐλεύθερος, έρα, ον *free, independent* as adj. and noun (= *a free man,* etc.) Mt 17:26; J 8:33, 36; 1 Cor 7:22, 39; Gal 4:31; Rv 6:15; 19:18.

ἐλευθερόω *free, set free* J 8:32, 36; Ro 6:18, 22; 8:2, 21; Gal 5:1.*

ἐλεύκανα 1 aor. act. ind. of λευκαίνω.

ἔλευσις, εως, ἡ *coming, advent* Ac 7:52; as v.l. in Lk 21:7 and 23:42.*

ἐλεύσομαι fut. mid. ind. of ἔρχομαι.

ἐλεφάντινος, η, ον *made of ivory* Rv 18:12.*

ἐλήλακα pf. act. ind. of ἐλαύνω.

ἐλήλυθα pf. act. ind. of ἔρχομαι.

ἐλθεῖν 2 aor. act. inf. of ἔρχομαι.

Ἐλιακίμ, ὁ indecl. *Eliakim* Mt 1:13; Lk 3:30; 3:23ff v.l.*

ἔλιγμα, ατος, τό *package, roll* J 19:39 v.l.*

Ἐλιέζερ, ὁ indecl. *Eliezer* Lk 3:29.*

Ἐλιούδ, ὁ indecl. *Eliud* Mt 1:14f; Lk 3:23ff v.l.*

Ἐλισάβετ, ἡ indecl. *Elizabeth* Lk 1:5, 7, 13, 24, 36, 40f, 57; 1:46 v.l.*

Ἐλισαῖος, ου, ὁ *Elisha* Lk 4:27.*

ἐλίσσω roll up Hb 1:12; Rv 6:14.*

ἕλκος, ους, τό sore, abscess, ulcer, wound Lk 16:21; Rv 16:2, 11.*

ἑλκόω pass. be covered with sores Lk 16:20.*

ἑλκύω and ἕλκω drag, pull, draw J 18:10; Ac 16:19; 21:30; haul J 21:6, 11; hale Js 2:6. Draw, attract J 6:44; 12:32.*

Ἑλλάς, άδος, ἡ Greece, Hellas Ac 20:2.*

Ἕλλην, ηνος, ὁ a Greek, a Hellene, one who speaks Greek Ro 1:14. Gentile, non-Jew Ac 11:20 v.l.; 20:21; 1 Cor 1:24; Gal 3:28. Of proselytes J 12:20. Of 'God-fearers' or people in sympathy with Israel's heritage Ac 17:4.

Ἑλληνικός, ή, όν Greek Lk 23:38 v.l.; supply 'language' Rv 9:11.*

Ἑλληνίς, ίδος, ἡ Gentile (lit. Greek) Ac 17:12; Gentile woman Mk 7:26.*

Ἑλληνιστής, οῦ, ὁ a Hellenist, a Greek-speaking Jew Ac 6:1; 9:29; 11:20.*

Ἑλληνιστί adv. in the Greek language J 19:20. Ἑ. γινώσκειν understand Greek Ac 21:37.*

ἐλλογάω or ἐλλογέω charge (to someone's account) Ro 5:13; Phlm 18.*

Ἐλμαδάμ, ὁ indecl. Elmadam Lk 3:28.*

ἑλόμενος 2 aor. mid. ptc. of αἱρέω.

ἐλπίζω hope, hope for, expect, foresee Lk 6:34; 23:8; Ac 26:7; 1 Cor 13:7; 2 Cor 8:5. Put one's hope (in) Mt 12:21; J 5:45; 2 Cor 1:10; 1 Pt 1:13.

ἐλπίς, ίδος, ἡ hope, expectation, prospect Ac 16:19; 23:6; Ro 4:18; 8:20, 24; 1 Cor 9:10; 2 Cor 1:7. Christian hope Ac 26:6; Ro 5:4f; 1 Cor 13:13; Eph 2:12; 1 Th 1:3; 1 Pt 1:3; (object of) hope 1 Th 2:19; 1 Ti 1:1; hope, something hoped for Ro 8:24; Col 1:5; Tit 2:13; Hb 6:18.

Ἐλύμας, α, ὁ Elymas Ac 13:8.*

ἐλωΐ Aramaic my God Mk 15:34; Mt 27:46 v.l.*

ἔμαθον 2 aor. act. ind. of μανθάνω.

ἐμαυτοῦ, ῆς reflexive pron. of the first pers. myself—1. in the genitive my own 1 Cor 10:33. ἀπ' or ἐξ ἐμαυτοῦ on my own authority, of my own free will J 5:30; 10:18; 12:49; 14:10.—2. in the dative ἔδοξα ἐμαυτῷ I once believed Ac

26:9. σύνοιδά τι ἐμαυτῷ I am aware of something 1 Cor 4:4.—3. in the accusative myself Lk 7:7; J 14:21; 1 Cor 9:19. ὑπ' ἐμαυτόν under my authority Mt 8:9.

ἐμβαίνω go in, step in J 5:4. Get into, embark Mt 8:23; Mk 8:10; Lk 8:22, 37; J 6:17, 24; Ac 21:6 v.l.

ἐμβάλλω throw (into) Lk 12:5.*

ἐμβαπτίζω dip (in, into) Mk 14:20 v.l.*

ἐμβάπτω dip (in, into) Mt 26:23; Mk 14:20.*

ἐμβάς 2 aor. act. ptc. of ἐμβαίνω.

ἐμβατεύω in N.T. only Col 2:18 ἃ ἑόρακεν ἐμβατεύων, where the meaning is in dispute. The verb can mean set foot upon, enter, go into detail, etc. Among the probabilities for Col 2:18 are entering at length upon the tale of what he has seen in a vision, or who enters (the sanctuary) which he saw (in ecstasy). Perhaps the text is not in order.*

ἐμβῆναι 2 aor. act. inf. of ἐμβαίνω.

ἐμβιβάζω put in, put on board Ac 27:6.*

ἐμβλέπω look at, fix one's gaze upon often with dative Mk 10:21, 27; Lk 20:17; J 1:36. With εἰς Mt 6: 26 (see below); Ac 1:11. Perh. be able to see Mk 8:25; Ac 22:11. Perh. consider Mt 6:26 (see above).

ἐμβριμάομαι w. dat. scold, censure Mk 14:5; warn sternly Mt 9:30; Mk 1:43. ἐ. τῷ πνεύματι or ἐν ἑαυτῷ be deeply moved lit. 'groan' J 11:33, 38.*

ἐμέ acc. sing. of ἐγώ.

ἔμεινα 1 aor. act. ind. of μένω.

ἐμέω spit out fig. Rv 3:16.* [emesis]

ἔμιξα 1 aor. act. ind. of μίγνυμι.

ἐμμαίνομαι be enraged Ac 26:11.*

Ἐμμανουήλ, ὁ indecl. Emmanuel Mt 1:23.*

Ἐμμαοῦς, ἡ Emmaus, a village approximately 11½ km. from Jerusalem Lk 24:13.*

ἐμμένω stay or live (in) Ac 28:30. Fig. persevere in, stand by, be true to 14:22; abide by Gal 3:10; Hb 8:9.*

ἐμμέσῳ v.l. for ἐν μέσῳ Rv 1:13; 2:1; 4:6; 5:6; 6:6; 22:2.*

'Εμμώρ, ὁ indecl. Hamor Ac 7:16.*

ἐμνήσθην 1 aor. pass. ind. of μιμνῄσκομαι.

ἐμοί dat. sing. of ἐγώ.

ἐμός, ή, όν possessive pron. my, mine without emphasis Mt 18:20; J 15:11; with emphasis my own Gal 6:11; Phlm 19. εἰς τὴν ἐμὴν ἀνάμνησιν in memory of me 1 Cor 11:24f. As noun τὸ ἐμόν what is mine, my property Mt 20:15; 25:27; J 16:14f.

ἐμπαιγμονή, ῆς, ἡ mocking 2 Pt 3:3.*

ἐμπαιγμός, οῦ, ὁ scorn, mocking, or derisive torture Hb 11:36.*

ἐμπαίζω ridicule, make fun of, mock w. dat. Mt 27:29, 31; Mk 10:34; Lk 22:63. Deceive, trick, make a fool of Mt 2:16.

ἐμπαίκτης, ου, ὁ mocker 2 Pt 3:3; Jd 18.*

ἐμπέμπω send (in) Lk 19:14 v.l.*

ἐμπεπλησμένος pf. pass. ptc. of ἐμπίμπλημι.

ἐμπεριπατέω walk about, move 2 Cor 6:16.*

ἐμπί(μ)πλημι or ἐμπι(μ)πλάω fill, satisfy Lk 1:53; 6:25; J 6:12; Ac 14:17; enjoy ὑμῶν your company Ro 15:24.*

ἐμπί(μ)πρημι set on fire, burn Mt 22:7. As v.l. in Ac 28:6, for which see πίμπρημι.*

ἐμπίπτω fall (in, into) lit. Lk 6:39. Fig. fall (into, among) 10:36; 1 Ti 3:6f; Hb 10:31. [impetus]

ἐμπλακείς 2 aor. pass. ptc. of ἐμπλέκω.

ἐμπλέκω pass. become entangled or involved in 2 Ti 2:4; 2 Pt 2:20.*

ἐμπλησθῶ 1 aor. pass. subj. of ἐμπί(μ)πλημι.

ἐμπλοκή, ῆς, ἡ braiding w. connotation of high fashion 1 Pt 3:3.*

ἐμπνέω breathe w. gen. Ac 9:1.*

ἐμπορεύομαι carry on business Js 4:13. Exploit, lit. 'sell' 2 Pt 2:3.*

ἐμπορία, ας, ἡ business, trade Mt 22:5.*

ἐμπόριον, ου, τό market οἶκος ἐμπορίου market house J 2:16.* [emporium]

ἔμπορος, ου, ὁ merchant, (wholesale) dealer Mt 13:45; Rv 18:3, 11, 15, 23.*

ἐμπρήθω alt. form for ἐμπίμπρημι.

ἔμπροσθεν—1. adv. in front, forward, ahead Lk 19:4, 28; Rv 4:6. τὰ ἔ. what lies ahead Phil 3:13.—2. functions as prep. w. gen. in front of, before Mt 5:24; 27:29; Lk 5:19; Ac 18:17. Before, in the presence of Mt 10:32f; 27:11; Gal 2:14; 1 Th 1:3; 2:19. Before, in the sight of Mt 6:1 Mk 2:12; Lk 19:27; J 12:37; Ac 10:4; in the face of Mt 23:13. Of rank before, higher than J 1:15, 30. For the simple gen. Mt 18:14, or dat. 11:26.

ἐμπτύω spit on or at w. dat. or εἰς and acc. Mt 27:30; Mk 10:34; 14:65; Lk 18:32.

ἐμφανής, ές visible Ac 10:40; ἐ. ἐγενόμην I have been revealed (= revealed myself) Ro 10:20.*

ἐμφανίζω—1. reveal J 14:21f; pass. become visible, appear Mt 27:53; Hb 9:24.—2. make known, explain, inform, make a report Ac 23:15, 22; 25:15; Hb 11:14; bring formal charges Ac 24:1; 25:2.*

ἔμφοβος, ον afraid, startled, terrified Lk 24:5, 37; Ac 10:4; 24:25; Rv 11:13.*

ἐμφυσάω breathe upon J 20:22.*

ἔμφυτος, ον implanted Js 1:21.*

ἐμφωνέω only as v.l. for φωνέω in Lk 16:24.*

ἐμώρανα 1 aor. act. ind. of μωραίνω.

ἐν prep. w. dat., most common prep. in N.T., used with greatest variety of meanings, of which the following are typical:—I. of place: in Mt 3:1; Lk 2:49; Ac 5:42; 1 Ti 3:15. On Mt 5:25; 6:5; J 4:20f; 2 Cor 3:3. At, near Lk 13:4; J 8:20; Eph 1:20. In the case of, for Mt 17:12; Mk 14:6; 1 Cor 4:2, 6; 9:15. In the presence of, before 1 Cor 2:6; in the judgment of 14:11. Among, in Mt 2:6; Mk 8:38; Gal 1:14. With (denoting accompaniment or association, merging into instrument) Mt 16:28; Lk 14:31; 1 Cor 4:21; 2 Cor 10:14; Hb 9:25; in the power of, under the influence of Mk 1:23; 12:36; 1 J 5:19. The sense into, where εἰς would be expected, is rare, but see Lk 9:46; Rv 11:11. In of interrelationship, esp. involving either Jesus or God or both J 10:38; 14:20; Ro 6:11, 23; 16:11; 1 Cor 1:30; 3:1; 4:15;

Gal 2:20; Phil 3:1; 4:1f.—**II.** of time—
1. of a period of time *in the course of,
within* Mt 2:1; 3:1; 27:40; J 2:19f. *ἐν τῷ
μεταξύ meanwhile* J 4:31.—**2.** denoting a point of time when something oc-
curs *in, at* Mt 8:13; Mk 12:23; J 11:9,
10, 24; 1 Cor 15:23, 52.—**3.** *when, while,
during* Mt 13:4, 25; 21:22; Mk 15:7;
12:38; Eph 6:20.—**III.** causal—**1.** expressing means or instrument *with, in,
by* Mt 5:13; 26:52; Lk 1:51; Ro 5:9; Rv
17:16; *with the help of* Mt 9:34; Ac
17:31. *ἐν τῷ ἐλαύνειν as they rowed*
(temporal) or *because of the rowing*
(instrumental) Mk 6:48.—**2.** kind and
manner *ἐν δυνάμει with power, powerfully* Mk 9:1; Col 1:29. *ἐν ἐκτενείᾳ
earnestly* Ac 26:7. *ἐν παρρησίᾳ freely,
openly* J 7:4.—**3.** cause or reason *because of, on account of* Mt 6:7; J 16:30;
Ac 24:16; Ro 1:24.—**IV.** various other
uses: *amounting to* Ac 7:14. *Consisting in* Eph 2:15. *ἐν* w. dat. stands for
the ordinary dative Lk 2:14; Ro 1:19;
Gal 1:16; very rarely for the genitive
Ro 5:15. With *ὄμνυμι by* Mt 5:34ff; Rv
10:6; with *ὁμολογεῖν* omit *ἐν* in translation Lk 12:8. *ἐν ᾧ* may mean *wherein*
Ro 14:22; *while, as long as* Mk 2:19;
Lk 5:34; *whereby* Ro 14:21; *because*
8:3; *under which circumstance* 1 Pt
3:19.

ἐναγκαλίζομαι *take in one's arms, hug,
embrace* Mk 9:36; 10:16.*

ἐνάλιος, ον *belonging to the sea* Js 3:7.*

ἐνάλλομαι *leap upon* Ac 19:16 v.l.*

ἐνανθρωπέω *take on human form* 1 J
4:17 v.l.*

ἔναντι adv. functions as prep. w. gen.
before, in the judgment of Lk 1:8; Ac
8:21; 7:10 v.l.*

ἐναντίον functions as prep. w. gen. *before, in the presence (of)* Lk 20:26; Ac
8:32; Mk 2:12 v.l. *In the sight* or *judgment (of)* Lk 1:6; 24:19; Ac 7:10. Adv.
with the article *τοὐναντίον on the other
hand* 2 Cor 2:7; Gal 2:7; 1 Pt 3:9.*

ἐναντιόομαι *oppose (oneself)* w. dat. Ac
13:45 v.l.*

ἐναντίος, α, ον *opposite, against, contrary* Mt 14:24; Mk 6:48; Ac 27:4; 28:17;
hostile 1 Th 2:15. *ἐναντία πράσσειν
πρός oppose* Ac 26:9. *ἐξ ἐναντίας op-*

posite Mk 15:39; *ὁ ἐξ ἐ. the opponent*
Tit 2:8.*

ἐναργής, ές *clear, evident, visible* Hb
4:12 v.l.*

ἐνάρχομαι *begin, make a beginning* Gal
3:3; Phil 1:6.*

ἔνατος, η, ον *ninth* Rv 21:20. *ἕ. ὥρα
ninth hour* = 3 P.M. Mt 20:5; Ac 10:3,
30.

ἐναφίημι *let, permit* Mk 7:12 v.l.*

ἐνγ- see **ἐγγ-**.

ἐνδεής, ές *poor, impoverished* Ac 4:34.*

ἔνδειγμα, ατος, τό *evidence, plain indication* 2 Th 1:5.*

ἐνδείκνυμι *show, demonstrate* Ro 9:17,
22; Eph 2:7; Hb 6:10. *Do* 2 Ti 4:14.
Appoint, designate Lk 10:1 v.l.

ἔνδειξις, εως, ἡ *proof* Ro 3:25f; 2 Cor
8:24. *Sign, omen* Phil 1:28.*

ἔνδεκα indecl. *eleven* Mt 28:16; Mk
16:14; Lk 24:9, 33; Ac 1:26; 2:14.* [Cf.
hendecagon.]

ἐνδέκατος, η, ον *eleventh* Rv 21:20. *ἕ.
ὥρα eleventh hour* = 5 P.M. Mt 20:9,
cf. 20:6.*

ἐνδέχομαι impers. *it is possible* Lk
13:33.*

ἐνδημέω *be at home* fig. 2 Cor 5:6, 8f.*
[Cf. *endemic.*]

ἐνδιδύσκω *dress* with double acc. Mk
15:17; mid. *dress oneself* Lk 16:19; 8:27
v.l.*

ἔνδικος, ον *just, deserved* Ro 3:8; Hb
2:2.*

ἐνδόμησις v.l. for *ἐνδώμησις* Rv 21:18.*

ἐνδοξάζομαι *be glorified, honored* 2 Th
1:10, 12.*

ἔνδοξος, ον *honored, distinguished* 1 Cor
4:10. *Splendid* Lk 7:25; 13:17; *glorious*
Eph 5:27.*

ἔνδυμα, ατος, τό *garment, clothing* Mt
3:4; 6:25, 28; 7:15; 22:11f; 28:3; Lk
12:23.*

ἐνδυναμόω *strengthen* Phil 4:13; 1 Ti
1:12; 2 Ti 4:17. Pass. *become strong*
Ac 9:22; Ro 4:20; Eph 6:10; 2 Ti 2:1.*

ἐνδύνω *go (in), creep (in)* 2 Ti 3:6 v.l.*

ἔνδυσις, εως, ἡ *putting on* 1 Pt 3:3.*

ἐνδύω act. *dress, clothe* lit. Lk 15:22; with double acc. Mt 27:31; Mk 15:20. Mid. *clothe oneself in, put on, wear* lit. Mt 6:25; Mk 6:9; Lk 8:27; Ac 12:21; Ro 13:12; Rv 19:14; fig., mid. and pass. Lk 24:49; Ro 13:14; 1 Cor 15:53f; 2 Cor 5:3; Col 3:12.

ἐνδώμησις, εως, ἡ *construction, material*, perh. *foundation* Rv 21:18.*

ἐνέβην 2 aor. act. ind. of ἐμβαίνω.

ἐνεγκ- unaugmented stem of aor. of φέρω.

ἐνεδειξάμην 1 aor. mid. ind. of ἐνδείκνυμι.

ἐνέδρα, ας, ἡ *plot, ambush* Ac 23:16; 25:3.*

ἐνεδρεύω *lie in wait (for), plot* Lk 11:54; Ac 23:21.*

ἔνεδρον, ου, τό a variant form for ἐνέδρα in Ac 23:16 v.l.*

ἐνειλέω *wrap up in* Mk 15:46.*

ἔνειμι ptc. τὰ ἐνόντα *what is inside, the contents* Lk 11:41.*

ἕνεκα, ἕνεκεν, and s. entries s.v. εἵνεκεν functions as prep. w. gen. *because of, on account of* Mt 5:10f; Ro 14:20; *for the sake of* Mt 16:25; 19:29. ἕ. τούτου *for this reason* 19:5. τίνος ἕ.; *why?* Ac 19:32. ἕ. τοῦ w. inf. *in order that* 2 Cor 7:12.

ἐνεκεντρίσθην 1 aor. pass. ind. of ἐγκεντρίζω.

ἐνέκοψα 1 aor. act. ind. of ἐγκόπτω.

ἐνέκρυψα 1 aor. act. ind. of ἐγκρύπτω.

ἐνέμεινα 1 aor. act ind. of ἐμμένω.

ἐνενήκοντα indecl. *ninety* Mt 18:12f; Lk 15:4, 7.*

ἐνεός, ά, όν *speechless* Ac 9:7.*

ἐνέπαιξα, ἐνεπαίχθην 1 aor. act. and pass. ind. of ἐμπαίζω.

ἐνέπεσον 2 aor. act. ind. of ἐμπίπτω.

ἐνέπλησα, ἐνεπλήσθην 1 aor. act. and pass. ind. of ἐμπί(μ)πλημι.

ἐνέπρησε 1 aor. act. ind. of ἐμπί(μ)πρημι.

ἐνέργεια, ας, ἡ *working, operation, activity* Col 2:12; 2 Th 2:9. *Manifestation* Eph 1:19; 3:7; 4:16; Col 1:29; *power* Phil 3:21. ἐ. πλάνης *a deluding influence* 2 Th 2:11.* [energy]

ἐνεργέω—1. intrans. *work, be at work, operate, be effective* act. Mk 6:14; Gal 2:8; Eph 2:2. τὸ θέλειν καὶ τὸ ἐ. *the will and the action* Phil 2:13b. Mid. *work, be at work* Ro 7:5; 2 Cor 4:12; Eph 3:20; 1 Th 2:13; *become effective* 2 Cor 1:6. δέησις ἐ. *effective prayer* Js 5:16.—2. transitive *work, produce, effect* 1 Cor 12:6; Eph 1:11; 2:2; Phil 2:13a.

ἐνέργημα, ατος, τό *working, activity* 1 Cor 12:6, 10.*

ἐνεργής, ές *effective, active, powerful* Phlm 6; Hb 4:12. θύρα ἐ. *a door* (fig.) *for effective service* 1 Cor 16:9.*

ἐνεστηκώς, ἐνεστώς first and second pf. act. participles of ἐνίστημι.

ἐνετειλάμην 1 aor. mid. ind. of ἐντέλλω.

ἐνετράπην 2 aor. pass. ind. of ἐντρέπω.

ἐνέτυχον 2 aor. act. ind. of ἐντυγχάνω.

ἐνευλογέω *bless* 1 fut. pass Ac 3:25; Gal 3:8.*

ἐνεχθ- stem of 1 aor. pass. ptc. of φέρω.

ἐνέχω *be hostile* Lk 11:53; w. dat. *have a grudge against* someone, with χόλον 'anger' understood Mk 6:19. Pass., w. dat. *be subject to, be loaded down with* Gal 5:1; 2 Th 1:4 v.l.*

ἐνθάδε adv. *here, to this place* J 4:15f; Ac 25:17. *Here, in this place* Lk 24:41; Ac 10:18; 16:28; 17:6; 25:24.*

ἔνθεν adv. *from here* Mt 17:20; Lk 16:26.*

ἐνθυμέομαι *reflect (on), consider, think* Mt 1:20; 9:4; Ac 10:19 v.l.* [enthymeme]

ἐνθύμησις, εως, ἡ *thought, reflection, idea* Mt 9:4; 12:25; Ac 17:29; Hb 4:12.*

ἔνι (for ἔνεστι) *there is* 1 Cor 6:5; Gal 3:28; Col 3:11; Js 1:17.*

ἐνιαυτός, οῦ, ὁ *year* Lk 4:19; J 11:49; Ac 11:26; Hb 9:7; Rv 9:15. Perh. certain *days of the year* Gal 4:10.

ἐνίοτε adv. *sometimes* Mt 17:15 v.l.*

ἐνίστημι—1. *be present, have come* 2 Th 2:2. The participles ἐνεστηκώς and ἐνεστώς mean *present* Ro 8:38; Gal 1:4; Hb 9:9.—2. *impend, be imminent* 1 Cor 7:26; 2 Ti 3:1; but meaning 1 is possible for these passages.

ἐνισχύω intrans. *grow strong, regain one's strength* Ac 9:19; 19:20 v.l. Trans. *strengthen* Lk 22:43.*

ἐνκ- see ἐγκ-.

ἐννέα indecl. *nine* Mt 18:12f; Lk 15:4, 7; 17:17.* [*ennead*]

ἐννεός see ἐνεός.

ἐννεύω *nod, make signs* Lk 1:62.*

ἔννοια, ας, ἡ *thought, knowledge, insight* Hb 4:12; 1 Pt 4:1.*

ἔννομος, ον *legal,* perh. *regular* Ac 19:39. *Subject to the law,* perh. *true to the law* 1 Cor 9:21.*

ἐννόμως adv. = ἐν νόμῳ *subject to* or *in possession of the law* Ro 2:12 v.l.*

ἔννυχος, ον *at night* neut. pl ἔννυχα as adv. *while it was still dark* Mk 1:35.*

ἐνοικέω *live* or *dwell (in)* Ro 7:17 v.l.; 8:11; 2 Cor 6:16; Col 3:16; 2 Ti 1:5, 14; Lk 13:4 v.l.*

ἐνορκίζω *adjure, cause to swear* w. double accusative 1 Th 5:27.*

ἑνότης, ητος, ἡ *unity* Eph 4:3, 13.*

ἐνοχλέω *trouble, annoy* Lk 6:18; *cause trouble* Hb 12:15.*

ἔνοχος, ον (= ἐνεχόμενος 'caught in') *subject to* Hb 2:15. *Liable, answerable, guilty* Mt 5:21f; Mk 3:29; *guilty (of a sin against)* 1 Cor 11:27. *Deserving* Mt 26:66; Mk 14:64; 3:29 v.l. γέγονεν πάντων ἔ. *has sinned against all* Js 2:10. ἔ. εἰς τ. γέενναν *guilty enough (to go) into hell* Mt 5:22 c.*

ἐνπ- see ἐμπ-.

ἐνστήσομαι fut. mid. ind. of ἐνίστημι.

ἔνταλμα, ατος, τό *commandment, precept* Mt 15:9; Mk 7:7; Col 2:22.*

ἐνταφιάζω *prepare for burial, bury* Mt 26:12; J 19:40.*

ἐνταφιασμός, οῦ, ὁ *preparation for burial* or *burial itself* Mk 14:8; J 12:7.*

ἐντειλάμενος, ἐντελεῖται aor. mid. ptc. and fut. mid. ind. of ἐντέλλω.

ἐντέλλω mid. *command, order, give orders* Mt 17:9; 19:7; J 14:31; Ac 1:2; 13:47; Hb 11:22; *ordain* 9:20.

ἐντέταλμαι pf. mid. ind. of ἐντέλλω.

ἐντεῦθεν adv. *from here* Lk 4:9; J 2:16; 7:3; 18:36. ἐντεῦθεν καὶ ἐντεῦθεν *on each side* 19:18. *From this* Js 4:1.

ἔντευξις, εως, ἡ *prayer* 1 Ti 2:1; 4:5.*

ἐντίθημι *put in, implant* Ac 18:4 v.l.*

ἔντιμος, ον *honored, respected, distinguished* Lk 14:8; *valuable, precious* 7:2; 1 Pt 2:4, 6. ἔ. ἔχειν *hold in esteem* Phil 2:29.*

ἐντολή, ῆς, ἡ *command(ment), writ, order, decree* Mt 22:36, 38, 40; Mk 10:19; J 11:57; 13:34; Ro 13:9; 1 Cor 7:19; Col 4:10; 1 Ti 6:14; 2 Pt 2:21. *Law* Lk 23:56; Hb 7:16.

ἐντόπιος, ία, ον *local, belonging to a certain place, resident* Ac 21:12.*

ἐντός functions as prep. w. gen. *inside, within* τὸ ἐντός *the inside* Mt 23:26. In Lk 17:21 ἐ. ὑμῶν may be *within you, in your hearts* or *among you, in your midst.** [*ento-,* combining form, as in *entoderm*]

ἐντραπῇ, ἐντραπήσομαι 2 aor. pass. subj. and 2 fut. pass. of ἐντρέπω.

ἐντρέπω *make ashamed* 1 Cor 4:14; pass. *be put to shame, be ashamed* 2 Th 3:14; Tit 2:8. W. mid. sense *have respect* or *regard for* Mt 21:37; Lk 20:13; Hb 12:9.

ἐντρέφω *bring up, rear, train* 1 Ti 4:6.*

ἔντρομος, ον *trembling* Lk 8:47 v.l.; Ac 7:32; 16:29; Hb 12:21.*

ἐντροπή, ῆς, ἡ *shame, humiliation* 1 Cor 6:5; 15:34.*

ἐντρυφάω *revel, carouse* 2 Pt 2:13.*

ἐντυγχάνω *approach, appeal, plead* Ac 25:24; Ro 8:27, 34; 11:2; Hb 7:25.*

ἐντυλίσσω *wrap (up)* Mt 27:59; Lk 23:53; *fold up* J 20:7.*

ἐντυπόω *carve, impress* 2 Cor 3:7.*

ἐνυβρίζω *insult, outrage* Hb 10:29.*

ἐνυπνιάζομαι *to dream, have visions* Ac 2:17; Jd 8.*

ἐνύπνιον, ου, τό *a dream* Ac 2:17.*

ἐνφ- see ἐμφ-.

ἐνώπιον functions as prep. w. gen.—1. *before* Lk 1:19; Ac 10:30; Rv 3:8; 7:15.—2. *in the sight* or *presence of* Lk 23:14; J 20:30; Ac 10:33; 1 Ti 6:12; Rv 3:5; 13:13.—3. *in the opinion* or *judgment of* Lk 16:15; 2 Cor 8:21.—4. Various uses: simply *to* Ac 6:5; 2 Cor 7:12. *Among* Lk 15:10. *Against* 15:18, 21. *By* the authority of, on behalf of Rv 13:12, 14.

Ἐνώς, ὁ indecl. Enos Lk 3:38.*

ἐνωτίζομαι give ear to, pay attention to Ac 2:14.*

Ἐνώχ, ὁ indecl. Enoch Lk 3:37; Hb 11:5; Jd 14; introduced by conjecture 1 Pt 3:19.*

ἐξ prep. see ἐκ.

ἕξ indecl. six Mt 17:1; Lk 4:25; J 12:1; Js 5:17. [hexa-, combining form, as in hexaemeron, hexagon]

ἐξαγγέλλω proclaim, report 1 Pt 2:9 and short ending of Mk.*

ἐξαγοράζω redeem (lit. 'buy back'), deliver Gal 3:13; 4:5. Mid. ἐξ. τ. καιρόν prob. make the most of the time Eph 5:16; Col 4:5.*

ἐξάγω lead out, bring out Lk 24:50; J 10:3; Ac 7:36, 40; 12:17; 21:38; Hb 8:9.

ἐξαιρέω—1. act. take out, tear out Mt 5:29; 18:9.—2. mid. set free, deliver, rescue Ac 7:10, 34; 12:11; 23:27; Gal 1:4. In Ac 26:17 deliver or select, choose out.*

ἐξαίρω remove, drive away 1 Cor 5:13; also 5:2 v.l.*

ἐξαιτέω mid. ask for, demand Lk 22:31.*

ἐξαίφνης adv. suddenly, unexpectedly Mk 13:36; Lk 2:13; 9:39; Ac 9:3; 22:6.*

ἐξακολουθέω follow, obey 2 Pt 1:16; 2:2; follow, pursue 2:15.*

ἐξακόσιοι, αι, α six hundred Rv 13:18; 14:20.*

ἐξαλείφω wipe away Rv 7:17; 21:4. Wipe out, erase 3:5. Remove, obliterate, blot out Ac 3:19; Col 2:14.*

ἐξάλλομαι leap up Ac 3:8; 14:10 v.l.*

ἐξανάστασις, εως, ἡ resurrection Phil 3:11.*

ἐξαναστήσῃ 1 aor. act. subj. 3 sing. of ἐξανίστημι.

ἐξανατέλλω spring up ἐξανέτειλε 1 aor. act. ind. 3 sing. Mt 13:5; Mk 4:5.

ἐξανέστησα 1 aor. act. ind. of ἐξανίστημι.

ἐξανίστημι trans. raise up Mk 12:19; Lk 20:28. Intrans. stand up Ac 15:5.*

ἐξανοίγω to open (fully) Ac 12:16 v.l.*

ἐξαπατάω deceive, cheat Ro 7:11; 16:18; 1 Cor 3:18; 2 Cor 11:3; 2 Th 2:3; 1 Ti 2:14.*

ἐξαπεστάλην, ἐξαπέστειλα 1 aor. pass. and 1 aor. act. ind. of ἐξαποστέλλω.

ἐξάπινα adv. suddenly Mk 9:8.*

ἐξαπορέω pass. be in great difficulty, despair 2 Cor 4:8. τοῦ ζῆν despair of living 1:8.*

ἐξαποστέλλω send out, send away Lk 1:53; 24:49 v.l.; Ac 7:12; 17:14; 22:21; Gal 4:4, 6.

ἐξάρατε, ἐξαρθῇ 1 aor. act. impv. and 1 aor. pass. subj. 3 sing. of ἐξαίρω.

ἐξαρτάω be attached to, be an adherent of Mk 3:21 v.l.*

ἐξαρτίζω finish, complete Ac 21:5. Equip, furnish 2 Ti 3:17.*

ἐξαστράπτω flash or gleam like lightning Lk 9:29.*

ἐξαυτῆς adv. at once, immediately, soon thereafter Mk 6:25; Ac 10:33; 21:32; Phil 2:23.

ἐξέβαλον, ἐξεβλήθην 2 aor. act. ind. and 1 aor. pass. ind. of ἐκβάλλω.

ἐξέβην 2 aor. act. ind. of ἐκβαίνω.

ἐξεγείρω awaken pass. wake up, awaken Mk 6:45 v.l. Raise from the dead 1 Cor 6:14. Cause to appear, bring into being Ro 9:17.*

ἐξεγερῶ fut. act. ind. of ἐγείρω.

ἐξέδετο 2 aor. mid. ind. of ἐκδίδωμι.

ἐξείλατο 2 aor. mid. ind. of ἐξαιρέω.

ἔξειμι (from εἶμι) go out, go away Ac 13:42; 20:7; 27:43.

ἔξειμι from εἰμί, see ἔξεστιν.

ἐξεκαύθην 1 aor. pass. ind. of ἐκκαίω.

ἐξεκλάσθην 1 aor. pass. ind. of ἐκκλάω.

ἐξεκόπην 2 aor. pass. ind. of ἐκκόπτω.

ἐξεκρέμετο impf. mid. ind. of ἐκκρεμάννυμι.

ἔξελε, ἐξελέσθαι 2 aor. act. impv. and mid. inf. of ἐξαιρέω.

ἐξελέγχω convict Jd 15 v.l.*

ἐξελέξω 1 aor. mid. 2 sing. of ἐκλέγω.

ἐξελεύσομαι, ἐξελήλυθα fut. mid. and pf. act. ind. of ἐξέρχομαι.

ἐξέλκω drag away Js 1:14.*

ἐξέμαξα 1 aor. act. ind. of ἐκμάσσω.

ἐξενεγκ- aor. stem of ἐκφέρω.

ἐξέπεσα 1 aor. act. ind. of ἐκπίπτω.

ἐξεπέτασα 1 aor. act. ind. of ἐκπετάννυμι.

ἐξεπλάγην 2 aor. pass. ind. of ἐκπλήσσω.

ἐξέπλει impf. act. ind. 3 sing. of ἐκπλέω.

ἐξέπλευσα 1 aor. act. ind. of ἐκπλέω.

ἐχέπνευσα 1 aor. act. ind. of ἐκπνέω.

ἐξέραμα, ατος, τό vomit, what has been vomited 2 Pt 2:22.*

ἐξεραυνάω Hellenistic for ἐξερευνάω inquire carefully 1 Pt 1:10.*

ἐχέρχομαι go out, come out, get out, go away Mt 8:28; 25:1; Mk 1:35; 5:2; J 13:3; Ac 12:9f; Js 3:10; Rv 19:21. Be released Lk 12:59. Appear Mk 8:11. Proceed, be descended Hb 7:5. Be gone Ac 16:19. ἐκ τ. κόσμου ἐ. leave the world = die 1 Cor 5:10.

ἐξεστακέναι, ἐξέστην, ἐξέστησα pf. act. inf., 2 aor. act. ind., and 1 aor. act. ind. of ἐξίστημι.

ἔξεστι impersonal 3 sing. of the unused verb ἔξειμι; it is permitted, it is possible or proper Mt 12:2; Mk 3:4; Lk 6:9; J 18:31; Ac 22:25; 1 Cor 6:12. The neut. participle of ἔ. is ἐξόν; with ἐστί expressed or understood, it = ἔξεστι Mt 12:4; Ac 2:29.

ἐξέστραπται pf. pass. ind. of ἐκστρέφω.

ἐξετάζω inquire Mt 10:11. ἐ. περί τινος make a careful search for someone 2:8. Question, examine J 21:12.*

ἐξετέθην 1 aor. pass. ind. of ἐκτίθημι.

ἐξέτεινα 1 aor. act. ind. of ἐκτείνω.

ἐξετράπην 2 aor. pass. ind. of ἐκτρέπω.

ἐξέφνης Hellenistic spelling of ἐξαίφνης.

ἐξέφυγον 2 aor. act. ind. of ἐκφεύγω.

ἐξέχεα, ἐξεχύθην 1 aor. act. and 1 aor. pass. ind. of ἐκχέω.

ἐξέχω stand out, be prominent Mt 20:28 v.l.*

ἐξέψυξα 1 aor. act. ind. of ἐκψύχω.

ἐξέωσαι 1 aor. act. inf. of ἐξωθέω.

ἐξήγαγον 2 aor. act. ind. of ἐξάγω.

ἐξήγγειλα 1 aor. act. ind. of ἐξαγγέλλω.

ἐξήγειρε 1 aor. act. ind. 3 sing. of ἐξεγείρω.

ἐξηγέομαι explain, interpret, tell, report, describe Lk 24:35; Ac 10:8; 15:12, 14; 21:19. Make known, bring news of J 1:18.*

ἐξῄειν, ἐξῄεσαν impf. act. ind. 1 sing. and 3 pl. of ἔξειμι (1).

ἐξήκοντα indecl. sixty Mt 13:8; Lk 24:13; 1 Ti 5:9; Rv 13:18.

ἐξῆλθον 2 aor. act. ind. of ἐξέρχομαι.

ἐξήρανε, ἐξηράνθη, ἐξήρανται 1 aor. act., 1 aor. pass., and pf. pass. ind. of ξηραίνω.

ἑξῆς adv. next Lk 9:37; Ac 21:1; 25:17; 27:18. ἐν τῷ ἑξῆς (soon) afterward Lk 7:11.*

ἐξητήσατο 1 aor. mid. ind. of ἐξαιτέω.

ἐξηχέω pass. be caused to sound forth, ring out 1 Th 1:8.* [echo]

ἐξιέναι pres. act. inf. of ἔξειμι.

ἕξις, εως, ἡ mature state Hb 5:14.* [cachexy (κακός + ἕξις), general ill health]

ἐξίστημι, ἐξιστάνω, ἐξιστάω—1. trans. confuse, amaze, astound Lk 24:22; Ac 8:9, 11.—2. intrans. (2 aor. and pf. act.; all of the mid.) be out of one's senses Mk 3:21; 2 Cor 5:13. Be amazed or overwhelmed Mt 12:23; Mk 5:42; Lk 2:47; Ac 2:7, 12. [ecstasy]

ἐξιστῶν pres. act. ptc. of ἐξίστημι (ἐξιστάω).

ἐξισχύω be able, be strong enough, be in a position Eph 3:18.*

ἔξοδος, ου, ἡ going out or away; the exodus Hb 11:22. Fig. departure, death Lk 9:31; 2 Pt 1:15.*

ἐξοίσουσι fut. act. ind. of ἐκφέρω.

ἐξολεθρεύω destroy utterly, root out Ac 3:23.*

ἐξομολογέω—1. act. promise, consent Lk 22:6.—2. mid.—a. confess, admit Mt 3:6; Mk 1:5; Ac 19:18; Js 5:16.—b. acknowledge Phil 2:11.—c. praise Mt 11:25; Lk 10:21; Ro 14:11; 15:9.* [exomologesis, public confession of sin] ἐξόν see ἔξεστιν.

ἐξορκίζω adjure, charge under oath Mt 26:63. Exorcise Ac 19:13 v.l., 14 v.l.*

ἐξορκιστής, οῦ, ὁ exorcist, one who drives out demons Ac 19:13.*

ἐξορύσσω dig out, tear out Gal 4:15; dig through Mk 2:4.*

ἐξουδενέω and ἐξουδενόω treat with contempt Mk 9:12.*

ἐξουθενέω and ἐξουθενόω—1. despise, disdain Lk 18:9; Ro 14:3, 10; 1 Cor 1:28; 16:11; Gal 4:14; consider of no account 1 Cor 6:4; amount to nothing 2 Cor 10:10.—2. reject with contempt Ac 4:11; 1 Th 5:20; treat with contempt Lk 23:11.*

ἐξουσία, ας, ἡ—1. freedom of choice, right to act, decide, etc. J 10:18; Ac 5:4; Ro 9:21; 1 Cor 9:4ff, 12; 2 Th 3:9; Hb 13:10; Rv 13:5; 22:14.—2. ability, capability, might, power Mt 9:8; Mk 1:22, 27; Lk 10:19; Ac 8:19; Rv 9:19; 20:6.—3. authority, absolute power Mt 21:23, 24, 27; 28:18; Mk 2:10; Ac 26:12.—4. power or authority exercised by rulers, etc., by virtue of their office—a. ruling power, official power Lk 7:8; 20:20; 17:12f.—b. domain, jurisdiction Lk 4:6; 23:7; Eph 2:2; Col 1:13.—c. bearers of authority in the state, authorities, officials, government Lk 12:11; Ro 13:1, 2, 3; cosmic powers above and beyond the human sphere but not unrelated to it 1 Cor 15:24; Eph 1:21; 3:10; Col 2:15.—5. means of exercising power, prob. a veil 1 Cor 11:10.

ἐξουσιάζω have power w. gen. over someone Lk 22:25; 1 Cor 7:4. Pass. be mastered 6:12.*

ἐξουσιαστικός, ή, όν authoritative Mk 1:27 v.l.*

ἐξοχή, ῆς, ἡ prominence ἄνδρες οἱ κατ᾽ ἐξοχήν the most prominent men Ac 25:23.*

ἐξυπνίζω wake up, arouse fig. J 11:11.*

ἔξυπνος, ον awake, aroused Ac 16:27.*

ἔξω—1. adv. outside Mt 12:46f; Mk 11:4; Lk 1:10; J 18:16. Out Mt 26:75; Lk 14:35; J 18:29; Rv 3:12. δεῦρο ἔξω come out! J 11:43. As a noun οἱ ἔξω those who are outside Mk 4:11; 1 Cor 5:12f.

As an adj. outer, outside 2 Cor 4:16; foreign Ac 26:11.—2. functions as prep. w. gen. outside Hb 13:11f; out of, out from Mt 10:14; Lk 4:29; Ac 4:15; 14:19.

ἔξωθεν—1. adv. from the outside Mk 7:18. Outside Mt 23:27f; 2 Cor 7:5. As noun οἱ ἔ. those on the outside 1 Ti 3:7. τὸ ἔ. the outside Mt 23:25; Lk 11:39f. As adj. external 1 Pt 3:3.—2. functions as prep. w. gen. from outside Mk 7:15; outside Rv 11:2f; 14:20.*

ἐξωθέω drive out, expel Ac 7:45. Beach, run ashore 27:39.*

ἐξῶσαι 1 aor. act. inf. of ἐξωθέω.

ἐξώτερος, α, ον comparative used as superlative farthest (out) Mt 8:12; 22:13; 25:30.*

ἔοικα be like, resemble w. dat. Js 1:6, 23.*

ἑόρακα pf. act. ind. of ὁράω.

ἑορτάζω celebrate a festival 1 Cor 5:8.*

ἑορτή, ῆς, ἡ festival, feast Mt 26:5; Mk 14:2; Lk 2:41f; 22:1; J 7:2, 8, 10f, 14; 13:1; Col 2:16.

ἐπαγαγεῖν 2 aor. act. inf. of ἐπάγω.

ἐπαγγελία, ας, ἡ promise Ac 2:39; 23:21; Ro 4:20; Gal 3:16, 18, 29; Hb 7:6; what was promised Ac 1:4; 2:33; Gal 3:14.

ἐπαγγέλλομαι—1. promise, offer Mk 14:11; Ro 4:21; Gal 3:19; Hb 6:13; Js 1:12.—2. profess, lay claim to 1 Ti 2:10; 6:21.

ἐπάγγελμα, ατος, τό promise 2 Pt 3:13; the thing promised 1:4.*

ἐπάγω bring on or upon Ac 5:28; 2 Pt 2:1, 5; stir up Ac 14:2 v.l.*

ἐπαγωνίζομαι fight, contend Jd 3.*

ἔπαθον 2 aor. act. ind. of πάσχω.

ἐπαθροίζω collect besides or in addition pass. Lk 11:29.*

Ἐπαίνετος, ου, ὁ Epaenetus Ro 16:5.*

ἐπαινέω praise Lk 16:8; Ro 15:11; 1 Cor 11:2, 17, 22.*

ἔπαινος, ου, ὁ praise, approval, recognition Ro 2:29; 1 Cor 4:5; Eph 1:6, 12, 14; 1 Pt 2:14; a thing worthy of praise Phil 4:8.

ἐπαίρω lift up, hold up Mt 17:8; Lk 6:20; 21:28; J 17:1; Ac 14:11; 1 Ti 2:8. Pass.

be taken up Ac 1:9; fig. rise up, be in opposition 2 Cor 10:5; be presumptuous, put on airs 2 Cor 11:20.

ἐπαισχύνομαι be ashamed (of) Mk 8:38; Lk 9:26; Ro 1:16; 6:21; 2 Ti 1:8, 12, 16; Hb 2:11; 11:16.*

ἐπαιτέω beg as a mendicant Lk 16:3; 18:35; Mk 10:46 v.l.*

ἐπακολουθέω follow, come after 1 Ti 5:24; 1 Pt 2:21; devote oneself (to) 1 Ti 5:10; accompany, authenticate Mk 16:20.*

ἐπακούω hear, listen to w. gen. 2 Cor 6:2.*

ἐπακροάομαι listen to w. gen. Ac 16:25.*

ἐπάν conj. w. subjunctive when, as soon as Mt 2:8; Lk 11:22, 34.*

ἐπαναγαγεῖν 2 aor. act. inf. of ἐπανάγω.

ἐπάναγκες adv. necessarily τὰ ἐ. the necessary things Ac 15:28.*

ἐπανάγω lead or bring up intrans.—1. push off from shore Lk 5:3f.—2. return Mt 21:18.*

ἐπαναμιμνῄσκω remind again Ro 15:15.*

ἐπαναπαήσομαι fut. pass. ind. of ἐπαναπαύομαι Lk 10:6.

ἐπαναπαύομαι rest Lk 10:6; 1 Pt 4:14 v.l. (ἐπαναπέπαυται pf. mid. 3 sing.); find rest or support in, rely on Ro 2:17.*

ἐπανέρχομαι return Lk 10:35; 19:15.*

ἐπανίστημι rise up in rebellion Mt 10:21; Mk 13:12.*

ἐπανόρθωσις, εως, ἡ correcting, improvement 2 Ti 3:16.*

ἐπάνω adv. above, over Lk 11:44; more than Mk 14:5; 1 Cor 15:6. Functions as prep. w. gen. over, above, on Mt 2:9; 5:14; 23:18, 20, 22; Lk 19:17, 19; J 3:31; Rv 20:3. ἐ. αὐτῆς at her head Lk 4:39.

ἐπάξας 1 aor. act. ptc. of ἐπάγω.

ἐπᾶραι, ἐπάρας, ἐπάρατε 1 aor. act. inf., ptc., and impv. of ἐπαίρω.

ἐπάρατος, ον accursed J 7:49.*

ἐπαρκέω help, aid w. dat. 1 Ti 5:10, 16.*

ἐπαρχεία, ας, ἡ province Ac 23:34; 25:1.*

ἐπάρχειος, ον belonging to an eparch ἡ ἐπάρχειος the province Ac 25:1 v.l.*

ἐπαρχικός, ή, όν pertaining to the eparch or prefect Phlm subscr.

ἔπαυλις, εως, ἡ farm, homestead, residence Ac 1:20.*

ἐπαύριον adv. tomorrow τῇ ἐ. on the next day Mk 11:12; J 1:29, 35, 43; Ac 20:7; 25:6, 23. εἰς τὴν ἐ. Ac 4:3 v.l.

Ἐπαφρᾶς, ᾶ, ὁ Epaphras Col 1:7; 4:12; Phlm 23.*

ἐπαφρίζω cause to splash up like foam Jd 13.*

Ἐπαφρόδιτος, ου, ὁ Epaphroditus Phil 2:25; 4:18.*

ἐπέβαλον 2 aor. act. ind. of ἐπιβάλλω.

ἐπέβην 2 aor. act. ind. of ἐπιβαίνω.

ἐπεγείρω rouse up fig. arouse, excite, stir up Ac 13:50; 14:2.*

ἐπέγνωκα, ἐπέγνων, ἐπεγνώσθην pf. act. ind., 2 aor. act. ind., and 1 aor. pass. ind. of ἐπιγινώσκω.

ἐπεδίδου, ἐπεδόθην, ἐπέδωκα impf. act. 3 sing., 1 aor. pass. ind., and 1 aor. act. ind. of ἐπιδίδωμι.

ἐπεθέμην, ἐπέθηκα 2 aor. mid. and 1 aor. act. ind. of ἐπιτίθημι.

ἐπεί conj.—1. when, after Lk 7:1 v.l.— 2. because, since, for Mt 18:32; Mk 15:42; Lk 1:34; J 19:31; 1 Cor 14:12; 2 Cor 13:3; Hb 5:2, 11; for otherwise Ro 3:6; 1 Cor 14:16; Hb 10:2.

ἐπειδή conj.—1. when, after Lk 7:1.— 2. since, since then, because Lk 11:6; 1 Cor 14:16; 15:21. Whereas Ac 15:24.

ἐπειδήπερ conj. inasmuch as, since, whereas Lk 1:1.*

ἐπεῖδον 2 aor. of ἐφοράω fix one's glance upon, look at, concern oneself (with) Lk 1:25; Ac 4:29.*

ἔπειμι (from εἶμι) ptc. ἐπιών, ἐπιοῦσα, ἐπιόν; τῇ ἐπιούσῃ ἡμέρᾳ on the next day Ac 7:26; cf. 16:11; 20:15; 21:18; 23:11. τῷ ἐπιόντι σαββάτῳ Ac 18:19 v.l.*

ἐπείπερ conj. since indeed Ro 3:30 v.l.*

ἐπειράσθην 1 aor. pass. ind. of πειράζω.

ἔπεισα 1 aor. act. ind. of πείθω.

ἐπεισαγωγή, ῆς, ἡ bringing in, introduction Hb 7:19.*

ἐπεισέρχομαι rush in suddenly Lk 21:35.*

ἔπειτα adv. then, thereupon Lk 16:7; 1 Cor 12:28; 15:46; Gal 1:21; 1 Th 4:17; Hb 7:2, 27; Js 3:17.

ἐπέκειλα 1 aor. act. ind. of ἐπικέλλω.

ἐπέκεινα adv. farther on, beyond w. gen. Ac 7:43.*

ἐπεκεκλήμην, ἐπεκλήθην plupf. pass. and 1 aor. pass. ind. of ἐπικαλέω.

ἐπεκτείνομαι stretch out, strain w. dat. Phil 3:13.*

ἐπελαβόμην 2 aor. mid. ind. of ἐπιλαμβάνομαι.

ἐπελαθόμην 2 aor. mid. ind. of ἐπιλανθάνομαι.

ἐπέλθοι, ἐπελθών 2 aor. act. opt. 3 sing. and 2 aor. act. ptc. of ἐπέρχομαι.

ἐπέμεινα 1 aor. act. ind. of ἐπιμένω.

ἐπενδύομαι put on (in addition) 2 Cor 5:2, 4.*

ἐπενδύτης, ου, ὁ outer garment, coat J 21:7.*

ἐπενεγκεῖν 2 aor. act. inf. of ἐπιφέρω.

ἐπέπεσον 2 aor. act. ind. of ἐπιπίπτω.

ἐπεποίθει plupf. act. ind. of πείθω.

ἐπέρχομαι come, come along, appear Ac 14:19. Come on, approach Eph 2:7. Come upon Lk 21:26; Ac 8:24; Js 5:1; from on high Lk 1:35; Ac 1:8. Come about Ac 13:40. Attack Lk 11:22.*

ἐπερωτάω ask a question, interrogate Mt 12:10; 22:46; Mk 9:32; 10:10; 12:18; Lk 2:46; Ac 5:27; 1 Cor 14:35. With two accusatives ask someone about something Mk 7:17, but ask someone for something Mt 16:1. Inquire after Ro 10:20.

ἐπερώτημα, ατος, τό request, appeal or pledge 1 Pt 3:21.*

ἔπεσα and ἔπεσον aor. act. ind. of πίπτω.

ἐπέστειλα 1 aor. act. ind. of ἐπιστέλλω.

ἐπέστην 2 aor. act. ind. of ἐφίστημι.

ἐπεστράφην 2 aor. pass. ind. of ἐπιστρέφω.

ἐπέσχον 2 aor. act. ind. of ἐπέχω.

ἐπετίθεσαν 3 pl. impf. act. ind. of ἐπιτίθημι.

ἐπετράπην 2 aor. pass. ind. of ἐπιτρέπω.

ἐπέτυχε 2 aor. act. ind. 3 sing. of ἐπιτυγχάνω.

ἐπεφάνην 2 aor. pass. ind. of ἐπιφαίνω.

ἐπέχω—1. trans. hold fast Phil 2:16; Lk 4:42 v.l.—2. intr. hold toward, aim at; fix one's attention Ac 3:5; take pains 1 Ti 4:16; notice Lk 14:7. Stop, stay Ac 19:22.* [epoch]

ἐπηγγειλάμην, ἐπήγγελμαι 1 aor. mid. and pf. mid. ind. of ἐπαγγέλλομαι.

ἐπήγειρα 1 aor. act. ind. of ἐπεγείρω.

ἐπῆλθον 2 aor. act. ind. of ἐπέρχομαι.

ἐπήνεσα 1 aor. act. ind. of ἐπαινέω.

ἔπηξα 1 aor. act. ind. of πήγνυμι.

ἐπῆρα, ἐπήρθην 1 aor. act. and pass. ind. of ἐπαίρω.

ἐπηρεάζω mistreat, abuse, revile Lk 6:28; 1 Pt 3:16; Mt 5:44 v.l.*

ἐπί prep. w. gen., dat., or acc.—I. with the genitive—1. of place, lit. and fig. on, upon Mt 1:11; Mk 4:26; 6:48f; Lk 17:31, 34; 1 Cor 11:10; Gal 3:13. At, near, by Mt 21:19; Lk 22:30; J 21:1; Ac 5:23. Before, in the presence of Mk 13:9; Ac 23:30; 1 Cor 6:1; 1 Ti 6:13. Over of power, authority, control Lk 12:42; Ac 6:3; Ro 9:5; Rv 5:10; 17:18; in charge of Ac 8:27. On the basis or evidence of Mk 12:14, 32; Ac 4:27; 1 Ti 5:19; Hb 7:11.—2. of time in the time of Mt 1:11; Mk 2:26; Lk 3:2; Ac 11:28; Eph 1:16; Jd 18.—II. with the dative—1. of place, lit. and fig. on, in, above Mt 9:16; 14:8, 11; 16:18; Mk 6:39; Lk 23:38; J 11:38; Ac 3:11; 27:44. Against Lk 12:52f. At, near, by Mk 13:29; J 4:6; Ac 3:10; Rv 9:14. Over of power, authority, control Mt 24:47; Lk 12:44. To, in addition to Lk 3:20; 1 Cor 14:16; 2 Cor 7:13; Col 3:14. On, on the basis of Lk 4:4; 5:5; Ac 3:16; Ro 8:20; Hb 8:6. At, because of, from, with Mk 1:22; Lk 1:29; Ac 3:10; 20:38; Ro 16:19; Phlm 7; Rv 12:17; 18:20. About J 12:16; Hb 11:4; Rv 22:16. For Gal 5:13; Eph 2:10; 1 Th 4:7; 2 Ti 2:14. ἐφ' ᾧ on the condition under which, a commercial term, is probable in Ro 5:12; Phil 3:12.—2. of time at, in, at the time of, during 2 Cor 1:4; Phil 1:3; 2:17; 1 Th 3:7b; Hb 9:15, 26. ἐπὶ τούτῳ in the meanwhile J 4:27.—III. with the accusative—1. of place, lit. and fig., often with motion implied across, over Mt 14:25, 28f; Lk 23:44; Ac 11:28. On, upon Mt 5:45; 13:5; Lk 6:29; 23:30; 1 Cor 14:25; Rv 7:11. To, upon Mt 22:9; Ac 8:26; Rv 7:1. To, up to, in the neighborhood of, on Mt 3:13; Mk 5:21; Lk 22:44; J 19:33; 21:20; before Lk 12:58; Ac 25:12. To, toward Mt 12:49; 2 Pt 2:22. Against with hostile intent Mt 10:21; Mk 14:48; Lk 11:17f; Ac 13:50. Simply on, over with no motion Mt 13:2; Mk 4:38; J 12:15; 2 Cor 3:15; Rv 4:4. ἐπὶ τὸ αὐτό at the same place, together Lk 17:35; Ac 1:15, but to the same place with verbs of motion Mt 22:34; 1 Cor 11:20; 14:23 and προσετίθει ἐπὶ τὸ αὐτό he added to their number Ac 2:47. Over of power, rule, control Mt 25:21, 23; Lk 1:33; Ac 7:10; Ro 5:14; Rv 6:8. To, in addition to Mt 6:27; Lk 12:25; Phil 2:27. On, upon, to, over Mt 12:28; 27:25; Lk 3:2; 10:6; J 1:32f; Ac 2:17f; 13:11; Ro 2:2, 9; 1 Pt 5:7; Rv 11:11. In, on, for, toward Mt 27:43; Mk 9:22; Ac 11:17; Ro 4:24; Eph 2:7; Hb 6:1; Rv 1:7.—2. of time: time when on, at Lk 10:35; Ac 3:1; 4:5. Of extension over a period for, over a period of Lk 4:25; Ac 13:31; 18:20; 28:6.

ἐπιβαίνω go up or upon, mount, board Mt 21:5; Ac 27:2; go on board, embark 21:2. Set foot (in) Ac 20:18; 21:4; 25:1.*

ἐπιβάλλω—1. act., trans. throw over 1 Cor 7:35. Lay on, put on Mt 9:16; Mk 14:46; Lk 9:62; J 7:44; Ac 21:27.—2. act., intrans. throw oneself, beat upon Mk 4:37. ἐπιβαλὼν ἔκλαιεν Mk 14:72 most likely = he began to weep or when he reflected on it, he wept. Fall to, belong to Lk 15:12.

ἐπιβαλῶ fut. act. ind. of ἐπιβάλλω.

ἐπιβαρέω weigh down, burden 1 Th 2:9; 2 Th 3:8. ἵνα μὴ ἐπιβαρῶ 2 Cor 2:5 is probably 'in order not to heap up too great a burden of words' = in order not to say too much.*

ἐπιβάς, ἐπιβέβηκα 2 aor. act. ptc. and pf. act. ind. of ἐπιβαίνω.

ἐπιβιβάζω put on, cause to mount Lk 10:34; 19:35; Ac 23:24.*

ἐπιβλέπω look at, consider, care about Lk 1:48; 9:38; Js 2:3.*

ἐπίβλημα, ατος, τό a patch Mt 9:16; Mk 2:21; Lk 5:36.*

ἐπιβοάω cry out loudly Ac 25:24 v.l.*

ἐπιβουλή, ῆς, ἡ plot Ac 9:24; 20:3, 19; 23:30.*

ἐπιγαμβρεύω marry as next of kin Mt 22:24.*

ἐπίγειος, ον earthly 1 Cor 15:40; 2 Cor 5:1; Phil 2:10; 3:19; Js 3:15. τὰ ἐπίγεια earthly things J 3:12.*

ἐπιγίνομαι come up Ac 28:13; come on 27:27 v.l.*

ἐπιγινώσκω—1. know exactly, completely Lk 1:4; Ro 1:32; 1 Cor 13:12; Col 1:6. Know again, recognize Lk 24:16, 31; Ac 12:14. Acknowledge Mt 17:12; 1 Cor 16:18.—2. know Mt 7:16, 20; Mk 6:54; 1 Ti 4:3. Learn, find out Mk 6:33; Lk 7:37; Ac 28:1. Ascertain 23:28; 24:11. Notice, perceive, learn of Mk 5:30; Ac 9:30. Understand, know Ac 25:10; 2 Cor 1:13f. Learn to know 2 Pt 2:21b.

ἐπιγνούς, ἐπιγνῶ 2 aor. act. ptc. and subj. of ἐπιγινώσκω.

ἐπίγνωσις, εως, ἡ insight, knowledge Col 1:9f; 1 Ti 2:4; Tit 1:1; Phlm 6; Hb 10:26; 2 Pt 1:2; consciousness Ro 3:20. ἔχειν ἐν ἐ. recognize 1:28.

ἐπιγνώσομαι fut. mid. ind. of ἐπιγινώσκω.

ἐπιγραφή, ῆς, ἡ inscription, superscription Mt 22:20; Mk 12:16; 15:26; Lk 20:24; 23:38.*

ἐπιγράφω write on or in, inscribe Mk 15:26; Ac 17:23; Rv 21:12; fig. Hb 8:10; 10:16.* [epigraph, epigram]

ἔπιδε 2 aor. act. impv. of ἐπεῖδον, which is in turn the 2 aor. of ἐφοράω.

ἐπιδείκνυμι show, point out Mt 16:1; 22:19; 24:1; Lk 17:14; Ac 9:39. Demonstrate, show Ac 18:28; Hb 6:17.*

ἐπιδείξατε 1 aor. act. impv. 2 pl. of ἐπιδείκνυμι.

ἐπιδέχομαι receive as a guest 3 J 10; accept, recognize 3 J 9. Take along Ac 15:40 v.l.*

ἐπιδημέω stay in a place as a stranger or visitor, be in town Ac 2:10; 17:21; 18:27 v.l.*

ἐπιδιατάσσομαι add a codicil to Gal 3:15.*

ἐπιδίδωμι give, hand over, deliver Mt 7:9f; Lk 4:17; 11:11f; 24:30, 42; Ac 15:30; give up 27:15.*

ἐπιδιορθόω correct (in addition) Tit 1:5.*

ἐπιδούς 2 aor. act. ptc. of ἐπιδίδωμι.

ἐπιδύω set Eph 4:26.*

ἐπιδῶ, ἐπιδώσω 2 aor. act. subj. 3 sing. and fut. act. ind. 1 sing. of ἐπιδίδωμι.

ἐπιείκεια, ας, ἡ gentleness, graciousness, clemency, tolerance Ac 24:4; 2 Cor 10:1.*

ἐπιεικής, ές gentle, kind, yielding, tolerant 1 Ti 3:3; Tit 3:2; Js 3:17; 1 Pt 2:18. τὸ ἐπιεικές = ἡ ἐπιείκεια Phil 4:5.*

ἐπιεικία another spelling for ἐπιείκεια.

ἐπιζητέω search for, seek after Lk 4:42; Ac 12:19; want to know 19:39. Wish (for) Mt 6:32; Phil 4:17; Hb 13:14. Demand, desire Mt 12:39; 16:4.

ἐπιθανάτιος, ον condemned to death 1 Cor 4:9.*

ἐπιθεῖναι, ἐπιθείς, ἐπίθες 2 aor. act. inf., ptc., and impv. of ἐπιτίθημι.

ἐπίθεσις, εως, ἡ laying on Ac 8:18; 1 Ti 4:14; 2 Ti 1:6; Hb 6:2.*

ἐπιθήσω fut. act. ind. of ἐπιτίθημι.

ἐπιθυμέω desire, long for w. gen. or acc. Mt 5:28; Ac 20:33; Gal 5:17; 1 Ti 3:1; Hb 6:11; Rv 9:6. ἐπιθυμίᾳ ἐπιθυμεῖν eagerly desire Lk 22:15.

ἐπιθυμητής, οῦ, ὁ one who desires ἐ. κακῶν desirous of evil 1 Cor 10:6.*

ἐπιθυμία, ας, ἡ desire, longing Mk 4:19; Lk 22:15; Gal 5:24; Phil 1:23; Col 3:5; 1 Th 2:17; 4:5; Js 1:14f; craving Gal 5:16. ἐ. μιασμοῦ defiling passion 2 Pt 2:10.

ἐπιθύω offer a sacrifice Ac 14:13 v.l.*

ἐπιθῶ 2 aor. act. subj. of ἐπιτίθημι.

ἐπικαθίζω sit or sit down (on) Mt 21:7.*

ἐπικαλέω—1. act. and pass. call, name, give a name or surname to Mt 10:25; Ac 1:23; 12:12; Hb 11:16. ἐφ' οὓς ἐπικέκληται τὸ ὄνομα upon whom the name has been invoked (to indicate that the persons involved belong to the one named) Ac 15:17.—2. mid. call upon someone for aid Ac 2:21; Ro 10:12f; 1 Cor 1:2; 2 Cor 1:23; 2 Ti 2:22; 1 Pt 1:17. Appeal to Ac 25:11f, 21, 25.

ἐπικάλυμμα, ατος, τό covering, veil 1 Pt 2:16.*

ἐπικαλύπτω cover Ro 4:7.*

ἐπικατάρατος, ον cursed Gal 3:10, 13; Lk 6:5 v.l.*

ἐπίκειμαι—1. lie upon lit. J 11:38; 21:9; fig. Ac 27:20; 1 Cor 9:16.—2. press around, press upon, be urgent Lk 5:1; 23:23. Be imposed Hb 9:10.*

ἐπικέκλημαι pf. pass. ind. of ἐπικαλέω.

ἐπικέλλω bring to shore, run aground Ac 27:41.*

ἐπικερδαίνω gain in addition Mt 25:20 v.l.; 22 v.l.*

ἐπικεφάλαιον, ου, τό poll tax Mk 12:14 v.l.*

ἐπικληθείς 1 aor. pass. ptc. of ἐπικαλέω.

Ἐπικούρειος, ου, ὁ an Epicurean Ac 17:18.*

ἐπικουρία, ας, ἡ help Ac 26:22.*

ἐπικράνθη 1 aor. pass. ind. of πικραίνω.

ἐπικράζω shout threats Ac 16:39 v.l.*

ἐπικρίνω decide, determine Lk 23:24.*

ἐπιλαθέσθαι 2 aor. mid. inf. of ἐπιλανθάνομαι.

ἐπιλαμβάνομαι—1. take hold of, grasp, catch w. gen. or acc. Mt 14:31; Mk 8:23; Lk 9:47; 14:4; Ac 17:19; 18:17.—2. fig. catch Lk 20:20, 26; take hold of 1 Ti 6:12; be concerned with, take an interest in, help Hb 2:16. [epilepsy, ἐπί + λαμβάνειν]

ἐπιλάμπω shine out, shine forth Ac 12:7 v.l.*

ἐπιλανθάνομαι forget Mk 8:14; Phil 3:13; Js 1:24. Neglect, overlook Lk 12:6; Hb 13:2, 16.

ἐπιλέγω pass. *be called* or *named* J 5:2; mid. *choose, select* Ac 15:40.*

ἐπιλείπω *leave behind*, hence *fail* in Hb 11:32.*

ἐπιλείχω *lick* Lk 16:21.*

ἐπιλελησμένος pf. mid. and pass. ptc. of ἐπιλανθάνομαι.

ἐπιλησμονή, ῆς, ἡ *forgetfulness* ἀκροατὴς ἐπιλησμονῆς *a forgetful hearer* Js 1:25.*

ἐπίλοιπος, ον *left, remaining* 1 Pt 4:2; Lk 24:43 v.l.*

ἐπίλυσις, εως, ἡ *explanation, interpretation* 2 Pt 1:20.*

ἐπιλύω *explain, interpret* Mk 4:34; *decide, settle* pass. Ac 19:39.*

ἐπιμαρτυρέω *bear witness* 1 Pt 5:12.*

ἐπιμεῖναι 1 aor. act. inf. of ἐπιμένω.

ἐπιμέλεια, ας, ἡ *care, attention* Ac 27:3.*

ἐπιμελέομαι *care for, take care of* w. gen. Lk 10:34f; 1 Ti 3:5.*

ἐπιμελῶς adv. *carefully, diligently* Lk 15:8.*

ἐπιμένω—**1.** *stay, remain* Ac 10:48; 21:4; 1 Cor 16:8; Gal 1:18.—**2.** *continue, persist (in), persevere* w. dat. Ro 6:1; 11:22; Col 1:23. With participle following *keep on, persist in doing something* J 8:7; Ac 12:16.

ἐπινεύω *give consent* (by a nod) Ac 18:20.*

ἐπίνοια, ας, ἡ *thought, intent* Ac 8:22.*

ἔπιον 2 aor. act. ind. of πίνω.

ἐπιορκέω *swear falsely* or *break one's oath* Mt 5:33.*

ἐπίορκος, ον *perjured* as noun *perjurer* 1 Ti 1:10.*

ἐπιοῦσα, ης, ἡ *the next day* see ἔπειμι.

ἐπιούσιος, ον an extremely rare word of debated meaning; among the probabilities are *daily, necessary for existence, for the following day, for the future.* Found in the N.T. only Mt 6:11; Lk 11:3.*

ἐπιπέπτωκα pf. act. ind. of ἐπιπίπτω.

ἐπιπίπτω—**1.** *fall upon, approach eagerly* often w. dat. Mk 3:10; Ac 20:10; ἐ. ἐπὶ τὸν τράχηλον *embrace* vs. 37.—

2. *come upon* Lk 1:12; Ac 8:16; 10:44; 19:17; Ro 15:3.

ἐπιπλήσσω *strike at, reprove, rebuke* 1 Ti 5:1.*

ἐπιποθέω *long for, desire* Ro 1:11; 2 Cor 9:14; Phil 1:8; 1 Th 3:6; 1 Pt 2:2.

ἐπιπόθησις, εως, ἡ *longing* 2 Cor 7:7, 11.*

ἐπιπόθητος, ον *longed for* Phil 4:1.*

ἐπιποθία, ας, ἡ *longing, desire* Ro 15:23.*

ἐπιπορεύομαι *go* or *journey (to)* Lk 8:4.*

ἐπι(ρ)ράπτω *sew (on)* Mk 2:21.*

ἐπι(ρ)ρίπτω *throw, cast* Lk 19:35; 1 Pt 5:7.*

ἐπισείω *urge on, incite* Ac 14:19 v.l.*

ἐπίσημος, ον *prominent, outstanding* Ro 16:7. *Notorious* Mt 27:16.*

ἐπισιτισμός, οῦ, ὁ *food, something to eat* Lk 9:12.*

ἐπισκέπτομαι—**1.** *look for, select* Ac 6:3.—**2.** *go to see, visit* Mt 25:36; Ac 7:23; 15:36; *look after* Js 1:27.—**3.** *visit for the purpose of bringing salvation* Lk 1:68; 7:16; *be concerned about* Ac 15:14.

ἐπισκευάζομαι *make preparations* Ac 21:15.*

ἐπισκηνόω *take up one's abode* 2 Cor 12:9.*

ἐπισκιάζω *cast a shadow, overshadow* Mt 17:5; Lk 1:35; Ac 5:15.

ἐπισκοπέω *take care, see to it* Hb 12:15. *Oversee, care for* 1 Pt 5:2.*

ἐπισκοπή, ῆς, ἡ—**1.** *visitation:* favorable Lk 19:44; favorable or unfavorable 1 Pt 2:12.—**2.** *position* or *office as an overseer* Ac 1:20; *office of a supervisor* 1 Ti 3:1.* [*episcopate*]

ἐπίσκοπος, ου, ὁ *overseer, guardian, supervisor* of Jesus 1 Pt 2:25. The usage in the N.T., in reference to officials, appears to be less technical than a rendering such as 'bishop' would suggest; thus *superintendent, supervisor* Ac 20:28; Phil 1:1; 1 Ti 3:2; Tit 1:7.* [Cf. *bishop.*]

ἐπισπάομαι *pull over* the foreskin to conceal circumcision 1 Cor 7:18.*

ἐπισπείρω sow (afterward) Mt 13:25.*

ἐπίσταμαι understand Mk 14:68; 1 Ti 6:4. Know, be acquainted with Ac 15:7; 19:15; 26:26; Hb 11:8; Jd 10.

ἐπιστάς 2 aor. act. ptc. of ἐφίστημι.

ἐπίστασις, εως, ἡ attack, onset Ac 24:12. For 2 Cor 11:28 pressure is probably best; other possibilities are attention, oversight, hindrance.*

ἐπιστάτης, ου, vocative ἐπιστάτα, ὁ master Lk 5:5; 8:24, 45; 9:33, 49; 17:13.*

ἐπιστεῖλαι 1 aor. act. inf. of ἐπιστέλλω.

ἐπιστέλλω inform or instruct by letter, write Ac 15:20; 21:25; Hb 13:22.*

ἐπιστῇ, ἐπίστηθι 2 aor. subj. 3 sing. and act. impv. 2 sing. of ἐφίστημι.

ἐπιστήμη, ης, ἡ understanding, knowledge Phil 4:8 v.l.* [epistemology]

ἐπιστήμων, ον, gen. ονος expert, learned, understanding Js 3:13.*

ἐπιστηρίζω strengthen Ac 14:22; 15:32, 41; 11:2 v.l.; 18:23 v.l.*

ἐπιστολή, ῆς, ἡ letter, epistle Ac 9:2; 23:25; Ro 16:22; 1 Cor 5:9; 2 Cor 3:1; 10:9; 1 Th 5:27.

ἐπιστομίζω stop the mouth of, silence Tit 1:11.*

ἐπιστραφείς 2 aor. pass. ptc. of ἐπιστρέφω.

ἐπιστρέφω turn lit. and fig. Lk 1:16; Js 5:20; turn around Mk 5:30; turn back, return Mt 10:13; 12:44. Be converted J 12:40 v.l.

ἐπιστροφή, ῆς, ἡ conversion, lit. 'turning' Ac 15:3.*

ἐπισυναγαγεῖν 2 aor. act. inf. of ἐπισυνάγω.

ἐπισυνάγω gather (together) Mt 23:37; Mk 13:27; Lk 17:37.

ἐπισυναγωγή, ῆς, ἡ meeting Hb 10:25; assembling 2 Th 2:1.*

ἐπισυνάξαι 1 aor. act. inf. of ἐπισυνάγω.

ἐπισυντρέχω run together Mk 9:25.*

ἐπισυρράπτω for ἐπι(ρ)ράπτω (q.v.) Mk 2:21 v.l.*

ἐπισύστασις, εως, ἡ uprising, disturbance, insurrection Ac 24:12 v.l. 2 Cor 11:28 v.l.*

ἐπισφαλής, ές unsafe, dangerous Ac 27:9.*

ἐπισχύω insist Lk 23:5.*

ἐπισωρεύω accumulate 2 Tj 4:3.*

ἐπιταγή, ῆς, ἡ command, order 1 Cor 7:25; authority Tit 2:15. κατ' ἐπιταγήν by command Ro 16:26; 1 Ti 1:1; Tit 1:3. κατ' ἐπιταγὴν λέγειν say as a command 1 Cor 7:6; 2 Cor 8:8.*

ἐπιτάσσω order, command with dat. Mk 1:27; 6:39; Lk 8:25; Ac 23:2; Phlm 8. Without dat. order, give orders Mk 6:27; Lk 14:22.

ἐπιτελέω—1. end, finish Ro 15:28; 2 Cor 8:6, 11.—2. complete, perform, bring about 2 Cor 7:1; Hb 9:6; erect 8:5; lay upon 1 Pt 5:9.

ἐπιτήδειος, εία, ον necessary, suitable Ac 24:25 v.l. As noun τὰ ἐ. what is necessary Js 2:16.*

ἐπιτιθέασιν, ἐπιτίθει pres. act. ind. 3 pl. and 2 sing. impv. of ἐπιτίθημι.

ἐπιτίθημι lay or put upon Mt 9:18; 27:29, 37; Mk 8:23; J 9:6 v.l., 15; Ac 19:6; 1 Ti 5:22. Inflict Ac 16:23. Bring upon, add Rv 22:18. Give Mk 3:16f; Ac 28:10. Set upon, attack 18:10. [epithet]

ἐπιτιμάω rebuke, censure, warn Mt 8:26; 16:20 v.l.; Mk 8:30; 10:13; Lk 18:15, 39; 23:40. In Jd 9 the meaning could be rebuke or punish.

ἐπιτιμία, ας, ἡ punishment 2 Cor 2:6.*

ἐπιτρέπω allow, permit w. dat. Mt 8:21; Mk 10:4; Lk 9:59, 61; Ac 27:3; 1 Ti 2:12; give permission Mk 5:13; J 19:38; 1 Cor 16:7; Hb 6:3.

ἐπιτροπεύω be procurator, governor Lk 3:1 v.l.*

ἐπιτροπή, ῆς, ἡ permission, full power Ac 26:12.*

ἐπίτροπος, ου, ὁ manager, foreman, steward Mt 20:8 and perhaps Lk 8:3, where the mng. may also be governor, procurator. Guardian Gal 4:2.*

ἐπιτυγχάνω obtain, attain to, reach w. gen. Hb 6:15; 11:33; w. acc. Ro 11:7; abs. Ac 13:29 v.l.; Js 4:2.*

ἐπιτυχεῖν 2 aor. act. inf. of ἐπιτυγχάνω.

ἐπιφαίνω act. and pass. appear, make an appearance, show oneself Lk 1:79; Ac 27:20; Tit 2:11; 3:4.*

ἐπιφᾶναι 1 aor. act. inf. of ἐπιφαίνω.

ἐπιφάνεια, ας, ἡ appearing, appearance, epiphany 2 Th 2:8; 1 Ti 6:14; 2 Ti 1:10; 4:1, 8; Tit 2:13.*

ἐπιφανής, ές splendid, glorious Ac 2:20.*

ἐπιφαύσκω arise, appear, shine Eph 5:14.*

ἐπιφαύσω fut. act. ind. of ἐπιφαύσκω.

ἐπιφέρω bring over or upon Ac 19:12 v.l. Bring, pronounce Ac 25:18 v.l.; Jd 9. Inflict Ro 3:5.*

ἐπιφωνέω cry out (loudly) Lk 23:21; Ac 12:22; 21:34; 22:24.*

ἐπιφώσκω shine forth, dawn, break perhaps draw on Mt 28:1; Lk 23:54.*

ἐπιχειρέω set one's hand to, attempt, try Lk 1:1; Ac 9:29; 19:13.*

ἐπιχείρησις, εως, ἡ attempt, attack Ac 12:3 v.l.*

ἐπιχέω pour over, pour on Lk 10:34.*

ἐπιχορηγέω furnish, provide 2 Pt 1:5. Give, grant 2 Cor 9:10; Gal 3:5; 2 Pt 1:11. Support Col 2:19.*

ἐπιχορηγία, ας, ἡ support Eph 4:16; Phil 1:19.*

ἐπιχρίω spread or smear (on) J 9:6; anoint 9:11.*

ἐπιψαύω touch, grasp, attain to w. gen. Eph 5:14 v.l.*

ἐπλάσθην 1 aor. pass. ind. of πλάσσω.

ἐπλήγην 2 aor. pass. of πλήσσω.

ἔπλησα, ἐπλήσθην 1 aor. act. and pass. ind. of πίμπλημι.

ἔπνευσα 1 aor. act. ind. of πνέω.

ἐποικοδομέω build (on, upon) fig. 1 Cor 3:10, 12, 14; Eph 2:20; Col 2:7; Jd 20; Ac 20:32 v.l.; 1 Pt 2:5 v.l.*

ἐποκέλλω run aground Ac 27:41 v.l.*

ἐπονομάζω call, name Ro 2:17.*

ἐποπτεύω observe, see 1 Pt 2:12; 3:2.*

ἐπόπτης, ου, ὁ eyewitness 2 Pt 1:16.*

ἔπος, ους, τό word ὡς ἔ. εἰπεῖν so to speak, one might almost say, perhaps to use just the right word Hb 7:9.* [epic]

ἐπουράνιος, ον heavenly, celestial 1 Cor 15:40, 48f; Eph 1:3, 20; Phil 2:10; Hb 3:1; 8:5.

ἐπράθην 1 aor. pass. ind. of πιπράσκω.

ἐπρίσθην 1 aor. pass. ind. of πρίζω.

ἑπτά indecl. seven Mt 12:45; Mk 8:5f; Lk 20:29; Ac 6:3; Rv 1:4, 11; 16:1; 17:9. [hepta-, combining form in numerous terms]

ἑπτάκις adv. seven times Mt 18:21f; Lk 17:4.*

ἑπτακισχίλιοι, αι, α seven thousand Ro 11:4.*

ἑπταπλασίων, ον, gen. ονος sevenfold Lk 18:30 v.l.*

ἐπύθετο 2 aor. ind. 3 sing. of πυνθάνομαι.

Ἔραστος, ου, ὁ Erastus—1. Ro 16:23.—2. Ac 19:22; 2 Ti 4:20.*

ἐραυνάω search, examine, investigate J 5:39; 7:52; Ro 8:27; 1 Cor 2:10; 1 Pt 1:11; Rv 2:23.*

ἐργάζομαι—1. intr. work, be active Mt 21:28; 25:16; Ro 4:4f; 1 Cor 4:12; 9:6; 1 Th 2:9.—2. trans. do, accomplish, carry out Mt 26:10; J 3:21; 6:28; Ac 13:41; Ro 2:10; 13:10; 1 Cor 16:10; Gal 6:10; 2 Th 3:11. Practice, perform 1 Cor 9:13. Bring about, give rise to 2 Cor 7:10; Js 1:20. Work (on) Rv 18:17. Work for, earn or prepare, assimilate J 6:27.

ἐργασία, ας, ἡ practice, pursuit Eph 4:19. Trade, business Ac 19:25. Profit, gain 16:16, 19; 19:24. δὸς ἐργασίαν take pains Lk 12:58.*

ἐργάτης, ου, ὁ worker, laborer lit. Mt 9:37f; 20:1f, 8; Ac 19:25; 1 Ti 5:18; Js 5:4. Fig. 2 Cor 11:13; Phil 3:2; 2 Ti 2:15. A doer, one who does Lk 13:27.

ἔργον, ου, τό work—1. deed, action Lk 24:19; Col 3:17; 2 Th 2:17; Hb 4:3, 4, 10; Js 2:14ff. Manifestation, practical proof, practice Ro 2:15; Eph 4:12; 1 Th 1:3; 2 Th 1:11; Js 1:4. Deed, accomplishment Mt 11:2; Mk 14:6; Lk 11:48; J 3:19, 20f; 6:28f; 7:3, 21; 10:25, 37f; Ac 9:36; Ro 3:20, 28; Col 1:10; Hb 6:1; Js 3:13; Rv 15:3.—2. work, occupation, task Mk 13:34; J 17:4, Ac 14:26; 15:38; 1 Cor 15:58; 2 Ti 4:5.—3. work in the passive sense, indicating what is produced by work Ac 7:41; 1 Cor 3:13, 14, 15; Hb 1:10; 2 Pt 3:10; 1 J 3:8.—4. thing, matter Ac 5:38; perhaps 1 Ti 3:1. [energy, ἐν + ἔργον] ἐρεθίζω arouse, provoke in a good sense 2 Cor 9:2; in a bad sense irritate, embitter Col 3:21.* [erethism, unusual or morbid excitement]

ἐρείδω jam or stick fast Ac 27:41.*

ἐρεύγομαι utter, proclaim Mt 13:35.*

ἐρευνάω classical form of ἐραυνάω.

ἐρημία, ας, ἡ uninhabited region, desert Mt 15:33; Mk 8:4; 2 Cor 11:26; Hb 11:38.*

ἔρημος, ον—1. as adj. abandoned, empty, desolate Mt 14:13, 15; Mk 1:35, 45; Ac 1:20; lonely 8:26. Deserted, desolate Gal 4:27.—2. as noun ἡ ἔρημος desert, grassland, wilderness Mt 24:26; Mk 1:4; Lk 15:4; J 11:54; Ac 7:30; 21:38; Rv 12:6, 14. Lonely places Lk 1:80. [eremite, hermit]

ἐρημόω lay waste, depopulate Mt 12:25; Lk 11:17; Rv 17:16; 18:19. Ruin Rv 18:17.*

ἐρήμωσις, εως, ἡ devastation, destruction, depopulation Mt 24:15; Mk 13:14; Lk 21:20.*

ἐρίζω quarrel, wrangle Mt 12:19.*

ἐριθεία, ας, ἡ strife or selfish ambition Ro 2:8; 2 Cor 12:20; Gal 5:20; Phil 1:17; 2:3; Js 3:14, 16.*

ἐριμμένος pf. pass. ptc. of ῥίπτω.

ἔριον, ου, τό wool Hb 9:19; Rv 1:14.*

ἔρις, ιδος, ἡ strife, discord, contention Ro 1:29; 1 Cor 3:3; Gal 5:20; Phil 1:15; Tit 3:9. Pl. quarrels 1 Cor 1:11.

ἐρίφιον, ου, τό goat lit. 'kid' Mt 25:33; Lk 15:29 v.l.*

ἔριφος, ου, ὁ kid Lk 15:29; goat Mt 25:32.*

Ἑρμᾶς, ᾶ, ὁ Hermas Ro 16:14.*

ἑρμηνεία, ας, ἡ translation, interpretation 1 Cor 12:10; 14:26.*

ἑρμηνευτής, οῦ, ὁ translator 1 Cor 14:28 v.l.* [hermeneutics]

ἑρμηνεύω explain, interpret Lk 24:27 v.l. Translate J 1:38 v.l., 42; 9:7; Hb 7:2.*

Ἑρμῆς, οῦ, ὁ Hermes—1. the Greek god Ac 14:12.—2. recipient of a greeting Ro 16:14.* [hermetic]

Ἑρμογένης, ους, ὁ Hermogenes 2 Ti 1:15.*

ἑρπετόν, οῦ, τό reptile Ac 10:12; 11:6; Ro 1:23; Js 3:7.* [herpetology; serpent]

ἔρραμμαι pf. mid. ind. of ῥαίνω Rv 19:13 v.l.

ἐρραντισμένος pf. pass. ptc. of ῥαντίζω Rv 19:13 v.l.

ἐρρέθην 1 aor. pass. ind. of εἶπον.

ἔ(ρ)ρηξα 1 aor. act. ind. of ῥήγνυμι.

ἐρρίζωμαι pf. pass. ind. of ῥιζόω.

ἐ(ρ)ριμμένος pf. mid. and pass. ptc. of ῥίπτω.

ἐρρυσάμην, ἐρρύσθην 1 aor. mid. and pass. ind. of ῥύομαι.

ἔρρωσο pf. pass. impv. 2 sing. of ῥώννυμι.

ἐρυθρός, ά, όν red Ac 7:36; Hb 11:29.* [erythrism, excessive redness]

ἔρχομαι—1. come—a. in a literal sense Mt 8:9; Mk 7:1, 31; Lk 19:5; J 10:10; Ac 16:37, 39; Ro 9:9; 2 Cor 13:1; Hb 6:7; Rv 18:10. Appear, come before the public Mt 21:9; Mk 9:11; Lk 3:16; 7:33; J 7:27, 31; Ac 1:11; 1 Cor 4:5; 1 Ti 1:15. In a hostile sense Lk 11:22 v.l.—b. in a nonliteral sense Mt 23:35; Lk 15:17; J 18:4; Eph 5:6. ἔ. ἐκ τ. θλίψεως have suffered persecution Rv 7:14. ἔ. εἰς κρίσιν submit to judgment J 5:24. εἰς προκοπήν result in furthering Phil 1:12.—2. go Mt 16:24; Mk 11:13; Lk 15:20; J 21:3.

ἐρῶ fut. act. ind. of εἶπον.

ἐρωτάω—1. ask, ask a question Mt 21:24; Mk 4:10; Lk 22:68; J 8:7.—2. ask, request Mt 15:23; Lk 14:32; J 14:16; Ac 10:48; Phil 4:3; 2 Th 2:1; beseech Lk 4:38.

ἔσβεσα 1 aor. act. ind. of σβέννυμι.

ἐσθής, ῆτος, ἡ clothing Lk 23:11; 24:4; Ac 1:10; 10:30; 12:21; Js 2:2, 3. The dat. pl. ἐσθήσεσι (Ac 1:10; Lk 24:4 v.l.) is not from a separate form ἔσθησις, but is the result of doubling the dat. ending.*

ἐσθίω and ἔσθω eat—1. lit. Mt 15:32; Mk 2:26; 7:28; Lk 22:30; Ac 10:14; Ro 14:2; 1 Cor 10:25, 27; 2 Th 3:12; Rv 19:18; get sustenance 1 Cor 9:7.—2. fig. consume, devour Hb 10:27; Js 5:3. [Cf. edible.]

ἐσήμανα 1 aor. act. ind. of σημαίνω.

ἐσκυλμένος pf. pass. ptc. of σκύλλω.

Ἐσλί, ὁ indecl. Esli Lk 3:25.*

ἐσόμενος fut. ptc. of εἰμί.

ἔσοπτρον, ου, τό mirror 1 Cor 13:12; Js 1:23.*

ἐσπαρμένος pf. pass. ptc. of σπείρω.

ἑσπέρα, ας, ἡ evening Lk 24:29; Ac 4:3; 20:15 v.l.; 28:23.*

ἑσπερινός, ή, όν of or pertaining to the evening φυλακή six to nine P.M. Lk 12:38 v.l.*

Ἑσρώμ, ὁ indecl. Hezron Mt 1:3; Lk 3:33.*

ἑσσόομαι be defeated, be overpowered, be worse off 2 Cor 12:13.*

ἐστάθην, ἑστάναι, ἕστηκα, ἑστηκώς, ἔστην, ἔστησα, ἑστώς 1 aor. pass. ind., pf. act. inf., pf. act. ind., pf. act. ptc., 2 aor. act. ind., 1 aor. act. ind., and pf. act. ptc. of ἵστημι.

ἐστράφην 2 aor. pass. ind. of στρέφω.

ἐστρωμένος, ἔστρωσα pf. pass. ptc. and 1 aor. act. ind. of στρώννυμι.

ἔστω, ἔστωσαν pres. impv., 3 sing. and 3 pl., of εἰμί.

ἐσφάγην, ἐσφαγμένος, ἔσφαξα 2 aor. pass. ind., pf. pass. ptc., and 1 aor. act. ind. of σφάζω.

ἔσχατος, η, ον last. Of place Lk 14:9f. τὸ ἔσχατον the end Ac 1:8; 13:47. Of rank and succession last, least, most insignificant Mt 20:16; Lk 13:30; 1 Cor 4:9. Of time least, last Mt 20:8, 12, 14; J 6:39f; 7:37; Ac 2:17; 1 Cor 15:26, 45, 52; 2 Ti 3:1; Js 5:3; Rv 2:19. [eschatology]

ἐσχάτως adv. finally ἐ. ἔχειν be at the point of death Mk 5:23.*

ἔσχηκα, ἔσχον pf. act. and 2 aor. act. ind. of ἔχω.

ἔσω in, into Mt 26:58; Mk 14:54; 15:16. Inside, within J 20:26; Ac 5:23; 1 Cor 5:12; inner Ro 7:22; 2 Cor 4:16; Eph 3:16.*

ἔσωθεν adv. from inside Mk 7:21, 23; Lk 11:7. Inside, within Mt 23:25, 27f; 2 Cor 7:5. τὸ ἔ. ὑμῶν your inner nature Lk 11:39.

ἐσώτερος, α, ον inner Ac 16:24. τὸ ἐσώτερον what is inside w. gen. (= behind) Hb 6:19.*

ἑταῖρος, ου, ὁ comrade, companion, friend Mt 11:16 v.l.; 20:13; 22:12; 26:50.*

ἐταράχθην 1 aor. pass. ind. of ταράσσω.

ἐτάφην 2 aor. pass. ind. of θάπτω.

ἐτέθην 1 aor. pass. ind. of τίθημι.

ἔτεκον 2 aor. act. ind. of τίκτω.

ἑτερόγλωσσος, ον speaking a foreign language 1 Cor 14:21.*

ἑτεροδιδασκαλέω offer different, divergent (i.e. sectarian) instruction 1 Ti 1:3; 6:3.*

ἑτεροζυγέω be unevenly yoked, be mismated 2 Cor 6:14.*

ἕτερος, α, ον other of two Lk 5:7; 7:41; 18:10; Ac 23:6; 1 Cor 4:6. Of more than two Mt 11:3; 12:45; J 19:37; Ac 15:35; Ro 2:1, 21; 1 Cor 12:9f; used interchangeably with ἄλλος Gal 1:6f; 2 Cor 11:4. Next Ac 20:15. Another, different Mk 16:12; Ro 7:23; 1 Cor 15:40. [hetero-, combining form in numerous words, such as heterodox, heterogeneous]

ἑτέρως adv. differently, otherwise Phil 3:15.*

ἐτέχθην 1 aor. pass. ind. of τίκτω.

ἔτι adv. yet, still Mt 12:46; Lk 14:32; 15:20; Ro 9:19; Gal 1:10; Rv 9:12. Again 2 Cor 1:10; Hb 12:26f; further Mk 14:63; Hb 7:11; other Mt 18:16.

ἐτίθει, ἐτίθεσαν, ἐτίθουν impf. act. 3 sing. and two impf. act. 3 pl. forms of τίθημι.

ἑτοιμάζω put or keep in readiness, prepare Mt 22:4; 25:34, 41; Mk 1:3; Lk 22:13; J 14:2f; Rv 9:7; 21:2; make preparations Lk 9:52.

Ἕτοιμας v.l. for Ἐλύμας in Ac 13:8.*

ἑτοιμασία, ας, ἡ readiness, preparation, equipment Eph 6:15.*

ἕτοιμος, η, ον ready, prepared Mt 22:4; 25:10; Mk 14:15; J 7:6; Ac 23:15, 21; 2 Cor 9:5; 1 Pt 1:5. τὰ ἕτοιμα what has been accomplished 2 Cor 10:16. ἐν ἑτοίμῳ ἔχειν be ready 10:6.

ἑτοίμως adv. *readily* ἑ. ἔχειν *be ready, be willing* Ac 21:13; 2 Cor 12:14; 13:1 v.l.; 1 Pt 4:5.*

ἔτος, ους, τό *year* Mt 9:20; Mk 5:42; Lk 4:25; Ac 7:30; Gal 1:18; Rv 20:4. κατ' ἔτος *annually* Lk 2:41. πεντήκοντα ἔτη ἔχειν *be fifty years old* J 8:57. πρὸ ἐτῶν δεκατεσσάρων *fourteen years ago* 2 Cor 12:2. [*etesian*, of winds in the Mediterranean area]

ἐτύθην 1 aor. pass. ind. of θύω.

εὖ adv. *well* εὖ ποιεῖν *do good, show kindness* Mk 14:7. εὖ πράσσειν *do well, act rightly* Ac 15:29. ἵνα εὖ σοι γένηται *that you may prosper* Eph 6:3. Used alone *well done! excellent!* Mt 25:21, 23; Lk 19:17.* [*eu-*, combining form as in *eugenics, euphemism*]

Εὖα, ας, ἡ *Eve* 2 Cor 11:3; 1 Ti 2:13.*

εὐαγγελίζω act. and mid. *bring* or *announce good news* Lk 1:19; Rv 14:6. *Proclaim, preach (the gospel)* Lk 4:43; Ac 13:32; Ro 15:20; 1 Cor 15:1; 2 Cor 10:16; Gal 1:11, 23; 1 Pt 1:12. Pass. *have good news (the gospel) preached to one* Mt 11:5; Hb 4:2, 6. [*evangelize*]

εὐαγγέλιον, ου, τό *good news, gospel* Mt 4:23; 26:13; Mk 1:1, 14, 15; 8:35; Ac 15:7; Ro 1:16; 1 Cor 9:12, 18, 23; 2 Cor 4:4; 11:7; Eph 6:15; Col 1:5, 23; 1 Pt 4:17. [*evangel*]

εὐαγγελιστής, οῦ, ὁ *preacher of the gospel, evangelist* Ac 21:8; Eph 4:11; 2 Ti 4:5.*

εὐαρεστέω *please, be pleasing* Hb 11:5f; *be pleased, be satisfied* 13:16.*

εὐάρεστος, ον *pleasing, acceptable* Ro 12:1f; 2 Cor 5:9; Eph 5:10; Tit 2:9; Hb 13:21.

εὐαρέστως adv. *in an acceptable manner* Hb 12:28.*

Εὔβουλος, ου, ὁ *Eubulus* 2 Ti 4:21.*

εὖγε adv. *well done! excellent!* Lk 19:17.*

εὐγενής, ές, gen. οῦς *well born, of the best families* 1 Cor 1:26. ἄνθρωπος εὐ. *nobleman* Lk 19:12. *Noble-minded, open-minded* Ac 17:11.* [*eugenics*]

εὐγλωττία, ας, ἡ *glibness, fluency of speech* Ro 16:18 v.l.*

εὐδία, ας, η *good, fine weather* Mt 16:2.*

εὐδοκέω *consider good, consent, resolve* Lk 12:32; Ro 15:26f; 2 Cor 5:8; Col 1:19; 1 Th 2:8. *Be well pleased, take delight* Mt 3:17; 12:18; 1 Cor 10:5; 2 Pt 1:17. *Delight in, approve, like* 2 Cor 12:10; 2 Th 2:12; Hb 10:6, 8.

εὐδοκία, ας, ἡ—1. *good will* Phil 1:15; 2:13; 2 Th 1:11 (see 3 below).—2. *favor, good pleasure* Mt 11:26; Lk 10:21; Eph 1:5, 9. ἐν ἀνθρώποις εὐδοκίας Lk 2:14 *among people on whom God's favor rests.*—3. *wish, desire* Ro 10:1, perh. 2 Th 1:11.*

εὐεργεσία, ας, ἡ *the doing of good service, beneficence* 1 Ti 6:2; *benefaction, good deed* Ac 4:9.*

εὐεργετέω *do good (to), confer a benefit* Ac 10:38.*

εὐεργέτης, ου, ὁ *benefactor* Lk 22:25.*

εὔθετος, ον *fit, suitable, usable* Lk 9:62; 14:35; Hb 6:7.*

εὐθέως adv. *at once, immediately* Mt 4:20, 22; 14:31; Lk 12:36; J 6:21; Ac 9:18, 20, 34; Gal 1:16; Rv 4:2.

εὐθυδρομέω *run a straight course* Ac 16:11; 21:1.*

εὐθυμέω *be cheerful* Js 5:13; *cheer up, keep up one's courage* Ac 27:22, 25.*

εὔθυμος, ον *cheerful, in good spirits, encouraged* Ac 27:36.*

εὐθύμως adv. *cheerfully* Ac 24:10.*

εὐθύνω *straighten, make straight* J 1:23. *Steer (straight)* ὁ εὐθύνων *the pilot* Js 3:4.*

εὐθύς, εῖα, ύ gen. έως *straight.* Lit. Mt 3:3; Mk 1:3; Lk 3:4f; Ac 9:11. Fig. Ac 13:10; 2 Pt 2:15; *right, upright* Ac 8:21.*

εὐθύς adv. *immediately, at once* Mt 13:20f; Mk 1:10, 12; Lk 6:49; J 13:30, 32; Ac 10:16. Perh. *then, so then* Mk 1:21, 23, 29.

εὐθύτης, ητος, ἡ *righteousness, uprightness,* lit. 'straightness.' ῥάβδος τῆς εὐθύτητος *the righteous scepter* Hb 1:8.*

εὐκαιρέω *have (a favorable) time, leisure, opportunity* Mk 6:31; 1 Cor 16:12; *spend one's time* Ac 17:21.*

εὐκαιρία, ας, ἡ *favorable opportunity, the right moment* Mt 26:16; Lk 22:6.*

εὔκαιρος, ον well timed, suitable Mk 6:21; εὐ. βοήθεια help in time of need Hb 4:16.*

εὐκαίρως adv. conveniently Mk 14:11; in season, when it is convenient 2 Ti 4:2. εὐ. ἔχειν have leisure Mk 6:31 v.l.*

εὔκοπος, ον easy comparative εὐκοπώτερος: εὐκοπώτερόν ἐστιν it is easier Mt 9:5; Mk 10:25; Lk 16:17; 18:25.

εὐλάβεια, ας, ἡ awe, reverence, fear of God Hb 12:28; piety 5:7.*

εὐλαβέομαι be afraid, be concerned Ac 23:10 v.l. For Hb 11:7 take care and reverence, respect are also possible.*

εὐλαβής, ές devout, God-fearing Lk 2:25; Ac 2:5; 8:2; 22:12.*

εὐλογέω—1. speak well of, praise, extol in recognition of divine benefits Lk 1:64; 24:53; Js 3:9; give thanks and praise Mt 14:19; Lk 24:30; 1 Cor 14:16; consecrate Mk 8:7; 1 Cor 10:16.—2. of God confer favor or benefit—a. act. bless Ac 3:26; Eph 1:3.—b. pass. be blessed Mt. 25:34; Lk 1:42.—3. request God's favor for someone, bless Lk 6:28; 24:50f; 1 Cor 4:12; Hb 7:1, 6f. [eulogize]

εὐλογητός, ή, όν blessed, praised Mk 14:61; Lk 1:68; Ro 9:5; Eph 1:3; 1 Pt 1:3.

εὐλογία, ας, ἡ praise Rv 5:12f. Flattery, false eloquence Ro 16:18. Blessing, benefaction Ro 15:29; Eph 1:3; Js 3:10; Hb 6:7. Consecration τὸ ποτήριον τῆς εὐ. the cup of blessing i.e. the cup whereby divine favor is shared 1 Cor 10:16. Bounty 2 Cor 9:6, perh. Hb 6:7. [eulogy]

εὐμετάδοτος, ον generous 1 Ti 6:18.*

Εὐνίκη, ης, ἡ Eunice 2 Ti 1:5.*

εὐνοέω be well disposed (to), make friends (with) Mt 5:25.*

εὔνοια, ας, ἡ good will, enthusiasm Eph 6:7.*

εὐνουχίζω emasculate, make a eunuch of Mt 19:12.*

εὐνοῦχος, ου, ὁ emasculated man, eunuch Mt 19:12; Ac 8:27, 34, 36, 38f.*

εὐξαίμην 1 aor. mid. opt. of εὔχομαι.

Εὐοδία, ας, ἡ Euodia Phil 4:2.*

εὐοδόω get along well, prosper, succeed Ro 1:10; 3 J 2; gain 1 Cor 16:2.*

εὐπάρεδρος, ον constant, devoted 1 Cor 7:35.*

εὐπειθής, ές gen. οὓς obedient, compliant, willing to give in Js 3:17.*

εὐπερίσπαστος, ον easily distracting Hb 12:1 v.l.*

εὐπερίστατος, ον easily ensnaring, constricting, obstructing Hb 12:1.*

εὐποιΐα, ας, ἡ the doing of good Hb 13:16.*

εὐπορέω have plenty, be well off καθὼς εὐπορεῖτό τις according to one's (financial) ability Ac 11:29.*

εὐπορία, ας, ἡ prosperity Ac 19:25.*

εὐπρέπεια, ας, ἡ beauty Js 1:11.*

εὐπρόσδεκτος, ον acceptable, pleasant, welcome Ro 15:16, 31; 2 Cor 6:2; 8:12; 1 Pt 2:5.*

εὐπρόσεδρος, ον constant 1 Cor 7:35 v.l.*

εὐπροσωπέω make a good showing Gal 6:12.*

εὐρακύλων, ωνος, ὁ Euraquilo, the northeast wind Ac 27:14.*

εὑρέθην, εὕρηκα, εὑρήσω 1 aor. pass., pf. act., and fut. act. ind. of εὑρίσκω.

εὑρίσκω find, discover, come upon Mt 7:7f; Mk 14:55; Lk 6:7; 11:24; J 7:34, 36; Ac 13:6, 28; 27:6; Ro 7:21; 2 Cor 12:20; Rv 20:15. Find, obtain Lk 1:30; 2 Ti 1:18; Hb 4:16; 9:12. Pass. be found, find oneself, be Ac 8:40; Phil 3:9; 1 Pt 2:22; prove to be Ro 7:10; be judged 2 Pt 3:10. [eureka, Archimedes' exclamation; heuristic]

εὕροιεν, εὗρον 2 aor. act. opt. 3 pl. and 2 aor. act. ind. of εὑρίσκω.

εὐροκλύδων, ωνος, ὁ Euroclydon, the southeast wind. Another form is εὐρυκλύδων; both as variant readings for εὐρακύλων in Ac 27:14.*

εὐρύχωρος, ον broad, spacious Mt 7:13.*

εὐσέβεια, ας, ἡ piety, godliness, religion Ac 3:12; 1 Ti 2:2; 3:16; 4:7f; 6:3, 5f, 11; 2 Ti 3:5; Tit 1:1; 2 Pt 1:3, 6f. Pl. godly acts 2 Pt 3:11.*

εὐσεβέω worship Ac 17:23. Show piety toward 1 Ti 5:4.*

εὐσεβής, ές devout, godly, pious, reverent Ac 10:2, 7; 2 Pt 2:9.* [Eusebius]

εὐσεβῶς adv. in a godly manner 2 Ti 3:12; Tit 2:12.*

εὔσημος, ον easily recognizable, clear, distinct 1 Cor 14:9.*

εὔσπλαγχνος, ον tenderhearted, compassionate Eph 4:32; 1 Pt 3:8.*

εὐσχημονέω behave in an affected manner 1 Cor 13:5 v.l.*

εὐσχημόνως adv. decently, becomingly, properly Ro 13:13; 1 Cor 14:40; 1 Th 4:12.*

εὐσχημοσύνη, ης, ἡ propriety, decorum, presentability 1 Cor 12:23.*

εὐσχήμων, ον, gen. ονος proper, presentable 1 Cor 12:24. Prominent, of high standing Mk 15:43; Ac 13:50; 17:12, 34 v.l. τὸ εὔ. good order 1 Cor 7:35.*

εὐτόνως adv. powerfully, vigorously, vehemently Lk 23:10; Ac 18:28.*

εὐτραπελία, ας, ἡ coarse jesting, buffoonery Eph 5:4.*

Εὔτυχος, ου, ὁ Eutychus Ac 20:9.*

εὐφημία, ας, ἡ good report 2 Cor 6:8.*

εὔφημος, ον praiseworthy, appealing Phil 4:8.* [euphemism]

εὐφορέω bear good crops, be fruitful Lk 12:16.* [euphoria, εὖ + φέρω]

εὐφραίνω act. gladden, cheer 2 Cor 2:2. Pass. be glad, enjoy oneself, rejoice, be merry Lk 12:19; 15:32; Ac 2:26; 7:41; Ro 15:10. [euphrasy, an herb]

εὐφρανθῆναι 1 aor. pass. inf. of εὐφραίνω.

Εὐφράτης, ου, ὁ the Euphrates river Rv 9:14; 16:12.*

εὐφροσύνη, ης, ἡ joy, gladness, cheerfulness Ac 2:28; 14:17.* [Euphrosyne, one of the Graces]

εὐχαριστέω give thanks, render or return thanks Mt 26:27; Mk 8:6; Lk 17:16; 18:11; Ac 27:35; 28:15; Ro 1:21; 1 Cor 14:17f; Col 1:3, 12; 1 Th 1:2; 2:13.

εὐχαριστία, ας, ἡ thankfulness, gratitude Ac 24:3. The rendering of thanks, thanksgiving 2 Cor 9:11; Eph 5:4; Col 2:7; 1 Th 3:9; Rv 4:9. Prayer of thanks-

giving 1 Cor 14:16; 2 Cor 9:12. Lord's Supper, Eucharist 1 Cor 10:16 v.l.

εὐχάριστος, ον thankful Col 3:15.*

εὐχή, ῆς, ἡ—1. prayer ἡ εὐ. τῆς πίστεως the prayer offered in faith Js 5:15.—2. oath, vow Ac 18:18; 21:23.*

εὔχομαι—1. pray (for) Ac 26:29; 2 Cor 13:7, 9; Js 5:16 v.l.—2. wish (for) Ac 27:29; Ro 9:3; 3 J 2.*

εὔχρηστος, ον useful, serviceable 2 Ti 2:21; 4:11; Phlm 11.*

εὐψυχέω be glad, have courage Phil 2:19.*

εὐωδία, ας, ἡ aroma, fragrance 2 Cor 2:15; Eph 5:2; Phil 4:18.*

εὐώνυμος, ον left, as opposed to 'right' Mt 20:21, 23; 25:33, 41; Mk 15:27; Ac 21:3; Rv 10:2.

εὐωχία, ας, ἡ banquet, feasting Jd 12 v.l.*

ἔφαγον 2 aor. act. ind. of ἐσθίω. [Cf. omophagous, eating raw flesh.]

ἐφάλλομαι leap (upon) Ac 19:16.*

ἐφαλόμην 2 aor. mid. ind. of ἐφάλλομαι.

ἐφάνην 2 aor. pass. ind. of φαίνω.

ἐφάπαξ adv.—1. at once, at one time 1 Cor 15:6.—2. once for all Ro 6:10; Hb 7:27; 9:12; 10:10.*

Ἐφέσιος, ία, ιον Ephesian Ac 19:28, 34f; 21:29.*

Ἔφεσος, ου, ἡ Ephesus, a seaport in w. Asia Minor, famous for the worship of Artemis. Ac 18:19, 21, 24; 19:1, 17, 26; 1 Cor 15:32; 16:8.

ἐφευρετής, οῦ, ὁ inventor, contriver Ro 1:30.*

ἔφη impf. 3 sing. or 2 aor. act. 3 sing. of φημί.

ἐφημερία, ας, ἡ class or division of priests Lk 1:5, 8.*

ἐφήμερος, ον for the day, daily Js 2:15.*

ἔφθασα 1 aor. act. ind. of φθάνω.

ἐφικέσθαι 2 aor. mid. inf. of ἐφικνέομαι.

ἐφικνέομαι come (to), reach 2 Cor 10:13f.*

ἐφίστημι—1. pres. and aor. (2 aor. act. ind. ἐπέστην) stand by or near, ap-

proach, appear Lk 4:39; 10:40; Ac 4:1; 6:12; 10:17; 1 Th 5:3. *Attack* Ac 17:5. ἐπίστηθι *stand by, be ready* 2 Ti 4:2.—2. pf. (act. ind. ἐφέστηκα, ptc. ἐφεστώς) *stand by, be present* Ac 22:20; 28:2. *Be imminent* 2 Ti 4:6.

Ἐφραίμ, ὁ indecl. *Ephraim*, a city J 11:54.*

ἔφυγον 2 aor. act. ind. of φεύγω.

ἐφφαθά Aramaic word *be opened* Mk 7:34.*

ἐχάρην 2 aor. pass. ind. of χαίρω.

ἐχθές adv. *yesterday* J 4:52; Ac 16:35 v.l.; 7:28; *of the past as a whole* Hb 13:8.*

ἔχθρα, ας, ἡ *enmity* Lk 23:12; Ro 8:7; Gal 5:20; Eph 2:14, 16. ἔ. τοῦ θεοῦ *enmity toward God* Js 4:4.*

ἐχθρός, ά, όν—1. as adj. *hated, hostile* Mt 13:28; Ro 11:28.—2. as noun ὁ ἐχθρός *the (personal) enemy* Mt 5:43f; Mk 12:36; Lk 1:74; 10:19; Ro 5:10; 12:20; 1 Cor 15:26; Gal 4:16; Phil 3:18; 2 Th 3:15.

ἔχιδνα, ης, ἡ *viper, snake* Mt 3:7; 12:34; 23:33; Lk 3:7; Ac 28:3.*

ἔχρησα 1 aor. act. ind. of κίχρημι.

ἔχω—I. act. transitive—1. *have, hold* Mt 26:7; Rv 1:16; 5:8. *Have on, wear* Mt 3:4; J 18:10; Rv 9:9, 17. *Keep, preserve* Lk 19:20; 1 Ti 3:9; Rv 6:9. *Seize* Mk 16:8.—2. *have as one's own, possess* lit. and fig. Mt 18:8f; 19:22; Lk 11:5; 15:4; 19:26; J 8:41; Ac 2:44; Ro 12:4; 1 Cor 4:7; 5:1; 7:2; Eph 5:5; Col 4:1; 1 J 2:23; Rv 18:19. *Of all conditions of body and soul have* Mt 11:18; J 5:42; Ac 28:9; Ro 10:2; 1 Cor 13:1; Hb 10:2, 19. *Have at hand, have at one's disposal* Mt 14:17; Mk 8:1; J 4:11; Phil 2:20; 1 J 2:1. *With indications of time and age* πεντήκοντα ἔτη ἔχειν *be fifty years old* J 8:57. πολὺν χρόνον ἔχειν *be for a long time* 5:6. ἡλικίαν ἔχειν *be of age* 9:21, 23. *Have = have something over one, be under something* ἀνάγκην ἔχειν *be under necessity* 1 Cor 7:37; *be compelled* Lk 14:18. χρείαν ἔ. *be in need* Eph 4:28; *need* Lk 19:31, 34. διακονίαν 2 Cor 4:1. *Have*

within oneself Mk 13:17; J 5:26; 2 Cor 1:9; Phil 1:7.—3. *have* or *include in itself, bring about, cause* Hb 10:35; Js 1:4; 2:17; 1 J 4:18.—4. *consider, look upon, view* Mt 14:5; 21:46; Mk 11:32; Lk 14:18f; Phil 2:29.—5. ἔ. *with inf. following have the possibility, can, be able, be in a position* Mt 18:25; Lk 12:4; Ac 4:14; 25:26; Hb 6:13; 2 Pt 1:15. *One must* Lk 12:50; 2 J 12.—6. *Special combinations:* ἔ. ἐν ἐπιγνώσει *acknowledge* Ro 1:28. ἐν ἐμοὶ οὐκ ἔχει οὐδέν *he has no hold on me* J 14:30. ἔ. κατὰ πρόσωπον *meet face to face* Ac 25:16. ἔ. ὁδόν *be situated* (a certain distance) *away* Ac 1:12.—II. act., intrans., with an adverb *be, be situated* πῶς ἔχουσιν *how they are* Ac 15:36. ἑτοίμως ἔχειν *be ready* 2 Cor 12:14. κακῶς ἔ. *be sick* Mt 4:24. καλῶς ἔ. *be well, healthy* Mk 16:18. ἐσχάτως ἔχειν *be at the point of death* 5:23. τὸ νῦν ἔχον *for the present* Ac 24:25. *Other expressions:* Ac 7:1; 12:15; 1 Ti 5:25.—III. mid. *hold oneself fast, cling to* τὰ ἐχόμενα σωτηρίας *things that belong to salvation* Hb 6:9. ἐχόμενος *neighboring* Mk 1:38. *Of time immediately following:* τῇ ἐχομένῃ ἡμέρᾳ *on the next day* Ac 21:26; cf. 20:15; Lk 13:33.

ἐψεύσω 1 aor. mid. ind. 2 sing. of ψεύδομαι.

ἐῶν pres. act. ptc. of ἐάω.

ἑώρακα, ἑώρων pf. act. ind. and impf. act. 3 pl. of ὁράω.

ἕως—1. temporal conjunction *till, until* Mt 2:9; Mk 6:10; Lk 21:32; J 21:22f; Ac 2:35; 1 Cor 4:5; 2 Th 2:7; Hb 10:13. *As long as, while* Mk 6:45; Lk 17:8; J 9:4.—2. functions as prep. w. gen.: *of time until, up to* Mt 11:13; 27:64; Mk 14:25; Lk 23:44; Ac 1:22; 1 Cor 1:8. ἕως οὗ *until* Mt 13:33; Ac 21:26; 25:21. ἕως πότε *how long* Mt 9:19; J 10:24; Rv 6:10. *Of place as far as, to* Lk 2:15; Ac 1:8; 2 Cor 12:2. ἕως ἑπτάκις *as many as seven times* Mt 18:21f. ἕως ἔσω *right into* Mk 14:54. οὐκ ἔστιν ἕως ἑνός *there is not even one* Ro 3:12.

ς

ς the stigma or vau, an obsolete letter, is used as the numeral *six* (ςʹ) in the

entry χξςʹ Rv 13:18 v.l.

Z

Ζαβουλών, ὁ indecl. *Zebulun,* an Israelite tribe Mt 4:13, 15; Rv 7:8; Lk 4:31 v.l.*

Ζακχαῖος, ου, ὁ *Zacchaeus* Lk 19:2, 5, 8.*

Ζάρα, ὁ indecl. *Zerah* Mt 1:3.*

ζαφθάνι the reading of ms. D for *σαβαχθάνι* in Mt 27:46; Mk 15:34.*

Ζαχαρίας, ου, ὁ *Zechariah*—**1.** father of John the Baptist Lk 1 passim; 3:2.—**2.** son of Barachiah Mt 23:35; Lk 11:51.—**3.** Z. the prophet, as v.l. for Jeremiah in Mt 27:9.*

[ζάω] contracted **ζῶ** *live*—**1.** of natural life Mt 4:4; Lk 24:5; Ro 7:1, 2, 3; 1 Cor 15:45; Phil 1:22. Of the conduct of life Lk 2:36; Ac 26:5; Ro 14:7; 2 Cor 5:15. *Be well, recover* Mk 5:23. Of God Mt 26:63; Hb 3:12; *ζῶ ἐγώ as surely as I live* Ro 14:11. *τὸ ζῆν life* 2 Cor 1:8. Fig. J 4:10f; Ac 7:38; 1 Pt 1:3; 2:4.—**2.** of the life of the child of God Lk 10:28; J 5:25; Ro 1:17; 2 Cor 13:4; Gal 2:20; 1 Th 5:10.

ζβέννυμι alternate form of *σβέννυμι.*

Ζεβεδαῖος, ου, ὁ *Zebedee,* father of the apostles James and John Mt 4:21; Mk 10:35; Lk 5:10; J 21:2.

ζεστός, ή, όν *hot* Rv 3:15f.*

ζεύγνυμι *connect, join* (lit. with a yoke) Mk 10:9 v.l.*

ζεῦγος, ους, τό *yoke,* of two animals united by a yoke Lk 14:19. *Pair* 2:24.*

ζευκτηρία, ας, ἡ *bands, ropes* ('pendant' or 'pennant,' nautical t.t.) that tied the rudders Ac 27:40.*

Ζεύς, Διός, acc. **Δία, ὁ** *Zeus,* king of the Greek gods Ac 14:12, 13.*

ζέω *boil, seethe* fig. *ζέων τῷ πνεύματι* with burning zeal Ac 18:25, but *τῷ πνεύματι ζέοντες maintain(ing) the spiritual glow* Ro 12:11.* [*eczema,* ἐκ + ζεῖν]

ζῇ pres. act. ind. 3 sing. of [ζάω].

ζηλεύω *be eager, earnest* Rv 3:19.*

ζῆλος, ου, ὁ and **ζῆλος, ους, τό**—**1.** in a good sense *zeal, ardor* Ro 10:2; 2 Cor 7:11; 9:2; Phil 3:6.—**2.** in a bad sense *jealousy, envy* Ac 5:17; Ro 13:13; Js 3:14, 16; *factionalism, party strife* 1 Cor 3:3; 2 Cor 12:20; Gal 5:20 [*zeal*].

ζηλόω—**1.** in a good sense *strive (for), desire* 1 Cor 12:31; 14:1, 39. *Be deeply concerned about* Gal 4:17. *Show zeal* 4:18.—**2.** in a bad sense *be filled with jealousy* or *envy (toward)* Ac 7:9; 1 Cor 13:4; Js 4:2.

ζηλωτής, οῦ, ὁ *zealot, enthusiastic adherent, one who is eager* or *zealous for* w. gen. Ac 22:3; 1 Cor 14:12; Tit 2:14; 1 Pt 3:13. Of Simon as a former member of a Jewish faction Lk 6:15; Ac 1:13.

ζημία, ας, ἡ *damage, loss* Ac 27:10, 21; Phil 3:7, 8.*

ζημιόω *inflict injury* or *punishment.* Pass. *suffer damage* or *loss, forfeit* with acc. of respect or specification Mt 16:26; Mk 8:36; Lk 9:25; Phil 3:8; without acc. 2 Cor 7:9. *Be punished* 1 Cor 3:15.*

ζῆν pres. act. inf. of [ζάω].

Ζηνᾶς, acc. -ᾶν, ὁ *Zenas* Tit 3:13.*

Ζήνων, ωνος, ὁ *Zeno* 2 Ti 4:19 v.l.*

ζητέω—1. *seek, look for* Mt 13:45; 18:12; Mk 1:37; Lk 19:10; J 18:4; Ac 10:19, 21; 2 Ti 1:17; *search for* Ac 17:27. *Investigate, examine, consider, deliberate* Mk 11:18; Lk 12:29; J 8:50; 16:19.— **2.** somewhat removed from the idea of seeking: *try to obtain, desire to possess* Mt 6:33; 26:59; Lk 22:6; J 5:44; Ro 2:7; Col 3:1. *Strive for, aim (at), desire, wish* Mt 12:46; Lk 17:33; J 1:38; Ac 16:10; 1 Cor 13:5; Gal 1:10. *Ask for, request, demand* Mk 8:11f; Lk 12:48; J 4:23; 2 Cor 13:3. Pass. *it is required* 1 Cor 4:2.

ζήτημα, ατος, τό *(controversial) question, issue* Ac 15:2; 18:15; 23:29; 25:19; 26:3.*

ζήτησις, εως, ἡ *investigation, controversial question, controversy, discussion, debate* J 3:25; Ac 15:2, 7; 25:20; 1 Ti 6:4; 2 Ti 2:23; Tit 3:9.*

ζιζάνιον, ου, τό *darnel, cheat* a troublesome weed resembling wheat Mt 13 passim.*

Ζμύρνα a variant of Σμύρνα.

Ζοροβαβέλ, ὁ, indecl. *Zerubbabel* (Ezra 2:2; 3:8) Mt 1:12f; Lk 3:27.*

ζόφος, ου, ὁ *darkness, gloom* Hb 12:18; in the nether regions, *hell* 2 Pt 2:4, 17; Jd 6, 13.*

ζυγός, οῦ, ὁ—1. *yoke* fig. Mt 11:29f; Ac 15:10; Gal 5:1; 1 Ti 6:1.—**2.** *balance, pair of scales* Rv 6:5.*

ζύμη, ης, ἡ *yeast, leaven* lit. Mt 16:12; Lk 13:21; 1 Cor 5:6; Gal 5:9. Fig. Mt 16:6, 11; Lk 12:1; 1 Cor 5:6–8. [*enzyme*]

ζυμόω *to ferment, leaven* Mt 13:33; Lk 13:21; 1 Cor 5:6; Gal 5:9.*

ζωγρέω *capture (alive)* Lk 5:10; 2 Ti 2:26.*

ζωή, ῆς, ἡ *life*—**1.** in the physical sense Lk 16:25; Ac 17:25; Ro 8:38; 1 Ti 4:8; Js 4:14.—**2.** of the life belonging to God, Christ, and the believer Mt 25:46; Mk 10:17, 30; J 1:4; 3:15f; 5:26; 6:35; Ac 5:20; Ro 6:4; 8:2; Eph 4:18; Phil 2:16; 1 Ti 6:19; Js 1:12; Rv 2:7; 13:8. [*Zoë*]

ζώνη, ης, ἡ *belt, girdle* Mt 3:4; 10:9; Mk 1:6; 6:8; Ac 21:11; Rv 1:13; 15:6.*

ζώννυμι or **ζωννύω** *gird* J 21:18; Ac 12:8.*

ζωογονέω *give life to, make alive* 1 Ti 6:13. *Keep* or *preserve alive* Lk 17:33; Ac 7:19.*

ζῷον, ου, τό *animal* in the usual sense Hb 13:11; 2 Pt 2:12; Jd 10. *Living thing* or *being* Rv 4:6–9; 6:1, 3, 5–7; 19:4. [*zoology*]

ζωοποιέω *make alive, give life to* J 5:21; 1 Cor 15:22, 36, 45; 2 Cor 3:6; 1 Pt 3:18; *bring to life* Ro 4:17.

ζῶσαι, ζώσω 1 aor. mid. impv. and fut. act. ind. of ζώννυμι.

Η

ἤ particle—**1.** disjunctive *or* Mt 5:17, 36; Mk 3:4; Ro 8:35; 14:13; Rv 3:15. ἤ . . . ἤ *either . . . or* Mt 6:24; Lk 16:13; 1 Cor 14:6. In interrogative sentences Mt 26:53; Lk 13:4; 1 Cor 9:7; Gal 1:10.— **2.** denoting comparison *than* Mt 10:15;

18:8, 9, 13; Mk 10:25; Lk 15:7; Ac 17:21; 1 Cor 9:15; 14:19. πρὶν ἤ before Mk 14:30; Lk 2:26; Ac 25:16.

ἤ adv. truly, perhaps the correct accentuation in 1 Cor 9:15.

ἤγαγον 2 aor. act. ind. of ἄγω.

ἤγγειλα 1 aor. act. ind. of ἀγγέλλω.

ἤγειρα 1 aor. act. ind. of ἐγείρω.

ἡγεμονεύω be leader, rule of a governor Lk 2:2 and a prefect 3:1.*

ἡγεμονία ας, ἡ leadership, chief command of the office of the Roman emperor Lk 3:1.* [hegemony]

ἡγεμών, όνος, ὁ prince Mt 2:6. Governor Mt 10:18; Mk 13:9; 1 Pt 2:14. Prefect, procurator Mt 27:2, 11, 14f; Lk 20:20; Ac 23:24; 24:1; 26:30.

ἡγέομαι—1. lead, guide pres. participle ὁ ἡγούμενος ruler, leader Mt 2:6; Lk 22:26; Ac 7:10; Hb 13:7, 17, 24. ὁ ἡγούμενος τοῦ λόγου the chief speaker Ac 14:12.—2. think, consider, regard Ac 26:2; 2 Cor 9:5; Phil 2:3; 3:8; Hb 10:29; Js 1:2; w. δίκαιον consider it a duty or responsibility. 2 Pt 1:13.

ἠγέρθην 1 aor. pass. ind. of ἐγείρω.

ἡγνικώς, ἡγνισμένος pf. act. ptc. and pf. pass. ptc. of ἁγνίζω.

ᾔδειν plupf. act. ind. 1 sing. of οἶδα.

ἡδέως adv. gladly 2 Cor 11:19. ἡ. ἀκούειν like to hear Mk 6:20; 12:37. Superlative ἥδιστα very gladly 2 Cor 12:9, 15.*

ἤδη adv. now, already, by this time, really Mt 5:28; 15:32; 17:12; Mk 4:37; 6:35; Lk 21:30; J 3:18; 4:35. ἤδη καί even now Lk 3:9. ἤδη ποτέ now at length Ro 1:10; Phil 4:10.

ἥδιστα see ἡδέως.

ἡδονή, ῆς, ἡ pleasure, enjoyment in an unfavorable sense Lk 8:14; Tit 3:3; Js 4:1, 3; 2 Pt 2:13.* [hedonist]

ἠδυνάσθην, ἠδυνήθην 1 aor. pass. ind. forms of δύναμαι.

ἡδύοσμον, ου, τό mint (garden plant) Mt 23:23; Lk 11:42.*

ἤθελον impf. act. of θέλω.

ἦθος, ους, τό custom, usage, habit 1 Cor 15:33.* [Cf. ἔθος.]

ἠκαιρεῖσθε impf. 2 pl. of ἀκαιρέομαι.

ἥκω have come, be present Mt 8:11; Mk 8:3; Lk 15:27; J 4:47; 8:42; Hb 10:37; Rv 15:4; 18:8.

ἡλάμην 1 aor. mid. ind. of ἄλλομαι.

ἠλεήθην, ἠλεημένος 1 aor. pass. ind. and pf. pass. ptc. of ἐλεέω.

ἦλθα, ἦλθον 2 aor. act. ind. forms of ἔρχομαι.

ἡλί (also spelled ἡλι, ἠλει, ἡλει) Hebrew my God Mt 27:46.*

Ἡλί, ὁ indecl. Heli Lk 3:23.*

Ἡλίας, ου, ὁ Elijah (1 Kings 17–20) Mt 11:14; 17:3f, 10–12; Mk 15:35f; Lk 1:17; 4:25f; J 1:21, 25; Js 5:17. ἐν Ἡλίᾳ in the story of Elijah Ro 11:2.

ἡλικία, ας, ἡ—1. age, time of life. This sense is possible in Mt 6:27 = Lk 12:25, but it is probable that hyperbolic humor about increasing one's height underlies the maxim; see 2. Mature age Eph 4:13. Years Lk 2:52. ἡλικίαν ἔχειν be of age J 9:21, 23. παρὰ καιρὸν ἡλικίας past the normal age Hb 11:11.—2. bodily stature Lk 19:3. This mng. is also possible for Lk 2:52 and Eph 4:13 above and is probable for Mt 6:27 = Lk 12:25.*

ἡλίκος, η, ον how great, how large Col 2:1; Js 3:5; Gal 6:11 v.l.*

ἥλιος, ου, ὁ the sun Mt 13:6, 43; Lk 21:25; 23:45; Ac 13:11; 27:20; 1 Cor 15:41; Rv 7:2, 16; 21:23.

ἧλος, ου, ὁ nail J 20:25.*

ἤλπικα, ἤλπισα pf. and 1 aor. act. ind. of ἐλπίζω.

ἡμάρτησα, ἥμαρτον 1 aor. and 2 aor. act. ind. of ἁμαρτάνω.

ἡμεῖς nom. pl. of ἐγώ.

ἡμέρα, ας, ἡ day—1. of the period of daylight Mt 4:2; Mk 4:27; Lk 4:42; 9:12; J 1:39; 11:9; 2 Pt 1:19; Rv 8:12. Fig. 1 Th 5:5.—2. of civil or legal day, including the night Mt 6:34; 28:15; Mk 2:1; Lk 17:4; Ac 13:31; Ro 8:36; 1 Cor 10:8; Hb 3:13; Rv 1:10; 9:15.—3. of a day appointed for a special purpose Mt 10:15; Lk 17:24, 30; Ac 28:23; 1 Cor 4:3; 5:5; Hb 10:25; Rv 16:14.—4. of a longer period time Mt 2:1; Lk 21:22; Ac 5:36; 2 Cor 6:2; 2 Ti 3:1; Hb 5:7; 8:9 [ephemeral, ἐπί + ἡμέρα] ἡμέτερος, α, ον *our* Ac 2:11; Ro 15:4; 1 J 1:3. τὸ ἡμ. *what is ours* Lk 16:12 v.l.

ἦ μήν see ἦ.

ἤμην impf. act. of εἰμί.

ἡμιθανής, ές *half dead* Lk 10:30.*

ἥμισυς, εια, υ *half* Lk 19:8. τὸ ἥ. *one half* Mk 6:23; Rv 11:9, 11; 12:14.*

ἡμίωρον, ου, τό *a half hour* Rv 8:1.*

ἠμφιεσμένος pf. pass. ptc. of ἀμφιέννυμι.

ἤν impf. of εἰμί.

ἤνεγκα, ἠνέχθην 1 aor. act. and pass. ind. of φέρω.

ἠνεῳγμένος, ἠνέῳξα, ἠνεῴχθην pf. mid. ptc., 1 aor. act., and 1 aor. pass. ind. of ἀνοίγω.

ἡνίκα particle denoting time *when, at the time when* with ἄν *whenever* 2 Cor 3:15; with ἐάν *when, every time that* vs. 16.*

ἠνοίγην, ἠνοίχθην 2 aor. pass. ind. and 1 aor. pass. ind. of ἀνοίγω.

ἠντληκώς pf. act. ptc. of ἀντλέω.

ἤπερ strengthened form of ἤ *than* J 12:43.*

ἤπιος, α, ον *gentle* 1 Th 2:7 v.l.; 2 Ti 2:24.*

ἠπίστησα, ἠπίστουν 1 aor. act. ind. and impf. act. of ἀπιστέω.

Ἤρ, ὁ indecl. *Er* Lk 3:28.*

ἦρα, ἤρθην 1 aor. act. and pass. ind. of αἴρω.

ἠργασάμην 1 aor. ind. of ἐργάζομαι.

ἤρεμος, ον *quiet, tranquil* 1 Ti 2:2.*

ἤρεσε 1 aor. act. ind. of ἀρέσκω.

ἤρθην, ἦρκα, ἦρμαι 1 aor. pass., pf. act., and pf. pass. ind. of αἴρω.

ἡρπάγην 2 aor. pass. ind. of ἁρπάζω.

ἠρχόμην impf. of ἔρχομαι.

Ἡρῴδης, ου, ὁ *Herod*—1. Herod I, the Great (41–4 B.C.) Mt 2:1–22.—2. Herod Antipas, son of Herod I Mk 6:14–22; Lk 3:1, 19; 13:31; 23:7; Ac 4:27.—3. Herod Agrippa I, grandson of Herod I Ac 12 passim.

Ἡρῳδιανοί, ῶν, οἱ *the Herodians*, partisans of Herod I and his family Mt 22:16; Mk 3:6; 8:15 v.l.; 12:13.*

Ἡρῳδιάς, άδος, ἡ *Herodias*, wife of Herod Antipas Mt 14:3, 6; Mk 6:17, 19, 22; Lk 3:19.*

Ἡρῳδίων, ωνος, ὁ *Herodion* Ro 16:11.*

Ἡσαΐας, ου, ὁ *Isaiah* the prophet and his book Mt 3:3; 13:14; Mk 1:2; Lk 4:17; J 12:38f; Ac 8:28; Ro 9:27, 29.

Ἡσαῦ, ὁ indecl. *Esau* (Gen 27 and 28) Ro 9:13; Hb 11:20; 12:16.*

ἦσθα impf. 2 sing. of εἰμί.

ἡσσώθην 1 aor. pass. ind. of ἑσσόομαι.

ἥσσων or ἥττων, ον, gen. ονος comparative without a positive *lesser, inferior, weaker* Mt 20:28 v.l. εἰς τὸ ἧσσον *for the worse* 1 Cor 11:17. The neut. as adv. *less* 2 Cor 12:15.*

ἡσυχάζω *be quiet, rest, abstain from work* Lk 23:56; 1 Th 4:11; *remain silent* Lk 14:4; Ac 11:18; 21:14; 22:2 v.l.*

ἡσυχία, ας, ἡ *quietness, rest.* Opposite of causing a disturbance *orderliness* 2 Th 3:12. *Quietness* as a listening posture 1 Ti 2:11f; Ac 21:40 v.l. παρέχειν ἡσυχίαν *quiet down, give a hearing, be orderly* Ac 22:2.*

ἡσύχιος, ον *quiet* 1 Ti 2:2; 1 Pt 3:4.*

ἤτοι strengthened form of ἤ; ἤτοι . . . ἤ *either . . . or* Ro 6:16.*

ἡττάομαι *be defeated (by), succumb (to)* 2 Pt 2:19f; *be inferior* 2 Cor 12:13 v.l.*

ἥττημα, ατος, τό *defeat* Ro 11:12; 1 Cor 6:7.*

ἤτω impv. 3 sing. of εἰμί.

ηὐξήθην, ηὔξησα 1 aor. pass. and act. ind. of αὐξάνω.

ηὐφράνθην 1 aor. pass. ind. of εὐφραίνω.

ἤφιε impf. 3 sing. of ἀφίημι.

ἠχέω *sound, ring out* 1 Cor 13:1. *Roar, thunder* Lk 21:25 v.l.*

ἤχθην 1 aor. pass. ind. of ἄγω.

ἦχος, ου, ὁ *sound, tone, noise* Ac 2:2; Hb 12:19. *Report, news* Lk 4:37.*

ἦχος, ους, τό *sound, tone, noise* Lk 21:25.*

ἠχώ, οῦς, ἡ *sound.* If the gen. in Lk 21:25 is accented ἠχοῦς, the form comes from this nominative. [echo]

ἡψάμην 1 aor. mid. ind. of ἅπτω.

Θ

θά an Aramaic term in the phrase μαράνα θά, q.v.

θάβιτα Mk 5:41 v.l.; see ραβιθά.

Θαδδαῖος, ου, ὁ Thaddaeus Mt 10:3; Mk 3:18.*

θάλασσα, ης, ἡ sea Mt 23:15; Mk 9:42; Ac 7:36; 10:6, 32; 2 Cor 11:26; Rv 8:8f; Lake (of Galilee) Mt 4:18; 8:24; J 6:1. [thalassic]

θάλπω cherish, comfort Eph 5:29; 1 Th 2:7.*

Θαμάρ, ἡ indecl. Tamar (Gen 38) Mt 1:3.*

θαμβέω intrans. be astounded Ac 9:6 v.l. Trans. pass. be astounded, amazed Mk 1:27; 10:24, 32; Ac 3:11 v.l.*

θάμβος, ους, τό and **θάμβος, ου, ὁ** astonishment, fear Lk 4:36; 5:9; Ac 3:10.*

θανάσιμος, ον deadly Mk 16:18.*

θανατηφόρος, ον death-bringing, deadly Js 3:8.*

θάνατος, ου, ὁ death—**1.** of natural death Mt 10:21; 20:18; J 11:4, 13; Ac 22:4; Ro 5:12, 14, 17; Phil 2:27, 30; Hb 7:23; Rv 18:8.—**2.** fig., of spiritual death Mt 4:16; J 8:51; Ro 1:32; 7:10, 13; 1 J 5:16f. [thanatopsis, θανατ- + ὄψις]

θανατόω put to death lit. Mt 10:21; Mk 14:55; Lk 21:16; 2 Cor 6:9. Be in danger of death Ro 8:36. Fig. Ro 7:4; 8:13.

θάπτω bury Mt 8:21f; Lk 9:59f; Ac 5:6, 9f; 1 Cor 15:4.

Θάρα, ὁ indecl. Terah, father of Abraham Lk 3:34.*

θαρρέω be confident, be courageous 2 Cor 5:6, 8; have confidence in someone 7:16; (speak) with confidence Hb 13:6; θ. εἴς τινα be bold toward someone 2 Cor 10:1.*

θαρσέω by-form of θαρρέω be cheerful, be courageous. θάρσει, θαρσεῖτε Courage! Cheer up! Don't be afraid! Mt 9:2, 22; 14:27; Mk 6:50; 10:49; J 16:33; Ac 23:11.*

θάρσος, ους, τό courage Ac 28:15.*

θαῦμα, ατος, τό a wonder, marvel 2 Cor 11:14. ἐθαύμασα θαῦμα I wondered in great amazement Rv 17:6.* [thaumaturgy, θαῦμα + ἔργον]

θαυμάζω wonder, marvel, be astonished Mt 8:10; Mk 15:5; Lk 11:38; Gal 1:6; Rv 17:6; esp. at divine epiphanies or deeds Mt 15:31; Lk 1:21, 63; J 5:20; 7:21; Ac 2:7; 7:31. Admire, wonder at Lk 7:9; J 5:28; 2 Th 1:10. Flatter Jd 16. Pass. wonder, be amazed Rv 13:3; 17:8.

θαυμάσιος, α, ον wonderful, remarkable Mt 21:15.*

θαυμαστός, ή, όν wonderful, marvelous, remarkable Mt 21:42; Mk 12:11; J 9:30; 1 Pt 2:9; Rv 15:1, 3.*

θεά, ᾶς, ἡ goddess Ac 19:27.*

θεάομαι see, look at Mt 11:7; Mk 16:11, 14; Lk 5:27; J 1:14, 32; 4:35; Ac 21:27; 1 J 1:1; come to see, visit Ro 15:24; greet Mt 22:11. Pass. be noticed Mt 6:1. [Cf. θέατρον.]

θεατρίζω put to shame, expose publicly Hb 10:33.*

θέατρον, ου, τό theater Ac 19:29, 31. Play, spectacle 1 Cor 4:9.*

θεῖον, ου, τό sulphur Lk 17:29; Rv 9:17f; 14:10; 19:20; 20:10; 21:8.*

θεῖος, θεία, θεῖον divine 2 Pt 1:3f. τὸ θεῖον divine being, divinity Ac 17:29, 27 v.l.; Tit 1:9 v.l.*

θειότης, ητος, ἡ divinity, divine nature as manifested in performance Ro 1:20.*

θείς 2 aor. act. ptc. of τίθημι.

θειώδης, ες sulphurous Rv 9:17.*

Θέκλα, ης, ἡ Thecla 2 Ti 3:11 v.l.*

θέλημα, ατος, τό will Mt 6:10; Lk 12:47; J 6:38–40; Ac 21:14; Ro 2:18; 12:2; 15:32; Eph 1:9; Hb 10:10; 2 Pt 1:21. Desire 1 Cor 7:37. τὰ θελήματα τ. σαρκός what the flesh desires Eph 2:3.

θέλησις, εως, ἡ will Hb 2:4.*

θέλω—1. *wish of desire, wish to have, desire, want* Mt 20:21; Mk 10:43; Lk 5:39; J 9:27; Ro 1:13; Gal 4:20. Js 2:20. τί θέλω *how I wish* Lk 12:49. τί θέλετε ποιήσω ὑμῖν; *what do you want me to do for you?* Mt 20:32.—**2.** *wish, will* of purpose or resolve, *wish to do* Mt 20:14; Mk 3:13; J 6:21, 67; Ac 18:21; Ro 7:15f, 19f; 2 Cor 8:10; Col 1:27; Rv 11:5. οὐ θέλω *I will not* Mt 21:30 v.l.—**3.** τί θέλει τοῦτο εἶναι *what does this mean?* Ac 2:12; cf. 17:20; Lk 15:26 v.l.—**4.** *take pleasure in, like* Mt 27:43; Mk 12:38; Lk 20:46; Col 2:18.—**5.** *maintain* 2 Pt 3:5. [*monotheletism,* μόνος + θέλειν]

θεμέλιον, ου, τό *foundation* Ac 16:26.*

θεμέλιος, ου, ὁ *foundation* lit. Lk 6:48f; 14:29; Hb 11:10; *foundation stone* Rv 21:14, 19. Fig. Ro 15:20; 1 Cor 3:10–12; Hb 6:1; *treasure, reserve* 1 Ti 6:19.

θεμελιόω *found* Mt 7:25; Lk 6:48 v.l.; Hb 1:10. Fig. *establish, strengthen* Eph 3:17; Col 1:23; 1 Pt 5:10.*

θεοδίδακτος, ον *taught by God* 1 Th 4:9.*

θεολόγος, ου, ὁ *one who speaks of God* or *divine things* Rv inscr. v.l.* [*theologian*]

θεομαχέω *fight against God* Ac 23:9 v.l.* [*theomachy*]

θεομάχος, ον *fighting against God* Ac 5:39.*

θεόπνευστος, ον *inspired by God* 2 Ti 3:16.*

θεός, οῦ, ὁ and ἡ *God, god* a term generally used in the ancient world of beings that have powers or confer benefits that lie beyond the capacity of mortals. In translation the capitalized term *God* refers to a specific deity and ordinarily to the One God of Israel.— **I.** God of Israel, as opposed to other so-called deities Gal 4:8; as revealed to the Patriarchs Lk 20:37; as Creator Mk 13:19; as the Father who sent Jesus Christ J 17:3; as Father uniquely of Jesus Christ Ro 15:6; as the Parent of believers 1:7; ἀστεῖος τῷ θεῷ *very beautiful* (lit. 'beautiful in the sight of God') Ac 7:20; ὁ θεός as a vocative *O God!* Lk 18:11.—**II.** Other than the God of Israel—**1.** of nonmortals, nonspec-

ified *so-called gods* 1 Cor 8:5 (in the heavens); Gal 4:8; God Raphia Ac 7:43; ἡ θεός *the Goddess* (Artemis), who is unique from the perspective of the non-Christian and non-Jewish Ephesians Ac 19:37; the Devil, *the God of this age* 2 Cor 4:4.—**2.** of human beings, nonspecified J 10:34f; 1 Cor 8:5 (on earth); Herod Ac 12:22; Paul 28:6.—**3.** of a thing, the belly Phil 3:19.—**III.** of Christ J 1:1, 18; 20:28; Hb 1:8 (vocative ὁ θεός); 2 Pt 1:1.

θεοσέβεια, ας, ἡ *reverence for God, piety, religion* 1 Ti 2:10.*

θεοσεβής, ές *God-fearing, devout* J 9:31.*

θεοστυγής, ές *hating God,* perhaps *God-forsaken* Ro 1:30.*

θεότης, ητος, ἡ *deity, divinity* Col 2:9.*

Θεόφιλος, ου, ὁ *Theophilus* Lk 1:3; Ac 1:1.*

θεραπεία, ας, ἡ *serving, care* hence *healing* Lk 9:11; Rv 22:2. ἡ θ. = οἱ θεράποντες *servants* Lk 12:42; Mt 24:45 v.l.* [*therapy*]

θεραπεύω *serve* Ac 17:25. *Care for,* then *heal, restore* Mt 4:23f; Mk 3:2, 10; Lk 4:23, 40; 14:3; Rv 13:3. [*therapeutic*]

θεράπων, οντος, ὁ *servant* Hb 3:5.*

θερίζω *reap, harvest* lit. Mt 6:26; J 4:36; Js 5:4. Fig. Lk 19:21f; J 4:37f; Gal 6:7–9; Rv 14:15f.

θερισμός, οῦ, ὁ *harvest* Mt 13:30, 39; Mk 4:29; J 4:35a. Fig. Mt 9:37f; Lk 10:2; J 4:35b; Rv 14:15.*

θεριστής, οῦ, ὁ *reaper, harvester* Mt 13:30, 39.*

θερμαίνω mid. *warm oneself, keep warm* Mk 14:54, 67; J 18:18, 25; Js 2:16.*

θέρμη, ης, ἡ *heat* Ac 28:3.* [*thermometer,* θέρμη + μέτρον]

θέρος, ους, τό *summer* Mt 24:32; Mk 13:28; Lk 21:30.*

θέσθε 2 aor. mid. impv. 2 pl. of τίθημι. [Cf. *thesis*.]

Θεσσαλία, ας, ἡ *Thessaly,* a region in northeast Greece Ac 17:15 v.l.*

Θεσσαλονικεύς, έως, ὁ *Thessalonian,* an inhabitant of Thessalonica Ac 20:4; 27:2; 1 Th 1:1, inscr.; 2 Th 1:1, inscr.*

Θεσσαλονίκη, ης, ἡ *Thessalonica*, a seaport city in Macedonia Ac 17:1, 11, 13; Phil 4:16; 2 Ti 4:10.*

Θευδᾶς, ᾶ, ὁ *Theudas* Ac 5:36.*

θεωρέω *see, look at, observe, perceive* Mt 27:55; Mk 12:41; Lk 14:29; J 12:45; 14:17; 20:12; Ac 7:56; 9:7; 17:22; *view* Mt 28:1; *catch sight of, notice* Mk 3:11; *experience* death J 8:51. [*theorem; theory*]

θεωρία, ας, ἡ *spectacle, sight* Lk 23:48.*

θήκη, ης, ἡ *sheath* J 18:11.*

θηλάζω *suck*—**1.** of a mother *nurse* (a baby at the breast) Mt 24:19; Mk 13:17; Lk 21:23.—**2.** of an infant *nurse* (at the breast) Lk 11:27; pl. ptc. as subst. *nursing babies* Mt 21:16.*

θῆλυς, εια, υ *female* Mt 19:4; Mk 10:6; Ro 1:26, 27; Gal 3:28.*

θήρα, ας, ἡ *net, trap* Ro 11:9.*

θηρεύω *hunt, catch* fig. Lk 11:54.*

θηριομαχέω *fight with wild animals* probably fig. 1 Cor 15:32.*

θηρίον, ου, τό *(wild) animal, beast* lit. Mk 1:13; Hb 12:20; Js 3:7; of animal-like beings Rv 11:7; 13:1ff; 20:4, 10. Fig. of persons, *beast, monster* Tit 1:12. [*therianthropic*, θήριον + ἄνθρωπος; *theriomorphic*, θ. + μορφή]

θησαυρίζω *store up, gather, save* lit. Mt 6:19; Lk 12:21; 1 Cor 16:2; 2 Cor 12:14; Js 5:3. Fig. Mt 6:20; Ro 2:5; *reserve* 2 Pt 3:7.*

θησαυρός, οῦ, ὁ *treasure* lit. Mt 6:19, 21; 13:44; Lk 12:34; Hb 11:26. Fig. Mt 6:20; Mk 10:21; Lk 6:45; 2 Cor 4:7; Col 2:3. *Treasure box* or *chest* Mt 2:11; *storehouse* 13:52. [*thesaurus*]

θήσω fut. act. ind. of τίθημι.

θιγγάνω *touch* Col 2:21; Hb 11:28; 12:20.*

θίγῃ 2 aor. act. subj. 3 sing. (Hb 12:20) of θιγγάνω.

θλίβω *press upon, crowd* Mk 3:9; *make narrow* Mt 7:14. *Oppress, afflict* pass. 2 Cor 1:6; 7:5; 1 Th 3:4; 1 Ti 5:10; Hb 11:37.

θλῖψις, εως, ἡ *oppression, affliction, tribulation* Mt 24:9, 21; Ac 11:19; Ro 12:12; 2 Cor 4:17; Col 1:24; 2 Th 1:6; Rv 2:9, 22; 7:14. *Difficult circum-*stances 2 Cor 8:13; Js 1:27. *Trouble* 2 Cor 2:4; Phil 1:17.

θνῄσκω *die* pf. τέθνηκα *have died, be dead* lit. Mk 15:44; Lk 8:49; J 19:33; Ac 14:19. Fig. 1 Ti 5:6.

θνητός, ή, όν *mortal* Ro 6:12; 8:11; 1 Cor 15:53f; 2 Cor 4:11; 5:4.*

θορυβάζω *cause trouble* pass. *be distracted* Lk 10:41.*

θορυβέω *throw into disorder* Ac 17:5; 21:13 v.l. Pass. *be troubled, aroused, distressed* Mt 9:23; Mk 5:39; 13:7 v.l.; Ac 20:10.*

θόρυβος, ου, ὁ *noise, clamor* Ac 21:34; *turmoil, excitement, uproar* Mt 26:5; 27:24; Mk 5:38; 14:2; Ac 20:1; 24:18.*

θραυματίζω *break* Lk 4:18 v.l.*

θραύω *break* pf. pass. ptc. τεθραυσμένοι *the downtrodden* Lk 4:18.*

θρέμμα, ατος, τό *(domesticated) animal*, esp. a sheep or goat J 4:12.*

θρηνέω *mourn (for), lament* Lk 23:27; J 16:20. *Sing a dirge* Mt 11:17; Lk 7:32.*

θρῆνος, ου, ὁ *dirge* Mt 2:18 v.l.* [*threnody*]

θρησκεία, ας, ἡ *religion, worship* Ac 26:5; Col 2:18; Js 1:26f.*

θρῆσκος, ον *religious* Js 1:26.*

θριαμβεύω *lead in a triumphal procession* Col 2:15. This may also be the mng. in 2 Cor 2:14, but in that passage the sense may be *cause to triumph* or *exhibit in a public procession.**

θρίξ, τριχός, ἡ *hair* Mt 3:4; 5:36; Lk 21:18; J 11:2; 1 Pt 3:3; Rv 9:8. [*trichinosis*]

θροέω pass. *be disturbed* or *frightened* Mt 24:6; Mk 13:7; 2 Th 2:2; Lk 24:37 v.l.*

θρόμβος, ου, ὁ *drop* Lk 22:44.*

θρόνος, ου, ὁ *throne* Mt 5:34; 19:28; 25:31; Lk 1:32, 52; Hb 4:16; Rv 2:13; 4:4; 12:5. *Dominion, sovereignty* of a class of supramundane beings Col 1:16.

θρύπτω *break in pieces* 1 Cor 11:24 v.l.*

Θυάτειρα, ων, τά *Thyatira*, a city in Lydia in Asia Minor, noted for the purple cloth it produced Ac 16:14; Rv 1:11; 2:18, 24.*

θυγάτηρ, τρός, ἡ daughter lit. Mt 10:35, 37; Mk 5:35; Lk 2:36; Ac 7:21; Hb 11:24. Fig. Mk 5:34; Lk 1:5; 23:28; J 12:15; 2 Cor 6:18.

θυγάτριον, ου, τό (little) daughter Mk 5:23; 7:25.*

θύελλα, ης, ἡ storm, whirlwind Hb 12:18.*

θύϊνος, η, ον from the citron tree, therefore scented (wood) Rv 18:12.*

θυμίαμα, ατος, τό incense Rv 5:8; 8:3f; 18:13; incense-burning, incense-offering Lk 1:10f.*

θυμιατήριον, ου, τό altar of incense Hb 9:4.*

θυμιάω make an incense offering Lk 1:9.*

θυμομαχέω be very angry Ac 12:20.*

θυμός, οῦ, ὁ anger, wrath, rage Lk 4:28; Ac 19:28; Ro 2:8; Gal 5:20; Hb 11:27; Rv 12:12; 14:10. Passion is probable for 14:8.

θυμόω make angry pass. become angry Mt 2:16.*

θύρα, ας, ἡ door lit. Mt 6:6; Mk 1:33; Lk 11:7; J 20:19, 26; Ac 5:19; entrance Mk 15:46; Rv 4:1. Fig. Mt 24:33; Lk 13:24; J 10:9; 1 Cor 16:9; Js 5:9; Rv 3:20.

θυρεός, οῦ, ὁ a long, oblong shield Eph 6:16.*

θυρίς, ίδος, ἡ window Ac 20:9; 2 Cor 11:33.*

θυρωρός, οῦ, ὁ and ἡ doorkeeper Mk 13:34; J 10:3; 18:16f.*

θυσία, ας, ἡ sacrifice, offering lit. Mt 9:13; Mk 12:33; Ac 7:41f; 1 Cor 10:18; Hb 10:1, 8, 12. Fig. Ro 12:1; Phil 2:17 (here act of offering is also possible); 4:18; Hb 13:15.

θυσιαστήριον, ου, τό altar lit. Mt 5:23f; Lk 1:11; 11:51; Hb 7:13; Js 2:21; Rv 11:1; 14:18. Fig. Hb 13:10.

θύω sacrifice Ac 14:13, 18; 1 Cor 10:20. Slaughter, kill Mt 22:4; Lk 15:23; J 10:10; Ac 10:13; 1 Cor 5:7. Celebrate Mk 14:12. [Cf. thyme.]

θῶ 2 aor. act. subj. of τίθημι.

Θωμᾶς, ᾶ, ὁ (Aramaic = 'twin') Thomas Mt 10:3; Mk 3:18; Lk 6:15; J 11:16; 14:5; 20:24, 26–28; 21:2; Ac 1:13.*

θώραξ, ακος, ὁ breastplate lit. Rv 9:9b, 17; fig. Eph 6:14; 1 Th 5:8. Probably chest Rv 9:9a.* [thorax]

Ι

Ἰάϊρος, ου, ὁ Jaïrus Mk 5:22; Lk 8:41.*

Ἰακώβ, ὁ indecl. Jacob—**1.** the patriarch, son of Isaac Mt 1:2; Mk 12:26; Lk 13:28; J 4:5f, 12; Ac 7:8, 46; Ro 9:13; 11:26.—**2.** the father of Joseph, in the genealogy of Jesus Mt 1:15f; Lk 3:23 v.l.

Ἰάκωβος, ου, ὁ (Grecized form of the preceding) James—**1.** son of Zebedee, brother of John, member of the Twelve Mt 4:21; Mk 3:17; Lk 9:28, 54; Ac 1:13a; 12:2.—**2.** son of Alphaeus Mt 10:3; Mk 3:18; Lk 6:15; Ac 1:13b. He is perhaps identical with—**3.** son of Mary Mt 27:56; Mk 16:1; Lk 24:10; in Mk 15:40 he is called Ἰ. ὁ μικρός James the small or the younger.—**4.** James, the Lord's brother Mt 13:55; Mk 6:3; 1 Cor 15:7; Gal 1:19; 2:9, 12; Ac 12:17; 15:13; 21:18; Js 1:1.—**5.** James, father of an apostle named Judas Lk 6:16a; Ac 1:13c.—**6.** In Mk 2:14 v.l. the tax collector is called James (instead of Levi).

ἴαμα, ατος, τό healing 1 Cor 12:9, 28, 30.*

Ἰαμβρῆς, ὁ Jambres, an Egyptian sorcerer 2 Ti 3:8.*

Ἰανναί, ὁ indecl. Jannai Lk 3:24.*

Ἰάννης, ὁ Jannes, an Egyptian sorcerer 2 Ti 3:8.*

ἰάομαι heal, cure lit. Mt 8:8, 13; Mk 5:29; Lk 5:17; 9:11, 42; J 4:47; 5:13. Fig. restore Mt 13:15; Lk 4:18 v.l.; J 12:40; Hb 12:13.

Ἰάρετ, ὁ indecl. Jared Lk 3:37.*

ἴασις, εως, ἡ healing, cure Lk 13:32; Ac 4:22, 30.*

ἴασπις, ιδος, ἡ jasper a precious stone found in various colors Rv 4:3; 21:11, 18f.*

Ἰάσων, ονος, ὁ Jason—1. Ac 17:5–7, 9.—2. Ro 16:21.—3. Ac 21:16 v.l.*

ἰατρός, οῦ, ὁ physician Mt 9:12; Mk 2:17; 5:26; Lk 4:23; 5:31; 8:43 v.l.; Col 4:14.* [psychiatry, ψυχή + ἰατρεία]

Ἰαχίν, ὁ indecl. Jachin Lk 3:23ff v.l.*

ιβ´ numeral twelve Mk 6:7 v.l.; Ac 1:26 v.l.*

ἴδε impv. of εἶδον, stereotyped as a particle (you) see Mk 2:24; 13:1; J 3:26; 5:14; 11:36; 12:19; 18:21; Gal 5:2. Here is (are) Mt 25:20; Mk 3:34; 16:6. There Mt 26:65. You hear Mk 15:4, cf. vs. 35.

ἰδέα, ας, ἡ appearance, aspect Lk 9:29 v.l. S. εἰδέα.* [ideo-, a combining form, as in ideogram, ideograph]

ἴδετε impv. 2 pl. of εἶδον, which serves as 2 aor. of ὁράω.

ἴδιος, ία, ον one's own, private, peculiar to oneself Mt 25:15; Lk 6:41, 44; J 10:3f; Ac 2:8; 4:32; Ro 10:3; 1 Cor 3:8; 4:12; Tit 1:3; 2:5, 9; 2 Pt 1:20; 2:22. As noun οἱ ἴδιοι one's own people of fellow-Christians Ac 4:23; 24:23; relatives J 1:11b; 1 Ti 5:8. τὰ ἴδια home Lk 18:28; J 1:11a; 16:32; Ac 21:6, but property, supply J 8:44 and one's own affairs 1 Th 4:11; the sing. J 15:19. ἰδίᾳ by oneself, privately 1 Cor 12:11. κατ᾽ ἰδίαν privately, by oneself Mt 14:13; Mk 9:2, 28; Lk 10:23; Ac 23:19; Gal 2:2. [idio-, a combining form, as in idiosyncrasy]

ἰδιώτης, ου, ὁ amateur, layperson in contrast to an expert, untrained person Ac 4:13. i. τῷ λόγῳ unskilled in speaking 2 Cor 11:6. Inquirer, of one seeking to know more about Christianity, prob. akin to the later catechumen 1 Cor 14:16, 23f.*

ἰδού aor. mid. impv. of εἶδον, used as a demonstrative particle when accented thus. Can be translated variously: (you) see, look, behold, or left untranslated Mt 2:1, 13; 13:3; Lk 1:20; 22:10; Ac 2:7; Js 5:9; Rv 9:12; and yet Mt 7:4; 2 Cor 6:9; remember, consider Mt 10:16; Lk 2:48; Ac 9:11; 2 Cor 7:11; i. δέκα κ. ὀκτὼ ἔτη eighteen (long) years Lk 13:16. Here or there is (are) or was (were) or comes (came) Mt 3:17; 12:10; Lk 7:34, 37; 13:11; J 19:5; Ac 8:27, 36; 2 Cor 6:2; Rv 12:3. i. ἐγώ here I am Ac 9:10.

Ἰδουμαία, ας, ἡ Idumaea (O.T. Edom) a mountainous district south of Judaea Mk 3:8; Ac 2:9 v.l.*

ἱδρώς, ῶτος, ὁ sweat, perspiration Lk 22:44.* [hidrosis; hyperhidrosis, excessive sweating]

ἰδών 2 aor. act. ptc. of εἶδον.

ἰδώς alt. act. ptc. of οἶδα.

Ἰεζάβελ, ἡ indecl. Jezebel (1 Kings 16:31 and subsequent chapters), applied to a woman who endangered orthodox teaching Rv 2:20.*

Ἰεράπολις, εως, ἡ Hierapolis, a city on the Lycus River in Asia Minor Col 4:13.*

ἱερατεία, ας, ἡ priestly office Lk 1:9; Hb 7:5; priesthood Rv 5:10 v.l.* [hieratic]

ἱεράτευμα, ατος, τό priesthood 1 Pt 2:5, 9.*

ἱερατεύω perform the service of a priest Lk 1:8.*

Ἰερεμίας, ου, ὁ Jeremiah the prophet Mt 2:17; 16:14; 27:9.*

ἱερεύς, έως, ὁ priest Mt 8:4; Mk 1:44; Lk 10:31; Ac 14:13; Hb 7:14f, 17, 20f, 23; 8:4; Rv 20:6.

Ἰεριχώ, ἡ indecl. Jericho, a city in the Jordan valley just north of the Dead Sea Mt 20:29; Mk 10:46; Lk 10:30; 18:35; 19:1; Hb 11:30.*

ἱερόθυτος, ον sacrificed to a deity as noun τὸ ἱερόθυτον meat sacrificed to idols 1 Cor 10:28.*

ἱερόν, οῦ, τό (neut. of the adj. ἱερός, used as a noun) temple, sanctuary Mt 12:6; 21:12; Mk 13:3; Lk 22:52; J 10:23; Ac 19:27.

ἱεροπρεπής, ές worthy of reverence, holy Tit 2:3.*

ἱερός, ά, όν set apart for the deity, holy 2 Ti 3:15; Col 4:13 v.l. τὸ ἱερὸν κήρυγμα the sacred proclamation Mk 16:8 shorter ending. τὰ ἱερά the holy things, i.e. services 1 Cor 9:13.* [hiero-, a combining form, as in hieroglyphics]

Ἱεροσόλυμα, τά and **ἡ**, and **Ἱερουσαλήμ, ἡ** indecl. Jerusalem the holy city Mt 2:1, 3; Mk 3:8; Lk 19:28; J 2:13; Ac 25:1; Gal 4:25; Hb 12:22; Rv 21:2.

Ἱεροσολυμίτης, ου, ὁ an inhabitant of Jerusalem Mk 1:5; J 7:25.*

ἱεροσυλέω rob temples Ro 2:22.*

ἱερόσυλος, ὁ temple robber or simply sacrilegious person Ac 19:37.*

ἱερουργέω perform holy service, act as a priest ἱ. τὸ εὐαγγέλιον serve the gospel as a priest Ro 15:16.*

Ἱερουσαλήμ see Ἱεροσόλυμα.

ἱερωσύνη, ης, ἡ priestly office, priesthood Hb 7:11f, 24.*

Ἱεσσαί, ὁ indecl. Jesse, father of David (1 Sam 16) Mt 1:5f; Lk 3:32; Ac 13:22; Ro 15:12.*

Ἱεφθάε, ὁ indecl. Jephthah (Judges 11f) Hb 11:32.*

Ἱεχονίας, ου, ὁ Jechoniah Mt 1:11f; Lk 3:23ff v.l.*

Ἱησοῦς, gen. οῦ, dat. οῦ, acc. οῦν, voc. οῦ, ὁ Jesus, Greek form of the Hebrew name Joshua or later Jeshua.—**1.** Joshua, successor to Moses Ac 7:45; Hb 4:8.—**2.** Jesus, son of Eliezer Lk 3:29.—**3.** Jesus Christ Mt 1:1, 21, 25 and often throughout the N.T.—**4.** Jesus Barabbas Mt 27:16f.—**5.** Jesus who is called Justus Col 4:11.

ἱκανός, ή, όν—**1.** sufficient, adequate, large enough or simply large, much. Large Mk 10:46; Ac 11:24, 26. ἀργύρια a large sum of money Mt 28:12. φῶς a very bright light Ac 22:6. ἱκανὸν ἡ ἐπι-τιμία the punishment is severe enough 2 Cor 2:6. Of time long, considerable Lk 8:27; 23:8; Ac 14:3; 27:9; many Ac 9:23, 43; Ro 15:23 v.l. ἱκανόν ἐστιν it is enough Lk 22:38. τὸ ἱκανὸν ποιεῖν satisfy Mk 15:15. τὸ ἱκανόν pledge, security, bond Ac 17:9. ἐφ᾿ ἱκανόν enough, as long as one wishes Ac 20:11.—**2.** fit, appropriate, competent, able, worthy Mt 3:11; Lk 7:6; J 1:27 v.l.; 1 Cor 15:9; 2 Cor 2:16; 3:5.

ἱκανότης, ητος, ἡ fitness, capability, qualification 2 Cor 3:5.*

ἱκανόω make sufficient, qualify, authorize Col 1:12; with double accusative 2 Cor 3:6.*

ἱκετηρία, ας, ἡ prayer, supplication Hb 5:7.*

ἱκμάς, άδος, ἡ moisture Lk 8:6.*

Ἱκόνιον, ου, τό Iconium, a city in central Asia Minor Ac 13:51; 14:1, 19, 21; 16:2; 2 Ti 3:11.*

ἱλαρός, ά, όν cheerful, without grudging the gift, gracious 2 Cor 9:7.*

ἱλαρότης, ητος, ἡ cheerfulness, graciousness. ἐν ἱ. without reluctance Ro 12:8.* [hilarity]

ἱλάσκομαι—**1.** be merciful pass. Lk 18:13.—**2.** expiate Hb 2:17.*

ἱλασμός, οῦ, ὁ expiation, sin offering 1 J 2:2; 4:10.*

ἱλαστήριον, ου, τό means of expiation, place of expiation Ro 3:25; Hb 9:5.*

ἵλεως, neut. ων (Attic second declension) gracious, merciful Hb 8:12. ἵλεώς σοι may God be gracious to you, God forbid Mt 16:22.*

Ἱλλυρικόν, οῦ, τό Illyricum, a district across the Adriatic Sea from Italy Ro 15:19.*

ἱμάς, άντος, ὁ leather strap or thong for sandals Mk 1:7; Lk 3:16; J 1:27. In Ac 22:25 ἱ. may mean thong or whip.*

ἱματίζω dress, clothe Mk 5:15; Lk 8:35.*

ἱμάτιον, ου, τό garment, clothing in general Mt 9:16; 27:35; Mk 5:28, 30; Lk 7:25; Hb 1:11f; 1 Pt 3:3. Cloak, robe of outer clothing Mt 5:40; 9:20f; Lk 6:29; 22:36; J 19:2; Ac 9:39; 12:8; 16:22; Rv 19:16. [himation] ἱματισμός, οῦ, ὁ *clothing, apparel* Lk 7:25; 9:29; J 19:24; Ac 20:33; 1 Ti 2:9.*

ἱμείρομαι *desire, long for* 1 Th 2:8 v.l.*

ἵνα conjunction—**1.** denoting purpose, aim, or goal *in order that, that* Mt 1:22; Mk 4:21; Lk 20:10; J 5:20; Ac 5:15; Ro 14:9; Gal 2:4; Eph 6:22; Rv 3:9.—**2.** as a substitute for the infinitive, as used in Greek and English ἀρκετὸν τῷ μαθητῇ ἵνα γένηται *it is enough for the disciple to become* Mt 10:25. τῷ θυρωρῷ ἐνετείλατο ἵνα γρηγορῇ *he gave orders to the doorkeeper to be on the alert* Mk 13:34. ἐδεήθην τῶν μαθητῶν ἵνα ἐκβάλωσιν αὐτό *I begged the disciples to cast it out* Lk 9:40. Cf. Mt 7:12; Mk 9:30; 11:16; Lk 7:6; J 6:29; 16:30; 1 Cor 1:10; 4:2; Rv 2:21; 9:5.— **3.** indicating result *so that* Lk 9:45; J 9:2; Gal 5:17; Rv 9:20. Sometimes purpose and result cannot be clearly differentiated Lk 11:50; J 4:36; Ro 3:19; 8:17.—**4.** as a periphrasis for the imperative ἵνα ἐπιθῇς τὰς χεῖρας αὐτῇ (please) *lay your hands on her* Mk 5:23. ἡ δὲ γυνὴ ἵνα φοβῆται τὸν ἄνδρα *the wife is to respect her husband* Eph 5:33. ἵνα ἀναπαήσονται *let them rest* Rv 14:13. Cf. Mt 20:33; Mk 10:51; 2 Cor 8:7; Gal 2:10.

ἱνατί (ἵνα + τί) *why? for what reason?* Mt 9:4; 27:46; Lk 13:7; Ac 4:25; 7:26; 1 Cor 10:29.*

Ἰόππη, ης, ἡ *Joppa,* modern Jaffa, a city on the s. coast of Palestine Ac 9:36, 38, 42f; 10:5, 8, 23, 32; 11:5, 13.*

Ἰορδάνης, ου, ὁ *the Jordan,* chief river of Palestine Mt 3:5f; 19:1; Mk 10:1; Lk 4:1; J 3:26; 10:40.

ἰός, οῦ, ὁ *poison, venom* Ro 3:13; Js 3:8. *Rust* Js 5:3.*

Ἰουδαία, ας, ἡ *Judaea,* the part of Palestine south of Samaria Mt 2:1, 5, 22; 24:16; Mk 1:5; Lk 1:65; 6:17; Ac 1:8; 12:19; 28:21; Ro 15:31; Gal 1:22. In a wider sense, the region occupied by the Jewish nation Mt 19:1; Lk 1:5; Ac 10:37; 1 Th 2:14.

ἰουδαΐζω *live as a Jew, according to Jewish customs* Gal 2:14.*

Ἰουδαϊκός, ή, όν *Jewish* Tit 1:14.*

Ἰουδαϊκῶς adv. *in a Jewish manner, according to Jewish customs* Gal 2:14.*

Ἰουδαῖος, αία, αῖον *Jewish* Mk 1:5; Ac 13:6; 19:13f; 21:39. As noun ὁ Ἰ. *the Jew* Mt 2:2; Mk 7:3; Lk 23:51; J 2:18, 20; 9:18, 22; 11:8; Ac 2:11; 18:4; Ro 2:9f, 17, 28f; 3:1; Gal 2:14. Of Jewish Christians Gal 2:13.

Ἰουδαϊσμός, οῦ, ὁ *Judaism* Gal 1:13f.*

Ἰούδας, α, ὁ *Judah* (Hebrew), *Judas* (Greek), *Jude* (see 8).—**1.** *Judah,* son of Jacob, and the tribe named for him Mt 1:2f; 2:6; Lk 1:39; Hb 7:14; Rv 5:5.— **2.** *Judas* in the genealogy of Jesus Lk 3:30.—**3.** *Judas* of Galilee, a revolutionary Ac 5:37.—**4.** *Judas* of Damascus, Paul's host Ac 9:11.—**5.** *Judas,* an apostle, son (or brother) of James Lk 6:16; J 14:22; Ac 1:13.—**6.** *Judas* Iscariot, betrayer of Jesus Mt 10:4; 26:14, 25, 47; 27:3; Mk 3:19; 14:10, 43; Lk 6:16; 22:3, 47f; J 6:71; 12:4; 13:2, 29; 18:2f, 5; Ac 1:16, 25.—**7.** *Judas* called Barsabbas, a Christian prophet Ac 15:22, 27, 32 (34).—**8.** *Judas,* the brother of Jesus Mt 13:55; Mk 6:3. Probably the same man is meant by the *Jude* in Jd 1.

Ἰουλία, ας, ἡ *Julia* Ro 16:15.*

Ἰούλιος, ου, ὁ *Julius* Ac 27:1, 3.*

Ἰουνία, ας, ἡ—**1.** *Junia* Ro 16:15 v.l.*— **2.** Perh. the fem. Ἰ. is to be read in 16:7.*

Ἰουνιᾶς, ᾶ, ὁ *Junias,* unless a woman's name Ἰουνία *Junia* is to be read Ro 16:7.*

Ἰοῦστος, ου, ὁ *Justus,* surname of—**1.** Joseph Barsabbas Ac 1:23.—**2.** Titius Ac 18:7.—**3.** Jesus, a Jewish Christian Col 4:11.*

ἱππεύς, έως, ὁ *horseman, cavalryman* Ac 23:23, 32.*

ἱππικός, ή, όν *pertaining to a horseman* τὸ ἱ. *the cavalry* Rv 9:16.*

ἵππος, ου, ὁ *horse, steed* Js 3:3; Rv 6:2, 4f, 8; 9:7, 17; 18:13; 19:11, 14. [*hippodrome,* ἵππος + δρόμος]

ἶρις, ιδος, ἡ *rainbow* Rv 10:1. *Halo, radiance* 4:3.* [*irido-,* combining form, as in *iridescent* and in *iridoplegia,* paralysis of the *iris*]

Ἰσαάκ, ὁ indecl. *Isaac* son of Abraham, father of Jacob Mt 8:11; Mk 12:26; Lk 3:34; Ac 7:8; Ro 9:7, 10; Gal 4:28; Hb 11:17.

ἰσάγγελος, ον *like an angel* Lk 20:36.*

ἴσασι pf. act. ind. 3 pl. of οἶδα.

ἴσθι impv. 2 sing. of εἰμί.

Ἰσκαριώθ indecl. and Ἰσκαριώτης, ου, ὁ *Iscariot* surname of Judas the betrayer and of his father Mt 10:4; 26:14; Mk 14:10; Lk 6:16; 22:3; J 6:71; 13:2, 26; 14:22.

ἴσος, η, ον *equal* Mt 20:12; J 5:18; Rv 21:16; *consistent* Mk 14:56, 59. ἡ ἴ. *the same* Ac 11:17; τὰ ἴσα *an equal amount* Lk 6:34. ἴσα (used as adv.) εἶναι *be equal* Phil 2:6.* [*iso-*, combining form, as in *isosceles*, ἴσος + σκέλος, leg]

ἰσότης, ητος, ἡ *equality* 2 Cor 8:14; ἐξ ἰσότητος *as a matter of equality* 8:13. *Fairness* Col 4:1.*

ἰσότιμος, ον *with the same privileges*, lit. *equal in value* or *prestige* 2 Pt 1:1.*

ἰσόψυχος, ον *of like soul* or *mind* Phil 2:20.*

Ἰσραήλ, ὁ indecl. *Israel*—1. the patriarch Jacob Mt 10:6; Lk 1:16; Ac 2:36; Phil 3:5; Hb 8:10.—2. the nation of *Israel* Mt 2:6; Mk 12:29; Lk 2:34; J 3:10; Ac 4:10; Ro 11:2; Rv 7:4.—3. of Christians as participants in the privileges of Israel Ro 9:6b; Gal 6:16.

Ἰσραηλίτης, ου, ὁ *the Israelite* J 1:47; Ro 11:1; 2 Cor 11:22. ἄνδρες Ἰσραηλῖται *men of Israel* Ac 2:22; 5:35; 21:28.

Ἰσσαχάρ, ὁ indecl. *Issachar* son of Jacob, and an Israelite tribe named after him Rv 7:7.*

ἴστε pf. act. ind. 2 pl. of οἶδα.

ἵστημι or ἱστάνω—1. trans. (pres., impf., fut., 1 aor. act.) *put, place, set, bring* Mt 25:33; Mk 9:36; Lk 4:9; Ac 5:27. *Put forward, propose* Ac 1:23; 6:13. *Establish, confirm* Ro 3:31; 10:3; Hb 10:9. *Cause to stand* Ro 14:4. *Set, fix* Ac 17:31. *Set out* or *weigh out* Mt 26:15.—2. intrans. (2 aor., pf., plupf. act.; fut. mid. and pass.; 1 aor. pass.) aor. and fut. *stand still, stop* Mt 20:32; Mk 10:49; Lk 6:17; 8:44; Ac 8:38; Js 2:3. *Come up, stand, appear* Mt 27:11; Mk 13:9; Lk 24:36; Ac 10:30; 11:13.

Resist Eph 6:11, 13. *Stand firm, hold one's ground* Mt 12:25f; Mk 3:26; Ro 14:4a; Eph 6:14; Rv 6:17. Pf. and plupf. *I stand, I stood* Mt 27:47; Lk 23:10; J 7:37; Ac 1:11. *Be, exist* Mt 12:46f; 26:73; Lk 18:13; J 11:56; Ac 7:55f; 21:40; Rv 18:10. Fig. *stand, stand firm* Ro 11:20; 1 Cor 7:37; 2 Ti 2:19. *Stand* or *be* Ro 5:2; 1 Cor 15:1; 2 Cor 1:24. *Attend upon, be in the service of* Rv 8:2.

ἱστίον, ου, τό *a sail* Ac 27:16 v.l.*

ἱστορέω *visit* Gal 1:18; Ac 17:23 v.l.*

ἰσχυρός, ά, όν *strong, mighty, powerful* Mt 3:11; Mk 3:27; 1 Cor 1:25; 4:10; 10:22; Rv 6:15; 18:8. *Severe* Lk 15:14; *loud* Hb 5:7; Rv 18:2; 19:6. *Forceful* 2 Cor 10:10.

ἰσχύς, ύος, ἡ *strength, power, might* Mk 12:30, 33; Eph 1:19; 2 Th 1:9; 2 Pt 2:11; Rv 5:12.

ἰσχύω *be strong, powerful, able* Mt 8:28; Mk 14:37; Lk 14:6, 29f; J 21:6; Ac 15:10. *Be strong enough* Lk 16:3. *Be in good health* Mk 2:17. *Win out, prevail* Ac 19:16; Rv 12:8. *Have meaning, be valid* Gal 5:6; Hb 9:17. ἰ. πολύ *be able to do much* Js 5:16. εἰς οὐδέν *be good for nothing* Mt 5:13.

ἴσως adv. *perhaps, probably* Lk 20:13.*

Ἰταλία, ας, ἡ *Italy* Ac 18:2; 27:1, 6; Hb 13:24; Hb subscription.*

Ἰταλικός, ή, όν *Italian* Ac 10:1.*

Ἰτουραῖος, αία, αῖον of Ἰ. χώρα *Ituraea* a region along the Lebanon and Anti-Lebanon ranges, part of the tetrarchy of Philip Lk 3:1.*

ἰχθύδιον, ου, τό *little fish* Mt 15:34; Mk 8:7.*

ἰχθύς, ύος, ὁ *fish* Mt 7:10; 17:27; Mk 6:38, 41, 43; Lk 5:6, 9; J 21:6, 8, 11; 1 Cor 15:39. [*ichthyology*]

ἴχνος, ους, τό *footprint, footstep* fig. Ro 4:12; 2 Cor 12:18; 1 Pt 2:21.* [*ichnography*, ground plan]

Ἰωαθάμ, ὁ indecl. *Jotham* Mt 1:9; Lk 3:23ff v.l.*

Ἰωακίμ, ὁ indecl. *Jehoiakim* Mt 1:11 v.l.; Lk 3:23ff v.l.*

Ἰωανάν, ὁ indecl. *Joanan* Lk 3:27.*

Ἰωάν(ν)α, ας, ἡ *Joanna* Lk 8:3; 24:10.*

Ἰωάν(ν)ης, ου, ὁ John—1. John the Baptist or Baptizer Mt 3:1, 4, 13f; 11:2, 4, 7, 11–13, 18; 21:25f; Mk 1:4; 6:14, 16–18; Lk 16:16; 20:4, 6; J 1:6, 15; 3:23–27; Ac 1:5, 22; 18:25; 19:3f.—2. John, son of Zebedee, brother of James, one of the Twelve Mt 4:21; Mk 1:19, 29; 5:37; Lk 8:51; Ac 3:1, 3f, 11; 12:2; Gal 2:9.—3. John of the Apocalypse, equated by church tradition with 2, the son of Zebedee Rv 1:1, 4, 9; 22:8.—4. John, father of Peter J 1:42; 21:15–17.—5. John an otherwise unknown member of the high council Ac 4:6.—6. John surnamed Mark Ac 12:12, 25; 13:5, 13; 15:37.

Ἰωάς, ὁ indecl. Joash, king of Judah (2 Kings 14:1) Mt 1:8 v.l.; Lk 3:23ff v.l.*

Ἰώβ, ὁ indecl. Job, hero of the book of the same name Js 5:11.*

Ἰωβήδ, ὁ indecl. Obed, David's grandfather Mt 1:5; Lk 3:32.*

Ἰωδά, ὁ indecl. Joda Lk 3:26.*

Ἰωήλ, ὁ indecl. Joel, the O.T. prophet Ac 2:16.*

Ἰωνάθας, ου, ὁ Jonathas Ac 4:6 v.l. of Ἰωάννης.*

Ἰωνάμ, ὁ indecl. Jonam Lk 3:30.*

Ἰωνᾶς, ᾶ, ὁ Jonah—1. the O.T. prophet Mt 12:39–41; 16:4; Lk 11:29f, 32.—2. a Galilean fisherman, father of Simon Peter and Andrew Mt 16:17 v.l. Also as v.l. in J 1:42; 21:15–17.*

Ἰωράμ, ὁ indecl. Joram or Jehoram, king of Judah (2 Kings 8:16ff) Mt 1:8; Lk 3:23ff v.l.*

Ἰωρίμ, ὁ indecl. Jorim Lk 3:29.*

Ἰωσαφάτ, ὁ indecl. Jehoshaphat, king of Judah (1 Kings 22:41ff) Mt 1:8; Lk 3:23ff v.l.*

Ἰωσῆς, ῆ or ῆτος, ὁ Joses—1. a brother of Jesus Mk 6:3; Mt 13:55 v.l.—2. son of a woman named Mary and brother of James the younger Mk 15:40, 47; Mt 27:56 v.l.—3. a member of the early church better known as Barnabas Ac 4:36 v.l.*

Ἰωσήφ, ὁ indecl. Joseph—1. the patriarch J 4:5; Ac 7:9, 13f, 18; Hb 11:21f. In Rv 7:8 the tribe of Joseph stands for the half-tribe Ephraim.—2. son of Jonam Lk 3:30.—3. son of Mattathias Lk 3:24.—4. husband of Mary the mother of Jesus Mt 1:16, 18–20, 24; 2:13, 19; Lk 1:27; 2:4, 16, 33 v.l.; 3:23; 4:22; J 1:45; 6:42.—5. a brother of Jesus Mt 13:55.—6. Joseph of Arimathea Mt 27:57, 59; Mk 15:43, 45; Lk 23:50; J 19:38.—7. Joseph, surnamed Barnabas Ac 4:36.—8. Joseph, surnamed Barsabbas, also called Justus 1:23.—9. son of a certain Mary Mt 27:56.*

Ἰωσήχ, ὁ indecl. Josech Lk 3:26.*

Ἰωσίας, ου, ὁ Josiah, king of Judah (2 Kings 22) Mt 1:10f; Lk 3:23ff v.l.*

ἰῶτα, τό indecl. iota, smallest letter of the Greek alphabet, corresponding to yod, the smallest in the Aramaic alphabet Mt 5:18.* [iotacism]

K

κάβος, ου, ὁ the cab, a dry measure equivalent to approximately two liters Lk 16:6 v.l.*

κἀγώ formed by crasis from καί plus ἐγώ, dat. κἀμοί, acc. κἀμέ and I Mt 11:28;

Lk 2:48; J 1:31, 33f; 6:56; 2 Cor 12:20; Gal 6:14. But I J 12:32; Ac 10:28; Js 2:18a. I also, I too Mt 2:8; Lk 1:3; J 5:17; Ac 8:19; 2 Cor 11:21f. I for my part, I in turn Mt 10:32f; Lk 11:9; 22:29;

Rv 3:10. *I in particular, I for instance* Ro 3:7. κἀγώ = ἐγώ 1 Cor 7:8; 10:33; 11:1; Eph 1:15.

κάδος, ου, ὁ *jar, container* Lk 16:6 v.l.*

καθά conj. *or adv. just as* Mt 6:12 v.l.; 27:10; Lk 1:2 v.l.*

καθαίρεσις, εως, ἡ *tearing down, destruction* 2 Cor 10:4, 8; 13:10.*

καθαιρέω—1. *take down, bring down* Mk 15:36, 46; Lk 1:52; 23:53; Ac 13:29.— 2. *tear down, overpower, destroy* Lk 12:18; Ac 13:19; 2 Cor 10:4; pass. *suffer the loss of* Ac 19:27.*

καθαίρω *make clean;* of a vine *clear, prune* by removing superfluous wood J 15:2.* [*cathartic*]

καθάπερ conj. *or adv. just as* Ro 3:4 v.l.; 11:8 v.l.; 1 Cor 10:10; 2 Cor 3:13, 18; 1 Th 2:11. καθάπερ καί *as also* Ro 4:6; 1 Th 3:6, 12.

καθάπτω *take hold of, seize* Ac 28:3.*

καθαριεῖ Attic fut. 3 sing. of καθαρίζω Hb 9:14.

καθαρίζω *make clean, cleanse, purify* lit. and fig. Mt 23:25f; Mk 7:19; Ac 10:15; 15:9; 2 Cor 7:1; Tit 2:14; Hb 9:22f; 10:2; Js 4:8. *Heal* Mt 8:3.

καθαρισμός, οῦ, ὁ *purification* Mk 1:44; Lk 2:22; 5:14; J 2:6; 3:25; Hb 1:3; 2 Pt 1:9.*

κάθαρμα, ατος, τό *offscouring, scapegoat* v.l. for περικάθαρμα (q.v.) in 1 Cor 4:13.*

καθαρός, ά, όν *clean, pure* lit. and fig., ceremonially and morally Mt 5:8; 23:26; 27:59; Lk 11:41; J 13:10; Ro 14:20; Hb 10:22; Js 1:27; Rv 15:6; 21:18. [S. καθαίρω]

καθαρότης, ητος, ἡ *purity* Hb 9:13.*

καθέδρα, ας, ἡ *chair, seat* Mt 21:12; 23:2; Mk 11:15.* [*cathedral*]

καθέζομαι *sit* Mt 26:55; Lk 2:46; J 11:20; Ac 6:15; 20:9; 3:10 v.l. *Sit there* J 20:12. *Sit down* 4:6; 6:3 v.l.*

καθεῖλον, καθελεῖν, καθελῶ, καθελόν 2 aor. act. ind., 2 aor. act. inf., 2 fut. act. ind., and 2 aor. act. ptc. of καθαιρέω.

καθεῖς = καθ' εἷς *individually* Ro 12:5 v.l.*

καθεξῆς adv. *in order, one after the other* with reference to time, space, or logic Lk 1:3; Ac 3:24; 11:4; 18:23; *afterward* Lk 8:1.*

καθερίζω variant form of καθαρίζω.

καθεύδω *sleep* lit. Mt 8:24; 13:25; Mk 4:27, 38; 14:37, 40f. The fig. meaning *die, be dead* is probable in Mt 9:24 (= Mk 5:39; Lk 8:52) and certain for 1 Th 5:10. Of spiritual indifference Eph 5:14; 1 Th 5:6.

κάθῃ pres. ind. 2 sing. of κάθημαι.

καθηγητής, οῦ, ὁ *teacher* Mt 23:10.*

καθῆκα 1 aor. act. ind. of καθίημι.

καθήκω *be proper* or *fitting* Ac 22:22. τὰ μὴ καθήκοντα *what is improper* Ro 1:28.*

κάθημαι *sit* Mt 26:64; 27:61; Mk 2:6; 13:3; Lk 10:13; 18:35; Ac 8:28; 23:3; Col 3:1; Rv 6:8, 16; *sit (there)* Lk 5:17; J 2:14; *be enthroned* Rv 18:7. *Stay, live, reside* Lk 1:79; 21:35; Rv 14:6. *Sit down* Mt 22:44; 28:2; Mk 4:1; Ac 2:34; Js 2:3.

καθημέραν = καθ' (κατὰ) ἡμέραν.

καθημερινός, ή, όν *daily* Ac 6:1.*

καθῆψα 1 aor. act. ind. of καθάπτω.

καθιέμενος pres. pass. ptc. of καθίημι Ac 10:11.

καθίζω—1. trans. *cause to sit down, seat, set* Ac 2:30; Eph 1:20. *Appoint* 1 Cor 6:4.—2. intrans. *sit down* Mt 5:1; 26:36; Mk 9:35; Lk 4:20; Ac 8:31; 13:14; 1 Cor 10:7; Hb 1:3; *rest* Ac 2:3. *Settle, stay, live* Lk 24:49; Ac 18:11. [Cf. *cathedral*.]

καθίημι *let down* Lk 5:19; Ac 9:25; 10:11; 11:5.*

καθιστάνω see καθίστημι.

καθίστημι and **καθιστάνω**—1. *bring, conduct, take* Ac 17:15.—2. *appoint, put in charge* Mt 24:45, 47; Ac 6:3; *authorize, appoint* Lk 12:14; Ac 7:10, 27; Tit 1:5; Hb 5:1.—3. *make, cause* 2 Pt 1:8. Pass. *be made, become* Ro 5:19; Js 4:4.

καθό adv. = καθ' ὅ. *as* Ro 8:26. *Insofar as, to the degree that* 2 Cor 8:12; 1 Pt 4:13.*

καθολικός, ή, όν *general, universal, catholic* Js inscription v.l.*

καθόλου adv. *entirely, completely* μὴ κ. *not at all* Ac 4:18.*

καθοπλίζω mid. *arm* or *equip oneself* Lk 11:21.*

καθοράω *perceive* Ro 1:20.*

καθότι *as, to the degree that* Ac 2:45; 4:35. *Because, in view of the fact that* Lk 1:7; 19:9; Ac 2:24; 17:31.*

κάθου pres. impv. 2 sing. of κάθημαι.

καθώς adv. *as, just as* Mt 21:6; 28:6; Mk 1:2; Lk 11:30; 24:24; J 1:23; Ac 15:8; Ro 1:17; 1 Cor 15:49; 2 Cor 1:5; 1 Ti 1:3; 1 J 3:2. *As, to the degree that* Mk 4:33; Ac 11:29; 1 Cor 12:11, 18; 1 Pt 4:10. *Since, insofar as* J 17:2; Ro 1:28; Eph 1:4; Phil 1:7. *When* Ac 7:17. *How, that* Ac 15:14; 3 J 3.

καθώσπερ adv. *just as* Hb 5:4; 2 Cor 3:18 v.l.*

καί conjunction—1. *and* Mt 13:55; 23:32; Lk 2:47; 3:14; Ro 7:12; Ac 5:29; Hb 1:1. *When* Mt 26:45; Mk 15:25; J 2:13; Hb 8:8. *That* = ὅτι Mk 6:14. καὶ ἐγένετο . . . καί *and it came about* . . .: *that* Mt 9:10; Mk 2:15; Lk 5:1, 12, 17. *But* Mt 12:43; Lk 13:7; Ro 1:13; 1 Th 2:18. *And so, that is, namely* Mt 8:33; J 1:16; Ro 1:5; 1 Cor 3:5. καί . . . καί *both* . . . *and, not only* . . . *but also* Mt 10:28; Mk 4:41; 9:13; J 7:28; Ac 26:29; 1 Cor 1:22; Phil 4:16. Sometimes καί may be left untranslated as πολλὰ . . . κ. ἄλλα σημεῖα *many other signs* J 20:30; cf. Lk 3:18; Ac 25:7.—2. used rather as an adverb *also, likewise* Mt 5:39f; 12:45; Mk 8:7. *Even* Mt 5:46f; Mk 1:27; Ac 5:39; 2 Cor 1:8; Phlm 21; Hb 7:25; Jd 23. ὁ καί with double names *who is also called* Ac 13:9.

Καϊάφας, α, ὁ *Caiaphas,* high priest 18–36 A.D.: Mt 26:3, 57; Lk 3:2; J 11:49; 18:13f, 24, 28; Ac 4:6.*

καίγε = καί + γε.

Κάϊν, ὁ indecl. *Cain,* son of Adam Hb 11:4; 1 J 3:12; Jd 11.*

Καϊνάμ, ὁ indecl. *Cainan*—1. son of Arphaxad Lk 3:36.—2. son of Enos 3:37.*

καινός, ή, όν *new* Mt 13:52; 27:60; Mk 2:21f; Lk 22:20; J 13:34; 2 Cor 3:6; 5:17; Hb 9:15; Rv 2:17; 5:9; 21:1, 5; *strange* Mk 1:27. Comparative τι καινότερον *something quite new* Ac 17:21.

καινότης, ητος, ἡ *newness* κ. ζωῆς a *new life* Ro 6:4; cf. 7:6.*

καινοφωνία see κενοφωνία.

καίπερ conjunction *although* Phil 3:4; Hb 5:8; 7:5; 12:17; 2 Pt 1:12.*

καιρός, οῦ, ὁ *time,* i.e. *point of time* as well as *period of time*—1. generally Lk 21:36; Ac 14:17; 2 Cor 6:2; Eph 6:18; 2 Ti 3:1; *present (time)* Ro 3:26; 13:11. κατὰ καιρόν *from time to time* J 5:4.—2. *the right, proper, favorable time* Mt 24:45; Mk 12:2; Lk 20:10; J 7:6, 8; Ac 24:25. *Opportunity* Gal 6:10; Col 4:5; Hb 11:15.—3. *definite, fixed time* Mt 13:30; 26:18; Mk 11:13; Lk 8:13; 19:44; Gal 4:10; 6:9; 2 Ti 4:6.—4. *the time of crisis, the last times* Mt 8:29; 16:3; Mk 10:30; 13:33; Lk 21:8; 1 Cor 7:29; Eph 1:10; Rv 1:3.

Καῖσαρ, ος, ὁ *Caesar, emperor* Mk 12:14, 16f; Lk 2:1; 3:1; 23:2; J 19:12; Ac 17:7; 25:10–12; Phil 4:22.

Καισάρεια, ας, ἡ *Caesarea*—1. Καισάρεια ἡ Φιλίππου *Caesarea Philippi,* a city at the foot of Mt. Hermon, in the tetrarchy of Philip Mt 16:13; Mk 8:27.—2. Caesarea 'by the sea,' south of Mt. Carmel, seat of the Roman procurators and capital of Palestine Ac 8:40; 10:1, 24; 18:22; 21:8, 16; 25:1, 4, 6, 13.

καίτοι particle *and yet* Ac 14:17; Hb 4:3.*

καίτοιγε or **καίτοι γε** particle *and yet* J 4:2; Ac 14:17 v.l.*

καίω—1. *light something, have* or *keep something burning* lit. Mt 5:15; Lk 12:35; J 5:35; Hb 12:18; Rv 8:8, 10; 21:8. Fig. Lk 24:32.—2. pass. *be burned* J 15:6; 1 Cor 13:3 v.l. [*caustic*]

κἀκεῖ = καὶ ἐκεῖ adv. *and there* Mt 5:23; 10:11; 28:10; J 11:54; Ac 14:7; 27:6. *There also* Mk 1:38 v.l.; Ac 17:13.

κἀκεῖθεν = καὶ ἐκεῖθεν adv. *and from there* Mk 9:30; Lk 11:53; Ac 7:4; 16:12; 27:4; 28:15. *And then* Ac 13:21.

κἀκεῖνος, η, ο = καὶ ἐκεῖνος *and that one, and he* Lk 11:7; J 10:16; Ac 18:19; *and he, and it* or *that* Mt 15:18; Mk 16:11; J 7:29. *That one also, also he, he too* Mk 12:4f; Lk 20:11; J 6:57; Ac 15:11; 1 Cor 10:6; 2 Ti 2:12.

κακία, ας, ἡ *badness, faultiness* in the sense *depravity, wickedness, vice* Ac

8:22; 1 Cor 14:20; Js 1:21; 1 Pt 2:16. Malice, ill will, malignity Ro 1:29; Col 3:8; 1 Pt 2:1. Trouble, misfortune Mt 6:34.

κακοήθεια, ας, ἡ malice, malignity, craftiness Ro 1:29.*

κακολογέω speak evil of, revile, insult Mt 15:4; Mk 7:10; 9:39; Ac 19:9.*

κακοπάθεια, ας, ἡ and **κακοπαθία, ας, ἡ** perseverance, strenuous effort Js 5:10.*

κακοπαθέω suffer misfortune 2 Ti 2:9; Js 5:13. Bear hardship patiently 2 Ti 4:5.*

κακοπαθία see κακοπάθεια.

κακοποιέω do wrong, be an evildoer or a criminal 1 Pt 3:17; 3 J 11. In Mk 3:4 = Lk 6:9 the meaning may be as above or harm, injure.*

κακοποιός, όν doing evil, as noun evildoer, criminal 1 Pt 2:12, 14; 4:15; J 18:30 v.l.*

κακός, ή, όν bad, evil Mt 21:41; 24:48; 27:23; Mk 7:21; J 18:23; Ro 7:19, 21; 1 Cor 15:33; Rv 2:2. Evil, wrong, harmful, as noun harm Ac 9:13; 16:28; 28:5; Ro 12:17; 13:10; 14:20; Js 3:8; 1 Pt 3:9. [caco-, a combining form in numerous words, such as cacophony (κακός + φωνή)]

κακοῦργος, ον as noun ὁ κ. criminal, evildoer Lk 23:32f, 39; 2 Ti 2:9.*

κακουχέω maltreat, torment Hb 11:37; 13:3.*

κακόω harm, mistreat Ac 7:6, 19; 12:1; 18:10; 1 Pt 3:13. Make angry, embitter Ac 14:2.*

κακῶς adv. badly, wrongly, wickedly J 18:23; Ac 23:5; Js 4:3. Severely Mt 15:22; 17:15 v.l. κ. ἔχειν be ill, sick Mt 4:24; Mk 6:55; Lk 5:31.

κάκωσις, εως, ἡ mistreatment, oppression Ac 7:34.*

καλάμη, ης, ἡ straw, perh. stubble 1 Cor 3:12.*

κάλαμος, ου, ὁ reed Mt 11:7; 12:20; Lk 7:24. Stalk, staff Mt 27:29f, 48; Mk 15:19, 36. Measuring rod Rv 11:1; 21:15f. Reed pen 3 J 13.* [calamus, the quill of a feather]

καλέω call, name, address as Mt 22:43, 45; 23:7f, 10; Lk 1:59f; 2:4; 10:39; Ac 14:12; Ro 9:26; 1 Pt 3:6. Almost equivalent to the verb 'to be' Mt 2:23; Lk 1:32, 35f; 1 Cor 15:9; Hb 3:13. Invite Mt 22:3, 9; J 2:2; 1 Cor 10:27; Rv 19:9; call together Mt 20:8; 25:14; Lk 19:13. Summon Mt 2:7, 15; Mk 3:31; Ac 4:18; 24:2. Fig., of God or Christ call to eternal salvation, repentance, etc. Mk 2:17; 1 Cor 1:9; Gal 5:8, 13; Eph 4:1; 1 Ti 6:12; Hb 9:15; 1 Pt 5:10. [ecclesia, ἐκ + καλεῖν]

καλλιέλαιος, ου, ἡ the cultivated olive tree Ro 11:24.*

κάλλιον comparative degree of καλῶς.

καλοδιδάσκαλος, ον teaching what is good Tit 2:3.*

Καλοὶ λιμένες, Καλῶν λιμένων, οἱ Fair Havens, a bay on the south coast of Crete, near the city of Lasaea Ac 27:8.*

καλοκαγαθία, ας, ἡ nobility of character, excellence a Graeco-Roman ideal Js 5:10 v.l.*

καλοποιέω do what is right or good 2 Th 3:13.*

καλός, ή, όν beautiful Lk 21:5. Good, useful, free from defects, fine Mt 7:17ff; 13:8, 23, 48; Mk 4:8, 20; Lk 14:34; J 2:10. Morally good, noble, praiseworthy Mt 5:16; Mk 14:6; Ro 7:18, 21; Gal 6:9; Hb 5:14; 10:24; 13:18; Js 2:7; 4:17; 1 Pt 4:10. καλόν (ἐστιν) it is good, pleasant, advantageous Mt 18:8f; Mk 9:5; 1 Cor 7:26a; morally good Mk 7:27; 1 Cor 7:1, 8, 26b; Hb 13:9. καλόν ἐστιν αὐτῷ μᾶλλον it is better for him Mk 9:42. καλὸν ἦν αὐτῷ it would have been better for him Mt 26:24. [calligraphy, καλός + γράφειν]

κάλυμμα, ατος, τό veil, covering lit. 2 Cor 3:13. Fig. 3:14, 15, 16.*

καλύπτω cover, hide, conceal lit. Mt 8:24; Lk 8:16; 23:30. Fig. Js 5:20; 1 Pt 4:8; 2 Cor 4:3. [apocalypse, ἀπό + καλύπτειν]

καλῶς adv. well Mk 7:37; Lk 6:48; Gal 5:7; rightly Mk 7:6; as exclamation well said! Mk 12:32; Ro 11:20; used ironically 2 Cor 11:4. κ. ποιεῖν do good Mt 12:12; Lk 6:27, but do what is right 1

Cor 7:37f; Js 2:8, 19. κ. ἔχειν be in good health Mk 16:18. Comparative κάλλιον Ac 25:10.

κάμέ = καὶ ἐμέ.

κάμηλος, ου, ὁ and ἡ camel Mt 3:4; 23:24; Mk 10:25; Lk 18:25. [camel, of Semitic origin]

κάμητε 2 aor. act. subj. 2 pl. of κάμνω.

κάμιλος, ου, ὁ rope, ship's cable as v.l. in Mt 19:24; Mk 10:25; Lk 18:25.*

κάμινος, ου, ἡ oven, furnace Mt 13:42, 50; Rv 1:15; 9:2.*

καμμύω close (the eyes) Mt 13:15; Ac 28:27.*

κάμνω κ. ψυχῇ be discouraged Hb 12:3. Be ill Js 5:15.*

κάμοί = καὶ ἐμοί.

κάμπτω bend, bow Ro 11:4; 14:11; Eph 3:14; Phil 2:10.*

κἄν = καὶ ἐάν and if Mk 16:18; Lk 12:38; J 8:55; Js 5:15. Even if Mt 21:21; J 8:14; Hb 12:20. (Even) if only, at least Ac 5:15; 2 Cor 11:16.

Κανά, ἡ indecl. Cana, a city in Galilee J 2:1, 11; 4:46; 21:2.*

Καναναῖος, ου, ὁ Cananaean, surname of the second Simon among the Twelve; it means enthusiast, zealot Mt 10:4; Mk 3:18.*

Κανανίτης, ου, ὁ Canaanite, man from Cana, as v.l. in Mt 10:4; Mk 3:18.*

Κανδάκη, ης, ἡ Candace, title of the queen of Ethiopia Ac 8:27.*

κανών, όνος, ὁ—1. rule, standard Gal 6:16; Phil 3:16 v.l.—2. sphere of action, province, limits 2 Cor 10:13, 15f.*

Καπερναούμ see Καφαρναούμ.

καπηλεύω trade in, peddle, huckster 2 Cor 2:17.*

καπνός, οῦ, ὁ smoke Ac 2:19; Rv 9:2f, 17f; 15:8.

Καππαδοκία, ας, ἡ Cappadocia, a province in the interior of Asia Minor Ac 2:9; 1 Pt 1:1.*

καραδοκία, ας, ἡ eager expectation Phil 1:20 v.l.*

καρδία, ας, ἡ heart as the seat of physical life Ac 14:17. Mainly as the center and source of the whole inner life Mt 18:35; Lk 16:15; 2 Cor 5:12; 1 Th 2:4; 1 Pt 1:22; 3:4. Of the emotions J 16:6, 22; Ro 1:24; Hb 10:22. Of the will Ac 11:23; Ro 2:5, 15; 2 Pt 2:14. καρδία may sometimes be translated mind Lk 24:25; Ac 7:23; Ro 1:21; 2 Cor 9:7, and approaches the sense conscience 1 J 3:20f. ἐν τῇ κ. to oneself Mt 24:48; Ro 10:6; Rv 18:7. Fig. καρδία in the sense interior, center Mt 12:40. [cardiac]

καρδιογνώστης, ου, ὁ knower of hearts Ac 1:24; 15:8.*

Κάρπος, ου, ὁ Carpus, a Christian 2 Ti 4:13.*

καρπός, οῦ, ὁ fruit—1. lit. Mt 12:33; 21:34; Mk 11:14; Lk 13:6f; Js 5:7, 18; Rv 22:2. Crop(s) Mk 4:29; Lk 12:17; J 4:36. Of offspring Lk 1:42; Ac 2:30.—2. fig. fruit in the sense result, outcome, deed Mt 7:16, 20; J 15:5, 8, 16; Gal 5:22; Eph 5:9; Phil 1:11; Js 3:18; Hb 12:11. In the sense advantage, gain Ro 1:13; Phil 1:22; 4:17. [carpo-, combining form, as in endocarp, mesocarp, pericarp]

καρποφορέω bear fruit or crops—1. lit. Mk 4:28.—2. fig. Mt 13:23; Mk 4:20; Lk 8:15; Ro 7:4f; Col 1:6, 10.*

καρποφόρος, ον fruitbearing, fruitful Ac 14:17; J 15:2 v.l.*

καρτερέω endure, persevere Hb 11:27.*

[ἀπὸ] Καρυώτου (from) Kerioth J 6:71 v.l.

κάρφος, ους, τό speck, chip, a small piece of straw, chaff, wood, etc. Mt 7:3ff; Lk 6:41f.*

κατά prep. w. gen. and acc.—I. with the genitive—1. of place down (from) Mk 5:13; throughout Lk 23:5; Ac 9:31, 42; 10:37.—2. fig. by Mt 26:63; Hb 6:13, 16. Against Mt 5:11; 10:35; Mk 14:55; Lk 11:23; J 19:11; Ac 25:3, 15, 27; Ro 8:31; 1 Cor 4:6; Gal 5:17; Rv 2:4, 14, 20.—II. with the accusative—1. of place—a. of extension in space along Ac 25:3; 27:5. Through Lk 8:39. Throughout Ac 11:1. Over 8:1. Among 21:21.—b. of direction toward Ac 8:26; Phil 3:14. Up to Lk 10:32; to Ac 16:7. κατὰ πρόσωπον to the face Gal 2:11.—c. serving to isolate or separate by Ac 28:16; Js 2:17; to Ro 14:22. κατὰ μόνας alone, by oneself Mk 4:10; Lk 9:18.—d. as a distributive κατὰ πόλιν in every

city Ac 15:21; 20:23; Tit 1:5. Cf. Lk
8:1; Ac 15:36.—**2.** of time *at* Ro 9:9;
in Hb 1:10; 3:8; *during* Mt 1:20; 2:12;
about Ac 16:25. Distributively κ. ἔτος
every year Lk 2:41; cf. Mt 26:55; Ac
2:46f; 17:17; 2 Cor 11:28; Rv 22:2.—**3.**
distributively (apart from place and time
as above) κ. δύο ἤ τρεῖς *two or three
at a time* 1 Cor 14:27. κ. ἕνα *one after
the other* 14:31. Cf. Mk 6:40; Ac 21:19.
κ. ὄνομα *by name* J 10:3; 3 J 15.—**4.**
of goal or purpose *for (the purpose of)*
J 2:6; *to* 2 Cor 11:21.—**5.** of the norm,
of similarity, homogeneity—**a.** to introduce the norm that governs something *according to, in accordance with*
Mt 2:16; Lk 2:22; 22:22; J 19:7; Ro 8:28;
1 Cor 3:8; 15:3; Hb 7:5. *As a result of,
on the basis of* Mt 19:3; Gal 2:2; Phil
4:11; Phlm 14.—**b.** of equality, similarity, example *(just) as, similar(ly) to*
Mt 23:3; Gal 4:28. κατὰ τὰ αὐτά *in (just)
the same way* Lk 6:23, 26; 17:30. κατὰ
τὸ αὐτό *together* Ac 14:1. καθ᾽ ὅν τρόπον *just as* 15:11; 27:25. Frequently the
κατά phrase is equivalent to an adverb:
κ. συγκυρίαν *by chance* Lk 10:31. κ.
κράτος *powerfully* Ac 19:20. κ. λόγον
reasonably 18:14.—**6.** denoting relationship to something *with respect to,
in relation to* Ac 17:22; Ro 1:3f; 9:3, 5;
Col 3:20, 22; Hb 2:17.—**7.** sometimes
the κατά phrase can function as an adj.,
a possessive pronoun, or the genitive
of a noun. Adj.: κατὰ φύσιν *natural*
Ro 11:21. κατὰ σάρκα *earthly* Eph 6:5.
Poss. pron.: καθ᾽ ὑμᾶς *your* Ac 17:28.
κατ᾽ ἐμέ *my* Ro 1:15. Gen. of a noun
κ. Ἰουδαίους *of the Jews* Ac 26:3. κ.
πίστιν *of faith* Hb 11:7. Cf. the title
εὐαγγέλιον κατὰ Ματθαῖον, etc. [*cat-,
cata-, cath-,* combining forms, as in
category, catastrophe, cathode]

κατάβα 2 aor. act. impv. 2 sing. of καταβαίνω.

καταβαίνω *come down, go down, climb
down* Mt 8:1; Mk 1:10; 9:9; 15:30, 32;
Lk 19:5f; Ac 25:7; J 2:12; 4:47, 49, 51;
Ro 10:7; Eph 4:10; Js 1:17; Rv 12:12.
Get out Mt 14:29. *Fall* 7:25, 27. Fig.
be brought down 11:23.

καταβάλλω act. and pass. *throw down,
strike down* 2 Cor 4:9; Rv 12:10 v.l.
Mid. *found, lay (a foundation)* fig. Hb

6:1.* [*catabolism,* destructive metab-
olism]

καταβαρέω *burden, be a burden to* 2
Cor 12:16.*

καταβαρύνω *weigh down, burden* pass.
be heavy Mk 14:40.*

καταβάς 2 aor. act. ptc. of καταβαίνω.

κατάβασις, εως, ἡ *slope, declivity* Lk
19:37.* [*catabasis,* of a disease in de-
cline]

καταβάτω 2 aor. act. impv. 3 sing. of
καταβαίνω.

**καταβέβηκα, καταβῇ, κατάβηθι, κα-
ταβῆναι, καταβήσομαι** pf. act. ind.,
2 aor. act. subj. 3 sing., 2 aor. act.
impv. 2 sing., 2 aor. act. inf., and fut.
ind. of καταβαίνω.

καταβιβάζω *bring down, make come
down* Mt 11:23 v.l.; Lk 10:15 v.l.; Ac
19:33 v.l.*

καταβοάω *cry out, bring charges, complain* Ac 18:13 v.l.*

καταβολή, ῆς, ἡ *foundation, beginning*
Mt 25:34; Lk 11:50; J 17:24; Eph 1:4;
Hb 11:11; Rv 17:8.

καταβραβεύω *decide against* (as um-
pire), *rob of a prize, condemn* Col 2:18.*

καταγαγεῖν 2 aor. act. inf. of κατάγω.

καταγγελεύς, έως, ὁ *proclaimer,
preacher* Ac 17:18.*

καταγγέλλω *proclaim* Ac 13:5; 16:21;
17:23; Ro 1:8; 1 Cor 9:14; 11:26; Phil
1:17f.

καταγελάω *laugh at, ridicule* w. gen.
Mt 9:24; Mk 5:40; Lk 8:53.*

καταγινώσκω *condemn, convict* w. gen.
Gal 2:11; 1 J 3:20f; Mk 7:2 v.l.*

κατάγνυμι *break* Mt 12:20; J 19:31–33.*

καταγράφω *write* J 8:6, also vs. 8 v.l.*

κατάγω *lead* or *bring down* Ac 9:30;
22:30; 23:15, 20, 28; Ro 10:6. Act. *bring
boats to land* Lk 5:11; pass. *put in* at
a harbor Ac 27:3; 28:12; 21:3 v.l.*

καταγωνίζομαι *conquer, defeat, overcome* Hb 11:33.*

καταδέω *bind up* Lk 10:34.*

κατάδηλος, ον *very clear, quite plain*
Hb 7:15.*

καταδικάζω condemn, find or pronounce guilty Mt 12:7, 37; Lk 6:37; Js 5:6.*

καταδίκη, ης, ἡ condemnation, sentence of condemnation Ac 25:15.*

καταδιώκω search for, hunt for Mk 1:36.*

καταδουλόω enslave, reduce to slavery fig. 2 Cor 11:20; Gal 2:4.*

καταδυναστεύω oppress, exploit, dominate w. gen. Ac:10:38; Js 2:6.*

κατάθεμα, ατος, τό accursed thing Rv 22:3.*

καταθεματίζω curse Mt 26:74.*

κατάθεσθαι 2 aor. mid. inf. of κατατίθημι.

καταισχύνω dishonor, disfigure 1 Cor 11:4f. Put to shame 1 Cor 1:27; pass. be put to shame, be humiliated Lk 13:17; 2 Cor 7:14; 9:4; 1 Pt 3:16; Mt 20:28 v.l. Humiliate 1 Cor 11:22. Disappoint Ro 5:5; pass. 9:33; 10:11; 1 Pt 2:6.*

κατακαήσομαι 2 fut. pass. ind. of κατακαίω.

κατακαίω burn up, burn down, consume by fire Mt 3:12; 13:30, 40; Ac 19:19; Hb 13:11; Rv 8:7; 18:8; 2 Pt 3:10 v.l.

κατακαλύπτω mid. cover oneself with a veil 1 Cor 11:6f.*

κατακανθήσομαι, κατακαῦσαι, κατακαύσει 1 fut. pass., 1 aor. act. inf., and fut. act. ind. 3 sing. of κατακαίω.

κατακαυχάομαι boast (against) Ro 11:18; Js 3:14; 4:16 v.l. Triumph over w. gen. Js 2:13.*

κατακαυχῶ pres. impv. 2 sing. of κατακαυχάομαι Ro 11:18.

κατάκειμαι lie down of sick people Mk 1:30; 2:4; cf. 5:40 v.l.; Lk 5:25; J 5:3, 6; Ac 9:33; 28:8. Recline on a couch at a dinner table, dine Mk 2:15; 14:3; Lk 5:29; 7:37; 1 Cor 8:10.*

κατακλάω break in pieces Mk 6:41; Lk 9:16.*

κατακλείω shut up, lock up Lk 3:20; Ac 26:10.*

κατακληροδοτέω parcel out by lot Ac 13:19 v.l.*

κατακληρονομέω give (over) as an inheritance Ac 13:19.*

κατακλίνω act. cause to lie down or sit down to eat Lk 9:14f. Pass. recline at dinner Lk 7:36; 14:8; 24:30.* [cataclinal, of descent in the direction toward which strata dip]

κατακλύζω flood, inundate pass. 2 Pt 3:6.*

κατακλυσμός, οῦ, ὁ flood, deluge Mt 24:38f; Lk 17:27; 2 Pt 2:5.* [cataclysm]

κατακολουθέω follow w. dat. Lk 23:55; Ac 16:17.*

κατακόπτω cut, bruise, beat Mk 5:5.*

κατακρημνίζω throw down (from) a cliff Lk 4:29.*

κατάκριμα, ατος, τό punishment, doom Ro 5:16, 18; 8:1.*

κατακρίνω condemn, pronounce sentence Mt 27:3; Mk 10:33; Lk 11:31f; Ro 2:1; 8:3, 34; Hb 11:7; 2 Pt 2:6.

κατάκρισις, εως, ἡ condemnation 2 Cor 3:9; 7:3.*

κατακύπτω bend down J 8:8.*

κατακυριεύω become master, gain dominion over, subdue w. gen. Ac 19:16. Be master, lord it (over), rule w. gen. Mt 20:25; Mk 10:42; 1 Pt 5:3.*

καταλαλέω speak against, speak evil of, slander w. gen. Js 4:11; 1 Pt 2:12; 3:16.*

καταλαλιά, ᾶς, ἡ evil speech, slander, defamation 2 Cor 12:20; 1 Pt 2:1.*

κατάλαλος, ον slanderous subst. ὁ κ. the slanderer Ro 1:30.*

καταλαμβάνω—1.—a. act. and pass. seize, win, attain, make one's own Ro 9:30; 1 Cor 9:24; Phil 3:12f; ending of Mk in the Freer Gospels 3. For J 1:5 there are two sets of possibilities: grasp, comprehend, appreciate and overcome, put out, master.—**b.** seize with hostile intent, overtake, come upon Mk 9:18; J 12:35; 6:17 v.l.; 1 Th 5:4.—**c.** catch, detect J 8:3f.—**2.** mid. grasp, find, understand Ac 4:13; 10:34; Eph 3:18; ἐγὼ δὲ κατελαβόμην I satisfied myself Ac 25:25.* [catalepsy, a condition of muscular rigidity]

καταλέγω select, enroll 1 Ti 5:9.* [catalogue]

κατάλειμμα, ατος, τό *remnant* Ro 9:27 v.l.*

καταλείπω *leave (behind)* Mt 16:4; 19:5; 21:17; Mk 12:19, 21; Lk 15:4; 20:31; Ac 18:19; 24:27; Hb 11:27. *Abandon, give up* Mk 14:52; Lk 5:28. *Neglect* Ac 6:2. *Keep* Ro 11:4. Pass. *remain behind* J 8:9; 1 Th 3:1; *be open* Hb 4:1.

καταλελειμμένος pf. pass. ptc. of καταλείπω.

καταλιθάζω *stone to death* Lk 20:6.*

καταλιπών 2 aor. act. ptc. of καταλείπω.

καταλλαγείς 2 aor. pass. ptc. of καταλλάσσω.

καταλλαγή, ῆς, ἡ *reconciliation* Ro 5:11; 11:15; 2 Cor 5:18f.*

καταλλάσσω *reconcile* Ro 5:10; 1 Cor 7:11; 2 Cor 5:18–20; Ac 12:22 v.l.* [*catalase*, an enzyme that decomposes hydrogen peroxide]

κατάλοιπος, ον *left, remaining* οἱ κ. *the rest* Ac 15:17.*

κατάλυμα, ατος, τό *guest room, dining room* Mk 14:14; Lk 22:11. Since Lk 10:34 uses the more specific term for *inn*, πανδοχεῖον, the term κ. in 2:7 is best understood as *guest room*.*

καταλύω—1. trans.—**a.** *throw down, detach* Mk 13:2.—**b.** *destroy, demolish, dismantle* lit. Mt 27:40; Mk 14:58; Ac 6:14. Fig. Ro 14:20; 2 Cor 5:1; Gal 2:18.—**c.** *do away with, annul, make invalid* Mt 5:17; Lk 23:2 v.l. *Ruin, bring to an end* Ac 5:38; *stop* 5:39.—**2.** intrans. *halt, rest, find lodging* Lk 9:12; 19:7. [*catalysis, catalytic*]

καταμάθετε 2 aor. act. impv. 2 pl. of καταμανθάνω.

καταμανθάνω *observe (well), notice* Mt 6:28.*

καταμαρτυρέω *bear witness against, testify against* Mt 26:62; 27:13; Mk 14:60.*

καταμένω *stay, live* Ac 1:13; 1 Cor 16:6 v.l.*

καταμόνας = κατὰ μόνας, see s.v. μόνος.

κατανάθεμα v.l. for κατάθεμα in Rv 22:3, with the same meaning.

καταναθεματίζω *curse* Mt 26:74 v.l.*

καταναλίσκω *consume* Hb 12:29.*

καταναρκάω *burden, be a burden to* w. gen. 2 Cor 11:9; 12:13f.*

κατανεύω *signal* by means of a nod Lk 5:7.*

κατανοέω *notice, observe* Mt 7:3; Lk 6:41; Ac 27:39. *Look at, consider, contemplate* Lk 12:24, 27; Ac 7:31f; Js 1:23f; Hb 3:1. *See through (one's) tricks* Lk 20:23.

καταντάω *come (to), arrive (at)* Ac 16:1; 18:19; 28:13; 1 Cor 10:11; 14:36. *Attain (to)* Ac 26:7; Eph 4:13; Phil 3:11.

κατάνυξις, εως, ἡ *stupefaction, stupor* Ro 11:8.*

κατανύσσομαι *be pierced, stabbed* fig. Ac 2:37.*

καταξιόω *consider worthy* pass. Lk 20:35; 21:36 v.l.; Ac 5:41; 2 Th 1:5.*

καταπατέω *trample under foot* lit. Mt 5:13; 7:6; Lk 8:5; 12:1. Fig. *treat with disdain* Hb 10:29.*

κατάπαυσις, εως, ἡ *rest* Ac 7:49. *Place of rest* Hb 3:11, 18; 4:1, 3, 5, 10f.*

καταπαύω—1. trans. *(cause to) stop, restrain* Ac 14:18. *Bring to a place of rest* Hb 4:8.—**2.** intrans. *stop, rest* 4:4, 10.*

καταπεσών 2 aor. act. ptc. of καταπίπτω.

καταπέτασμα, ατος, τό *curtain* Mt 27:51; Mk 15:38; Lk 23:45; Hb 6:19; 9:3; 10:20.*

καταπιεῖν, καταπίῃ 2 aor. act. inf. and subj. 3 sing. of καταπίνω.

καταπίνω *swallow up*—**1.** lit. though more or less transferred Mt 23:24; Rv 12:16. *Devour* 1 Pt 5:8. Pass. *be drowned* Hb 11:29; *be overwhelmed* 2 Cor 2:7.—**2.** fig. *swallow up* 1 Cor 15:54; 2 Cor 5:4.*

καταπίμπρημι *burn to ashes* κατέπρησεν 1 aor. act. ind. 3 sing. 2 Pt 2:6 v.l.*

καταπίπτω *fall (down)* Lk 8:6; Ac 26:14; 28:6.*

καταπλέω *sail (toward,* lit.. *down)* Lk 8:26.*

καταποθῇ 1 aor. pass. subj. 3 sing. of καταπίνω.

καταπονέω subdue, wear out, oppress pres. pass. ptc. 2 Pt 2:7; Ac 4:2 v.l. As noun one who is oppressed Ac 7:24.*

καταποντίζω throw into the sea, pass. be sunk, be drowned Mt 18:6; sink 14:30.*

κατάρα, ας, ἡ a curse, an imprecation Gal 3:10, 13; Hb 6:8; Js 3:10; 2 Pt 2:14.*

καταράομαι to curse Mt 25:41; Mk 11:21; Lk 6:28; Ro 12:14; Js 3:9.*

καταργέω—1. make ineffective, powerless lit. use up, waste Lk 13:7. Fig. make ineffective, nullify Ro 3:3; 4:14; 1 Cor 1:28; Gal 3:17; make invalid Ro 3:31; Eph 2:15.—**2.** abolish, set aside, do away with, bring to an end Ro 6:6; 1 Cor 6:13; 13:11; 15:24, 26; 2 Th 2:8; 2 Ti 1:10; Hb 2:14. Pass. cease, pass away 1 Cor 2:6; 13:8, 10; 2 Cor 3:7, 11, 13f; Gal 5:11.—**3.** καταργοῦμαι ἀπό τινος be released from, have nothing more to do with Ro 7:2, 6; be estranged Gal 5:4.*

καταριθμέω count pass. belong to Ac 1:17.*

καταρτίζω—1. put in order, restore 2 Cor 13:11; Gal 6:1; mend Mt 4:21; Mk 1:19. Complete, make complete 1 Cor 1:10; 1 Th 3:10; Hb 13:21; 1 Pt 5:10. κατηρτισμένος fully trained Lk 6:40.—**2.** prepare, make, create, design Mt 21:16; Ro 9:22; Hb 10:5; 11:3.*

κατάρτισις, εως, ἡ being made complete 2 Cor 13:9.*

καταρτισμός, οῦ, ὁ equipping or training Eph 4:12.*

κατασείω shake, wave Ac 19:33. Motion, signal 12:17; 13:16; 21:40.*

κατασκάπτω tear down, raze to the ground Ro 11:3; Ac 15:16.*

κατασκευάζω make ready, prepare Mk 1:2; Lk 1:17. Build, construct, create Hb 3:3f; 11:7; 1 Pt 3:20. Furnish, equip Hb 9:2, 6.

κατασκηνοῦν pres. act. inf. of κατασκηνόω.

κατασκηνόω live, dwell Ac 2:26. Nest Mt 13:32; Mk 4:32; Lk 13:19.*

κατασκήνωσις, εως, ἡ a place to live, a nest Mt 8:20; Lk 9:58.*

κατασκιάζω overshadow Hb 9:5.*

κατασκοπέω spy out, lie in wait for Gal 2:4.*

κατάσκοπος, ου, ὁ a spy Hb 11:31; Js 2:25 v.l.*

κατασοφίζομαι take advantage of by trickery Ac 7:19.*

κατασταθήσομαι fut. pass. of καθίστημι.

καταστείλας 1 aor. act. ptc. of καταστέλλω.

καταστέλλω restrain, quiet Ac 19:35f.*

κατάστημα, ατος, τό behavior, demeanor Tit 2:3.*

καταστήσω fut. act. ind. of καθίστημι.

καταστολή, ῆς, ἡ deportment 1 Ti 2:9.*

καταστρέφω upset, overturn Mt 21:12; Mk 11:15; J 2:15 v.l. τὰ κατεστραμμένα ruins Ac 15:16 v.l.*

καταστρηνιάω be filled with desires that conflict with affection for someone 1 Ti 5:11.*

καταστροφή, ῆς, ἡ ruin, destruction 2 Ti 2:14; 2 Pt 2:6.* [catastrophe]

καταστρώννυμι lay low, kill pass. 1 Cor 10:5.*

κατασύρω drag (away by force) Lk 12:58.*

κατασφάζω or **κατασφάττω** slaughter, strike down Lk 19:27.*

κατασφραγίζω seal (up) Rv 5:1.*

κατάσχεσις, εως, ἡ possession, taking into possession Ac 7:5, 45; 13:33 v.l. Holding back, restraining, delay 20:16 v.l.*

κατάσχωμεν 2 aor. act. subj. 1 pl. of κατέχω.

κατατίθημι—1. lay, place Mk 15:46 v.l.—**2.** mid. with χάρις as object, grant or do a favor Ac 24:27; 25:9.*

κατατομή, ῆς, ἡ mutilation Phil 3:2.*

κατατοξεύω shoot down Hb 12:20 v.l.*

κατατρέχω run down Ac 21:32.*

καταυγάζω shine upon, illuminate 2 Cor 4:4 v.l.*

καταφαγεῖν, καταφάγομαι 2 aor. act. inf. and fut. ind. of κατεσθίω.

καταφέρω cast a vote against Ac 26:10; bring charges 25:7. Pass. sink into sleep 20:9a; overwhelmed by sleep 20:9b.*

καταφεύγω *flee* Ac 14:6. *Take refuge* Hb' 6:18.*

καταφθείρω *destroy* 2 Pt 2:12 v.l. *Ruin, corrupt, deprave* 2 Ti 3:8.*

καταφιλέω *kiss* Mt 26:49; Mk 14:45; Lk 7:38, 45; 15:20; Ac 20:37.*

καταφρονέω—1. *look down on, despise, scorn* w. gen. Mt 6:24; 18:10; Lk 16:13; 1 Cor 11:22; 1 Ti 4:12; 2 Pt 2:10; Tit 2:15 v.l. *Entertain wrong ideas about* Ro 2:4; 1 Ti 6:2.—2. *care nothing for, disregard, be unafraid of* Hb 12:2.*

καταφρονητής, οῦ, ὁ *despiser, scoffer* Ac 13:41.*

καταφυγών 2 aor. act. ptc. of κατα-φεύγω.

καταφωνέω v.l. for ἐπιφωνέω with the same meaning Ac 22:24.*

καταχέω *pour out* or *down over* w. gen. Mt 26:7; Mk 14:3.*

καταχθείς 1 aor. pass. ptc. of κατάγω.

καταχθόνιος, ον *under the earth, subterranean* Phil 2:10.*

καταχράομαι *use, be absorbed in* or *with* 1 Cor 7:31; *make full use of, exploit* 9:18.* [catachresis]

καταψηφίζομαι *be enrolled* Ac 1:26 v.l.*

καταψύχω *cool (off)* Lk 16:24.*

κατεάγην, κατεαγῶσιν, κατέαξα, κατεάξω 2 aor. pass., 2 aor. pass. subj. 3 pl., 1 aor. act. ind., and fut. act. ind. of κατάγνυμι.

κατέβην 2 aor. act. ind. of καταβαίνω.

κατεγέλων impf. act. of καταγελάω.

κατέγνωσμαι pf. pass. ind. of κατα-γινώσκω.

κατέδραμον 2 aor. act. ind. of κατα-τρέχω.

κατέθηκα 1 aor. act. ind. of κατατίθημι.

κατείδωλος, ον *full of images* or *idols* Ac 17:16.*

κατειλημμένος, κατείληφα pf. mid. and pass. ptc., and pf. act. ind. of κα-ταλαμβάνω.

κατεκάην 2 aor. pass. ind. of κατακαίω.

κατεκρίθην 1 aor. pass. ind. of κατα-κρίνω.

κατέλαβον 2 aor. act. ind. of καταλαμ-βάνω.

κατέλειψα 1 aor. act. ind. of κατα-λείπω.

κατελήμφθην 1 aor. pass. ind. of κα-ταλαμβάνω.

κατελθεῖν 2 aor. act. inf. of κατέρχο-μαι.

κατέλιπον 2 aor. act. ind. of κατα-λείπω.

κατέναντι adv. *opposite* Lk 19:30. Functions as prep. w. gen. *opposite* Mk 13:3; *in the presence of* Mt 27:24 v.l.; *before* Ro 4:17; 2 Cor 2:17; 12:19.

κατενεχθείς 1 aor. pass. ptc. of κατα-φέρω.

κατενύγην 2 aor. pass. ind. of κατα-νύσσομαι.

κατενώπιον adv. functions as prep. w. gen. *in the presence of* Jd 24; *before* Eph 1:4; Col 1:22.*

κατεξουσιάζω *exercise authority over, domineer* w. gen. Mt 20:25; Mk 10:42.*

κατέπεσον 2 aor. act. ind. of κατα-πίπτω.

κατέπιον 2 aor act. ind. of καταπίνω.

κατεπέστησαν 2 aor. act. ind. 3 pl. of κατεφίστημι.

κατέπλευσα 1 aor. act. ind. of κατα-πλέω.

κατεπόθην 1 aor. pass. ind. of κατα-πίνω.

κατέπρησα 1 aor. act. ind. formed from πρήθω + κατά, s. καταπίμπρημι 2 Pt 2:6 v.l.

κατεργάζομαι—1. *achieve, accomplish, do* Ro 1:27; 7:15, 17f, 20; 1 Cor 5:3; 1 Pt 4:3; perh. Eph 6:13 (see 3 below).—2. *bring about, produce, create* Ro 4:15; 7:8, 13; 2 Cor 7:10f; 9:11; Js 1:3. *Work out* Phil 2:12. *Prepare* 2 Cor 5:5.—3. *subdue, conquer* perh. Eph 6:13 (see 1 above).

κατέρχομαι *come down* Lk 4:31; 9:37; Ac 8:5; 15:1, 30; 21:10; Js 3:15. Of ships *arrive, put in* Ac 18:22; 27:5.

κατεσθίω and **κατέσθω** *eat up, consume, devour* lit. Mt 13:4; Rv 10:9f; 12:4. Fig. *destroy, consume* Mk 12:40; Lk 15:30; J 2:17; 2 Cor 11:20; Gal 5:15; Rv 11:5; 20:9.

κατεστάθην 1 aor. pass. ind. of καθίστημι.

κατέσταλμαι pf. pass. ind. of καταστέλλω.

κατέστησα 1 aor. act. ind. of καθίστημι.

κατεστρώθην 1 aor. pass. ind. of καταστρώννυμι.

κατευθύναι, κατευθῦναι 1 aor. act. opt. 3 sing. and inf. of κατευθύνω.

κατευθύνω lead, direct Lk 1:79; 1 Th 3:11; 2 Th 3:5.*

κατευλογέω bless Mk 10:16.*

κατέφαγον 2 aor. act. ind. of κατεσθίω.

κατεφθαρμένος pf. pass. ptc. of καταφθείρω.

κατεφίσταμαι rise up against w. dat. Ac 18:12.*

κατέφυγον 2 aor. act. ind. of καταφεύγω.

κατεφώνουν impf. act. of καταφωνέω.

κατέχεεν 1 aor. act. ind. 3 sing. of καταχέω Mt 26:7.

κατέχω—1. trans.—a. hold back, hinder Lk 4:42; keep Phlm 13; suppress Ro 1:18; restrain, check 2 Th 2:6f.—b. hold fast Lk 8:15; 1 Cor 11:2; 15:2; 1 Th 5:21; Hb 3:6, 14; 10:23; possess 1 Cor 7:30; 2 Cor 6:10; occupy Lk 14:9.—c. pass. be bound Ro 7:6; J 5:4 v.l.—2. intrans. of a ship, head for, steer toward Ac 27:40.*

κατήγαγον 2 aor. act. ind. of κατάγω.

κατήγγειλα, κατηγγέλην 1 aor. act. and 2 aor. pass. ind. of καταγγέλλω.

κατηγορείτωσαν pres. act. impv. 3 pl. of κατηγορέω.

κατηγορέω accuse Mt 12:10; 27:12; Mk 15:3f; Lk 23:2, 10, 14; J 5:45; Ac 24:2, 8, 13, 19; 25:5; Ro 2:15; Rv 12:10.

κατηγορία, ας, ἡ accusation J 18:29; 1 Ti 5:19; Tit 1:6; Lk 6:7 v.l.* [category]

κατήγορος, ου, ὁ accuser Ac 23:30, 35; 24:8 v.l.; 25:16, 18; Rv 12:10 v.l.*

κατήγωρ, ορος, ὁ accuser Rv 12:10.*

κατῆλθον 2 aor. act. ind. of κατέρχομαι.

κατηλλάγην 2 aor. pass. ind. of καταλλάσσω.

κατήνεγκα 1 aor. act. ind. of καταφέρω.

κατηραμένος pf. pass. ptc. of καταράομαι.

κατηράσω 1 aor. mid. ind. 2 sing. of καταράομαι.

κατήργηκα pf. act. ind. of καταργέω.

κατήφεια, ας, ἡ gloominess, dejection Js 4:9.*

κατηχέω inform Lk 1:4; Ac 21:21, 24. Teach, instruct Ac 18:25; Ro 2:18; 1 Cor 14:19; Gal 6:6.* [catechize]

κατηχήθημεν 1 aor. pass. ind. 1 pl. of κατάγω.

κατ᾽ ἰδίαν see ἴδιος.

κατιόω pass. become rusty, tarnished, corroded Js 5:3.*

κατισχύω be dominant, prevail Lk 23:23; be able 21:36. Win a victory over w. gen. Mt 16:18.*

κατίωται pf. pass. ind. 3 sing. of κατιόω.

κατοικέω—1. intrans. live, reside, settle Mt 2:23; 12:45; Ac 1:20; 2:5; 7:2, 4a, 48; 17:24, 26; 22:12; Eph 3:17; Col 2:9; Hb 11:9; 2 Pt 3:13; Rv 3:10; 17:8.—2. trans. inhabit, dwell in Mt 23:21; Lk 13:4; Ac 1:19; 2:14; Rv 17:2.

κατοίκησις, εως, ἡ living quarters, dwelling Mk 5:3.*

κατοικητήριον, ου, τό dwelling place Eph 2:22; Rv 18:2.*

κατοικία, ας, ἡ habitation Ac 17:26.*

κατοικίζω place in, cause to live in Js 4:5.*

κατοπτρίζω mid. look at as in a mirror, contemplate 2 Cor 3:18.*

κατόρθωμα, ατος, τό success, prosperity, good order Ac 24:2 v.l.*

κάτω adv.—1. below Mk 14:66; Ac 2:19; under Mt 2:16 v.l. τὰ κάτω this world J 8:23.—2. downward, down Mt 4:6; Lk 4:9; J 8:6; Ac 20:9. ἕως κάτω to bottom Mt 27:51; Mk 15:38.*

κατῴκισα 1 aor. act. ind. of κατοικίζω.

κατώτερος, α, ον lower Eph 4:9.*

κατωτέρω adv. lower, under. Mt 2:16.*

Καῦδα Cauda, a small island south of Crete Ac 27:16.*

καυθήσομαι fut. pass. ind. of καίω.

καῦμα, ατος, τό burning, heat Rv 7:16; 16:9.*

καυματίζω burn Mt 13:6; Mk 4:6; Rv 16:8f.*

καυματόω be scorched by the heat Mt 13:6 v.l.*

καῦσις, εως, ἡ burning Hb 6:8.*

καυσόω pass. be consumed by heat, burn up 2 Pt 3:10, 12.*

καυστηριάζω brand with a red-hot iron, sear pass., fig. 1 Ti 4:2.*

καύσων, ωνος, ὁ heat, burning (sun) Mt 20:12; a hot day Lk 12:55; scorching heat Js 1:11.* [caustic, s. καίω]

καυτηριάζω v.l. for καυστηριάζω.

καυχάομαι—1. intrans. boast, glory, pride oneself Ro 2:17, 23; 1 Cor 1:31; 4:7; 13:3; 2 Cor 10:13, 15–17; 12:5; Gal 6:13f; Phil 3:3; Js 1:9; 4:16.—2. trans. boast about 2 Cor 7:14; 9:2; 10:8; 11:16, 30.

καύχημα, ατος, τό—1. boast, object of boasting, something to boast about Ro 4:2; 1 Cor 5:6; 9:15f; Gal 6:4; Phil 1:26; Hb 3:6; pride 2 Cor 1:14; Phil 2:16.—2. boast, what is said in boasting 2 Cor 5:12; 9:3.*

καύχησις, εως, ἡ boasting, pride Ro 3:27; 15:17; 1 Cor 15:31; 2 Cor 7:4, 14; 8:24; 11:10, 17; Js 4:16; 1 Th 2:19. Object of boasting, reason for boasting 2 Cor 1:12.*

Καφαρναούμ, ἡ indecl. Capernaum, a city on the Sea of Galilee Mt 4:13; Mk 1:21; Lk 4:23, 31; 7:1; J 2:12; 4:46.

Κεγχρεαί, ῶν, αἱ Cenchreae, the seaport of Corinth Ac 18:18; Ro 16:1; subscription.*

κέδρος, ου, ἡ cedar tree J 18:1 v.l.*

Κεδρών, ὁ indecl. Kidron, a valley near Jerusalem J 18:1.*

κεῖμαι lie, recline (can serve as passive of τίθημι)—1. lit. Mt 5:14; Lk 2:12, 16; 23:53; J 20:5f, 12; 2 Cor 3:15; stand J 2:6; Rv 4:2; be stored up Lk 12:19; be laid Mt 3:10; 1 Cor 3:11; be laid out Rv 21:16.—2. fig. be appointed, set, destined Lk 2:34; Phil 1:16; 1 Th 3:3. Be given, be valid 1 Ti 1:9. Find oneself, be 1 J 5:19.

κειρία, ας, ἡ bandage, graveclothes J 11:44.*

κείρω shear Ac 8:32. Mid. have one's hair cut 18:18; 1 Cor 11:6.*

κεκαθαρμένος pf. pass. ptc. of καθαίρω.

κεκάθικα pf. act. ind. of καθίζω.

κέκαυμαι, κεκαυμένος pf. pass. ind. and ptc. of καίω.

κεκερασμένος pf. pass. ptc. of κεράννυμι.

κέκληκα pf. act. ind. of καλέω.

κέκλικα pf. act. ind. of κλίνω.

κέκμηκα pf. act. ind. of κάμνω.

κεκορεσμένος pf. pass. ptc. of κορέννυμι.

κέκραγα pf. act. ind. of κράζω.

κέκρικα pf. act. ind. of κρίνω.

κέκρυμμαι pf. pass. ind. of κρύπτω.

κέλευσμα, ατος, τό signal, (cry of) command 1 Th 4:16.*

κελεύω command, order, urge Mt 8:18; 14:19, 28; 18:25; 27:58; Lk 18:40; Ac 4:15; 8:38; 12:19; 16:22; 21:34; 23:10; 25:23.

κενεμβατεύω step on emptiness, make a misstep in ropewalking, conjectural v.l. in Col 2:18.*

κενοδοξία, ας, ἡ empty conceit Phil 2:3.*

κενόδοξος, ον conceited, boastful Gal 5:26.*

κενός, ή, όν empty—1. lit. empty-handed Mk 12:3; Lk 1:53; 20:10f.—2. fig. empty in the sense without any basis, without truth or power 1 Cor 15:14; Eph 5:6; Col 2:8; Js 2:20 v.l. In the sense without effect, without reaching its goal, (in) vain Ac 4:25; 1 Cor 15:10, 58; 1 Th 2:1. Foolish, senseless Js 2:20. εἰς κενόν in vain 2 Cor 6:1; Gal 2:2; Phil 2:16; 1 Th 3:5.* [cenotaph, κενός + τάφος]

κενοφωνία, ας, ἡ chatter, empty talk 1 Ti 6:20; 2 Ti 2:16.*

κενόω to empty Phil 2:7. Destroy, render void or invalid 1 Cor 9:15; pass. Ro 4:14; 1 Cor 1:17; lose its justification 2 Cor 9:3.* [kenosis, of Christ humbling himself]

κέντρον, ου, τό the sting of an animal Rv 9:10; fig. 1 Cor 15:55f. A goad, a pointed stick Ac 26:14; 9:5 v.l.* [center; centri-, combining form, as in centrifugal, centripetal]

κεντυρίων, ωνος, ὁ (Latin loanword) centurion a Roman army officer, roughly equivalent to our captain Mk 15:39, 44f.*

Κενχρεαί see Κεγχρεαί.

κενῶς adv. in vain, to no purpose Js 4:5.*

κεραία, ας, ἡ projection, hook as part of a letter, serif, lit. 'horn' Mt 5:18; Lk 16:17.*

κεραμεύς, έως, ὁ potter Mt 27:7, 10; Ro 9:21.*

κεραμικός, ή, όν belonging to the potter or made of clay Rv 2:27.* [ceramic]

κεράμιον, ου, τό earthenware vessel, jar Mk 14:13; Lk 22:10.*

κέραμος, ου, ὁ a roof tile made of clay Lk 5:19.*

κεράννυμι mix Rv 18:6; pour 14:10.* [crasis]

κέρας, ατος, τό horn lit. Rv 5:6; 17:3, 7, 12, 16; corners, ends of the altar 9:13. Fig., for might, power Lk 1:69. [rhinoceros, ῥίς + κέρας]

κεράτιον, ου, τό carob pod Lk 15:16.*

κερδαίνω—1. to gain lit. Mt 16:26; 25:16f, 20, 22; Mk 8:36; Lk 9:25; make a profit Js 4:13. Fig. Mt 18:15; 1 Cor 9:19–22; Phil 3:8; pass. 1 Pt 3:1.—2. avoid Ac 27:21.*

κερδάνω aor. subj. act. of κερδαίνω.

κερδῆσαι, κερδήσω 1 aor. act. inf. and fut. act. ind. of κερδαίνω.

κέρδος, ους, τό a gain Phil 1:21; 3:7; Tit 1:11.*

κερέα another spelling of κεραία.

κέρμα, ατος, τό coin, small change J 2:15.*

κερματιστής, οῦ, ὁ money changer J 2:14.*

κεφάλαιον, ου, τό—1. main thing, main point Hb 8:1.—2. financial capital, sum of money Ac 22:28.*

κεφαλαιόω in the text of Mk 12:4 is better spelled κεφαλιόω; see the latter entry.

κεφαλή, ῆς, ἡ head—1. lit. Mt 5:36; 8:20; 27:29f; Mk 6:24f, 27f; 15:29; Lk 21:28; J 13:9; Ac 21:24; Ro 12:20; 1 Cor 11:4f, 7, 10; Rv 10:1; 17:3, 7, 9; 18:19; 19:12.—2. fig.—a. head denoting one of superior rank 1 Cor 11:3; Eph 1:22; 4:15; 5:23; Col 1:18; 2:10.—b. head as extremity, end κ. γωνίας cornerstone Mt 21:42; Mk 12:10; Lk 20:17; Ac 4:11; 1 Pt 2:7. Capital or frontier city Ac 16:12 v.l. [cephalic]

κεφαλιόω strike on the head Mk 12:4.*

κεφαλίς, ίδος, ἡ roll of a book Hb 10:7.*

κέχρημαι pf. mid. and pass. ind. of χράομαι.

κηδεύω take care of, bury a corpse Mk 6:29 v.l.*

κημόω to muzzle 1 Cor 9:9.*

κῆνσος, ου, ὁ tax, poll tax Mt 17:25; 22:17, 19; Mk 12:14.* [Latin loanword, census]

κῆπος, ου, ὁ garden Lk 13:19; J 18:1, 26; 19:41.*

κηπουρός, οῦ, ὁ gardener J 20:15.*

κηρίον, ου, τό wax, honeycomb Lk 24:42 v.l.* [Cf. ceruse.]

κήρυγμα, ατος, τό proclamation, preaching Mt 12:41; Mk 16:8 shorter ending; Lk 11:32; Ro 16:25; 1 Cor 1:21; 2:4; 15:14; 2 Ti 4:17; Tit 1:3.*

κῆρυξ, υκος, ὁ proclaimer, preacher, lit. 'herald' 1 Ti 2:7; 2 Ti 1:11; 2 Pt 2:5.*

κηρύσσω proclaim aloud, announce, mention publicly, preach most often in reference to God's saving action Mt 10:27; Mk 1:4, 39, 45; 5:20; 7:36; 13:10; Lk 8:39; 9:2; 12:3; 24:47; Ac 15:21; Ro 2:21; 1 Cor 9:27; 15:12; 2 Cor 4:5; Gal 2:2; 5:11; 1 Th 2:9; 2 Ti 4:2; Rv 5:2. Proclaim victory 1 Pt 3:19.

κῆτος, ους, τό sea monster Mt 12:40.*

Κηφᾶς, ᾶ, ὁ (Aramaic = 'rock') Cephas, surname of Simon J 1:42; 1 Cor 1:12; 3:22; 9:5; 15:5; Gal 1:18; 2:9, 11, 14.*

κιβώριον, ου, τό ciborium, the seed vessel of the Egyptian bean, also a vessel of similar shape Ac 19:24 v.l.*

κιβωτός, οῦ, ἡ box, chest, the ark of Noah Mt 24:38; Lk 17:27; Hb 11:7; 1 Pt 3:20. The ark in the Holy of Holies Hb 9:4; Rv 11:19.*

κιθάρα, ας, ἡ *lyre, harp* 1 Cor 14:7; Rv 5:8; 14:2; 15:2.* [*zither*]

κιθαρίζω *play the lyre* or *harp* 1 Cor 14:7; Rv 14:2.*

κιθαρῳδός, οῦ, ὁ *lyre player, harpist* Rv 14:2; 18:22.*

Κιλικία, ας, ἡ *Cilicia,* a province in the southeast corner of Asia Minor; Tarsus is its capital Ac 6:9; 15:23, 41; 21:39; 22:3; 23:34; 27:5; Gal 1:21.*

Κίλιξ, ικος, ὁ *a Cilician* Ac 23:34 v.l.*

κινδυνεύω *be in danger, run a risk* Lk 8:23; Ac 19:27, 40; 1 Cor 15:30.*

κίνδυνος, ου, ὁ *danger, risk* Ro 8:35; 2 Cor 11:26.*

κινέω *move, move away, remove* Mt 23:4; Rv 2:5; 6:14. *Shake* Mt 27:39; Mk 15:29. *Arouse* Ac 21:30; 14:7 v.l. *Cause, bring about* 24:5. Pass. *be moved, move* Ac 17:28.* [*cinema*]

κίνησις, εως, ἡ *motion* J 5:3 v.l.* [*kinetic*]

κιννάμωμον, ου, τό Hebrew loanword *cinnamon* Rv 18:13.*

Κίς, ὁ indecl. *Kish,* father of Saul Ac 13:21.*

κίχρημι *lend* Lk 11:5.*

κλάδος, ου, ὁ *branch* Mt 13:32; 21:8; 24:32; Mk 4:32; 13:28; Lk 13:19. Fig. Ro 11:16–19, 21.* [*phylloclade, φυλή* + *κλάδος,* a flattened stem, as of cacti]

κλαίω *weep, cry* Mk 14:72; Lk 7:13, 32, 38; 19:41; 22:62; J 20:11, 13, 15; Ac 9:39; 1 Cor 7:30; Js 4:9; Rv 5:5; 18:9. *Weep for, bewail* Mt 2:18; Rv 18:9 v.l.

κλάσις, εως, ἡ *breaking* Lk 24:35; Ac 2:42; Phlm subscr.*

κλάσμα, ατος, τό *fragment, piece, crumb* Mt 14:20; 15:37; Mk 6:43; 8:8, 19f; Lk 9:17; J 6:12f.*

Κλαῦδα alt. form of Καῦδα, q.v., Ac 27:16 v.l.*

Κλαυδία, ας, ἡ *Claudia* 2 Ti 4:21.*

Κλαύδιος, ου, ὁ *Claudius*—1. Roman emperor 41–54 A.D. Ac 11:28; 18:2.—2. Claudius Lysias, Roman official in Jerusalem 23:26.*

κλαυθμός, οῦ, ὁ *weeping, crying* Mt 2:18; 13:42, 50; 25:30; Ac 20:37.

κλαύσω fut. act. ind. of κλαίω.

κλάω *break* Mt 14:19; 26:26; Mk 8:6, 19; Lk 24:30; Ac 20:7, 11; 1 Cor 11:24. [*iconoclast, εἰκών* + *κλάω*]

κλείς, κλειδός, ἡ *key* Mt 16:19; Lk 11:52; Rv 1:18; 3:7; 9:1; 20:1.* [*clef;* cf. Latin *clavis.*]

κλείω *shut, lock, close* lit. and fig. Mt 6:6; 23:13; 25:10; Lk 11:7; J 20:19, 26; Ac 21:30; 1 J 3:17; Rv 3:7f; 11:6; 20:3; 21:25. Pass. Ac 5:23; Lk 4:25.*

κλέμμα, ατος, τό *stealing, theft* Rv 9:21; Mk 7:22 v.l.*

Κλεοπᾶς, ᾶ, ὁ *Cleopas* Lk 24:18.*

κλέος, ους, τό *fame, credit* 1 Pt 2:20.*

κλέπτης, ου, ὁ *thief* Mt 6:19f; J 10:1, 8, 10; 1 Cor 6:10; 1 Pt 4:15; Rv 3:3.

κλέπτω *steal* Mt 6:19f; 27:64; Mk 10:19; Ro 2:21; Eph 4:28. [*kleptomaniac, κλέπτω* + *μανία*]

κληθήσομαι 1 fut. pass. ind. of καλέω.

κλῆμα, ατος, τό *branch,* especially of a vine J 15:2, 4–6.*

Κλήμης, εντος, ὁ *Clement* Phil 4:3.*

κληρονομέω—1. *inherit, be an heir* Gal 4:30.—2. *acquire, obtain, come into possession of* Mt 5:5; 25:34; 1 Cor 6:9f; 15:50; Gal 5:21. *Receive, share in* Mt 19:29; Mk 10:17; Lk 10:25; Hb 1:4, 14; 12:17; Rv 21:7.

κληρονομία, ας, ἡ—1. *inheritance* Mt 21:38; Mk 12:7; Lk 12:13; 20:14. *Possession, property* Ac 7:5; 13:33 v.l.; Hb 11:8. *The heirs* Ro 11:1 v.l.—2. in a specifically Christian usage *salvation* Ac 20:32; Gal 3:18; Col 3:24; Eph 1:14, 18; Hb 9:15; 1 Pt 1:4; *share* Eph 5:5.*

κληρονόμος, ου, ὁ *heir*—1. lit. Mt 21:38; Mk 12:7; Lk 20:14; Gal 4:1.—2. fig. Ro 4:13f; 8:17; Gal 3:29; 4:7; Tit 3:7; Hb 1:2; 6:17; 11:7; Js 2:5.*

κλῆρος, ου, ὁ—1. *lot* (i.e. a pebble, small stick, etc., thrown or drawn to arrive at a decision) Mt 27:35; Mk 15:24; Lk 23:34; J 19:24; Ac 1:26.—2. *that which is assigned by lot, portion, share, place* Ac 1:17, 25 v.l.; 8:21; 26:18; Col 1:12. κλῆρος in 1 Pt 5:3 means a *portion* of God's people, namely a congregation or group of congregations.* [*clergy; clerk*]

κληρόω act. *appoint by lot* pass. *be appointed by lot* ἐν ᾧ ἐκληρώθημεν *in whom our lot is cast* Eph 1:11.*

κλῆσις, εως, ἡ—1. *call, calling, invitation* Ro 11:29; 1 Cor 1:26; Eph 4:1, 4; Phil 3:14; 2 Th 1:11; 2 Ti 1:9; Hb 3:1; 2 Pt 1:10; Lk 11:42 v.l. ἡ ἐλπὶς τῆς κ. αὐτοῦ *the hope to which he calls* Eph 1:18.—2. *station in life, position, vocation* 1 Cor 7:20.*

κλητός, ἡ, όν *called, invited* Mt 20:16 v.l.; 22:14; Ro 1:1, 7; 8:28; 1 Cor 1:1f, 24; Jd 1; Rv 17:14. κλητοὶ Ἰησοῦ Χριστοῦ *called to belong to Jesus Christ* Ro 1:6.*

κλίβανος, ου, ὁ *oven, furnace* Mt 6:30; Lk 12:28; Rv 2:22 v.l.*

κλίμα, ατος, τό *district,* pl. *region* Ro 15:23; 2 Cor 11:10; Gal 1:21.* [*climate*]

κλινάριον, ου, τό *bed* Ac 5:15.*

κλίνη, ης, ἡ *bed, couch* Mk 4:21; 7:30; Lk 8:16; 17:34; *dining couch* Mk 7:4 v.l. *Pallet, stretcher* Mt 9:2, 6; Lk 5:18. *Sickbed* Rv 2:22.* [*clinic*]

κλινίδιον, ου, τό *bed* = *pallet, stretcher* Lk 5:19, 24.*

κλίνω—1. trans. *incline, bend, bow* Lk 24:5; J 19:30. *Lay (down)* Mt 8:20; Lk 9:58. *Turn to flight* Hb 11:34.—2. intrans. *decline, be far spent* Lk 9:12; 24:29.* [*enclitic,* ἐν + κλίνειν]

κλισία, ας, ἡ *a group of people eating together* Lk 9:14.*

κλοπή, ῆς, ἡ *theft, stealing* Mt 15:19; Mk 7:21.* [S. κλέπτω.]

κλύδων, ωνος, ὁ *(a succession of) waves* Lk 8:24; *surf* Js 1:6.*

κλυδωνίζομαι *be tossed here and there by waves* fig. Eph 4:14.*

Κλωπᾶς, ᾶ, ὁ *Clopas* J 19:25.*

κνήθω *itch* pass. *feel an itching* fig. 2 Ti 4:3.*

Κνίδος, ου, ἡ *Cnidus,* a peninsula with a city of the same name on the coast of Caria in s.w. Asia Minor Ac 27:7.*

κοδράντης, ου, ὁ (Latin loanword: quadrans) *quadrans, penny,* smallest Roman coin (= ¼ of an as) Mt 5:26; Mk 12:42; Lk 12:59 v.l.*

κοιλία, ας, ἡ *body cavity, belly*—1. *stomach, belly* Mt 12:40; 15:17; Mk

7:19; Lk 15:16 v.l.; Ro 16:18; 1 Cor 6:13; Phil 3:19; Rv 10:9f.—2. *womb, uterus* Mt 19:12; Lk 1:41f, 44; 2:21; 11:27; 23:29; J 3:4. ἐκ κοιλίας etc. *from birth* Lk 1:15; Ac 3:2; 14:8; Gal 1:15.—3. in reference to the depths of personality = 'heart' ἐκ τῆς κ. αὐτοῦ *from within* J 7:38.* [*coeliac,* pertaining to the cavity of the abdomen]

κοιμάω pass. *sleep, fall asleep*—1. lit. Mt 28:13; Lk 22:45; J 11:12; Ac 12:6.—2. fig., of death, *fall asleep, die, pass away* Mt 27:52; J 11:11; Ac 7:60; 13:36; 1 Cor 7:39; 11:30; 15:6, 18, 20, 51; 1 Th 4:13–15; 2 Pt 3:4.* [Cf. *cemetery.*]

κοίμησις, εως, ἡ *sleep* J 11:13.*

κοινός, ἡ, όν *common*—1. *communal, common* Ac 2:44; 4:32; Tit 1:4; Jd 3.—2. *common, ordinary, ceremonially unclean, impure* Mk 7:2, 5; Ac 10:14, 28; 11:8; Ro 14:14; Hb 10:29; Rv 21:27.* [*coenobite* or *cenobite* (κοινός + βίος), a member of a religious order living in community; opposite of anchorite (s. ἀναχωρέω); Koine, the Greek language commonly spoken and written in the Near East in the Hellenistic and Roman periods]

κοινόω *make common* or *impure, defile* ceremonially Mt 15:11, 18, 20; Mk 7:15, 18, 20, 23; Hb 9:13. *Profane, desecrate* Ac 21:28. *Consider* or *declare unclean* Ac 10:15; 11:9.*

κοινωνέω—1. *share in, have a share in* w. gen. Hb 2:14. W. dat. Ro 12:13; 15:27; 1 Ti 5:22; 1 Pt 4:13; 2 J 11.—2. *give a share* Gal 6:6; Phil 4:15.—3. κ. is found in the same sense as κοινόω *make impure* as v.l. in Mt 15:11, 18, 20.*

κοινωνία, ας, ἡ—1. *association, communion, fellowship, close relationship* Ac 2:42; Ro 15:26; 1 Cor 1:9; 2 Cor 6:14; 13:13; Gal 2:9; Phil 1:5; 2:1; 1 J 1:3, 6f.—2. *generosity, fellow feeling* 2 Cor 9:13; Hb 13:16; perh. Phil 2:1.—3. *sign of fellowship, gift* perh. Ro 15:26 and 1 Cor 10:16.—4. *participation, sharing* 2 Cor 8:4; Phil 3:10; Phlm 6; perh. 1 Cor 1:9; 10:16; 2 Cor 13:13.* [*koinonia*]

κοινωνικός, ἡ, όν *sharing* what is one's own, *liberal, generous* 1 Ti 6:18.*

κοινωνός, οῦ, ὁ and **ἡ** *companion, partner, sharer* often w. gen. or dat. Mt 23:30; Lk 5:10; 1 Cor 10:18, 20; 2 Cor 1:7; 8:23; Phlm 17; Hb 10:33; 1 Pt 5:1; 2 Pt 1:4.*

κοινῶς adv. *in the common language or dialect* Mk 3:17 v.l.*

κοίτη, ης, ἡ—1. *bed* Lk 11:7; *marriage bed* Hb 13:4.—**2.** euphemistically for *sexual intercourse* pl. *sexual excesses* Ro 13:13. *Conception of a child* 9:10.*

κοιτών, ῶνος, ὁ *bedroom* ὁ ἐπὶ τοῦ κοιτῶνος *the chamberlain* Ac 12:20.*

κόκκινος, η, ον *red, scarlet* Mt 27:28; Hb 9:19; Rv 17:3; *scarlet cloth or garment* 17:4; 18:12, 16.*

κόκκος, ου, ὁ *seed, grain* Mt 13:31; 17:20; Mk 4:31; Lk 13:19; 17:6; J 12:24; 1 Cor 15:37.* [*coccus*, term in botany and bacteriology]

κολάζω *punish* Ac 4:21; 1 Pt 2:20 v.l.; 2 Pt 2:9.*

κολακεία, ας, ἡ *flattery* 1 Th 2:5.*

κόλασις, εως, ἡ *punishment* Mt 25:46; 1 J 4:18.*

Κολασσαεύς, έως, ὁ *a Colossian* only as v.l. in the title of Col.

Κολασσαί v.l. for Κολοσσαί Col 1:2.

κολαφίζω *strike with the fist, beat—1.* lit. Mt 26:67; Mk 14:65; 1 Pt 2:20; *be roughly treated* 1 Cor 4:11.—**2.** fig., of *attacks of illness* 2 Cor 12:7.*

κολλάω *join closely together, unite* pass. *cling* Lk 10:11. *Join oneself to, join, cling to, associate with* Mt 19:5; Ac 5:13; 8:29; 9:26; 10:28; Ro 12:9; 1 Cor 6:16f. *Become a follower of* Ac 17:34. *Hire oneself out to* Lk 15:15. *Touch, reach* Rv 18:5.* [Cf. *colloid*.]

κολλούριον, ου, τό *eye salve* Rv 3:18.* [*collyrium*]

κολλυβιστής, οῦ, ὁ *money changer* Mt 21:12; Mk 11:15; Lk 19:45 v.l.; J 2:15.*

κολλύριον a variant spelling of κολλούριον.

κολοβόω *shorten, curtail* Mt 24:22; Mk 13:20.*

Κολοσσαεύς, έως, ὁ *the Colossian,* title of Col.*

Κολοσσαί, ῶν, αἱ *Colossae,* a city in Phrygia, in w. Asia Minor Col 1:2; Phlm subscr. v.l.*

κόλπος, ου, ὁ—1. *bosom, breast, chest* ἀνακεῖσθαι ἐν τῷ κόλπῳ τινός *recline* (at a meal) with one's head *on someone's breast* J 13:23. Similarly Lk 16:22f; J 1:18.—**2.** *the fold of a garment,* formed as it falls from the chest over the girdle, used as a pocket Lk 6:38.—**3.** *bay, gulf* of the sea Ac 27:39.*

κολυμβάω *swim,* lit. 'dive' Ac 27:43.*

κολυμβήθρα, ας, ἡ *pool, swimming pool* J 5:2, 4, 7; 9:7.*

κολωνία, ας, ἡ (Latin loanword: colonia) *colony* Ac 16:12.*

κομάω *wear long hair, let one's hair grow long* 1 Cor 11:14f.*

κόμη, ης, ἡ *hair* 1 Cor 11:15.*

κομιοῦμαι, κομιεῖται fut. mid. ind. 1 and 3 sing. of κομίζω.

κομίζω—1. act. *bring* Lk 7:37.—**2.** mid. *carry off, get, receive, obtain* 2 Cor 5:10, 39; 1 Pt 1:9; 5:4; 2 Pt 2:13 v.l. *Get back, recover* Mt 25:27; Hb 11:19.*

κομίσομαι fut. mid. ind. of κομίζω.

κομψότερον adv. *better* κ. ἔσχεν *he began to improve* J 4:52.*

κονιάω *to whitewash* Mt 23:27; Ac 23:3.*

κονιορτός, οῦ, ὁ *dust* Mt 10:14; Lk 9:5; 10:11; Ac 13:51; 22:23.*

κοπάζω *abate,* of wind *fall* Mt 14:32; Mk 4:39; 6:51.*

κοπετός, οῦ, ὁ *mourning, lamentation* Ac 8:2.*

κοπή, ῆς, ἡ *cutting down, defeat* Hb 7:1.*

κοπιάω—1. *become weary, tired* Mt 11:28; J 4:6; Rv 2:3.—**2.** *work hard, toil, strive, struggle* Mt 6:28; J 4:38b; Ac 20:35; Ro 16:6, 12; 1 Cor 4:12; Phil 2:16; Col 1:29; 1 Ti 5:17. *Labor for* J 4:38a.

κόπος, ου, ὁ—1. *trouble, difficulty* Mk 14:6; Lk 11:7; Gal 6:17.—**2.** *work, labor, toil* J 4:38; 1 Cor 15:58; 2 Cor 6:5; 11:23, 27; 1 Th 1:3; 3:5; 2 Th 3:8; Rv 14:13.

κοπρία, ας, ἡ *dunghill, rubbish heap* Lk 14:35.*

κόπριον, ου, τό dung, manure Lk 13:8.*

κόπρος, ου, ἡ dung, manure Lk 13:8 v.l.* [coprolite, fossil dung]

κόπτω—1. act. cut (off) Mt 21:8; Mk 11:8.—**2.** mid. beat one's breast, mourn Mt 11:17; 24:30; Lk 8:52; 23:27; Rv 1:7; 18:9.* [pericope, περί + κόπτειν; syncopate]

κόραξ, ακος, ὁ crow, raven Lk 12:24.*

κοράσιον, ου, τό girl Mt 9:24f; 14:11; Mk 5:41f; 6:22, 28.*

κορβᾶν indecl. (Hebrew word) corban, a gift consecrated to God Mk 7:11.*

κορβανᾶς, ᾶ, ὁ (Hebrew) temple treasury Mt 27:6.*

Κόρε, ὁ indecl. Korah (Numbers 16) Jd 11.*

κορέννυμι satiate, fill pass. have enough Ac 27:38; 1 Cor 4:8.*

κορεσθείς 1 aor. pass. ptc. of κορέννυμι.

Κορίνθιος, ου, ὁ the Corinthian Ac 18:8, 27 v.l.; 2 Cor 6:11; titles of 1 and 2 Cor; Ro subscr.*

Κόρινθος, ου, ἡ Corinth, an important commercial city on the isthmus joining central and southern Greece. Ac 18:1, 27 v.l.; 19:1; 1 Cor 1:2; 2 Cor 1:1, 23; 2 Ti 4:20; Ro and 1 Th subscr.*

Κορνήλιος, ου, ὁ Cornelius Ac 10:1, 3, 17, 22, 24f, 30f.*

κόρος, ου, ὁ cor, a dry measure amounting to between ten and twelve bushels Lk 16:7.*

κοσμέω—1. put in order Mt 12:44; Lk 11:25; trim Mt 25:7.—**2.** adorn, decorate lit. Mt 23:29; Lk 21:5; 1 Ti 2:9; Rv 21:2, 19; perh. Mt 12:44; Lk 11:25. Fig. make beautiful or attractive 1 Pt 3:5; adorn, do credit to Tit 2:10.* [cosmetic]

κοσμικός, ή, όν earthly Hb 9:1. Worldly Tit 2:12.* [cosmic]

κόσμιος, (ία), ον respectable, honorable 1 Ti 3:2; modest 2:9.*

κοσμίως adv. modestly 1 Ti 2:9 v.l.*

κοσμοκράτωρ, ορος, ὁ world-ruler Eph 6:12.*

κόσμος, ου, ὁ—1. adornment, adorning 1 Pt 3:3.—**2.** world, in many senses— **a.** the world in its most inclusive sense, the (orderly) universe Mt 25:34; J 17:5; Ac 17:24; Ro 1:20; 1 Cor 8:4; Phil 2:15; Hb 4:3.—**b.** the world as the earth, the planet on which we live Mt 4:8; Mk 14:9; Lk 12:30; J 10:36; 11:9, 27; 16:21, 28; 18:36; 1 Ti 6:7; 1 Pt 5:9; Rv 11:15.— **c.** the world as humanity in general Mt 18:7; J 1:29; 3:16; 4:42; 6:33, 51; 8:12; 12:19; 17:6; 18:20; Ro 3:6, 19; 1 Cor 4:13; 2 Pt 2:5.—**d.** the world as the scene of earthly possessions, joys, sufferings, etc. Mt 16:26; Mk 8:36; Lk 9:25; 1 Cor 7:31a, 33f; 1 J 2:15f; 3:17.—**e.** the world is sometimes spoken of as that which is hostile to God, lost in sin, ruined, depraved J 7:7; 8:23; 12:31; 15:18f; 16:33; 17:25; 18:36; 1 Cor 2:12; 3:19; 11:32; 2 Cor 5:19; Gal 6:14; Js 1:27; 1 J 4:17; 5:4f, 19.—**f.** the world as totality, sum total Js 3:6. [cosmos]

Κούαρτος, ου, ὁ Quartus Ro 16:23; 1 Cor subscr.*

κοῦμ Aramaic word meaning stand up Mk 5:41.*

κοῦμι an alternate form of κοῦμ.

κουστωδία, ας, ἡ a guard composed of soldiers Mt 27:65f; 28:11.* [Latin loanword: custodia, custody]

κουφίζω make light, lighten Ac 27:38.*

κόφινος, ου, ὁ a large, heavy basket Mt 14:20; 16:9; Mk 6:43; 8:19; Lk 9:17; 13:8 v.l.; J 6:13.*

κράβαττος, ου, ὁ mattress, pallet, the poor man's bed Mk 2:4, 9, 11f; 6:55; J 5:8–11; Ac 5:15; 9:33.*

κράζω—1. cry out, scream wordlessly Mt 14:26; 27:50; Mk 5:5; 9:26; Lk 9:39; Ac 7:57; Rv 12:2.—**2.** call, call out, cry—**a.** lit. Mt 15:23; 20:30f; Mk 10:48; 15:14; Lk 18:39; J 7:28; Ac 7:60; 16:17; 19:32; 24:21; Rv 6:10.—**b.** fig. Lk 19:40; Ro 8:15; 9:27; Gal 4:6; Js 5:4.

κραιπάλη, ης, ἡ dissipation Lk 21:34.* [crapulous, intemperate in drinking habits]

κρανίον, ου, τό skull κρανίου τόπος the place that is called (a) skull Mt 27:33; Mk 15:22; J 19:17; cf. Lk 23:33.* [cranium]

κράσπεδον, ου, τό—1. edge, border, hem of a garment Mt 9:20; 14:36; Mk

6:56; Lk 8:44; mng. 2 is also possible for all these passages.—**2.** *tassel* (Deut 22:12) Mt 23:5.*

κραταιός, ά, όν *powerful, mighty* 1 Pt 5:6.*

κραταιόω *strengthen* pass. *become* or *be strong* Lk 1:80; 2:40; 1 Cor 16:13; Eph 3:16.*

κρατέω—1. *take into one's possession* or *custody*—**a.** *arrest, apprehend* Mt 26:4, 48, 50, 55, 57; Mk 3:21; 6:17; Ac 24:6; Rv 20:2.—**b.** *take hold of, grasp, seize* w. acc. or gen. Mt 12:11; 22:6; 28:9; Mk 1:31; 9:27; Lk 8:54. *Attain* Ac 27:13.—**2.** *hold* Ac 3:11; Rv 2:1. *Hold back, restrain* 7:1; pass. *be prevented* Lk 24:16. *Hold fast* Mk 7:3f, 8; Ac 2:24; Col 2:19; Rv 2:13–15. *Keep* Mk 9:10. *Retain* J 20:23. [*democratic,* δῆμος + κρατεῖν]

κράτιστος, η, ον *most noble, most excellent* used in addressing a person of social or political prominence Ac 23:26; 24:3; 26:25. In polite address, with no official connotation Lk 1:3.*

κράτος, ους, τό *power, might, sovereignty* Ac 19:20; Eph 1:19; 6:10; Col 1:11; 1 Ti 6:16; Hb 2:14; Rv 1:6. *Mighty deed* Lk 1:51.

κραυγάζω *cry (out), cry loudly* Mt 12:19; Lk 4:41; J 11:43; 12:13; 18:40; 19:6, 12, 15; Ac 22:23.*

κραυγή, ῆς, ἡ *shout(ing), clamor* Mt 25:6; Lk 1:42; Ac 23:9; Eph 4:31; Hb 5:7. *Crying* Rv 21:4.*

κρέας, κρέως, and **κρέατος, τό,** in the pl. **κρέα** *meat* Ro 14:21; 1 Cor 8:13.*
[*creosote,* κρέας + σωτ(ηρία)]

κρείσσων and **κρείττων, ον,** gen. **ονος** *better*—**1.** in the sense *more prominent, higher in rank, preferable* Hb 1:4; 7:7, 19, 22; 11:16, 35, 40.—**2.** in the sense *more useful, more advantageous* 1 Cor 7:9; 11:17; Phil 1:23; Hb 6:9; 1 Pt 3:17; 2 Pt 2:21.—**3.** as adv. *better* 1 Cor 7:38; Hb 12:24.

κρέμαμαι see κρεμάννυμι 2.

κρεμάννυμι—1. trans. *hang (up)* Ac 5:30; 10:39. Pass. Mt 18:6; Lk 23:39.—**2.** intrans. mid. κρέμαμαι *hang* lit. Ac 28:4; Gal 3:13. Fig. *depend* Mt 22:40.*

κρεμάσας, κρεμάσθεις 1 aor. act. and pass. ptc. of κρεμάννυμι.

κρεπάλη a different spelling for κραιπάλη.

κρημνός, οῦ, ὁ *steep slope* or *bank, cliff* Mt 8:32; Mk 5:13; Lk 8:33.*

Κρής, ητός, ὁ pl. **Κρῆτες** *a Cretan* Ac 2:11; Tit 1:12; Tit subscr.*

Κρήσκης, εντος, ὁ *Crescens* 2 Ti 4:10.*

Κρήτη, ης, ἡ *Crete,* a large island at the south end of the Aegean Sea Ac 27:7, 12f, 21; Tit 1:5.*

κριθή, ῆς, ἡ *barley* Rv 6:6.*

κριθήσομαι fut. pass. ind. of κρίνω.

κρίθινος, η, ον *made of barley flour* J 6:9, 13.*

κρίμα, ατος, τό *lawsuit* 1 Cor 6:7. *Decision, decree* Ro 11:33. *Judging, judgment* Mt 7:2; Ac 24:25; Hb 6:2; 1 Pt 4:17; *authority to judge* Rv 20:4. *Verdict* Ro 5:16. Mostly *condemnation, sentence, punishment* Mk 12:40; Lk 24:20; Ro 2:2f; 3:8; 1 Cor 11:29, 34; 1 Ti 5:12; 2 Pt 2:3; Rv 17:1.

κρίνον, ου, τό *lily* Mt 6:28; Lk 12:27.*
[*Crinum,* genus of bulbous plants]

κρίνω—1. *separate, distinguish,* then *select, prefer* Ro 14:5a; in 14:5b κ. prob. means *hold in esteem.*—**2.** *judge, think, consider, look upon* Lk 7:43; Ac 4:19; 13:46; 16:15; 26:8; 1 Cor 11:13; 2 Cor 5:14.—**3.** *reach a decision, decide, propose, intend* Ac 3:13; 16:4; 20:16; 21:25; 27:1; 1 Cor 2:2; 5:3; 7:37; Ro 14:13.—**4.** as legal term, of human or divine courts *judge, decide, hale before a court, condemn, sentence, hand over for punishment* Mt 5:40; 7:1b, 2b; Lk 19:22; J 5:30; 7:51; 18:31; Ac 13:27; 17:31; 23:3; 25:9; 26:6; Ro 2:16, 27; 1 Cor 5:12f; 6:2f, 6; 2 Ti 4:1; Js 2:12; 1 Pt 1:17; Rv 6:10; 20:12f. *Condemn, punish* J 3:17f; 12:47f; 16:11; Ro 2:12; 1 Cor 11:31f; Hb 10:30; Rv 18:8.—**5.** *judge, pass judgment on, express an opinion about* Mt 7:1a, 2a; Lk 6:37a; J 7:24; 8:15. In an unfavorable sense *find fault with, condemn* Ro 2:1, 3; 14:3f, 10, 13a, 22; 1 Cor 4:5; 10:29; Col 2:16; Js 4:11f.

κρίσις, εως, ἡ—1. *judging, judgment* Mt 10:15; Lk 10:14; J 5:30; 2 Th 1:5;

Hb 9:27; 2 Pt 2:9; Jd 6. κρίσιν ποιεῖν act as judge J 5:27. Condemnation, punishment Mt 23:33; J 5:24, 29; Hb 10:27; Js 5:12; Rv 18:10; 19:2.—2. board of judges, local court Mt 5:21f.—3. right in the sense of justice, righteousness Mt 12:18, 20; 23:23; Lk 11:42. This meaning is also possible for J 7:24; 12:31; Ac 8:33 and others. [crisis]

Κρίσπος, ου, ὁ Crispus Ac 18:8; 1 Cor 1:14; 2 Ti 4:10 v.l.*

κριτήριον, ου, τό—1. law court, tribunal Js 2:6.—2. lawsuit, legal action is prob. for 1 Cor 6:2, 4, though mng. 1 is possible.* [criterion]

κριτής, οῦ, ὁ judge Mt 5:25; 12:27; Lk 18:2, 6; Ac 10:42; 24:10; 2 Ti 4:8; Hb 12:23; Js 2:4; 4:11f. A leader of the people in the period of the Judges Ac 13:20.

κριτικός, ή, όν able to discern or judge Hb 4:12.* [critic]

κρούω knock (at) Mt 7:7f; Lk 11:9f; 12:36; 13:25; Ac 12:13, 16; Rv 3:20.*

κρυβῆναι 2 aor. pass. inf. of κρύπτω.

κρύπτη, ης, ἡ a dark and hidden place, a cellar Lk 11:33.*

κρυπτός, ή, όν hidden, secret as adj. Mt 10:26; Mk 4:22; Lk 12:2; 1 Pt 3:4. As noun a hidden thing Lk 8:17; Ro 2:16; 1 Cor 4:5; 14:25. τὰ κ. τῆς αἰσχύνης the things that are hidden out of a sense of shame 2 Cor 4:2. A hidden place J 7:4; 18:20. ἐν τῷ κ. in secret Mt 6:4, 6, 18 v.l., but inwardly Ro 2:29. ὡς ἐν κ. privately, as it were J 7:10 [cryptic]

κρύπτω hide, conceal, cover lit. Mt 13:44; 25:18, 25; Lk 13:21; J 12:36; Rv 6:15f. Fig. Mt 11:25; Lk 18:34; J 19:38; Col 3:3; 1 Ti 5:25.

κρυσταλλίζω shine like crystal, be as transparent as crystal Rv 21:11.* [crystallize]

κρύσταλλος, ου, ὁ rock crystal Rv 4:6; 22:1.* [crystal]

κρυφαῖος, αία, αῖον hidden ἐν τῷ κ. in secret Mt 6:18.*

κρυφῇ adv. in secret Eph 5:12.*

κρύφιος, ία, ιον hidden, secret Mt 6:18 v.l.*

κτάομαι procure for oneself, acquire, get Mt 10:9; Lk 18:12; 21:19; Ac 1:18; 8:20; 22:28; 1 Th 4:4.*

κτῆμα, ατος, τό property, possession Mt 19:22; Mk 10:22; Ac 2:45. Field, piece of ground 5:1.*

κτῆνος ους, τό animal, domesticated animal 1 Cor 15:39; used for riding Lk 10:34; Ac 23:24. Pl. cattle Rv 18:13.*

κτήτωρ, ορος, ὁ owner Ac 4:34.*

κτίζω create Mt 19:4; Mk 13:19; 1 Cor 11:9; Eph 2:10, 15; 4:24; 1 Ti 4:3; Rv 10:6.

κτίσις, εως, ἡ—1. creation—a. the act of creation Ro 1:20.—b. creation in the sense that which is created, creature Mk 10:6; 13:19; Ro 1:25; 8:19–22, 39; 2 Cor 5:17; Col 1:15, 23; Hb 4:13; 2 Pt 3:4.—2. institution, governmental authority 1 Pt 2:13.

κτίσμα, ατος, τό that which is created (by God), creature 1 Ti 4:4; Js 1:18; Rv 5:13; 8:9.*

κτίστης, ου, ὁ Creator of God 1 Pt 4:19.*

κυβεία, ας, ἡ craftiness, trickery, lit. 'dice-playing' Eph 4:14.* [cube]

κυβέρνησις, εως, ἡ administration 1 Cor 12:28.*

κυβερνήτης, ου, ὁ captain, steersman, pilot Ac 27:11; Rv 18:17.* [cybernetics]

κυβία a different spelling for κυβεία.

κυκλεύω surround Rv 20:9; J 10:24 v.l.*

κυκλόθεν adv. all around, from all sides Rv 4:8. Functions as prep. w. gen. around 4:3f.*

κυκλόω surround, encircle Lk 21:20; J 10:24; Ac 14:20. Go around, circle round pass. Hb 11:30.*

κύκλῳ dat. of κύκλος fixed as an adv. around, all around, lit. in a circle Mk 3:34; 6:6; Ro 15:19. Used as an adj. nearby Mk 6:36; around here Lk 9:12. Functions as prep. w. gen. around Rv 4:6; 5:11; 7:11.* [cycle]

κύλισμα, ματος, τό v.l. for κυλισμός.

κυλισμός, οῦ, ὁ rolling, wallowing 2 Pt 2:22.*

κυλίω act. roll Lk 23:53 v.l. Pass. roll (oneself) Mk 9:20.* [Cf. cylinder.]

κυλλός, ή, όν crippled, deformed Mt 18:8; Mk 9:43. As noun cripple Mt 15:30f.*

κῦμα, ατος, τό wave lit. Mt 8:24; 14:24; Mk 4:37; Ac 27:41 v.l. Fig. Jd 13.* [cyma, molding]

κύμβαλον, ου, τό cymbal 1 Cor 13:1.*

κύμινον, ου, τό cum(m)in, the tiny fruit or seed of the cumin, a dwarf plant native to Egypt and Syria Mt 23:23.*

κυνάριον, ου, τό little dog or simply dog Mt 15:26f; Mk 7:27f.*

Κύπριος, ου, ὁ a Cypriot, an inhabitant of Cyprus Ac 4:36; 11:20; 21:16.*

Κύπρος, ου, ἡ Cyprus, an island south of Asia Minor Ac 11:19; 13:4; 15:39; 21:3; 27:4.*

κύπτω bend (oneself) down Mk 1:7; J 8:6, 8 v.l.*

Κυρεῖνος variant spelling of Κυρήνιος.

Κυρηναῖος, ου, ὁ a Cyrenian Mt 27:32; Mk 15:21; Lk 23:26; Ac 6:9; 11:20; 13:1.*

Κυρήνη, ης, ἡ Cyrene, an important Greek city in N. Africa, west of Egypt Ac 2:10.*

Κυρήνιος and Κυρίνιος, ου, ὁ Quirinius (P. Sulpicius Q.), imperial governor of Syria Lk 2:2.*

κυρία, ας, ἡ lady, mistress in 2 J verses 1 and 5 may refer to an individual or, more likely, to a leading congregation.*

κυριακός, ή, όν belonging to the Lord, the Lord's 1 Cor 11:20. κ. ἡμέρα the Lord's Day, Sunday Rv 1:10.*

κυριεύω be lord or master, rule, lord it (over), control w. gen. Lk 22:25; Ac 19:16 v.l.; Ro 6:9, 14; 7:1; 14:9; 2 Cor 1:24; 1 Ti 6:15.*

κύριος, ου, ὁ lord, Lord, master—**1.** generally—**a.** owner, master Mt 6:24; 20:8; 24:48; Lk 12:46; 19:33; J 13:16; Ro 14:4; Gal 4:1; lord, master, one who has full control of something Mt 9:38; Mk 2:28.—**b.** as a respectful designation used in addressing persons of varying social or political rank, often equivalent to our sir Mt 27:63; J 12:21; Ac 16:30; Rv 7:14. (My) master 1 Pt 3:6.—**2.** in specialized usage—**a.** as a desig-

nation of God Mt 5:33; Mk 12:29f; Lk 1:11, 15, 17, 32; 2:15, 22; Ac 7:31; 1 Ti 6:15; Hb 8:2; Js 1:7; 2 Pt 2:9.—**b.** as a designation of the Roman emperor Ac 25:26.—**c.** as a designation of Jesus Christ, with emphasis on his authority and frequently in contrast to δοῦλος. Because of the editorial interests of the Evangelists it is difficult to determine the precise level of social recognition or status awareness in reported dialogue. Mt 20:31; Mk 11:3; Lk 7:13; 10:1, 39, 41; J 20:18, 20, 28; Ac 2:36; 9:10f, 42; 10:36; Ro 1:4; 10:9; 12:11; 16:12; 1 Cor 4:17; 6:13f, 17; 11:23; Eph 6:8; Col 1:10; Phlm 25; Hb 2:3; 7:14; 1 Pt 1:3; 2 Pt 1:2; Rv 22:20.—**d.** In some passages it is not clear whether God or Christ is meant, e.g. 1 Cor 4:19; 7:17; 2 Cor 8:21; 1 Th 4:6; 2 Th 3:16.—**e.** as designation of a divine messenger Ac 10:4.—**f.** in general of beings or persons who elicit devotion appropriate to deity (deities) 1 Cor 8:5.

κυριότης, ητος, ἡ—**1.** ruling power, lordship, dominion 2 Pt 2:10; Jd 8.—**2.** a special class of angelic powers, bearers of the ruling power, dominions Eph 1:21; Col 1:16.*

κυρόω—**1.** confirm, ratify, validate Gal 3:15.—**2.** conclude, decide in favor of, perh. reaffirm 2 Cor 2:8.*

κυσί dat. pl. of κύων.

κύων, κυνός, ὁ dog lit. Mt 7:6; Lk 16:21; 2 Pt 2:22. Fig. Phil 3:2; Rv 22:15.* [cynic]

κῶλον, ου, τό pl. dead body, corpse, lit. 'limbs' Hb 3:17.*

κωλύω—**1.** hinder, prevent, forbid Mt 19:14; Mk 9:38f; Lk 9:49f; Ac 8:36; 11:17; 27:43; Ro 1:13; 1 Cor 14:39; 1 Th 2:16; 2 Pt 2:16.—**2.** refuse, deny, withhold, keep back Lk 6:29; Ac 10:47.

κώμη, ης, ἡ village, small town Mt 9:35; Mk 6:36, 56; 8:23, 26; Lk 13:22; 17:12; J 11:1, 30.

κωμόπολις, εως, ἡ market town Mk 1:38.*

κῶμος, ου, ὁ carousing, revelry Ro 13:13; Gal 5:21; 1 Pt 4:3.* [comic]

κώνωψ, ωπος, ὁ gnat, mosquito Mt 23:24.*

Κῶς, Κῶ, ἡ acc. Κῶ Cos, an island in the Aegean Sea Ac 21:1.*

Κωσάμ, ὁ indecl. Cosam Lk 3:28.*

κωφός, ή, όν—1. unable to articulate or speak, mute Mt 15:30f; of Zechariah Lk 1:22; with special reference to demonic interference Mt 9:32f; 12:22; Lk 11:14.—2. deaf Mt 11:5; Mk 7:32, 37; 9:25; Lk 7:22.*

Λ

λ΄ numeral = 30 Lk 3:23 v.l.

λάβε, λαβεῖν, λάβοι, λαβών 2 aor. act. impv., inf., opt. 3 sing., and ptc. of λαμβάνω.

λαγχάνω—1. receive, obtain (by lot or by divine will) Ac 1:17; 2 Pt 1:1.—2. be appointed or chosen by lot Lk 1:9.—3. cast lots J 19:24.*

Λάζαρος, ου, ὁ Lazarus—1. brother of Mary and Martha J 11:1f, 5, 11, 14, 43; 12:1f, 9f, 17.—2. name of a beggar in the parable Lk 16:20, 23–25.*

λαθεῖν 2 aor. act. inf. of λανθάνω.

λάθρα adv. secretly Mt 1:19; 2:7; Mk 5:33 v.l.; J 11:28; Ac 16:37.*

λαῖλαψ, απος, ἡ whirlwind, hurricane 2 Pt 2:17. λ. ἀνέμου a fierce gust of wind Mk 4:37; Lk 8:23.*

λακάω burst open Ac 1:18.*

λακτίζω kick Ac 26:14; 9:5 v.l.*

λαλέω—1. sound, give forth sounds or tones of inanimate things Hb 11:4; 12:24; Rv 4:1; 10:4.—2. speak Mt 12:34, 46f; 13:3; Mk 1:34; Lk 1:19, 55; Ac 13:45; 18:9; 1 Cor 13:11; 14:29; Hb 2:5; Rv 13:11. Be able to speak Mk 7:35, 37; Lk 1:20, 64. Proclaim, say Mt 12:36; Mk 2:2; J 3:34; 16:25a; 1 Cor 2:6f.

λαλιά, ᾶς, ἡ speech, speaking J 4:42. Form of speech, way of speaking Mt 26:73; J 8:43.*

λαμά (Hebrew) lama = why? Mt 27:46 v.l.; Mk 15:34 v.l.*

λαμβάνω—1. in a more or less active sense take, take hold of, grasp Mt 26:26a; Mk 12:19–21; 15:23; J 19:30; Js 5:10; Rv 5:8f. Seize Mt 21:35, 39; Lk 5:26; 9:39; 1 Cor 10:13. Catch Lk 5:5. Draw Mt 26:52. Put on J 13:12; Phil 2:7. Take up, receive Mt 13:20; J 6:21; 12:48; 13:20; 19:27. Collect Mt 17:24; 21:34; Mk 12:2; Hb 7:8f. Choose, select Hb 5:1. Sometimes the ptc. can be translated with λαβὼν τὴν σπεῖραν ἔρχεται he came with a detachment J 18:3.—2. in a more or less passive sense receive, get, obtain Mk 10:30; 12:40; Lk 11:10; Ac 1:20; 10:43; 20:35; 1 Cor 4:7; 9:24f; Js 1:12; Rv 22:17. Accept a bribe Mt 28:15. As a periphrasis for the pass. οἰκοδομὴν λ. be edified 1 Cor 14:5. Cf. J 7:23; Ro 5:11.

Λάμεχ, ὁ indecl. Lamech Lk 3:36.*

λαμπάς, άδος, ἡ torch J 18:3; Rv 4:5; 8:10. Lamp, but not the very small household type, may be meant in Mt 25:1, 3f, 7f; Ac 20:8.*

λαμπρός, ά, όν bright, shining, radiant Lk 23:11; Ac 10:30; Js 2:2f; Rv 15:6; 19:8; 22:16. Clear, transparent Rv 22:1. τὰ λαμπρά splendor 18:14.*

λαμπρότης, ητος, ἡ brightness Ac 26:13.*

λαμπρῶς adv. splendidly, sumptuously Lk 16:19.*

λάμπω shine lit. Mt 5:15; Ac 12:7; gleam Mt 17:2; flash Lk 17:24; shine forth 2 Cor 4:6a. Fig Mt 5:16; 2 Cor 4:6b.* [lamp]

λανθάνω escape notice, be hidden Mk 7:24; Lk 8:47; Ac 26:26; Hb 13:2; 2 Pt 3:5, 8.*

λαξευτός, ή, όν hewn in the rock Lk 23:53.*

Λαοδίκεια, ας, ἡ Laodicea, a city in Phrygia in Asia Minor Col 2:1; 4:13, 15f; subscr. of 1 and 2 Ti; Rv 1:11; 3:14.*

Λαοδικεύς, έως, ὁ a Laodicean Col 4:16.*

λαός, οῦ, ὁ people Mt 26:5; Lk 7:29; 19:48; Ac 3:23; 4:10, 25; 15:14; Ro 9:25; Hb 2:17; 4:9; 1 Pt 2:9; Jd 5; Rv 5:9; 17:15; populace Mt 27:64. [lay, laity]

λάρυγξ, γγος, ὁ throat, gullet Ro 3:13.* [larynx]

Λασαία, ας, or **Λασέα, ας, ἡ** Lasaea, a city on the south coast of Crete. Ac 27:8.*

λάσκω a form erroneously thought to be the source of ἐλάκησεν Ac 1:18, which is 1 aor. act. ind. of λακάω.

λατομέω hew out of the rock Mt 27:60; Mk 15:46; Lk 23:53 v.l.*

λατρεία, ας, ἡ religious service, worship (of God) J 16:2; Ro 9:4; 12:1; Hb 9:1; pl. rites 9:6.* [latria; idolatry]

λατρεύω serve by carrying out religious duties, w. dat. Mt 4:10; Lk 1:74; Ac 7:7, 42; 26:7; Ro 1:9; 2 Ti 1:3; Hb 9:9, 14; Rv 7:15.

λάχανον, ου, τό garden herb, vegetable Mt 13:32; Mk 4:32; Lk 11:42; Ro 14:2.*

λαχοῦσιν dat. pl., 2 aor. act. ptc. of λαγχάνω.

λάχωμεν, λαχών 2 aor. act. subj. 1 pl. and ptc. of λαγχάνω.

Λεββαῖος, ου, ὁ Lebbaeus Mt 10:3 v.l. and Mk 3:18 v.l.*

λεγιών, ῶνος, ἡ (Latin loanword: legio) legion, a unit of about 6,000 Roman soldiers Mt 26:53; Mk 5:9, 15 (masc. because the demon is masc.); Lk 8:30.* [The Latin legio is derived from λέγω.]

λέγω say—1. generally, say, tell, give expression to orally, but also in writing Mt 1:20; 9:34; 21:45; Mk 1:15; Lk 13:6, 24; J 2:3; 18:34; Ac 14:11; Ro 10:16, 20; Hb 8:8; 11:32. Make reference to Mk 14:71. Mean(s) of foreign terms and names Mt 27:33b; J 20:16; 1 Cor 10:29; of statements made Gal 3:17; 4:1. Bring charges Ac 23:30.—2. more specifi-

cally, of special forms of saying etc. Ask Mt 9:14; Mk 14:14. Answer Mt 4:10; 19:8; J 1:21. Order, command, direct Mk 13:37; Lk 6:46; J 2:7f; Rv 10:9. Assure, assert Mt 11:22; Mk 11:24; Lk 9:27. Maintain, declare, proclaim Mt 22:23; Mk 15:2; Ro 15:8; 1 Cor 15:12; Gal 4:1. Speak, report, tell of Mk 7:36; Lk 9:31; Ac 1:3; Eph 5:12. Call, name Mk 10:18; 12:37; J 5:18; Col 4:11; Rv 2:20. [legend]

λεῖμμα, ατος, τό remnant Ro 11:5.*

λεῖος, α, ον smooth, level Lk 3:5.*

λείπω mid. and pass., and intrans act. fall short, lack Lk 18:22; Tit 1:5; 3:13; Js 1:4. Be in need or want of Js 1:5; 2:15.*

λειτουργέω The λειτουργ- family in Graeco-Roman usage denotes various types of public or civic service, cultic and secular. N.T. writers adopt the terminology in ref. to Christian understanding of responsibility to God and generous concern for human beings.—1. perform a (religious) service Hb 10:11; Tit 1:9 v.l. Ac 13:2.—2. serve Ro 15:27.*

λειτουργία, ας, ἡ—1. service of a ritual or other cultic nature Lk 1:23; Phil 2:17; Hb 8:6; 9:21.—2. service rendered to one in need 2 Cor 9:12; Phil 2:30.* [liturgy]

λειτουργικός, ή, όν engaged in holy service Hb 1:14.* [liturgical]

λειτουργός, οῦ, ὁ—1. servant, minister with special ref. to accountability before God Ro 13:6; 15:16; Hb 1:7; 8:2.—2. In Phil 2:25 the term λ. refers to the role of Epaphroditus as personal aide to Paul.* [liturgist]

λείχω lick Lk 16:21 v.l.*

Λέκτρα, ας, ἡ Lectra 2 Ti 4:19 v.l.*

λεμά (Aramaic) lema = why? Mt 27:46; Mk 15:34.*

λέντιον, ου, τό (Latin loanword: linteum) linen towel J 13:4f.*

λεπίς, ίδος, ἡ scale Ac 9:18.* [lepidopterous, having wings (πτερά) like butterfly wings, covered with scales.]

λέπρα, ας, ἡ a general term for such diseases of the skin as psoriasis, lupus, ringworm, and favus, popularly known

118   λεπρός–λιπαρός

in the transliterated form *leprosy*, but probably not Hansen's disease. Mt 8:3; Mk 1:42; Lk 5:12f.*

λεπρός, ά, όν *leprous* Lk 17:12. As noun *leper* Mt 10:8; 11:5; Mk 1:40; 14:3; Lk 4:27.

λεπτός, ή, όν *small, thin.* As noun τὸ λεπτόν *small copper coin* Mk 12:42; Lk 12:59; 21:2.* [*lepto-*, combining form, as in *leptodactylous*, having slender toes]

Λευί, ὁ indecl. and **Λευίς, gen. Λευί,** acc. **Λευίν** *Levi*—**1.** son of Jacob Hb 7:5, 9; Rv 7:7.—**2.** son of Melchi Lk 3:24.—**3.** son of Symeon 3:29.—**4.** the tax collector, a disciple of Jesus Mk 2:14; Lk 5:27, 29. Called Matthew Mt 9:9.*

Λευίτης, ου, ὁ *a Levite*, one of a group that performed the lowlier services in the temple ritual Lk 10:32; J 1:19; Ac 4:36.*

Λευιτικός, ή, όν *Levitical* Hb 7:11.*

λευκαίνω *whiten, make white* lit. Mk 9:3; fig. Rv 7:14.*

λευκάναι 1 aor. act. inf. of λευκαίνω.

λευκοβύσσινος v.l. for βύσσινον λευκόν *white linen* Rv. 19:14b.*

λευκός, ή, όν—**1.** *bright, shining, gleaming* Mt 17:2; Lk 9:29.—**2.** *white* Mt 5:36; Mk 9:3; 16:5; Lk 9:29; J 4:35; Ac 1:10; Rv 1:14; 2:17; 6:2; 7:9, 13; 19:11, 14; 20:11. [*leucite, leukemia, lucid*]

λέων, οντος, ὁ *lion* lit. Hb 11:33; 1 Pt 5:8; Rv 4:7; 9:8, 17; 10:3; 13:2. Fig. 2 Ti 4:17; Rv 5:5.*

λήθη, ης, ἡ *forgetfulness* λήθην λαμβάνειν *forget* 2 Pt 1:9.* [*Lethe*]

λῆμψις, εως, ἡ *receiving, credit* Phil 4:15.*

λήμψομαι fut. mid. ind. of λαμβάνω.

ληνός, οῦ, ἡ *winepress* Mt 21:33; Rv 14:19f; 19:15.*

λῆρος, ου, ὁ *idle talk, nonsense* Lk 24:11.*

ληστής, οῦ, ὁ—**1.** *robber, highwayman, bandit* Mt 27:38; Mk 11:17; 15:27; Lk 10:30, 36; J 10:1, 8; 2 Cor 11:26.—**2.** *revolutionary, insurrectionist* J 18:40

and probably Mt 26:55; Mk 14:48; Lk 22:52.

λῆψις variant form of λῆμψις.

λίαν adv. *very (much), exceedingly* Mt 2:16; 8:28; 27:14; Mk 1:35; 16:2; Lk 23:8; 2 J 4; *vehemently* 2 Ti 4:15.

λίβα acc. sing. of λίψ.

λίβανος, ου, ὁ *frankincense*, an aromatic resinous gum Mt 2:11; Rv 18:13.*

λιβανωτός, οῦ, ὁ *censer* Rv 8:3, 5.*

Λιβερτῖνος, ου, ὁ *Freedman* Ac 6:9.*

Λιβύη, ης, ἡ *Libya*, a district in N. Africa near Cyrene Ac 2:10.*

Λιβυστῖνος, ου, ὁ *Libyan* v.l. for Λιβερτῖνος in Ac 6:9.*

λιθάζω *to stone* J 8:5; 10:31–33; 11:8; Ac 5:26; 14:19; 2 Cor 11:25; Hb 11:37.*

λίθινος, ίνη, ον *(made of) stone* J 2:6; 2 Cor 3:3; Rv 9:20.*

λιθοβολέω *throw stones at* Mt 21:35; Mk 12:4 v.l.; Ac 14:5. *Stone (to death)* Mt 23:37; Lk 13:34; J 8:5 v.l.; Ac 7:58f; Hb 12:20.*

λίθος, ου, ὁ *stone* lit. Mt 3:9; 24:2; Mk 5:5; 15:46; Lk 4:3, 11; 21:5; J 8:7, 59; Ac 17:29; Rv 17:4; 18:21; 21:11, 19. Fig. Lk 20:17f; Ac 4:11; Ro 9:32f; 1 Pt 2:4–8. [*lithograph; monolith*]

λιθόστρωτος, ον *paved with blocks of stone*, as noun *stone pavement* or *mosaic* J 19:13.*

λικμάω *crush* Mt 21:44; Lk 20:18.*

λιμήν, ένος, ὁ *harbor* Ac 27:12. For the place name Καλοὶ λιμένες 27:8 see this as a separate entry.*

λίμμα a different spelling for λεῖμμα.

λίμνη, ης, ἡ *lake* Lk 5:1f; Rv 20:14f; 21:8. [*limnology*, scientific study of fresh waters]

λιμός, οῦ, ὁ and **ἡ**—**1.** *hunger* Lk 15:17; Ro 8:35; 2 Cor 11:27.—**2.** *famine* Mk 13:8; Lk 4:25; 15:14; Ac 7:11; Rv 6:8. [*limosis*]

λίνον, ου, τό *flax, linen*, then something made of them: *lampwick* Mt 12:20; *linen garment* Rv 15:6.*

Λίνος, ον, ὁ *Linus* 2 Ti 4:21.*

λιπαρός, ά, όν *bright, costly, rich* as noun τὰ λιπαρά *luxury* Rv 18:14.*

λίτρα, ας, ἡ (Latin loanword: libra) *a* (Roman) *pound* (12 ounces; 327.45 grams) J 12:3; 19:39.*

λίψ, λιβός, ὁ *the southwest* Ac 27:12.*

λογεία, ας, ἡ *collection* of money 1 Cor 16:1f.*

λογίζομαι—**1.** *reckon, calculate*—**a.** *count, take into account* Ro 4:8; 1 Cor 13:5; 2 Cor 5:19; 2 Ti 4:16. *Credit* Ro 4:3f, 5f, 9, 11; 2 Cor 12:6; Js 2:23.—**b.** *evaluate, estimate, look upon as, consider* Ac 19:27; Ro 2:26; 9:8; 1 Cor 4:1; 2 Cor 10:2b. *Class* Lk 22:37.—**2.** *think (about), consider, let one's mind dwell on* J 11:50; 2 Cor 10:11; Hb 11:19. *Propose* 2 Cor 10:2a. *Reason, make plans* 1 Cor 13:11.—**3.** *think, believe, be of the opinion* Ro 2:3; 3:28; 14:14; 2 Cor 11:5; Phil 3:13; 1 Pt 5:12.

λογικός, ή, όν *spiritual*, lit. *rational* Ro 12:1; 1 Pt 2:2.* [*logical*]

λόγιον, ου, τό *saying* pl. *sayings, oracles* Ac 7:38; Ro 3:2; Hb 5:12; 1 Pt 4:11.* [*Logia*]

λόγιος, ία, ιον *eloquent* or *learned* Ac 18:24.*

λογισμός, οῦ, ὁ *thought* Ro 2:15; *reasoning, sophistry* 2 Cor 10:4.*

λογομαχέω *dispute about words, split hairs* 2 Ti 2:14.* [*logomachy*]

λογομαχία, ας, ἡ *word battle, dispute about words* 1 Ti 6:4; Tit 3:9 v.l.*

λόγος, ου, ὁ—**1.** *word*—**a.** generally Mt 12:37; 13:19–23; 22:46; Mk 7:13; Lk 5:1; 24:19; Ac 15:27; 2 Cor 11:6; Eph 5:6; Phil 2:16; Col 3:17; 1 Ti 1:15; Tit 2:5; 1 Pt 1:23; Rv 6:9. εἰπὲ λόγῳ *say the word* Mt 8:8.—**b.** *subject* under discussion, *matter, thing* Mt 5:32; Mk 9:10; Ac 8:21; 15:6; *complaint* 19:38.—**c.** *statement, assertion, declaration* Mt 12:32; 15:12; 19:11, 22; 22:15; Mk 5:36; 7:29; Lk 1:29; J 4:39, 50; 19:8; Ac 6:5; 1 Th 4:15.—**d.** The translation of λ. will often vary according to the context: *what you say* Mt 5:37. *Question* 21:24. *Prayer* Mk 14:39. *Preaching* 1 Ti 5:17. *Prophecy* J 2:22. *Command* Lk 4:36. *Report, story* 5:15; J 21:23; Ac 11:22. *Proverb* J 4:37. *Proclamation, instruction, teaching, message* Lk 4:32; J 4:41; Ac 10:44; 1 Cor 1:17. *A speech* Ac 15:32; 20:2.—**2.** The *Word* or *Logos*, the personified 'Word' (of God) J 1:1, 14; 1 J 1:1; Rv 19:13.—**3.** *computation, reckoning*—**a.** *account(s), reckoning* Mt 12:36; Lk 16:2; Ac 19:40; Ro 14:12; 1 Pt 3:15; 4:5. In a transferred sense ἐν τῷ λόγῳ τούτῳ *under this entry* Ro 13:9; cf 9:6.—**b.** *settlement* (of an account) Mt 18:23; 25:19; Phil 4:15, 17.—**c.** *reason, motive* Ac 10:29; 18:14; perhaps Mt 5:32 (see **1b** above).—**d.** πρὸς ὅν ἡμῖν ὁ λόγος *with whom we have to reckon* Hb 4:13. [*log-, logo-*, combining forms, as in *logarithm; logogriph,* riddle or anagram]

λόγχη, ης, ἡ *spear, lance* J 19:34; Mt 27:49 v.l.*

λοιδορέω *revile, abuse* J 9:28; Ac 23:4; 1 Cor 4:12; 1 Pt 2:23.*

λοιδορία, ας, ἡ *reviling, reproach,* verbal *abuse* 1 Ti 5:14; 1 Pt 3:9.*

λοίδορος, ου, ὁ *reviler, abusive person* 1 Cor 5:11; 6:10.*

λοιμός, οῦ, ὁ *pestilence* Lk 21:11; Mt 24:7 v.l. Fig. *a plague spot, i.e. a public menace* Ac 24:5.*

λοιπός, ή, όν *remaining*—**1.** *left* Rv 8:13; 9:20; 11:13.—**2.** *other,* sometimes in pl. *the rest* Ac 2:37; Ro 1:13; 1 Cor 9:5; Gal 2:13; Phil 4:3. As noun Mt 22:6; Lk 8:10; 12:26; Ac 5:13; Ro 11:7; 2 Cor 13:2; 1 Th 4:13; 5:6; Rv 3:2; 19:21.—**3.** adverbial uses (τὸ) λοιπόν *from now on, in the future, henceforth* 1 Cor 7:29; 2 Ti 4:8; Hb 10:13; *finally* Ac 27:20; perh. *still* Mk 14:41. τὸ λοιπόν can also mean *as far as the rest is concerned, beyond that, in addition, finally* 1 Cor 1:16; 2 Cor 13:11; Phil 4:8; 1 Th 4:1. *Furthermore* 1 Cor 4:2. τοῦ λοιποῦ *from now on, in the future* Gal 6:17; *finally* Eph 6:10.

Λουκᾶς, ᾶ, ὁ *Luke* Col 4:14; Phlm 24; 2 Ti 4:11; title of third gospel; 2 Cor subscr.*

Λούκιος, ου, ὁ *Lucius*—**1.** from Cyrene, at Antioch Ac 13:1.—**2.** sender of a greeting Ro 16:21.*

λουτρόν, οῦ, τό *bath, washing* of baptism Eph 5:26; Tit 3:5.*

λούω *wash, bathe*—**1.** act., lit. Ac 9:37; 16:33; Rv 1:5 v.l.—**2.** mid. *I wash my-*

self or for myself J 13:10; Hb 10:22; 2 Pt 2:22.* [Cf. lotion.]

Λύδδα, gen. ας or ης, acc. **Λύδδα**, ἡ Lydda, a city about 18 km. southeast of Joppa Ac 9:32, 35, 38.*

Λυδία, ας, ἡ Lydia, a merchant Ac 16:14, 40.*

Λυκαονία, ας, ἡ Lycaonia, a province in the interior of Asia Minor, in which were located the cities of Lystra, Iconium, and Derbe. Ac 14:6.*

Λυκαονιστί adv. in (the) Lycaonian (language) Ac 14:11.*

Λυκία, ας, ἡ Lycia, a projection on the south coast of Asia Minor Ac 27:5.*

λύκος, ου, ὁ wolf lit. Mt 10:16; Lk 10:3; J 10:12. Fig. Mt 7:15; Ac 20:29.* [lycanthrope (λύκος + ἄνθρωπος), werewolf]

λυμαίνω harm, damage, ruin, destroy; impf. ἐλυμαίνετο he was trying to destroy Ac 8:3.*

λυπέω grieve, pain—**1.** act. vex, irritate, offend, insult 2 Cor 2:2, 5; 7:8; Eph 4:30.—**2.** pass. become sad, sorrowful, distressed Mt 14:9; 18:31; J 16:20; 21:17; 2 Cor 2:4; 1 Pt 1:6. Be sad, be distressed, grieve Mk 10:22; 14:19; Ro 14:15; 2 Cor 6:10; 1 Th 4:13.

λύπη, ης, ἡ grief, sorrow, pain, affliction Lk 22:45; J 16:6, 20–22; Ro 9:2; 2 Cor 2:1, 3, 7; 7:10; 9:7; Phil 2:27; Hb 12:11; 1 Pt 2:19.*

Λυσανίας, ου, ὁ Lysanias Lk 3:1.*

Λυσίας, ου, ὁ (Claudius) Lysias Ac 23:26; 24:7, 22.*

λύσις, εως, ἡ divorce 1 Cor 7:27.*

λυσιτελέω be advantageous impersonal it is better Lk 17:2.*

Λύστρα, acc. **Λύστραν**, dat. **Λύστροις**, ἡ or τά Lystra, a city in Lycaonia in Asia Minor Ac 14:6, 8, 21; 16:1f; 27:5 v.l.; 2 Ti 3:11.*

λύτρον, ου, τό price of release, ransom Mt 20:28; Mk 10:45.*

λυτρόω free by paying a ransom, redeem fig. 1 Pt 1:18. Set free, redeem, rescue Lk 24:21; Tit 2:14; Ac 28:19 v.l.*

λύτρωσις, εως, ἡ ransoming, releasing, redemption Lk 1:68; 2:38; Hb 9:12.*

λυτρωτής, οῦ, ὁ redeemer Ac 7:35.*

λυχνία, ας, ἡ lampstand Mk 4:21; Lk 8:16; Hb 9:2; Rv 1:12f, 20; 11:4.

λύχνος, ου, ὁ lamp lit. Mt 5:15; Mk 4:21; Lk 11:33, 36; 15:8; J 5:35; Rv 18:23; 22:5. Fig. Mt 6:22; Rv 21:23.

λύω—1. loose, untie, set free lit. Mt 21:2; Mk 1:7; Lk 13:15; J 11:44; Ac 7:33; 22:30; Rv 9:14f; 20:3; break 5:2. Fig. untie, free, release Mk 7:35; Lk 13:16; 1 Cor 7:27; Rv 1:5; permit Mt 16:19; 18:18.—**2.** break up, tear down J 2:19; Ac 13:43; 27:41; Eph 2:14; 2 Pt 3:10–12.—**3.** destroy, bring to an end, abolish, do away with Ac 2:24; 1 J 3:8; repeal, annul, abolish Mt 5:19; J 5:18; 7:23; 10:35. [-lysis, a combining form, as in analysis, paralysis]

Λωΐς, ΐδος, ἡ Lois 2 Ti 1:5.*

Λώτ, ὁ indecl. Lot (Gen 11:27) Lk 17:28f, 32; 2 Pt 2:7.*

M

μ´ numeral = forty Ac 10:41 v.l.*

Μάαθ, ὁ indecl. Maath Lk 3:26.*

Μαγαδάν, ἡ indecl. Magadan, a place on Lake Gennesaret Mt 15:39; Mk 8:10 v.l.*

Μαγδαληνή, ῆς, ἡ Magdalene, woman from Magdala, a town on the west side of Lake Gennesaret Mt 27:56, 61; 28:1; Mk 15:40, 47; 16:1, 9; Lk 8:2; 24:10; J 19:25; 20:1, 18.*

Μαγεδών see Ἁρμαγεδ(δ)ών.

μαγεία, ας, ἡ magic Ac 8:11.*

μαγεύω practice magic Ac 8:9.*

μαγία a different spelling for μαγεία.

μάγος, ου, ὁ—1. a Magus, pl. Magi, a wise man or astrologer Mt 2:1, 7, 16.—**2.** magician Ac 13:6, 8.*

Μαγώγ, ὁ indecl. Magog (Ezekiel 38:2–39:16) Rv 20:8.*

Μαδιάμ, ὁ indecl. Midian, a people in Arabia Ac 7:29.*

μαζός, οῦ, ὁ breast Rv 1:13 v.l.*

μαθεῖν 2 aor. act. inf. of μανθάνω.

μαθητεύω—1. intrans. act. and pass. deponent be or become a pupil or disciple Mt 13:52; 27:57 (both pass.); 27:57 v.l. (act.).—**2.** trans. act. make a disciple of, teach Mt 28:19; Ac 14:21.* [Cf. μανθάνω, μαθεῖν.]

μαθητής, οῦ, ὁ learner, pupil, disciple—**1.** pupil, apprentice Mt 10:24f; Lk 6:40.—**2.** disciple, adherent Mt 10:1; 22:16; Mk 2:18; 5:31; Lk 6:17; 8:9; J 1:35, 37; 6:66; Ac 9:1; practically = Christian Ac 6:1f, 7; 13:52.

μαθήτρια, ας, ἡ a (woman) disciple, Christian woman Ac 9:36.*

Μαθθάθ see Μαθθάτ.

Μαθθαῖος, ου, ὁ Matthew Mt 9:9; 10:3; Mk 3:18; Lk 6:15; Ac 1:13; title of the First Gospel.*

Μαθθάν see Μαθθάτ.

Μαθθάτ, ὁ indecl. Matthat—**1.** Lk 3:24.—**2.** 3:29.*

Μαθθίας Matthias Ac 1:23, 26.*

Μαθουσαλά, ὁ indecl. Methuselah Lk 3:37.*

Μαϊνάν see Μεννά.

μαίνομαι be mad, be out of one's mind J 10:20; Ac 12:15; 26:24f; 1 Cor 14:23.*

μακαρίζω call or consider blessed, happy, fortunate Lk 1:48; Js 5:11.*

μακάριος, ία, ιον blessed, fortunate, happy usually in the sense of privileged recipient of divine favor Mt 11:6; 13:16; Lk 11:27; 23:29; J 13:17; Js 1:25; 1 Pt 3:14. μακάριος ὁ blessed is one who Mt 5:3–11; Lk 6:20–22; J 20:29; Rv 1:3; 22:7, 14. Of God as the source of all benefaction 1 Ti 6:15.

μακαρισμός, οῦ, ὁ blessing Ro 4:6, 9; Gal 4:15.* [macarism]

Μακεδονία, ας, ἡ Macedonia Ac 16:9f, 12; 19:21f; Ro 15:26; 1 Cor 16:5; 2 Cor 2:13; 8:1; Phil 4:15; 1 Ti 1:3.

Μακεδών, όνος, ὁ a Macedonian Ac 16:9; 19:29; 27:2; 2 Cor 9:2, 4.*

μάκελλον, ου, τό meat market, food market 1 Cor 10:25.*

μακράν far (away) adv. Mt 8:30; Mk 12:34; Lk 15:20; J 21:8; Ac 17:27; Eph 2:13, 17. As prep. w. gen. Lk 7:6 v.l.

μακρόθεν adv. from far away, from a distance, at a distance, sometimes with ἀπό Mt 26:58; 27:55; Mk 11:13; 14:54; Lk 18:13; 22:54; Rv 18:10, 15, 17. Far away Mk 8:3.

μακροθυμέω have patience, wait Hb 6:15; Js 5:7f. Be patient, forbearing Mt 18:26, 29; 1 Cor 13:4; 1 Th 5:14; 2 Pt 3:9. μακροθυμεῖ ἐπ' αὐτοῖς; Lk 18:7 is probably will he delay long over them?*

μακροθυμία, ας, ἡ patience, steadfastness, endurance, forbearance Ro 2:4; 9:22; 2 Cor 6:6; Gal 5:22; Eph 4:2; Col 1:11; 3:12; 1 Ti 1:16; 2 Ti 3:10; 4:2; Hb 6:12; Js 5:10; 1 Pt 3:20; 2 Pt 3:15.*

μακροθύμως adv. patiently Ac 26:3.*

μακρός, ά, όν long Mt 23:14 v.l.; Mk 12:40; Lk 20:47. Far away, distant Lk 15:13; 19:12.* [macron; macrocosm, μακρός + κόσμος]

μακροχρόνιος, ον long-lived Eph 6:3.*

μαλακία, ας, ἡ ailment, sickness, lit. 'softness' Mt 4:23; 9:35; 10:1.*

μαλακός, ή, όν soft Mt 11:8; Lk 7:25; effeminate, of the passive partner in a same-sex relationship. 1 Cor 6:9.*

Μαλελεήλ, ὁ indecl. Maleleel Lk 3:37.*

μάλιστα adv. especially, above all, particularly, (very) greatly Ac 20:38; 26:3; Gal 6:10; Phil 4:22; 1 Ti 5:8, 17; 2 Ti 4:13; Phlm 16.

μᾶλλον adv. more, rather—**1.** more, to a greater degree Mk 9:42; 10:48; 1 Cor 12:22; 14:18; Phil 1:9, 12; 3:4; now more than ever Lk 5:15; Ac 5:14; 2 Cor 7:7. Superfluous, with other comparative expressions Mt 6:26; Phil 1:23.—**2.** for a better reason—**a.** rather, sooner 1 Cor 7:21; Phil 2:12; 1 Ti 6:2; Hb 12:9.—**b.**

more (surely), more (certainly) Mt 6:30; 7:11; Lk 11:13; Ro 5:9f, 15, 17; 1 Cor 9:12; Phlm 16; Hb 9:14.—**3.** *rather* in the sense *instead* Mt 10:6, 28; 25:9; Mk 15:11; J 3:19; Ro 8:34; 1 Cor 5:2; 2 Cor 12:9; Eph 4:28; Phlm 9; Hb 12:13.

Μάλχος, ου, ὁ *Malchus* J 18:10.*

μάμμη, ης, ἡ *grandmother* 2 Ti 1:5.*

μαμωνᾶς, ᾶ, ὁ (Aramaic) *wealth, property* Lk 16:9, 11. Personified, 'Money' Mt 6:24; Lk 16:13.* [*mammon*]

Μαναήν, ὁ indecl. *Manaen* Ac 13:1.*

Μανασσῆς, ῆ, acc. **ῆ, ὁ** *Manasseh*—**1.** an Israelite tribe Rv 7:6.—**2.** Hebrew king Mt 1:10; Lk 3:23ff v.l.*

μανθάνω *learn* Mt 11:29; Mk 13:28; J 7:15; Ro 16:17; 1 Cor 14:31; Phil 4:11; Col 1:7; 1 Ti 2:11; Hb 5:8; *find out* Ac 23:27; Gal 3:2; *learn,* apparently by inquiry, 1 Cor 14:35. μαθεῖν in Rv 14:3 may mean *hear,* but *learn* and *understand* are also probable. [*mathematics*]

μανία, ας, ἡ *madness, delirium,* also in weakened sense *eccentricity, queerness* Ac 26:24.* [*mania*]

μάννα, τό indecl. *manna* (Exodus 16:32ff) J 6:31, 49; Hb 9:4; fig. Rv 2:17.*

μαντεύομαι *prophesy, divine, give an oracle* Ac 16:16.* [*mantic*]

μαραίνω *quench, destroy,* pass. *die out, fade, disappear, wither* Js 1:11.*

μαράνα θά (Aramaic) (our) *Lord, come!* 1 Cor 16:22.*

μαρανθήσομαι 1 fut. pass. ind. of μαραίνω.

μαργαρίτης, ου, ὁ *pearl* Mt 7:6; 13:45f; 1 Ti 2:9; Rv 17:4; 18:12, 16; 21:21.* [*Margaret* and variant forms]

Μάρθα, ας, ἡ *Martha* Lk 10:38, 40f; J 11:1, 5, 19–21, 24, 30, 39; 12:2.*

Μαρία, ας, ἡ and **Μαριάμ,** indecl. *Mary*—**1.** the mother of Jesus Christ Mt 1:16, 18, 20; 2:11; 13:55; Mk 6:3; Lk 1:27–56 passim; 2:5, 16, 19, 34; Ac 1:14.*—**2.** *Mary Magdalene* (see Μαγδαληνή)Mt 27:56, 61; 28:1; Mk 15:40, 47; 16:1, 9; Lk 8:2; 24:10; J 19:25; 20:1, 11, 16, 18.*—**3.** the 'other' *Mary,* mother of James and Joses Mt 27:56, 61; 28:1; Mk 15:40, 47; 16:1; Lk 24:10.* She could be identical with—**4.** *Mary,*

the wife of Clopas J 19:25.*—**5.** *Mary,* sister of Martha and Lazarus Lk 10:39, 42; J 11:1–45 passim; 12:3.*—**6.** *Mary,* mother of John Mark Ac 12:12.*—**7.** *Mary,* recipient of a greeting Ro 16:6.*

Μᾶρκος, ου, ὁ *Mark,* surname of John, son of Mary of Jerusalem Ac 12:12, 25; 15:37, 39; Col 4:10; Phlm 24; 2 Ti 4:11; 1 Pt 5:13; title of the second gospel.*

μάρμαρος, ου, ὁ *marble* as precious material Rv 18:12.* [*marmoreal*]

μαρτυρέω—**1.** act.—**a.** *bear witness, be a witness, testify* Mt 23:31; J 1:7f, 15; 5:33; 8:13f, 18; 15:27; Ac 22:5; 26:5; 2 Cor 8:3; Gal 4:15; 1 Ti 6:13; Hb 11:4; Rv 22:18.—**b.** *bear witness to, declare, confirm* J 3:11, 32; 1 J 1:2; 5:10; Rv 1:2; 22:20.—**c.** *testify favorably, speak well (of), approve (of)* w. dat. Lk 4:22; J 3:26; Ac 13:22; 14:3; 3 J 12b.—**2.** pass.—**a.** *be witnessed, have witness borne* Ro 3:21; Hb 7:8, 17.—**b.** *be well spoken of, be approved* Ac 6:3; 10:22; 16:2; 22:12; Hb 11:2, 4f, 39; 3 J 12a. [*martyrize*]

μαρτυρία, ας, ἡ *testimony* Mk 14:55f, 59; J 1:7, 19; 3:11; 8:13f, 17; 19:35; Ac 22:18; Tit 1:13; Rv 1:2, 9; 6:9; 11:7; 12:11, 17; 20:4. Standing 1 Ti 3:7.

μαρτύριον, ου, τό *testimony, proof* Mt 10:18; 24:14; Mk 1:44; 6:11; 13:9; Lk 21:13; Ac 4:33; 7:44; 2 Cor 1:12; 2 Th 1:10; 1 Ti 2:6; Hb 3:5; Js 5:3.

μαρτύρομαι *testify, bear witness* Ac 20:26; 26:22; Gal 5:3. *Affirm, insist, implore* Eph 4:17; 1 Th 2:12.*

μάρτυς, μάρτυρος, ὁ *witness*—**1.** in a legal sense Mt 18:16; Mk 14:63; Ac 6:13; 7:58; Hb 10:28.—**2.** in a nonlegal sense, esp. in reference to attestation in response to noteworthy performance or communication Lk 11:48; Ac 1:8, 22; 26:16; Ro 1:9; 2 Cor 1:23; 1 Ti 6:12; Hb 12:1; 1 Pt 5:1; Rv 11:3.—**3.** of one whose witness or attestation ultimately leads to death (the background for the later technical usage 'martyr') Ac 22:20; Rv 1:5; 2:13; 3:14; 17:6.

μασάομαι *bite* Rv 16:10.*

μασθός v.l. for μαστός.

μαστιγόω whip, flog, scourge lit. Mt 10:17; 20:19; 23:34; Mk 10:34; Lk 18:33; J 19:1. Fig. punish, chastise Hb 12:6.*

μαστίζω scourge Ac 22:25.*

μάστιξ, ιγος, ή whip, lash lit. Ac 22:24; Hb 11:36. Fig. torment, suffering, illness Mk 3:10; 5:29, 34; Lk 7:21.*

μαστός, οῦ, ὁ breast Lk 11:27; 23:29; Rv 1:13.* [masto-, combining form, as in mastectomy, mastitis]

ματαιολογία, ας, ή empty, fruitless talk 1 Ti 1:6.*

ματαιολόγος, ον talking idly as noun an idle talker Tit 1:10.*

μάταιος, αία, αιον idle, empty, worthless, foolish 1 Cor 3:20; 15:17; Tit 3:9; Js 1:26; 1 Pt 1:18. τὰ μάταια idols Ac 14:15.*

ματαιότης, ητος, ή emptiness, futility, frustration, transitoriness Ro 8:20; Eph 4:17; 2 Pt 2:18.*

ματαιόω render futile pass. be given over to worthlessness, think about worthless things Ro 1:21.*

μάτην adv. in vain, to no end Mt 15:9; Mk 7:7.*

Ματθαῖος see Μαθθαῖος.

Ματθάν, ὁ indecl. Matthan Mt 1:15; Lk 3:24 v.l.*

Ματθάτ see Μαθθάτ.

Ματταθά, ὁ indecl. Mattatha Lk 3:31.*

Ματταθίας, ου, ὁ Mattathias—1. Lk 3:25.—2. 3:26.*

μάχαιρα, ης, ή sword, saber lit. Mt 26:52; Mk 14:43, 47f; Lk 21:24; 22:36, 38, 49; J 18:10f; Ac 16:27; Hb 4:12; 11:34, 37; Rv 13:10, 14. Fig. Mt 10:34; Ro 8:35 of violent death; 13:4; Eph 6:17.

μάχη, ης, ή pl. fighting, quarrels, strife, disputes 2 Cor 7:5; 2 Ti 2:23; Tit 3:9; Js 4:1.* [logomachy, λόγος + μάχη]

μάχομαι to fight lit. Ac 7:26. Fig. be quarrelsome 2 Ti 2:24; dispute J 6:52; Js 4:2.*

μέ acc. of ἐγώ.

μεγαλαυχέω become proud, boast Js 3:5 v.l.*

μεγαλεῖος, α, ον magnificent, splendid as noun τὰ μ. the mighty deeds Ac 2:11; cf. Lk 1:49 v.l.*

μεγαλειότης, ητος, ή grandeur, sublimity, majesty Lk 9:43; Ac 19:27; 2 Pt 1:16.*

μεγαλοπρεπής, ές magnificent, sublime, majestic 2 Pt 1:17.*

μεγαλύνω make large or long, magnify—1. lit. Mt 23:5; Lk 1:58; pass. increase, grow 2 Cor 10:15.—2. fig. exalt, glorify, praise, extol Lk 1:46; Ac 5:13; 10:46; pass. Ac 19:17; Phil 1:20.*

μεγάλως adv. greatly Phil 4:10; heartily Ac 15:4 v.l.*

μεγαλωσύνη, ης, ή majesty Jd 25; as a periphrasis for God Majesty Hb 1:3; 8:1.*

μέγας, μεγάλη, μέγα large, great—1. lit. Mk 4:32; 5:11; 16:4; Lk 14:16; 22:12; 2 Ti 2:20; Rv 8:8, 10; 12:3; 14:19. Long Rv 6:4; 20:1. Wide 1 Cor 16:9.—2. fig.—a. of measure, intensity Mt 8:26; 28:2; Mk 5:7; Lk 2:9f; 21:11; J 6:18; Ac 4:33; 11:28; Hb 10:35; 11:24; Rv 11:18; 15:3. Loud Mt 27:46; Mk 15:37; Lk 19:37; Ac 7:57; 23:9; Rv 5:2. Bright Mt 4:16. Intense Rv 16:9. Severe Ac 8:1.—b. of rank and dignity great, etc. Mt 20:25; Mk 10:43; Lk 7:16; J 19:31; Ac 2:20; 19:27f, 34f; Eph 5:32; Tit 2:13; Hb 4:14. μεγάλα proud words Rv 13:5.—For μείζων and μέγιστος see them as separate entries. [megalo-, a combining form in such words as megalomania, megaphone]

μέγεθος, ους, τό greatness Eph 1:19.*

μεγιστάν, ᾶνος, ὁ great man, courtier, magnate Mk 6:21; Rv 6:15; 18:23.*

μέγιστος superlative of μέγας very great 2 Pt 1:4.*

μεθερμηνεύω translate Mt 1:23; Mk 5:41; 15:22, 34; J 1:38, 41; Ac 4:36; 13:8.*

μέθη, ης, ή drunkenness Lk 21:34; Ro 13:13; Gal 5:21.*

μεθίστημι or μεθιστάνω remove Ac 13:22; 1 Cor 13:2; transfer Col 1:13; pass. be discharged Lk 16:4. Turn away, mislead Ac 19:26.*

μεθοδεία, ας, ή scheming, craftiness Eph 4:14; pl. wiles, stratagems 6:11, 12 v.l.* [method]

μεθόριον, ου, τό boundary, pl. region Mk 7:24 v.l.*

μεθύσκω cause to become intoxicated pass. become intoxicated, get drunk Lk 12:45; Eph 5:18; 1 Th 5:7; Rv 17:2; drink freely, be drunk J 2:10.*

μέθυσος, ου, ὁ drunkard 1 Cor 5:11; 6:10.*

μεθύω be drunk lit. Mt 24:49; Ac 2:15; 1 Cor 11:21; 1 Th 5:7; fig. Rv 17:6.*

μείγνυμι or **μειγνύω** mix, mingle Mt 27:34; Lk 13:1; Rv 8:7; 15:2.*

μειζότερος, α, ον comparative of μέγας greater 3 J 4.*

μείζων, ον comparative of μέγας greater Mt 11:11; 12:6; Lk 22:26f; J 4:12; 14:28; 1 Cor 12:31; 14:5; Hb 6:13; 1 J 3:20; 4:4. ὁ μ. the older Ro 9:12. μεῖζον as adv. all the more Mt 20:31. μείζων as superlative greatest Mt 18:1, 4; Mk 9:34; 1 Cor 13:13.

μεῖναι, μεῖνον 1 aor. act. inf. and impv. of μένω.

μέλαν, τό see μέλας.

μέλας, μέλαινα, μέλαν gen. **ανος, αίνης, ανος** black Mt 5:36; Rv 6:5, 12. Neut. τὸ μέλαν ink 2 Cor 3:3; 2 J 12; 3 J 13.* [melano-, a combining form, as in melanoma]

Μελεά, ὁ indecl. Melea Lk 3:31.*

μέλει third pers. sing. of μέλω, used mostly impersonally, but sometimes personally; w. dat. it is a care or concern to someone, i.e. someone cares Mt 22:16; Mk 4:38; 12:14; Lk 10:40; J 10:13; 12:6; 1 Cor 9:9; 1 Pt 5:7. Personal Ac 18:17. μή σοι μελέτω never mind 1 Cor 7:21.*

μελετάω practice, cultivate 1 Ti 4:15. Think about, meditate upon Ac 4:25; rack one's brains Mk 13:11 v.l.*

μέλι, ιτος, τό honey Mt 3:4; Mk 1:6; Rv 10:9f.* [Cf. mellifluous.]

μελίσσιος, ιον pertaining to the bee μ. κηρίον honeycomb Lk 24:42 v.l. The other v.l. ἀπὸ μελισσίου κηρίον belongs to μελισσ(ε)ίον, ου, τό beehive.*

Μελίτη, ης, ἡ Malta an island south of Sicily Ac 28:1.*

Μελιτήνη v.l. for Μελίτη.

μέλλω—**1.** be about to, be on the point of Mk 13:4; Lk 7:2; 19:4; 22:23; Ac 12:6; 16:27; Ro 8:18; 1 Ti 1:16; 1 Pt 5:1; Rv 3:2, 16.—**2.** be destined, must Mt 17:12, 22; J 11:51; Ac 26:22; Gal 3:23; Hb 1:14; Rv 1:19.—**3.** intend Mt 2:13; Lk 10:1; J 6:15, 71; 7:35; Ac 17:31; 20: 3, 7, 13.—**4.** the participle often means future, to come Mt 12:32; Ro 8:38; Eph 1:21; Col 2:17; 1 Ti 6:19; Hb 2:5; 13:14.—**5.** delay Ac 22:16.

μέλος, ους, τό member, part, limb lit. Mt 5:29f; Ro 7:5, 23; 12:4; 1 Cor 12:18–20; Js 3:5. Fig. Ro 12:5; 1 Cor 6:15a; 12:27; Eph 5:30.

Μελχί, ὁ indecl. Melchi—**1.** Lk 3:24.—**2.** 3:28.*

Μελχισέδεκ, ὁ indecl. Melchizedek (Gen 14:18) Hb 5:6, 10; 6:20; 7:1, 10f, 15, 17.*

μέλω see μέλει.

μεμάθηκα pf. act. ind. of μανθάνω.

μεμβράνα, ης, ἡ parchment, used for making books 2 Ti 4:13.* [Latin loanword: membrana; membrane]

μεμενήκεισαν plupf. act. 3 pl. of μένω.

μεμίαμμαι pf. pass. ind. of μιαίνω.

μέμιγμαι pf. pass. ind. of μίγνυμι.

μέμνημαι pf. mid. and pass. ind. of μιμνήσκομαι.

μέμφομαι find fault with, blame Ro 9:19; Hb 8:8; Mk 7:2 v.l.*

μεμψίμοιρος, ον fault-finding, complaining Jd 16.*

μέμψις, εως, ἡ reason for complaint Col 3:13 v.l.*

μέν affirmative particle—**1.** used correlatively with other particles—**a.** frequently indicating a (strong) contrast between two clauses. μὲν . . . δέ, μὲν . . . ἀλλά may be translated to be sure . . . but or on the one hand . . . on the other hand, though this scheme will not always fit Mt 3:11; 9:37; Mk 9:12f; 14:21; J 19:32; Ro 14:20; 1 Cor 14:17.—**b.** When used with conjunctions μέν is often left untranslated Lk 13:9; 1 Cor 11:7; Hb 11:15. μέν may sometimes be left untranslated even when unaccompanied by a conjunction Lk 11:48; 1 Cor 1:12, 18, 23; Phil 3:1.—**c.** When it is used with the definite article ὁ μὲν . . . ὁ δέ or the relative pronoun ὃς μὲν

... ὅς δέ the combination means *the one ... the other*, but pl. *some ... others* Mt 21:35; 25:15; Lk 23:33; Ac 14:4; 17:32; 27:44; Ro 14:5; Gal 4:23; Eph 4:11; Phil 1:16; Jd 22. ὁ μὲν οὕτως, ὁ δὲ οὕτως *one in one way, one in another* 1 Cor 7:7.—**2.** Sometimes the second clause of the contrast is omitted altogether, though it can be supplied from the context 1 Cor 6:7; 2 Cor 12:12; Col 2:23.

Μεννά, ὁ indecl. *Menna* Lk 3:31.*

μενοῦν Lk 11:28; Ro 9:20 v.l.; Phil 3:8 v.l. and **μενοῦνγε** (μενοῦν γε) particles *rather, on the contrary* Lk 11:28. *Indeed* Ro 10:18. ἀλλὰ μενοῦνγε *more than that* Phil 3:8. μενοῦνγε σὺ τίς εἶ; *on the contrary, who are you?* Ro 9:20.*

μέντοι particle—**1.** *really, actually* Js 2:8.—**2.** *though, to be sure, indeed* J 4:27; 7:13; 20:5; 21:4. *Nevertheless* 2 Ti 2:19. ὅμως μ. *yet, despite that* J 12:42. *But* Jd 8.*

μένω—**1.** intrans. *remain, stay* J 7:9; 12:24; 15:4b; Ac 27:31; 1 Cor 7:11, 40; Hb 7:3. *Live, dwell* Lk 8:27; J 1:38; Ac 28:16. *Continue, abide* J 6:56; 12:46; 14:10; 15:4–7, 9f; 1 J passim; 2 J 9. *Last, persist, continue to live* or *exist* Mt 11:23; J 9:41; 21:22f; 1 Cor 13:13; 15:6; 2 Cor 3:11; Phil 1:25; Hb 13:1, 14; Rv 17:10.—**2.** trans. *wait for, await* Ac 20:5, 23. [Cf. *permanent.*]

μερίζω *divide, separate*—**1.** *divide* act. and pass., fig. Mt 12:25f; Mk 3:24–26; 1 Cor 1:13; 7:34; mid. *share* Lk 12:13.—**2.** *distribute* Mk 6:41; *assign, apportion* Ro 12:3; 1 Cor 7:17; 2 Cor 10:13; Hb 7:2.*

μέριμνα, ης, ἡ *anxiety, worry, care* Mt 13:22; Mk 4:19; Lk 8:14; 21:34; 2 Cor 11:28; 1 Pt 5:7.*

μεριμνάω—**1.** *have anxiety, be anxious, be (unduly) concerned* Mt 6:25, 27f, 31, 34a; 10:19; Lk 10:41; 12:11, 22, 25f; Phil 4:6.—**2.** *care for, be concerned about* Mt 6:34b v.l.; 1 Cor 7:32–34; 12:25; Phil 2:20.*

μερίς, ίδος, ἡ—**1.** *part, district* Ac 16:12.—**2.** *share* Ac 8:21; Col 1:12; *portion* Lk 10:42. τίς μερὶς πιστῷ μετὰ ἀπίστου; *what has a believer in common with an unbeliever?* 2 Cor 6:15.*

μερισμός, οῦ, ὁ *separation* Hb 4:12. *Distribution, apportionment* 2:4.*

μεριστής, οῦ, ὁ *arbitrator, divider* Lk 12:14.*

μέρος, ους, τό—**1.** *part* Lk 11:36; 15:12; Ac 5:2; Eph 4:16; Rv 16:19. Specialized uses: *side* J 21:6; *piece* Lk 24:42; *party* Ac 23:6, 9; *line of business* 19:27; *matter, affair* 2 Cor 3:10; 9:3; pl. *region, district* Mt 2:22; 15:21; Ac 2:10; 19:1.—With prepositions: ἀνὰ μέρος *one after the other* 1 Cor 14:27.—ἀπὸ μέρους *in part* Ro 11:25; 15:15; 2 Cor 1:14; 2:5; *for a while* Ro 15:24.—ἐκ μέρους *individually* 1 Cor 12:27; *in part* 13:9f, 12.—ἐν μέρει *in the matter of, with regard to* Col 2:16.—κατὰ μέρος *in detail* Hb 9:5.—μέρος τι as adverbial acc. *in part, partly* 1 Cor 11:18.—**2.** *share* Rv 20:6; 22:19. *Place* Mt 24:51; Lk 12:46; J 13:8; Rv 21:8. [*-merous*, as in *dimerous, pentamerous*]

μεσάζω *be in* or *at the middle* J 7:14 v.l.*

μεσημβρία, ας, ἡ *midday, noon* Ac 22:6. κατὰ μεσημβρίαν 8:26 may. be *about noon*, but is more likely used of place *toward the south.**

μεσιτεύω *mediate, guarantee* Hb 6:17.*

μεσίτης, ου, ὁ *mediator, arbitrator* Gal 3:19f; 1 Ti 2:5; Hb 8:6; 9:15; 12:24.*

μεσονύκτιον, ου, τό *midnight* Mk 13:35; Lk 11:5; Ac 16:25; 20:7.* [μέσος + νύξ]

Μεσοποταμία, ας, ἡ *Mesopotamia,* country between the Tigris and Euphrates rivers Ac 2:9; 7:2.*

μέσος, η, ον *middle, in the middle*—**1.** as adj. Mt 25:6; Lk 23:45; J 19:18; Ac 1:18; 26:13. μέσος αὐτῶν *among them* Lk 22:55; cf. J 1:26.—**2.** (τὸ) μέσον as noun *the middle:* ἀνὰ μέσον w. gen. *among* Mt 13:25; *within* Mk 7:31; *between* 1 Cor 6:5 (the expression is incomplete); *on the center* Rv 7:17.—ἐν (τῷ) μέσῳ *before* Mt 14:6; Mk 6:47; J 8:3; Ac 4:7, but *in the middle* J 8:9; *within* Lk 21:21; *among* 22:27.—ἐκ μέσου *from among* Col 2:14.—With other prepositions Mk 3:3; 14:60; Lk 4:30, 35.—**3.** the neut. μέσον serves as an adv., which functions as a prep. w. gen. *in the middle* or *midst of* Mt 14:24 v.l.;

Phil 2:15. [*meso-*, combining form, as in *mesoplast*, the nucleus of a cell; *Mesopotamia*]

μεσότοιχον, ου, τό *dividing wall* Eph 2:14.*

μεσουράνημα, ατος, τό *zenith, midheaven* Rv 8:13; 14:6; 19:17.*

μεσόω *be at the midpoint* J 7:14.*

Μεσσίας, ου, ὁ (Hebrew) *the Messiah* = *the Anointed One*, translated into Greek as Χριστός J 1:41; 4:25.*

μεστός, ή, όν *full* lit. J 19:29; 21:11. Fig. Mt 23:28; Ro 1:29; 15:14; Js 3:8, 17; 2 Pt 2:14.*

μεστόω *fill* pass. *be filled* Ac 2:13.*

μετά prep.—**1.** w. genitive *with*—**a.** generally Mk 3:5; 10:30; Ac 13:17; 2 Cor 7:15; 8:4; Eph 6:7; 1 Ti 2:9; 1 Pt 3:16.— **b.** *with, in company with* Mt 2:3; 8:11; 20:20; 26:18, 38, 40; Mk 11:11; Lk 22:59; J 11:54; Gal 2:1; 4:25; 2 Ti 4:11; 1 J 2:19; Rv 22:12.—**c.** *among* Mt 24:51; Mk 1:13; 14:54; Lk 22:37; 24:5; J 6:43; Rv 1:7.—**d.** be *with* someone, to aid or help Lk 1:28; J 3:2; Ac 11:21; 1 Cor 16:24; 2 Cor 13:11; Gal 6:18.—**e.** *with* of hostile or friendly association Lk 23:12; J 16:19; Ro 12:18; 1 Cor 6:6; 1 J 1:3a, 7; Rv 2:16; 11:7.—**2.** w. accusative *after* Mt 17:1; 25:19; 26:32; Mk 1:14; 8:31; 13:24; Ac 20:29; 27:14. *Behind* Hb 9:3. [*meta-*, combining form, as in *metaphor, metaphysical*]

μετάβα 2 aor. act. impv. 2 sing. of μεταβαίνω.

μεταβαίνω—**1.** lit. *go* or *pass over (from one place to another)* Mt 8:34; 17:20; J 7:3; 13:1; Ac 18:7; *change one's residence, move* Lk 10:7.—**2.** fig. *pass, move* J 5:24; 1 J 3:14.

μεταβάλλω mid. *change one's mind* Ac 28:6.* [*metabolic*]

μεταβαλόμενος 2 aor. mid. ptc. of μεταβάλλομαι.

μεταβάς, μεταβέβηκα, μεταβήσομαι 2 aor. act. ptc., pf. act. ind., and fut. ind. of μεταβαίνω.

μετάβηθι 2 aor. act. impv. 2 sing. of μεταβαίνω.

μετάγω *guide, steer* Js 3:3f; pass. *be brought back* Ac 7:16 v.l.*

μεταδιδόναι, μεταδιδούς pres. act. inf. and ptc. of μεταδίδωμι.

μεταδίδωμι *impart, share, give* Lk 3:11; Ro 1:11; 12:8; Eph 4:28; 1 Th 2:8.*

μεταδότω, μεταδοῦναι, μεταδῶ 2 aor. act. impv., inf., and subj. of μεταδίδωμι.

μετάθεσις, θέσεως, ἡ *removal* Hb 12:27. *Taking up* or *translation* 11:5. *Change, transformation* 7:12.* [*metathesis*]

μεταίρω *go away* Mt 13:53; 19:1.*

μετακαλέω mid. *call to oneself, summon* Ac 7:14; 10:32; 20:17; 24:25.*

μετακινέω *shift, remove* fig. Col 1:23.*

μεταλαβεῖν 2 aor. act. inf. of μεταλαμβάνω.

μεταλαμβάνω *receive one's share, share in, receive* Ac 2:46; 27:33f; 2 Ti 2:6; Hb 6:7; 12:10. καιρὸν μ. *find time* Ac 24:25.*

μετάλημψις, εως, ἡ *sharing, receiving* 1 Ti 4:3.*

μεταλλάσσω *exchange* Ro 1:25f.*

μεταμέλομαι *regret, repent* Mt 21:29; 32; 27:3; 2 Cor 7:8; Hb 7:21.-

μεταμορφόω pass. *be changed in form, be transformed* Ro 12:2; 2 Cor 3:18. *Be transfigured* Mt 17:2; Mk 9:2.* [*metamorphosis*]

μετανοέω *feel remorse, repent*, lit. 'change one's mind' Mt 11:21; 12:41; Mk 1:15; Lk 11:32; 13:3, 5; Ac 3:19; 8:22; 2 Cor 12:21; Rv 9:20f; 16:9.

μετάνοια, ας, ἡ *remorse, repentance, turning about*, lit. 'change of mind' Mt 3:8, 11; Mk 1:4; Lk 15:7; Ac 5:31; 20:21; 26:20; 2 Cor 7:9f; Hb 6:1; 12:17.

μεταξύ adv.—**1.** used as adv. *between* ἐν τῷ μεταξύ *in the meanwhile* J 4:31. *Afterward, next* Ac 13:42.—**2.** functions as prep. w. gen. *between* Mt 18:15; 23:35; Lk 16:26; Ac 12:6; 15:9; *among* Ro 2:15.

μεταπέμπω mid. and pass. *send for, summon* Ac 10:5, 22, 29; 11:13; 20:1; 24:24, 26; 25:3.*

μετάπεμψαι 1 aor. mid. impv. 2 sing. of μεταπέμπω.

μεταστρέφω *change* Ac 2:20; Js 4:9 v.l.* *Pervert* Gal 1:7.*

μετασχηματίζω change (the form of), transform Phil 3:21. Mid. change or disguise oneself 2 Cor 11:13–15. The act. in 1 Cor 4:6 means something like apply.*

μετατίθημι change (the position of)— **1.** lit. bring back Ac 7:16. Be taken up, translated Hb 11:5.—**2.** nonliterally change, alter Hb 7:12. Pervert Jd 4. Mid. turn away Gal 1:6.* [metathesis]

μετατρέπω turn around pass. be turned Js 4:9.*

μεταφυτεύω transplant Lk 17:6 v.l.*

μετέβη 2 aor. act. ind. 3 sing. of μεταβαίνω.

μετέπειτα adv. afterward Hb 12:17.*

μετέχω share (in), have a share (of), participate (in) w. gen. 1 Cor 10:21; Hb 2:14; belong to 7:13. Eat, drink, enjoy 1 Cor 9:10, 12; 10:17, 30; Hb 5:13. Have Lk 1:34 v.l.*

μετεωρίζομαι be anxious, worry Lk 12:29.*

μετήλλαξα 1 aor. act. ind. of μεταλλάσσω.

μετῆρα 1 aor. act. ind. of μεταίρω.

μετοικεσία, ας, ἡ deportation, captivity Mt 1:11f, 17.*

μετοικίζω remove (to another place of habitation) Ac 7:4. Deport 7:43.* [metic, immigrant or settler in ancient Greece]

μετοικιῶ fut. act. ind. of μετοικίζω.

μετοχή, ῆς, ἡ sharing, participation 2 Cor 6:14.*

μέτοχος, ον sharing or participating in w. gen. Hb 3:1, 14; 6:4; 12:8. As noun ὁ μ. the partner, companion Lk 5:7; Hb 1:9.*

μετρέω measure—**1.** take the dimensions of, measure—**a.** lit. Rv 11:1f; 21:15–17.—**b.** fig. 2 Cor 10:12.—**2.** give out, deal out, apportion Mt 7:2; Mk 4:24; Lk 6:38.* [metric]

μετρητής, οῦ, ὁ a liquid measure amounting to about 40 liters J 2:6.*

μετριοπαθέω moderate one's feelings, deal gently w. dat. Hb 5:2.*

μετρίως adv. moderately οὐ μ. immeasurably Ac 20:12.*

μέτρον, ου, τό measure Mk 4:24; Ro 12:3; Eph 4:7, 13, 16; Rv 21:15. κατὰ τὸ μέτρον τοῦ κανόνος within the limits 2 Cor 10:13; οὐκ ἐκ μέτρου not from a measure, that is, without measure J 3:34. [metronome]

μετῴκισα 1 aor. act. ind. of μετοικίζω.

μέτωπον, ου, τό forehead Lk 23:48 v.l.; Rv 7:3; 14:1, 9; 22:4.

μέχρι or **μέχρις** until—**1.** prep. w. gen. Mt 11:23; 28:15; Lk 16:16; Ac 10:30; 20:7; Hb 3:6 v.l., 14; 9:10; as far as Ro 15:19; to the point of 2 Ti 2:9; Hb 12:4; unto Phil 2:8, 30.—**2.** conjunction until Mk 13:30; Gal 4:19; Eph 4:13.

μή negative particle not—**1.** as a neg. particle Mt 5:20; 18:25; 24:22; Mk 3:9; Lk 20:27; J 20:17; Ac 23:8; Ro 5:13; 14:21; 2 Cor 3:7; Gal 5:26; 6:14; Eph 4:26; Col 2:21; 1 Pt 3:10.—**2.** as a conjunction, that . . . (not), lest Mk 13:5, 36; Gal 6:1; Col 2:8; Hb 12:15.—**3.** as an interrogative particle when a negative answer is expected μή τινος ὑστερήσατε; you did not lack anything, did you? Lk 22:35; cf. Mt 7:9f; J 3:4; Ac 7:28; 1 Cor 1:13.—**4.** οὐ μή strengthens the negation, never, certainly not, etc. Mt 5:18, 20, 26; 16:22; Lk 6:37; J 13:8; 18:11; 1 Cor 8:13; Hb 13:5. On the other hand, in the combination μή οὐ, μή is an interrogative word and οὐ negatives the word; an affirmative answer is expected Ro 10:18f; 1 Cor 9:4f.

μήγε = μή + γε.

μηδαμῶς adv. by no means, certainly not Ac 10:14; 11:8.*

μηδέ negative particle and not, but not Mt 22:29; Mk 6:11; J 14:27; Ro 9:11; 1 Cor 5:8; 1 Pt 3:14. Not even Mk 2:2; 3:20; 8:26; 1 Cor 5:11; Eph 5:3.

μηδείς, μηδεμία, μηδέν or **μηθείς,** etc.—**1.** adj. no Ac 13:28; 25:17; 28:18; 1 Cor 1:7; 1 Ti 5:14; Hb 10:2; with another negative no . . . at all 2 Cor 6:3; 13:7; 1 Pt 3:6.—**2.** substantive μηδείς nobody Mt 8:4; Mk 7:36; Ac 9:7; 11:19; Ro 12:17; 1 Cor 10:24; Rv 3:11. μηδέν nothing Mk 1:44; Lk 9:3; Ac 8:24; Ro 13:8; 1 Cor 10:25; Gal 6:3; not . . . at all, in no way Mk 5:26; Lk 4:35; Ac 4:21; Phil 4:6; Js 1:6.

μηδέποτε adv. *never* 2 Ti 3:7.*

μηδέπω adv. *not yet* Hb 11:7.*

Μῆδος, ου, ὁ *a Mede*, inhabitant of Media Ac 2:9.*

μηθαμῶς see μηδαμῶς.

μηθέν see μηδείς.

μηκέτι adv. *no longer, not from now on* Mk 1:45; 11:14; J 5:14; Ac 13:34; 25:24; Ro 6:6; 2 Cor 5:15; 1 Pt 4:2.

μῆκος, ους, τό *length* Eph 3:18; Rv 21:16.*

μηκύνω *make long*, pass. *become long, grow (long)* Mk 4:27.*

μηλωτή, ῆς, ἡ *sheepskin* Hb 11:37.*

μήν particle; see εἰ μήν as a separate entry.

μήν, μηνός, ὁ *month* Lk 1:24, 26, 56; Ac 7:20; 18:11; Js 5:17; Rv 9:5; 13:5; 22:2. *New moon* (festival) Gal 4:10. [*menology; menopause*, μήν + παύειν]

μηνύω *make known, reveal* Lk 20:37; Ac 23:30; *report* J 11:57; *inform* 1 Cor 10:28.*

μὴ οὐ see μή 4.

μήποτε—1. negative particle *never* Hb 9:17.—2. conjunction *that . . . not, lest* Lk 21:34; Hb 3:12; 4:1; *(in order) that . . . not* Mt 5:25; Mk 4:12; Ac 5:39; Hb 2:1.—3. interrogative particle *whether perhaps* J 7:26; 2 Ti 2:25.

μήπου or μή που conj. *lest* or *that . . . somewhere* Ac 27:29.*

μήπω adv. *not yet* Ro 9:11; Hb 9:8.*

μήπως or μή πως conj.—1. denoting purpose, etc. *so that . . . (perhaps) not, lest somehow, that perhaps* 1 Cor 8:9; 9:27; 2 Cor 2:7; 9:4; Gal 4:11; 1 Th 3:5.—2. introducing an indirect question *that perhaps* Gal 2:2.

μηρός, οῦ, ὁ *thigh* Rv 19:16.*

μήτε negative copula *and not*, after μή *not . . . and not, neither . . . nor*, etc. Lk 7:33; 9:3; Ac 23:8, 12, 21; Hb 7:3; Js 5:12; Rv 7:1, 3.

μήτηρ, τρός, ἡ *mother* lit. Mt 1:18; 2:11, 13f, 20f; 10:37; 12:46; Mk 5:40; 6:24, 28; 2 Ti 1:5. Fig. Mt 12:49f; J 19:27; Gal 4:26; Rv 17:5. [Cf. *maternal*.]

μήτι interrogative particle in questions that expect a negative answer, often left untranslated, but cf. μήτι συλλέγουσιν *surely they do not gather . . . do they?* Mt 7:16; also cf. 26:22, 25; Mk 14:19; J 18:35; Ac 10:47; 2 Cor 12:18. Perhaps Mt 12:23; J 4:29.

μήτιγε = μήτι γε *not to speak of, let alone* 1 Cor 6:3.*

μήτρα, ας, ἡ *womb* Lk 2:23; Ro 4:19.* [*endometriosis*]

μητραλῴας or μητρολῴας, ου, ὁ *one who murders his mother, a matricide* 1 Ti 1:9.*

μητρόπολις, εως, ἡ *capital city* 1 Ti subscr.* [*metropolis*, μητήρ + πόλις]

μιαίνω *stain, defile* fig., of ceremonial or moral defilement J 18:28; Tit 1:15; Hb 12:15; Jd 8; Ac 5:38 v.l.*

μιανθῶ 1 aor. pass. subj. of μιαίνω.

μίασμα, ατος, τό *shameful deed, misdeed, crime* 2 Pt 2:20.* [*miasma*]

μιασμός, οῦ, ὁ *pollution, corruption* 2 Pt 2:10.*

μίγμα, ατος, τό *mixture, compound* J 19:39.* [Cf. μείγνυμι.]

μίγνυμι see μείγνυμι.

μικρός, ά, όν *small* Mt 13:32; Lk 12:32; Js 3:5; Rv 3:8. *Small* or *young* Mk 15:40. *Little one, child* Mt 18:6, 10, 14; cf. Ac 8:10; Rv 11:18. *Humble* Mk 9:42; ὁ μικρότερος *the one of least importance* Mt 11:11. *Short* J 7:33. *Little* 1 Cor 5:6. The neut. (τὸ) μικρόν: μικρόν τι *a little* 2 Cor 11:1, 16. (ἔτι) μικρὸν καί *soon* J 16:16–19. μικρόν alone *a short distance* Mt 26:39; *a short time* Mk 14:70; J 13:33. [*microbe*, μικρός + βίος]

Μίλητος, ου, ἡ *Miletus*, a seaport city on the west coast of Asia Minor, 60 km south of Ephesus Ac 20:15, 17; 2 Ti 4:20.*

μίλιον, ου, τό (Latin loanword: mille) a Roman *mile*, 1,478.5 meters or about 4,854 feet Mt 5:41.*

μιμέομαι *imitate, emulate, follow, use as a model* 2 Th 3:7, 9; Hb 13:7; 3 J 11.* [*mime*]

μιμητής, οῦ, ὁ *imitator* w. ref. to the use of a model for exemplary living 1 Cor 4:16; 11:1; Eph 5:1; 1 Th 1:6; 2:14; Hb 6:12; 1 Pt 3:13 v.l.* [*mimetic*] μιμνῄσκομαι—1. reflexive remind oneself, recall to mind, remember w. gen. Mt 5:23; 27:63; Lk 24:6, 8; J 2:17, 22; Ac 11:16; 1 Cor 11:2; 2 Ti 1:4. Remember in the sense think of, be concerned about Lk 1:72; 23:42; Hb 2:6; 8:12.—2. pass. be mentioned or be called to remembrance Ac 10:31; Rv 16:19.

μισέω hate detest, abhor Mt 5:43; 24:10; Mk 13:13; Lk 1:71; 14:26; J 3:20; 15:18f, 23f, 25; Ro 7:15; 9:13; Eph 5:29; Hb 1:9; Jd 23; Rv 2:6; 18:2. [misanthrope, μῖσος + ἄνθρωπος]

μισθαποδοσία, ας, ἡ reward Hb 10:35; 11:26; punishment, penalty 2:2.* [μισθός + ἀποδίδωμι]

μισθαποδότης, ου, ὁ rewarder Hb 11:6.*

μίσθιος, ου, ὁ, day laborer, hired man Lk 15:17, 19, 21 v.l.*

μισθός, οῦ, ὁ pay, wages lit. Mt 20:8; Lk 10:7; J 4:36; Ac 1:18; 1 Ti 5:18; 2 Pt 2:13, 15. Personified Js 5:4. μισθοῦ for pay Jd 11. Fig. reward Mt 5:46; 6:2, 5, 16; Mk 9:41; Lk 6:23, 35; Ro 4:4; 1 Cor 3:8, 14; Rv 11:18; reward or punishment 22:12.

μισθόω mid. hire, engage Mt 20:1, 7.*

μίσθωμα, ατος, τό in Ac 28:30 the word means either expense or rented lodging.*

μισθωτός, οῦ, ὁ hired hand Mk 1:20; J 10:12f.*

Μιτυλήνη, ης, ἡ Mitylene, chief city of the island of Lesbos, off the northwest coast of Asia Minor Ac 20:14.*

Μιχαήλ, ὁ indecl. Michael, an archangel Jd 9; Rv 12:7.*

μνᾶ, μνᾶς, ἡ (Semitic loanword) mina, a Greek monetary unit = 100 drachmas Lk 19:13, 16, 18, 20, 24f.*

μνάομαι woo or court for one's bride; pf. ptc. μεμνησμένη engaged, betrothed Lk 1:27 v.l.*

Μνάσων, ωνος, ὁ Mnason Ac 21:16.*

μνεία, ας, ἡ—1. remembrance, memory Ro 12:13 v.l.; 2 Ti 1:3; μνείαν ἔχειν think kindly 1 Th 3:6.—2. mention Ro 1:9; Eph 1:16; Phil 1:3; 1 Th 1:2; Phlm 4.*

μνῆμα, ατος, τό grave, tomb Mk 5:3, 5; Lk 8:27; 23:53; 24:1; Ac 2:29; 7:16; Rv 11:9; v.l. in Mk 15:46 and 16:2.*

μνημεῖον, ου, τό monument, memorial Lk 11:47. Grave, tomb Mt 23:29; 27:52f; Mk 5:2; 6:29; 15:46; 16:2, 3, 5, 8; Lk 11:44; 24:2, 9, 12; J 11:17, 31, 38; 20:1–4, 6, 8, 11; Ac 13:29.

μνήμη, ης, ἡ remembrance, memory μνήμην ποιεῖσθαι recall to mind 2 Pt 1:15.*

μνημονεύω remember, keep in mind, think of, mention w. gen. or acc. Mt 16:9; Lk 17:32; J 15:20; Ac 20:31, 35; Gal 2:10; 1 Th 1:3; 2 Ti 2:8; Hb 13:7; Rv 2:5. [mnemonic]

μνημόσυνον, ου, τό memory, remembrance Mt 26:13; Mk 14:9. Memorial offering Ac 10:4.* [Cf. Mnemosyne, goddess of memory and mother of the Muses.]

μνησθήσομαι, μνήσθητι 1 fut. ind. and 1 aor. impv. of μιμνῄσκομαι.

μνηστεύω woo and win, betroth pass. be betrothed, become engaged Mt 1:16 v.l., 18; Lk 1:27; 2:5.*

μογγιλάλος, ον speaking in a hoarse or hollow voice Mk 7:32 v.l.*

μογιλάλος, ον speaking with difficulty or impaired in speech Mk 7:32, 33 v.l.*

μόγις adv. scarcely, with difficulty Lk 9:39; 23:53 v.l.; Ac 14:18 v.l.; Ro 5:7 v.l.*

μόδιος, ίου, ὁ a peck measure, a grain measure containing about 8.75 liters, almost one peck Mt 5:15; Mk 4:21; Lk 11:33.*

μοί dat. of ἐγώ.

μοιχαλίς, ίδος, ἡ adulteress lit. Ro 7:3; 2 Pt 2:14. Fig. Js 4:4; as adj. adulterous Mt 12:39; 16:4; Mk 8:38.*

μοιχάω cause to commit adultery pass. commit adultery Mt 5:32 in text and v.l.; 19:9 in text and v.l.; Mk 10:11f.*

μοιχεία, ας, ἡ adultery Mt 15:19; Mk 7:22; J 8:3.*

μοιχεύω commit adultery Mt 5:27f, 32; Mk 10:19; Lk 16:18; J 8:4; Ro 2:22; Rv 2:22.

μοιχός, οῦ, ὁ adulterer lit. Lk 18:11; 1 Cor 6:9; Hb 13:4; fig. Js 4:4 v.l.*

μόλις adv. *scarcely, with difficulty* Lk 9:39 v.l.; Ac 14:18; 23:29 v.l.; 27:7f, 16; 1 Pt 4:18; *not readily, only rarely* or *hardly* Ro 5:7.*

Μόλοχ, ὁ indecl. *Moloch*, the Canaanite-Phoenician god of sky and sun Ac 7:43.*

μολύνω *stain, defile, make impure, soil* 1 Cor 8:7; Rv 3:4; 14:4; Ac 5:38 v.l.*

μολυσμός, οῦ, ὁ *defilement* 2 Cor 7:1.*

μομφή, ῆς, ἡ *blame, (cause for) complaint* Col 3:13.*

μονή, ῆς, ἡ *staying, tarrying* μονὴν ποιεῖσθαι *live, stay* J 14:23. *Dwelling (place), room, abode* 14:2.*

μονογενής, ές *only* Lk 7:12; 8:42; 9:38; Hb 11:17. *Only, unique* J 1:14, 18; 3:16, 18; 1 J 4:9.*

μόνον see μόνος 2.

μόνος, η, ον *only, alone*—1. adj. Mt 4:4; 14:23; Mk 9:8; Lk 9:36; 24:12, 18; J 8:9; 17:3; Ro 16:27; 1 Th 3:1; 1 Ti 1:17; Hb 9:7; Rv 15:4; *alone, deserted, helpless* J 8:29; 16:32.—2. adv., the neut. μόνον Mt 9:21; Lk 8:50; J 11:52; Ac 19:26; Ro 4:12, 16; Gal 1:23; 5:13; Hb 9:10; Js 1:22.—3. κατὰ μόνας *alone* Mk 4:10; Lk 9:18. [*mon-, mono-*, combining forms, as in *monody, monogamy*]

μονόφθαλμος, ον *one-eyed* Mt 18:9; Mk 9:47.*

μονόω *make solitary* pass. *be left alone* 1 Ti 5:5.*

μορφή, ῆς, ἡ *form, outward appearance, shape* Mk 16:12; Phil 2:6f.* [*morphology*]

μορφόω *to form, shape* pass. *take on form, be formed* Gal 4:19.*

μόρφωσις, εως, ἡ—1. *embodiment, formulation* Ro 2:20.—2. *outward form, appearance* 2 Ti 3:5.* [*metamorphosis*]

μοσχοποιέω *make a calf* Ac 7:41.*

μόσχος, ου, ὁ *calf, young bull* or *ox* Lk 15:23, 27, 30; Hb 9:12, 19; Rv 4:7.*

μοῦ gen. of ἐγώ.

μουσικός, ή, όν *pertaining to music* ὁ μουσικός as noun *the musician* Rv 18:22.*

μόχθος, ου, ὁ *labor, exertion, hardship* 2 Cor 11:27; 1 Th 2:9; 2 Th 3:8.*

μυελός, οῦ, ὁ *marrow* Hb 4:12.* [*myelin*, soft material in nerve fibers]

μυέω *initiate (into the mysteries)* pass. *be initiated, learn the secret* Phil 4:12.*

μῦθος, ου, ὁ *tale, story*, with special ref. to unreliability or fanciful character 1 Ti 1:4; 4:7; 2 Ti 4:4; Tit 1:14; 2 Pt 1:16.* [*myth*]

μυκάομαι *roar* Rv 10:3.*

μυκτηρίζω *treat with contempt, mock* Gal 6:7.*

μυλικός, ή, όν *belonging to a mill* Mk 9:42 v.l.; Lk 17:2; Rv 18:21 v.l.*

μύλινος, η, ον *belonging to a mill* Rv 18:21.*

μύλος, ου, ὁ—1. *mill* Mt 24:41; Rv 18:22.—2. *millstone* Mt 18:6; Mk 9:42; Rv 18:21 v.l.*

μυλών, ῶνος, ὁ *millhouse* Mt 24:41 v.l.*

μυλωνικός, ή, όν *belonging to the millhouse* Mk 9:42 v.l.*

Μύρα, ων, τά *Myra*, a city on the south coast of Asia Minor Ac 27:5; 21:1 v.l.*

μυριάς, άδος, ἡ *myriad (ten thousand)* lit., as a number Ac 19:19. A very large number, not exactly defined, pl. *myriads* Lk 12:1; Ac 21:20; Hb 12:22; Jd 14; Rv 5:11; 9:16.*

μυρίζω *anoint* Mk 14:8.*

μύριοι, αι, α *ten thousand* Mt 18:24.*

μυρίος, α, ον *innumerable, countless* 1 Cor 4:15; 14:19.*

μύρον, ου, τό *ointment, perfume* Mk 14:3–5; J 11:2; 12:3, 5; Rv 18:13. [*myrrh*, of Semitic origin]

Μύρρα a variant form of Μύρα.

Μυσία, ας, ἡ *Mysia*, a province in northwest Asia Minor Ac 16:7f.*

μυστήριον, ου, τό *secret, secret teaching, mystery* with reference to something previously unknown but now revealed Mk 4:11; Ro 11:25; 1 Cor 2:7; 13:2; 15:51; Eph 3:3f, 9; Col 1:26f; 4:3; Rv 10:7. *Secret truths* 1 Cor 14:2. Allegorical significance Rv 1:20; 17:7. τὸ τ. εὐσεβείας μ. the Christian religion 1 Ti 3:16. [*mystery*]

μυωπάζω *be nearsighted* fig. 2 Pt 1:9.*

μώλωψ, ωπος, ὁ *welt, bruise, wound* 1 Pt 2:24.*

μωμάομαι mid. dep. *find fault with,
blame* 2 Cor 8:20; pass. *have fault found
with it* 6:3.*

μῶμος, ου, ὁ *blemish* 2 Pt 2:13.*

μωραίνω—1. *show to be foolish* 1 Cor
1:20; pass. *become foolish* Ro 1:22.—
2. *make tasteless* pass. *become tasteless, insipid* Mt 5:13; Lk 14:34.*

μωράνθω 1 aor. pass. subj. of μωραίνω.

μωρία, ας, ἡ *foolishness* 1 Cor 1:18, 21,
23; 2:14; 3:19.*

μωρολογία, ας, ἡ *foolish, silly talk* Eph
5:4.*

μωρός, ά, όν *foolish, stupid* Mt 7:26;
23:17; 25:2f, 8; 1 Cor 1:25, 27; 3:18;
4:10; 2 Ti 2:23; Tit 3:9. μωρέ *you fool*
Mt 5:22 (s. BAGD s.v́., 3).* [*moron*]

Μωσῆς variant form of Μωϋσῆς.

Μωϋσῆς, έως, ὁ *Moses* Mt 19:7f; Mk
1:44; Lk 20:37; J 7:19; Ac 7:20ff; 2 Cor
3:7; Hb 3:5; Jd 9. *Book of Moses* 2 Cor
3:15.

N

Ναασσών, ὁ indecl. *Nahshon* Mt 1:4;
Lk 3:32.*

Ναγγαί, ὁ indecl. *Naggai* Lk 3:25.*

Ναζαρά, Ναζαρέτ, Ναζαρέθ, ἡ indecl. *Nazareth,* a village in Galilee,
home of Jesus' parents Mt 2:23; 4:13;
21:11; Mk 1:9; Lk 1:26; 2:4, 39, 51;
4:16; J 1:45f; Ac 10:38.*

Ναζαρηνός, ή, όν *coming from Nazareth* only as noun ὁ Ν. *the Nazarene*
Mk 1:24; 10:47; 14:67; 16:6; Lk 4:34;
24:19; J 18:5 v.l.*

Ναζωραῖος, ου, ὁ *Nazorean, Nazarene*
Mt 2:23; 26:69 v.l., 71; Lk 18:37; J 18:5,
7; 19:19; Ac 2:22; 3:6; 4:10; 6:14; 22:8;
24:5; 26:9.*

Ναθάμ, ὁ indecl. *Nathan* Lk 3:31.*

Ναθαναήλ, ὁ indecl. *Nathanael,* a disciple of Jesus J 1:45–49; 21:2.*

ναί affirmative particle *yes, yes indeed*
Mt 5:37; 11:9, 26; 17:25; Lk 7:26; 12:5;
J 11:27; 21:15f; Ac 22:27; 2 Cor 1:17–
20; Phlm 20; Js 5:12. *Certainly, indeed*
Mt 15:27; Mk 7:28 v.l.; Rv 14:13; *surely*
22:20.

Ναιμάν, ὁ indecl. *Naaman* (2 Kings
5:1ff) Lk 4:27.*

Ναΐν, ἡ indecl. *Nain,* a city in Galilee
Lk 7:11.*

ναός, οῦ, ὁ *temple* lit. Mt 23:17, 35; Mk
14:58; 15:38; Lk 1:21f; J 2:20; Ac 17:24;
19:24 (here perhaps *shrine*); Rv 11:2,
19; 15:6, 8; 21:22. Fig. J 2:19–21; 1 Cor
3:16, 17; 6:19. [*naos,* architectural term
= *cella,* innermost part of a temple]

Ναούμ, ὁ indecl. *Nahum* Lk 3:25.*

νάρδος, ου, ἡ *oil of (spike)nard,* ex-
tracted from the root of the nard plant,
used as perfume Mk 14:3; J 12:3.*

Νάρκισσος, ου, ὁ *Narcissus* Ro 16:11.*

ναυαγέω *suffer shipwreck* lit. 2 Cor 11:25;
fig. 1 Ti 1:19.*

ναύκληρος, ου, ὁ *ship owner* or *captain*
Ac 27:11.*

ναῦς, acc. **ναῦν, ἡ** *ship* Ac 27:41.*

ναύτης, ου, ὁ *sailor* Ac 27:27, 30; Rv
18:17.* [*nautical*]

Ναχώρ, ὁ indecl. *Nahor* Lk 3:34.*

νεανίας, ου, ὁ *young man* Ac 7:58; 20:9;
23:17, 18 v.l., 22 v.l.*

νεανίσκος, ου, ὁ *young man* Mt 19:20,
22; Mk 14:51; Lk 7:14; Ac 23:18, 22; 1
J 2:13f.

Νεάπολις see νέος, end.

Νεεμάν variant spelling of Ναιμάν.

νεῖκος in 1 Cor 15:54f v.l. is itacistic
form of νῖκος, q.v.

νεκρός, ά, όν *dead*—**1.** adj., lit. Mt 28:4; Mk 9:26; Ac 5:10; 28:6; Rv 1:17f. Fig. Ro 6:11; Eph 2:1, 5; Hb 6:1; Js 2:17, 26; Rv 3:1.—**2.** as noun ὁ νεκρός *the dead person, corpse* lit. Mt 10:8; Mk 9:9f; Lk 7:15; J 2:22; Ac 10:42; Ro 10:7; 1 Cor 15:20f; Col 2:12; 2 Ti 4:1; Hb 13:20; Rv 16:3. Fig. Mt 8:22; Eph 5:14. [*necrology*]

νεκρόω *put to death* Col 3:5. Pass. *be worn out, as good as dead* Ro 4:19; Hb 11:12.*

νέκρωσις, εως, ή—**1.** *death, putting to death* 2 Cor 4:10.—**2.** *deadness* of Sarah's unproductive womb Ro 4:19; *deadening* Mk 3:5 v.l.*

νενικήκατε pf. act. ind. 2 pl. of νικάω.

νενομοθέτητο unaugmented plupf. pass. 3 sing. of νομοθετέω.

νεομηνία, ας, ή *new moon* festival, *first of the month* Col 2:16.*

νέος, α, ον comparative νεώτερος—**1.** adj. *new, fresh* Lk 5:37–39; 1 Cor 5:7; Col 3:10; Hb 12:24. *Young,* comp. *younger* Lk 15:12f; 1 Ti 5:11.—**2.** as noun (οἱ) νέοι *the young people,* fem. Tit 2:4. Comp., with little comp. force Ac 5:6; 1 Ti 5:1, 2; 1 Pt 5:5, but equal to superlative Lk 22:26.—**3.** Νέα πόλις *Neapolis* (New City), the harbor of Philippi in Macedonia Ac 16:11. [*neo-,* combining form, as in *neo-Hellenic, neolithic*]

νεοσσός another form of νοσσός.

νεότης, τητος, ή *youth* Mk 10:20; Lk 18:21; Ac 26:4; 1 Ti 4:12.*

νεόφυτος, ον *newly converted,* lit. 'newly planted' 1 Ti 3:6.* [*neophyte*]

Νέρων, ωνος, ὁ *Nero,* Roman emperor 54–68 A.D. 2 Ti subscr.*

Νεύης name of the rich man Lk 16:19 v.l.

νεύω *nod* as a signal J 13:24; Ac 24:10.*

νεφέλη, ης, ή *cloud* Mt 17:5; Mk 13:26; Lk 12:54; Ac 1:9; 1 Cor 10:1f; Jd 12; Rv 14:14–16. [*nephelometer,* νεφέλη + μέτρον]

Νεφθαλίμ, ὁ indecl. *Naphtali,* a Hebrew tribe and its ancestor Mt 4:13, 15; Lk 4:31 v.l.; Rv 7:6.*

νέφος, ους, τό *cloud,* fig. *host* Hb 12:1.*

νεφρός, οῦ, ὁ *kidney,* fig. of the inner life *mind* Rv 2:23.* [*nephritic*]

νεωκόρος, ον, ὁ lit. *temple keeper,* in Ac 19:35 *guardian of the temple.**

νεωτερικός, ή, όν *youthful* 2 Ti 2:22.* [*neoteric,* modern]

νεώτερος see νέος.

νή particle of strong affirmation *by* w. acc. 1 Cor 15:31.*

νήθω *spin* Mt 6:28; Lk 12:27.*

νηπιάζω *be (as) a child* 1 Cor 14:20.*

νήπιος, ία, ιον *infant, minor*—**1.** lit. of very small children: *child* Mt 21:16; 1 Cor 13:11 (five times). Fig. *immature* Ro 2:20; 1 Cor 3:1; Eph 4:14; Hb 5:13. *Childlike, innocent* Mt 11:25; Lk 10:21.—**2.** *minor, not yet of age* Gal 4:1, 3; 1 Th 2:7 v.l.*

Νηρεύς, έως, ὁ *Nereus* Ro 16:15.*

Νηρί, ὁ indecl. *Neri* Lk 3:27.*

νησίον, ου, τό *little island* Ac 27:16.*

νῆσος, ου, ἡ *island* Ac 13:6; 27:26; 28:1, 7, 9, 11; Rv 1:9; 6:14; 16:20.* [*Peloponnesus,* Pelops' island; *Polynesia,* 'of many islands']

νηστεία, ας, ἡ *fasting, abstention from food*—**1.** of necessity, *hunger* 2 Cor 6:5; 11:27.—**2.** as a cultic rite Mt 17:21; Mk 9:29 v.l.; Lk 2:37; Ac 14:23; 27:9; 1 Cor 7:5 v.l.*

νηστεύω *to fast* as a cultic rite Mt 4:2; 6:16–18; Mk 2:18–20; Lk 18:12; Ac 13:2f.

νῆστις, ὁ, ἡ gen. ιος or ιδος, acc. pl. νήστεις *not eating, hungry* Mt 15:32; Mk 8:3.*

νηφαλέος, α, ον variant form of νηφάλιος.

νηφάλιος, ία, ον *temperate* in the use of alcoholic beverages, *sober, clearheaded, self-controlled* 1 Ti 3:2, 11; Tit 2:2.*

νήφω *be sober, be well balanced, self-controlled* 1 Th 5:6, 8; 2 Ti 4:5; 1 Pt 1:13; 4:7; 5:8.*

νήψατε 1 aor. act. impv. 2 pl. of νήφω.

Νίγερ, ὁ *Niger* (dark-complexioned), surname of Simeon Ac 13:1.* [Latin loanword: niger; *Negro*]

Νικάνωρ, ορος, ὁ *Nicanor* Ac 6:5.*

νικάω—**1.** intrans. *be victor, prevail, conquer* Rv 2:7; 6:2; in a legal action Ro 3:4.—**2.** trans. *conquer, overcome, vanquish* Lk 11:22; J 16:33; Ro 12:21b; 1 J 5:4f; Rv 11:7. Pass., *let oneself be overcome* Ro 12:21a. [Cf. *Nicholas.*]

νίκη, ης, ή *victory* 1 J 5:4.*

Νικόδημος, ου, ὁ *Nicodemus* J 3:1, 4, 9; 7:50; 19:39.*

Νικολαΐτης, ου, ὁ *Nicolaitan,* a follower of Nicolaus, an otherwise unknown founder of a sect Rv 2:6, 15.*

Νικόλαος, ου, ὁ *Nicolaus* Ac 6:5.*

Νικόπολις, εως, ή *Nicopolis;* most probably the city bearing this name in Epirus (northwest of Greece) Tit 3:12; subscriptions of 1 Ti and Tit.*

νῖκος, ους, τό *victory* Mt 12:20; 1 Cor 15:54f, 57.*

νικοῦντι = **νικῶντι,** pres. act. ptc. dat.

Νινευή, ή indecl. *Nineveh,* capital of the later Assyrian empire Lk 11:32 v.l.*

Νινευίτης, ου, ὁ *Ninevite, inhabitant of Nineveh* Mt 12:41; Lk 11:30, 32.*

νιπτήρ, ῆρος, ὁ *(wash)basin* J 13:5.*

νίπτω *wash* act. J 13:5f; 1 Ti 5:10. Mid. *wash oneself* J 9:7b, 11, 15; *bathe* 9:7a; *wash (for oneself)* Mt 6:17; 15:2; Mk 7:3; J 13:10 (if εἰ μὴ τ. πόδας is accepted).*

νίψαι 1 aor. mid. impv. 2 sing. of νίπτω.

νοέω—**1.** *perceive, understand, gain an insight into* Mt 16:9, 11; Mk 7:18; J 12:40; Ro 1:20; 1 Ti 1:7; Hb 11:3.—**2.** *consider, take note of, think over* Mk 13:14; 2 Ti 2:7.—**3.** *think, imagine* Eph 3:20. [*noetic*]

νόημα, ατος, τό—**1.** *thought, mind* 2 Cor 3:14; 4:4; 11:3; Phil 4:7.—**2.** *purpose, design, plot* 2 Cor 2:11; 10:5.*

νόθος, η, ον *born out of wedlock, illegitimate* Hb 12:8.*

νομή, ῆς, ή—**1.** *pasture* J 10:9.—**2.** fig. *spreading* νομὴν ἕξει *it will spread* 2 Ti 2:17.*

νομίζω—**1.** *have in common use,* pass. *be the custom* Ac 16:13 v.l.—**2.** *think, believe, suppose, consider* Mt 5:17; 10:34; Lk 2:44; Ac 7:25; 8:20; 16:13, 27; 1 Cor 7:26, 36.

νομικός, ή, όν *pertaining to the law* Tit 3:9. ὁ νομικός *legal expert, jurist, lawyer* Mt 22:35; Lk 7:30; 10:25; 11:45f, 52, 53 v.l.; 14:3; Tit 3:13.*

νομίμως adv. *in accordance with rules* 2 Ti 2:5. *Lawfully* 1 Ti 1:8.*

νόμισμα, ατος, τό *coin* Mt 22:19.*

νομοδιδάσκαλος, ου, ὁ *teacher of the law* Lk 5:17; Ac 5:34; 1 Ti 1:7.*

νομοθεσία, ας, ή *legislation, law* Ro 9:4.*

νομοθετέω *function as lawgiver* pass. *receive law(s)* Hb 7:11. *Be enacted* 8:6.* [*nomothetic*]

νομοθέτης, ου, ὁ *lawgiver* Js 4:12.*

νόμος, ου, ὁ *law*—**1.** *rule, principle, norm* Ro 7:21, 23; 8:2b; Hb 7:16.—**2.** of any kind of law Ro 3:27; perh. 7:1f.—**3.** of the Mosaic law Mt 22:36; Lk 2:22; 16:17; J 7:23, 51; 18:31; Ac 13:38; 18:13; 21:24; Ro 2:25; 3:19; 4:14; 7:2; Gal 3:12f, 17, 19; 5:23; 1 Ti 1:9; Hb 7:19. Almost equivalent to *(Jewish) religion* Ac 23:29. Specifically of the written law, the Pentateuch Mt 7:12; 12:5; Lk 2:23; 24:44; 1 Cor 9:9; Gal 3:10; 4:21b. Of the scriptures generally Mt 5:18; J 10:34; Ro 3:19.—**4.** of Christianity as a 'new law' Ro 3:27b; 8:2a; Gal 6:2; Js 1:25; 2:8f, 12. [*-nomy,* a combining form, as in *agronomy, astronomy, theonomy*]

νοσέω *be sick, ailing* fig. 1 Ti 6:4.*

νόσημα, ατος, τό *disease* J 5:4 v.l.*

νόσος, ου, ή *disease, illness* Mt 8:17; 9:35; Mk 1:34; Lk 7:21; 9:1; Ac 19:12. [*nosophobia*]

νοσσιά, ᾶς, ή *brood* Lk 13:34.*

νοσσίον, ου, τό *the young* of a bird Mt 23:37.*

νοσσός, οῦ, ὁ *the young* of a bird Lk 2:24.*

νοσφίζω mid. *put aside for oneself, misappropriate* Ac 5:2f; Tit 2:10.*

νότος, ου, ὁ *south* or *southwest wind* Lk 12:55; Ac 27:13; 28:13. *South* Lk 13:29; Rv 21:13. A country in the *south* Mt 12:42; Lk 11:31.*

νουθεσία, ας, ή *admonition, instruction, warning* 1 Cor 10:11; Eph 6:4; Tit 3:10.*

νουθετέω admonish, warn, instruct Ac 20:31; Ro 15:14; 1 Cor 4:14; Col 1:28; 3:16; 1 Th 5:12, 14; 2 Th 3:15; Tit 1:11 v.l.*

νουμηνία contract form of νεομηνία.

νουνεχῶς adv. wisely, thoughtfully Mk 12:34.*

νοῦς, gen. **νοός**, dat. **νοΐ**, acc. **νοῦν**, **ὁ**—**1.** the understanding, the mind as the faculty of thinking Lk 24:45; 1 Cor 14:14, 15, 19; Phil 4:7; Rv 13:18; 17:9; composure 2 Th 2:2; intellect Ro 7:23, 25.—**2.** mind, attitude, way of thinking Ro 1:28; 12:2; 1 Cor 1:10; Eph 4:17, 23; Col 2:18; 1 Ti 6:5; 2 Ti 3:8; Tit 1:15.—**3.** mind as the result of thinking, thought Ro 11:34; 14:5; 1 Cor 2:16 (in the latter passage νοῦς is practically equivalent to πνεῦμα, vs. 14f).* [nous, philosophical term = mind, reason]

Νύμφαν is an accusative form in Col 4:15; it is not clear whether it is from the feminine name Νύμφα, ας, Nympha, or from the masculine name Νυμφᾶς, ᾶ, Nymphas.*

νύμφη, **ης**, **ἡ**—**1.** bride Mt 25:1 v.l.; J 3:29; Rv 18:23; 21:2, 9; 22:17.—**2.** daughter-in-law Mt 10:35; Lk 12:53.* [nymph]

νυμφίος, **ου**, **ὁ** bridegroom Mt 25:1, 5f, 10; Mk 2:19f; Lk 5:34f; J 2:9; 3:29; Rv 18:23. [Cf. nuptial.]

νυμφών, **ῶνος**, **ὁ**—**1.** wedding hall Mt 22:10 v.l.—**2.** bridal chamber οἱ υἱοὶ τοῦ νυμφῶνος the bridegroom's attendants Mt 9:15; Mk 2:19; Lk 5:34.*

νῦν adv. now—**1.** lit., of time Mt 27:42f; Lk 16:25; 22:36; J 9:21; 13:31; Ac 12:11; 16:36; Ro 5:11; 8:1; 1 Cor 3:2; Eph 5:8; 1 Pt 2:10, 25. Just now J 11:8; Ac 7:52; Phil 1:20.—**2.** as things now stand Ac 15:10; 1 Th 3:8. νῦν δέ sometimes contrasts the real state of affairs with something unreal but, as a matter of fact Lk 19:42; J 8:40; 9:41; 1 Cor 5:11; 12:20; Hb 11:16; Js 4:16.—**3.** used with the article: ὁ, ἡ, τὸ νῦν the present as adj. Ro 3:26; 8:18; 2 Cor 8:14; Gal 4:25; 1 Ti 4:8; 2 Ti 4:10; Tit 2:12; 2 Pt 3:7. As noun τὸ νῦν the present time, now Mt 24:21; Lk 1:48; 5:10; Ac 18:6; Ro 8:22; Phil 1:5. As adv. τὰ νῦν as far as the present situation is concerned = now Ac 4:29; 17:30; 27:22. τὸ νῦν ἔχον for the present Ac 24:25.

νυνί adv., emphatic form of νῦν now—**1.** lit., of time Ac 22:1; 24:13; Ro 3:21; 15:23, 25; 2 Cor 8:22; Eph 2:13; Col 3:8; Phlm 9.—**2.** with the idea of time weakened or entirely absent νυνί δέ but now, but, as a matter of fact Ro 7:17; 1 Cor 5:11 v.l.; 12:18; 13:13; 15:20; Hb 9:26.

νύξ, **νυκτός**, **ἡ** night—**1.** lit. Mt 4:2; 14:25; 28:13; Mk 5:5; 14:30; Lk 5:5; 21:37; J 13:30; 19:39; Ac 16:33; 20:31; 23:11; Rv 8:12.—**2.** fig. J 9:4; Ro 13:12; 1 Th 5:5. [Cf. nocturnal.]

νύσσω prick, stab, pierce J 19:34; Mt 27:49 v.l. Nudge Ac 12:7 v.l.*

νυστάζω nod, become drowsy, doze lit. Mt 25:5; fig. be sleepy, idle 2 Pt 2:3.*

νυχθήμερον, **ου**, **τό** a day and a night = 24 hours 2 Cor 11:25.*

Νῶε, **ὁ** indecl. Noah Mt 24:37f; Lk 3:36; 17:26f; Hb 11:7; 1 Pt 3:20; 2 Pt 2:5.*

νωθρός, **ά**, **όν** lazy, sluggish Hb 6:12. ν. ταῖς ἀκοαῖς hard of hearing 5:11.*

νῶτος, **ου**, **ὁ** back Ro 11:10.* [noto-, combining form, as in notochord, back support or backbone, esp. in higher forms of vertebrates]

Ξ

ξαίνω comb, card wool Mt 6:28 v.l.*

ξενία, ας, ἡ hospitality, or more likely guest room Ac 28:23; Phlm 22.*

ξενίζω—1. receive as a guest, entertain Ac 10:23; 28:7; Hb 13:2. Pass. be entertained, stay Ac 10:6, 18, 32; 21:16; 1 Cor 16:19 v.l.—2. surprise, astonish Ac 17:20. Pass. be surprised, wonder 1 Pt 4:4, 12.*

ξενοδοχέω show hospitality 1 Ti 5:10.*

ξένος, η, ον—1. adj. strange, foreign Ac 17:18; Hb 13:9; surprising, unheard of 1 Pt 4:12. ξ. τῶν διαθηκῶν estranged from the covenants Eph 2:12.—2. as noun ὁ ξένος the stranger, alien Mt 25:35, 38, 43f; 27:7; Ac 17:21; Eph 2:19; Hb 11:13; 3 J 5. Host, one who extends hospitality Ro 16:23.* [xenophobia]

ξέστης, ου, ὁ pitcher, jug Mk 7:4, 8 v.l.*

ξηραίνω dry, dry out Js 1:11. Become dry, dry up, wither Mt 21:19f; Mk 3:1,

3 v.l.; 4:6; 5:29; Lk 8:6; J 15:6; 1 Pt 1:24; Rv 14:15; 16:12; become stiff Mk 9:18.

ξηρός, ά, όν dry, dried (up) Lk 23:31; Hb 11:29; dry land Mt 23:15. Withered, paralyzed 12:10; Mk 3:3; Lk 6:6, 8; J 5:3.* [xerophagy, ξηρός + φαγεῖν, strict diet of dry food]

ξύλινος, η, ον wooden 2 Ti 2:20; Rv 9:20.*

ξύλον, ου, τό—1. wood 1 Cor 3:12; Rv 18:12.—2. of objects made of wood: stocks Ac 16:24. Club, cudgel Mt 26:47, 55; Mk 14:43, 48; Lk 22:52. Cross Ac 5:30; 10:39; 13:29; Gal 3:13; 1 Pt 2:24.—3. tree Lk 23:31; Rv 2:7; 22:2, 14, 19.* [xylo-, combining form, as in xylophone]

ξυν—alternate form of συν-.

ξυράω, ξυρέω, ξύρω mid. have oneself shaved Ac 21:24; 1 Cor 11:5f.*

Ο

ὁ, ἡ, τό pl. οἱ, αἱ, τά the definite article, the—1. as a demonstrative pronoun this one, that one τοῦ γὰρ καὶ γένος ἐσμέν for we are also his (lit. 'this One's') offspring Ac 17:28.—ὁ μὲν . . . ὁ δέ the one . . . the other, pl. οἱ μὲν . . . οἱ δέ some . . . others Ac 14:4; 17:32; 1 Cor 7:7; Hb 7:5f, 20f. ὁ δέ, οἱ δέ frequently indicate a change in subject and he, and they Mt 2:9, 14; sometimes with suggestion of contrast, but he, but they 4:4; 9:31.—2. as definite article, the, in a great variety of uses. It will

suffice to say here that the definite article is omitted in translation in the following expressions—a. when it is used between a demonstrative adjective (οὗτος, this; ἐκεῖνος, that) and a noun, or when this adj. follows its noun Mt 15:8; Mk 7:6; 14:71; Lk 14:30; J 9:24.—b. when it is placed before the nominative of a noun, thus making it a vocative ὁ πατήρ (O) father Mt 11:26; cf. 7:23; Lk 8:54; 18:11, 13; J 19:3.—c. when the neuter of the article is used with an infinitive τὸ φαγεῖν to eat, eat-

ing Mt 15:20; cf. Mk 12:33; Ro 7:18; 2 Cor 8:10f. In the genitive case with a variety of uses, including purpose Mt 13:3; Lk 1:77; Ro 6:6; Phil 3:10 or result Mt 21:32; Ac 7:19; Ro 7:3.—**d.** when it precedes personal names Mt 27:21; Mk 1:14.

ὀγδοήκοντα indecl. *eighty* Lk 2:37; 16:7.*

ὄγδοος, η, ον *the eighth* Lk 1:59; Ac 7:8; 2 Pt 2:5; Rv 17:11; 21:20.* [*ogdoad*]

ὄγκος, ου, ὁ *weight, burden, impediment* Hb 12:1.*

ὅδε, ἥδε, τόδε *this (one)* Lk 10:39; Ac 21:11; Rv 2:1, 8, 12, 18; 3:1, 7, 14. εἰς τήνδε τὴν πόλιν *into such and such a city* Js 4:13.*

ὁδεύω *travel* Lk 10:33.*

ὁδηγέω *lead, guide* lit. Mt 15:14; Lk 6:39; Rv 7:17. Fig. *lead, guide, instruct* J 16:13; Ac 8:31.*

ὁδηγός, οῦ, ὁ *leader, guide* Mt 15:14; 23:16, 24; Ac 1:16; Ro 2:19.*

ὁδοιπορέω *travel, be on the way* Ac 10:9.*

ὁδοιπορία, ας, ἡ *walking, journey* J 4:6; 2 Cor 11:26.*

ὁδοποιέω *make a path* Mk 2:23 v.l.*

ὁδός, οῦ, ἡ *way*—**1.** lit.—**a.** as a place: *way, road, highway* Mt 2:12; 3:3; Mk 10:46; Lk 8:5; Ac 8:26, 36. ὁδόν w. gen. *toward* Mt 4:15.—**b.** as an action: *way, journey* Mt 10:10; Mk 8:3; Lk 12:58; 24:35; Ac 9:27. σαββάτου ὁδός *a Sabbath day's journey* Ac 1:12.—**2.** fig.— **a.** *way* Mt 7:13f; 10:5; Lk 1:79; J 14:6; Ac 2:28; 16:17; Ro 3:17.—**b.** *way of life* or *acting, conduct* Mt 21:32; Lk 20:21; Ro 11:33; Js 5:20; Hb 3:10; 2 Pt 2:21; Rv 15:3.—**c.** *the Way* or *teaching,* of Christianity Ac 9:2; 19:9, 23; 22:4; 24:14, 22; 1 Cor 4:17; 2 Pt 2:2. [*odometer,* ὁδός + μέτρον]

ὀδούς, ὀδόντος, ὁ *tooth* Mt 5:38; 8:12; 13:42, 50; Mk 9:18; Lk 13:28; Ac 7:54; Rv 9:8. [*odontology; orthodontist*]

ὀδυνάω *cause pain* pass. *feel pain* Lk 16:24f; Ac 20:38; *be anxious* Lk 2:48.*

ὀδύνη, ης, ἡ *pain, grief* Ro 9:2; 1 Ti 6:10; Mt 24:8 v.l.*

ὀδυρμός, οῦ, ὁ *lamentation, mourning* Mt 2:18; 2 Cor 7:7.*

Ὀζίας, ου, ὁ *Uzziah,* Hebrew king Mt 1:8f; Lk 3:23ff v.l.*

ὄζω *smell, give off an unpleasant odor* J 11:39.* [Cf. *odor.*]

ὅθεν adv. *from where, whence* Mt 12:44; 25:24, 26; Lk 11:24; Ac 14:26; 28:13. *From which fact* 1 J 2:18. *For which reason, therefore, hence* Mt 14:7; Ac 26:19; Hb 2:17; 3:1; 11:19.

ὀθόνη, ης, ἡ *linen cloth, sheet* Ac 10:11; 11:5.*

ὀθόνιον, ου, τό *linen cloth, bandage* J 19:40; 20:5ff; Lk 24:12.*

οἶδα—**1.** *know (about)* Mt 6:32; 20:22; 25:13; Mk 1:34; 6:20; Lk 4:41; 11:44; J 4:25; 9:25; Ac 2:22; 3:16; Ro 8:27; 1 Cor 13:2; 16:15; 2 Cor 12:2; Gal 4:8; Col 4:6; 1 Ti 1:8; 2 Pt 1:12. ἴστε J 1:19 can be either indicative *you know* or imperative *know!*—**2.** *be* (intimately) *acquainted with, stand in a close relation to* Mt 26:72, 74; Lk 22:57; J 8:19; 2 Cor 5:16; 2 Th 1:8; Tit 1:16.—**3.** *know* or *understand how, can, be able* Mt 7:11; 27:65; Lk 12:56; Phil 4:12; 1 Th 4:4; 1 Ti 3:5; Js 4:17.—**4.** *understand, recognize, come to know* Mt 26:70; Mk 4:13; 12:15; Lk 22:60; J 6:61; 16:18; 1 Cor 2:11; Eph 1:18.—**5.** various other uses: *remember* 1 Cor 1:16. *Respect* or *take an interest in* 1 Th 5:12.

οἰέσθω pres. impv. 3 sing. of οἴομαι.

οἰκεῖος, (α), ον *belonging to the house* οἱ οἰκεῖοι *members of the household* Gal 6:10; Eph 2:19; 1 Ti 5:8.*

οἰκετεία, ας, ἡ *the slaves in a household* Mt 24:45.*

οἰκέτης, ου, ὁ *house slave, domestic, slave* generally Lk 16:13; Ac 10:7; Ro 14:4; 1 Pt 2:18.*

οἰκέω intrans. *live, dwell, have one's habitation* Ro 7:17f, 20; 8:9, 11; 1 Cor 3:16; 7:12f. Trans. *inhabit, dwell in* 1 Ti 6:16.—On οἰκουμένη see it as a separate entry.*

οἴκημα, ατος, τό *room,* euphemistically for *prison* Ac 12:7.*

οἰκητήριον, ου, τό *dwelling, habitation* lit. Jd 6; fig. 2 Cor 5:2.*

οἰκία, ας, ἡ—1. *house* lit. Mt 7:24–27; 9:28; 19:29; Mk 1:29; 6:10; 13:34f; Lk 18:29; 20:47; J 8:35; 12:3; Ac 4:34; 10:6; 1 Cor 11:22. Fig J 14:2; 2 Cor 5:1.—2. *household, family* Mt 12:25; Mk 3:25; 6:4; J 4:53; 1 Cor 16:15.—3. a kind of middle position between mngs. 1 and 2 is held by Mt 10:12f and Phil 4:22; in the latter passage οἰκία refers to the servants and slaves in the emperor's court.

οἰκιακός, οῦ, ὁ *member of a household* Mt 10:25, 36.*

οἰκοδεσποτέω *manage one's household, keep house* 1 Ti 5:14.*

οἰκοδεσπότης, ου, ὁ *the master of the house* Mt 10:25; 13:52; 20:1; 21:33; 24:43; Mk 14:14; Lk 13:25; 22:11.

οἰκοδομέω *build*—1. lit. *build, erect* Mt 7:24, 26; 23:29; Mk 12:1; Lk 6:48; 12:18; 1 Pt 2:7. *Build up again, restore* Mt 27:40; Mk 15:29.—2. fig. Mt 16:18; Ro 15:20; Gal 2:18; 1 Pt 2:5.—3. also in a nonliteral sense, with little consciousness of the central meaning *build up, edify, benefit, strengthen* Ac 9:31; 20:32; 1 Cor 8:1, 10; 10:23; 14:4, 17; 1 Th 5:11.

οἰκοδομή, ῆς, ἡ—1. lit. *building, edifice* Mt 24:1; Mk 13:1f.—2. fig. *building* 1 Cor 3:9; 2 Cor 5:1; Eph 2:21. In the sense *edifying, edification, building up* 1 Cor 14:3, 12; 2 Cor 12:19; 13:10; Ro 15:2; Eph 4:12, 16.

οἰκοδομία, ας, ἡ *edification* 1 Ti 1:4 v.l.*

οἰκοδόμος, ου, ὁ *builder* Ac 4:11.*

οἰκονομέω *be manager* Lk 16:2.*

οἰκονομία, ας, ἡ *management* of a household, *administration, office* Lk 16:2–4; Col 1:25; *commission* 1 Cor 9:17; *stewardship* Eph 3:2. *Plan* of salvation 1:10; 3:9. *Training* in the way of salvation 1 Ti 1:4.* [economy]

οἰκονόμος, ου, ὁ *(house) steward, manager*—1. lit. Lk 12:42; 16:1, 3, 8; 1 Cor 4:2; Gal 4:2. ὁ οἰκ. τῆς πόλεως *the city treasurer* Ro 16:23.—2. fig. *administrator* 1 Cor 4:1; Tit 1:7; 1 Pt 4:10.* [economics]

οἶκος, ου, ὁ—1. *house, home*—a. lit. Mt 9:7; 11:8; 21:13; Mk 2:1; 5:38; 8:3; Lk 6:4; 11:17; 15:6; Ac 2:2; 7:47, 49; Ro

16:5; Phlm 2. κατ' οἶκον *in the various private homes* Ac 2:46; 5:42. οἶκος = *city* Mt 23:38; Lk 13:35.—b. fig. 1 Pt 2:5; perh. 1 Ti 3:15; 1 Pt 4:17. *Dwelling, habitation* Mt 12:44; Lk 11:24.—2. *household, family* Lk 10:5; 19:9; Ac 10:2; 16:31; 1 Cor 1:16; 1 Ti 3:4f; 2 Ti 1:16; 4:19; Tit 1:11; Hb 3:2–6.—3. *house* = *descendants, nation* Mt 10:6; 15:24; Lk 1:27, 69; 2:4; Ac 2:36; 7:42; Hb 8:8, 10.—4. *property, possessions* Ac 7:10. [ecology]

οἰκουμένη, ης, ἡ lit. 'inhabited,' with γῆ supplied—1. *the inhabited earth, the world* Mt 24:14; Lk 4:5; 21:26; Ac 11:28; Ro 10:18; Hb 1:6; Rv 3:10; 16:14. *World* in the sense *humankind* Lk 2:1; Ac 17:31; 19:27; Rv 12:9.—2. *the Roman Empire* Ac 24:5; *its inhabitants* 17:6.—3. ἡ οἰκ. ἡ μέλλουσα *the world to come* Hb 2:5.* [ecumenical]

οἰκουργός, όν *working at home, domestic* Tit 2:5.*

οἰκουρός, όν *staying at home, domestic* Tit 2:5 v.l.*

οἰκτείρω a different spelling for οἰκτίρω.

οἰκτιρμός, οῦ, ὁ *pity, mercy, compassion* Ro 12:1; 2 Cor 1:3; Col 3:12; Phil 2:1; Hb 10:28.*

οἰκτίρμων, ον *merciful, compassionate* Lk 6:36; Js 5:11.*

οἰκτίρω *have compassion on* Ro 9:15.*

οἶμαι see οἴομαι.

οἰνοπότης, ου, ὁ *wine-drinker, drunkard* Mt 11:19; Lk 7:34.*

οἶνος, ου, ὁ *wine*—1. lit. Mt 9:17; Mk 15:23; Lk 1:15; 7:33; 10:34; J 2:3, 9f; Ro 14:21; Eph 5:18; 1 Ti 3:8; 5:23; Tit 2:3; Rv 18:13.—2. fig. Rv 14:8, 10; 18:3; 19:15.—3. *vineyard* 6:6.

οἰνοφλυγία, ας, ἡ *drunkenness* 1 Pt 4:3.*

οἴομαι contracted οἶμαι *think, suppose, expect* J 21:25; Phil 1:17; Js 1:7.*

οἷος, α, ον *relative pron. of what sort, (such) as* Mt 24:21; Mk 9:3; 13:19; 2 Cor 12:20; 2 Ti 3:11; Rv 16:18. οἷος . . . τοιοῦτος 1 Cor 15:48; cf. 2 Cor 10:11. *Which* Phil 1:30. οὐχ οἷον ὅτι *it is by no means as if* Ro 9:6. οἴῳ δηποτοῦν κατείχετο νοσήματι *no matter what disease he had* J 5:4 v.l.

οἱοσδηποτοῦν see οἷος.

οἴσω fut. act. ind. of φέρω.

ὀκνέω hesitate, delay Ac 9:38.*

ὀκνηρός, ά, όν idle, lazy, indolent Mt 25:26; Ro 12:11. Troublesome Phil 3:1.*

ὀκταήμερος, ον on the eighth day Phil 3:5.*

ὀκτώ eight Lk 2:21; 13:16; J 20:26; 1 Pt 3:20. [octo-, combining form, as in octogenarian]

ὀλεθρευτής, ὀλεθρεύω different spellings for ὀλοθρευτής, ὀλοθρεύω.

ὀλέθριος, ον deadly, destructive 2 Th 1:9 v.l.*

ὄλεθρος, ου, ὁ destruction, ruin, death 1 Cor 5:5; 1 Th 5:3; 2 Th 1:9; 1 Ti 6:9.*

ὀλιγοπιστία, ας, ἡ littleness or poverty of faith Mt 17:20.*

ὀλιγόπιστος, ον of little faith or trust Mt 6:30; 8:26; 14:31; 16:8; Lk 12:28.*

ὀλίγος, η, ον—1. plural few, a few Mt 9:37; 22:14; 25:21, 23; Mk 8:7; Lk 12:48; 13:23; Ac 17:4; Hb 12:10; 1 Pt 5:12; Rv 2:14; 3:4.—2. singular little, small, short Lk 7:47; Ac 12:18; 15:2; 19:24; 2 Cor 8:15; 1 Ti 5:23; Rv 12:12.—3. the neut. ὀλίγον in adverbial expressions a little Mk 1:19; 6:31; Lk 5:3; 7:47b; 1 Pt 1:6; 5:10; Rv 17:10. ἐν ὀλίγῳ in brief Eph 3:3, but in a short time Ac 26:28, cf. vs. 29. πρὸς ὀλίγον for a short time Js 4:14, but for (a) little 1 Ti 4:8. [oligarchy, ὀλίγος + ἄρκειν]

ὀλιγόψυχος, ον fainthearted, discouraged 1 Th 5:14.*

ὀλιγωρέω think lightly of, make light of w. gen. Hb 12:5.*

ὀλίγως adv. scarcely, barely 2 Pt 2:18.*

ὀλοθρευτής, οῦ, ὁ the destroyer 1 Cor 10:10.*

ὀλοθρεύω destroy Hb 11:28.*

ὁλοκαύτωμα, ατος, τό whole burnt offering Mk 12:33; Hb 10:6, 8.* [holocaust]

ὁλοκληρία, ας, ἡ wholeness, completeness, soundness Ac 3:16.*

ὁλόκληρος, ον whole, complete, intact 1 Th 5:23; Js 1:4.*

ὀλολύζω cry out, wail Js 5:1.*

ὅλος, η, ον whole, entire, complete Mt 14:35; 16:26; Mk 6:55; Lk 5:5; 13:21; J 4:53; 7:23; Ac 11:26; Ro 1:8; 8:36; Tit 1:11; 1 J 5:19; all Ac 21:31. δι᾽ ὅλου throughout J 19:23. [holo-, combining form, as in holophrastic, expressing a phrase or sentence in a single word]

ὁλοτελής, ές a quantitative term complete; in 1 Th 5:23 wholly.*

Ὀλυμπᾶς, ᾶ, ὁ Olympas Ro 16:15.*

ὄλυνθος, ου, ὁ late or summer fig Rv 6:13.*

ὅλως adv. generally speaking, actually, everywhere 1 Cor 5:1; 6:7; w. neg. not at all Mt 5:34; 1 Cor 15:29.*

ὄμβρος, ου, ὁ rainstorm Lk 12:54.*

ὁμείρομαι have a kindly feeling for, long for w. gen. 1 Th 2:8.*

ὁμιλέω talk, converse Lk 24:14f; Ac 20:11; 24:26.* [homily; homiletics]

ὁμιλία, ας, ἡ association, company 1 Cor 15:33.*

ὅμιλος, ου, ὁ crowd, throng Rv 18:17 v.l.*

ὁμίχλη, ης, ἡ mist, fog 2 Pt 2:17.*

ὄμμα, ατος, τό eye Mt 20:34; Mk 8:23.*

ὀμνύναι pres. act. inf. of ὄμνυμι (s. ὀμνύω) Mk 14:71.

ὄμνυμι see the by-form ὀμνύω.

ὀμνύω swear, take an oath; the person or thing by which one swears may be expressed by: the simple acc. Js 5:12; ἐν with the dat. Mt 5:34, 36; Rv 10:6; κατά with the gen. Hb 6:13. In other constructions Mk 6:23; Lk 1:73; Ac 2:30; Hb 3:18.

ὁμοθυμαδόν adv. with one mind or purpose or impulse Ac 1:14; 4:24; 8:6; 15:25; 19:29; Ro 15:6; together Ac 5:12.

ὁμοιάζω be like, resemble only as v.l. in Mt 23:27; 26:73; and Mk 14:70.*

ὁμοιοπαθής, ές with the same nature w. dat. as someone Ac 14:15; Js 5:17.* [homeopathic]

ὅμοιος, οία, οιον of the same nature, like, similar with the person or thing compared in the dative: Mt 11:16; 13:31, 33, 44f; Lk 6:47–49; J 8:55; 9:9; Ac 17:29; Gal 5:21; 1 J 3:2; Rv 4:3, 6f; 21:11, 18. With the genitive J 8:55 v.l. In an extraordinary construction with the accusative Rv 1:13; 14:14. In a special sense *as powerful as, equally important, equal to* w. dat. Mt 22:39; Mk 12:31 v.l.; Rv 13:4; 18:18. [*homoeoteleuton*, ὅμοιος + τελευτή; *Homoiousian*, ὅμοιος + οὐσία]

ὁμοιότης, ητος, ἡ *likeness, similarity* καθ' ὁμοιότητα *in (quite) the same way* Hb 4:15; 7:15.*

ὁμοιόω—1. *make like* pass. *become like, be like* Mt 7:24, 26; 22:2; Ac 14:11; Ro 9:29; Hb. 2:17.—2. *compare* Mt 11:16; Mk 4:30; Lk 7:31; 13:20.

ὁμοίωμα, ατος, τό—1. *likeness* Ro 5:14; 6:5; 8:3; Phil 2:7.—2. *image, copy* Ro 1:23.—3. *form, appearance* Rv 9:7.*

ὁμοίως adv. *likewise, so, similarly, in the same way* Mt 22:26; Mk 4:16 v.l.; Lk 3:11; 5:10; 13:3; Ro 1:27; 1 Cor 7:3f; 1 Pt 3:1, 7; Jd 8. *Also* J 5:19; 6:11; 21:13.

ὁμοίωσις, εως, ἡ *likeness* Js 3:9.*

ὁμολογέω—1. *promise, assure* Mt 14:7; Ac 7:17.—2. *agree, admit* Hb 11:13.—3. *confess* J 1:20; Ac 24:14; 1 J 1:9.—4. *declare (publicly), acknowledge, confess* Lk 12:8; J 9:22; Ac 23:8; Ro 10:9; 1 Ti 6:12; 1 J 4:2f, 15; Rv 3:5; *say plainly* Mt 7:23; *claim* Tit 1:16.—5. *praise*, w. dat. Hb 13:15. [*homologate*, approve, be in accord]

ὁμολογία, ας, ἡ *confessing* 2 Cor 9:13. *Confession, acknowledgment* 1 Ti 6:12f; Hb 3:1; 4:14; 10:23.* [*homology*, of correspondence in structure]

ὁμολογουμένως adv. *confessedly, undeniably, most certainly* 1 Ti 3:16.*

ὁμόσαι 1 aor. act. inf. of ὀμνύω.

ὁμόσε adv. *together* Ac 20:18 v.l.*

ὁμότεχνος, ον *practicing the same trade* Ac 18:3.*

ὁμοῦ adv. *together* J 4:36; 20:4; 21:2; Ac 2:1.*

ὁμόφρων, ον *like-minded* 1 Pt 3:8.*

ὅμως adv. *all the same, nevertheless, yet* J 12:42. This may also be the sense in 1 Cor 14:7 and Gal 3:15, but *likewise, also* is possible.* [Cf. *hom-*, a combining form in such words as *homocentric, homogamy, homogeneous*.]

ὀναίμην 2 aor. mid. opt. of ὀνίνημι.

ὄναρ, τό (found only in nom. and acc. sing.) *dream* κατ' ὄναρ *in a dream* Mt 1:20; 2:12f, 19, 22; 27:19.* [Cf. *oneiric*.]

ὀνάριον, ου, τό *(young) donkey* J 12:14.*

ὀνειδίζω *reproach, revile, heap insults upon* Mt 5:11; 27:44; Mk 15:32; 16:14; Lk 6:22; Ro 15:3; Js 1:5; 1 Pt 4:14; *reproach* justifiably Mt 11:20; Mk 16:14.*

ὀνειδισμός, οῦ, ὁ *reproach, reviling, disgrace, insult* Ro 15:3; 1 Ti 3:7; Hb 10:33; 11:26; 13:13.*

ὄνειδος, ους, τό *disgrace* Lk 1:25.*

Ὀνήσιμος, ου, ὁ *Onesimus, slave of* Philemon Col 4:9; Phlm 10: subscr. of Col and Phlm.*

Ὀνησίφορος, ου, ὁ *Onesiphorus* 2 Ti 1:16; 4:19.*

ὀνικός, ή, όν *pertaining to a donkey* μύλος ὄν. *a millstone worked by donkeypower* Mt 18:6; Mk 9:42; Lk 17:2 v.l.*

ὀνίνημι 2 aor. mid. opt. ὀναίμην *as a formula* *may I have joy* or *benefit*, in a play on words Phlm 20.*

ὄνομα, ατος, τό—1. *name*—a. generally Mt 10:2; Mk 14:32; Lk 8:30, 41; 10:20; Hb 1:4; Rv 9:11. ὀνόματι *by name, named* Mt 27:32; Lk 5:27; Ac 5:1, 34.—b. in combination with God or Jesus Mt 6:9; Lk 1:49; Ro 2:24; 2 Th 1:12; Hb 2:12; 13:15; Rv 2:13; 11:18. The following uses with prepositions are noteworthy: ἐν τῷ ὀνόματι *with* or *at the mention of the name* Mk 9:38; Lk 10:17; Ac 4:7, 10; 10:48; Phil 2:10; Js 5:14, but *at the command of, commissioned by* Mt 21:9; J 5:43; 12:13.—ἐπὶ τῷ ὀνόματι *when the name is mentioned, using the name* Mt 24:5; Mk 9:39; Lk 24:47; Ac 2:38; 4:17f. πρὸς τὸ ὄνομα *in opposition to the name* Ac 26:9.—2. *title, category* ὁ δεχόμενος προφήτην εἰς ὄνομα προφήτου *whoever receives a prophet within the category 'prophet', i.e. as a prophet* Mt 10:41a; cf. 41b, 42; Mk 9:41. *For the sake of* 1 Pt 4:14. *In the capacity* 4:16.—3. *person* Ac 1:15; 18:15; Rv 3:4; 11:13.—4. *reputation, fame* Mk 6:14; Rv 3:1. [Cf. *onomasticon*, systematic collection of names and nouns.]

ὀνομάζω give a name, call, name Mk 3:14; Lk 6:13f; 2:21 v.l.; 1 Cor 5:11; Eph 3:15. Use a name or word Ac 19:13; Eph 1:21; 5:3; 2 Ti 2:19. Pass. be named, in the sense be known Ro 15:20; 1 Cor 5:1 v.l.*

ὄνος, ου, ὁ and ἡ donkey (male or female), ass, she-ass Mt 21:2, 5, 7; Lk 13:15; 14:5 v.l.; J 12:15.*

ὄντως adv. really, certainly, in truth Mk 11:32; Lk 23:47; 24:34; J 8:36; 1 Cor 14:25; Gal 3:21. As adj. real 1 Ti 5:3, 5, 16; 6:19; 2 Pt 2:18 v.l.* [Cf. ontology.]

ὄξος, ους, τό sour wine, wine vinegar Mt 27:48; Mk 15:36; Lk 23:36; J 19:29f.*

ὀξύς, εῖα, ύ—1. sharp Rv 1:16; 2:12; 14:14, 17f; 19:15.—2. quick, swift Ro 3:15.* [oxy-, combining form, as in oxymoron; oxytone]

ὀπή, ῆς, ἡ opening, hole Hb 11:38; Js 3:11.*

ὄπισθεν adv.—1. as adv. from behind Mt 9:20; Mk 5:27; Lk 8:44. Behind Rv 4:6; on the back 5:1.—2. functions as prep. w. gen. behind, after Mt 15:23; Lk 23:26; Rv 1:10 v.l.* [opisth-, combining form, as in opisthograph, with writing on the back]

ὀπίσω adv.—1. as adv. behind Lk 7:38. τὰ ὀπίσω what lies behind Phil 3:13. εἰς τὰ ὀπ. back J 18:6; 20:14; backwards Lk 9:62.—2. functions as prep. w. gen. after Mt 3:11; 16:24; Mk 8:34; Lk 9:23; 14:27; J 1:15, 27, 30; Jd 7; Rv 12:15. δεῦτε ὀπ. μου come, follow me Mk 1:17.

ὁπλίζω equip, arm mid., fig. arm oneself with w. acc. 1 Pt 4:1.*

ὅπλον, ου, τό weapon—1. lit. J 18:3; Ro 6:13 (here tool is possible).—2. fig. Ro 13:12; 2 Cor 6:7; 10:4.* [hoplite]

ὁποῖος, οία, οἶον correlative pron. of what sort, as Ac 26:29; 1 Cor 3:13; Gal 2:6; 1 Th 1:9; Js 1:24.*

ὁπότε particle when Lk 6:3 v.l.*

ὅπου particle where Mt 6:19f; 26:57; Mk 9:48; J 1:28; 6:62; 8:21f; Ro 15:20; Col 3:11; Hb 9:16; Js 3:16; Rv 2:13; insofar as 1 Cor 3:3. ὅπου ἄν or ἐάν wherever, whenever Mt 26:13; Lk 9:57; Rv 14:4.

ὀπτάνομαι appear Ac 1:3.*

ὀπτασία, ας, ἡ a vision Lk 1:22; 24:23; Ac 26:19; 2 Cor 12:1.* [optic]

ὀπτός, ή, όν broiled Lk 24:42.*

ὀπώρα, ας, ἡ fruit Rv 18:14.*

ὅπως conjunction indicating purpose, etc. (in order) that Mt 5:45; 23:35; Lk 2:35; 16:26, 28; Ac 9:17, 24; 15:17; 2 Cor 8:11; Hb 9:15. After verbs of asking that Mt 8:34; 9:38; Ac 25:3; Js 5:16.

ὅραμα, ατος, τό vision as opposed to figment of the imagination Mt 17:9; Ac 7:31; 10:3, 17, 19; 18:9. [panorama, πᾶν + ὅραμα]

ὅρασις, εως, ἡ appearance Rv 4:3. Vision Ac 2:17; Rv 9:17.*

ὁρατός, ή, όν visible Col 1:16.*

ὁράω—1. trans.—a. see, catch sight of, notice Mt 24:30; 28:7, 10; Mk 14:62; Lk 1:22; J 1:18; Ac 2:17; 22:15; 1 Cor 9:1; Col 2:1, 18; 1 J 1:1–3; 3:2; visit Hb 13:23. Pass. become visible, appear Ac 2:3; 7:2; 16:9; 1 Ti 3:16; Rv 11:19.—b. experience, witness Lk 3:6; 17:22; J 1:50; 3:36.—c. mentally and spiritually see, perceive, look at Ac 8:23; Ro 15:21; Hb 2:8; Js 2:24.—2. intrans. look J 19:37. See to, take care, be on guard Mt 16:6; 27:4, 24; Lk 12:15; Ac 18:15; Hb 8:5; Rv 19:10.

ὀργή, ῆς, ἡ anger, wrath, indignation Mk 3:5; J 3:36; Ro 12:19; 13:4f; Eph 4:31; 1 Ti 2:8; Hb 3:11; Js 1:19. Judgment Lk 21:23; Ro 5:9; Eph 2:3; Col 3:6; Rv 6:16f; 14:10; punishment Ro 3:5.

ὀργίζω pass. be angry Mk 1:41 v.l.; Mt 5:22; 18:34; 22:7; Lk 14:21; 15:28; Eph 4:26; Rv 11:18; 12:17.*

ὀργίλος, η, ον inclined to anger, quick-tempered Tit 1:7.*

ὀργυιά, ᾶς, ἡ fathom (= 6 feet or 1.83 meters) Ac 27:28.*

ὀρέγω mid. aspire to, strive for, desire, long for w. gen. 1 Ti 3:1; 6:10; Hb 11:16.*

ὀρεινός, ή, όν hilly ἡ ὀρεινή the hill country Lk 1:39, 65.*

ὄρεξις, εως, ἡ desire Ro 1:27.*

ὀρθοποδέω act rightly, be straightforward Gal 2:14, though progress, advance are also possible.*

ὀρθός, ή, όν straight Hb 12:13; upright Ac 14:10.* [ortho-, combining form, as in orthodontic; orthoepy; orthography]

ὀρθοτομέω guide along a straight path 2 Ti 2:15.*

ὀρθρίζω be up or get up very early in the morning Lk 21:38.*

ὀρθρινός, ή, όν early in the morning Lk 24:22.*

ὄρθριος, ία, ιον early in the morning Lk 24:22 v.l.*

ὄρθρος, ου, ὁ dawn, early morning Lk 24:1; J 8:2; Ac 5:21.*

ὀρθῶς adv. rightly, correctly Lk 7:43; 10:28; 20:21; normally Mk 7:35.*

ὁρίζω determine, fix, set Ac 2:23; 11:29; 17:26; Hb 4:7. τὸ ὡρισμένον Lk 22:22. Appoint, designate, declare Ac 10:42; 17:31; Ro 1:4.* [Cf. aorist; horizon.]

ὅριον, ου, τό boundary pl. boundaries = region, district Mt 2:16; 4:13; 8:34; 15:22, 39; 19:1; Mk 5:17; 7:24, 31; 10:1; Ac 13:50.*

ὁρκίζω adjure, implore Mk 5:7; Ac 19:13; Mt 26:63 v.l.; 1 Th 5:27 v.l.*

ὅρκος, ου, ὁ oath Mt 5:33; 14:7, 9; 26:72; Mk 6:26; Lk 1:73; Ac 2:30; Hb 6:16f; Js 5:12.*

ὁρκωμοσία, ας, ἡ oath, taking an oath Hb 7:20f, 28.*

ὁρμάω set out, rush (headlong) Mt 8:32; Mk 5:13; Lk 8:33; Ac 7:57; 19:29.*

ὁρμή, ῆς, ἡ impulse, inclination, desire Ac 14:5; Js 3:4.*

ὅρμημα, ατος, τό violent rush Rv 18:21.*

ὄρνεον, ου, τό bird Rv 18:2; 19:17, 21.*

ὄρνιξ v.l. for ὄρνις Lk 13:34.*

ὄρνις, ιθος, ὁ and ἡ bird, specifically cock or hen Mt 23:37; Lk 13:34.* [ornithology]

ὁροθεσία, ας, ἡ fixed boundary Ac 17:26.*

ὄρος, ους, τό mountain, hill Mt 5:1, 14; 17:1; 28:16; Mk 5:5, 11; 14:26; Lk 3:5; J 4:20f; Ac 7:30, 38; 1 Cor 13:2; Hb 11:38; 12:22; Rv 6:15f; 8:8. [orology, science of mountains]

ὅρος, ου, ὁ limit ending of Mk in the Freer manuscript 7.*

ὀρύσσω dig (up) Mt 25:18. Dig out, prepare by digging 21:33; Mk 12:1. Dig (a hole) Mt 25:18 v.l.*

ὀρφανός, ή, όν orphaned lit. deprived of one's parents as noun orphan Mk 12:40 v.l.; Js 1:27. Fig. J 14:18.*

ὀρχέομαι dance Mt 11:17; 14:6; Mk 6:22; Lk 7:32.* [Cf. orchestra.]

ὅς, ἥ, ὅ relative pronoun who, which, what, that usually agreeing with its antecedent in gender and number; its case is determined by the construction within its own clause Mt 2:9; Lk 9:9; J 1:47; Ac 13:6; 17:3; Ro 2:29. At times, however, the relative is attracted to or assimilated to the case of its antecedent Mt 18:19; 24:50b; Lk 2:20; J 7:31; Ac 1:22; 3:25; 1 Cor 6:19.—With prepositions: ἀντί: ἀνθ᾽ ὧν because Lk 1:20; 19:44; Ac 12:23; 2 Th 2:10, but therefore Lk 12:3. εἰς: εἰς ὅ to this end 2 Th 1:11. ἐπί: ἐφ᾽ ᾧ because, under what terms Ro 5:12; 2 Cor 5:4; Phil 3:12, but for 4:10. χάριν: οὗ χάριν therefore Lk 7:47.—At times there is a demonstrative pronoun 'concealed' within the relative pronoun, so that it means the one who, etc. Mt 10:27, 38; Mk 9:40; 15:12; J 5:21; 18:26; Ro 6:16; 1 Cor 10:30; Gal 1:8. In still other instances the relative pronoun functions as a demonstrative ὅς δέ but he (lit. that one) Mk 15:23; J 5:11. ὅς μὲν . . . ὅς δέ the one . . . the other, etc. Mt 22:5; Lk 23:33; Ac 27:44; Ro 14:5; 1 Cor 11:21; 2 Cor 2:16; Jd 22f. ὅ μὲν . . . ὃ δέ this . . that Ro 9:21. ἃ μὲν . . . ἃ δέ some . . . others 2 Ti 2:20.

ὁσάκις adv. as often as 1 Cor 11:25f; Rv 11:6.*

ὅσγε = ὅς γε.

ὅσιος, ία, ον devout, pleasing to God, holy 1 Ti 2:8; Tit 1:8. Of God or Christ holy Ac 2:27; 13:35; Hb 7:26; Rv 15:4; 16:5. τὰ ὅσια divine decrees Ac 13:34.*

ὁσιότης, τητος, ἡ holiness of life Lk 1:75; Eph 4:24.*

ὁσίως adv. in a holy manner 1 Th 2:10.*

ὀσμή, ῆς, ἡ fragrance, odor lit. J 12:3. Fig. 2 Cor 2:14, 16; Eph 5:2; Phil 4:18.* [osmium, a metallic element of the platinum group] ὅσος, η, ον as great, how great; as far, how far; as long, how long; as much, how much correlative with πόσος, τοσοῦτος.—1. of space and time: τὸ μῆκος αὐτῆς (τοσοῦτόν ἐστιν), ὅσον τὸ πλάτος its length is as great as its breadth Rv 21:16. ἐφ᾽ ὅσ. χρόνον as long as Ro 7:1; 1 Cor 7:39; Gal 4:1; also ἐφ᾽ ὅσον Mt 9:15; 2 Pt 1:13 and ὅσον χρόνον Mk 2:19 with the same meaning. ἔτι μικρὸν ὅσον ὅσον in a very little while Hb 10:37. ὅσον ὅσον a short distance Lk 5:3 v.l.—2. of quantity and number how much (many), as much (many) as ὅσον ἤθελον as much as they wanted J 6:11. With πάντες (ἅπαντες) all who Lk 4:40; J 10:8; Ac 3:24; 5:36f, πάντα ὅσα everything that Mt 13:46; Mk 11:24; Lk 18:12, 22. Even without πάντες, ὅσοι has the meaning all that or all who J 1:12; Ac 9:13, 39; Ac 10:45; Ro 8:14; Gal 6:12, 16; Phil 4:8. ὅσοι alone all those who Mt 14:36; Mk 6:56; Ac 4:6, 34; Ro 2:12. ὅσα everything that, whatever Mt 17:12; Mk 5:19f; Lk 8:39; Ac 14:27; 2 Ti 1:18.—3. of measure and degree: ὅσον . . . , μᾶλλον περισσότερον as much as . . . , so much the more Mk 7:36. πλείονος . . . , καθ᾽ ὅσον πλείονα as much more . . . as Hb 3:3. τοσούτῳ . . . ὅσῳ (by) as much . . . as 1:4. ὅσα . . . τοσοῦτον to the degree that . . . to the same degree Rv 18:7.

ὅσπερ a slightly strengthened form of ὅς.

ὀστέον, ου, contracted ὀστοῦν, οῦ, τό bone Mt 23:27; Lk 24:39; J 19:36; Hb 11:22; Eph 5:30 v.l.* [osteo-, combining form, as in osteopath]

ὅστις, ἥτις, ὅ τι whoever, whatever, every one who, everything that Mt 5:39, 41; 13:12; 23:12; Lk 14:27; Ro 11:4; Gal 5:4, 10; Js 2:10. Often equivalent to ὅς, ἥ, ὅ who Mt 27:62; Mk 15:7; Lk 2:4; 8:26; Ac 16:12; 21:4; 23:14, 21, 33; Hb 9:2, 9, though at times ὅστις emphasizes a characteristic quality οἵτινες μετήλλαξαν since indeed they had exchanged Ro 1:25; cf. 2:15; 6:2. οἵτινες οὐκ ἔγνωσαν who, to be sure, have not learned Rv 2:24.

ὀστράκινος, η, ον made of earth or clay, earthen(ware) 2 Cor 4:7; 2 Ti 2:20.*

ὄσφρησις, εως, ἡ sense of smell 1 Cor 12:17.*

ὀσφῦς, ύος, ἡ—1. waist Mt 3:4; Mk 1:6; Lk 12:35; Eph 6:14; 1 Pt 1:13.—2. loins as the place of the reproductive organs Ac 2:30; Hb 7:5, 10.*

ὅταν temporal particle at the time that, whenever, when Mt 5:11; 24:15; 26:29; Mk 3:11; J 8:28; 2 Cor 12:10; 1 Th 5:3; Rv 4:9. Whenever, as often as, every time that Mt 6:2, 5f, 16; Mk 13:11; 14:7; Lk 12:11; 14:12f.

ὅτε temporal particle when, while, as long as Mt 9:25; 21:34; Mk 1:32; 14:12; 15:41; Lk 6:3; 13:35; 17:22; J 4:21, 23; Ac 12:6; Ro 13:11; 1 Cor 13:11; Gal 1:15; Hb 9:17.

ὅτι conjunction—1. that, introducing an indirect statement, etc. Mt 26:54; 28:7; Mk 11:32; Ac 20:26; 27:10; 1 Cor 1:15; 16:15; 2 Cor 1:23; 1 J 4:9, 10, 13. So that expressing result J 7:35; 14:22; 1 Ti 6:7; Hb 2:6. τί ὅτι; what (is it) that, why? Lk 2:49; Ac 5:4, 9; Mk 2:16 v.l. οὐχ ὅτι not that, not as if J 6:46; 7:22; 2 Cor 1:24; Phil 3:12; 2 Th 3:9.—2. introducing direct discourse. In this case it is not to be translated into English, but to be represented by quotation marks: ὁμολογήσω αὐτοῖς ὅτι οὐδέποτε ἔγνων ὑμᾶς I will declare to them, 'I never knew you' Mt 7:23. Cf. Mt 26:72, 74f; Mk 1:37; 2:16; Lk 1:25, 61; J 1:20, 32; Ac 15:1; Ro 3:8; 1 J 4:20.—3. as a causal conjunction because, since Mt 5:3ff; Mk 5:9; Lk 10:13; J 1:30, 50a; 20:29; Ro 6:15; 9:32; 1 Cor 12:15f. For Mt 7:13; Lk 9:12; J 1:16f; 1 Cor 1:25; 4:9; 2 Cor 4:6; 7:8, 14.

ὅτου gen. sing. masc. and neut. of ὅστις.

οὗ the genitive of ὅς, functioning as an adv. where Mt 2:9; 18:20; Lk 4:16f; 10:1; 23:53; Ac 1:13; 16:13; Ro 4:15; 5:20; 2 Cor 3:17; to which Mt 28:16; Lk 24:28.

οὐ (before consonants), οὐκ (before a vowel with smooth breathing), οὐχ (before a vowel with rough breathing) negative adv.—1. οὔ with an accent means no Mt 5:37; Mk 12:14; Lk 14:3; J 1:21; 7:12; 21:5; 2 Cor 1:17–19; Js 5:12; cf. Ro 7:18.—2. οὐ as an enclitic means not in a wide variety of uses, examples of which may be found in the following passages: Mt 1:25; 7:21; Mk 4:25; Ac 12:9; 13:10; 17:4, 12; Ro 7:7; 1 Cor 15:51; 2 Cor 2:11; Hb 12:25.— οὐ is regularly used with the indicative, but it is found with the participle in the following passages Mt 22:11; Lk 6:42; Gal 4:8, 27; Hb 11:1, 35; 1 Pt 2:10.— **3.** οὐ is used in direct questions when an affirmative answer is expected οὐκ ἀκούεις; *you hear, do you not?* Mt 27:13. Cf. 6:26, 30; 17:24; Mk 6:3; Lk 11:40; J 6:70; Ac 9:21.—**4.** in combination with other negatives—**a.** strengthening the negation Mt 22:16; Mk 5:37; esp. Lk 23:53; J 6:63; 15:5; Ac 8:39; 2 Cor 11:9. For οὐ μή see μή 4.—**b.** destroying the force of the negation. In questions, if the verb is already negatived (by οὐ), the negation can be invalidated by μή used as an interrogative particle (see μή 3); the stage is thus set for an affirmative answer: μὴ οὐκ ἤκουσαν *surely they have heard, have they not?* Ro 10:18, cf. μὴ οἰκίας οὐκ ἔχετε; *you have houses, do you not?* 1 Cor 11:22; cf. 9:4f.

οὐά interjection *aha!* as an expression of scornful wonder Mk 15:29. Cf. Mt 11:26 v.l.*

οὐαί interjection *woe, alas!* Mt 11:21; Mk 14:21; Lk 6:24f; 17:1; 21:23; Jd 11; Rv 12:12; 18:10, 16, 19. As noun 1 Cor 9:16; Rv 9:12; 11:14.

οὐδαμῶς adv. *by no means* Mt 2:6.*

οὐδέ negative conjunction—**1.** *and not, nor* Mt 6:20, 26, 28; Mk 8:17; Lk 6:43f; J 8:42; Ac 4:12, 34; Rv 5:3.—**2.** *also not, not either, neither* Mt 6:15; Mk 16:13; Lk 16:31; 23:15; J 15:4; Ro 4:15; 1 Cor 15:13, 16.—**3.** *not even* Mt 6:29; 24:36; Lk 12:26; 18:13; J 1:3; 21:25; Ac 19:2; 1 Cor 5:1; 14:21; Hb 8:4.

οὐδείς, οὐδεμία, οὐδέν—**1.** as an adj. *no* Lk 4:24; 16:13; J 16:29; 18:38; Ac 25:18; 27:22; 1 Cor 8:4a; Phil 4:15.—**2.** as a substantive—**a.** οὐδείς *no one, nobody* Mt 6:24; Mk 7:24; Lk 5:36f, 39; 23:53; J 1:18; 13:28; 16:5; Ac 5:13.— **b.** οὐδέν *nothing* Mt 5:13; 17:20; Mk 7:15; 14:60f; Lk 18:34; J 3:27 v.l.; Ac 18:17; 1 Cor 9:15a.—The acc. οὐδέν in *no respect, in no way* Ac 15:9; 25:10;

1 Cor 13:3; 2 Cor 12:11a; Gal 4:1, 12.— In the sense *worthless, meaningless, invalid* Mt 23:16, 18; J 8:54; Ac 21:24; 1 Cor 7:19; 2 Cor 12:11b.

οὐδέποτε adv. *never* Mt 7:23; 21:16, 42; 26:33; Mk 2:12; Lk 15:29; J 7:46; Ac 10:14; 1 Cor 13:8; Hb 10:1, 11.

οὐδέπω adv. *not yet* J 7:39; 20:9. οὐ . . . οὐδεὶς οὐδέπω *no one ever* Lk 23:53 v.l. οὐδέπω οὐδείς J 19:41; cf. Ac 8:16.*

οὐθείς a late Greek form for οὐδείς.

οὐκέτι adv. *no more, no longer, no further*—**1.** lit., of time Mt 19:6; Mk 9:8; Lk 15:19, 21; J 4:42; 6:66; 14:19; *never again* Ro 6:9a; Ac 20:25, 38; 2 Cor 1:23. οὐκέτι οὐ μή *never again* Mk 14:25; Rv 18:14.—**2.** in a nontemporal use *then* not Ro 11:6a; 14:15; Gal 3:18. Likewise νυνὶ οὐκέτι Ro 7:17.

οὐκοῦν adv., introducing a question *so, then* J 18:37.*

Οὐλαμμαούς v.l. for Ἐμμαοῦς in Lk 24:13, influenced by the earlier name of Bethel in the LXX of Gen 28:19.*

οὐ μή see μή 4.

οὖν particle, never found at the beginning of a clause; its sense is inferential and transitional. Its meaning varies with the context, and sometimes οὖν may be left untranslated.—**1.** inferential *therefore, consequently, accordingly, then* Mt 1:17; Mk 10:9; Lk 11:35; J 6:13; Ac 5:41; 21:22; Ro 3:9; 1 Cor 3:5; Hb 4:16; 3 J 8.—**2.** In historical narrative οὖν serves—**a.** to resume a subject *so, as has been said* Lk 3:7 (connecting with vs. 3). Cf. J 19:12; J 4:6, 28; Ac 8:25; 12:5; 1 Cor 8:4; 11:20.—**b.** to indicate a transition to something new *now, then* J 1:22; Ac 25:1.—**c.** to indicate a response *in reply, in turn* is possible in J 4:9, 48; 6:53 and elsewhere.—**3.** Other possible meanings are *certainly, really,* etc. Mt 3:10; J 20:30; 1 Cor 3:5 and *but, however* J 9:18; Ac 23:21; 25:4; 28:5; Ro 10:14.

οὔπω adv. of time *not yet* Mt 24:6; J 2:4; 6:17; 8:20, 57; 1 Cor 3:2; Phil 3:13 v.l.; Hb 2:8; Rv 17:10, 12. οὐδεὶς οὔπω *no one ever* Mk 11:2; Lk 23:53.

οὐρά, ᾶς, ἡ *tail* Rv 9:10, 19; 12:4.*

οὐράνιος, ον heavenly, coming from or living in heaven Mt 5:48; 6:14, 26, 32; 15:13; 18:35; 23:9; Lk 2:13; Ac 26:19; 1 Cor 15:47 v.l.*

οὐρανόθεν adv. of place from heaven Ac 14:17; 26:13.*

οὐρανός, οῦ, ὁ heaven Mt 5:16, 18, 45; 23:22; Mk 1:10; 13:31; Lk 2:15; J 3:13, 31; Ac 7:55f; Hb 12:23; Col 1:5; Rv 3:12; of more than one heaven 2 Cor 12:2; Eph 4:10; Hb 1:10. Sky Mt 11:23; 16:2f; Lk 4:25; 10:18; 17:29; Ac 2:19; Rv 16:21. Fig., synonymous with God Mt 3:2; 21:25; 22:2; Lk 15:18, 21. [uranium]

Οὐρβανός, οῦ, ὁ Urbanus Ro 16:9.*

Οὐρίας, ου, ὁ Uriah (2 Sam 11; 12:24) Mt 1:6.*

οὖς, ὠτός, τό ear—1. lit. Mk 7:33; Lk 12:3; 22:50; Ac 7:57; 1 Cor 2:9; Js 5:4; 1 Pt 3:12.—2. transferred to mental and spiritual understanding τοῖς ὠσὶ βαρέως ἀκούειν be hard of hearing = comprehend slowly or not at all Mt 13:15. Cf. 11:15; Mk 8:18; Lk 9:44; Ac 7:51; Rv 2:7, 11. [otology]

οὐσία, ας, ἡ property, wealth Lk 15:12f.*

οὔτε adv. and not. οὔτε . . . οὔτε neither . . . nor Mt 6:20; 12:32; Mk 12:25; Lk 20:35; J 5:37; Ac 25:8; Ro 8:38f; 1 Th 2:5f; Rv 9:20. οὔτε ἄντλημα ἔχεις you have no bucket J 4:11; cf. 3 J 10.

οὗτος, αὕτη, τοῦτο demonstrative pronoun, used as adjective and as substantive this.—1. as substantive Mt 3:17; 26:26, 28; Lk 5:21; J 6:29, 39f; Ac 7:35; 9:21; 25:25; 1 Cor 1:12; Gal 4:24; Eph 3:14; Hb 2:14; Js 1:23; 1 Pt 5:12. This one, he, etc. Mt 3:3; Lk 1:32; J 1:2, 41; Ac 21:24; 1 Cor 2:2; 2 Ti 3:5f, 8; Hb 8:3. This (very) one J 9:9; Ac 4:10; 9:20; 1 J 5:6; 2 Pt 2:17. καὶ τοῦτο and at that, and especially Ro 13:11; 1 Cor 6:6, 8; Eph 2:8. Elliptically, τοῦτο δέ the point is this 2 Cor 9:6. τοῦτο μὲν . . . τοῦτο δέ sometimes . . . sometimes, not only . . . but also Hb 10:33.— 2. as an adj., coming before the substantive with the article between ἐν τούτῳ τῷ αἰῶνι in this age Mt 12:32. Cf. 16:18; Lk 7:44; J 4:15; Ac 1:11; Hb 7:1; Rv 20:14. Following a substantive that has the article ἐκ τῶν λίθων τούτων

from these stones Mt 3:9. Cf. 5:19; Mk 12:16; Lk 11:31; 21:3; Ro 15:28; 1 Cor 11:26; Eph 3:8; Rv 2:24.—When the article is lacking, either the demonstrative or the noun belongs to the predicate τρίτην ταύτην ἡμέραν this is the third day Lk 24:21. Cf. 1:36; J 2:11; 4:54; 2 Cor 13:1.

οὕτω and οὕτως adv. in this manner, thus, so Mt 5:16, 19; 12:40; Mk 7:18; 10:43; 14:59; Lk 11:30; 24:24; J 3:8; 11:48; 21:1; Ac 8:32; Ro 1:15; 12:5; Gal 3:3; Rv 16:18. As follows Mt 2:5. Without further ado, simply J 4:6, perh. 13:25. ὁ μὲν οὕτως, ὁ δὲ οὕτως the one in one way, the other in another 1 Cor 7:7.

οὐχ see οὐ.

οὐχί (strengthened form of οὐ) negative adv.—1. not J 13:10f; 14:22; 1 Cor 5:2; 6:1; 10:29.—2. no, by no means Lk 1:60; 12:51; 13:3, 5; 16:30; J 9:9; Ro 3:27.— 3. interrogative word in questions that expect an affirmative answer not Mt 5:46; 6:25; 10:29; Lk 6:39; 12:6; 17:8; J 11:9; Ro 3:29.

ὀφειλέτης, ου, ὁ debtor—1. lit. Mt 18:24.—2. fig. one who is obligated ὀφειλέτην εἶναι be under obligation Ro 1:14; 8:12; 15:27; Gal 5:3. One who is guilty of a misdeed, one who is culpable or at fault Mt 6:12; sinner Lk 13:4.*

ὀφειλή, ῆς, ἡ debt—1. lit. Mt 18:32.— 2. fig. obligation, duty, one's due 1 Cor 7:3. Pl., of taxes, etc. Ro 13:7.*

ὀφείλημα, ατος, τό debt, what is owed, one's due Ro 4:4. Debt = sin Mt 6:12.*

ὀφείλω owe, be indebted—1. lit., of financial debts Mt 18:28, 30, 34; Lk 7:41; 16:5, 7; Phlm 18.—2. fig.—a. generally owe, be indebted Ro 13:8.—Be obligated, one must, one ought Lk 17:10; J 19:7; Ac 17:29; Ro 15:1; 1 Cor 9:10; 11:7; 2 Cor 12:11, 14; 2 Th 1:3.—b. ὀφείλει he is obligated, bound (by his oath) Mt 23:16, 18. Commit a sin Lk 11:4.

ὄφελον (2 aor. act. ptc. of ὀφείλω) a fixed form, functioning as a particle to introduce unattainable wishes O that, would that 1 Cor 4:8; 2 Cor 11:1; Gal 5:12; Rv 3:15.*

ὄφελος, ους, τό benefit, good 1 Cor 15:32; Js 2:14, 16.*

ὀφθαλμοδουλία, ας, ἡ eyeservice, service performed only when one is being watched Eph 6:6; Col 3:22.*

ὀφθαλμός, οῦ, ὁ eye—1. lit. Mt 6:23; Lk 11:34; 1 Cor 2:9; 12:16f; 15:52; Hb 4:13; 1 J 1:1; 2:16; Rv 4:6, 8; 19:12.—2. transferred to mental and spiritual understanding: Mt 13:16; Mk 8:18; Lk 19:42; Ro 11:8; Eph 1:18. [ophthalmology]

ὀφθείς, ὀφθήσομαι 1 aor. pass. ptc. and fut. pass. ind. of ὁράω.

ὄφις, εως, ὁ snake, serpent—1. lit. Mt 7:10; 10:16; Mk 16:18; Lk 10:19; 11:11; J 3:14; 1 Cor 10:9; Rv 9:19.—2. fig. and symbolic Mt 23:33; 2 Cor 11:3; Rv 12:9, 14f; 20:2.* [Ophites, members of a Gnostic sect]

ὀφρῦς, ύος, ἡ lit. eyebrow, then brow, edge of a cliff or hill Lk 4:29.*

ὀχετός, οῦ, ὁ drain, sewer Mk 7:19 v.l.*

ὀχλέω trouble, disturb pass. Ac 5:16; Lk 6:18 v.l.*

ὀχλοποιέω form a mob Ac 17:5.*

ὄχλος, ου, ὁ—1. crowd, throng, multitude (of people) Mt 9:23, 25; 21:8; Mk 2:4, 13; 6:34; Lk 5:1; 12:13; 19:3; Ac 8:6; 14:11, 13, 18f; 21:27; Rv 17:15.—2. the (common) people, populace Mt 14:5; 15:10; 21:26, 46; Mk 11:18; 12:12; Ac 24:12; rabble J 7:49.—3. large number Lk 5:29; 6:17; Ac 1:15; 6:7. [ochlocracy, ὄχλος + κρατεῖν]

Ὀχοζίας, ου, ὁ Ahaziah (2 Kings 8:24) Mt 1:8 v.l.; Lk 3:23ff v.l.*

ὀχύρωμα, ατος, τό stronghold, fortress 2 Cor 10:4.*

ὀψάριον, ου, τό fish J 6:9, 11; 21:9f, 13.*

ὀψέ adv. late (in the day), in the evening Mk 11:19; 13:35. Functions as prep. w. gen. after Mt 28:1.* [opsimathy, ὀψέ + μάθη]

ὀψία, ας, ἡ see ὄψιος 2.

ὄψιμος, ον late in the season ὑετὸς ὄψιμος the late (i.e. spring) rain Js 5:7 v.l. The text has the substantive (ὁ) ὄψιμος in the same meaning.*

ὄψιος, α, ον late—2. as substantive ἡ ὀψία evening Mt 8:16; Mk 1:32; J 6:16; 20:19.

ὄψις, εως, ἡ—1. outward appearance, aspect J 7:24.—2. face J 11:44. Either appearance or face is possible for Rv 1:16.* [synopsis]

ὄψομαι fut. mid. ind. of ὁράω.

ὀψώνιον, ου, τό wages, pay, salary, compensation Lk 3:14; Ro 6:23; 1 Cor 9:7; 2 Cor 11:8.* [Cf. opsonin, a constituent of blood serum.]

Π

παγιδεύω entrap fig. Mt 22:15.*

παγίς, ίδος, ἡ trap, snare lit. Lk 21:35. Fig. Ro 11:9; 1 Ti 3:7; 6:9; 2 Ti 2:26.*

πάγος see Ἄρειος πάγος.

παθεῖν, παθών 2 aor. inf. and ptc. of πάσχω.

πάθημα, ατος, τό—1. suffering, misfortune Ro 8:18; 2 Cor 1:5–7; Phil 3:10; Col 1:24; 2 Ti 3:11; Hb 2:9f; 10:32; 1 Pt 4:13; 5:1, 9. τὰ εἰς Χριστὸν παθήματα the sufferings of Christ 1:11.—2. passion Ro 7:5; Gal 5:24.*

παθητός, ή, όν subject to suffering Ac 26:23.*

πάθος, ους, τό passion, especially of a sexual nature Ro 1:26; Col 3:5; 1 Th 4:5.* [patho-, path-, -pathia, -pathic, combining forms]

παθοῦσα, παθών 2 aor. act. ptc. fem. and masc. of πάσχω.

παιδαγωγός, οῦ, ὁ attendant (slave), custodian, guide, lit. 'boy-leader,' whose duty it was to superintend the conduct of the boys in the family to which he was attached and to conduct them to and from school (frequently viewed as a repressive figure) 1 Cor 4:15; Gal 3:24f.* [pedagogue]

παιδάριον, ου, τό little boy, boy, child Mt 11:16 v.l. For J 6:9 youth or young slave are also possible.*

παιδεία, ας, ἡ training, discipline Eph 6:4; 2 Ti 3:16; Hb 12:5, 7, 8, 11.*

παιδευτής, οῦ, ὁ instructor, teacher Ro 2:20; one who disciplines, a corrector Hb 12:9.* [Cf. propaedeutic, preliminary instruction.]

παιδεύω—1. instruct, train, educate Ac 7:22; 22:3.—2. correct, give guidance to 2 Ti 2:25; Tit 2:12.—3. discipline with punishment 1 Cor 11:32; 2 Cor 6:9; 1 Ti 1:20; Hb 12:6f, 10; Rv 3:19. Whip, scourge Lk 23:16, 22 (Jesus is to be 'taught a lesson').*

παιδιόθεν adv. from childhood Mk 9:21.*

παιδίον, ου, τό—1. very young child, infant Mt 2:8f, 11; Lk 1:59, 66; 2:17; J 16:21; Hb 11:23.—2. child Mt 14:21; 18:2, 4f; Mk 5:39–41; 9:24, 36f; Lk 18:17; J 4:49.—3. fig. child Mt 18:3; J 21:5; 1 Cor 14:20; Hb 2:13f; 1 J 2:18.

παιδίσκη, ης, ἡ maid, servant girl, female slave Mt 26:69; Mk 14:66, 69; Lk 12:45; 22:56; J 18:17; Ac 12:13; 16:16, 19 v.l.; Gal 4:22f, 30f.*

παιδόθεν adv. from childhood Mk 9:21 v.l.*

παίζω play, amuse oneself, dance 1 Cor 10:7.*

παῖς, παιδός, ὁ or **ἡ** child—1. ὁ παῖς—**a.** with reference to a relation between two human beings boy, youth Mt 2:16; 17:18; 21:15; Mk 9:21 v.l.; Lk 2:43; 9:42; Ac 20:12. Son J 4:51; son is also possible for Mt 8:6, 8, 13, but even more probable is servant, slave Lk 7:7; 12:45; 15:26. Courtier, attendant Mt 14:2.—**b.** in relation to God: of men as God's servants, slaves Lk 1:54, 69; Ac 4:25.—

Of Christ: servant Mt 12:18. For Ac 3:13, 26; 4:27, 30 either servant or son is possible.—2. ἡ παῖς girl Lk 8:51, 54.* [pedo-, combining form, as in pediatrics, pedobaptism, pedology]

παίω strike, hit, wound Mt 26:68; Mk 14:47; Lk 22:64; J 18:10; sting Rv 9:5.*

Πακατιανός, ή, όν Pacatian, in Pacatia a later name for the part of Phrygia in which Laodicea was located 1 Ti subscription.*

πάλαι adv. long ago Mt 11:21; Lk 10:13; Hb 1:1; Jd 4; former 2 Pt 1:9. For a long time 2 Cor 12:19. Already Mk 15:44.

παλαιός, ά, όν old Mt 13:52; Mk 2:21f; Lk 5:39; Ro 6:6; 1 Cor 5:7f; 2 Cor 3:14; Eph 4:22; Col 3:9; 1 J 2:7. [paleo-, combining form, as in paleography, paleolithic]

παλαιότης, ητος, ἡ age, obsoleteness Ro 7:6.*

παλαιόω act. declare or treat as obsolete Hb 8:13a. Pass. become old Lk 12:33; Hb 1:11; 8:13b.*

πάλη, ης, ἡ struggle fig. Eph 6:12.*

παλιγγενεσία, ας, ἡ rebirth, regeneration Mt 19:28; Tit 3:5.*

πάλιν adv.—1. back Mk 5:21; 14:39; J 6:15; 11:7; Ac 18:21; 2 Cor 1:16; Gal 1:17; 4:9; Phil 1:26.—2. again, once more, anew Mt 4:8; 20:5; 26:42; 27:50; Mk 2:13; Lk 23:20; Ac 17:32; Ro 8:15; 1 Cor 7:5; Gal 2:18.—3. furthermore, thereupon Mt 5:33; 19:24; Lk 13:20; J 12:39; 19:37; Ro 15:10–12; Hb 1:5; 2:13.—4. on the other hand, in turn Mt 4:7; Lk 6:43; 1 Cor 12:21; 2 Cor 10:7.—5. πάλιν in Mk 15:13; J 18:40 refers to responses made in turn. [as prefix in palimpsest, palindrome, palinode]

παλιγγενεσία see παλιγγενεσία.

παμπληθεί adv. all together Lk 23:18.*

πάμπολυς, παμπόλλη, πάμπολυ very great Mk 8:1 v.l.*

Παμφυλία, ας, ἡ Pamphylia, a province along the Mediterranean seacoast of Asia Minor Ac 2:10; 13:13; 14:24; 15:38; 16:6 v.l.; 27:5.*

πανδοκεῖον see πανδοχεῖον.

πανδοκεύς see πανδοχεύς.

πανδοχεῖον, ου, τό inn Lk 10:34.*

πανδοχεύς, έως, ὁ innkeeper Lk 10:35.* [πᾶς + δέχομαι, i.e. one who receives everyone]

πανήγυρις, εως, ἡ festal gathering Hb 12:22.* [panegyric]

πανοικεί or πανοικί with one's whole household Ac 16:34.*

πανοπλία, ας, ἡ full armor of a heavy-armed soldier, panoply lit. Lk 11:22. Fig. Eph 6:11, 13.*

πανουργία, ας, ἡ cunning, craftiness, trickery, skulduggery Lk 20:23; 1 Cor 3:19; 2 Cor 4:2; 11:3; Eph 4:14.*

πανοῦργος, ον clever, crafty, sly 2 Cor 12:16.*

πανπληθεί see παμπληθεί.

πανταχῆ adv. everywhere Ac 21:28.*

πανταχόθεν adv. from every direction Mk 1:45 v.l.*

πανταχοῦ adv. everywhere Mk 16:20; Lk 9:6; Ac 17:30; 24:3; 28:22; 1 Cor 4:17. In all directions Mk 1:28.*

παντελής, ές complete, perfect, absolute; εἰς τὸ παντελές can mean completely, wholly or forever, for all time in Hb 7:25. In Lk 13:11 it may mean fully or at all.*

πάντῃ adv. in every way Ac 24:3.*

πάντοθεν adv. from all directions Mk 1:45; Lk 19:43; on all sides, entirely Hb 9:4.*

παντοκράτωρ, ορος, ὁ the Almighty, All-Powerful, Omnipotent (One) only of God 2 Cor 6:18; Rv 1:8; 4:8; 11:17; 15:3; 16:7, 14; 19:6, 15; 21:22.*

πάντοτε adv. always, at all times Mt 26:11; Lk 15:31; J 7:6; Ro 1:10; 1 Cor 1:4; 2 Cor 2:14; Hb 7:25.

πάντως adv.—1. by all means, certainly, probably, doubtless Lk 4:23; Ac 18:21 v.l.; 21:22; 28:4; 1 Cor 9:10.—2. at least or by any and all means 1 Cor 9:22.—3. with a neg. not at all Ro 3:9; 1 Cor 16:12; by no means 5:10.*

παρά prep. with three cases—1. w. gen. from (the side of) Mt 18:19; Mk 12:2; 14:43; Lk 2:1; J 6:46; 8:26, 40; 16:27; Ac 9:2, 14; Gal 1:12; Eph 6:8; 2 Ti 3:14; Js 1:5; Rv 3:18. παρὰ κυρίου at the Lord's command Lk 1:45. παρὰ θεοῦ by God J 1:6. τὰ παρ' αὐτῆς her property, what she had Mk 5:26; τὰ παρ' αὐτῶν their gifts, what they give Lk 10:7. οἱ παρ' αὐτοῦ his family, his relatives Mk 3:21.—2. w. dat. at or by the side of, beside, near, with Mt 6:1; 22:25; Lk 2:52; 9:47; 11:37; J 14:25; 19:25; Ac 9:43; 21:7, 16; Ro 2:11; 1 Cor 16:2; Eph 6:9; Col 4:16. For Mt 19:26. In the sight or judgment of Ro 2:13; 12:16; 1 Pt 2:4, 20.—3. w. acc.—a. of space to (the side of) Mt 15:29; Mk 2:13; Ac 16:13. By, along Mt 4:18; Mk 4:1; Ac 10:6, 32. Near, at Lk 7:38; 17:16; Ac 5:2; 22:3. On Mt 13:4, 19; Mk 4:15; Lk 18:35; Hb 11:12.—b. in a comparative sense: in comparison to, more than, beyond Lk 3:13; 13:2, 4; Ro 14:5; Hb 2:7, 9; 9:23; 12:24. Instead of, rather than, to the exclusion of Lk 18:14; Ro 1:25; Hb 1:9. Beyond 2 Cor 8:3.—c. other uses: because of 1 Cor 12:15f. Against, contrary to Ac 18:13; Ro 1:26; 4:18; 11:24; 16:17; Gal 1:8f. Less 2 Cor 11:24. [para-, combining form, as in parody; parenthesis]

παραβαίνω—1. turn aside Ac 1:25.—2. transgress, break Mt 15:2f; 2 J 9 v.l.*

παραβάλλω—1. compare Mk 4:30 v.l.—2. come near (by ship) Ac 20:15.* [S. παραβολή.]

παράβασις, εως, ἡ overstepping, transgression, violation Ro 2:23; 4:15; 5:14; Gal 3:19; 1 Ti 2:14; Hb 2:2; 9:15.*

παραβάτης, ου, ὁ transgressor Ro 2:25, 27; Gal 2:18; Js 2:9, 11.*

παραβιάζομαι urge strongly, prevail upon Lk 24:29; Ac 16:15.*

παραβολεύομαι expose to danger, risk w. dat. Phil 2:30.*

παραβολή, ῆς, ἡ—1. symbol, type, figure Hb 9:9; 11:19.—2. parable, illustration Mt 13:18; 21:45; Mk 4:2; 7:17; Lk 8:9; 13:6; 18:1. [parable; parabola]

παραβουλεύομαι be careless, have no concern Phil 2:30 v.l.*

παραγγείλας 1 aor. act. ptc. of παραγγέλλω.

παραγγελία, ας, ἡ order, command Ac 5:28; 16:24. Instruction 1 Th 4:2; 1 Ti 1:5, 18.*

παραγγέλλω give orders, command, instruct, direct Mt 10:5; Mk 6:8; 8:6; Ac 15:5; 16:18, 23; 23:22; 1 Cor 11:17; 1 Th 4:11; 2 Th 3:4; 1 Ti 6:13.

παραγένωμαι 2 aor. mid. subj. of παραγίνομαι.

παραγίνομαι—1. come, arrive, be present Mt 2:1; 3:13; Lk 11:6; 22:52; Ac 9:26, 39; 20:18; 24:17, 24; 1 Cor 16:3.—2. appear, make a public appearance Mt 3:1; Lk 12:51; Hb 9:11.— 3. stand by, come to the aid of 2 Ti 4:16.

παράγω pass by Mt 20:30; Mk 1:16; 2:14; 15:21; J 9:1. Go away Mt 9:9, 27; J 8:59 v.l. Pass away act. 1 Cor 7:31; passive 1 J 2:8, 17.* [paragogic]

παραδέδομαι, παραδεδώκεισαν pf. mid. and plupf. act. ind. 3 pl. of παραδίδωμι, without augment.

παραδειγματίζω hold up to contempt Hb 6:6; expose, make an example of Mt 1:19 v.l.* [paradigm]

παράδεισος, ου, ὁ paradise, a place of blessedness above the earth Lk 23:43; 2 Cor 12:4; Rv 2:7.*

παραδέχομαι receive, accept, acknowledge (as correct) Mk 4:20; Ac 15:4; 16:21; 22:18; 1 Ti 5:19. Receive favorably = love Hb 12:6.*

παραδιατριβή, ῆς, ἡ useless occupation 1 Ti 6:5 v.l.*

παραδιδοῖ, παραδιδόναι, παραδιδούς pres. act. subj. 3 sing., pres. act. inf., and pres. act. ptc. of παραδίδωμι.

παραδίδωμι—1. hand over, give (over), deliver, give up Mt 10:19; 25:20, 22; 26:2, 15; Mk 13:11f; 15:15; Lk 4:6; 21:12; 22:22; J 19:11, 30; Ac 3:13; 12:4; 28:17; Ro 1:24, 26, 28; 1 Cor 5:5; 13:3; Eph 4:19. Risk Ac 15:26. ὁ παραδιδούς the betrayer Mt 26:25, 46, 48; Lk 22:21; J 18:2, 5.—2. give over, commend, commit Ac 14:26; 15:40; 1 Pt 2:23.—3. hand down, pass on, transmit, relate, teach oral or written tradition Mk 7:13; Lk 1:2; Ac 6:14; 16:4; 2 Pt 2:21; Jd 3.— 4. allow, permit Mk 4:29.

παραδίδως, παραδοθείς, παραδοθῆναι, παραδοθήσομαι, παραδοῖ, παραδοθῶ pres. act. ind. 2 sing., 1 aor. pass. ptc., 1 aor. pass. inf., 1

fut. pass., 2 aor. act. subj. 3 sing., and 1 aor. pass. subj. of παραδίδωμι.

παράδοξος, ον strange, wonderful, remarkable Lk 5:26.* [paradox]

παράδοσις, εως, ἡ tradition Mt 15:2f, 6; Mk 7:3, 5, 8f, 13; 1 Cor 11:2; Gal 1:14; Col 2:8; 2 Th 2:15; 3:6.*

παραδοῦναι, παραδούς, παραδῶ, παραδώσω 2 aor. act. inf., 2 aor. act. ptc., 2 aor. act. subj. 3 sing., and fut. act. ind. of παραδίδωμι.

παραζηλόω provoke to jealousy Ro 10:19; 11:11, 14; 1 Cor 10:22.*

παραθαλάσσιος, ία, ον (located) by the sea or lake Mt 4:13; Lk 4:31 v.l.*

παραθεῖναι 2 aor. act. inf. of παρατίθημι.

παραθεωρέω overlook, neglect Ac 6:1.*

παραθήκη, ης, ἡ deposit, property entrusted to another fig. 1 Ti 6:20; 2 Ti 1:12, 14.*

παραθήσω, παράθου, παραθῶσιν fut. act. ind., 2 aor. mid. impv. 2 sing., and 2 aor. act. subj. 3 pl. of παρατίθημι.

παραινέω advise, recommend, urge Ac 27:9, 22; Lk 3:18 v.l.*

παραιτέομαι—1. ask for, request, intercede for Mk 15:6. Excuse ἔχε με παρῃτημένον consider me excused Lk 14:18b, 19; cf. 18a.—2. decline—a. reject, refuse 1 Ti 5:11; Tit 3:10; Hb 12:25.—b. reject, avoid Ac 25:11; 1 Ti 4:7; 2 Ti 2:23.—c. beg Hb 12:19.*

παρακαθέζομαι sit beside Lk 10:39.*

παρακαθίζω sit down beside Lk 10:39 v.l.*

παρακαλέω—1. call to one's side, summon, invite Lk 8:41; Ac 8:31; 9:38; 16:9, 15. Summon to one's aid, call upon for help Mt 26:53; 2 Cor 12:8.—2. appeal to, urge, exhort, encourage Ac 14:22; 16:40; 20:1f; Ro 12:1, 8; 1 Cor 4:16; 2 Cor 10:1; 1 Th 5:11; Hb 3:13; 1 Pt 5:1.— 3. request, implore, appeal to, entreat Mt 8:5; Mk 1:40; Lk 7:4; 8:31f; Ac 19:31; 2 Cor 12:18; Phlm 9.—4. comfort, encourage, cheer up Mt 5:4; Lk 16:25; 2 Cor 1:4; 7:6; Eph 6:22; 1 Th 3:2; 4:18; Tit 1:9.—5. in some passages π. may mean try to console or conciliate Ac 16:39; 1 Cor 4:13; 1 Th 2:12 and possibly others. [S. παράκλητος.]

παρακαλύπτω hide, conceal Lk 9:45.*

παρακαταθήκη, ης, ἡ deposit v.l. in 1 Ti 6:20 and 2 Ti 1:14.*

παράκειμαι be at hand, ready Ro 7:18, 21.*

παρακέκλημαι, παρακληθῶ pf. mid. and pass. ind. and 1 aor. pass. subj. of παρακαλέω.

παράκλησις, εως, ἡ—1. encouragement, exhortation Ac 13:15; Ro 12:8; 1 Cor 14:3; Phil 2:1; 1 Th 2:3; 1 Ti 4:13; Hb 6:18; 12:5; 13:22.—**2.** appeal, request 2 Cor 8:4, 17.—**3.** comfort, consolation Lk 2:25; 6:24; Ac 4:36; 9:31; 15:31; Ro 15:4f; 2 Cor 1:3–7; 7:4, 7, 13; Phil 2:1; 2 Th 2:16; Phlm 7.*

παράκλητος, ου, ὁ Helper, Intercessor J 14:16, 26; 15:26; 16:7; 1 J 2:1.* [Paraclete]

παρακοή, ῆς, ἡ unwillingness to hear, disobedience Ro 5:19; 2 Cor 10:6; Hb 2:2.*

παρακολουθέω follow fig.—**1.** follow, accompany, attend Mk 16:17.—**2.** understand, make one's own or follow faithfully w. dat. 1 Ti 4:6; 2 Ti 3:10.—**3.** follow, trace, investigate w. dat. Lk 1:3.*

παρακούω overhear Mk 5:36. Refuse to listen to w. gen. Mt 18:17.*

παρακύπτω bend over lit. Lk 24:12; J 20:5; bend over and look 20:11. Fig. look, glance Js 1:25; 1 Pt 1:12.*

παράλαβε 2 aor. impv. 2 sing. of παραλαμβάνω.

παραλαμβάνω—1. take (to oneself), take with or along Mt 1:20, 24; 2:13f, 20f; 12:45; 24:40f; Mk 4:36; Lk 9:28; 11:26; J 14:3; Ac 15:39; 21:24, 26, 32. Take into custody, arrest Ac 16:35 v.l.—**2.** take over, receive Mk 7:4; 1 Cor 11:23; 15:3; Gal 1:9; Col 4:17; 1 Th 4:1; Hb 12:28.—**3.** receive with favor, accept J 1:11; 1 Cor 15:1; Phil 4:9.

παραλέγομαι sail past, coast along Ac 27:8, 13.*

παραλημφθήσομαι, παραλήμψομαι 1 fut. pass. ind. and fut. mid. ind. of παραλαμβάνω.

παράλιος, ον (located) by the sea ἡ παράλιος (χώρα) the seacoast (district) Lk 6:17.*

παραλλαγή, ῆς, ἡ change, variation Js 1:17.* [Cf. parallax.]

παραλογίζομαι deceive, delude Col 2:4; Js 1:22.* [paralogism]

παραλυτικός, ή, όν lame only as noun (ὁ) π. the lame person, the paralytic Mt 4:24; 8:6; 9:2, 6; Mk 2:3–5, 9f; Lk 5:24 v.l.; J 5:3 v.l.*

παράλυτος, ον lame as noun ὁ π. the paralytic Mk 2:9 v.l.*

παραλύω undo, weaken, disable, paralyze Lk 5:18; Ac 9:33; Hb 12:12. ὁ παραλελυμένος the paralytic Lk 5:24; Ac 8:7.*

παραμείνας 1 aor. act. ptc. of παραμένω.

παραμένω remain, stay (at someone's side) 1 Cor 16:6. Continue Phil 1:25; Hb 7:23; Js 1:25.*

παραμυθέομαι encourage, cheer up 1 Th 2:12; 5:14. Console, comfort J 11:19, 31.*

παραμυθία, ας, ἡ comfort, consolation 1 Cor 14:3.*

παραμύθιον, ου, τό solace Phil 2:1.*

παράνοια, ας, ἡ madness, foolishness 2 Pt 2:16 v.l.* [paranoia]

παρανομέω act contrary to the law Ac 23:3.*

παρανομία, ας, ἡ lawlessness, evildoing 2 Pt 2:16.*

παραπικραίνω be disobedient, rebellious Hb 3:16.*

παραπικρασμός, οῦ, ὁ embitterment, then revolt, rebellion Hb 3:8, 15.*

παραπίπτω fall away, commit apostasy Hb 6:6.*

παραπλεῦσαι 1 aor. act. inf. of παραπλέω.

παραπλέω sail past w. acc. Ac 20:16.*

παραπλήσιος, ία, ιον coming near, resembling, similar. The neut. παραπλήσιον as adv. ἠσθένησεν παραπλήσιον θανάτῳ he was so ill that he nearly died Phil 2:27.*

παραπλησίως adv. in just the same way Hb 2:14.*

παραπορεύομαι go or pass by Mt 27:39; Mk 11:20; 15:29. Simply go Mk 2:23; 9:30.*

παράπτωμα, ατος, τό false step, transgression, sin Mt 6:14f; Mk 11:25; Ro 4:25; 5:15–18, 20; 11:11f; 2 Cor 5:19; Gal 6:1; Eph 1:7; 2:1, 5; Col 2:13.*

παραρρέω flow by, slip away fig. drift away Hb 2:1.*

παραρυῶμεν 2 aor. pass. subj. 1 pl. of παραρρέω.

παράσημος, ον distinguished, marked παρασήμῳ Διοσκούροις marked by the Dioscuri, i.e. with the D. as the ship's insignia Ac 28:11.*

παρασκευάζω prepare act. Ac 10:10; 1 Pt 2:8 v.l. Mid. prepare (oneself) 1 Cor 14:8; perf. be ready 2 Cor 9:2f.*

παρασκευή, ῆς, ἡ preparation, i.e. day of preparation for a festival, Friday Mt 27:62; Mk 15:42; Lk 23:54; J 19:14, 31, 42.*

παραστάτις, ιδος, ἡ a supporter, of Phoebe Ro 16:2 v.l.*

παραστήσομαι 1 fut. mid. ind. of παρίστημι.

παρασχών 2 aor. act. ptc. of παρέχω.

παρατείνω extend, prolong Ac 20:7.*

παρατηρέω watch closely, observe carefully—**1.** watch (maliciously), lie in wait for Mk 3:2; Lk 6:7; 14:1. Watch one's opportunity 20:20. Watch, guard Ac 9:24.—**2.** observe cultically Gal 4:10.*

παρατήρησις, εως, ἡ observation Lk 17:20.*

παρατίθημι place beside, place before—**1.** act. set before Mk 6:41; 8:6f; Lk 9:16; 10:8; 11:6; Ac 16:34; 1 Cor 10:27. Put before Mt 13:24, 31.—**2.** mid. give over, entrust, commend Lk 12:48; 23:46; Ac 14:23; 20:32; 1 Ti 1:18; 2 Ti 2:2; 1 Pt 4:19. Demonstrate, point out Ac 17:3; 28:23 v.l.*

παρατυγχάνω happen to be there Ac 17:17.*

παραυτίκα adv. immediately, for the present as adj. momentary 2 Cor 4:17.*

παραφέρω take or carry away Hb 13:9; Jd 12. Take away, remove Mk 14:36; Lk 22:42.*

παραφρονέω be beside oneself, lose one's wits 2 Cor 11:23.*

παραφρονία, ας, ἡ madness, insanity 2 Pt 2:16.*

παραφροσύνη, ης, ἡ madness, insanity 2 Pt 2:16 v.l.*

παραχειμάζω spend the winter Ac 27:12; 28:11; 1 Cor 16:6; Tit 3:12.*

παραχειμασία, ας, ἡ wintering Ac 27:12.*

παραχράομαι misuse 1 Cor 7:31 v.l.

παραχρῆμα adv. at once, immediately Mt 21:19f; Lk 1:64; 13:13; Ac 3:7; 13:11.

πάρδαλις, εως, ἡ leopard Rv 13:2.*

παρέβαλον 2 aor. act. ind. of παραλαμβάνω.

παρέβην 2 aor. act. ind. of παραβαίνω.

παρεγενόμην 2 aor. mid. ind. of παραγίνομαι.

παρεδίδοσαν and **παρεδίδουν** impf. act. ind. 3 pl. of παραδίδωμι.

παρεδόθην, παρέδοσαν 1 aor. pass. ind. and 2 aor. act. ind. of παραδίδωμι.

παρεδρεύω sit beside, serve regularly 1 Cor 9:13.*

παρέδωκα 1 aor. act. ind. of παραδίδωμι.

παρέθηκα, παρεθέμην 1 aor. act. ind. and 2 aor. mid. of παρατίθημι.

παρεῖδον 2 aor. act. ind. of παροράω.

παρειμένος pf. pass. ptc. of παρίημι.

πάρειμι—1. be present J 7:6; 11:28; Ac 10:33; 24:19; 1 Cor 5:3; Gal 4:18, 20; Col 1:6; Rv 17:8.—The pres. 'be here' can take on the perfect sense have come Mt 26:50; Lk 13:1; Ac 10:21; 12:20; 17:6.—τὸ παρόν the present Hb 12:11.—**2.** πάρεστίν τί μοι something is at my disposal, I have something 2 Pt 1:9, 12. τὰ παρόντα one's possessions Hb 13:5.

παρεῖναι serves as pres. inf. of πάρειμι (Ac 24:19; Gal 4:18, 20) and as 2 aor. inf. of παρίημι (Lk 11:42).

παρεισάγω bring in secretly or maliciously 2 Pt 2:1.*

παρείσακτος, ον secretly brought in, smuggled in Gal 2:4.*

παρεισδύ(ν)ω slip in stealthily, sneak in Jd 4.*

παρεισενέγκας 1 aor. act. ptc. of παρεισφέρω.

παρεισέρχομαι slip in, come in as a side issue Ro 5:20. Slip in, sneak in Gal 2:4.*

παρεισῆλθον 2 aor. act. ind. of παρεισέρχομαι.

παρειστήκειν plupf. act. of παρίστημι.

παρεισφέρω apply, bring to bear 2 Pt 1:5.*

παρεῖχαν impf. act. 3 pl. of παρέχω.

παρεκλήθην 1 aor. pass. ind. of παρακαλέω.

παρεκτός adv.—1. used as adv. besides, outside 2 Cor 11:28.—2. used as prep. w. gen. apart from, except for Mt 5:32; 19:9 v.l.; Ac 26:29.*

παρέλαβον, παρελάβοσαν 2 aor. act. ind. forms of παραλαμβάνω.

παρελεύσομαι, παρεληλυθέναι, παρεληλυθώς, παρεθλεῖν fut. mid. ind., pf. act. inf., pf. act. ptc., and 2 aor. act. inf. of παρέρχομαι.

παρεμβάλλω, fut. παρεμβαλῶ put or throw up Lk 19:43.*

παρεμβολή, ῆς, ἡ—1. a (fortified) camp Hb 13:11, 12 v.l., 13; Rv 20:9.—2. barracks, headquarters Ac 21:34, 37; 22:24; 23:10, 16, 32; 28:16 v.l.—3. army, battle line Hb 11:34.*

παρένεγκε aor. act. impv. of παραφέρω.

παρενοχλέω cause difficulty (for), trouble, annoy w. dat. Ac 15:19.*

παρέξῃ fut. mid. ind. 2 sing. of παρέχω.

παρεπίδημος, ον sojourning as noun ὁ π. stranger, exile, visiting stranger Hb 11:13; 1 Pt 1:1; 2:11.*

παρεπίκρανα 1 aor. act. ind. of παραπικραίνω Hb 3:16.

παρέρχομαι—1. go by, pass by—a. lit. Mt 8:28; Mk 6:48; Lk 18:37. Pass Mt 14:15; Ac 27:9; 1 Pt 4:3.—b. fig. pass away, come to an end, disappear Mt 5:18a; Mk 13:31; Lk 21:32; 2 Cor 5:17; Js 1:10; 2 Pt 3:10; in the sense lose force, become invalid Mt 5:18b; Lk 21:33b. Pass by, neglect, disobey Lk 11:42; 15:29. Pass Mt 26:39, 42; Mk 14:35.—2. go through, pass through Ac

16:8; 17:15 v.l.—3. come to, come here, come Lk 12:37; 17:7; Ac 24:7 v.l.

πάρεσις, εως, ἡ passing over, letting go unpunished Ro 3:25.*

παρέστηκα, παρέστην, παρέστησα, παρεστώς, παρεστηκώς pf. act. ind., 2 aor. act. ind., 1 aor. act. ind., and two forms of the pf. act. ptc. of παρίστημι.

παρέσχον 2 aor. act. ind. of παρέχω.

παρέτεινεν 1 aor. act. ind. 3 sing. of παρατείνω Ac 20:7.

παρέχω—1. act.—a. give up, offer, present Lk 6:29.—b. grant, show Ac 17:31; 22:2; 28:2; 1 Ti 6:17.—c. cause, bring about Mt 26:10; Mk 14:6; Lk 11:7; 18:5; Ac 16:16; Gal 6:17; 1 Ti 1:4.—2. mid. ἑαυτόν τι π. show oneself to be something Tit 2:7. Grant Lk 7:4; Col 4:1. Get for oneself Ac 19:24.*

παρήγγειλα 1 aor. act. ind. of παραγγέλλω.

παρηγορία, ας, ἡ comfort Col 4:11.*

παρηκολούθηκώς pf. act. ptc. of παρακολουθέω.

παρῆλθον 2 aor. act. ind. of παρέρχομαι.

παρήνει impf. act. 3 sing. of παραινέω Ac 27:9.

παρῆσαν impf. 3 pl. of πάρειμι.

παρῃτημένος, παρῃτοῦντο pf. pass. ptc. (Lk 14:18f) and impf. mid. 3 pl. (Mk 15:6) of παραιτέομαι.

παρθενία, ας, ἡ virginity Lk 2:36.*

παρθένος, ου, ἡ—1. virgin Mt 1:23; 25:1, 7, 11; Lk 1:27; Ac 21:9; 1 Cor 7:25, 28, 34, 36–38; 2 Cor 11:2.—2. chaste man Rv 14:4.* [parthenogenesis, παρθένος + γένεσις; Parthenon, temple of Athena Parthenos at Athens]

Πάρθοι, ων, οἱ Parthians (Parthia was east of the Euphrates) Ac 2:9.*

παρίημι leave undone, neglect Lk 11:42. Slacken, weaken pf. pass. ptc. παρειμένος weakened, listless, drooping Hb 12:12.*

παριστάνω see παρίστημι.

παρίστημι and παριστάνω—1. trans.—a. place beside, put at someone's disposal Mt 26:53; Ac 23:24; Ro 6:13, 16, 19.—b. present Lk 2:22; Ac

1:3; 9:41; 23:33; 2 Cor 11:2. *Offer, present* Ro 12:1.—**c.** *make, render* Eph 5:27; Col 1:22, 28; 2 Ti 2:15. *Prove, demonstrate* Ac 24:13.—**2.** intrans. (all mid. forms, also pf., plupf., 2 aor. act.)—**a.** pres., fut., aor. *approach, stand before* w. dat. Ac 9:39; 27:23f; Ro 14:10. *Stand by, help, be supportive, come to the aid of* Ro 16:2; 2 Ti 4:17.—**b.** pf. and plupf. *stand, be present* Mk 15:39; Lk 1:19; J 18:22; 19:26. *Have come* Mk 4:29.

Παρμενᾶς, ᾶ, ὁ acc. -ᾶν *Parmenas* Ac 6:5.*

πάροδος, ου, ἡ *passing by* 1 Cor 16:7.*

παροικέω *live as a stranger* Lk 24:18 v.l. followed by ἐν. *Migrate* Hb 11:9. Simply *inhabit, live in* Lk 24:18.*

παροικία, ας, ἡ *alien residence, the stay* or *sojourn of one who is not a citizen in a strange place* Ac 13:17; 1 Pt 1:17.* [*parish*]

πάροικος, ον *strange* Ac 7:6. ὁ π. as noun *stranger, resident alien* 7:29; Eph 2:19; 1 Pt 2:11.* [*paroecious*, a botanical term]

παροιμία, ας, ἡ *proverb, maxim* 2 Pt 2:22. *Dark saying, figure of speech* J 10:6; 16:25, 29.*

πάροινος, ον *drunken, addicted to wine* 1 Ti 3:3; Tit 1:7.*

παροίχομαι *pass by, be gone* Ac 14:16.*

παρομοιάζω *be like* Mt 23:27.*

παρόμοιος, (α), ον *like, similar* Mk 7:8 v.l., 13.*

παρόν, τό see πάρειμι 2.

παροξύνω *urge on, provoke to wrath, irritate* pass. *become irritated, angry* 1 Cor 13:5. *Be aroused* Ac 17:16.*

παροξυσμός, οῦ, ὁ *stirring up, encouraging* Hb 10:24. *Irritation, sharp disagreement* Ac 15:39.* [*paroxysm*]

παροράω *overlook, take no notice of* Ac 17:30 v.l.*

παροργίζω *make angry* Ro 10:19; Eph 6:4; Col 3:21 v.l.*

παροργισμός, οῦ, ὁ *angry mood, anger* Eph 4:26.*

παροργιῶ fut. act. ind. of παροργίζω.

παροτρύνω *arouse, incite* Ac 13:50.*

παρουσία, ας, ἡ—1. *presence* 1 Cor 16:17; 2 Cor 10:10; Phil 2:12.—**2.** *coming, advent*—**a.** of human beings 2 Cor 7:6f; Phil 1:26.—**b.** of Christ and his Messianic Advent at the end of this age Mt 24:3, 27, 37, 39; 1 Cor 1:8 v.l.; 15:23; 1 Th 2:19; 3:13; 4:15; 5:23; 2 Th 2:1, 8f; Js 5:7f; 2 Pt 1:16; 3:4, 12; 1 J 2:28.—**c.** of the Antichrist 2 Th 2:9.* [*parousia*]

παροψίς, ίδος, ἡ *dish* Mt 23:25, 26 v.l.*

παρρησία, ας, ἡ—1. *outspokenness, frankness, plainness of speech* J 16:29; Ac 2:29; 2 Cor 3:12. παρρησίᾳ *plainly, openly* Mk 8:32; J 7:13; 10:24; 11:14; 16:25, 29 v.l.—**2.** *openness to the public* παρρησίᾳ *in public, publicly* J 7:26; 11:54; 18:20. Similarly J 7:4; Ac 14:19 v.l.; 28:31; Phil 1:20; Col 2:15.—**3.** *courage, confidence, boldness, fearlessness* Ac 2:29; 4:13, 29, 31; 6:10 v.l.; 16:4 v.l.; 2 Cor 7:4; Eph 6:19; Phlm 8. *Joyousness, confidence* Eph 3:12; 1 Ti 3:13; Hb 3:6; 4:16; 10:19, 35; 1 J 2:28; 3:21; 4:17; 5:14.* [πᾶς + ῥῆσις]

παρρησιάζομαι—1. *speak freely, openly, fearlessly; express oneself freely* Ac 9:27f; 13:46; 14:3; 18:26; 19:8; 26:26; Eph 6:20.—**2.** *have the courage, venture* 1 Th 2:2.*

παρών pres. ptc. of πάρειμι.

παρῳχημένος pf. ptc. of παροίχομαι.

πᾶς, πᾶσα, πᾶν gen. παντός, πάσης, παντός—**1.** adj., used with a noun—**a.** with the noun in the sing. without the article *every, each* πᾶν δένδρον *every tree* Mt 3:10; Lk 3:9. Similarly Mt 15:13; Lk 3:5; J 1:9; Ac 5:42; Ro 3:4; 1 Cor 15:24; Hb 3:4; Rv 1:7a. *All* Mk 13:20; Lk 3:6; Hb 12:11.—*Every kind of, all sorts of* Mt 4:23; 23:27; Ac 2:5; 7:22; Ro 1:18; 1 Cor 6:18; Eph 1:3, 8; Tit 1:16; Js 1:17.—*Every, any and every, just any* Mt 4:4; 18:19; 2 Cor 1:4b; Eph 4:14; 1 J 4:1; *any at all* Mt 19:3.—*Full, greatest, all* Ac 4:29; 5:23; 23:1; 2 Cor 12:12; Eph 6:18c; 1 Ti 3:4; 5:2; Js 1:2.—*Before proper names all, the whole* Mt 2:3; Ac 17:26b; Ro 11:26.—**b.** with a noun in the pl. without the article πάντες ἄνθρωποι *all people, everyone* Ac 22:15; Ro 5:18;

12:17f; 1 Cor 15:19; Tit 2:11. Cf. Hb 1:6.—**c.** with a noun in the sing. with the article *the whole, all (the)* πᾶσα ἡ Ἰουδαία καὶ πᾶσα ἡ περίχωρος *all Judaea and the whole region around* Mt 3:5. Cf. 8:32, 34; 27:25, 45; Mk 5:33; 16:15; Ac 3:9, 11; Ro 8:22; 9:17; 1 Cor 13:2b, c; Hb 9:19b, c.—*All* 2 Cor 1:4a; 7:4; Phil 1:3; 1 Th 3:7; 1 Pt 5:7.—πᾶς with the article is often used with a participle *every one who, whoever* Mt 5:22; cf. 7:8, 26; Lk 19:26; J 3:8, 15f, 20; Ac 13:39; Ro 2:1, 10; Hb 5:13. πᾶν τό *everything that* Mt 15:17; Mk 7:18; 1 Cor 10:25, 27; 1 J 5:4. Also πᾶς ὅς, etc. *every one who* Mt 7:24; 19:29; Lk 14:33; J 6:37, 39; Ro 14:23.—**d.** with a noun, pronoun, participle, etc. in the plural with the article *all* Mt 1:17; 4:24; 25:7; Mk 4:13, 31f; Lk 2:47; J 10:8; Ac 1:18; 2:7, 14, 32; 16:32; Ro 1:7f; 9:6; 1 Cor 12:26; Phil 1:4, 7f; Hb 11:13, 39; Rv 7:11; 13:8.—**e.** πᾶς stands between article and noun: sing. *the whole* Ac 20:18; Gal 5:14; pl. *all the* Ac 21:21; Ro 16:15; Gal 1:2.—**2.** substantive—**a.** without the article πᾶς *every one* i.e. *without exception* Lk 16:16. διὰ παντός *always, continually* Mt 18:10; Mk 5:5. ἐν παντί *in every respect, in everything* 1 Cor 1:5; 2 Cor 7:5, 11, 16; 1 Th 5:18.—πάντες, πᾶσαι *all, everyone* Mt 10:22; Mk 1:37; Lk 1:63; Ro 5:12.—πάντα *all things, everything* Mt 11:27; 18:26; J 1:3; 3:35; 1 Cor 2:10; 3:21. πάντα as accusative of specification *in all respects, in every way, altogether* Ac 20:35; 1 Cor 9:25b. Cf. 2 Cor 2:9.—**b.** with the article: οἱ πάντες *all (of them)* Ro 11:32a, b; 1 Cor 9:22; Phil 2:21. *(We, they) all* Mk 14:64; 1 Cor 10:17; Eph 4:13.—τὰ πάντα *all things, the universe* Ro 11:36; 1 Cor 8:6; Eph 1:10; 3:9; Hb 1:3; 2:10; Rv 4:11. *All this* 2 Cor 4:15; Col 3:8. As accusative of specification *in all respects* Eph 4:15. [*pan-, panto-,* combining forms in numerous terms, such as *pantheist, pantheon, pantograph*]

πάσχα, τό indecl. *the Passover*—**1.** a Jewish festival Mt 26:2; Mk 14:1; Lk 2:41; 22:1; J 2:13, 23; 6:4; 11:55; 12:1; 13:1; 18:39; 19:14; Ac 12:4.—**2.** *the Paschal lamb* Mt 26:17; Mk 14:12, 14;

Lk 22:7, 11, 15; J 18:28. Fig. 1 Cor 5:7.—**3.** *the Passover meal* Mt 26:18f; Mk 14:16; Lk 22:8, 13; Hb 11:28.* [*paschal*]

πάσχω—**1.** *have an experience* Gal 3:4; cf. Mt 17:15.—**2.** *suffer, endure*—**a.** *suffer,* sometimes *suffer death* Mt 17:12; Lk 22:15; 24:46; Ac 1:3; 17:3; 1 Cor 12:26; Phil 1:29; 2 Th 1:5; Hb 2:18; 9:26; 1 Pt 2:19–21, 23; 3:14, 17; 4:19. *Undergo punishment* 1 Pt 4:15.—**b.** *endure, undergo* Mt 27:19; Mk 8:31; 9:12; Lk 9:22; 17:25; Ac 9:16; 28:5; 2 Cor 1:6; 1 Th 2:14; 2 Ti 1:12; Hb 5:8; Rv 2:10. [See *patho-, -pathia,* etc., s.v. πάθος.]

Πάταρα, ων, τά *Patara,* a city in Lycia, on the southwest coast of Asia Minor Ac 21:1.*

πατάσσω *strike, hit* Mt 26:51; Lk 22:49f; Ac 12:7, 23; Rv 11:6; 19:15. *Strike down, slay* Mt 26:31; Mk 14:27; Ac 7:24.*

πατέω *tread (on)*—**1.** trans. *tread* Rv 14:20; 19:15. *Tread on, trample* Lk 21:24; Rv 11:2.—**2.** intrans. *walk, tread* Lk 10:19.*

πατήρ, πατρός, ὁ *father, parent*—**1.** lit.—**a.** of the immediate ancestor Mt 2:22; 10:21; Mk 5:40; 15:21; J 4:53; Ac 7:14; 1 Cor 5:1; Hb 12:9a. Plural *parents* 11:23.—**b.** *forefather, ancestor, progenitor* Mt 3:9; 23:30, 32; Mk 11:10; Lk 1:73; 16:24; J 4:20; 8:39, 53, 56; Ac 3:13, 25; Ro 9:10; Hb 1:1.—**2.** fig. of spiritual parenthood or used in respectful address, etc. Ac 7:2a; Ro 4:11, 12a; 1 Cor 4:15; 10:1; 2 Pt 3:4.—**3.** of God—**a.** as Parent of humanity Mt 6:4; Lk 6:36; J 8:41f; 20:17c; Ro 1:7; 2 Cor 1:2, 3b; Col 1:2; Tit 1:4.—**b.** as Parent of Jesus Christ Mt 7:21; Mk 8:38; 14:36; Lk 2:49; J 4:21; 6:40; Ro 15:6; 2 Cor 11:31; Eph 1:3; Rv 2:28.—**c.** Often God is called simply (ὁ) πατήρ *(the) Father, (the) Parent* Gal 1:1; Eph 1:17; 2:18; 3:14; Phil 2:11; 1 J 1:2; 2:1, 15.—**4.** of Satan J 8:44.

Πάτμος, ου, ὁ *Patmos,* a small, rocky island in the Aegean Sea Rv 1:9.*

πατραλώας a variant form of πατρολώας.

πατριά, ᾶς, ἡ *family, clan* Lk 2:4; Eph 3:15. *People, nation* Ac 3:25.*

πατριάρχης, ου, ὁ *father of a nation, patriarch* Ac 7:8f; Hb 7:4. *Ancestor* Ac 2:29.*

πατρικός, ή, όν *derived from* or *handed down by one's father, paternal* Gal 1:14.*

πατρίς, ίδος, ἡ—1. *fatherland, homeland* J 4:44; fig. Hb 11:14.—2. *home town, one's own part of the country* Mt 13:54, 57; Mk 6:1, 4; Lk 2:3 v.l.; 4:23f; Ac 18:25 v.l., 27 v.l.*

Πατροβᾶς, ᾶ, ὁ *Patrobas* Ro 16:14.*

πατρολῴας, ου, ὁ *one who kills one's father, a parricide* 1 Ti 1:9.*

πατροπαράδοτος, ον *inherited from one's father* or *ancestors* 1 Pt 1:18.*

πατρῷος, α, ον *paternal, belonging to one's father* or *ancestors* Ac 22:3; 28:17. ὁ π. θεός *the God of my ancestors* 24:14.*

Παῦλος, ου, ὁ *Paul*, a Roman name—1. Sergius Paulus, see Σέργιος.—2. Paul, an apostle of Jesus Christ Ac chapters 13–28 passim; Ro 1:1; 1 Cor 1:1, 12f; 3:4f, 22; 16:21; 2 Cor 1:1; 10:1; Gal 1:1; 5:2; Eph 1:1; 3:1; Phil 1:1; Col 1:1, 23; 4:18; 1 Th 1:1; 2:18; 2 Th 1:1; 3:17; 1 Ti 1:1; 2 Ti 1:1; Tit 1:1; Phlm 1, 9, 19; 2 Pt 3:15.*

παύω—1. act. *stop, cause to stop, hinder, keep* 1 Pt 3:10.—2. mid. *stop* (oneself), *cease* Lk 5:4; 8:24; 11:1; Ac 5:42; 6:13; 13:10; 20:1, 31; 21:32; 1 Cor 13:8; Eph 1:16; Col 1:9; Hb 10:2. *Cease from* w. gen. 1 Pt 4:1.* [*pause*]

Πάφος, ου, ἡ *Paphos*, a city on the west coast of Cyprus Ac 13:6, 13.*

παχύνω *make fat* fig., pass. *become dull* Mt 13:15; Ac 28:27.* [*pachyderm*, παχύς (here, 'thick') + δέρμα]

πέδη, ης, ἡ *fetter, shackle* Mk 5:4; Lk 8:29.*

πεδινός, ή, όν *flat, level* Lk 6:17.*

πεζεύω *travel by land* or *on foot* Ac 20:13.*

πεζῇ adv. *by land*, lit. 'on foot' Mt 14:13; Mk 6:33.*

πεζός, ή, όν *going by land* Mt 14:13 v.l.* [*pedestrian*, via Latin *pedester*]

πειθαρχέω *obey* w. dat. Ac 5:29, 32; *follow the advice of* 27:21. *Be obedient* Tit 3:1.*

πειθός, ή, όν *persuasive* 1 Cor 2:4.*

πειθώ, οῦς, ἡ dat. pl. πειθοῖς; ἐν πειθοῖ[ς] σοφίας [λόγοις] *with the persuasive words of wisdom* 1 Cor 2:4.*

πείθω—1. act., except for 2 pf. and plupf.—a. *convince* Ac 18:4; 19:8, 26; 28:23.—b. *persuade, appeal to* Mt 27:20; Ac 13:43; 2 Cor 5:11. The difficult passage Ac 26:28 ἐν ὀλίγῳ με πείθεις Χριστιανόν ποιῆσαι may be rendered *you are in a hurry to persuade me and make a Christian of me.*—c. *win over, strive to please* Ac 12:20; 14:19; Gal 1:10.—d. *conciliate, set at ease* 1 J 3:19. *Conciliate, satisfy* Mt 28:14.—2. The 2 pf. πέποιθα and plupf. ἐπεποίθειν have pres. and past meaning—a. *depend on, trust in, put one's confidence* in w. dat. Mt 27:43; Lk 11:22; 18:9; 2 Cor 1:9; 2:3; Phil 1:14; 3:3f; 2 Th 3:4; Phlm 21; Hb 2:13.—b. *be convinced, be sure, certain* Ro 2:19; 2 Cor 10:7; Phil 1:6, 25.—3. pass., except for the pf.—a. *be persuaded, be convinced, come to believe, believe* Lk 16:31; Ac 17:4; 21:14; 26:26; 28:24.—b. *obey, follow* w. dat. Ro 2:8; Gal 5:7; Hb 13:17; Js 3:3.—c. Some passages stand between mngs. a and b and allow either translation Ac 5:36f; 23:21; 27:11; ἐπείσθησαν δὲ αὐτῷ *so they took* (Gamaliel's) *advice* 5:39.—4. pf. pass. πέπεισμαι *be convinced, be certain* Lk 20:6; Ro 8:38; 15:14; 2 Ti 1:5, 12; Hb 6:9.

Πειλᾶτος a variant spelling of Πιλᾶτος.

πεῖν 2 aor. act. inf. of πίνω.

πεινάω *hunger, be hungry* lit. Mt 4:2; 12:1; Mk 11:12; Lk 6:3; 1 Cor 11:21, 34; Phil 4:12; Rv 7:16. Fig. Mt 5:6; J 6:35.

πεῖρα, ας, ἡ *attempt, trial* Hb 11:29. *Experience* 11:36.* [*empirical*, ἐν + πεῖρα]

πειράζω—1. *try, attempt* Ac 9:26; 16:7; 24:6.—2. *try, make trial of, put to the test*—a. generally Mt 16:1; 22:18, 35; Mk 10:2; J 6:6; 1 Cor 10:13; 2 Cor 13:5; Hb 2:18; 11:17; Rv 2:2; 3:10. Of making trial of God Ac 5:9; 15:10; 1 Cor 10:9;

Hb 3:9.—**b.** *tempt, entice to sin* Mt 4:1, 3; Mk 1:13; Lk 4:2; Gal 6:1; 1 Th 3:5; Js 1:13f; Rv 2:10.

πειρασμός, οῦ, ὁ—1. *test, trial* 1 Pt 4:12. Of testing God Hb 3:8.—**2.** *temptation, enticement to sin* Mt 6:13; 26:41; Mk 14:38; Lk 8:13; 11:4; 22:40, 46; Ac 15:26 v.l.; 1 Ti 6:9; 2 Pt 2:9; Rv 3:10; *way of tempting* Lk 4:13.

πειράω mid. *πειράομαι try, attempt, endeavor* Ac 26:21; 9:26 v.l. *πεπειραμένος κατὰ πάντα who was experienced in all respects* Hb 4:15 v.l.*

πεισθήσομαι 1 fut. pass. of *πείθω.*

πεισμονή, ῆς, ἡ *persuasion* Gal 5:8.*

πέλαγος, ους, τό *the open sea, the depths (of the sea)* Mt 18:6. *Sea* Ac 27:5.* [*pelagic,* pertaining to the ocean]

πελεκίζω *behead* Rv 20:4.*

πεμπταῖος, α, ον *on the fifth day* Ac 20:6 v.l.*

πέμπτος, η, ον *fifth* Rv 6:9; 9:1; 16:10; 21:20.*

πέμπω *send* Mt 2:8; Mk 5:12; Lk 4:26; J 1:22; Ac 10:5, 32f; Ro 8:3; Eph 6:22; Phil 4:16; Tit 3:12; 1 Pt 2:14; Rv 1:11.

πένης, ητος, ὁ *poor person* 2 Cor 9:9.*

πενθερά, ᾶς, ἡ *mother-in-law* Mt 8:14; 10:35; Mk 1:30; Lk 4:38; 12:53.*

πενθερός, οῦ, ὁ *father-in-law* J 18:13.*

πενθέω—1. intrans. *be sad, grieve, mourn* Mt 5:4; 9:15; Mk 16:10; Lk 6:25; 1 Cor 5:2; Js 4:9; Rv 18:11, 15, 19.—**2.** trans. *mourn over* 2 Cor 12:21.*

πένθος, ους, τό *grief, sadness, mourning* Js 4:9; Rv 18:7f; 21:4.*

πενιχρός, ά, όν *poor, needy* Lk 21:2.*

πεντάκις adv. *five times* 2 Cor 11:24.*

πεντακισχίλιοι, αι, α *five thousand* Mt 14:21; 16:9; Mk 6:44; 8:19; Lk 9:14; J 6:10.*

πεντακόσιοι, αι, α *five hundred* Lk 7:41; 1 Cor 15:6.*

πέντε indecl. *five* Mt 14:17, 19; 16:9. [*pentateuch, πέντε + τεῦχος*]

πεντεκαιδέκατος, η, ον *fifteenth* Lk 3:1.*

πεντήκοντα indecl. *fifty* Mk 6:40; Lk 7:41; 9:14; 16:6; J 8:57; 21:11; Ac 13:20.*

πεντηκοστή, ῆς, ἡ *Pentecost,* lit. 'fiftieth,' i.e. the festival celebrated on the fiftieth day after Passover Ac 2:1; 20:16; 1 Cor 16:8.*

πέπεισμαι pf. pass. ind. of *πείθω.*

πεπιστεύκεισαν plupf. act. ind. 3 pl. of *πιστεύω,* without augment.

πέποιθα 2 pf. act. ind. of *πείθω.*

πεποιήκεισαν plupf. act. ind. 3 pl. of *ποιέω,* without augment.

πεποίθησις, εως, ἡ *trust, confidence* 2 Cor 1:15; 3:4; 8:22; 10:2; Eph 3:12; Phil 3:4.*

πέπονθα 2 pf. act. ind. of *πάσχω.*

πέπρακα and **πεπραμένος** 1 pf. act. ind. and pass. ptc. of *πιπράσκω.*

πέπραχα 1 pf. act. ind. of *πράσσω.*

πέπτωκα 1 pf. act. ind. of *πίπτω.*

πέπωκα 1 pf. act. ind. of *πίνω.*

περ enclitic particle, with intensive and extensive force, strengthening the word to which it is added; see *διόπερ, ἐάνπερ, εἴπερ, ἐπειδήπερ, ἐπείπερ, ἤπερ, καθάπερ, καίπερ, ὅσπερ, ὥσπερ, ὡσπερεί.*

Πέραια, ας, ἡ *Peraea,* part of Palestine east of the Jordan Lk 6:17 v.l.*

περαιτέρω adv. *further, beyond* Ac 19:39.*

πέραν adv. *on the other side—1.* subst. *τὸ πέραν the shore* or *land on the other side* Mt 8:18, 28; Mk 6:45; 8:13.—**2.** functions as prep. w. gen. *to the other side* J 6:1, 17; 10:40. *On the other side* Mt 19:1; Mk 5:1; J 1:28; 6:22, 25. *πέραν τοῦ Ἰορδάνου on the other side* (= east) *of the Jordan,* i.e. *Peraea* Mt 4:15, 25; Mk 3:8; 10:1.

πέρας, ατος, τό *end, limit, boundary* Mt 12:42; Lk 11:31; Ro 10:18; Hb 6:16; Ac 13:33 v.l.*

Πέργαμος, ου, ἡ or **Πέργαμον, ου, τό** *Pergamus* or *Pergamum,* an important city in northwest Asia Minor Rv 1:11; 2:12.*

Πέργη, ης, ἡ *Perga,* a city in Pamphylia, near the south central coast of Asia Minor Ac 13:13f; 14:25.*

περί prep. w. gen. and acc.—**1.** with the genitive *about, concerning* Mt 18:19; 22:42; Lk 2:17; 9:9; J 8:13f, 18; Ac 17:32;

24:24; 1 Cor 7:1; 2 Cor 9:1; Jd 3.—On account of, because of Lk 3:15; 19:37; 24:4; J 8:26; 10:33.—With regard to, with reference to Ac 15:2; 1 Cor 7:37; Col 4:10; Hb 11:20.—For Lk 6:28; Ac 12:5; Ro 8:3; Col 1:3; 2 Th 1:11; 3:1; Hb 10:18, 26; 13:18; 1 Pt 3:18.—2. with the accusative around, about, near Mt 8:18; 18:6; 20:3, 5f, 9; Mk 1:6; 3:34; 4:10; Lk 13:8; Ac 10:3; 28:7. οἱ περὶ Παῦλον Paul and his companions Ac 13:13.—With Lk 10:40f; Ac 19:25.—With regard or respect to 1 Ti 6:21; 2 Ti 2:18; Tit 2:7.—τὰ περὶ ἐμέ how I am getting along Phil 2:23. [peri-, combining form, as in peripatetic, periscope]

περιάγω—1. trans. lead around, have someone with oneself or accompanying oneself 1 Cor 9:5.—2. intrans. go around, go about Mt 4:23; 9:35; 23:15; Mk 6:6; Ac 13:11.*

περιαιρέω take away (from around), remove 2 Cor 3:16; Hb 10:11. Cast off or slip an anchor Ac 27:40. Pass. be abandoned 27:20.

περιάπτω kindle Lk 22:55.*

περιαστράπτω trans. shine around Ac 9:3; 22:6 v.l. Intrans. shine 22:6.*

περιβάλλω throw, lay, or put around Lk 19:43 v.l. Put on an article of clothing Mt 6:31; Mk 14:51; Lk 12:27; J 19:2; Ac 12:8; Rv 19:8. περιβέβλημαί τι have put something on, wear Mk 16:5; Rv 7:9, 13; 11:3.

περιβαλοῦ, περιβαλῶ, περιβέβλημαι 2 aor. mid. impv., fut. act. ind., and pf. pass. ind. of περιβάλλω.

περιβλέπω look around (at) Mk 3:5, 34; 5:32; 9:8; 10:23; 11:11; Lk 6:10.*

περιβόλαιον, ου, τό covering, wrap, cloak: cloak Hb 1:12; covering 1 Cor 11:15.*

περιδέω bind or wrap around J 11:44.*

περιέβαλον 2 aor. act. ind. of περιβάλλω.

περιεδέδετο plupf. pass. ind. 3 sing. of περιδέω.

περιέδραμον 2 aor. act. ind. of περιτρέχω.

περιεζωσμένος pf. pass. ptc. of περιζώννυμι.

περιέθηκα 1 aor. act. ind. of περιτίθημι.

περιελεῖν, περιελεών 2 aor. act. inf. and ptc. of περιαιρέω.

περιέπεσον 2 aor. act. ind. of περιπίπτω.

περιεργάζομαι be a busybody 2 Th 3:11.*

περίεργος, ον meddlesome, curious as noun a busybody 1 Ti 5:13. τὰ περίεργα magic Ac 19:19.*

περιέρχομαι go from place to place Ac 19:13; wander about Hb 11:37; cf. Ac 13:6 v.l. π. τὰς οἰκίας go about from house to house 1 Ti 5:13. Sail around Ac 28:13.*

περιέστησαν, περιεστώς 2 aor. act. ind. 3 pl. and pf. act. ptc. of περιίστημι.

περιέσχον 2 aor. act. ind. of περιέχω.

περιέτεμον, περιετμήθην 2 aor. act. ind. and 1 aor. pass. ind. of περιτέμνω.

περιέχω—1. seize, come upon lit. 'encircle' Lk 5:9.—2. contain trans. Ac 15:23 v.l.; 23:25 v.l. Intrans. περιέχει it stands or says 1 Pt 2:6.*

περιζώννυμι and περιζωννύω gird about—1. act., with double acc. gird someone (about) with something pass. Lk 12:35; Rv 1:13; 15:6.—2. mid. gird oneself Lk 12:37; 17:8; Ac 12:8 v.l. Fig. Eph 6:14.*

περιζωσάμενος, περιζώσομαι 1 aor. mid. ptc. and fut. mid. ind. of περιζώννυμι.

περιῆλθον 2 aor. act. ind. of περιέρχομαι.

περιῃρεῖτο impf. pass. 3 sing. of περιαιρέω.

περιθείς 2 aor. act. ptc. of περιτίθημι.

περίθεσις, εως, ἡ putting on 1 Pt 3:3.*

περιΐστασο pres. mid. impv. 2 sing. (2 Ti 2:16; Tit 3:9) of περιΐστημι.

περιΐστημι—1. stand around J 11:42; Ac 25:7.—2. avoid, shun 2 Ti 2:16; Tit 3:9.*

περικάθαρμα, ατος, τό refuse, offscouring, scapegoat 1 Cor 4:13.*

περικαθίζω sit around Lk 22:55 v.l.*

περικαλύπτω *conceal, cover* Mk 14:65; Lk 22:64; Hb 9:4.*

περίκειμαι—**1.** *lie* or *be placed around* Mk 9:42; Lk 17:2. *Surround* Hb 12:1.— **2.** περίκειμαί τι *wear something, have something on* Ac 28:20. Fig. *be subject to* Hb 5:2.*

περικεφαλαία, ας, ἡ *helmet* fig. Eph 6:17; 1 Th 5:8.*

περικρατής, ές *having power, being in command* περικρατεῖς γενέσθαι τῆς σκάφης *to get the boat under control* Ac 27:16.*

περικρύβω *hide, conceal* Lk 1:24.*

περικυκλόω *surround, encircle* Lk 19:43.*

περιλάμπω *shine around* Lk 2:9; Ac 26:13.*

περιλείπομαι *remain, be left behind* 1 Th 4:15, 17.*

περιλείχω *lick all around, lick off* Lk 16:21 v.l.*

περίλυπος, ον *very sad, deeply grieved* Mt 26:38; Mk 6:26; 14:34; Lk 18:23f.*

περιμένω *wait for* Ac 1:4; *wait* 10:24 v.l.*

πέριξ adv. *(all) around* Ac 5:16.*

περιοικέω *live in the neighborhood of* Lk 1:65.*

περίοικος, ον *living around* οἱ π. *the neighbors* Lk 1:58.*

περιούσιος, ον *chosen, special* Tit 2:14.*

περιοχή, ῆς, ἡ in Ac 8:32 can mean either *content, wording,* or *portion.**

περιπατέω *go about, walk around*—**1.** lit. *walk around, go about, walk, go* Mt 9:5; Mk 11:27; Lk 11:44; J 6:19; 1 Pt 5:8; Rv 2:1; 3:4.—**2.** fig. *walk in the sense live, conduct oneself* Mk 7:5; J 8:12; Ac 21:21; Ro 6:4; 8:4; 1 Cor 7:17; 2 Cor 5:7; Gal 5:16; Eph 4:1; Col 3:7; 1 Th 2:12; 2 Th 3:6; Hb 13:9; 1 J 2:6; 2 J 4; 3 J 4. [peripatetic]

περιπείρω *pierce through* fig. 1 Ti 6:10.*

περιπεσών 2 aor. act. ptc. of περι-πίπτω.

περιπίπτω *fall in with, encounter* w. dat., lit. *fall into the hands of* Lk 10:30; *strike* Ac 27:41. Fig. *become involved in* Js 1:2.*

περιποιέω mid.—**1.** *save, preserve* Lk 17:33.—**2.** *acquire, obtain, gain for oneself* Ac 20:28; 1 Ti 3:13.*

περιποίησις, εως, ἡ *saving* Hb 10:39. *Gaining* 1 Th 5:9; 2 Th 2:14. *Possession, property* Eph 1:14; 1 Pt 2:9.*

περιρεραμμένον, περιρεραντισμένον pf. pass. ptc. forms of περι(ρ)ραίνω and περι(ρ)ραντίζω, respectively Rv 19:13 v.l.

περι(ρ)ραίνω and **περι(ρ)ραντίζω** *sprinkle (all around)* Rv 19:13 v.l.*

περι(ρ)ρήγνυμι *tear off* Ac 16:22.*

περισπάω *be* or *become distracted, overburdened* Lk 10:40.*

περισσεία, ας, ἡ *surplus, abundance* Ro 5:17; 2 Cor 8:2; 10:15; Js 1:21.*

περίσσευμα, ατος, τό—**1.** *abundance, fullness* Mt 12:34; Lk 6:45; 2 Cor 8:14.— **2.** *what remains, scraps* Mk 8:8.*

περισσεύω—**1.** intrans.—**a.** of things *be more than enough, be left over* Mt 14:20; 15:37; Lk 9:17; J 6:12f.—*Be present in abundance* Mt 5:20; Mk 12:44; Lk 21:4; Ro 5:15; 2 Cor 1:5; Phil 1:26.—*Be extremely rich* or *abundant, overflow* Ro 3:7; 2 Cor 3:9; 8:2; 9:12.— *Grow* Ac 16:5; Phil 1:9.—**b.** of persons *have an abundance, abound, be rich* w. gen. *of* or *in something* Ro 15:13; 1 Cor 8:8; 2 Cor 9:8b; Phil 4:12, 18.—*Be outstanding, be prominent, excel* 1 Cor 14:12; 15:58; 2 Cor 8:7; Col 2:7. *Progress* 1 Th 4:1, 10.—**2.** trans. *cause to abound, make extremely rich* Mt 13:12; 25:29; Lk 15:17; 2 Cor 4:15; 9:8a; Eph 1:8; 1 Th 3:12.

περισσός, ή, όν *exceeding the usual number* or *size*—**1.** *extraordinary, remarkable* Mt 5:47. τὸ περισσόν *the advantage* Ro 3:1.—**2.** *abundant, profuse* J 10:10. *Superfluous, unnecessary* 2 Cor 9:1.—**3.** in the comparative sense τὸ περισσὸν τούτων *whatever is more than this* Mt 5:37.—ἐκ περισσοῦ *extremely* Mk 6:51.*

περισσότερος, τέρα, ον *greater, more*—**1.** with a subst. Mk 12:40; Lk 20:47; 1 Cor 12:23f; 2 Cor 2:7.—**2.** *even more* Lk 12:48; 1 Cor 15:10. Cf. Mt 11:9; Mk 12:33; Lk 7:26; 12:4; 2 Cor 10:8.—**3.** the neut. sing. as adv. *even* *more* Hb 6:17; 7:15. *So much more* Mk 7:36.

περισσοτέρως adv.—**1.** *(even) more* Mk 15:14 v.l.; *to a much greater degree* 2 Cor 11:23; Gal 1:14; cf. 2 Cor 12:15. *So much (the) more* Phil 1:14; Hb 2:1; 13:19.—**2.** *especially* 2 Cor 1:12; 2:4; 7:13, 15; 1 Th 2:17.*

περισσῶς adv. *exceedingly, beyond measure, very* Ac 26:11.—*More, even more* Mt 27:23; Mk 10:26; 15:14.*

περιστερά, ᾶς, ἡ *pigeon, dove* Mt 3:16; Mk 11:15; Lk 3:22; J 1:32.

περιτεμεῖν 2 aor. act. inf. of *περιτέμνω.*

περιτέμνω *circumcise*—**1.** lit. Lk 1:59; 2:21; J 7:22; Ac 7:8; 15:1, 5; 16:3; 21:21; 1 Cor 7:18; Gal 2:3; 5:2f; 6:12f.—**2.** fig. of baptism Col 2:11.*

περιτέτμημαι pf. pass. ind. of *περιτέμνω.*

περιτιθέασιν pres. act. ind. 3 pl. of *περιτίθημι.*

περιτίθημι *put* or *place around, on* Mt 21:33; 27:28, 48; Mk 12:1; 15:17, 36; J 19:29. Fig. *grant, show* 1 Cor 12:23.*

περιτμηθῆναι 1 aor. pass. inf. of *περιτέμνω.*

περιτομή, ῆς, ἡ *circumcision*—**1.** lit. J 7:22f; Ac 7:8; Ro 3:11; 1 Cor 7:19; Gal 5:11.—**2.** fig., *of spiritual circumcision* Ro 2:29; Col 2:11.—**3.** *those who are circumcised,* lit., *of Jews* Ac 10:45; Ro 3:30; Gal 2:7–9; Col 3:11. Fig., *of Christians* Phil 3:3.

περιτρέπω *turn, drive* (εἰς μανίαν) *insane* Ac 26:24.*

περιτρέχω *run about, go about in* Mk 6:55.*

περιφέρω *carry about, carry here and there* Mk 6:55; 2 Cor 4:10. Fig., pass. Eph 4:14; Hb 13:9 v.l.* [*periphery*]

περιφρονέω *look down on, despise* w. gen. Tit 2:15.*

περίχωρος, ον *neighboring* as subst. ἡ περίχωρος (γῆ) *the region around, neighborhood* with its inhabitants Mt 14:35; Mk 1:28; Lk 4:14, 37; 8:37; Ac 14:6.

περίψημα, ατος, τό *dirt, offscouring* fig. 1 Cor 4:13.*

περπερεύομαι *boast, brag* 1 Cor 13:4.*

Περσίς, ίδος, ἡ *Persis* Ro 16:12.*

πέρυσι adv. *last year, a year ago ἀπὸ πέρυσι a year ago, since last year* 2 Cor 8:10; 9:2.*

πεσεῖν, πεσών, πεσοῦμαι 2 aor. act. inf. and ptc. and fut. mid. ind. of *πίπτω.*

πετεινόν, οῦ, τό *bird* Mt 6:26; 13:32; Mk 4:4; Lk 12:24; 13:19; Ac 10:12; Ro 1:23; Js 3:7.

πέτομαι *fly* Rv 4:7; 8:13; 12:14; 14:6; 19:17.*

πέτρα, ας, ἡ *rock* lit. Mt 7:24f; 27:51, 60; Lk 8:6, 13; Ro 9:33; 1 Cor 10:4; 1 Pt 2:8; Rv 6:15f. Fig. Mt 16:18. [Cf. *petrify.*]

Πέτρος, ου, ὁ *Peter,* surname of the head of the twelve disciples; his name was originally Simon, q.v. The name Π. appears 156 times. The following passages illustrate some aspects of his role in the N.T.: Mt 16:16, 18; Mk 3:16; Lk 5:8; J 18:10; Ac 15:7; Gal 2:8; 1 Pt 1:1; 2 Pt 1:1.

πετρώδης, ες *rocky, stony* τὸ πετρῶδες and τὰ πετρώδη *rocky ground* Mt 13:5, 20; Mk 4:5, 16.*

πεφίμωσο pf. pass. impv. 2 sing. of *φιμόω.*

πήγανον, ου, τό *rue* (Ruta graveolens), a garden herb Lk 11:42.*

πηγή, ῆς, ἡ *spring* of water, *fountain*—**1.** lit. Mk 5:29; Js 3:11; 2 Pt 2:17; Rv 8:10; 14:7; 16:4. *Well* J 4:6.—**2.** symbolic J 4:14; Rv 7:17; 21:6.*

πήγνυμι *set up* Hb 8:2.*

πηδάλιον, ου, τό *steering paddle, rudder* Ac 27:40; Js 3:4.*

πηλίκος, η, ον interrogative pron. used in exclamatory statements: *how large* Gal 6:11. *How great* Hb 7:4.*

πηλός, οῦ, ὁ *clay* Ro 9:21. *Mud* J 9:6, 11, 14f.*

πήρα, ας, ἡ *knapsack, traveler's bag* Mt 10:10; Mk 6:8; Lk 9:3; 10:4; 22:35f.*

πηρόω *disable, maim* only as v.l. in the following passages: Mk 8:17; J 12:40; Ac 5:3; Ro 11:7.*

πήρωσις, εως, ἡ *nearsightedness, blindness* fig. Mk 3:5 v.l.*

πῆχυς, εως, ὁ *cubit*, a measure of length, about 18 inches or .462 of a meter J 21:8; Rv 21:17. For usage in Mt 6:27 and Lk 12:25 see ἡλικία 1.*

πιάζω *take (hold of)* Ac 3:7. *Seize, arrest, take into custody* J 7:30, 32, 44; 8:20; 10:39; 11:57; Ac 12:4; 2 Cor 11:32. *Catch* J 21:3, 10; Rv 19:20.*

πίε, πιεῖν 2 aor. act. impv. and inf. of πίνω.

πιέζω *press down* pass. Lk 6:38.*

πίεσαι fut. mid. ind. 2 sing. (Lk 17:8) of πίνω.

πιθανολογία, ας, ἡ *persuasive speech, plausible* (but false) *argument* Col 2:4.*

πιθός another spelling for πειθός.

πικραίνω *make bitter* lit. Rv 8:11; 10:9f. Fig. *embitter* Col 3:19.*

πικρανῶ fut. act. ind. of πικραίνω.

πικρία, ας, ἡ *bitterness* lit. Ac 8:23; Hb 12:15. Fig. *bitterness, animosity, anger* Ro 3:14; Eph 4:31.*

πικρός, ά, όν *bitter* lit. Js 3:11; fig. 3:14.* [*picr-, picro-*, combining forms in such words as *picrite, picrotoxin*]

πικρῶς adv. *bitterly* Mt 26:75; Lk 22:62.*

Πιλᾶτος, ου, ὁ Pontius *Pilate*, Roman prefect of Judaea 26–36 A.D. Mt 27 and Mk 15 passim; Lk 3:1; 13:1; ch. 23 passim; J 18–19 passim; Ac 3:13; 4:27; 13:28, 29 v.l.; 1 Ti 6:13.*

πίμπλημι *fill* lit. Mt 22:10; Lk 1:15, 41, 67; Ac 3:10. Fig. *be fulfilled* Lk 21:22; *come to an end* Lk 1:23, 57; 2:6, 21f.

πίμπρημι in Ac 28:6 the pres. pass. inf. πίμπρασθαι may mean either *burn with fever* or *become distended, swell up*.*

πινακίδιον, ου, τό *little* (wooden) *tablet* for writing notes Lk 1:63.*

πινακίς, ίδος, ἡ *little* (wooden) *writing tablet* Lk 1:63 v.l.*

πίναξ, ακος, ὁ *platter, dish* Mt 14:8, 11; Mk 6:25, 28; Lk 11:39.*

πίνω *drink*—**1.** lit. Mt 6:25, 31; 11:18; Mk 16:18; Lk 1:15; J 6:53f, 56; 1 Cor 10:21.—**2.** fig. Mk 10:38f; J 7:37; Hb 6:7; Rv 14:10.

πιότης, τητος, ἡ *fatness, richness* Ro 11:17.*

πιπράσκω *sell* Mt 13:46; 18:25; 26:9; Ac 2:45; 4:34; 5:4. Fig. Ro 7:14.

πίπτω *fall*, the passive of the idea conveyed in βάλλω—**1.** lit. Mt 15:27; Mk 9:20; Lk 8:7; 21:24; Ac 20:9; Rv 1:17. *Fall down* as a sign of devotion Mt 2:11; 18:26, 29; Rv 5:14. *Fall to pieces, collapse* Mt 7:25, 27; Lk 13:4; Hb 11:30; Rv 11:13.—**2.** fig. Ac 1:26; 13:11; Rv 7:16. *Fail, become invalid* Lk 16:17; 1 Cor 13:8. *Be destroyed* Rv 14:8; 18:2. In a moral or cultic sense *go astray, be ruined, fall* Ro 11:11, 22; Hb 4:11; 1 Cor 10:12; Rv 2:5.

Πισιδία, ας, ἡ *Pisidia*, a region in central Asia Minor Ac 14:24; 13:14 v.l.*

Πισίδιος, ία, ιον *Pisidian* Ac 13:14.*

πιστεύω—**1.** *believe, believe in, be convinced of, give credence to* Mt 21:25, 32; Mk 16:14; Lk 1:20; J 2:22; 8:24; Ac 8:37b; Ro 4:18; 1 Cor 13:7; Gal 3:6; 2 Th 1:10b.—**2.** *believe (in), trust* in a special sense, with God or Christ as object: J 6:30; 14:1; 16:9; Ac 5:14; 16:34; Ro 4:5, 24; 1 Cor 14:22; Gal 2:16; 3:22; 1 Ti 3:16; Hb 4:3; 1 Pt 2:7. *Have confidence* Mt 8:13; 9:28; 21:22; Mk 9:23f; 2 Cor 4:13.—**3.** *entrust* Lk 16:11; J 2:24. Pass. Ro 3:2; 1 Cor 9:17; Gal 2:7.—**4.** *think, hold*, or *consider (possible)* J 9:18; Ro 14:2; cf. 1 Cor 13:7.

πιστικός, ή, όν may mean *genuine, unadulterated*, or it may designate a certain kind of nard, e.g. pistachio Mk 14:3; J 12:3.*

πίστις, εως, ἡ *faith, trust, commitment*—**1.** as a characteristic or quality *faithfulness, reliability, loyalty, commitment* Mt 23:23; Ro 3:3; Gal 5:22; Tit 2:10.—**2.** that which evokes confidence, *solemn promise, oath* 1 Ti 5:12; *proof, pledge* Ac 17:31; τὴν π. τετήρηκα *I have honored my obligation* 2 Ti 4:7.—**3.** *trust, confidence, faith* in the active sense = 'believing,' esp. of relation to God and Christ Mt 9:2; Mk 11:22; Lk 18:42; Ac 14:9; 26:18; Ro 4:5, 9, 11–13; Gal 2:16; Eph 1:15; Col 2:12; Hb 12:2; Js 1:6; 1 Pt 1:21. *Faith* as commitment, Christianity Lk 18:8; Ro 1:5, 8; 1 Cor 2:5; 13:13; 2 Cor 1:24; Gal 3 passim; Js 1:3; 1 Pt 1:9. *Conviction* Ro 14:22f. Faith defined Hb 11:1.—**4.**

160 πιστός—πλῆθος

That which is believed, *body of faith* or *belief, doctrine* Gal 1:23; Jd 3, 20; cf. 1 Ti 1:19.

πιστός, ή, όν—1. *trustworthy, faithful, dependable, inspiring trust* or *faith* Mt 25:21, 23; Lk 16:10–12; 1 Cor 1:9; 7:25; Col 4:7; 1 Ti 1:12, 15; 2 Ti 2:2, 13; Tit 3:8; Hb 2:17; 10:23; Rv 2:13.—2. *trusting, cherishing faith* or *trust*, also *believing, faithful* J 20:27; Ac 16:15; Gal 3:9; Eph 1:1. Of Christian *believers* Ac 10:45; 16:1; 1 Ti 4:3, 12; 6:2.

πιστόω *feel confidence, be convinced* 2 Ti 3:14.*

πίω 2 aor. act. subj. of πίνω.

πλανάω—1. *lead astray, cause to wander* fig. *mislead, deceive* Mt 24:4f, 11; J 7:12; 1 J 1:8; Rv 2:20; 20:3, 8, 10.—2. *go astray, be misled* or *deluded, wander about* lit. and fig. Mt 18:12f; Lk 21:8; 1 Cor 15:33; 2 Ti 3:13; Tit 3:3; Hb 11:38; Js 5:19; 1 Pt 2:25; 2 Pt 2:15; Rv 18:23. *Be mistaken, deceive oneself* Mk 12:24, 27; Gal 6:7.

πλάνη, ης, ή *wandering* from the path of truth, *error, delusion, deception* Mt 27:64; Ro 1:27; Eph 4:14; 1 Th 2:3; 2 Th 2:11; Js 5:20; 2 Pt 2:18; 3:17; 1 J 4:6; Jd 11.*

πλάνης, ητος, ό v.l. in Jd 13 for πλανήτης, with the same meaning.*

πλανήτης, ου, ό *wanderer* ἀστέρες πλανῆται *wandering stars* Jd 13.* [*planet*]

πλάνος, ον *leading astray, deceitful* 1 Ti 4:1. ὁ πλάνος as noun *deceiver, impostor* Mt 27:63; 2 Cor 6:8; 2 J 7.*

πλάξ, πλακός, ή *flat stone, tablet, table* 2 Cor 3:3; Hb 9:4.*

πλάσας 1 aor. act. ptc. of πλάσσω.

πλάσμα, ατος, τό *that which is formed* or *molded* Ro 9:20.*

πλάσσω *form, mold* Ro 9:20; 1 Ti 2:13.*

πλαστός, ή, όν *made up, fabricated, false* 2 Pt 2:3.* [*plastic*]

πλατεῖα, ας, ή *wide road, street* Mt 6:5; 12:19; Lk 10:10; 13:26; 14:21; Ac 5:15; Rv 11:8; 21:21; 22:2.*

πλάτος, ους, τό *breadth, width* Eph 3:18; Rv 20:9; 21:16.*

πλατύνω *make broad, enlarge* lit. Mt 23:5. Fig. 2 Cor 6:11, 13.*

πλατύς, εῖα, ύ *broad, wide* Mt 7:13.*

πλέγμα, ατος, τό *anything woven* or *braided* of hair 1 Ti 2:9.*

πλείων, πλειόνως, πλεῖστος see πολύς.

πλέκω *weave, plait* Mt 27:29; Mk 15:17; J 19:2.*

πλέον see πολύς. [*pleonasm*]

πλεονάζω—1. intrans. *be* or *become more, be present in abundance, grow, increase* Ro 5:20; 6:1; 2 Cor 4:15; Phil 4:17; 2 Th 1:3; 2 Pt 1:8. *Have more than is necessary* 2 Cor 8:15.—2. trans. *cause to increase* 1 Th 3:12.*

πλεονάσαι 1 aor. act. opt. 3 sing. of πλεονάζω.

πλεονεκτέω *take advantage of, outwit, defraud, cheat* 2 Cor 2:11; 7:2; 12:17f; 1 Th 4:6.*

πλεονέκτης, ου, ό *one who is greedy, a covetous person* 1 Cor 5:10f; 6:10; Eph 5:5.*

πλεονεξία, ας, ή *greediness, insatiableness, avarice, covetousness* Mk 7:22; Lk 12:15; Ro 1:29; 2 Cor 9:5; Eph 4:19; 5:3; Col 3:5; 1 Th 2:5; 2 Pt 2:3, 14.*

πλευρά, ᾶς, ή *side* Mt 27:49 v.l.; J 19:34; 20:20, 25, 27; Ac 12:7.* [*pleurisy*]

πλέω *travel by sea, sail* Lk 8:23; Ac 21:3; 27:2, 6, 24; Rv 18:17.*

πληγή, ῆς, ή *blow, stroke*—1. lit. Lk 12:48; Ac 16:23; 2 Cor 11:23.—2. *wound, bruise* Ac 16:33; Rv 13:12, 14.—3. *plague, misfortune* Rv 9:18, 20; 18:4, 8; 22:18.

πλῆθος, ους, τό—1. *quantity* or *number* Hb 11:12.—2. *large number, multitude*—a. of things w. gen. Lk 5:6; *bundle* Ac 28:3; *host* Js 5:20.—b. of persons—α. *crowd, throng, host* Mk 3:7f; Lk 2:13; 6:17; Ac 5:14; 21:36.—β. *a meeting, assembly* Lk 23:1; Ac 23:7.—γ. *people, populace, population* Lk 8:37; Ac 2:6; 5:16; 14:4; 25:24.—δ. *community, church, fellowship* Lk 1:10; 19:37; Ac 4:32; 6:5; 15:12, 30; 19:9. [*plethora*]

πληθύνω—1. trans., act. and pass. *increase, multiply* Mt 24:12; Ac 6:7; 9:31; 12:24; 2 Cor 9:10; Hb 6:14; 1 Pt 1:2.— **2.** intrans. *grow, increase* Ac 6:1.

πλήκτης, ου, ὁ *pugnacious man, bully* 1 Ti 3:3; Tit 1:7.*

πλήμμυρα, ης, ἡ *high water, flood* Lk 6:48.*

πλήν adv.—**1.** used as a conjunction *only, nevertheless, however, but* Mt 11:22, 24; 26:39; Lk 6:24, 35; 11:41; 22:21f, 42; 23:28.—*Only, in any case, however, but* 1 Cor 11:11; Eph 5:33; Phil 3:16; 4:14; Rv 2:25.—πλήν ὅτι *except that* Ac 20:23.—**2.** used as prep. w. gen. *except* Mk 12:32; Ac 8:1; 15:28; 20:23; 27:22.

πλήρης, ες—1. *filled, full* Mt 15:37; Mk 8:19; Lk 4:1; 5:12; J 1:14; Ac 7:55; 9:36; 11:24; 13:10.—**2.** *complete, full, in full* 2 J 8. πλήρης σῖτος *fully ripened grain* Mk 4:28.

πληροφορέω—1. *fill (completely), fulfill* 2 Ti 4:5, 17; *accomplish* Lk 1:1.—**2.** *convince fully* pass. Ro 4:21; 14:5; Col 4:12.*

πληροφορία, ας, ἡ *full assurance, certainty* Col 2:2; 1 Th 1:5; Hb 6:11; 10:22. For the passages from Col and Hb and Ro 15:29 v.l. *fullness* is also possible.*

πληρόω—1. *fill, make full* Mt 13:48; Lk 3:5; J 12:3; 16:6; Ac 2:2, 28; 5:28; Ro 1:29; Eph 5:18; Phil 4:18; 2 Ti 1:4.—**2.** of time *fill up, complete, reach its end* pass. Mk 1:15; J 7:8; Ac 7:23, 30; 9:23; 24:27.—**3.** *bring to completion, finish* something already begun J 3:29; 17:13; 2 Cor 10:6; Phil 2:2; Col 1:25. Gal 5:14 may be classed here or under 4 below.—**4.** *fulfill* a prophecy, promise, etc. Mt 1:22; 5:17; 13:35; 26:54, 56; Mk 14:49; Lk 9:31; 22:16; J 18:9, 32; 19:24, 36; Ro 13:8; Gal 5:14 (see 3 above); Col 4:17.—**5.** *complete, finish, bring to an end* Lk 7:1; 21:24; Ac 12:25; 13:25; 14:26; 19:21.

πλήρωμα, ατος, τό—1. *that which fills*—**a.** *that which fills (up), content* or *contents.* ἡ γῆ καὶ πλ. αὐτῆς *the earth and everything that is in it* 1 Cor 10:26. κλάσματα δώδεκα κοφίνων πληρώματα (enough) *pieces to fill twelve baskets* Mk 6:43; cf. 8:20.—**b.** *that which* makes something *full* or *complete, supplement, complement* lit. *patch* Mt 9:16; Mk 2:21. Perh. *complement* for Eph 1:23, though mng. 2 is more likely.—**2.** *that which is full of something;* in this case Eph 1:23 would mean *(that) which is full of him who.*—**3.** *that which is brought to fullness* or *completion*—**a.** *full number* Ro 11:25. The word in Ro 11:12 may belong here or under 4 below.—**b.** *sum total, fullness, abundance* Ro 15:29. πᾶν τὸ πλ. τῆς θεότητος *the full measure of deity* Col 2:9; cf. 1:19.—J 1:16; Eph 3:19. For Eph 4:13 see μέτρον and ἡλικία.—**4.** *fulfilling, fulfillment* Ro 13:10; perh. 11:12 (see 3a above).—**5.** *the state of being full, fullness* of time Gal 4:4; Eph 1:10.* [*pleroma*]

πλήσας, πλησθείς, πλησθῆναι, πλησθήσομαι 1 aor. participles act. and pass., 1 aor. pass. inf., and 1 fut. pass. of πίμπλημι.

πλησίον adv. *near, close by*—**1.** as noun (ὁ) πλησίον *the neighbor, the one who is near* or *close by, the fellow human being* Mt 5:43; Mk 12:31, 33; Lk 10:27, 29, 36; Ac 7:27; Ro 13:9f; 15:2; Gal 5:14; Js 4:12.—**2.** as prep. w. gen. *near, close to* J 4:5.

πλησμονή, ῆς, ἡ *gratification, indulgence* Col 2:23.*

πλήσσω *strike* pass. Rv 8:12.*

πλοιάριον, ου, τό diminutive of πλοῖον, though the diminutive sense is not always present: *small ship, boat, skiff* Mk 3:9 (cf. 4:1); 4:36 v.l.; Lk 5:2 v.l.; J 6:22–24; 21:8.*

πλοῖον, ου, τό *ship* of rather large seafaring vessels Ac 20:13, 38; 21:2f, 6; 27 passim; Js 3:4; Rv 8:9; 18:19. *Boat* of fishing vessels on Lake Gennesaret Mt 4:21f; 9:1; Mk 1:19f; 6:51, 54; J 6:19, 21f; 21:3.

πλοκή, ῆς, ἡ *braiding, braid* 1 Pt 3:3 v.l.*

πλόος, contracted πλοῦς, gen. πλοός, acc. πλοῦν, ὁ *voyage, navigation* Ac 21:7; 27:9f.*

πλούσιος, ία, ιον *rich, wealthy*—**1.** lit. Mt 19:23f; 27:57; Mk 12:41; Lk 12:16; 16:1, 19; 18:23; 19:2. As noun *rich man* Lk 16:21f; 21:1; Js 1:10f; 2:6; 5:1; Rv

6:15.—2. fig. 2 Cor 8:9; Eph 2:4; Js 2:5; Rv 2:9.

πλουσίως adv. *richly, abundantly* Col 3:16; 1 Ti 6:17; Tit 3:6; 2 Pt 1:11.*

πλουτέω *be rich;* aor. *become rich;* pf. *have become rich*—**1.** lit. Lk 1:53; 1 Ti 6:9; Rv 18:3, 15, 19.—2. fig. Lk 12:21; Ro 10:12; 1 Cor 4:8; 2 Cor 8:9; 1 Ti 6:18; Rv 3:17f.*

πλουτίζω *make rich* fig. 1 Cor 1:5; 2 Cor 6:10; 9:11.*

πλοῦτος, ου, ὁ or in nom. and acc. only **πλοῦτος, τό** *wealth, riches*—**1.** lit. Mt 13:22; Mk 4:19; Lk 8:14; 1 Ti 6:17; Js 5:2; Rv 18:17.—**2.** fig. *a wealth, abundance* Ro 9:23; 11:12, 33; 2 Cor 8:2; Eph 1:7, 18; 3:8, 16; Phil 4:19; Hb 11:26; Rv 5:12. [*plutocrat,* πλοῦτος + κρατεῖν]

πλύνω *wash* lit. and symbolically Lk 5:1; Rv 7:14; 22:14.*

πνεῦμα, ατος, τό—**1.** *blowing, breathing*—**a.** *wind* J 3:8a; Hb 1:7.—**b.** *the breathing out of air, breath* 2 Th 2:8.—**2.** *breath, (life-)spirit, soul,* that which gives life to the body Mt 27:50; Lk 8:55; 23:46; J 19:30; Ac 7:59; Js 2:26; Hb 12:23; 1 Pt 3:19; Rv 11:11.—**3.** *spirit* as part of the human personality—**a.** the immaterial part 1 Cor 5:3–5; 7:34; 2 Cor 7:1; Col 2:5; 1 Th 5:23; Hb 4:12.—**b.** the representative part of the inner life Mt 5:3; 26:41; Mk 2:8; 8:12; Lk 1:47; J 4:23; 11:33; 13:21; Ro 1:9; 2 Cor 2:13. One's *very self* Ro 8:16; Phil 4:23.—**c.** *spiritual state, state of mind, disposition* 1 Cor 4:21; Gal 6:1; Eph 4:23; 1 Pt 3:4.—**4.** *a spirit* as an independent being that cannot be perceived by the physical senses—**a.** as a description of God J 4:24a.—**b.** *lesser good spirits* or *spirit-beings* Ac 23:8f; Hb 1:14; 12:9; Rv 1:4; 5:6.—*Ghost* Lk 24:37, 39.—**c.** *evil spirits* Mk 1:23, 26f; Lk 11:24, 26; Ac 5:16; 16:18; 19:15f; Rv 18:2.—**5.** *the Spirit* as that which differentiates God from everything that is not God—**a.** the Spirit of God or Christ Mt 3:16; Lk 4:18; Ac 5:9; 16:7; Ro 8:9f; 1 Cor 2:11b, 12b, 14; Gal 4:6; Eph 3:16; 1 Pt 1:11.—**b.** *(the Holy) Spirit* Mt 3:11; 12:32; Mk 1:8, 10, 12; 3:29; Lk 2:26; 10:21; 12:10; J 1:32f; 3:34; 14:17; 16:13; Ac 1:8, 16; 8:15, 17, 19; 19:2; Ro 5:5; 1 Cor 3:16; 6:19; Eph 4:30; Col 1:8; 1 Th 1:6; Hb 10:15; 2 Pt 1:21.—Clearly with independent identity Mt 28:19; cf. 2 Cor 13:13.—**c.** of a *spirit* that is not from God 1 Cor 12:10; 2 Cor 11:4; 2 Th 2:2; 1 J 4:1–3. [*pneumatology*]

πνευματικός, ή, όν *pertaining to the spirit, spiritual*—**1.** *caused by* or *filled with the* (divine) *Spirit, pertaining* or *corresponding to the* (divine) *Spirit*—**a.** as adj. Ro 1:11; 7:14; 1 Cor 10:3f; 15:44; Eph 1:3; 5:19; Col 1:9; 3:16; 1 Pt 2:5. ὁ πνευματικὸς (ἄνθρωπος) in 1 Cor 2:15 means *the spiritual person,* whose powers of judgment are directed by the divine πνεῦμα. Cf. also 1 Cor 15:47 v.l.—**b.** subst. τὰ πνευματικά *spiritual things* or *matters* Ro 15:27; 1 Cor 2:13; 9:11; 15:46. *Spiritual gifts* 1 Cor 12:1; 14:1. ὁ πνευματικός *the one who possesses the Spirit* 1 Cor 3:1; 14:37; Gal 6:1.—**2.** *pertaining to* (evil) *spirits* subst. *spirit-forces* Eph 6:12.* [*pneumatic*]

πνευματικῶς adv. *spiritually, in a manner consistent with the* (divine) *Spirit* 1 Cor 2:14; 2:13 v.l. *In a spiritual* (allegorical) *way* Rv 11:8.*

πνέω *blow* of wind Mt 7:25, 27; Lk 12:55; J 3:8; 6:18; Ac 27:15 v.l.; 27:40; Rv 7:1.*

πνίγω *choke, strangle* Mt 13:7; 18:28. *Drown* Mk 5:13.*

πνικτός, ή, όν *strangled, choked to death* of animals killed for food without having the blood drained from them Ac 15:20, 29; 21:25.*

πνοή, ῆς, ἡ *wind* Ac 2:2. *Breath* 17:25.*

ποδαπός an older form of ποταπός.

ποδήρης, ες *reaching to the feet* as noun ὁ π. *the robe reaching to the feet* Rv 1:13.*

ποδονιπτήρ, ῆρος, ὁ *basin for washing the feet* J 13:5 v.l.

πόθεν adv. *from where, from which, whence?*—**1.** *from what place? from where?* Mt 15:33; Mk 8:4; Lk 13:25, 27; J 3:8; 9:29f; 19:9; Rv 2:5.—**2.** *from what source? brought about* or *given by whom? born of whom?* Mt 13:27, 54, 56; Lk 20:7; J 2:9; 7:27; Js 4:1.—

3. *how, why, in what way?* Mk 12:37; Lk 1:43; J 1:48; 6:5.

ποία, ας, ἡ *grass, herb.* This meaning was formerly assumed by some for Js 4:14; the form is better taken as the feminine of ποῖος.*

ποιέω I. act.—**1.** *do, make*—**a.** of external things *make, manufacture, produce* J 18:18; Ac 7:40; 9:39; Ro 9:21; Hb 8:5. *Create* Mk 10:6; Ac 7:50; 17:24; Rv 14:7.—**b.** *do, cause, accomplish,* also *keep, carry out, practice,* etc. Mt 7:22; Mk 1:17; 2:23; 11:3; Lk 19:18; J 2:23; 3:21; 8:39, 41; 12:16; Ac 3:12; 24:12; Ro 13:3f; 1 Cor 6:18; 2 Ti 4:5.— *Do with* Mt 27:22. *Establish* Eph 2:15. *Give* Lk 14:12, 16. *Celebrate* Hb 11:28. *Yield, bear* Mt 3:10; Rv 22:2. *Claim, pretend* J 19:7, 12. *Exercise* Rv 13:12a.—**c.** specialized expressions: *get, gain* Lk 12:33; 16:9; J 4:1.—*Assume, suppose* Mt 12:33.—*Take* outside Ac 5:34.—*Spend, stay* Ac 15:33; 18:23; 20:3; 2 Cor 11:25; Js 4:13.—**2.** *do, act, proceed* Mt 12:12; 20:5; Mk 15:8; Lk 2:27; 16:8; Ac 10:33. *Work, be active* Mt 20:12a; Rv 13:5.—**II.** mid. *make* or *do* something *for oneself* or *of oneself* Lk 5:33; J 14:23; Ro 1:9; Phil 1:4; 2 Pt 1:10. *Form* Ac 23:13. σπουδὴν π. *be eager* Jd 3.

ποίημα, ατος, τό *what is made, creation* Ro 1:20; Eph 2:10.* [*poem*]

ποίησις, εως, ἡ *doing, working* Js 1:25.* [*poesy*]

ποιητής, οῦ, ὁ *one who does, a doer* Ro 2:13; Js 1:22f, 25; 4:11. *Poet* Ac 17:28.*

ποικίλος, η, ον *of various kinds, diversified, manifold* Mk 1:34; 2 Ti 3:6; Js 1:2; 1 Pt 4:10. W. connotation of *ambiguous, crafty, deceitful* Hb 13:9. [*poikilitic,* mottled, of rock]

ποιμαίνω *herd, tend, (lead to) pasture*—**1.** lit. 1 Cor 9:7; *tend sheep* Lk 17:7.—**2.** fig.—**a.** in the sense 'lead,' 'guide,' 'rule' Mt 2:6; J 21:16; Ac 20:28; 1 Pt 5:2; Rv 2;27; 12:5; 19:15.—**b.** *care for, look after* Jd 12; Rv 7:17.*

ποιμάνατε 1 aor. act. impv. 2 pl. of ποιμαίνω.

ποιμήν, ένος, ὁ *shepherd*—**1.** lit. Mt 9:36; 25:32; Mk 6:34; 14:27; Lk 2:8, 15, 18, 20; as a symbol Mt 26:31; J 10:2,

11f, 14, 16.—**2.** fig. Hb 13:20; 1 Pt 2:25. *Pastor* Eph 4:11.* [*poimenic*]

ποίμνη, ης, ἡ *flock* lit. Lk 2:8; 1 Cor 9:7; as a symbol Mt 26:31; J 10:16.*

ποίμνιον, ου, τό *flock* fig. Lk 12:32; Ac 20:28f; 1 Pt 5:2f.*

ποῖος, α, ον—**1.** *of what kind?* Lk 6:32-34; J 12:33; 21:19; Ac 7:49; Ro 3:27; 1 Cor 15:35; Js 4:14; 1 Pt 1:11.—**2.** *which, what?* Mt 19:18; 21:23f, 27; 22:36; Mk 11:28; Lk 5:19; 12:39; J 10:32; Ac 23:34; Rv 3:3.

πολεμέω *make war, fight* lit. Rv 2:16; 12:7; 13:4; 17:14; 19:11. Fig. Js 4:2.*

πόλεμος, ου, ὁ—**1.** lit. *armed conflict*—**a.** *war* Mt 24:6; Lk 14:31; Hb 11:34; Rv 11:7; 13:7.—**b.** *battle, fight* 1 Cor 14:8; Rv 9:7, 9; 16:14.—**2.** fig. *strife, conflict, quarrel* Js 4:1. [*polemic*]

πόλις, εως, ἡ *city, city-state* Mt 8:33; Lk 10:8, 10; J 4:8, 28, 30. *Capital city, main city* Ac 8:5; Lk 8:27. The heavenly *city,* the New Jerusalem Hb 11:10, 16; Rv 21:2, 10, 14–16, 18f.—Fig., *city* for its inhabitants Mt 8:34; Mk 1:33; Lk 4:43; Ac 14:21; 21:30. [*-polis,* suffix in such words as *metropolis, necropolis*]

πολιτάρχης, ου, ὁ *civic magistrate, politarch,* five or six of whom formed the city council in Thessalonica Ac 17:6, 8.*

πολιτεία, ας, ἡ *citizenship* Ac 22:28, but *commonwealth, state, body politic* Eph 2:12.* [*polity*]

πολίτευμα, ατος, τό *commonwealth, state,* perh. with allusion to relocated veterans Phil 3:20.*

πολιτεύομαι *live, conduct oneself, lead one's life* Ac 23:1; Phil 1:27.*

πολίτης, ου, ὁ *citizen* Lk 15:15; Ac 21:39. *Fellow citizen* Lk 19:14; Hb 8:11.* [*political*]

πολλά see πολύς.

πολλάκις adv. *many times, often, frequently* Mt 17:15; Mk 5:4; Ac 26:11; Ro 1:13; 2 Cor 8:22; Hb 6:7; 9:25f.

πολλαπλασίων, ον gen. ονος neut. pl. *many times as much* Mt 19:29 v.l.; Lk 18:30.*

πολυεύσπλαγχνος, ον rich in compassion Js 5:11 v.l.*

πολύλαλος, ον talkative, garrulous; it has been suspected that πολύλαλοι was once read for πολλοί in Js 3:1.*

πολυλογία, ας, ἡ much speaking, wordiness Mt 6:7; Lk 11:2 v.l.*

πολυμερῶς adv. in many ways Hb 1:1.*

πολυπλήθεια, ας, ἡ large crowd Ac 14:7 v.l.*

πολυποίκιλος, ον (very) many-sided Eph 3:10.*

πολύς, πολλή, πολύ gen. πολλοῦ, ῆς, οῦ—I. positive degree of comparison much, many—1. adj.—a. with a noun, etc., in the plural many, numerous, large, great Mt 4:25; 7:13, 22; Mk 6:13; Lk 15:13; J 20:30; Ac 1:3; 24:10; Ro 4:17f; 1 Cor 8:5; Hb 2:10; Rv 5:11. κτήματα πολλά a great deal of property Mk 10:22. πολλοί χρόνοι long periods of time Lk 8:29.—b. with a noun in the singular much, large, great, strong, severe Mt 20:29; Ac 6:7; 11:21; 18:10; 23:10; 27:21; Ro 9:22; Eph 2:4; 1 Th 2:2. Long J 5:6; Ac 15:32. ὥρα πολλή late hour Mk 6:35.—2. substantively—a. πολλοί many persons Mk 2:2; 10:45; Lk 1:1, 14, 16; Gal 3:16; 2 Cor 12:21; 2 Pt 2:2. οἱ πολλοί the many Mk 6:2; Ro 12:5; 1 Cor 10:33; the majority, most Mt 24:12; Hb 12:15; the crowd 2 Cor 2:17.—b. πολλά many things, much, at length Mt 13:3; Mk 4:2; Lk 9:22; 2 Cor 8:22a.—πολλά in the acc. as adv. greatly, earnestly, strictly, loudly, often, etc. Mk 5:38, 43; 6:20; 1 Cor 16:12, 19; Js 3:2; hard Ro 16:6, 12.—c. πολύ much Mt 6:30; Lk 12:48; Ac 28:6; Ro 3:2; Phil 2:12; Hb 12:9, 25. πολλοῦ gen. of price for a large sum of money Mt 26:9. πολύ acc. as adv. greatly, very much Mk 12:27; Lk 7:47b.—II. comparative degree πλείων, neut. πλεῖον or πλέον, genitive of all genders πλείονος; nom. pl. masc. and fem. πλείονες, contracted πλείους; neut. πλείονα, contracted πλείω; more.—1. adj. Mt 21:36; J 4:1; 7:31; 15:2; Ac 2:40; 4:22; Hb 3:3; Rv 2:19; longer Ac 18:20; many 13:31.—2. subst.—a. (οἱ) πλείονες, (οἱ) πλείους the majority, most Ac 19:32; 27:12; 1

Cor 10:5; 15:6.—(Even) more J 4:41; Ac 28:23.—b. πλεῖον, πλέον more τὸ πλεῖον the greater sum, etc. Mt 6:25; Mk 12:43; Lk 7:43; 9:13.—Acc. as adv. more, to a greater degree Mt 5:20; Lk 7:42; J 21:15.—III. superlative πλεῖστος, η, ον most—1. adj. most of Mt 11:20. Very great, very large Mt 21:8; Mk 4:1.—2. subst. οἱ πλεῖστοι the majority, most Ac 19:32 v.l. Neut. acc. as adv. τὸ πλεῖστον at the most 1 Cor 14:27. [poly-, combining form in such words as polygamy, polymath]

πολύσπλαγχνος, ον compassionate, merciful Js 5:11.*

πολυτελής, ές (very) expensive, costly Mk 14:3; 1 Ti 2:9; 1 Pt 3:4.*

πολύτιμος, ον very precious, valuable Mt 13:46; 26:7 v.l.; J 12:3; 1 Pt 1:7.*

πολυτρόπως adv. in various ways Hb 1:1.*

πόμα, ατος, τό a drink Hb 9:10. Symbolically 1 Cor 10:4; 12:13 v.l.*

πονηρία, ας, ἡ wickedness, baseness, maliciousness, sinfulness Mt 22:18; Lk 11:39; Ac 3:26; Ro 1:29; 1 Cor 5:8; Eph 6:12; pl. malicious acts Mk 7:22.*

πονηρός, ά, όν—1. adj.—a. in the physical sense in poor condition, sick Mt 6:23; Lk 11:34 (for other possibilities see ὀφθαλμός). Painful, serious Rv 16:2. Bad, spoiled Mt 7:17f.—b. in the ethical sense wicked, evil, bad, vicious, degenerate Mt 12:35; 16:4; Lk 19:22; J 3:19; Ac 19:15f; Gal 1:4; 2 Ti 4:18; Hb 3:12; 10:22; Js 2:4. Arrogant Js 4:16. Envious Mt 20:15.—2. subst.—a. wicked or evil-intentioned person, evildoer Mt 5:39, 45; Lk 6:35; 1 Cor 5:13.—ὁ πονηρός the evil one = the Devil Mt 13:19; J 17:15; Eph 6:16; 1 J 3:12; 5:18f. The genitives in Mt 5:37 and 6:13 may be masc. the evil one, or neut. evil.—τὸ πονηρόν (that which is) evil Mt 5:11; Mk 7:23; Lk 6:45c; Ac 25:18; Ro 12:9 (see Mt 5:37 and 6:13 above).

πόνος, ου, ὁ (hard) labor, toil Col 4:13. Pain, distress, affliction Rv 16:10f; 21:4.*

Ποντικός, ή, όν from Pontus (see Πόντος) Ac 18:2.* [Pontic]

Πόντιος, ου, ὁ Pontius, the tribal (middle) name of Pilate Mt 27:2 v.l.; Lk 3:1; Ac 4:27; 1 Ti 6:13.*

πόντος, ου, ὁ the (high) sea Rv 18:17 v.l.*

Πόντος, ου, ὁ Pontus, a district in northeast Asia Minor Ac 2:9; 1 Pt 1:1.*

Πόπλιος, ου, ὁ Publius, a Roman personal name Ac 28:7f.*

πορεία, ας, ἡ journey, trip Lk 13:22; Js 1:11; for the latter passage way of life, conduct is also possible.*

πορεύω only as mid. and pass. **πορεύ-ομαι** go, proceed, travel—**1.** lit. Mt 2:20; 22:15; 25:41; Lk 7:50; 9:56; Ac 8:39; 20:1, 22; 25:12; Ro 15:24f; 1 Cor 10:27; 16:6; I am about to go J 14:12, 28.—**2.** fig.—**a.** as a euphemism go to one's death, die Lk 22:22.—**b.** π. ὀπίσω follow, i.e. indulge, w. gen. 2 Pt 2:10.— **c.** conduct oneself, live, walk Lk 1:6; Ac 9:31; 14:16; 1 Pt 4:3; 2 Pt 3:3; Jd 11, 16, 18.—**d.** pass by Lk 8:14.

πορθέω pillage, destroy, annihilate Ac 9:21; Gal 1:13, 23.*

πορία a variant spelling for πορεία.

πορισμός, οῦ, ὁ means of gain 1 Ti 6:5, 6.*

Πόρκιος, ου, ὁ Porcius, tribal name of Festus Ac 24:27.*

πορνεία, ας, ἡ unchastity, prostitution, fornication, of various kinds of unlawful sexual intercourse—**1.** lit. Mt 5:32; 19:9; Mk 7:21; J 8:41; Ac 15:20; 1 Cor 6:13, 18; 7:2; 2 Cor 12:21; Gal 5:19; Col 3:5.—**2.** fig., of idolatry immorality Rv 2:21; 14:8; 17:2, 4; 19:2.

πορνεύω to prostitute, practice prostitution or sexual immorality in general—**1.** lit. Mk 10:19 v.l.; 1 Cor 6:18; 10:8; Rv 2:14, 20.—**2.** fig., of idolatry Rv 17:2; 18:3, 9.*

πόρνη, ης, ἡ prostitute, whore.—**1.** lit. Mt 21:31f; Lk 15:30; 1 Cor 6:15f; Hb 11:31; Js 2:25.—**2.** fig. Rv 17:1, 5, 15f; 19:2.* [porno-, as prefix in pornographic]

πόρνος, ου, ὁ one who practices sexual immorality, a fornicator 1 Cor 5:9–11; Eph 5:5; 1 Ti 1:10; Hb 12:16; Rv 22:15.

πόρρω adv. far (away) Mt 15:8; Mk 7:6; Lk 14:32.—As comparative degree we have in the text of Lk 24:28 πορρώτερον and as v.l. πορρωτέρω farther.*

πόρρωθεν adv. from a distance Hb 11:13. At a distance Lk 17:12.*

πορρώτερον and **πορρωτέρω** see πόρρω.

πορφύρα, ας, ἡ purple (cloth) Lk 16:19; purple (garment) Rv 18:12; cf. 17:4 v.l. Of the reddish purple cloak of the Roman soldier Mk 15:17, 20.* [porphyry]

πορφυρόπωλις, ιδος, ἡ a businesswoman dealing in purple cloth Ac 16:14.*

πορφυροῦς, ᾶ, οῦν purple J 19:2, 5. Purple (clothing) Rv 17:4; 18:16.*

ποσάκις adv. how many times? how often? Mt 18:21; 23:37; Lk 13:34.*

πόσις, εως, ἡ (the act of) drinking Ro 14:17; Col 2:16. A drink J 6:55.*

πόσος, η, ον pron.—**1.** how great(?) Mt 6:23; 7:11; Mk 9:21; Lk 11:13; Ro 11:12, 24; 2 Cor 7:11; Hb 10:29.—**2.** how much, how many(?) Mt 27:13; Mk 6:38; Lk 15:17; 16:5, 7; Ac 21:20.

ποταμός, οῦ, ὁ river, stream Mt 3:6; Lk 6:48f; J 7:38; Ac 16:13; 2 Cor 11:26; Rv 9:14; 22:1f. Mountain or winter torrent Mt 7:25, 27. [Cf. Mesopotamia.]

ποταμοφόρητος, ον swept away by a river Rv 12:15.*

ποταπός, ή, όν of what sort or kind Mt 8:27; Lk 1:29; 7:39; 2 Pt 3:11. How great Mk 13:1; how glorious 1 J 3:1.*

ποταπῶς adv. in what way, how Ac 20:18 v.l.*

πότε adv. when(?) Mt 25:37–39, 44; Mk 13:4, 35; Lk 17:20; J 6:25. ἕως π. how long? Mt 17:17; Lk 9:41; J 10:24; Rv 6:10.

ποτέ enclitic particle at some time or other, of the past once, formerly J 9:13; Ro 7:9; 11:30; 1 Cor 9:7; Gal 1:13, 23; Eph 2:2f; of the fut. once Lk 22:32. ἤδη ποτέ now at last Ro 1:10; Phil 4:10.

πότερον interrogative word whether J 7:17.*

ποτήριον, ου, τό cup, drinking vessel—**1.** lit. Mt 10:42; 26:27; Mk 7:4; 9:41;

14:23; Lk 11:39; 22:17, 20a; 1 Cor 10:16, 21; 11:25a, 27f; Rv 17:4. The cup stands, by metonymy, for what it contains Lk 22:20b; 1 Cor 11:25b, 26.—2. fig., of undergoing a violent death Mt 20:22f; 26:39, 42 v.l.; Mk 10:38f; 14:36; Lk 22:42; J 18:11; Rv 14:10; 16:19; 18:6.

ποτίζω—1. of persons *give to drink, cause someone to drink* Mt 10:42; 25:35; Mk 15:36; 1 Cor 3:2; 12:13; Rv 14:8.— **2.** of animals and plants Lk 13:15; 1 Cor 3:6–8. [Cf. *potion.*]

Ποτίολοι, ων, οἱ *Puteoli,* a city on the Gulf of Naples in Italy Ac 28:13.*

πότος, ου, ὁ *drinking party, carousal* 1 Pt 4:3.*

ποῦ adv.—**1.** *where(?), at which place(?)* Mt 2:2, 4; 8:20; Mk 14:12, 14; 15:47; Lk 17:17, 37; J 20:2, 13, 15; Ro 3:27; 1 Cor 1:20; 2 Pt 3:4; Rv 2:13.—**2.** *where(?), whither(?), to what place(?)* J 3:8; 7:35; 8:14; 13:36; Hb 11:8.

πού enclitic adv. *somewhere* Hb 2:6; 4:4. *About, approximately* Ro 4:19.*

Πούδης, εντος, ὁ *Pudens,* a Roman personal name 2 Ti 4:21.*

πούς, ποδός, ὁ *foot*—**1.** lit. Mt 7:6; Lk 7:46; 8:35; 24:39f; J 13:5f; 20:12; Ac 4:35, 37; 5:10; Eph 6:15; Rv 3:9; 19:10. *Leg* Rv 10:1. The *foot* as a measure of length Ac 7:5.—**2.** fig. Mt 5:35; 22:44; Lk 1:79; Ro 3:15; 16:20; 1 Cor 15:25, 27; Hb 1:13. [*podium; platypus,* πλατύ + πούς]

πρᾶγμα, ατος, τό—1. *deed, thing, event, occurrence* Lk 1:1; Ac 5:4; Hb 6:18; *matter* 2 Cor 7:11.—**2.** *undertaking, occupation, task* Ro 16:2.—**3.** *thing, affair* Mt 18:19; Hb 10:1; 11:1; Js 3:16.—**4.** *lawsuit* 1 Cor 6:1.—**5.** perh. as a euphemism for *illicit sexual intercourse* 1 Th 4:6. [*pragmatic*]

πραγματεία, ας, ἡ *affair, undertaking* 2 Ti 2:4.*

πραγματεύομαι *conduct* or *be engaged in a business* Lk 19:13.*

πραθείς, πραθῆναι 1 aor. pass. ptc. and inf. of πιπράσκω.

πραιτώριον, ου, τό (Latin loanword: praetorium) *the praetorium, governor's official residence* Mt 27:27; Mk 15:16; J 18:28, 33; 19:9; Ac 23:35. This

may also be the meaning in Phil 1:13, but here *praetorian guard* is also probable.*

πράκτωρ, ορος, ὁ *bailiff, constable* Lk 12:58.*

πρᾶξις, εως, ἡ—1. *activity, function* Mt 16:27; Ro 12:4.—**2.** *act, action, deed* generally in the title of Ac. *Evil* or *disgraceful deed* Lk 23:51; Ac 19:18; Ro 8:13; Col 3:9.* [*praxis*]

πρᾶος variant of πραΰς.

πραότης variant form of πραΰτης.

πρασιά, ᾶς, ἡ *garden plot* fig. πρασιαὶ πρασιαί *group by group* Mk 6:40.*

πράσσω—1. trans.—**a.** *do, accomplish* Ac 5:35; 26:20, 26; 2 Cor 5:10. *Do, commit* Lk 22:23; 23:15; Ac 16:28; 19:36; Ro 2:1–3; 7:19; 1 Cor 5:2. *Practice, busy oneself with, mind* Ac 19:19; 1 Th 4:11; *observe* Ro 2:25.—**b.** *collect* taxes, etc. Lk 3:13; 19:23.—**2.** intrans.—**a.** *act* Ac 3:17; 17:7.—**b.** *be, be situated, fare* Eph 6:21; εὖ πράξετε *a bureaucratic term you will fare well,* i.e. the addressees of the letter will share in the further goodwill of the leadership in Jerusalem.

πραϋπαθία, ας, ἡ *gentleness* 1 Ti 6:11.*

πραΰς, πραεῖα, πραΰ *gentle, humble, considerate* Mt 5:5; 11:29; 21:5; 1 Pt 3:4.*

πραΰτης, ητος, ἡ and **πραότης, ητος, ἡ** *gentleness, humility, courtesy, considerateness* 1 Cor 4:21; 2 Cor 10:1; Gal 5:23; 6:1; Eph 4:2; Col 3:12; 2 Ti 2:25; Tit 3:2; Js 1:21; 3:13; 1 Pt 3:15.*

πρέπω *be fitting, be seemly* or *suitable* Mt 3:15; 1 Cor 11:13; 1 Ti 2:10; Tit 2:1; Hb 7:26. Impersonal constr. w. dat. *it is fitting for someone* Eph 5:3; Hb 2:10.*

πρεσβεία, ας, ἡ *embassy, ambassador(s)* Lk 14:32; 19:14.*

πρεσβευτής, οῦ, ὁ see πρεσβύτης.

πρεσβεύω *be an ambassador, travel* or *work as an ambassador* 2 Cor 5:20; Eph 6:20.*

πρεσβυτέριον, ου, τό *council of elders*—**1.** *the Sanhedrin,* the highest Jewish council in Jerusalem Lk 22:66; Ac 22:5.—**2.** *the presbytery,* a Christian church council, including all the elders 1 Ti 4:14.*

πρεσβύτερος, α, ον—1. of age *older*, often subst. *old(er) person* Lk 15:25; J 8:9; Ac 2:17; 1 Ti 5:1f. Of a period of time οἱ π. *the men of old, our ancestors* Mt 15:2; Mk 7:3, 5; Hb 11:2.—**2.** as a designation of an official *elder, presbyter*—**a.** among the Jews Mt 16:21; 27:41; Mk 14:43, 53; Lk 7:3; 9:22; Ac 4:23; 6:12.—**b.** among the Christians Ac 11:30; 14:23; 1 Ti 5:17, 19; Tit 1:5; Js 5:14; 1 Pt 5:1; 5:5; 2 J 1; 3 J 1; Rv 4:4; 7:11. [Cf. *priest*, Old English preost via Latin presbyter.]

πρεσβύτης, ου, ὁ an *elderly* or *old man* Lk 1:18; Tit 2:2; Phlm 9. In the last-named passage some prefer the emendation πρεσβευτής *ambassador*.*

πρεσβῦτις, ιδος, ἡ *old(er)* or *elderly woman* Tit 2:3.*

πρηνής, ές gen. **οῦς** *headfirst, headlong* Ac 1:18. *Swollen, distended* is also possible.*

πρησθείς 1 aor. pass. ptc. of πίμπρα-μαι (πίμπρημι).

πρίζω or **πρίω** *saw (in two)* Hb 11:37.*

πρίν—1. conj. *before* Mt 1:18; 26:34, 75; Lk 2:26; 22:61; J 8:58; 14:29; Ac 7:2.— **2.** with ἤ, functions as prep. w. gen. *before* Mt 26:34 v.l.

Πρίσκα and its diminutive **Πρίσκιλλα, ης, ἡ** *Prisca, Priscilla*, tentmaker and, together with her husband Aquila, instructor of Apollos. The form Πρί-σκιλλα Ac 18:2, 18, 26; Πρίσκα Ro 16:3; 1 Cor 16:19; 2 Ti 4:19.*

πρίω see πρίζω.

πρό prep. w. gen. *before*—**1.** of place *before, in front of, at* Mt 11:10; Lk 9:52; Ac 12:6; 14:13; Js 5:9.—**2.** of time Mt 6:8; 24:38; Lk 11:38; J 11:55; Ac 23:15; Ro 16:7; 1 Cor 4:5; Gal 1:17; Eph 1:4; Col 1:17; 2 Ti 4:21.—**3.** of precedence Js 5:12; 1 Pt 4:8. [*pro-*, combining form, as in *prognathous*, πρό + γνάθος, with jaws projecting beyond the upper part of the face]

προαγαγεῖν 2 aor. act. inf. of προάγω.

προάγω—1. trans. *lead forward, lead* or *bring out* Ac 12:6; 16:30; 17:5; 25:26.— **2.** intrans. *go before, lead the way, pre-*

cede—**a.** in space Mt 2:9; Mk 11:9; *walk ahead of* Mk 10:32.—**b.** in time *go* or *come before* Mt 14:22; Mk 6:45; 14:28; 1 Ti 1:18; 5:24; Hb 7:18; *get in before* Mt 21:31.

προαιρέω mid. *choose (for oneself), determine, decide* 2 Cor 9:7.*

προαιτιάομαι *accuse, bring an accusation beforehand* Ro 3:9.*

προακούω *hear beforehand* Col 1:5.*

προαμαρτάνω *sin beforehand* 2 Cor 12:21; 13:2.*

προαύλιον, ου, τό *forecourt, gateway* Mk 14:68.*

προβαίνω *go ahead, go on* lit. Mt 4:21; Mk 1:19. Fig. *be advanced* Lk 1:7, 18; 2:36.*

προβάλλω *put forward, cause to come forward* Ac 19:33. *Put out* Lk 21:30.* [*problem*]

προβάς 2 aor. act. ptc. of προβαίνω.

προβατικός, ή, όν *pertaining to sheep* ἡ προβατική *the sheep gate* J 5:2.*

προβάτιον, ου, τό *lamb* or *sheep* J 21:16f v.l.*

πρόβατον, ου, τό *sheep*—**1.** lit. Mt 7:15; 12:11f; Mk 14:27; Lk 15:4, 6; J 2:14f; Ro 8:36; Rv 18:13.—**2.** symbolically and allegorically Mt 25:32f; J 10:1–16, 26f; Hb 13:20; 1 Pt 2:25.

προβεβηκώς pf. act. ptc. of προβαίνω.

προβιβάζω *put forward, cause to come forward* Mt 14:8; Ac 19:33 v.l.*

προβλέπω *see beforehand* mid. *select, provide* Hb 11:40.*

προγίνομαι *happen* or *be done before* Ro 3:25.*

προγινώσκω *know beforehand* or *in advance, have foreknowledge (of)* 1 Pt 1:20; 2 Pt 3:17. *Choose beforehand* Ro 8:29; 11:2. *Know from time past* Ac 26:5.*

πρόγνωσις, εως, ἡ *foreknowledge* Ac 2:23; 1 Pt 1:2.* [*prognosis*]

πρόγονος, ον *born early* οἱ πρόγονοι *parents, forefathers, ancestors* 1 Ti 5:4; 2 Ti 1:3.*

προγράφω *write before(hand)* Ro 15:4; Eph 3:3; *mark out* Jd 4. *Show forth,* advertise, placard publicly, proclaim Gal 3:1.* [Cf. program.]

πρόδηλος, ον clear, evident, known to all 1 Ti 5:24f; Hb 7:14.*

προδίδωμι give in advance Ro 11:35. Hand over, betray Mk 14:10 v.l.*

προδότης, ου, ὁ traitor, betrayer Lk 6:16; Ac 7:52; 2 Ti 3:4.*

προδραμών 2 aor. act. ptc. of προτρέχω.

πρόδρομος, ον going before subst. forerunner Hb 6:20.* [prodrome, in medicine a premonitory symptom]

προέγνων 2 aor. act. ind. of προγινώσκω.

προέδωκα 1 aor. act. ind. of προδίδωμι.

προεθέμην 2 aor. mid. ind. of προτίθημι.

προεῖδον 2 aor. act. ind. of προοράω.

προεῖπον, προείρηκα foretell, tell beforehand—1. of prophetic utterances Mt 24:25; Mk 13:23; Ac 1:16; Ro 9:29; 2 Cor 13:2; Gal 5:21; 2 Pt 3:2; Jd 17.— 2. have said before or previously, have already said or mentioned 2 Cor 7:3; Gal 1:9; 1 Th 4:6; Hb 4:7; 10:15 v.l. Also s. προλέγω.*

προείρηκα, προείρημαι pf. ind. act. and mid. of προεῖπον.

προέλαβον 2 aor. act. ind. of προλαμβάνω.

προελθών, προελεύσομαι 2 aor. act. ptc. and fut. mid. ind. of προέρχομαι.

προελπίζω hope before, be the first to hope, or be in the first stage of expectation Eph 1:12.*

προενάρχομαι begin (beforehand) 2 Cor 8:6, 10.*

προεπαγγέλλω mid. and pass. promise beforehand, previously Ro 1:2; 2 Cor 9:5.*

προεπηγγείλατο (Ro 1:2), προεπηγγελμένη (2 Cor 9:5) 1 aor. mid. ind. 3 sing. and pf. pass. ptc. fem. of προεπαγγέλλω.

προέρχομαι—1. go forward, advance, proceed Mt 26:39; Mk 14:35; Ac 12:10.—2. go before as forerunner or leader Lk 1:17; 22:47.—3. come or go before someone, go on before or ahead

Mk 6:33; Ac 20:5, 13; 2 Cor 9:5. Come out Ac 12:13 v.l.*

προεστώς pf. act. ptc. of προΐστημι.

προετοιμάζω prepare beforehand Ro 9:23; Eph 2:10.*

προευαγγελίζομαι proclaim good news in advance Gal 3:8.*

προέχω in Ro 3:9 προεχόμεθα if mid. can mean have an advantage or protect oneself. If it is pass., be excelled.*

προήγαγον 2 aor. act. ind. of προάγω.

προηγέομαι go before; in Ro 12:10 outdo or consider better, esteem more highly.*

προῆλθον 2 aor. act. ind. of προέρχομαι.

προήλπικα pf. act. ind. of προελπίζω.

προημαρτηκόσιν, προημαρτηκότων pf. act. ptc. dat. and gen. pl. of προαμαρτάνω.

προήρηται pf. mid. ind. 3 sing. of προαιρέω.

πρόθεσις, εως, ἡ—1. setting forth, putting out, presentation οἱ ἄρτοι τῆς προθέσεως loaves of presentation, sacred bread Mt 12:4; Mk 2:26; Lk 6:4; cf. Hb 9:2.—2. plan, purpose, resolve, will Ac 11:23; 27:13; Ro 8:28; 9:11; Eph 1:11; 3:11; 2 Ti 1:9; 3:10.* [prothesis]

προθεσμία, ας, ἡ appointed day, fixed or limited time Gal 4:2.*

προθυμία, ας, ἡ goodwill, willingness, readiness Ac 17:11; 2 Cor 8:11f, 19; 9:2.*

πρόθυμος, ον ready, willing, eager Mt 26:41; Mk 14:38. τὸ πρόθυμον desire, eagerness Ro 1:15.*

προθύμως adv. willingly, eagerly, freely 1 Pt 5:2.*

προΐδών 2 aor. act. ptc. of προοράω.

πρόϊμος, ον early as subst. early rain (about October) Js 5:7.*

προϊνός a variant spelling of πρωϊνός.

προΐστημι—1. be at the head (of), rule, direct w. gen. 1 Ti 3:4f, 12; 5:17. Perh. Ro 12:8; 1 Th 5:12.—2. be concerned about, care for, give aid perh. Ro 12:8; 1 Th 5:12. Busy oneself with, engage in w. gen. Tit 3:8, 14.*

προκαλέω mid. *provoke, challenge* Gal 5:26.*

προκαταγγείλαντας (Ac 7:52), **προκατήγγειλεν** (Ac 3:18) 1 aor. act. ptc. masc. acc. pl. and 1 aor. act. ind. 3 sing. of *προκαταγγέλλω.*

προκαταγγέλλω *announce beforehand, foretell* Ac 3:18, 24 v.l.; 7:52; 2 Cor 9:5 v.l.*

προκαταρτίζω *get ready* or *arrange for in advance* 2 Cor 9:5.*

προκατέχω *gain possession of* or *occupy previously* προκατέχομεν περισσόν; *do we have a previous advantage?* Ro 3:9 v.l.*

πρόκειμαι *be set before*—**1.** *be exposed to* public *view* Jd 7.—**2.** *lie before, be present, be set before* 2 Cor 8:12; Hb 6:18; 12:1f.*

προκηρύσσω *proclaim beforehand* Ac 13:24; pass. 3:20 v.l.*

προκοπή, ῆς, ἡ *progress, advancement* Phil 1:12, 25; 1 Ti 4:15.*

προκόπτω *go forward, make progress, advance, go on* Lk 2:52; Gal 1:14; 2 Ti 2:16; 3:9, 13. *Be advanced, be far gone* Ro 13:12.*

πρόκριμα, ατος, τό *prejudgment, discrimination* 1 Ti 5:21.*

προκυρόω *ratify previously* Gal 3:17.*

προλαμβάνω *take before(hand). Do something before the usual time* προέλαβεν μυρίσαι *she had anointed beforehand* Mk 14:8. Simply *take* 1 Cor 11:21. *Detect, overtake, surprise* Gal 6:1.* [*prolepsis*, anticipation; adj., *proleptic*]

προλέγω *tell beforehand* or *in advance* 2 Cor 13:2; Gal 5:21; 1 Th 3:4. Also see προεῖπον.* [*prologue*]

προλημφθῇ 1 aor. pass. subj. 3 sing. of προλαμβάνω.

προμαρτύρομαι *bear witness to beforehand, predict* 1 Pt 1:11.*

προμελετάω *practice beforehand, prepare* Lk 21:14.*

προμεριμνάω *concern oneself* or *be anxious beforehand* Mk 13:11.*

προνοέω *think of beforehand, take care*—**1.** *care for, provide for* w. gen. 1 Ti 5:8.—**2.** *take into consideration, have*

regard for w. gen. Ro 12:17; 2 Cor 8:21.*

πρόνοια, ας, ἡ *foresight, care, provision* Ac 24:2; Ro 13:14.*

πρόοιδα *know beforehand* or *previously* Ac 2:31 v.l.*

προοράω—**1.** *see previously* Ac 21:29.— **2.** *foresee, see in advance* Ac 2:31; Gal 3:8.—**3.** mid. *see before one, have before one's eyes* Ac 2:25.*

προορίζω *decide upon beforehand, predestine* Ac 4:28; Ro 8:29f; 1 Cor 2:7; Eph 1:5, 11.*

προπάσχω *suffer previously* προπαθόντες 2 aor. act. ptc. masc. pl. 1 Th 2:2.*

προπάτωρ, ορος, ὁ *ancestor* Ro 4:1.*

προπέμπω—**1.** *accompany, escort* Ac 20:38; 21:5.—**2.** *help on one's journey, send on one's way* Ac 15:3; Ro 15:24; 1 Cor 16:6, 11; 2 Cor 1:16; Tit 3:13; 3 J 6.*

προπετής, ές gen. **οὖς** *rash, reckless, thoughtless* Ac 19:36; 2 Ti 3:4.*

προπορεύομαι *go on before* w. gen. Lk 1:76; Ac 7:40.*

πρός prep. w. gen., dat., or acc.—**I.** with the genitive *to the advantage of, necessary for* Ac 27:34.—**II.** with the dative *near, at, by* Mk 5:11; Lk 19:37; J 18:16; 20:11f; *around* Rv. 1:13.—**III.** with the accusative—**1.** of place *toward, to* Mt 26:57; Mk 1:33; Lk 16:26; J 11:15; Ac 25:21; Ro 10:1; 1 Cor 12:2; Eph 2:18; *with* Ac 3:25.—**2.** of time *toward* Lk 24:29. *For* Lk 8:13; J 5:35; 1 Cor 7:5; Gal 2:5a; Hb 12:10; Js 4:14.— **3.** of a goal *for, for the purpose of, in order (to), on behalf of* Mt 23:5; Mk 13:22; Ac 3:10; 27:12; Ro 3:26; 1 Cor 7:35a; Cor 1:20; Eph 4:29; 1 Pt 4:12. Of result *so that, etc.* J 4:35; 1 Cor 14:26; 1 J 5:16f.—**4.** denoting a hostile or friendly relationship—**a.** hostile *against, with* Ac 11:2; 24:19; 1 Cor 6:1; Eph 6:12; Col 3:13; Rv 13:6.—**b.** friendly Ro 5:1; 2 Cor 6:14f; 7:4; Gal 6:10; Phlm 5; 1 J 3:21; 2 Ti 2:24.—**5.** to indicate a connection—**a.** *with reference to* Mt 19:8; Mk 12:12; Lk 12:41; 18:1; J 13:28; Ac 24:16; Hb 1:7f.—**b.** *as far as . . . is concerned, with regard to* Ro 15:17; 2 Cor 4:2; Hb 6:11. τὰ πρός τι that which belongs to something or is necessary for something Lk 14:32; Ac 28:10; 2 Pt 1:3.—c. elliptically τί πρὸς ἡμᾶς; what is that to us? Mt 27:4. τί πρὸς σέ; how does it concern you? J 21:22f.—d. in accordance with Lk 12:47; 2 Cor 5:10; Gal 2:14; Eph 3:4. In comparison with Ro 8:18.— 6. adverbial expression πρὸς φθόνον jealously Js 4:5.—7. (in company) with Mt 13:56; Mk 14:49; J 1:1f; Gal 1:18; 4:18, 20; Phil 1:26; 1 Th 3:4; 2 Th 3:10; Phlm 13; 1 J 1:2. πρὸς ἑαυτούς among or to themselves Mk 9:10; cf. Lk 18:11.

προσάββατον, ου, τό the day before the Sabbath, i.e. Friday Mk 15:42.*

προσαγαγεῖν 2 aor. act. inf. of προσάγω.

προσαγορεύω call, name, designate pass. Hb 5:10.*

προσάγω—1. trans. bring (forward) lit. Lk 9:41; Ac 12:6 v.l.; 16:20; pass. Mt 18:24 v.l. Fig. 1 Pt 3:18.—2. intrans. come near, approach Ac 27:27.*

προσαγωγή, ῆς, ἡ approach, access Ro 5:2; Eph 2:18; 3:12.*

προσαιτέω beg J 9:8; Mk 10:46 v.l.; Lk 18:35 v.l.*

προσαίτης, ου, ὁ beggar Mk 10:46; J 9:8.*

προσαναβαίνω go up, move up προσανάβηθι 2 aor. act. impv. Lk 14:10.*

προσαναλαμβάνω take in besides, welcome Ac 28:2 v.l.*

προσαναλίσκω or προσαναλόω spend lavishly (in addition) Lk 8:43.*

προσαναπληρόω fill up or replenish besides 2 Cor 9:12; 11:9.*

προσανατίθημι mid. add or contribute, lay before Gal 2:6. Consult with w. dat. 1:16.*

προσανεθέμην 2 aor. mid. ind. of προσανατίθημι.

προσανέχω rise up toward w. dat. Ac 27:27 v.l.*

προσαπειλέω threaten further or in addition Ac 4:21.*

προσαχέω resound of the surf Ac 27:27 v.l.*

προσδαπανάω spend in addition Lk 10:35.*

προσδέομαι need w. gen. Ac 17:25.*

προσδέχομαι—1. take up, receive, welcome Lk 15:2; Ro 16:2; Phil 2:29. Receive willingly, put up with Hb 10:34; accept Hb 11:35.—2. wait for, anticipate Mk 15:43; Lk 2:25, 38; 12:36; 23:51; Ac 23:21; 24:15; Tit 2:13; Jd 21; Lk 1:21 v.l.; Ac 10:24 v.l.*

προσδίδωμι give (over) Lk 24:30 v.l.*

προσδοκάω wait for, look for, expect Mt 11:3; 24:50; Lk 7:19f; 12:46; Ac 10:24; 27:33; 2 Pt 3:12–14.

προσδοκία, ας, ἡ expectation Lk 21:26; Ac 12:11.*

προσδραμών 2 aor. act. ptc. of προστρέχω.

προσεάω permit to go farther Ac 27:7.*

προσεγγίζω approach, come near Mk 2:4 v.l.; Ac 10:25 v.l.; 27:27 v.l.*

προσεδρεύω serve, wait upon w. dat. 1 Cor 9:13 v.l.*

προσεθέμην, προσέθηκα 2 aor. mid. and 1 aor. act. ind. of προστίθημι.

προσεκλίθη 1 aor. pass. ind. 3 sing. of προσκλίνω.

προσελαβόμην 2 aor. mid. ind. of προσλαμβάνω.

προσελεύσομαι, προσελήλυθα, πρόσελθε fut. mid. ind., pf. act. ind., and 2 aor. act. impv. of προσέρχομαι.

προσενέγκαι, προσένεγκε, προσενεγκεῖν, προσένεγκον, προσενεχθείς, προσενήνοχα 1 aor. act. inf., 2 aor. act. impv., 2 aor. act. inf., 1 aor. act. impv., 1 aor. pass. ptc., and 2 pf. act. ind. of προσφέρω.

προσέπεσον 2 aor. act. ind. of προσπίπτω.

προσεργάζομαι make more, earn in addition Lk 19:16.*

προσέρχομαι come or go to, approach—1. lit. Mt 4:3, 11; 5:1; 9:14; 24:1; Mk 6:35; Lk 23:52; J 12:21; Ac 9:1; Hb 12:18, 22.—2. fig.—a. of coming to a deity Hb 4:16; 7:25; 10:1, 22; 11:6; 1 Pt 2:4.—b. agree with, accede to 1 Ti 6:3.

προσέρηξα 1 aor. act. ind. of προσρήσσω (προσρήγνυμι).

προσέσχηκα, προσέσχον pf. act. ind. and 2 aor. act. ind. of προσέχω.

προσέταξα 1 aor. act. ind. of προσ-τάσσω.

προσετέθην, προσετίθει 1 aor. pass. ind. and impf. act. 3 sing. of προσ-τίθημι.

προσευχή, ῆς, ἡ—1. prayer Mt 17:21; Mk 9:29; Lk 6:12; Ac 3:1; Ro 12:12; Phil 4:6; Rv 8:3f.—**2.** place of prayer, chapel Ac 16:13, 16.

προσεύχομαι pray Mt 5:44; 6:5–7; Mk 1:35; 14:38; Lk 1:10; 20:47; Ac 6:6; Ro 8:26; 1 Cor 11:4f, 13; 14:14a, 15; Hb 13:18; Js 5:17.

προσέχω—1. act. turn one's mind to—**a.** pay attention to, give heed to, follow w. dat. Ac 8:6, 10f; 16:14; 1 Ti 1:4; 4:1; Tit 1:14; Hb 2:1; 2 Pt 1:19.—**b.** be concerned about, care for, pay attention to w. dat. Ac 20:28. προσέχειν ἑαυτῷ be careful, be on one's guard Lk 12:1; 17:3; Ac 5:35; cf. Mt 7:15; 10:17.—**c.** occupy oneself with, devote or apply oneself to w. dat. 1 Ti 4:13; Hb 7:13; be addicted 1 Ti 3:8.—**2.** mid. cling to w. dat. 1 Ti 6:3 v.l.

προσῆλθον 2 aor. act. ind. of προσέρχομαι.

προσηλόω nail (fast) Col 2:14.*

προσήλυτος, ου, ὁ proselyte, convert Mt 23:15; Ac 2:11; 6:5; 13:43.*

προσήνεγκα, προσηνέχθην 1 aor. act. ind. and 1 aor. pass. ind. of προσφέρω.

προσήχθειν 1 aor. pass. ind. of προσ-άγω.

προσθεῖναι, προσθείς, πρόσθες 2 aor. act. inf., 2 aor. act. ptc., and 2 aor. act. impv. 2 sing. of προστίθημι.

πρόσθεσις, εως, ἡ only as v.l. for πρό-θεσις presentation, with the same meaning Mt 12:4; Mk 2:26; Lk 6:4.*

προσθῶ 2 aor. subj. of προστίθημι.

πρόσκαιρος, ον lasting only for a time, temporary, transitory Mt 13:21; Mk 4:17; 2 Cor 4:18; Hb 11:25.*

προσκαλέω mid. summon—**1.** lit. summon, call to oneself, invite Mt 10:1; Mk 3:13, 23; Lk 15:26; Ac 5:40; 23:17f, 23; Js 5:14.—**2.** fig. Ac 2:39; 13:2; 16:10.

προσκαρτερέω adhere to, persist in—**1.** w. dat. attach oneself to, wait on, be faithful to Ac 8:13; 10:7; stand ready

Mk 3:9.—**2.** w. dat.—**a.** busy oneself with, be busily engaged in, be devoted to Ac 1:14; 6:4; Ro 12:12; Col 4:2.— With εἴς τι Ro 13:6.—**b.** hold fast to, continue or persevere in Ac 2:42.—**3.** spend much time with ἐν Ac 2:46.*

προσκαρτέρησις, εως, ἡ perseverance, patience Eph 6:18.*

προσκέκλημαι pf. mid. ind. of προσκαλέω.

προσκεφάλαιον, ου, τό pillow, cushion Mk 4:38.*

προσκληρόω allot, assign pass. be attached to, join w. dat. Ac 17:4.*

πρόσκλησις, εως, ἡ summons, invitation 1 Ti 5:21 v.l.*

προσκλίνω pass. intrans. incline toward w. dat. attach oneself to, join Ac 5:36.*

πρόσκλισις, εως, ἡ partiality 1 Ti 5:21.*

προσκολλάω pass. fig. adhere closely to, be devoted to, join Eph 5:31; Mt 19:5 v.l.; Mk 10:7; Ac 5:36 v.l.*

πρόσκομμα, ατος, τό stumbling, offense—**1.** stumbling λίθος προσκόμματος a stone that causes people to stumble Ro 9:32f; 1 Pt 2:8. διὰ προσ-κόμματος with offense Ro 14:20.—**2.** the opportunity to take offense, obstacle, hindrance Ro 14:13; 1 Cor 8:9.*

προσκοπή, ῆς, ἡ an occasion for taking offense 2 Cor 6:3.*

προσκόπτω—1. lit.—**a.** trans. strike Mt 4:6; Lk 4:11.—**b.** intrans. stumble J 11:9f. Beat against Mt 7:27.—**2.** fig. take offense at, feel repugnance for, reject Ro 9:32; 14:21; 1 Pt 2:8.*

προσκυλίω roll (up to) Mt 27:60; Mk 15:46; Lk 23:53 v.l.*

προσκυνέω (fall down and) worship, do obeisance to, prostrate oneself before, do reverence to, welcome respectfully depending on the object—**1.** to human beings Mt 18:26; Ac 10:25; Rv 3:9.—**2.** to God Mt 4:10; J 4:20f, 23f; 12:20; Ac 24:11; 1 Cor 14:25; Hb 11:21; Rv 4:10; 14:7; 19:4.—**2.** to foreign deities Ac 7:43.—**3.** to the Devil and Satanic beings Mt 4:9; Lk 4:7; Rv 9:20; 13:4; 14:9, 11.—**4.** to angels Rv 22:8.—**5.** to Christ Mt 2:2, 8, 11; 8:2; 9:18; 14:33; 20:20; 15:25; 28:9, 17; Mk 5:6; 15:19; Lk 24:52.

προσκυνητής, οῦ, ὁ *worshiper* J 4:23.*

προσλαβοῦ 2 aor. mid. impv. of *προσ-λαμβάνω.*

προσλαλέω *speak to* or *with* Ac 13:43; 28:20.*

προσλαμβάνω—1. act. *take, partake* w. gen. Ac 27:34 v.l.—**2.** mid.—**a.** *take aside* Mt 16:22; Mk 8:32; Ac 18:26.— **b.** *receive* or *accept in one's society, home,* or *circle of acquaintances* Ro 14:1; 15:7a. Of God or Christ *accepting* the believer 14:3; 15:7b.—Ac 28:2; Phlm 12 v.l., 17.—**c.** *take along* Ac 17:5.—**d.** *take* 27:33, 36.*

προσλέγω *answer, reply* ending of Mk in the Freer ms. 6.*

πρόσλημψις or **πρόσληψις, εως, ἡ** *acceptance* Ro 11:15.*

προσμεῖναι 1 aor. act. inf. of *προσ-μένω.*

προσμένω—1. *remain* or *stay with* w. dat., lit. Mt 15:32; Mk 8:2. Fig. Ac 11:23. *Continue in* Ac 13:43; 11:23 v.l.; 1 Ti 5:5.—**2.** *remain longer, further* Ac 18:18; 1 Ti 1:3.*

προσορμίζω pass. *come into (the) harbor, come to anchor* Mk 6:53.*

προσοφείλω *owe besides* Phlm 19.*

προσοχθίζω *be angry, offended, provoked* w. dat. Hb 3:10, 17.*

προσπαίω *strike* or *beat against* w. dat.; the aor. *προσέπαισαν* is a conjectural emendation for *προσέπεσαν* in Mt 7:25.*

πρόσπεινος, ον *hungry* Ac 10:10.*

προσπεσοῦσα 2 aor. act. ptc. fem. (Lk 8:47) of *προσπίπτω.*

προσπήγνυμι *fix* or *fasten to, nail to (a cross)* *προσπήξαντες* (1 aor. act. ptc. pl.) Ac 2:23.*

προσπίπτω—1. *fall down before* or *at the feet of* w. dat. Mk 3:11; 5:33; 7:25; Lk 5:8; 8:28, 47; Ac 16:29.—**2.** *fall upon, strike against* w. dat. Mt 7:25.*

προσποιέω mid.—**1.** *make* or *act as though, pretend* Lk 24:28.—**2.** *take notice* J 8:6 v.l.*

προσπορεύομαι *come up to, approach* Mk 10:35.*

προσρήγνυμι and **προσρήσσω** w. dat. *burst upon* Lk 6:48; cf. 49; Mt 7:27 v.l.*

προστάσσω *command, order, prescribe* Mt 1:24; 8:4; 21:6 v.l.; Mk 1:44; Lk 5:14; Ac 10:33, 48; 17:26.*

προστάτις, ιδος, ἡ *protector, patron, helper* of Phoebe Ro 16:2.* [*prostate* (gland)]

προστεθῆναι, προστεθήσομαι 1 aor. pass. inf. and 1 fut. pass. ind. of *προσ-τίθημι.*

προστεταγμένος pf. pass. ptc. of *προστάσσω.*

προστῆναι 2 aor. act. inf. of *προΐστημι.*

προστίθημι—1. *add, put to*—**a.** gener. Mt 6:27; Mk 4:24; Lk 3:20; 12:25; Ac 2:41, 47 v.l.; 5:14; 13:36; Gal 3:19; Hb 12:19; pass. *be brought* Ac 11:24.—**b.** in accordance with Hebrew usage *π.* is used as a paraphrase for *again, further,* etc. *προσθεὶς εἶπεν παραβολήν again* he told a parable, or *he proceeded to tell a parable* Lk 19:11. Cf. 20:11f; Ac 12:3; Mk 14:25 v.l.—**2.** *provide, give, grant, do* Mt 6:33; Lk 12:31; 17:5.* [*prosthesis*]

προστρέχω *run up (to)* Mk 9:15; 10:17; Ac 8:30; J 20:16 v.l.*

προσφάγιον, ου, τό *fish* J 21:5.*

πρόσφατος, ον *new* Hb 10:20.*

προσφάτως adv. *recently* Ac 18:2.*

προσφέρω—1. act. and pass. *bring (to)* Mt 4:24; 9:2, 32; 17:16; 19:13; 25:20; Mk 2:4; Lk 18:15; 23:14, 36; J 19:29; Ac 8:18.—**2.** *bring, offer, present*—**a.** lit. Mt 2:11; 5:23f; Mk 1:44; Ac 7:42; Hb 5:1, 3; 8:3f; 9:7, 9, 14, 25, 28; 11:4, 17.—**b.** fig. J 16:2; Hb 5:7.—**3.** pass. *meet, deal with* Hb 12:7.

προσφιλής, ές *pleasing, agreeable, lovely* Phil 4:8.*

προσφορά, ᾶς, ἡ—1. *presenting, offering, sacrificing* Ac 24:17; Hb 10:10, 14, 18.—**2.** *that which is brought, gift, offering* Ac 21:26; Ro 15:16; Eph 5:2; Hb 10:5, 8.*

προσφωνέω—1. *call out, address* w. dat. Mt 11:16; Lk 7:32; 23:20; Ac 22:2; cf. 21:40.—**2.** *call to oneself* Lk 6:13; 13:12; Ac 11:2 v.l.*

προσχαίρω be glad Mk 9:15 v.l.*

πρόσχυσις, εως, ἡ pouring, sprinkling Hb 11:28.*

προσψαύω touch w. dat. Lk 11:46.*

προσωπολημπτέω show partiality Js 2:9.*

προσωπολήμπτης, ου, ὁ one who shows partiality Ac 10:34.*

προσωπολημψία, ας, ἡ partiality Ro 2:11; Eph 6:9; Col 3:25; Js 2:1.*

πρόσωπον, ου, τό—1. face, countenance—a. lit. Mt 6:16f; 26:67; Mk 14:65; Lk 9:29; Ac 6:15; 1 Cor 14:25; 2 Cor 3:7, 13, 18; Js 1:23; Rv 4:7; 9:7; 10:1.— b. fig., in more or less symbolic expressions Mt 18:10; Lk 9:51, 53; 24:5; 1 Cor 13:12; Ac 20:25, 38; Gal 1:22; Hb 9:24; 1 Pt 3:12; Rv 22:4. προσώπῳ outwardly 1 Th 2:17. θαυμάζειν πρόσωπον flatter Jd 16. λαμβάνειν πρόσωπον show partiality or favoritism Lk 20:21; cf. Gal 2:6.—c. governed by prepositions, where π. may sometimes be translated presence or omitted altogether Mt 11:10; Lk 2:31; Ac 3:13, 20; 5:41; 13:24; 2 Th 1:9. εἰς π. before 2 Cor 8:24. κατὰ π. face to face Ac 25:16; 2 Cor 10:1; to one's face Gal 2:11.—d. appearance Mt 16:3; Lk 12:56; 2 Cor 5:12; Js 1:11.— e. face = surface Lk 21:35; Ac 17:26.— 2. person ἐκ πολλῶν προσώπων by many persons 2 Cor 1:11. [prosopopoeia, πρόσωπον + ποιεῖν, personification]

προτάσσω fix, determine, allot (beforehand) Ac 17:26 v.l.*

προτείνω stretch out, spread out Ac 22:25.* [Cf. protasis.]

πρότερος, α, ον—1. adj. earlier, former Eph 4:22.—2. neut. πρότερον as adv. earlier, formerly, in former times— a. without the article J 7:50, 51 v.l.; 2 Cor 1:15; 1 Ti 1:13 v.l.; Hb 4:6; 7:27.— b. with the art.—as adj. former Hb 10:32; 1 Pt 1:14.—As adv. τὸ πρ. before, once, formerly J 6:62; 9:8; 1 Ti 1:13. For Gal 4:13 the first time and once are both possible.* [Cf. hysteron proteron, reversal of natural order of statement or reason]

προτίθημι mid.—1. display publicly Ro 3:25.—2. to plan, purpose, intend 1:13; Eph 1:9.*

προτρέπω urge (on), encourage, persuade Ac 18:27.*

προτρέχω run ahead Lk 19:4; J 20:4; Ac 10:25 v.l.*

προϋπάρχω be, exist before προϋπῆρχεν μαγεύων he had practiced magic Ac 8:9.—Lk 23:12.*

πρόφασις, εως, ἡ—1. real motive, valid excuse J 15:22.—2. falsely alleged motive, pretext, excuse Mt 23:14 v.l.; Mk 12:40; Lk 20:47; Ac 27:30; Phil 1:18; 1 Th 2:5.* [prophasis, prognosis]

προφέρω bring out, produce Lk 6:45.*

προφητεία, ας, ἡ prophecy—1. prophetic activity Rv 11:6.—2. the gift of prophecy Ro 12:6; 1 Cor 12:10; 13:2, 8; 14:22; 1 Th 5:20; Rv 19:10.—3. the utterance of the prophet, prophecy Mt 13:14; 1 Cor 14:6; 1 Th 5:20; 1 Ti 1:18; 4:14; 2 Pt 1:20f; Rv 1:3; 22:7, 10, 18f.*

προφητεύω prophesy—1. proclaim or interpret a divine revelation Mt 7:22; 11:13; J 11:51; Ac 2:17f; 19:6; 21:9; 1 Cor 11:4f; 13:9; 14:1, 3–5, 24, 31, 39; Rv 10:11; 11:3.—2. prophetically reveal Mt 26:68; Mk 14:65; Lk 22:64.— 3. foretell the future, prophesy Mt 15:7; Mk 7:6; Lk 1:67; 1 Pt 1:10; Jd 14.

προφήτης, ου, ὁ prophet—1. in the Old Testament Mt 2:17, 23; Mk 1:2; 6:15; Lk 13:28; 24:44; J 1:23; Ac 2:16; 7:48; Ro 1:2; 3:21; Hb 11:32; 1 Pt 1:10; 2 Pt 2:16.—2. John the Baptist is called a prophet or greater than a prophet Mt 11:9; 14:5; 21:26; Mk 11:32; Lk 1:76; 7:26; 20:6.—3. Jesus is called a prophet Mt 13:57; 16:14; 21:11, 46; Mk 6:4, 15; 8:28; Lk 4:24; 7:16, 39; 9:8, 19; 24:19; J 4:19, 44; 6:14; 7:40, 52; 9:17; cf. 1:21, 25.—Ac 3:22f; 7:37.—4. gener. of people who proclaim a divine message Mt 11:9; 13:57; 23:30, 34, 37; Lk 10:24; 11:49; 13:33f; Ac 7:52; Rv 11:10.—5. of Christian prophets Ac 11:27; 13:1; 15:32; 21:10; 1 Cor 12:28f; 14:29, 32, 37; Eph 2:20; 3:5; 4:11; Rv 11:18; 16:6; 18:20, 24; Rv 22:6, 9.—6. of a Cretan poet Tit 1:12.

προφητικός, ή, όν prophetic Ro 16:26;
2 Pt 1:19.*

προφῆτις, ιδος, ή prophet Lk 2:36; Rv
2:20.*

προφθάνω come before, anticipate Mt
17:25.*

προχειρίζω mid. choose for oneself, select, appoint Ac 22:14; 26:16. Pass.
3:20.*

προχειροτονέω choose or appoint beforehand Ac 10:41.*

Πρόχορος, ου, ὁ Prochorus Ac 6:5.*

πρύμνα, ης, ή the stern (of a ship) Mk
4:38; Ac 27:29, 41.*

πρωΐ adv. early, early in the morning Mt
16:3; 20:1; Mk 1:35; 16:2, 9; J 18:28;
20:1; Ac 28:23. In Mk 13:35 π. refers
to the fourth and last watch of the night,
3–6 A.M.

πρωΐα, ας, ή (early) morning Mt 27:1;
21:18 v.l.; J 21:4; 18:28 v.l.*

πρώϊμος a variant spelling of πρόϊμος.

πρωϊνός, ή, όν early, belonging to the
morning ὁ ἀστὴρ ὁ πρ. the morning
star, Venus Rv 2:28; 22:16.*

πρῷρα, ης, ή the prow or bow (of a ship)
Ac 27:30, 41.*

πρωτεύω be first, have first place Col
1:18.*

πρωτοκαθεδρία, ας, ή place of honor,
best seat Mt 23:6; Mk 12:39; Lk 11:43;
20:46.*

πρωτοκλισία, ας, ή the place of honor
at a dinner Mt 23:6; Mk 12:39; Lk 14:7f;
20:46.*

πρωτόμαρτυς, υρος, ὁ first martyr Ac
22:20 v.l.*

πρῶτος, η, ον—1. first—a. first, earliest,
earlier Mt 12:45; 21:28; Mk 12:20; Lk
2:2; 20:29; J 1:15, 30 (both = earlier);
5:4 v.l.; 20:4; Ac 1:1; 20:18; 26:23; Phil
1:5; 2 Ti 4:16; Hb 9:15; 10:9; Rv 1:17.—
b. first, foremost, most important, most
prominent Mt 20:27; Mk 6:21; 12:28;
Lk 13:30; Ac 25:2; 1 Cor 15:3; Eph 6:2;
1 Ti 1:15.—c. outer, anterior Hb 9:2,
6, 8.—2. the neut. πρῶτον as adv.—a.
of time or sequence first, in the first
place, before, earlier, to begin with Mt
5:24; 8:21; Mk 4:28; 13:10; Lk 12:1; J
15:18; 18:13; Ac 7:12; Ro 1:8; 15:24; 1

Cor 12:28; 15:46.—b. of degree in the
first place, above all, especially Mt 6:33;
Ac 3:26; Ro 1:16; 2:9f; 2 Cor 8:5; 1 Ti
2:1; 2 Pt 1:20. [proto-, a combining
form, in protomartyr, protomorphic,
protozoa; proton]

πρωτοστάτης, ου, ὁ leader, ringleader
Ac 24:5.*

πρωτοτόκια, ων, τά the birthright of the
oldest son, right of primogeniture Hb
12:16.*

πρωτότοκος, ον firstborn—1. lit. Mt 1:25
v.l.; Lk 2:7; Hb 11:28.—2. fig. of Christ
Ro 8:29; Col 1:15, 18; Hb 1:6; Rv 1:5;
2:8 v.l.—Of people Hb 12:23.*

πρώτως adv. for the first time Ac 11:26.*

πταίω stumble, trip, then also make a
mistake, sin Ro 11:11; Js 2:10; 3:2; be
ruined or lost is also possible for 2 Pt
1:10.*

πτέρνα, ης, ή heel J 13:18.*

πτερύγιον, ου, τό end, edge, pinnacle,
summit Mt 4:5; Lk 4:9.*

πτέρυξ, υγος, ή wing Mt 23:37; Lk 13:34;
Rv 4:8; 9:9; 12:14.* [pterygoid, wing-
like]

πτηνός, (ή), όν feathered, winged τὰ
πτηνά the birds 1 Cor 15:39.*

πτοέω terrify pass. be terrified, be
alarmed, frightened, startled Lk 12:4
v.l.; 21:9; 24:37.*

πτόησις, εως, ή terrifying, intimidation
or fear, terror; either meaning is possible in 1 Pt 3:6.*

Πτολεμαΐς, ΐδος, ή Ptolemais, a seaport city in Phoenicia Ac 21:7.*

πτύξας 1 aor. act. ptc. of πτύσσω.

πτύον, ου, τό winnowing shovel Mt 3:12;
Lk 3:17.*

πτύρω frighten pass. let oneself be in-
timidated Phil 1:28.*

πτύσμα, ατος, τό saliva, spit(tle) J 9:6.*

πτύσσω fold or roll up Lk 4:20.*

πτύω to spit Mk 7:33; 8:23; J 9:6.* [Cf.
ptyalin, the amylase of saliva.]

πτῶμα, ατος, τό (dead) body, corpse Mt
14:12; 24:28; Mk 6:29; 15:45; Rv 11:8f.*

πτῶσις, εως, ή falling, fall Mt 7:27; Lk
2:34.* [ptosis, prolapse of an anatom-
ical part; cf. πίπτω.]

πτωχεία, ας, ἡ (extreme) poverty 2 Cor 8:2, 9; Rv 2:9.*

πτωχεύω be or become (extremely) poor 2 Cor 8:9.*

πτωχός, ή, όν—1. poor in this world's goods, lit. begging, which sometimes plays a part in the word's meaning in the N.T.: Mk 12:42f. As a noun Mk 10:21; 14:7; Lk 6:20; 14:13, 21; 16:20, 22; J 12:6, 8; Ro 15:26; 2 Cor 6:10; Gal 2:10; Js 2:2f, 5f.—Poor, oppressed Mt 11:5; Lk 4:18; 7:22.—Fig. Mt 5:3; Rv 3:17.—**2.** poor, miserable, beggarly, impotent Gal 4:9; 1 Cor 15:10 v.l.

πυγμή, ῆς, ἡ fist. In Mk 7:3 πυγμῇ with the fist is variously interpreted.* [Cf. pygmy.]

Πύθιος a variant for Pyrrhus Ac 20:4.

πυθόμενος 2 aor. mid. ptc. of πυνθάνομαι.

πύθων, ωνος, ὁ a spirit of divination πνεῦμα πύθωνα a spirit of divination or prophecy, fortune-teller Ac 16:16.*

πυκνός, ή, όν frequent, numerous 1 Ti 5:23. Neut. pl. πυκνά as adv. often, frequently Mk 7:3 v.l. (for πυγμῇ); Lk 5:33.—Neut. of the comparative πυκνότερον as adv. rather frequently Ac 24:26.*

πυκτεύω fight with fists, box symbolically 1 Cor 9:26.*

πύλη, ης, ἡ gate—1. lit. Mt 16:18; Lk 7:12; Ac 3:10; 9:24; 12:10; 16:13; Hb 13:12—2. fig. and symbolically Mt 7:13f; Lk 13:24 v.l.*

πυλών, ῶνος, ὁ—1. gate, esp. of a palace or temple Lk 16:20; Ac 14:13; Rv 21:12f, 15, 21, 25; 22:14.—**2.** gateway, portal, vestibule Ac 10:17; 12:13f.—**3.** gateway, entrance separated from the house by a court Mt 26:71.* [pylon]

πυνθάνομαι—1. inquire, ask, seek to learn Mt 2:4; Lk 15:26; 18:36; J 4:52; Ac 4:7; 10:18, 29; 21:33; 23:19f.—**2.** learn by inquiry Ac 23:34.*

πῦρ, ός, τό fire—1. lit. Mt 13:40; 17:15; Lk 17:29; Ac 2:3; 7:30; 28:5; 1 Cor 3:15; Js 5:3; Hb 12:18; 2 Pt 3:7; Rv 1:14; 4:5; 8:7; 17:16; 19:20.—2. metaphorically Mt 5:22 (εἰς τὴν γέενναν τοῦ πυρός = 'hell'); Mk 9:49; Lk 12:49; Js 3:6. [pyre]

πυρά, ᾶς, ἡ fire, pile of combustible or burning material Ac 28:2f; Lk 22:55 v.l.*

πύργος, ου, ὁ tower Mt 21:33; Mk 12:1; Lk 13:4; for 14:28 either tower or farm building is possible.*

πυρέσσω suffer with a fever Mt 8:14; Mk 1:30.* [pyrexia, fever]

πυρετός, οῦ, ὁ fever Mt 8:15; Mk 1:31; Lk 4:38f; J 4:52; Ac 28:8.* [pyretology, of treatment of fever]

πύρινος, η, ον fiery, the color of fire Rv 9:17.*

πυρόω set on fire, burn up pass.—1. burn—a. lit. 2 Pt 3:12; symbolically Eph 6:16.—b. fig. burn, be inflamed 1 Cor 7:9; 2 Cor 11:29.—2. make red hot, heat thoroughly Rv 1:15; 3:18.*

πυρράζω be (fiery) red Mt 16:2f.*

πυρρός, ά, όν red (as fire) Rv 6:4; 12:3.*

Πύρρος, ου, ὁ Pyrrhus Ac 20:4.*

πύρωσις, εως, ἡ lit., the process of burning Rv 18:9, 18. Fiery ordeal 1 Pt 4:12.*

πωλέω sell Mt 10:29; 13:44; 25:9; Mk 10:21; 11:15; Lk 17:28; 18:22; 22:36; Ac 5:1; 1 Cor 10:25; Rv 13:17. [monopoly]

πῶλος, ου, ὁ colt, young donkey Mt 21:2, 5, 7; Mk 11:2, 4f, 7; Lk 19:30, 33, 35; J 12:15. The meaning horse is possible for the passages in Mk and Lk.*

πώποτε adv. ever, at any time Lk 19:30; J 1:18; 5:37; 6:35; 8:33; 1 J 4:12.*

πωρόω make dull or obtuse or blind, lit. 'harden' Mk 6:52; 8:17; J 12:40; Ro 11:7; 2 Cor 3:14.*

πώρωσις, εως, ἡ dullness, insensibility, obstinacy, being of closed mind Mk 3:5; Ro 11:25; Eph 4:18.*

πῶς interrogative particle how? in what way? Mt 23:33; 26:54; Mk 11:18; Lk 1:34; Ro 4:10; 10:14f; 1 Cor 7:32–34; Eph 5:15; Rv 3:3.—With what right? in what sense? Mt 22:12, 43; Mk 12:35; J 12:34.—How is it (possible) that? Mt 16:11; Mk 4:40 v.l.; J 4:9; Ac 2:8; Gal 4:9.—How (could or should)? = by no means Mt 12:26, 29, 34; Ro 3:6; 1 Cor 14:7, 9, 16; 2 Cor 3:8; Hb 2:3.—In exclamations how! Mk 10:23f; Lk 12:50; 18:24; J 11:36.

πώς enclitic particle *somehow, in some way, perhaps* in combination with εἰ

Ac 27:12; Ro 1:10 (see εἰ, end). See also μήπως.

P

Ῥαάβ, ἡ indecl. *Rahab* (Josh 2 and 6:17, 25) Hb 11:31; Js 2:25.*

ῥαββί (Hebrew = *my lord*) *rabbi*, a form of address, then an honorary title for outstanding teachers of the law: gener. Mt 23:7f. Of John the Baptist J 3:26. Otherwise always of Jesus Mt 26:25, 49; Mk 9:5; 10:51 v.l.; 11:21; 14:45; J 1:38 (translated *teacher*), 49; 3:2; 4:31; 6:25; 9:2; 11:8.*

ῥαββουνί (Hebrew, heightened form of ῥαββί) *my Lord, my Master* as a form of address to Jesus in Mk 10:51; J 20:16.*

ῥαβδίζω *beat with a rod* Ac 16:22; 2 Cor 11:25.*

ῥάβδος, ου, ἡ *rod, staff, stick* Mt 10:10; Mk 6:8; Lk 9:3; 1 Cor 4:21; Hb 1:8; 9:4; 11:21; Rv 2:27; 11:1; 12:5; 19:15.* [*rhabdomancy*, divination by rods]

ῥαβδοῦχος, ου, ὁ the Roman *lictor*, roughly equivalent to *constable, policeman* Ac 16:35, 38.*

ῥαβιθά. In Mk 5:41 codex D reads ραββι ταβιτα; this is meant for ῥαβιθά *girl* (see ταλιθά).*

Ῥαγαύ, ὁ indecl. *Reu* Lk 3:35.*

ῥᾳδιούργημα, ατος, τό *knavery, crime* Ac 18:14.*

ῥᾳδιουργία, ας, ἡ *wickedness, unscrupulousness* Ac 13:10.*

ῥαίνω *sprinkle* pass. Rv 19:13 v.l.*

Ῥαιφάν, ὁ indecl. *Rephan*, an ancient deity Ac 7:43.

ῥακά a term of abuse; among the most likely meanings are *empty-head, numskull, fool* Mt 5:22.*

ῥάκος, ους, τό *piece of cloth, patch* Mt 9:16; Mk 2:21.*

Ῥαμά, ἡ indecl. *Rama*, a city about 10 km. north of Jerusalem Mt 2:18.*

ῥαντίζω—1. *(be)sprinkle* for purposes of purification Hb 9:13, 19, 21; Rv 19:13 v.l.—2. mid. *cleanse, purify: wash oneself* Mk 7:4 v.l.; *purify for oneself* Hb 10:22.*

ῥαντισμός, οῦ, ὁ *sprinkling* Hb 12:24; 1 Pt 1:2.*

ῥαπίζω *strike, slap* Mt 5:39; 26:67.*

ῥάπισμα, ατος, τό *blow, slap* Mk 14:65; J 18:22; 19:3.*

ῥάσσω *strike, dash, throw down* Mk 9:18 v.l.*

ῥαφίς, ίδος, ἡ *needle* Mt 19:24; Mk 10:25; Lk 18:25 v.l.*

ῥαχά a variant form of ῥακά.

Ῥαχάβ, ἡ indecl. *Rahab* Mt 1:5.*

Ῥαχήλ, ἡ indecl. *Rachel*, Jacob's wife Mt 2:18.*

Ῥεβέκκα, ας, ἡ *Rebecca*, wife of Isaac Ro 9:10.*

ῥέδη, ης, ἡ *a* (four-wheeled) *carriage* Rv 18:13.*

Ῥεμφάν, Ῥεφάν, Ῥομφά variant forms of Ῥαιφάν.

ῥέραμμαι pf. pass. ind. of ῥαίνω.

ῥεραντισμένος pf. pass. ptc. (Rv 19:13 v.l.) of ῥαντίζω.

ῥεριμμένος pf. mid. and pass. ptc. of ῥίπτω.

ῥεύσω fut. act. ind. of ῥέω.

ῥέω *flow* symbolically J 7:38.* [Cf. *rhythm*.]

Ῥήγιον, ου, τό Rhegium, a city at the 'toe' of Italy Ac 28:13.*

ῥῆγμα, ατος, τό wreck, ruin, collapse Lk 6:49.*

ῥήγνυμι and its by-form **ῥήσσω**—**1.** tear (in pieces), break, burst Mt 7:6; 9:17; Mk 2:22; Lk 5:6 v.l., 37.—**2.** break out, break forth Gal 4:27.*

ῥηθείς 1 aor. pass. ptc. of εἶπον.

ῥῆμα, ατος, τό—**1.** that which is said, word, saying, expression Mt 12:36; Mk 9:32; Lk 2:17, 50; J 5:47; 6:68; Ac 2:14; 28:25; Ro 10:8, 17; 2 Cor 12:4; Eph 6:17; Hb 1:3; 12:19; Jd 17. Threat Ac 6:13.—**2.** thing, object, matter, event Mt 18:16; Lk 1:37, 65; 2:15, 19, 51; Ac 5:32; 10:37; 13:42; 2 Cor 13:1.

ῥῆξον 1 aor. act. impv. of ῥήγνυμι.

ῥήξω fut. act. ind. of ῥήγνυμι.

Ῥησά, ὁ indecl. Rhesa Lk 3:27.*

ῥήσσω—**1.** by-form of ῥήγνυμι.—**2.** the epic ῥήσσω (cf. προσρήσσω) throw down, dash to the ground Mk 9:18; Lk 9:42.*

ῥήτωρ, ορος, ὁ orator, advocate, attorney Ac 24:1.* [rhetor]

ῥητῶς adv. expressly, explicitly 1 Ti 4:1.*

ῥίζα, ης, ἡ—**1.** root—**a.** lit. Mt 3:10; 13:6; Mk 4:6; 11:20; Lk 3:9.—**b.** fig. Mt 13:21; Mk 4:17; Lk 8:13; Ro 11:16–18; 1 Ti 6:10; Hb 12:15.—**2.** shoot, scion Ro 15:12; Rv 5:5; 22:16.* [rhizome, underground rootlike stem]

ῥιζόω cause to take root fig., pass. be or become firmly rooted Eph 3:17; Col 2:7.*

ῥιπή, ῆς, ἡ rapid movement, twinkling 1 Cor 15:52.*

ῥιπίζω blow here and there, toss pass. Js 1:6.*

ῥίπτω and **ῥιπτέω**—**1.** throw Mt 27:5; Lk 17:2; Ac 27:19, 29; throw off 22:23; throw down Lk 4:35.—**2.** put or lay down Mt 15:30. Pf. pass. ptc. ἐρριμμένοι lying down 9:36.*

ῥίψας 1 aor. act. ptc. of ῥίπτω.

Ῥοβοάμ, ὁ indecl. Rehoboam, son and successor of Solomon Mt 1:7; Lk 3:23ff v.l.*

Ῥόδη, ης, ἡ Rhoda, a maidservant Ac 12:13.*

Ῥόδος, ου, ἡ Rhodes, an island off the southwest point of Asia Minor Ac 21:1.*

ῥοιζηδόν adv. with a roar, with great suddenness 2 Pt 3:10.*

Ῥομφά, ὁ indecl. Rompha, a variant form for Ῥαιφάν, an ancient deity Ac 7:43 v.l.*

ῥομφαία, ας, ἡ sword Lk 2:35; Rv 1:16; 2:12, 16; 6:8; 19:15, 21; Lk 21:24 v.l.*

ῥοπή, ῆς, ἡ downward movement, twinkling 1 Cor 15:52 v.l.*

Ῥουβήν, ὁ indecl. Reuben (Gen 29:32) Rv 7:5.*

Ῥούθ, ἡ indecl. Ruth Mt 1:5.*

Ῥοῦφος, ου, ὁ Rufus—**1.** son of Simon of Cyrene Mk 15:21.—**2.** recipient of a greeting Ro 16:13.*

ῥύμη, ης, ἡ (narrow) street, lane, alley Mt 6:2; Lk 14:21; Ac 9:11; 12:10.*

ῥύομαι save, rescue, deliver Mt 6:13; 27:43; Lk 1:74; 11:4 v.l.; Ac 5:15 v.l.; Ro 7:24; 11:26; 15:31; 2 Cor 1:10; Col 1:13; 1 Th 1:10; 2 Th 3:2; 2 Ti 3:11; 4:17f; 2 Pt 2:7, 9.*

ῥυπαίνω befoul, soil fig. defile, pollute ῥυπανθήτω 1 aor. pass. impv. 3 sing. Rv 22:11.*

ῥυπαρεύω befoul, defile Rv 22:11 v.l.*

ῥυπαρία, ας, ἡ dirt fig. moral uncleanness, sordid avarice Js 1:21.*

ῥυπαρός, ά, όν dirty lit. Js 2:2. Fig. unclean, defiled Rv 22:11.*

ῥύπος, ου, ὁ dirt 1 Pt 3:21.*

ῥυπόω defile, pollute Rv 22:11 v.l.*

ῥῦσαι, ῥυσάσθω, ῥυσθῶ 1 aor. mid. impv. (Mt 6:13), 1 aor. mid. impv. 3 sing. (Mt 27:43), and 1 aor. pass. subj. 1 sing. of ῥύομαι.

ῥύσις, εως, ἡ flowing, flow Mk 5:25; Lk 8:43f.*

ῥυτίς, ίδος, ἡ wrinkle Eph 5:27.*

Ῥωμαϊκός, ή, όν Roman, Latin Lk 23:38 v.l.*

Ῥωμαῖος, α, ον Roman ὁ Ῥ. subst. the Roman, the Roman citizen J 11:48; Ac 2:10; 16:21, 37f; 22:25–27, 29; 23:27; 25:16; 28:17; Phlm subscr. Roman Christians Ro inscr.*

Ῥωμαϊστί adv. *in (the) Latin (language)* J 19:20; subscr. after Mk in minuscule 13 et al.*

Ῥώμη, ης, ἡ *Rome* Ac 18:2; 19:21; 23:11; 28:14, 16; Ro 1:7, 15; 2 Ti 1:17; 1 Pt 5:13 v.l.; subscriptions of Gal, Eph, Phil, Col, 2 Th, 2 Ti, Phlm, Hb.*

ῥώννυμι *be strong* pf. pass. impv. ἔρρωσο, ἔρρωσθε *farewell, goodbye* Ac 15:29; 23:30 v.l.*

Σ

σαβαχθάνι (Aramaic) *thou hast forsaken me* Mt 27:46; Mk 15:34.*

Σαβαώθ indecl. (Hebrew) *Sabaoth,* i.e. *armies, hosts* Ro 9:29; Js 5:4.*

σαββατισμός, οῦ, ὁ *Sabbath rest, Sabbath observance* fig. Hb 4:9.*

σάββατον, ου, τό—1. *Sabbath,* the seventh day of the week, held sacred by the Jews—a. sing. Mt 12:8; Mk 2:27f; Lk 6:7, 9; J 5:9f, 18; Ac 1:12; 13:27, 44.—b. pl., of more than one Sabbath Ac 17:2.—τὰ σάββατα for a single Sabbath day Mt 28:1a; Mk 1:21; 2:23f; Lk 4:16; 13:10; Ac 16:13.—2. *week*—a. sing. Mk 16:2 v.l., 9; Lk 18:12; 1 Cor 16:2.—b. pl., of a single week Mt 28:1b; Mk 16:2; Lk 24:1; J 20:1, 19; Ac 20:7; 1 Cor 16:2 v.l.

σαγήνη, ης, ἡ a large *dragnet* Mt 13:47.*

Σαδδουκαῖος, ου, ὁ *the Sadducee,* member of a Jewish party Mt 3:7; 16:1, 6, 11f; 22:23, 34; Mk 12:18; Lk 20:27; Ac 4:1; 5:17; 23:6–8.*

Σαδώκ, ὁ indecl. *Zadok* Mt 1:14; Lk 3:23ff v.l.*

σαίνω *fawn upon, flatter,* lit., of dogs 'wag the tail.' The pass. in 1 Th 3:3 may be rendered *be shaken* or *disturbed;* less likely, *be deceived.**

σάκκος, ου, ὁ *sack, sackcloth* Mt 11:21; Lk 10:13; Rv 6:12; 11:3.*

Σαλά, ὁ indecl. *Shelah*—1. Lk 3:32.—2. 3:35.*

Σαλαθιήλ, ὁ indecl. *Shealtiel, Salathiel* father of Zerubbabel Mt 1:12; Lk 3:27.*

Σαλαμίς, ῖνος, ἡ *Salamis,* a city on the east coast of Cyprus Ac 13:5.*

σαλεύω *shake, cause to move to and fro, cause to waver* or *totter, disturb*—1. lit. Mt 11:7; 24:29; Mk 13:25; Lk 6:38, 48; 7:24; 21:26; Ac 4:31; 16:26; Hb 12:26; Rv 6:13 v.l.—2. fig. Ac 2:25; 2 Th 2:2; Hb 12:27. *Upset, incite* Ac 17:13.*

Σαλήμ, ἡ *Salem* (Hebrew = peace) Hb 7:1f.*

Σαλίμ, τό indecl. *Salim,* a locality in Samaria J 3:23.*

Σαλμών, ὁ indecl. *Salmon* Mt 1:4f; Lk 3:32 v.l.*

Σαλμώνη, ης, ἡ *Salmone,* a promontory on the northeast corner of Crete Ac 27:7.*

σάλος, ου, ὁ *rolling* or *tossing motion, waves* in a rough sea Lk 21:25.*

σάλπιγξ, ιγγος, ἡ *trumpet*—1. the instrument itself 1 Cor 14:8; Hb 12:19; Rv 1:10; 4:1; 8:2, 6, 13; 9:14; Mt 24:31 v.l.—2. the sound made by the instrument, *trumpet call, (sound of the) trumpet* Mt 24:31; 1 Cor 15:52; 1 Th 4:16.* [*salpinx,* a Eustachian or a Fallopian tube]

σαλπίζω *sound the trumpet, trumpet (forth)* Mt 6:2; 1 Cor 15:52; Rv 8:6–8, 10, 12f; 9:1, 13; 10:7; 11:15.*

σαλπιστής, οῦ, ὁ *trumpeter* Rv 18:22.*

Σαλώμη, ης, ἡ *Salome,* a Galilean woman who followed Jesus Mk 15:40; 16:1; see also Mt 27:56. Salome was

Σαλωμών–Σάρρα   179

also the name of the daughter of Herodias who is mentioned but not named in Mk 6:22ff; Mt 14:6ff.*

Σαλωμών a variant of Σολομών Ac 7:47.*

Σαμάρεια, ας, ἡ Samaria, the province in west central Palestine Lk 17:11; J 4:4f, 7; Ac 1:8; 8:1, 5, 9, 14; 9:31; 15:3.*

Σαμαρία a different spelling for Σαμάρεια.

Σαμαρίτης, ου, ὁ Samaritan Mt 10:5; Lk 9:52; 10:33; 17:16; J 4:9, 39f; 8:48; Ac 8:25.*

Σαμαρῖτις, ιδος, ἡ adj. and subst. Samaritan (fem.) ἡ γυνὴ ἡ Σ. the Samaritan woman J 4:9.*

Σαμοθρᾴκη, ης, ἡ Samothrace, an island in the northern Aegean Sea Ac 16:11.*

Σάμος, ου, ἡ Samos, an island off the west coast of Asia Minor Ac 20:15.*

Σαμουήλ, ὁ indecl. Samuel (1 Samuel 1–25) Ac 3:24; 13:20; Hb 11:32.*

Σαμφουρειν indecl. J 11:54 v.l. = Sepphoris.*

Σαμψών, ὁ indecl. Samson (Judges 13–16) Hb 11:32.*

σανδάλιον, ου, τό sandal Mk 6:9; Ac 12:8.*

σανίς, ίδος, ἡ board, plank Ac 27:44.*

Σαούλ, ὁ indecl. Saul—1. first king of Israel Ac 13:21.—2. Jewish name of the Apostle Paul Ac 9:4, 17; 22:7, 13; 26:14. See Σαῦλος.*

σαπρός, ά, όν decayed, rotten—1. lit. Mt 7:17f; 12:33; Lk 6:43. Decayed or unusable Mt 13:48.—2. fig. bad, evil, unwholesome Eph 4:29.* [sapro-, a combining form meaning 'rotten,' as in saprogenic]

Σάπφιρα, gen. ης, dat. ῃ, ἡ Sapphira, a member of the church in Jerusalem, wife of Ananias Ac 5:1.*

σάπφιρος, ου, ἡ the sapphire Rv 21:19.*

σαργάνη, ης, ἡ basket, rope basket 2 Cor 11:33.*

Σάρδεις, εων, αἱ Sardis, the capital city of Lydia, in western Asia Minor Rv 1:11; 3:1, 4.*

σάρδινος, ου, ὁ late form of σάρδιον Rv 4:3 v.l. See σάρδιον.*

σάρδιον, ου, τό carnelian, sard(ius), a reddish precious stone Rv 4:3; 21:20.* [sard, a variety of carnelian]

σαρδόνυξ, υχος, ὁ sardonyx, a variety of agate Rv 21:20.*

Σάρεπτα, ων, τά Zarephath, a city on the Phoenician coast Lk 4:26.*

σαρκικός, ή, όν fleshly, in the manner of the flesh.—1. belonging to the order of earthly things, material Ro 15:27; 1 Cor 9:11.—2. belonging to the realm of the flesh, i.e. weak, sinful, transitory 1 Cor 3:3; 2 Cor 1:12; 10:4; 1 Pt 2:11. Also as v.l. in Ro 7:14; 1 Cor 3:1; Hb 7:16.*

σάρκινος, η, ον—1. fleshy, (made) of flesh 2 Cor 3:3.—2. fleshly, belonging to the realm of the flesh, i.e. weak, sinful, transitory Ro 7:14; 1 Cor 3:1; Hb 7:16; 2 Cor 1:12 v.l.*

σάρξ, σαρκός, ἡ flesh—1. lit. Lk 24:39; J 6:51–56; Ro 2:28; 1 Cor 15:39; 2 Cor 12:7; Gal 6:13; Js 5:3; Rv 19:18, 21.—2. the body Mk 10:8; Ac 2:26, 31; Gal 4:13; Eph 5:29; Col 2:5; Hb 9:10; 10:20; 1 Pt 4:1.—3. one having flesh and blood, a person Mt 16:17; Lk 3:6; J 1:14; Ro 3:20; Gal 1:16; 2:16.—4. human or mortal nature, earthly descent Ro 1:3; 4:1; 9:3, 5, 8; 1 Cor 10:18; Hb 2:14; 12:9.—5. corporeality, physical limitation(s), life here on earth 1 Cor 7:28; Gal 2:20; Phil 1:22, 24; Col 1:22, 24; 1 Pt 4:2.—6. the external or outward side of life, that which is natural or earthly J 8:15; 1 Cor 1:26; 2 Cor 5:16; 11:18; Eph 6:5; Phil 3:3f. ἐν σαρκί as a man Phlm 16.—7. the flesh, esp. in Paul's thought, is often the willing instrument of sin Mk 14:38; J 3:6; Ro 6:19; 7:5, 18, 25; 8:3–9, 12f; 2 Cor 1:17; Gal 5:13, 16f, 19, 24; Eph 2:3; Col 2:11, 18; Jd 23.—8. the flesh is the source of the sexual urge, with no suggestion of sinfulness J 1:13. [sarcous; sarcophagus, σάρξ + φαγεῖν]

Σαρούχ variant form of Σερούχ.

σαρόω sweep (clean) Mt 12:44; Lk 11:25; 15:8.*

Σάρρα, ας, ἡ Sarah, wife of Abraham Ro 4:19; 9:9; Hb 11:11; 1 Pt 3:6.*

Σαρών, ῶνος, ὁ (the accent is probable) *Sharon*, a plain along the north coast of Palestine Ac 9:35.*

σατάν, ὁ indecl. and **σατανᾶς, ᾶ, ὁ** *the Adversary, Satan*, the enemy of God and his people Mt 4:10; 12:26; Mk 1:13; 3:23, 26; 4:15; Lk 10:18; 11:18; 13:16; 22:3, 31; J 13:27; Ac 5:3; 26:18; Ro 16:20; 1 Cor 5:5; 7:5; 2 Cor 2:11; 11:14; 12:7; 1 Th 2:18; 2 Th 2:9; 1 Ti 1:20; 5:15; Rv 2:9, 13, 24; 3:9; 12:9; 20:2, 7.—In Mt 16:23; Mk 8:33 Peter is called Satan by Jesus because he is tempting the Master to abandon his role as Savior.*

σάτον, ου, τό *seah*, a Hebrew *measure* for grain, about a peck and a half Mt 13:33; Lk 13:21.*

Σαῦλος, ου, ὁ *Saul*, Grecized form of the Jewish name of the Apostle Paul (see Σαούλ) Ac 7:58; 8:1, 3; 9:1, 8, 11, 22, 24; 11:25, 30; 12:25; 13:1f, 7, 9; 22:7 v.l.; 26:14 v.l.*

σβέννυμι *extinguish, put out*—**1.** lit. Mt 12:20; 25:8; Mk 9:44, 46, 48; Eph 6:16; Hb 11:34.—**2.** fig. *quench, stifle, suppress* 1 Th 5:19.* [asbestos]

σβέσαι, σβέσει 1 aor. act. inf. and fut. act. ind. 3 sing. of σβέννυμι.

σέ acc. of σύ.

σεαυτοῦ, ῆς reflexive pron., only in gen., dat., and acc. *yourself*—**1.** gen. J 1:22; 2 Ti 4:11.—**2.** dat. Ac 9:34; 16:28; Ro 2:5.—**3.** acc. Mt 4:6; Mk 1:44; Lk 5:14; Ro 2:21; Gal 6:1.

σεβάζομαι *worship* pass. in act. meaning Ro 1:25.*

σέβασμα, ατος, τό *an object of worship, sanctuary* Ac 17:23; 2 Th 2:4.*

σεβαστός, ή, όν *revered, worthy of reverence, august*, as a translation of Lat. Augustus, designating the Roman emperor ὁ Σεβαστός *His Majesty the Emperor* Ac 25:21, 25. σπεῖρα Σεβαστή *imperial cohort* 27:1.*

σέβω mid. *worship* Mt 15:9; Mk 7:7; Ac 18:13; 19:27. σεβόμενοι τὸν θεόν *Godfearers, worshipers of God*, unconverted Gentiles who were attracted to the legacy of Israel but did not assume all the obligations of the Jewish law Ac 16:14; 18:7; cf. 13:43, 50; 17:4, 17.*

σειρά, ᾶς, ἡ *chain* 2 Pt 2:4.*

σειρός a variant spelling for σιρός.

σεισμός, οῦ, ὁ *shaking:* of a *storm* at sea Mt 8:24. *Earthquake* 24:7; 27:54; 28:2; Mk 13:8; Lk 21:11; Ac 16:26; Rv 6:12; 8:5; 11:13, 19; 16:18.* [seismic]

σείω *shake, cause to quake, agitate*—**1.** lit. Hb 12:26. Pass. Mt 27:51; Rv 6:13.—**2.** fig. *stir up* pass. *be stirred* Mt 21:10. *Tremble* 28:4.*

Σεκοῦνδος, ου, ὁ (a Latin name) *Secundus* Ac 20:4.*

Σελεύκεια, ας, ἡ *Seleucia*, the port city of Antioch in Syria Ac 13:4.*

σελήνη, ης, ἡ *moon* Mt 24:29; Mk 13:24; Lk 21:25; Ac 2:20; 1 Cor 15:41; Rv 8:12. [selenite, a variety of gypsum]

σεληνιάζομαι *be moonstruck* Mt 4:24; 17:15.*

Σεμεῖν, ὁ indecl. *Semein* Lk 3:26.*

σεμίδαλις, εως, ἡ *fine flour* Rv 18:13.*

σεμνός, ή, όν *worthy of respect, dignified, serious* 1 Ti 3:8, 11; Tit 2:2. *Honorable, worthy, holy, above reproach* Phil 4:8.*

σεμνότης, τητος, ἡ *reverence, dignity, seriousness, probity* 1 Ti 2:2; 3:4; Tit 2:7.*

Σέργιος, ου, ὁ *Sergius*, a Roman tribal name Ac 13:7.*

Σερούχ, ὁ indecl. *Serug* Lk 3:35.*

σέσηπα 2 pf. act. ind. of σήπω (Js 5:2).

σέσωκα 1 pf. act. ind. of σώζω.

Σήθ, ὁ indecl. *Seth* (Gen 4:25f) Lk 3:38.*

Σήμ, ὁ indecl. *Shem* (Gen 5:32) Lk 3:36.*

σημαίνω—**1.** *make known, report, communicate* Ac 25:27; Rv 1:1.—**2.** *indicate (beforehand), foretell* J 12:33; 18:32; 21:19; Ac 11:28.* [semantic]

σημᾶναι 1 aor. act. inf. of σημαίνω.

σημεῖον, ου, τό *sign*—**1.** *the sign* or *(distinguishing) mark* by which something is known, *token, indication* Mt 16:3; 24:3, 30; Mk 13:4; Lk 2:12, 34; 11:29f; 21:7; Ro 4:11; 1 Cor 14:22; 2 Th 3:17. *Signal* Mt 26:48.—**2.** *a sign* consisting of a *miracle* or *wonder*—**a.** *miracle* of divine origin Mt 12:38f; 16:1, 4; Mk 8:11f; 16:17, 20; Lk 11:16, 29; 23:8; J 2:11, 18; 3:2; 4:48; 6:2, 14; 7:31; 9:16;

Ac 2:22, 43; 4:16, 22; 14:3; Ro 15:19; 1 Cor 1:22; 2 Cor 12:12a; Hb 2:4.—b. *miracle* of a demonic nature Mk 13:22; 2 Th 2:9; Rv 13:13f; 16:14; 19:20.—c. *portent* Lk 21:11, 25; Ac 2:19; Rv 12:1, 3; 15:1. [*semio-*, combining form as in *semiology, semiotic*]

σημειόω mid. *mark, take special notice* of 2 Th 3:14.*

σήμερον adv. *today* Mt 6:11; Lk 23:43; Ac 4:9; Js 4:13. *ἡ σήμερον ἡμέρα today, this very day* Mt 28:15; Ac 20:26; Ro 11:8; 2 Cor 3:14.

σημικίνθιον another spelling for *σιμικίνθιον*.

σήπω *cause to rot* 2 pf. *σέσηπα rot, decay* Js 5:2.*

σηρικός another spelling for *σιρικός*.

σής, σητός, ὁ *the moth*, whose larvae eat clothing Mt 6:19f; Lk 12:33.*

σητόβρωτος, ον *motheaten* Js 5:2.*

σθενόω *strengthen* 1 Pt 5:10.*

σιαγών, όνος, ἡ *cheek* Mt 5:39; Lk 6:29.*

σιαίνομαι *be disturbed* or *annoyed* 1 Th 3:3 v.l.*

σιγάτωσαν pres. act. impv. 3 pl. of *σιγάω*.

σιγάω—**1.** intrans. *be silent, keep still*—**a.** *say nothing, keep silent* Lk 20:26; Ac 15:12; 1 Cor 14:28, 30, 34.—**b.** *stop speaking, become silent* Lk 18:39; Ac 15:13; 1 Cor 14:30.—**c.** *hold one's tongue* Lk 9:36.—**2.** trans. *keep secret, conceal* pass. Ro 16:25.*

σιγή, ῆς, ἡ *silence* Ac 21:40; Rv 8:1.*

σίδηρος, ου, ὁ *iron* Rv 18:12.*

σιδηροῦς, ᾶ, οῦν *(made of) iron* Ac 12:10; Rv 2:27; 9:9; 12:5; 19:15.* [*siderite*, a mineral popularly known as lodestone]

Σιδών, ῶνος, ἡ *Sidon*, an ancient royal city in Phoenicia Mt 11:21f; Mk 3:8; 7:31; Lk 6:17; Ac 27:3.

Σιδώνιος, ία, ιον *Sidonian, from Sidon* Ac 12:20. *ἡ Σιδωνία the country around Sidon* Lk 4:26.*

σικάριος, ου, ὁ (Latin loanword: sicarius) *dagger man, assassin, terrorist* Ac 21:38.*

σίκερα, τό indecl. Akkadian loanword *strong drink, beer* Lk 1:15.* [Cf *cider*.]

Σίλας, α or **Σιλᾶς, ᾶ, ὁ** *Silas*, friend and companion of Paul, mentioned 12 times Ac 15:22 to 18:5.—The same person as *Σιλουανός*.*

Σιλουανός, οῦ, ὁ *Silvanus* 2 Cor 1:19; 1 Th 1:1; 2 Th 1:1; 1 Pt 5:12.—The same person as *Σίλας*.*

Σιλωάμ, ὁ indecl. *Siloam*, a system of water supply in Jerusalem Lk 13:4; J 9:7, 11.*

Σιμαίας, ου, ὁ *Simaias* 2 Ti 4:19 v.l.*

σιμικίνθιον, ου, τό (Latin loanword: semicinctium) *an apron*, such as is used by workmen Ac 19:12.*

Σίμων, ωνος, ὁ *Simon*—**1.** Simon Peter = Cephas Mt 4:18; Mk 1:16; Lk 4:38 and often. See Πέτρος.—**2.** Simon, another of the 12 disciples, called ὁ Καναναῖος Mt 10:4; Mk 3:18 or (ὁ) ζηλωτής Lk 6:15; Ac 1:13.—**3.** name of a brother of Jesus Mt 13:55; Mk 6:3.—**4.** Simon of Cyrene, who carried Jesus' cross Mt 27:32; Mk 15:21; Lk 23:26.—**5.** father of Judas Iscariot J 6:71; 12:4 v.l.; 13:2, 26.—**6.** Simon the leper Mt 26:6; Mk 14:3.—**7.** Simon the Pharisee Lk 7:40, 43f.—**8.** Simon the tanner in Joppa Ac 9:43; 10:6, 17, 32b.—**9.** Simon the magician Ac 8:9, 13, 18, 24.

Σινά indecl. *Sinai*, a mountain on the peninsula of the same name Ac 7:30, 38; Gal 4:24f.*

σίναπι, εως, τό *mustard* Mt 13:31; 17:20; Mk 4:31; Lk 13:19; 17:6.*

σινδών, όνος, ἡ *linen cloth* or *sheet* Mt 27:59; Mk 15:46; Lk 23:53; *sheet* or *tunic* Mk 14:51f.*

σινιάζω *shake in a sieve, sift* fig. Lk 22:31.*

σιρικός, ή, όν *silk(en)* subst. *τὸ σιρικόν silk* cloth or garments Rv 18:12.*

σιρός, οῦ, ὁ *pit, cave* 2 Pt 2:4 v.l.*

σιτευτός, ή, όν *fattened* Lk 15:23, 27, 30.*

σιτίον, ου, τό pl. *food (made from grain)* Ac 7:12.*

σιτιστός, ή, όν *fattened* subst. *τὰ σιτιστά cattle that have been fattened* Mt 22:4.*

σιτομέτριον, ου, τό a measured allowance of grain or food, a ration Lk 12:42.*

σῖτος, ου, ὁ wheat, grain in general Mt 3:12; 13:25, 29; Mk 4:28; Lk 16:7; 22:31; J 12:24; 1 Cor 15:37; Rv 6:6. The form τὰ σῖτα Ac 7:12 v.l. [parasite, παρά + σῖτος]

Σιχάρ a variant of Συχάρ.

Σιών, ἡ indecl. Zion—1. Mount Zion, a hill within the city of Jerusalem Hb 12:22; Rv 14:1.—2. in poetic usage: the daughter of Zion in ref. to Jerusalem and its inhabitants Mt 21:5; J 12:15.— Of the people of Israel Ro 9:33; 11:26.— Of the New Jerusalem of Christianity 1 Pt 2:6.*

σιωπάω be silent—1. keep silent, say nothing Mt 26:63; Mk 3:4; 9:34; 14:61; Ac 18:9.—2. stop speaking, be or become quiet Mt 20:31; Mk 10:48; Lk 18:39 v.l.; 19:40. Lose the ability to speak Lk 1:20.—Symbolically Mk 4:39.* [aposiopesis, ἀπό + σιωπᾶν, breaking off in the expression of a thought]

σιωπῇ adv. quietly, privately J 11:28 v.l.*

σκανδαλίζω—1. cause to be caught or to fall, i.e. cause to sin—a. someone Mt 5:29f; Mk 9:42f, 45, 47; 1 Cor 8:13. Pass. be led into sin perh. 2 Cor 11:29 (see below). Be led into sin, fall away Mt 13:21; 24:10; J 16:1.—b. σκανδαλίζεσθαι ἔν τινι be led into sin or repelled by someone, take offense at someone Mt 11:6; 26:31, 33; Mk 6:3.— 2. give offense to, anger, shock Mt 17:27; J 6:61. Pass. Mt 15:12. τίς σκανδαλίζεται; perh. who has any reason to take offense? 2 Cor 11:29 (see 1a above). [scandalize]

σκάνδαλον, ου, τό—1. trap symbolically Ro 11:9.—2. temptation to sin, enticement Mt 16:23; 18:7; Lk 17:1; Ro 14:13; 16:17; Rv 2:14.—3. that which gives offense or causes revulsion, that which arouses opposition, an object of anger or disapproval, a stain, fault, etc. Mt 13:41; 1 Cor 1:23; Gal 5:11; 1 J 2:10. πέτρα σκανδάλου a stone that causes people to fall Ro 9:33; 1 Pt 2:8.* [scandal]

σκάπτω dig Lk 6:48; 13:8; 16:3.*

Σκαριώθ is the reading of ms. D in Mk 3:19; J 6:71 and Σκαριώτης is the reading of the same ms. in Mt 10:4; 26:14; Mk 14:10 for Ἰσκαριώθ or Ἰσκαριώτης.*

σκάφη, ης, ἡ (small) boat, skiff Ac 27:16, 30, 32.* [Cf. scaphoid, boat-shaped.]

σκέλος, ους, τό leg J 19:31-33.*

σκέπασμα, ατος, τό covering, shelter, clothing, house 1 Ti 6:8.*

Σκευᾶς, ᾶ, ὁ Sceva Ac 19:14.*

σκευή, ῆς, ἡ equipment, ship's gear Ac 27:19.*

σκεῦος, ους, τό—1. lit.—a. generally thing, object Mk 11:16; Ac 10:11, 16; 11:5; Hb 9:21; Rv 18:12. Pl. property Mt 12:29; Mk 3:27; Lk 17:31. Perh. kedge or driving anchor Ac 27:17.—b. vessel, jar, dish, etc. Lk 8:16; J 19:29; Ro 9:21; 2 Ti 2:20f; Rv 2:27.—2. fig., often of the human body, vessel, etc. Ro 9:22f; 2 Cor 4:7; 1 Pt 3:7. σκεῦος ἐκλογῆς a chosen instrument Ac 9:15. τὸ ἑαυτοῦ σκεῦος 1 Th 4:4 may refer either to one's own body or one's own wife.*

σκηνή, ῆς, ἡ tent, booth Mt 17:4; Mk 9:5; Lk 9:33; Hb 11:9.—The Tent of Testimony or Tabernacle Ac 7:44; Hb 8:2, 5; 9:11, 21; 13:10; Rv 15:5. The tabernacle consists of the Holy Place Hb 9:2, 6, 8 and the Holy of Holies 9:3, cf. 7. Of another sanctuary Ac 7:43.— Dwelling generally Lk 16:9; Ac 15:16; Rv 13:6; 21:3.* [scene]

σκηνοπηγία, ας, ἡ the building of tents or booths, hence the Festival of Booths or Tabernacles, Succoth, celebrated in autumn J 5:1 v.l.; 7:2.*

σκηνοποιός, οῦ, ὁ tentmaker Ac 18:3.*

σκῆνος, ους, τό tent, lodging fig. 2 Cor 5:1, 4.*

σκηνόω live, dwell J 1:14; Rv 7:15; 12:12; 13:6; 21:3.*

σκήνωμα, ατος, τό dwelling place, lodging Ac 7:46; 2 Pt 1:13f.*

σκιά, ᾶς, ἡ—1. shade, shadow lit. Mk 4:32; Ac 5:15. Fig. Mt 4:16; Lk 1:79; 1 J 2:8 v.l.—2. shadow, foreshadowing Col 2:17; Hb 8:5; 10:1.*

σκιρτάω leap, spring about Lk 1:41, 44; 6:23.*

σκληροκαρδία, ας, ἡ hardness of heart, obstinacy Mt 19:8; Mk 10:5; 16:14.*

σκληρός, ά, όν hard (to the touch) fig. hard, harsh, unpleasant J 6:60; Jd 15; rough, strong Js 3:4; strict, harsh, cruel Mt 25:24. σκληρόν σοι it is hard for you Ac 9:4 v.l.; 26:14.*

σκληρότης, ητος, ἡ hardness (of heart), stubbornness Ro 2:5.* [Cf. arteriosclerosis.]

σκληροτράχηλος, ον stiff-necked, stubborn Ac 7:51.*

σκληρύνω harden, fig. make stubborn Ac 19:9; Ro 9:18; Hb 3:8, 13, 15; 4:7.*

σκολιός, ά, όν crooked lit. Lk 3:5. Fig. crooked, unscrupulous, dishonest Ac 2:40; Phil 2:15; 1 Pt 2:18.*

σκόλοψ, οπος, ὁ thorn, splinter 2 Cor 12:7.*

σκοπέω look (out) for, notice, keep one's eyes on, consider Lk 11:35; Ro 16:17; 2 Cor 4:18; Gal 6:1; Phil 2:4; 3:17.*

σκοπός, οῦ, ὁ goal, mark Phil 3:14.* [scope]

σκορπίζω scatter, disperse Mt 12:30; Lk 11:23; J 10:12; 16:32. Distribute 2 Cor 9:9.*

σκορπίος, ου, ὁ scorpion Lk 10:19; 11:12; Rv 9:3, 5, 10.*

σκοτεινός, ή, όν dark Mt 6:23; Lk 11:34, 36.*

σκοτία, ας, ἡ darkness, gloom lit. or fig. Mt 4:16 v.l.; 10:27; Lk 12:3; J 1:5; 6:17; 8:12; 12:35, 46; 20:1; 1 J 1:5; 2:8f, 11.*

σκοτίζομαι pass. be or become dark, be darkened lit. or fig. Mt 24:29; Mk 13:24; Lk 23:45 v.l.; Ro 1:21; 11:10; Rv 8:12; Eph 4:18 v.l.*

σκότος, ους, τό darkness, gloom—1. lit. Mt 8:12; Mk 15:33; Ac 13:11; 2 Pt 2:17. Masculine form as v.l. Hb 12:18.—2. fig. Mt 4:16; 6:23; Lk 1:79; J 3:19; Ac 26:18; Ro 13:12; 1 Cor 4:5; 2 Cor 6:14; Col 1:13. [scoto-, a combining form, as in scotophobia, scotoscope]

σκοτόω pass. be or become darkened lit. or fig. Eph 4:18; Rv 9:2; 16:10.*

σκύβαλον, ου, τό refuse, rubbish, dirt, dung Phil 3:8.*

Σκύθης, ου, ὁ the Scythian, living in what is now southern Russia Col 3:11.*

σκυθρωπός, (ή), όν with a sad, gloomy, or sullen look Mt 6:16; Lk 24:17.*

σκύλλου pres. mid. impv. 2 sing. of σκύλλω.

σκύλλω trouble, bother, annoy Mk 5:35; Lk 8:49. Pass. be weary or harassed Mt 9:36. Mid. trouble oneself Lk 7:6.*

σκῦλον, ου, τό pl. booty, spoils Lk 11:22.*

σκωληκόβρωτος, ον eaten by worms Ac 12:23.*

σκώληξ, ηκος, ὁ worm Mk 9:44 v.l., 46 v.l., 48.*

σμαράγδινος, η, ον (of) emerald Rv 4:3.*

σμάραγδος, ου, ὁ emerald Rv 21:19.*

σμῆγμα, ατος, τό ointment, salve J 19:39 v.l.*

σμίγμα, ατος, τό v.l. for μίγμα J 19:39.*

σμύρνα, ης, ἡ myrrh an aromatic resinous gum Mt 2:11; J 19:39.*

Σμύρνα, ης, ἡ Smyrna, a large city on the west coast of Asia Minor Rv 1:11; 2:8.*

Σμυρναῖος, α, ον coming from Smyrna ὁ Σ. the Smyrnaean Rv 2:8 v.l.*

σμυρνίζω treat or flavor with myrrh Mk 15:23.*

Σόδομα, ων, τά Sodom (Gen 19:24) Mt 11:23f; Lk 17:29; Ro 9:29; 2 Pt 2:6; Rv 11:8.

σοί dat. sing of σύ.

Σολομών, ῶνος, ὁ and Σολομῶν, ῶντος, ὁ Solomon, son and successor of David Mt 1:6f; 6:29; Lk 11:31; J 10:23; Ac 3:11; 7:47.

σορός, οῦ, ἡ coffin, bier Lk 7:14.*

σός, σή, σόν your, yours (sing.); in older and formal usage thy, thine Mt 7:3, 22; Mk 2:18; J 4:42; 18:35; Ac 5:4; 1 Cor 8:11; Phlm 14. οἱ σοί your own people Mk 5:19. τὸ σόν, τὰ σά what is yours Mt 20:14; Lk 6:30; J 17:10.

σοῦ gen. sing. of σύ.

σουδάριον, ου, τό (Latin loanword: sudarium) facecloth, handkerchief Lk 19:20; J 11:44; 20:7; Ac 19:12.*

Σουσάννα, ης or ας, ἡ Susanna Lk 8:3.*

σοφία, ας, ἡ *wisdom*—**1.** the *wisdom* found among people, whether natural or imparted by God Mt 12:42; Ac 6:3, 10; 7:10, 22; 1 Cor 1:19f; 2:13; Col 1:28; Js 3:13, 15, 17; 2 Pt 3:15.—**2.** *wisdom* of Christ and of God Mk 6:2; Lk 2:40, 52; 1 Cor 1:21a, 24, 30; Col 2:3.—**3.** *Wisdom*, probable personification in Mt 11:19; Lk 7:35; 11:49. [*philosophy*, φιλεῖν + σοφία]

σοφίζω *make wise, teach* 2 Ti 3:15. *Reason out, devise craftily* pass. 2 Pt 1:16.* [*sophism*]

σοφός, ή, όν—**1.** *clever, skillful, experienced* 1 Cor 3:10; 6:5.—**2.** *wise, learned* of wisdom from a natural or divine source Mt 23:34; Lk 10:21; Ro 1:14, 22; 1 Cor 1:19f, 26f; 3:18; Eph 5:15; Js 3:13.—**3.** God is called *wise* in the absolute sense Ro 16:27; 1 Cor 1:25. [*sophomore*, σοφός + μωρός]

Σπανία, ας, ἡ *Spain* Ro 15:24, 28.*

σπαράσσω *tear, pull to and fro, convulse* Mk 1:26; 9:20 v.l., 26; Lk 9:39.*

σπαργανόω *wrap (up) in (swaddling) cloths* Lk 2:7, 12.*

σπαρείς 2 aor. pass. ptc. of σπείρω.

σπαταλάω *live luxuriously* or *indulgently* 1 Ti 5:6; Js 5:5.*

σπάω mid. *draw* Mk 14:47; Ac 16:27.*

σπεῖρα, ης, ἡ *cohort* (normally about 600 soldiers) Mt 27:27; Mk 15:16; J 18:3, 12; Ac 10:1; 21:31; 27:1.*

σπείρω *sow seed*—**1.** lit. Mt 6:26; Mk 4:3, 31; Lk 8:5; 1 Cor 15:36f.—**2.** fig. Mt 25:24, 26; Mk 4:14; J 4:36f; 1 Cor 15:42–44; Gal 6:7; Js 3:18.

σπεκουλάτωρ, ορος, ὁ *executioner* Mk 6:27.* [Latin loanword: speculator, meaning spy, explorer; *speculator*]

σπένδω *offer a libation* or *drink offering* pass. and fig. *be offered up* Phil 2:17; 2 Ti 4:6.*

σπέρμα, ατος, τό *seed*—**1.** lit. Mt 13:24, 27, 37f; Mk 4:31; J 7:42; 1 Cor 15:38; 2 Cor 9:10 v.l.; Hb 11:11.—**2.** fig. *survivors* Ro 9:29. *Descendants, children, posterity* Mt 22:24; Mk 12:20, 22; Lk 1:55; J 8:33, 37; Ac 13:23; Ro 9:7f; 11:1; Gal 3:16, 19; Hb 2:16. *Nature* 1 J 3:9. [*sperm*]

σπερμολόγος, ον *picking up seeds,* subst. a bird *the rook,* fig. *gossip, chatterer, ragpicker* Ac 17:18.*

σπεύδω—**1.** intrans. *hurry, make haste* Lk 2:16; 19:5f; Ac 20:16; 22:18.—**2.** trans. *hasten* or *strive for* 2 Pt 3:12.*

σπήλαιον, ου, τό *cave, hideout* Mt 21:13; Mk 11:17; Lk 19:46; J 11:38; Hb 11:38; Rv 6:15.* [*speleology*]

σπιλάς, άδος, ἡ either *a rock washed by the sea, a (hidden) reef* or *spot, stain* symbolically Jd 12.*

σπίλος, ου, ὁ *spot* fig. *stain, blemish* Eph 5:27; 2 Pt 2:13.*

σπιλόω *stain, defile* fig. Js 3:6; Jd 23.*

σπλαγχνίζομαι *have pity, feel sympathy* Mt 14:14; 18:27; Mk 1:41; 6:34; 8:2; Lk 7:13; 15:20.

σπλάγχνον, ου, τό pl.—**1.** lit. *inward parts, entrails* Ac 1:18.—**2.** fig., of the seat of the emotions, in our usage *heart* Lk 1:78; 2 Cor 6:12; 7:15; Phil 2:1; Col 3:12; Phlm 7, 20; 1 J 3:17. *Love, affection* Phil 1:8; *object of affection, beloved* Phlm 12.* [*splanchnic*]

σπόγγος, ου, ὁ *sponge* Mt 27:48; Mk 15:36; J 19:29.*

σποδός, οῦ, ἡ *ashes* Mt 11:21; Lk 10:13; Hb 9:13.*

σπορά, ᾶς, ἡ *seed* 1 Pt 1:23.* [*spore*]

σπόριμος, ον *sown,* subst. τὰ σπόριμα *standing grain, grain fields* Mt 12:1; Mk 2:23; Lk 6:1.*

σπόρος, ου, ὁ *seed* Mk 4:26f; Lk 8:5, 11; 2 Cor 9:10.*

σπουδάζω—**1.** *hasten, hurry* 2 Ti 4:9, 21; Tit 3:12, though mng. 2 is acceptable in these passages.—**2.** *be zealous* or *eager, take pains, make every effort* Gal 2:10; Eph 4:3; 1 Th 2:17; 2 Ti 2:15; Hb 4:11; 2 Pt 1:10, 15; 3:14.*

σπουδαῖος, α, ον *eager, zealous, earnest* 2 Cor 8:22a; comp. σπουδαιότερος *very earnest, more zealous* 8:17, 22b. Cf 2 Ti 1:17 v.l.*

σπουδαίως adv.—**1.** *with haste* comp. σπουδαιοτέρως *with special urgency* Phil 2:28.—**2.** *diligently, earnestly, zealously* 2 Ti 1:17; Tit 3:13; *strongly* Lk 7:4. Comp. *very eagerly* σπου-

δαιότερον and σπουδαιοτέρως both as
v.l. in 2 Ti 1:17.*

σπουδή, ῆς, ἡ—1. haste, speed Mk 6:25;
Lk 1:39.—2. eagerness, enthusiasm,
diligence, zeal Ro 12:8, 11; 2 Cor 7:11;
8:7f; Hb 6:11; 2 Pt 1:5; Jd 3. Good will,
devotion 2 Cor 7:12; 8:16.*

σπυρίς, ίδος, ἡ basket, hamper Mt
15:37; 16:10; Mk 8:8, 20; Ac 9:25.*

στάδιον, ου, τό—1. stade as a measure
of distance = about 192 meters. Mt
14:24; Lk 24:13; J 6:19; 11:18; Rv 14:20;
21:16.—2. arena, stadium 1 Cor 9:24.*

σταθείς, σταθῆναι, σταθήσομαι 1
aor. pass. ptc., 1 aor. pass. inf., and 1
fut. pass. of ἵστημι.

στάμνος, ου, ὁ or ἡ jar Hb 9:4.*

στασιαστής, οῦ, ὁ rebel, revolutionary
Mk 15:7.*

στάσις, εως, ἡ—1. existence, continu-
ance Hb 9:8.—2. uprising, riot, revolt,
rebellion Mk 15:7; Lk 23:19, 25; Ac
19:40.—3. strife, discord, dissension
Ac 15:2; 24:5; dispute 23:7, 10.* [stasis]

στατήρ, ῆρος, ὁ the stater, a silver coin
= four drachmas Mt 17:27; 26:15 v.l.
for the neut. pl. ἀργύρια.*

σταυρός, οῦ, ὁ the cross—1. lit. Mt 27:32,
40, 42; Mk 15:21, 30, 32; Lk 23:26; J
19:17, 19, 25, 31; Phil 2:8; Hb 12:2.—
2. symbolically, of suffering and death
Mt 10:38; 16:24; Mk 8:34; 10:21 v.l.;
Lk 9:23; 14:27.—3. the cross of Christ
as one of the most important elements
in Christian teaching 1 Cor 1:17f; Gal
5:11; 6:12, 14; Eph 2:16; Phil 2:8; 3:18;
Col 1:20; 2:14.*

σταυρόω nail to the cross, crucify—1.
lit. Mk 15 passim; 16:6; J 19:6, 10, 15f;
Ac 2:36; 4:10; 1 Cor 2:8; 2 Cor 13:4;
Rv 11:8.—2. fig. Gal 5:24; 6:14.

σταφυλή, ῆς, ἡ (a bunch of) grapes Mt
7:16; Lk 6:44; Rv 14:18.* [staphyloma]

στάχυς, υος, ὁ head or ear (of grain) Mt
12:1; Mk 2:23; 4:28; Lk 6:1.*

Στάχυς, υος, ὁ Stachys Ro 16:9.*

στέγη, ης, ἡ roof Mt 8:8; Mk 2:4; Lk
7:6.*

στέγω—1. cover, pass over in silence
perh. keep confidential 1 Cor 13:7,
though mng. 2 is also possible.—2.

bear, stand, endure 1 Cor 9:12; perh.
13:7 (see 1 above); 1 Th 3:1, 5.* [Cf.
Stegosaurus, a genus of dinosaur.]

στεῖρα, ας, ἡ (a) barren (woman), one
incapable of bearing children Lk 1:7,
36; 23:29; Gal 4:27; Hb 11:11.* [Cf.
sterile.]

στέλλω mid.—1. keep away, stand aloof
2 Th 3:6.—2. avoid, try to avoid 2 Cor
8:20.*

στέμμα, ατος, τό wreath or garland Ac
14:13.*

στεναγμός, οῦ, ὁ sigh, groan, groaning
Ac 7:34; Ro 8:26.*

στενάζω sigh, groan Mk 7:34; Ro 8:23;
2 Cor 5:2, 4; Hb 13:17; complain Js
5:9.*

στενός, ή, όν narrow Mt 7:13f; Lk
13:24.* [stenography, στένος + γρά-
φειν]

στενοχωρέω crowd, cramp, confine, re-
strict pass., fig. 2 Cor 6:12; be crushed
4:8.*

στενοχωρία, ας, ἡ fig. distress, difficulty, anguish, trouble Ro 2:9; 8:35; 2
Cor 6:4; 12:10.*

στερεός, ά, όν—1. lit. firm, solid, strong
2 Ti 2:19; Hb 5:12, 14.—2. fig. steadfast, firm 1 Pt 5:9.* [stereo-, combining
form, as in stereotype]

στερεόω make strong, make firm—1. lit.
Ac 3:7, 16.—2. fig. 16:5.*

στερέωμα, ατος, τό firmness, steadfastness Col 2:5.*

Στεφανᾶς, ᾶ, ὁ Stephanas, a Corinthian
Christian 1 Cor 1:16; 16:15, 17; subscr.*

Στέφανος, ου, ὁ Stephen, first Christian
martyr Ac 6:5, 8f; 7:1 v.l., 59; 8:2; 11:19;
22:20.*

στέφανος, ου, ὁ wreath, crown—1. lit.
Mt 27:29; Mk 15:17; J 19:2, 5; 1 Cor
9:25; Rv 4:4, 10; 6:2; 9:7; 12:1; 14:14.—
2. fig.—a. prize, reward 2 Ti 4:8; Js
1:12; 1 Pt 5:4; Rv 2:10; 3:11.—b.
adornment, pride Phil 4:1; 1 Th 2:19.*
[stephanotis, a genus of shrub]

στεφανόω crown, wreathe lit. 2 Ti 2:5.
Fig. honor, reward, crown Hb 2:7, 9.*

στῆθι 2 aor. act. impv. of ἵστημι.

στῆθος, ους, τό chest, breast Lk 18:13; 23:48; J 13:25; 21:20; Rv 15:6.* [stetho-, combining form, as in stethoscope]

στήκω—1. lit. stand Mk 3:31; 11:25; J 1:26; 8:44 is best taken as a form of ἵστημι; Rv 12:4 v.l.—2. fig. stand firm, be steadfast Ro 14:4; 1 Cor 16:13; Gal 5:1; Phil 1:27; 4:1; 1 Th 3:8; 2 Th 2:15.*

στῆναι 2 aor. act. inf. of ἵστημι.

στηριγμός, οῦ, ὁ firmness 2 Pt 3:17.*

στηρίζω set up, fix (firmly), establish, support—1. lit. Lk 16:26; set 9:51.—2. fig. confirm, establish, strengthen Lk 22:32; Ac 18:23 v.l.; Ro 1:11; 16:25; 1 Th 3:2, 13; 2 Th 2:17; 3:3; Js 5:8; 1 Pt 5:10; 2 Pt 1:12; Rv 3:2.*

στήσομαι fut. mid. ind. of ἵστημι.

στιβάς, άδος, ἡ leaves, leafy branches Mk 11:8.*

στίγμα, ατος, τό mark, brand Gal 6:17.* [stigma]

στιγμή, ῆς, ἡ moment Lk 4:5.*

στίλβω shine, be radiant Mk 9:3.*

στοά, ᾶς, ἡ (roofed) colonnade or cloister, portico J 5:2; 10:23; Ac 3:11; 5:12.*

στοιβάς a variant spelling of στιβάς.

Στοϊκός, ή, όν Stoic Ac 17:18.*

στοιχεῖον, ου, τό pl.—1. elements (of learning), fundamental principles, letters of the alphabet, ABCs Hb 5:12. This meaning is also possible in passages from Gal and Col under 3 below.—2. elemental substances, elements from which everything is made 2 Pt 3:10, 12.—3. elemental spirits may be the meaning in Gal 4:3, 9; Col 2:8, 20, but mng. 1 above is also possible.* [Cf. stoichiology, στοιχεῖον + λόγος, relating to the elements composing animal tissues.]

στοιχέω hold to, agree with, follow w. dat. Ac 21:24; Ro 4:12; Gal 5:25; 6:16; Phil 3:16.*

στολή, ῆς, ἡ robe, esp. a long, flowing robe Mk 12:38; Lk 15:22; Rv 6:11; 7:9; 22:14. [stole]

στόμα, ατος, τό—1. mouth Mt 4:4; 12:34; 15:11, 17f; Lk 1:64; 4:22; 21:15; Ac 8:32; 2 Cor 13:1; Col 3:8; Hb 11:33; Js 3:3, 10; Rv 9:17–19; 14:5.—2. edge of a sword Lk 21:24; Hb 11:34. [stoma,

mouthlike opening in lower animals or in the epidermis of plants]

στόμαχος, ου, ὁ stomach 1 Ti 5:23.*

στρατεία, ας, ἡ campaign fig. warfare 2 Cor 10:4; flight 1 Ti 1:18.*

στράτευμα, ατος, τό army Rv 19:14, 19. Of a smaller detachment Ac 23:10, 27. τὰ στρατεύματα the troops Mt 22:7; Lk 23:11; Rv 9:16.*

στρατεύομαι do military service, serve in the army—1. lit. Lk 3:14; 1 Cor 9:7; 2 Ti 2:4.—2. fig. 2 Cor 10:3; 1 Ti 1:18; Js 4:1; 1 Pt 2:11.*

στρατηγός, οῦ, ὁ—1. praetor, chief magistrate at Philippi Ac 16:20, 22, 35f, 38.—2. captain Lk 22:4, 52; Ac 4:1; 5:24, 26.* [strategy]

στρατιά, ᾶς, ἡ army Lk 2:13; host Ac 7:42. Equivalent to στρατεία warfare 2 Cor 10:4 v.l.*

στρατιώτης, ου, ὁ soldier lit. Mt 8:9; 27:27; 28:12; Mk 15:16; Lk 7:8; J 19:2; Ac 10:7. Fig. 2 Ti 2:3.

στρατολογέω gather an army, enlist soldiers 2 Ti 2:4.*

στρατοπεδάρχης or στρατοπέδαρχος, ου, ὁ military commander, commandant of a camp Ac 28:16 v.l.*

στρατόπεδον, ου, τό army, body of troops Lk 21:20.*

στραφείς 2 aor. pass. ptc. of στρέφω.

στρεβλόω twist, distort 2 Pt 3:16.*

στρέφω—1. act.—a. trans. turn Mt 5:39; perh. Ac 7:42 (see 1b below). Turn, change Rv 11:6. Bring back, return Mt 27:3.—b. intrans. turn (away) perh. Ac 7:42 (see 1a above).—2. pass.—a. turn around, turn toward lit. Mt 7:6; 9:22; Lk 22:61; 23:28; J 1:38. Fig. Ac 7:39; 13:46.—b. turn, change inwardly, be converted Mt 18:3; J 12:40.

στρέψον 1 aor. act. impv. 2 sing. of στρέφω.

στρηνιάω live in luxury, live sensually Rv 18:7, 9.*

στρῆνος, ους, τό sensuality, luxury Rv 18:3.*

στρουθίον, ου, τό sparrow Mt 10:29, 31; Lk 12:6f.*

στρωννύω = στρώννυμι spread (out) Mt 21:8; Mk 11:8. The pf. pass. ptc.

ἐστρωμένον Mk 14:15; Lk 22:12 may mean *paved* or *furnished*. στρῶσον σεαυτῷ *make your own bed* Ac 9:34.*

στρῶσον 1 aor. act. impv. 2 sing. of στρωννύω.

στυγητός, ή, όν *hated, hateful* Tit 3:3.*

στυγνάζω—1. *be shocked, appalled* perh. Mk 10:22 (see 2 below).—2. *be* or *become gloomy, dark, sad* perh. Mk 10:22 (see 1 above). Of the sky Mt 16:3.*

στῦλος, ου, ὁ *pillar, column* lit. Rv 10:1. Fig. Gal 2:9; 1 Ti 3:15; Rv 3:12.* [*stylite; peristyle*]

Στωϊκός a different spelling for Στοϊκός.

σύ, gen. σοῦ (σου), dat. σοί (σοι), acc. σέ (σε); pl. ὑμεῖς, ὑμῶν, ὑμῖν, ὑμᾶς *you* (older and more formal sing. *thou*).—1. the nominative Mt 2:6; 3:14; 11:3; J 4:9; Ac 1:24; 2 Cor 13:9; Js 2:18. For emphasis Mt 16:16, 18; Mk 14:30, 68; Lk 1:42; Ro 11:17; Gal 6:1.—2. The accented forms are used in the oblique cases of the sing. for emphasis or contrast Lk 2:35; Ro 11:18; Phil 4:3; also with prepositions Mt 6:23; Lk 1:35.—3. σου and ὑμῶν *your* Mt 1:20; 4:6; 9:6; Lk 7:48; Ro 1:8; Phil 1:19; 1 Ti 4:12.

συγγένεια, ας, ή *relationship, kinship,* the relatives Lk 1:61; Ac 7:3, 14.*

συγγενεῦσιν dat. pl. of συγγενής Mk 6:4; Lk 2:44.

συγγενής, ές *related, akin to* subst. *relative* Mk 6:4; Lk 1:36 v.l., 58; 2:44; 14:12; 21:16; J 18:26; Ac 10:24; *fellow countryman, fellow citizen* Ro 9:3; 16:7, 11, 21.*

συγγενίς, ίδος, ή *(female) relative, kinswoman* Lk 1:36.*

συγγνώμη, ης, ή *concession* 1 Cor 7:6.*

συγκάθημαι *sit (with)* Mk 14:54; Ac 26:30.*

συγκαθίζω—1. trans. *cause to sit down with* Eph 2:6.—2. intrans. *sit down with others* Lk 22:55.*

συγκακοπαθέω *suffer together with someone* 2 Ti 2:3; cf. 1:8.*

συγκακουχέομαι *suffer* or *be mistreated with* Hb 11:25.*

συγκαλέω *call together*—1. act. Mk 15:16; Lk 15:6, 9; Ac 5:21.—2. mid. *call to one's side, summon* Lk 9:1; 15:6

v.l., 9 v.l.; 23:13; Ac 5:21 v.l.; 10:24; 13:7 v.l.; 28:17.*

συγκαλύπτω *cover (completely), conceal* Lk 12:2.*

συγκάμπτω *(cause to) bend* Ro 11:10.*

συγκαταβαίνω *go down with someone* Ac 25:5.*

συγκαταβάς 2 aor. act. ptc. of συγκαταβαίνω.

συγκατάθεσις, εως, ή *agreement* 2 Cor 6:16.*

συγκατανεύω *agree, consent* by a nod Ac 18:27 v.l.*

συγκατατίθημι mid. *agree with, consent to* συγκατατιθειμένος pf. mid. ptc. Lk 23:51 (συγκατατιθέμενος pres. mid. ptc., v.l. here and in Ac 4:18; 15:12).*

συγκαταψηφίζομαι pass. *be chosen together with, be added* Ac 1:26.*

σύγκειμαι *recline together* Mt 9:10 v.l.*

συγκεκερασμένος or συγκεκραμένος pf. pass. ptc. of συγκεράννυμι.

συγκεράννυμι *mix (together), blend, unite* fig. *compose* 1 Cor 12:24; *unite* Hb 4:2.*

συγκεχυμένος pf. pass. ptc. of συγχέω.

συγκινέω *arouse* Ac 6:12.*

συγκλείω *close up together, hem in, enclose*—1. lit. Lk 5:6.—2. fig. *confine, imprison* Ro 11:32; Gal 3:22f.*

συγκληρονόμος, ον *inheriting together with* or *jointly* Eph 3:6. Subst. *fellow heir* Ro 8:17; Hb 11:9; 1 Pt 3:7.*

συγκοινωνέω *participate in with* someone, *be connected with* Eph 5:11; Phil 4:14; Rv 18:4.*

συγκοινωνός, οῦ, ὁ *participant, partner* Ro 11:17; 1 Cor 9:23; Phil 1:7; Rv 1:9.*

συγκομίζω *bury* Ac 8:2.*

συγκρίνω *compare* 2 Cor 10:12. For 1 Cor 2:13 *compare, bring together,* and *explain, interpret* are all possible.* [*syncrisis,* comparison, esp. of contraries or opposites]

συγκύπτω *be bent over* Lk 13:11.*

συγκυρία, ας, ή *coincidence, chance* Lk 10:31.*

συγχαίρω—1. *rejoice with, feel joy with* Lk 1:58 (see 2 below); 15:6, 9 (συγχάρητε 2 aor. pass. impv. 2 pl.); 1 Cor

188   συγχέω—συμβούλιον

12:26; 13:6; Phil 2:17f (see 2 below).—
2. congratulate w. dat. is also possible
for Lk 1:58; Phil 2:17f (see 1 above).*
συγχέω and συγχύ(ν)νω confuse, confound, trouble, stir up Ac 9:22; 19:29
v.l., 32; 21:27, 31; pass. be amazed,
excited 2:6.*
συγχράομαι have dealings with, associate on friendly terms with J 4:9.*
συγχύ(ν)νω see συγχέω.
σύγχυσις, εως, ἡ confusion, tumult Ac
19:29.*
συγχωρέω permit Ac 21:39 v.l.*
συζάω live with Ro 6:8; 2 Cor 7:3; 2 Ti
2:11.*
συζεύγνυμι join together Mt 19:6; Mk
10:9.*
συζητέω—1. discuss, carry on a discussion Mk 1:27; 9:10; Lk 24:15.—2. dispute, debate, argue w. dat. Mk 8:11;
9:14, 16; 12:28; Lk 22:23; Ac 6:9; 9:29.*
συζήτησις, εως, ἡ dispute, discussion
v.l. in Ac 15:2, 7; 28:29.*
συζητητής, οῦ, ὁ disputant, debater 1
Cor 1:20.*
σύζυγος, ου, ὁ comrade, lit. 'yoke fellow' Phil 4:3.* [syzygy]
συζωοποιέω make alive together with
someone Eph 2:5; Col 2:13.*
συκάμινος, ου, ἡ the mulberry tree Lk
17:6.*
συκῆ, ῆς, ἡ the fig tree Mt 21:19–21;
24:32; Mk 11:13, 20f; Lk 13:6f; J 1:48,
50; Js 3:12.
συκομορέα, ας, ἡ the fig-mulberry tree,
sycamore fig Lk 19:4.* [sycamore, σῦκον + μόρον]
σῦκον, ου, τό the fig, ripe fig Mt 7:16;
Mk 11:13; Lk 6:44; Js 3:12.* [sycosis,
disease relating to the hair]
συκοφαντέω—1. accuse falsely, annoy,
harass, oppress, blackmail Lk 3:14.—
2. extort Lk 19:8.* [sycophant, σῦκον
+ φαίνειν]
συλαγωγέω carry off as captive fig. Col
2:8.*
συλάω rob fig. 2 Cor 11:8.*
συλλαβεῖν 2 aor. act. inf. of συλλαμβάνω.

συλλαλέω talk or converse with, discuss
with Mt 17:3; Mk 9:4; Lk 4:36; 9:30;
22:4; Ac 18:12 v.l.; 25:12.*
συλλαμβάνω—1. act. and fut. mid.—a.
seize, grasp, apprehend, arrest Mt
26:55; Mk 14:48; Lk 22:54; J 18:12; Ac
1:16; 12:3; 23:27. Catch Lk 5:9.—b.
conceive, become pregnant Lk 1:24,
31, 36; 2:21. Fig. Js 1:15.—2. mid.—a.
seize, arrest Ac 26:21.—b. come to the
aid of, help, assist w. dat. Lk 5:7; Phil
4:3.* [syllabus]
συλλέγω collect, gather (in), pick Mt
7:16; 13:28–30, 40f, 48; Lk 6:44.*
συλλημφθῆναι, συλλήμψομαι 1 aor.
pass. inf. and fut. ind. of συλλαμβάνω.
συλλογίζομαι reason, discuss, debate
Lk 20:5.* [syllogism]
συλλυπέω hurt or grieve with pass. be
grieved (at) Mk 3:5.*
συμβαίνω meet, happen, come about
Mk 10:32; Ac 20:19; 21:35; 1 Cor 10:11;
1 Pt 4:12; 2 Pt 2:22. τὸ συμβεβηκός
what has happened Ac 3:10; cf. Lk
24:14.*
συμβαλεῖν 2 aor. act. inf. of συμβάλλω.
συμβάλλω—1. act.—a. trans. converse,
confer Ac 4:15; 17:18.—Consider,
ponder, draw conclusions about Lk
2:19.—b. intrans. meet, fall in with Ac
20:14.—Engage, fight w. dat. Lk
14:31.—Quarrel, dispute w. dat. 11:53
v.l.—2. mid. help, be of assistance Ac
18:27.* [symbol]
συμβάς 2 aor. act. ptc. of συμβαίνω.
συμβασιλεύω rule (as king) with (someone) 1 Cor 4:8; 2 Ti 2:12.*
συμβέβηκα pf. act. ind. of συμβαίνω.
συμβιβάζω—1. bring together, unite—
a. lit. hold together pass. Eph 4:16; Col
2:19.—b. fig. unite, knit together pass.
Col 2:2.—2. conclude, infer Ac 16:10.—
3. demonstrate, prove 9:22.—4. instruct, teach, advise 19:33; 1 Cor 2:16.*
συμβουλεύω—1. act. advise, give advice to J 18:14; Rv 3:18.—2. mid. consult, plot Mt 26:4; J 11:53 v.l.; Ac 9:23.*
συμβούλιον, ου, τό—1. plan, purpose
σ. λαμβάνειν or διδόναι form a plan,
consult, plot Mt 12:14; 22:15; 27:1, 7;

28:12; Mk 3:6. σ. ἐτοιμάζειν reach a decision 15:1.—2. council as a body Ac 25:12.*

σύμβουλος, ου, ὁ adviser, counselor Ro 11:34.*

Συμεών, ὁ indecl. Symeon, Simeon, a Semitic name.—1. son of Jacob, ancestor of the tribe of Simeon Rv 7:7.—2. Lk 3:30.—3. a devout old man 2:25, 34.—4. Simeon surnamed Niger Ac 13:1.—5. The original name of Peter (Σίμων) is occasionally written in this way Ac 15:14; 2 Pt 1:1.*

συμμαθητής, οῦ, ὁ fellow disciple J 11:16.*

συμμαρτυρέω confirm, testify in support of someone or something Ro 2:15; 8:16; 9:1; Rv 22:18 v.l.*

συμμερίζομαι share with 1 Cor 9:13.*

συμμέτοχος, ον sharing with someone Eph 3:6; 5:7.*

συμμιμητής, οῦ, ὁ fellow imitator Phil 3:17.*

συμμορφίζω invest with the same form pass. be conformed to, take on the same form as Phil 3:10.*

σύμμορφος, ον having the same form, similar in form Ro 8:29; Phil 3:21.*

συμμορφόω give the same form Phil 3:10 v.l.*

συμπαθέω sympathize with, have sympathy with Hb 4:15; 10:34.* [sympathy, σύν + πάθος]

συμπαθής, ές sympathetic 1 Pt 3:8.*

συμπαραγίνομαι come together Lk 23:48. Come to the aid of w. dat. 2 Ti 4:16 v.l.*

συμπαρακαλέω encourage together συμπαρακληθῆναι 1 aor. pass. inf. Ro 1:12.*

συμπαραλαβεῖν 2 aor. act. inf. of συμπαραλαμβάνω.

συμπαραλαμβάνω take along (with oneself) Ac 12:25; 15:37f; Gal 2:1.*

συμπαραμένω stay with someone to help Phil 1:25 v.l.*

συμπάρειμι be present with Ac 25:24.*

συμπάσχω suffer with, suffer the same thing as Ro 8:17; 1 Cor 12:26.*

συμπέμπω send with 2 Cor 8:18, 22.*

συμπεριέχω surround, stand around (together) Lk 12:1 v.l.*

συμπεριλαμβάνω throw one's arms around, embrace συμπεριλαβών 2 aor. act. ptc. Ac 20:10.*

συμπίνω drink with Ac 10:41.*

συμπίπτω fall together, collapse Lk 6:49.*

συμπληρόω fill completely, pass. become quite full—1. be swamped Lk 8:23.—2. fig. be fulfilled, approach, come Lk 9:51; Ac 2:1.*

συμπνίγω—1. (crowd together and) choke Mt 13:22; Mk 4:7, 19; Lk 8:14.—2. crowd around, press upon Lk 8:42; 12:1 v.l.*

συμπολίτης, ου, ὁ fellow citizen Eph 2:19.*

συμπορεύομαι—1. go (along) with Lk 7:11; 14:25; 24:15.—2. come together, flock Mk 10:1.*

συμποσία, ας, ἡ a common meal Mk 6:39 v.l.*

συμπόσιον, ου, τό a party, or group of people eating συμπόσια συμπόσια in groups Mk 6:39.* [symposium]

συμπρεσβύτερος, ου, ὁ fellow elder, fellow presbyter 1 Pt 5:1.*

συμφέρω—1. bring together Ac 19:19.—2. help, confer a benefit, be advantageous or profitable or useful—a. impersonal construction συμφέρει (it) is good, etc. Mt 5:29; 19:10; J 11:50; 18:14; 1 Cor 6:12; 2 Cor 8:10.—b. the participle συμφέρων profitable, etc. τὰ συμφέροντα what is good for you Ac 20:20; cf. 2 Cor 12:1. τὸ συμφέρον profit, advantage 1 Cor 10:33 v.l.; 12:7; Hb 12:10.

σύμφημι agree with Ro 7:16.*

σύμφορος, ον beneficial, advantageous τὸ σύμφορον benefit, advantage 1 Cor 7:35; 10:33.*

συμφορτίζω burden together with others Phil 3:10 v.l.*

συμφυείς 2 aor. pass. ptc. of συμφύω.

συμφυλέτης, ου, ὁ compatriot, pl. one's own people 1 Th 2:14.*

σύμφυτος, ον grown together Ro 6:5.*

συμφύω grow up with Lk 8:7.* [symphysis, articulation, as of bones] συμφωνέω agree Mt 18:19; Ac 5:9; 15:15; come to an agreement Mt 20:2, 13. Fit in with, match Lk 5:36.*

συμφώνησις, εως, ἡ agreement 2 Cor 6:15.*

συμφωνία, ας, ἡ in Lk 15:25 may be music, orchestra, or an instrument, perh. the double flute.* [symphony]

σύμφωνος, ον agreeing ἐκ συμφώνου by agreement 1 Cor 7:5.* [symphonious]

συμψηφίζω count up, compute Ac 19:19; pass. be counted 1:26 v.l.*

σύμψυχος, ον harmonious or united in spirit Phil 2:2.*

σύν prep. w. dat. with Mt 25:27; 26:35; Mk 2:26; Lk 1:56; Ac 5:1, 26; Ro 6:8; 1 Cor 15:10; Phil 1:23. Nearly equivalent to καί Lk 20:1; Ac 3:4; Phil 1:1. Beside(s), in addition to Lk 24:21.

συναγαγεῖν 2 aor. act. inf. of συνάγω.

συνάγω—1. gather (in), gather up Mt 13:47; 25:24, 26; Lk 3:17; 15:13; J 6:12f; 15:6.—2. bring or call together, gather Mt 22:10; 25:32; Mk 2:2; 7:1; J 11:47; 18:2; Ac 13:44; 14:27; 1 Cor 5:4.—3. invite or receive as a guest Mt 25:35, 38, 43.—4. advance, move Mt 20:28 v.l.

συναγωγή, ῆς, ἡ—1. place of assembly—a. the Jewish synagogue Mt 4:23; 10:17; Mk 6:2; Lk 6:6; 21:12; J 18:20; Ac 17:1, 10, 17; 22:19.—b. a Christian synagogue can also be meant in Js 2:2 (see 4 below).—2. (the congregation of a) synagogue Ac 6:9; 9:2.—3. συναγωγὴ τοῦ Σατανᾶ synagogue of Satan Rv 2:9; 3:9.—4. a meeting of Jews for worship Ac 13:43. The preferred interpretation for Js 2:2 is that it refers to the meeting of a Christian congregation (see 1b above).

συναγωνίζομαι help, assist Ro 15:30.*

συναθλέω fight or contend beside Phil 1:27; 4:3.*

συναθροίζω gather, bring together Lk 24:33 v.l.; Ac 12:12; 19:25.*

συναίρω settle (accounts) Mt 18:23f; 25:19.*

συναιχμάλωτος, ου, ὁ fellow prisoner Ro 16:7; Col 4:10; Phlm 23.*

συνακολουθέω follow, accompany w. dat. Mk 5:37; 14:51; Lk 23:49; J 13:36 v.l.*

συναλίζω in Ac 1:4 this word is variously understood: συναλίζω eat (salt) with; συναλίζω bring together, pass. come together; as another spelling for συναυλίζω mid. spend the night with, stay with.*

συναλίσκομαι be made captive together with Ac 1:4 v.l.*

συναλλάσσω reconcile Ac 7:26.*

συναναβαίνω come or go up with Mk 15:41; Ac 13:31.*

συνανάκειμαι recline (at table) with, eat with Mt 9:10; 14:9; Mk 2:15; 6:22; Lk 7:49; 14:10, 15.*

συναναμείγνυμι mix up together, pass. mingle or associate with 1 Cor 5:9, 11; 2 Th 3:14.*

συναναπαύομαι rest or find rest with Ro 15:32.*

συναναστρέφομαι associate, go about with Ac 10:41 v.l.*

συναντάω meet w. dat.; lit. Lk 9:18 v.l., 37; 22:10; Ac 10:25; Hb 7:1, 10. Fig. happen Ac 20:22.*

συνάντησις, εως, ἡ meeting εἰς συνάντησίν τινι to meet someone Mt 8:34 v.l.; J 12:13 v.l.*

συναντιλαμβάνομαι help, come to the aid of w. dat. Lk 10:40; Ro 8:26.*

συναπάγω pass., fig. be led or carried away Gal 2:13; 2 Pt 3:17. τοῖς ταπεινοῖς συναπαγόμενοι Ro 12:16 may mean accommodate yourself to humble ways or associate with humble folk.*

συναπαχθείς, συναπήχθην 1 aor. pass. ptc. and 1 aor. pass. ind. of συναπάγομαι.

συναπέθανον 2 aor. act. ind. of συναποθνῄσκω.

συναπέστειλα 1 aor. act. of συναποστέλλω.

συναποθανεῖν 2 aor. act. inf. of συναποθνῄσκω.

συναποθνῄσκω die with Mk 14:31; 2 Cor 7:3; 2 Ti 2:11.*

συναπόλλυμι destroy with mid. perish with Hb 11:31.*

συναποστέλλω send at the same time
2 Cor 12:18.*

συναπώλετο 2 aor. mid. ind. 3 sing. of συναπόλλυμι.

συνᾶραι 1 aor. act. inf. of συναίρω.

συναρμολογέω fit or join together pass. Eph 2:21; 4:16.*

συναρπάζω seize violently, drag away Lk 8:29; Ac 6:12; 19:29; 27:15.*

συναυλίζομαι see συναλίζω.

συναυξάνω pass. grow together, grow side by side Mt 13:30.*

συναχθήσομαι 1 fut. pass. ind. of συνάγω.

συνβ- see συμβ-.

συνγ- see συγγ-.

σύνδεσμος, ου, ὁ that which binds together—1. bond that holds something together—a. lit., of sinews Col 2:19.— b. fig. Eph 4:3; Col 3:14.—2. In Ac 8:23 σύνδεσμος may mean bond, fetter, or bundle.* [syndesmosis, articulation of bones by a ligament]

συνδέω bind (with) or imprison (with) Hb 13:3.* [syndetic, connecting]

συνδοξάζω pass. be glorified with someone, share in someone's glory Ro 8:17.*

σύνδουλος, ου, ὁ fellow slave lit. and fig. Mt 18:28f, 31, 33; 24:49; Col 1:7; 4:7; Rv 6:11; 19:10; 22:9.*

συνδρομή, ῆς, ἡ running together, forming of a mob Ac 21:30.* [syndrome]

συνεβαλόμην 2 aor. mid. ind. of συμβάλλω.

συνέβη 2 aor. act. ind. 3 sing. of συμβαίνω.

συνεγείρω cause someone to rise up with another fig. Eph 2:6; Col 2:12; 3:1.*

συνέδραμον 2 aor. act. ind. of συντρέχω.

συνέδριον, ου, τό the high council, the Sanhedrin, the highest indigenous governing body in Judaea Mt 5:22; Mk 14:55; Lk 22:66; J 11:47; Ac 5:21, 27, 34, 41; 23:1, 6, 15, 20, 28. Local council Mt 10:17; Mk 13:9.

συνέδριος Ac 5:35 v.l. is probably an error for σύνεδρος, ου, ὁ member of a council.*

συνέζευξα 1 aor. act. ind. of συζεύγνυμι.

συνέθεντο 2 aor. mid. ind. 3 pl. of συντίθημι.

συνείδησις, εως, ἡ—1. consciousness 1 Cor 8:7a v.l.; Hb 10:2; 1 Pt 2:19.—2. moral consciousness, conscience, scruples J 8:9 v.l.; Ac 23:1; 24:16; Ro 2:15; 9:1; 13:5; 1 Cor 8:7b, 10, 12; 10:25, 27–29; 2 Cor 1:12; 4:2; 5:11; 1 Ti 1:5, 19; 3:9; 4:2; 2 Ti 1:3; Tit 1:15; Hb 9:9, 14; 10:22; 13:18; 1 Pt 3:16, 21.*

συνεῖδον 2 aor. act. ind. of συνοράω.

συνειδυῖα pf. act. fem. ptc. of σύνοιδα.

συνείληφα pf. act. ind. of συλλαμβάνω.

I. σύνειμι (from εἰμί) be with Lk 9:18; Ac 22:11.*

II. σύνειμι (from εἶμι) come together Lk 8:4.*

συνείπετο impf. mid. ind. 3 sing. of συνέπομαι.

συνεισέρχομαι enter with, go in(to) with Mk 6:33 v.l.; J 6:22; 18:15.*

συνεισῆλθον 2 aor. act. ind. of συνέρχομαι.

συνείχετο impf. pass. ind. 3 sing. of συνέχω.

συνέκδημος, ου, ὁ traveling companion Ac 19:29; 2 Cor 8:19.*

συνεκέρασα 1 aor. act. ind. of συγκεράννυμι.

συνεκλεκτός, ή, όν chosen together with subst. the one who is chosen 1 Pt 5:13.*

συνεκπορεύομαι go out with Ac 3:11 v.l.*

συνέλαβον 2 aor. act. ind. of συλλαμβάνω.

συνελαύνω drive, force, bring Ac 7:26 v.l.*

συνελήλυθα, συνελθεῖν pf. act. ind. and 2 aor. inf. of συνέρχομαι.

συνελογισάμην 1 aor. act. ind. of συλλογίζομαι.

συνενέγκας 1 aor. act. ptc. of συμφέρω.

συνεπέθεντο 2 aor. mid. ind. 3 pl. of συνεπιτίθεμαι.

συνέπεσον 2 aor. act. ind. of συμπίπτω.

συνεπιμαρτυρέω testify at the same time Hb 2:4.*

συνέπιον 2 aor. act. ind. of συμπίνω.

συνεπίσκοπος, ου, ὁ fellow overseer Phil 1:1 v.l.*

συνεπιτίθεμαι join with others in an attack Ac 24:9.*

συνέπομαι accompany w. dat. Ac 20:4.*

συνεργέω work (together) with, cooperate (with), help Mk 16:20; 1 Cor 16:16; 2 Cor 6:1; Js 2:22. τοῖς ἀγαπῶσιν τὸν θεὸν πάντα συνεργεῖ εἰς ἀγαθόν Ro 8:28 means everything helps (or works with or for) those who love God to obtain what is good or (the Spirit) assists . . . in everything for what is beneficial unless ὁ θεός is read after συνεργεῖ, in which case the sense is in everything God helps (or works for or with) those who love God to obtain what is good.*

συνεργός, οῦ, ὁ fellow worker, helper Ro 16:3; 1 Cor 3:9; 2 Cor 1:24; Phil 2:25; 1 Th 3:2; Phlm 1, 24. [Cf. synergism.]

συνέρχομαι—1. come together, assemble, gather Mt 1:18; Mk 3:20; Lk 5:15; Ac 1:6; 16:13; 22:30; 1 Cor 11:17f, 20; 14:26.—**2.** come, go or travel with Lk 23:55; J 11:33; Ac 1:21; 10:23, 45; 21:16; 25:17.

συνεσθίω eat with Lk 15:2; Ac 10:41; 11:3; 1 Cor 5:11; Gal 2:12.*

σύνεσις, εως, ἡ—1. the faculty of comprehension, intelligence, shrewdness Mk 12:33; Lk 2:47; 1 Cor 1:19.—**2.** insight, understanding Eph 3:4; Col 1:9; 2:2; 2 Ti 2:7.* [synesis, syntactical construction according to sense]

συνεσπάραξα 1 aor. act. ind. of συσπαράσσω.

συνεσταλμένος, συνέστειλα pf. pass. ptc. and 1 aor. act. ind. of συστέλλω.

συνέστηκα, συνέστησα, συνεστώς pf. act. ind., 1 aor. act. ind., and pf. act. ptc. of συνίστημι.

συνέσχον 2 aor. act. ind. of συνέχω.

συνετάφην 2 aor. pass. ind. of συνθάπτω.

σύνετε 2 aor. act. impv. 2 pl. of συνίημι.

συνετέθειντο plupf. mid. ind. 3 pl. of συντίθημι.

συνετός, ή, όν intelligent, wise, with good sense Mt 11:25; Lk 10:21; Ac 13:7; 1 Cor 1:19.*

συνευδοκέω agree with, approve of, consent to, be willing Lk 11:48; Ac 8:1; 22:20; Ro 1:32; 1 Cor 7:12f.*

συνευωχέομαι feast together 2 Pt 2:13; Jd 12.*

συνέφαγον 2 aor. act. ind. of συνεσθίω.

συνεφίστημι join in an attack Ac 16:22.*

συνεφωνήθην 1 aor. pass. ind. of συμφωνέω.

συνέχεον, συνεχύθη, συνέχυννεν impf. act., 1 aor. pass. ind. 3 sing., and impf. act. 3 sing. of συγχέω.

συνέχω—1. close by holding, stop Ac 7:57.—**2.** press hard, crowd Lk 8:45; 19:43.—**3.** hold in custody Lk 22:63.—**4.** pass. be tormented by, suffer from Mt 4:24; Lk 4:38; 8:37; Ac 28:8. Be distressed, be hard pressed Lk 12:50; Phil 1:23.—**5.** pass. be occupied with, be absorbed in Ac 18:5.—**6.** For 2 Cor 5:14 urge on, impel or hold within bounds, control. Cf. Ac 18:5 v.l.*

συνζ- see συζ-.

συνήγαγον, συνηγμένος 2 aor. act. ind. and pf. pass. ptc. of συνάγω.

συνηγέρθην 1 aor. pass. ind. of συνεγείρω.

συνήδομαι (joyfully) agree with Ro 7:22.*

συνήθεια, ας, ἡ custom, habit J 18:39; 1 Cor 11:16; being accustomed 8:7.*

συνῆκα 1 aor. act. ind. of συνίημι.

συνήλασα 1 aor. act. ind. of συνελαύνω.

συνῆλθον 2 aor. ind. act. of συνέρχομαι.

συνηλικιώτης, ου, ὁ a person of one's own age, a contemporary Gal 1:14.*

συνηρπάκει, συνηρπάσα plupf. act. 3 sing. and 1 aor. act. ind. of συναρπάζω.

συνῆσαν impf. act. 3 pl. of σύνειμι.

συνῆτε 2 aor. act. subj. 2 pl. of συνίημι.

συνήχθην 1 aor. pass. ind. of συνάγω.

συνθάπτω *bury with* Ro 6:4; Col 2:12.*

συνθλάω *crush (together), dash to pieces* Mt 21:44; Lk 20:18.*

συνθλίβω *press together, press upon* Mk 5:24, 31.*

συνθρύπτω *break* fig. Ac 21:13.*

συνιᾶσιν pres. act. ind. 3 pl. of συνίημι.

συνιδών 2 aor. act. ptc. of συνοράω.

συνιείς, συνιέναι pres. act. ptc. and inf. of συνίημι.

συνίημι or συνίω *understand, comprehend, gain an insight into* Mt 13:13–15, 51; 15:10; 16:12; Mk 4:9 v.l.; 6:52; 8:17, 21; Lk 2:50; 18:34; Ac 7:25; Ro 3:11; 2 Cor 10:12; Eph 5:17.

συνίστημι, συνιστάνω, ουνιστάω—I. transitive, act. and pass.—1. *present, introduce, (re)commend* Ro 16:1; 2 Cor 3:1; 4:2; 5:12; 6:4; 10:12, 18; 12:11.—2. *demonstrate, show, bring out* Ro 3:5; 5:8; 2 Cor 7:11; Gal 2:18.—II. intransitive, pres. mid. and pf. act.—1. *stand with* or *by* Lk 9:32.—2. *continue, endure, exist, consist, be composed, hold together* Col 1:17; 2 Pt 3:5.* [*system*]

συνίων, συνιῶσιν pres. act. ptc. and pres. act. subj. 3 pl. of συνίω (see συνίημι).

συνκ- see συγκ-.

συνλ- see συλλ-.

συνμ- see συμμ-.

συνοδεύω *travel with* Ac 9:7.*

συνοδία, ας, ἡ *caravan, group of travelers* Lk 2:44.* [Cf. *synod.*]

σύνοιδα *share knowledge with, be implicated* Ac 5:2. σύνοιδα ἐμαυτῷ I *know with myself, I am conscious* 1 Cor 4:4.*

συνοικέω *live with* 1 Pt 3:7.*

συνοικοδομέω *build together with* pass., fig. *be built up* Eph 2:22.*

συνομιλέω *talk, converse with* Ac 10:27. *Live with* 1 Pt 3:7 v.l.*

συνομορέω *be next (door) to* Ac 18:7.*

συνοράω *perceive, become aware of, realize* Ac 12:12; 14:6.*

συνορία, ας, ἡ *neighboring country* Mt 4:24 v.l.*

συνοχή, ῆς, ἡ *distress. dismay, anguish* Lk 21:25; 2 Cor 2:4.*

συνπ- see συμπ-.

συνρ- see συρρ-.

συνσ- see συσσ-.

συνσπ- see συσσπ-.

συνστ- see συστ-.

συνταράσσω *throw into confusion, disturb* Lk 9:42 v.l.*

συντάσσω *order, direct, prescribe* Mt 21:6; 26:19; 27:10.* [Cf. *syntax.*]

συνταφείς 2 aor. pass. ptc. of συνθάπτω.

συντέλεια, ας, ἡ *completion, close, end* Mt 13:39f, 49; 24:3; 28:20; Hb 9:26.*

συντελέω—1. *bring to an end, complete, finish, close* Mt 7:28 v.l.; Lk 4:13.—Of time *come to an end, be over* Lk 2:21 v.l.; 4:2; Ac 21:27; perh. Mk 13:4 (see 2 below).—2. *carry out, fulfill, accomplish* Ro 9:28; Hb 8:8; perh. Mk 13:4 (see 1 above).—3. pass. *give out* J 2:3 v.l.*

συντέμνω *cut short, shorten, limit* Ro 9:28.*

συντετμημένος pf. pass. ptc. of συντέμνω.

συντετριμμένος, συντετρῖφθαι pf. pass. ptc. and inf. of συντρίβω.

συντεχνίτης, ου, ὁ *one who follows the same trade* Ac 19:25 v.l.*

συντηρέω—1. *protect, defend* Mk 6:20. Pass. *be saved, preserved* Mt 9:17; Lk 5:38 v.l.—2. *hold* or *treasure up (in one's memory)* Lk 2:19.* [*synteresis*]

συντίθημι mid. *agree* Lk 22:5; *decide* J 9:22; Ac 23:20. *Consent* Ac 24:9 v.l.* [Cf. *synthesis.*]

συντόμως adv. *briefly* Ac 24:4; *short ending of Mk.*

συντρέχω *run together* Mk 6:33; Ac 3:11. *Run with, go with* 1 Pt 4:4.*

συντρίβω *break, shatter, crush—1.* lit. Mt 12:20; Mk 5:4; 14:3; J 19:36; Ro 16:20; Rv 2:27. *Bruise, wear out* Lk 9:39.—2. fig. Lk 4:18 v.l.*

σύντριμμα, ατος, τό *destruction, ruin* Ro 3:16.*

σύντροφος, ου, ὁ *foster brother, intimate friend* Ac 13:1.*

συντυγχάνω *come together with, meet, join* Lk 8:19; Ac 11:26 v.l.*

συντυχεῖν 2 aor. act. inf., of συν-τυγχάνω.

Συντύχη, ης, ἡ Syntyche, a Christian woman Phil 4:2.*

συντυχία, ας, ἡ chance, incident Lk 10:31 v.l.*

συνυποκρίνομαι join in playing the hypocrite w. dat. Gal 2:13.*

συνυπουργέω join in helping 2 Cor 1:11.*

συνφ- see συμφ-.

συνχ- see συγχ-.

συνψ- see συμψ-.

συνωδίνω suffer agony together Ro 8:22.*

συνωμοσία, ας, ἡ conspiracy, plot Ac 23:13.*

συνών pres. ptc. of σύνειμι.

συνῶσιν 2 aor. act. subj. 3 pl. of συν-ίημι.

Σύρα, ας, ἡ the Syrian woman Mk 7:26 v.l.*

Συράκουσαι, ῶν, αἱ Syracuse, a city on the east coast of Sicily Ac 28:12.*

Συρία, ας, ἡ Syria Mt 4:24; Lk 2:2; Ac 15:23, 41; 18:18; 20:3; 21:3; Gal 1:21.*

Σύρος, ου, ὁ the Syrian Lk 4:27.*

Συροφοινίκισσα, ης, ἡ the Syro-Phoenician woman Mk 7:26.*

συρρήγνυμι dash (together) Lk 6:49 v.l.*

Σύρτις, εως, ἡ the Syrtis, two shallow gulfs along the Libyan coast in North Africa Ac 27:17.*

σύρω drag (away) J 21:8; Ac 8:3; 14:19; 17:6; sweep away Rv 12:4.*

συσπαράσσω pull about, convulse Mk 9:20; Lk 9:42.*

σύσσημον, ου, τό signal Mk 14:44.*

σύσσωμος, ον belonging to the same body Eph 3:6.*

συστασιαστής, οῦ, ὁ fellow insurrectionist Mk 15:7 v.l.*

συστατικός, ή, όν introducing, commendatory συστατικὴ ἐπιστολή a letter of recommendation 2 Cor 3:1.*

συσταυρόω crucify (together) with pass., lit. Mt 27:44; Mk 15:32; J 19:32. Fig. Ro 6:6; Gal 2:19.*

συστέλλω—1. draw together, limit, shorten 1 Cor 7:29.—2. The mng. of σ. in Ac 5:6, 10 v.l. is probably cover up, wrap up, but other possibilities are snatch up and take away.* [systaltic]

συστενάζω lament or groan together (with) Ro 8:22.*

συστοιχέω correspond Gal 4:25.*

συστρατιώτης, ου, ὁ fellow soldier Phil 2:25; Phlm 2.*

συστρέφω—1. gather up, bring together Ac 28:3; 17:5 v.l.—2. be gathered, gather, come together Mt 17:22; v.l. in Ac 10:41; 11:28; and 16:39.*

συστροφή, ῆς, ἡ disorderly or seditious gathering, commotion Ac 19:40. For 23:12 mob and plot are possible.*

συσχηματίζω form or mold after pass. be conformed to, be guided by Ro 12:2; 1 Pt 1:14.*

Συχάρ, ἡ indecl. Sychar, a city in Samaria J 4:5.*

Συχέμ indecl. Shechem—1. fem., a city in Samaria Ac 7:16.—2. masc., son of Hamor Ac 7:16 v.l.*

σφαγή, ῆς, ἡ slaughter Ac 8:32; Ro 8:36; Js 5:5.*

σφάγιον, ου, τό victim to be sacrificed, offering Ac 7:42.*

σφάζω to slaughter Rv 5:6, 12; 13:8. Murder 1 J 3:12; Rv 5:9; 6:4, 9; 13:3; 18:24.*

σφάλλω pass. slip, stumble, fall Mt 15:14 v.l.*

σφάξω fut. of σφάζω.

σφόδρα adv. very (much), extremely, greatly Mt 2:10; 17:6, 23; 19:25; Mk 16:4; Lk 18:23; Ac 6:7.

σφοδρῶς adv. very much, violently Ac 27:18.*

σφραγίζω (provide with a) seal—1. lit. Mt 27:66; Rv 20:3.—2. fig.—a. seal up to keep something secret Rv 10:4; 22:10.—b. mark (with a seal) to identify Eph 1:13; 4:30; Rv 7:3, 4f, 8. In J 6:27; 2 Cor 1:22 there is the added connotation 'endue with power from heaven.'—c. attest, certify, acknowledge J 3:33.—d. σφραγισάμενος αὐτοῖς τὸν καρπὸν τοῦτον Ro 15:28 may be translated when I have placed the sum that was collected safely (sealed) in their hands.*

σφραγίς, ῖδος, ἡ seal, signet—**1.** lit.— **a.** seal Rv 5:1f, 5, 9; 6:1, 3, 5, 7, 9, 12; 8:1.—**b.** the instrument with which one seals, a signet Rv 7:2.—**c.** the mark or impression of a seal 2 Ti 2:19; Rv 9:4.— **2.** fig. that which confirms, attests, or authenticates, certification Ro 4:11; 1 Cor 9:2.* [sphragistic]

σφυδρόν, οῦ, τό ankle Ac 3:7.*

σφυρίς, ίδος, ἡ an alternative form of σπυρίς.

σφυρόν, οῦ, τό ankle or heel Ac 3:7 v.l.*

σχεδόν adv. nearly, almost Ac 13:44; 19:26; Hb 9:22.*

σχῆμα, ατος, τό form, outward appearance 1 Cor 7:31; Phil 2:7.* [scheme]

σχίζω split, tear, divide—**1.** lit. Mt 27:51; Mk 1:10; 15:38; Lk 5:36; 23:45; J 19:24; 21:11.—**2.** fig., pass. become divided or disunited Ac 14:4; 23:7.* [schizophrenia, σχίζω + φρήν]

σχίσμα, ατος, τό split, division—**1.** lit. tear Mt 9:16; Mk 2:21.—**2.** fig. division, dissension, schism J 7:43; 9:16; 10:19; 1 Cor 1:10; 11:18; 12:25.*

σχοινίον, ου, τό rope or cord J 2:15; Ac 27:32.*

σχολάζω have time or leisure—**1.** devote oneself to, give one's time to 1 Cor 7:5.—**2.** be unoccupied, stand empty Mt 12:44; Lk 11:25 v.l.*

σχολή, ῆς, ἡ school Ac 19:9.*

σχῶ 2 aor. subj. act. of ἔχω.

σῴζω rescue, liberate, keep from harm, heal, preserve—**1.** preserve or rescue from natural dangers and afflictions— **a.** from death Mt 14:30; 27:40, 42, 49; Mk 13:20; Lk 6:9; 9:24; J 11:12; Ac 27:20, 31.—**b.** bring out safely J 12:27; Hb 5:7; Jd 5.—**c.** free from disease or from demonic possession Mt 9:22; Mk 5:23, 28, 34; 10:52; Lk 8:48, 50; 17:19; 18:42; Ac 4:9; 14:9; Js 5:15.—**2.** rescue or preserve from eternal death, from judgment, sin, bring salvation, bring to salvation—**a.** act. Mt 18:11; Lk 7:50; J 12:47; Ro 11:14; 1 Cor 1:21; 7:16; Tit 3:5; Hb 7:25; Js 4:12; 5:20; 1 Pt 3:21.— **b.** pass. be rescued or saved, attain salvation Mt 24:13; Mk 10:26; Lk 13:23;

18:26; J 3:17; 5:34; Ac 11:14; 15:1, 11; Ro 8:24; 11:26; 1 Cor. 3:15; 5:5; Eph 2:5, 8; 1 Ti 2:4.—**3.** Certain passages belong under 1 and 2 at the same time Mk 8:35; Lk 9:24; 9:56 v.l.; Ro 9:27.

σῶμα, ατος, τό body—**1.** body of a human being or animal—**a.** dead body, corpse Mt 27:52, 58f; Lk 17:37; J 19:31, 38, 40; Ac 9:40.—**b.** the living body Mt 5:29f; 6:25; Mk 14:22; Lk 11:34; Ro 4:19; 7:24; 8:10, 13; 12:1; 1 Cor 5:3; 6:20; 11:24, 27, 29; 15:44; 2 Cor 5:6, 8, 10; Gal 6:17; Col 2:11; Hb 13:3; Js 3:3.— **2.** pl. σώματα slaves Rv 18:13.—**3.** Paul speaks of various kinds of bodies in 1 Cor 15:35, 37f, 40.—**4** the body as the thing itself, the reality Col 2:17.—**5.** The church is pictured as a body, or the body of Christ Ro 12:5; 1 Cor 12:13, 27; Eph 4:4, 12, 16; Col 1:18, 24.

σωματικός, ή, όν bodily, corporeal Lk 3:22; 1 Ti 4:8.* [somatic]

σωματικῶς adv. bodily, corporeally Col 2:9.*

Σώπατρος, ου, ὁ Sopater, a Christian from Beroea Ac 20:4. See Σωσίπατρος.*

σωρεύω heap or pile up Ro 12:20. Pass. be filled with 2 Ti 3:6.* [sorites]

Σωσθένης, ους, ὁ Sosthenes—**1.** leader of a synagogue in Corinth Ac 18:17.— **2.** a 'brother' of Paul 1 Cor 1:1. It is possible that 1 and 2 are the same man.*

Σωσίπατρος, ου, ὁ Sosipater, a friend of Paul Ro 16:21. He may be the same man as Σώπατρος (Ac 20:4).*

σωτήρ, ῆρος, ὁ Savior, Deliverer, Preserver—**1.** of God Lk 1:47; 1 Ti 1:1; 2:3; 4:10; Tit 1:3; 2:10; 3:4; Jd 25.—**2.** of Christ Lk 2:11; J 4:42; Ac 5:31; 13:23; Eph 5:23; Phil 3:20; 2 Ti 1:10; Tit 1:4; 2:13; 3:6; 1 J 4:14; 2 Pt 1:1, 11; 2:20; 3:2, 18.*

σωτηρία, ας, ἡ salvation, deliverance, preservation—**1.** generally, preservation, deliverance Lk 1:71; Ac 7:25; 27:34; Hb 11:7.—**2.** salvation brought by Jesus Christ as Savior Lk 1:69, 77; 19:9; short ending of Mk; J 4:22; Ac 13:26, 47; Ro 1:16; 10:1, 10; 2 Cor 1:6; 6:2; Eph 1:13; Phil 1:28; 2:12; 1 Th 5:8f; 2 Th 2:13; 2 Ti 2:10; Hb 1:14; 2:3, 10;

9:28; 1 Pt 1:5, 9f; 2 Pt 3:15; Jd 3; Rv 7:10.

σωτήριος, ον saving, delivering, bringing salvation Tit 2:11. Neut. as subst. τὸ σωτήριον salvation Lk 2:30; 3:6; Ac 28:28; Eph 6:17.* [soteriology]

σωφρονέω—1. be of sound mind, be in one's right mind Mk 5:15; Lk 8:35; 2 Cor 5:13.—**2.** be reasonable, sensible, serious Ro 12:3; Tit 2:6; 1 Pt 4:7.*

σωφρονίζω encourage, advise, urge Tit 2:4.*

σωφρονισμός, οῦ, ὁ moderation, self-discipline, prudence 2 Ti 1:7.*

σωφρόνως adv. soberly, moderately, showing self-control Tit 2:12.*

σωφροσύνη, ης, ἡ—1. reasonableness, mental soundness Ac 26:25.—**2.** good judgment, self-control specifically decency, chastity 1 Ti 2:9, 15.*

σώφρων, ον, gen. **ονος** prudent, thoughtful, self-controlled 1 Ti 3:2; Tit 1:8; 2:2. Chaste, modest 2:5.*

Τ

ταβέρναι, ῶν, αἱ (Latin loanword: tabernae) tavern, shop, store Τρεῖς ταβέρναι Three Taverns, a place on the Appian Way, 33 Roman miles from Rome Ac 28:15.*

Ταβιθά, ἡ indecl. Tabitha, a Christian woman Ac 9:36, 40.*

τάγμα, ατος, τό class, group 1 Cor 15:23.*

τακήσομαι 2 fut. pass. ind. of τήκω.

τακτός, ή, όν fixed, appointed Ac 12:21.*

ταλαιπωρέω lament, complain Js 4:9.*

ταλαιπωρία, ας, ἡ distress, trouble, misery Ro 3:16; Js 5:1.*

ταλαίπωρος, ον miserable, wretched Ro 7:24; Rv 3:17.*

ταλαντιαῖος, α, ον weighing a talent (the weight varies from 26 to 36 kg.) Rv 16:21.*

τάλαντον, ου, τό talent; first a measure of weight (26 to 36 kg.), then a monetary unit whose value differed considerably in various times and places. The figure cited in Mt 18:24 is rhetorical = 'millions of dollars.' Mt 25:15–28.*

ταλιθά (Aramaic) girl, little girl Mk 5:41.*

ταμεῖον, ου, τό—1. storeroom Lk 12:24.—**2.** innermost, hidden, or secret room Mt 6:6; 24:26; Lk 12:3.*

ταμιεῖον, ου, τό hidden, secret room Mt 24:26 v.l.*

τανῦν see νῦν.

τάξις, εως, ἡ—1. fixed succession or order Lk 1:8.—**2.** (good) order 1 Cor 14:40; Col 2:5.—**3.** nature, quality κατὰ τὴν τάξιν according to the nature of = just like Melchisedek Hb 5:6, 10; 6:20; 7:11, 17, 21 v.l.* [tactic; taxonomy (τάξις + νόμος)]

ταπεινός, ή, όν low fig.—**1.** of low position, poor, lowly, undistinguished, of no account Lk 1:52; Ro 12:16; 2 Cor 7:6; Js 1:9.—**2.** of emotional states, etc. subservient, abject 2 Cor 10:1. In a good sense lowly, humble Mt 11:29. Subst. Js 4:6; 1 Pt 5:5.*

ταπεινοφροσύνη, ης, ἡ humility, modesty Ac 20:19; Eph 4:2; Phil 2:3; Col 2:18, 23; 3:12; 1 Pt 5:5.*

ταπεινόφρων, ον, gen. **ονος** humble 1 Pt 3:8.*

ταπεινόω lower, make low—**1.** lit. level Lk 3:5.—**2.** fig.—**a.** humble, humiliate Mt 23:12; Lk 14:11; 18:14; 2 Cor 11:7; 12:21; Phil 2:8.—**b.** humble, make *humble* in a good sense Mt 18:4; Js 4:10; 1 Pt 5:6.—**c.** pass. *discipline oneself* Phil 4:12.*

ταπείνωσις, εως, ἡ—1. *humiliation* Ac 8:33; Js 1:10.—**2.** *humility, humble station* Lk 1:48; Phil 3:21; Hb 11:20 v.l.*

ταράσσω—1. lit. *stir up* J 5:4 v.l., 7.— **2.** fig. *stir up, disturb, trouble, throw into confusion* Mt 2:3; Mk 6:50; Lk 24:38; J 11:33; 12:27; 13:21; 14:1; Ac 15:24; 17:8; Gal 1:7; 1 Pt 3:14.

ταραχή, ῆς, ἡ *disturbance*—**1.** lit. *the stirring up* of the water J 5:4 v.l.—**2.** fig. *disturbance, tumult, rebellion* Mk 13:8 v.l.*

ταραχθῶ 1 aor. pass. subj. of ταράσσω.

τάραχος, ου, ὁ *disturbance, commotion* Ac 19:23. *Mental agitation, consternation* 12:18.*

Ταρσεύς, έως, ὁ *(a man) from Tarsus* Ac 9:11; 21:39.*

Ταρσός, οῦ, ὁ *Tarsus,* capital of Cilicia in southwest Asia Minor Ac 9:30; 11:25; 21:39 v.l.; 22:3.*

ταρταρόω *hold captive in Tartarus,* thought of as a place of divine punishment lower than Hades 2 Pt 2:4.*

τάσσω—1. *place* or *station*—**a.** *appoint to* or *establish in an office* Ro 13:1.— **b.** used with a preposition *put* someone *in charge of* Mt 8:9 v.l.; Lk 7:8. *Assign,* pass. *belong to* Ac 13:48. *Devote* 1 Cor 16:15.—**2.** *order, fix, determine, appoint*—**a.** act. and pass. Ac 15:2; 18:2 v.l.; 22:10.—**b.** mid. = act. Mt 28:16; Ac 28:23.* [Cf. *tactics*.]

ταῦρος, ου, ὁ *bull, ox* Mt 22:4; Ac 14:13; Hb 9:13; 10:4.* [*tauromachy,* ταῦρος + μάχη]

ταυτά = τὰ αὐτά *the same things,* only as v.l. in Lk 6:23, 26; 17:30; 1 Th 2:14.*

ταφή, ῆς, ἡ *burial place* Mt 27:7.*

τάφος, ου, ὁ *grave, tomb*—**1.** lit. Mt 23:27, 29; 27:61, 64, 66; 28:1.—**2.** fig. Ro 3:13.* [*epitaph,* ἐπί + τάφος]

τάχα adv. *perhaps, possibly, probably* Ro 5:7; Phlm 15.*

τάχειον a variant spelling for τάχιον (ταχέως 2).

ταχέως adv.—**1.** positive ταχέως *quickly, without delay, soon* Lk 14:21; 16:6; J

11:31; 1 Cor 4:19; Phil 2:19, 24; 2 Ti 4:9. *Too quickly, too easily, hastily* Gal 1:6; 2 Th 2:2; 1 Ti 5:22.—**2.** comparative τάχιον—**a.** *more quickly, faster* Hb 13:19. With gen. of comparison J 20:4.—**b.** *without comparative meaning quickly, soon, without delay* J 13:27; 1 Ti 3:14 v.l.; Hb 13:23.—**3.** superlative τάχιστα ὡς τάχιστα *as soon as possible* Ac 17:15.*

ταχινός, ή, όν *imminent, swift,* 2 Pt 1:14; 2:1.*

τάχιον, τάχιστα see ταχέως 2 and 3.

τάχος, ους, τό *speed, quickness, swiftness, haste* Lk 18:8; Ac 12:7; 22:18; 25:4; Ro 16:20; 1 Ti 3:14; Rv 1:1; 22:6.* [*tachometer,* τάχος + μέτρον]

ταχύς, εῖα, ύ—1. adj. *quick, swift* Js 1:19.—**2.** the neut. sing. ταχύ as adv. *quickly, without delay, soon* Mt 28:7f; Mk 9:39; Lk 15:22; J 11:29; Rv 2:16; 22:7, 12, 20. [*tachygraphy*]

τέ enclitic particle—**1.** used alone *and* J 4:42; Ac 2:37, 40; 4:33; 6:7, 12f; 10:22; 23:10; 1 Cor 4:21; Hb 6:4f; 12:2.—**2.** τὲ . . . τέ, τὲ . . . καί *as . . . so, not only . . . but also* ἐάν τε οὖν ζῶμεν ἐάν τε ἀποθνήσκωμεν *so, not only if we live, but also if we die* Ro 14:8b. Ἰουδαίοις τε καὶ Ἕλλησιν *not only to Jews but also to Greeks* 1 Cor 1:24. Cf. Ac 2:46; 17:4; 26:10, 16. τὲ καί often means simply *and* Lk 23:12; J 2:15; Ac 1:1; 4:27; 5:24; 21:30; Ro 1:12; Hb 5:1, 7; 10:33; Js 3:7.

τέθεικα, τεθεικώς, τέθειται, τεθῆναι pf. act. ind., pf. act. ptc., pf. pass. ind. 3 sing., and 1 aor. pass. inf. of τίθημι.

τεθλιμμένος pf. pass. ptc. of θλίβω.

τεθνάναι, τέθνηκα pf. act. inf. and ind. of θνῄσκω.

τεθραμμένος pf. pass. ptc. of τρέφω.

τεθῶ 1 aor. pass. subj. of τίθημι.

τεῖχος, ους, τό *wall, city wall* Ac 9:25; 2 Cor 11:33; Hb 11:30; Rv 21:12, 14f, 17–19.*

τεκεῖν 2 aor. act. inf. of τίκτω.

τεκμήριον, ου, τό *convincing proof* Ac 1:3.*

τεκνίον, ου, τό (little) child fig. J 13:33; Gal 4:19 v.l.; 1 J 2:1, 12, 28; 3:7, 18; 4:4; 5:21.*

τεκνογονέω bear or beget children 1 Ti 5:14.*

τεκνογονία, ας, ἡ the bearing of children 1 Ti 2:15.*

τέκνον, ου, τό child—1. lit. Mt 7:11; Mk 13:12; Lk 1:7; 15:31; Ac 7:5; 1 Cor 7:14; 2 Cor 12:14; Col 3:20; Rv 12:4f. More generally, descendants, posterity Mt 2:18; 27:25; Ac 2:39; 13:33; Ro 9:8a.— 2. fig. Mt 3:9; 23:37; Mk 2:5; J 1:12; Ro 8:16f, 21; 9:7; 1 Cor 4:14, 17; Gal 4:19, 25; Eph 5:8; Phlm 10; Tit 1:4; 1 J 3:1f; 2 J 1.

τεκνοτροφέω bring up children 1 Ti 5:10.*

τεκνόω bear (a child) Hb 11:11 v.l.*

τέκτων, ονος, ὁ carpenter, woodworker, builder Mt 13:55; Mk 6:3.*

τέλειος, α, ον having attained the end or purpose, complete, perfect—1. of things Js 1:4a, 17, 25; Hb 9:11; 1 J 4:18. τὸ τέλειον what is perfect Ro 12:2; 1 Cor 13:10.—2. of persons—a. full-grown, mature, adult adj. 1 Cor 14:20; Eph 4:13; subst. Hb 5:14. For 1 Cor 2:6 the sense may be adult, or it may belong under b below.—b. the initiate into mystic rites, perh. 1 Cor 2:6 (see a above); probably Phil 3:15; Col 1:28.—c. perfect, fully developed in a moral sense Mt 5:48a; 19:21; Col 4:12; Js 1:4b; 3:2.—d. of God as absolutely perfect Mt 5:48b.* [teleo-, combining form, as in teleology]

τελειότης, ητος, ἡ perfection, completeness Col 3:14; maturity Hb 6:1.*

τελειόω—1. complete, finish, accomplish, bring to its goal, perfect J 4:34; 5:36; Ac 20:24; Hb 2:10; 5:9; 7:28.— Make perfect J 17:23; Hb 9:9; 10:1; 11:40; 12:23; Js 2:22; 1 J 2:5; 4:12, 17.— Spend Lk 2:43. Fulfill J 19:28.—Pass. reach one's goal Lk 13:32.—2. consecrate, initiate Phil 3:12; such passages as Hb 2:10; 5:9; 7:28 may perhaps be classed here (see 1 above.)

τελείως adv. fully, perfectly, completely 1 Pt 1:13.*

τελείωσις, εως, ἡ perfection Hb 7:11. Fulfillment Lk 1:45.*

τελειωτής, οῦ, ὁ perfecter Hb 12:2.*

τελεσφορέω bear fruit to maturity Lk 8:14, 15 v.l.*

τελευτάω die Mt 2:19; 22:25; Mk 7:10; Lk 7:2; Ac 7:15; Hb 11:22.

τελευτή, ῆς, ἡ end, a euphemism for death Mt 2:15.*

τελέω—1. bring to an end, finish, complete Mt 7:28; 11:1; 13:53; Lk 2:39; 2 Ti 4:7; Rv 11:7. Come to an end Rv 20:3, 5, 7. Find consummation 2 Cor 12:9.—2. carry out, accomplish, keep Lk 18:31; Ac 13:29; Ro 2:27; Gal 5:16; Js 2:8.—3. pay Mt 17:24; Ro 13:6.

τέλος, ους, τό—1. end—a. in the sense termination, cessation, conclusion Mk 3:26; 13:7; Lk 1:33; 22:37; Ro 10:4; Hb 7:3; 1 Pt 4:7; probably 1 Cor 10:11 (see 2 below).—b. end, goal, outcome Mt 26:58; Ro 6:21f; 1 Ti 1:5; Hb 6:8; Js 5:11; 1 Pt 1:9.—c. adverbial expressions. τὸ τέλος as adverbial acc. 1 Cor 15:24; 1 Pt 3:8.—ἄχρι τέλους, ἕως τέλους to the end, to the last 1 Cor 1:8; 2 Cor 1:13; Hb 3:6 v.l., 14; Rv 2:26.— εἰς τέλος in the end, finally Lk 18:5. To the end Mt 10:22; Mk 13:13. For 1 Th 2:16 forever or decisively, fully. In J 13:1 the mngs. to the end and to the uttermost are combined.—2. (indirect) tax, customs duties Mt 17:25; Ro 13:7; perhaps 1 Cor 10:11 (see 1a above). [Cf. teleology.]

τελωνεῖον a variant spelling for τελώνιον.

τελώνης, ου, ὁ tax collector, revenue officer Mt 5:46; 10:3; 21:31f; Mk 2:15f; Lk 3:12; 5:27; 7:29, 34; 18:10f, 13.

τελώνιον, ου, τό revenue or tax office Mt 9:9; Mk 2:14; Lk 5:27.*

τέξομαι fut. mid. ind. of τίκτω.

τέρας, ατος, τό portent, omen, wonder Mk 13:22; J 4:48; Ac 5:12; 14:3; Ro 15:19; 2 Cor 12:12. [teratology]

Τέρτιος, ου, ὁ Tertius, a Christian, helper of Paul Ro 16:22.*

Τέρτουλλος, ου, ὁ Tertullus, the Roman eparch under whom Onesimus was martyred Phlm subscr.*

Τέρτυλλος, ου, ὁ Tertullus, an attorney Ac 24:1f.*

τεσσαράκοντα or τεσσεράκοντα indecl. forty Mt 4:2; J 2:20; Ac 1:3; 23:13, 21; Hb 3:9; Rv 11:2; 21:17.

τεσσαρακονταετής, ές forty years (old) τ. χρόνος a period of forty years Ac 7:23; 13:18.*

τέσσαρες, neut. τέσσαρα, gen. τεσσάρων four Mt 24:31; Mk 2:3; Lk 2:37; J 11:17; Rv 4:4. [Diatessaron, διά + τεσσάρων]

τεσσαρεσκαιδέκατος, η, ον fourteenth Ac 27:27, 33.*

τεσσερ- see τεσσαρ-.

τεταγμέναι, τέτακται pf. pass. ptc. fem. pl. (Ro 13:1) and pf. pass. ind. 3 sing. (Ac 22:10) of τάσσω.

τεταραγμένοι, τετάρακται pf. pass. ptc. masc. pl. (Lk 24:38) and pf. pass. ind. 3 sing. (J 12:27) of ταράσσω.

τεταρταῖος, α, ον happening on the fourth day τεταρταῖός ἐστιν he has been dead four days J 11:39.*

τέταρτος, η, ον fourth Mt 14:25; Mk 6:48; Ac 10:30; Rv 4:7. τὸ τέταρτον the fourth part, quarter 6:8.

τετραα- see τετρα-.

τετράγωνος, ον (four)square or shaped like a cube Rv 21:16.* [tetragonal]

τετράδιον, ου, τό a squad of four soldiers Ac 12:4.*

τετρακισχίλιοι, αι, α four thousand Mt 15:38; 16:10; Mk 8:9, 20; Ac 21:38.*

τετρακόσιοι, αι, α four hundred Ac 5:36; 7:6; 13:20; 21:38 v.l.; Gal 3:17.*

τετράμηνος, ον lasting four months of a period of time J 4:35.*

τετραπλοῦς, ῆ, οῦν four times (as much), fourfold Lk 19:8.*

τετράπους, ουν, gen. ποδος four-footed, subst. τὰ τετράποδα four-footed animals, quadrupeds Ac 10:12; 11:6; Ro 1:23.* [Cf. tetrapody, a verse or group of four feet.]

τετραρχέω be tetrarch Lk 3:1.*

τετράρχης, ου, ὁ tetrarch, title of a petty dependent prince, whose rank and authority were lower than those of a king Mt 14:1; Lk 3:19; 9:7; Ac 13:1.*

τέτυχε pf. act. ind. 3 sing. of τυγχάνω.

τεφρόω cover with or reduce to ashes 2 Pt 2:6.*

τεχθείς 1 aor. pass. ptc. of τίκτω.

τέχνη, ης, ἡ skill, trade Ac 17:29; 18:3; Rv 18:22.* [technic; techno-, a combining form, as in technology]

τεχνίτης, ου, ὁ craftsman, artisan, designer Ac 19:24, 25 v.l., 38; Hb 11:10; Rv 18:22.*

τήκομαι melt, be melted, dissolve 2 Pt 3:12.*

τηλαυγῶς adv. (very) plainly, clearly Mk 8:25.*

τηλικοῦτος, αύτη, οῦτο so great, so large, so important 2 Cor 1:10; Hb 2:3; Js 3:4; Rv 16:18.*

τηνικαῦτα adv. at that time, then Phlm subscr.*

τηρέω—1. keep watch over, guard Mt 27:36, 54; 28:4; Ac 12:5; 24:23.—2. keep, hold, reserve, preserve J 2:10; 17:11f, 15; Ac 25:21; 1 Cor 7:37; 1 Ti 6:14; 2 Ti 4:7; 1 Pt 1:4; Jd 1, 13; Rv 3:10; 16:15.—3. keep, observe, pay attention to Mt 23:3; 28:20; Mk 7:9 v.l.; J 9:16; 14:15, 21; 1 J 3:22, 24; Rv 3:8, 10; 12:17; 22:7.

τήρησις, εως, ἡ—1. custody, imprisonment or prison Ac 4:3; 5:18.—2. keeping, observance 1 Cor 7:19.*

Τιβεριάς, άδος, ἡ Tiberias, a city on the west shore of Lake Gennesaret; the lake is sometimes named after the city J 6:1, 23; 21:1.*

Τιβέριος, ου, ὁ Tiberius, Roman emperor 14–37 A.D., Lk 3:1.*

τιθέασιν, τιθείς pres. act. ind. 3 pl. and pres. act. ptc. of τίθημι.

τίθημι and τιθέω—I. active and passive—1. put, place, lay—a. generally lay (away), set up, put (away) Mt 12:18; 27:60; Mk 16:6; Lk 11:33; 14:29; J11:34; Ac 3:2; 13:29; Ro 9:33; 14:13; 2 Cor 3:13; 2 Pt 2:6.—b. special expressions—τιθέναι τὰ γόνατα bend the knee, kneel down Mk 15:19; Ac 7:60; 21:5.—Place before someone, serve J 2:10.—Put aside, store up, deposit Lk 19:21f; 1 Cor 16:2.—Take off, remove J 13:4. Give (up) 10:11, 15, 17f; 1 J

3:16.—θέτε ἐν ταῖς καρδίαις make up (your) minds Lk 21:14.—Present Mk 4:30.—2. make Lk 20:43; Ac 13:47; Ro 4:17; 1 Ti 2:7; Hb 1:2. Appoint J 15:16.—II. middle—1. put, place, lay— a. arrange, fix, establish, set Ac 1:7; 1 Cor 12:18; 2 Cor 5:19. Put Ac 5:18, 25.—b. ἔθεντο ἐν τῇ καρδίᾳ they kept in mind Lk 1:66, but the same expression in the 2 sing. contrive in your mind Ac 5:4. Similarly resolve 19:21.—2. make Ac 20:28; 1 Cor 12:28. Reach Ac 27:12. Destine or appoint 1 Th 5:9; 1 Ti 1:12.

τίκτω bear, give birth (to)—1. lit. Mt 1:21, 23; Lk 2:6f, 11; J 16:21; Gal 4:27; Rv 12:2, 4f.—2. symbolically bring forth Hb 6:7; Js 1:15.

τίλλω pluck, pick Mt 12:1; Mk 2:23; Lk 6:1.*

Τιμαῖος, ου, ὁ Timaeus Mk 10:46.*

τιμάω—1. set a price on, estimate, value mid. for oneself Mt 27:9b. Pass. 27:9a.—2. honor, revere Mt 15:4, 8; Mk 7:6; 10:19; J 5:23; Eph 6:2; 1 Ti 5:3; 1 Pt 2:17. (Show) honor (to), reward J 12:26.

τιμή, ῆς, ἡ—1. price, value Mt 27:6, 9; Ac 5:2f; 7:16; 19:19. τιμῆς for a price 1 Cor 6:20; 7:23.—2. honor, reverence, respect J 4:44; Ac 28:10; Ro 2:7, 10; 12:10; 13:7; 1 Ti 6:1; 2 Ti 2:20f; 1 Pt 3:7; Rv 4:9; 5:13; 21:26. Privilege 1 Pt 2:7. Respectability 1 Th 4:4. Place of honor, office Hb 5:4. Honorarium, compensation may be the sense in 1 Ti 5:17, though honor and respect are also possible.—The expression οὐκ ἐν τιμῇ τινι Col 2:23 is probably they are of no value in. [timocracy, τιμή + κρατεῖν]

τίμιος, α, ον valuable, precious, costly, of great worth or value 1 Cor 3:12; Js 5:7; 1 Pt 1:19; Rv 17:4; 18:12, 16. Held in honor, respected Ac 5:34; Hb 13:4.

τιμιότης, ητος, ἡ costliness, abundance of costly things Rv 18:19.*

Τιμόθεος, ου, ὁ Timothy, son of Eunice, a friend, traveling companion, and co-worker of Paul Ac 16:1; 17:14f; 18:5; 19:22; 20:4; Ro 16:21; 1 Cor 4:17; 2 Cor 1:1; Phil 1:1; Col 1:1; 1 Th 1:1; 2 Th 1:1; 1 Ti 1:2; 2 Ti 1:2; Phlm 1; Hb 13:23.

Τίμων, ωνος, ὁ Timon Ac 6:5.*

τιμωρέω punish Ac 22:5; 26:11.*

τιμωρία, ας, ἡ punishment Hb 10:29.*

τίνω pay, undergo 2 Th 1:9.*

τίς, τί gen. τίνος (the acute accent on this word never changes to a grave) interrogative pron. who? which (one)? what?—1. subst.—a. τίς; who? which one? Mt 3:7; 22:42; 26:68; Mk 2:7; 11:28; J 18:4, 7; Ro 7:24; 1 Cor 9:7; Hb 1:5; 3:16–18.—Who? in the sense what sort of person? Lk 5:21a; J 1:19; 21:12; Ac 11:17; Ro 14:4.—Who, what as a substitute for the relative pron. Ac 13:25 v.l.; perh. Js 3:13.—b. τί; what? Mt 17:25a; 21:28, 40; Mk 10:3, 17; Lk 10:25f; J 18:38; Ro 10:8.—διὰ τί; εἰς τί; πρὸς τί; χάριν τίνος; all mean why?— What sort of thing? Mk 1:27; Col 1:27; Eph 1:19; 3:18.—Which of two? Mt 9:5; Mk 2:9; Lk 5:23; 1 Cor 4:21; Phil 1:22.— Elliptical expressions J 1:21; 11:47; Ro 3:3; 1 Cor 5:12. On τί ἐμοὶ καὶ σοί; see ἐγώ.—What as a substitute for the relative pron. Mk 14:36; Lk 17:8; Ac 13:25; 1 Ti 1:7.—2. adj. what? Mt 5:46; Lk 14:31; J 2:18; Ac 10:29; 2 Cor 6:14–16; 1 Pt 1:11.—3. adv.—a. τί; why? Mt 6:28; 7:3; Mk 4:40; Lk 19:33; J 18:23; Ac 14:15; 1 Cor 10:30; 15:29b, 30.—b. τί in an exclamation how! Mt 7:14 v.l.; Lk 12:49.

τὶς, τὶ, gen. τινός enclitic, indefinite pron. Anyone, anything; someone, something; many a one or thing.—1. subst.— a. τὶς, τινές someone, anyone, somebody Mt 12:29, 47; Lk 7:36; J 2:25; 6:46; Ac 5:25; 2 Cor 11:20. Pl. some Lk 13:1; Ac 15:1; 1 Cor 6:11; 2 Th 3:11.—τὶς a certain man, etc. Lk 9:49; J 11:1; Ac 18:7; Ro 3:8; 1 Cor 4:18; 2 Cor 2:5; 11:21. A person of importance Ac 5:36.—b. τὶ, τινά something, anything Mt 5:23; Mk 13:15; Lk 7:40; J 13:29; Ac 4:32; Ro 15:18; 1 Cor 10:31. εἶναί τι be or amount to something 1 Cor 3:7; Gal 2:6; 6:3.—2. adj.—a. some, any, a certain, often omitted in translation into English Mt 18:12; Lk 1:5; 17:12; 23:26; Ac 3:2; 8:34; 10:5f; Ro 9:11; 1 Cor 1:16; Hb 4:7.—b. serving to moderate or heighten ἀπαρχήν τινα a kind of firstfruits Js 1:18. δύο τινάς perhaps two Lk 7:18. Cf. Hb 10:27. βραχύ τι (only) a little 2:7, 9.—c. some, considerable Ac 18:23; Ro 1:11, 13; 1 Cor 11:18; 16:7.—**d.** τινές several Lk 8:2; Ac 9:19; 10:48; 15:2; 17:5f.

Τίτιος, ου, ὁ Titius Ac 18:7.*

τίτλος, ου, ὁ inscription, notice, giving the reason for condemnation J 19:19f.* [Latin loanword: titulus; title]

Τίτος, ου, ὁ Titus—**1.** friend and helper of Paul 2 Cor 2:13; 7:6; 8:6; 12:18; Gal 2:1, 3; 2 Ti 4:10; Tit 1:4.—**2.** surnamed Justus Ac 18:7 v.l.

τοιγαροῦν inferential particle for that very reason, then, therefore 1 Th 4:8; Hb 12:1.*

τοίνυν inferential particle hence, so, indeed Lk 20:25; 1 Cor 9:26; Hb 13:13; Js 2:24 v.l.*

τοιόσδε, άδε, όνδε such as this, of this kind τοιᾶσδε fem. gen. sing. 2 Pt 1:17.*

τοιοῦτος, αὕτη, οὗτον and οὗτο of such a kind, such (as this) Mt 9:8; Mk 6:2; 9:37; Ac 26:29; 1 Cor 5:1; 15:48; 2 Cor 12:3; Gal 6:1; Eph 5:27; Tit 3:11; Phlm 9; Hb 7:26; 11:14; Js 4:16.

τοῖχος, ου, ὁ wall Ac 23:3.*

τόκος, ου, ὁ interest on money loaned Mt 25:27; Lk 19:23.*

τολμάω—**1.** followed by the inf.—**a.** dare, have the courage, be brave enough Mt 22:46; Mk 12:34; Lk 20:40; J 21:12; Ac 5:13; 7:32; Ro 5:7; Phil 1:14.—**b.** bring oneself, presume Ro 15:18; 1 Cor 6:1; 2 Cor 10:12; Jd 9.—**2.** abs. dare, be courageous Mk 15:43; 2 Cor 10:2; 11:21.*

τολμηροτέρως Ro 15:15 v.l. and **τολμηρότερον** 15:15 both mean rather boldly.*

τολμητής, οῦ, ὁ bold, audacious man 2 Pt 2:10.*

τομός, ή, όν cutting, sharp comparative **τομώτερος** sharper fig. Hb 4:12.* [-tomy, from τομή, a combining form in such words as anatomy, appendectomy, dichotomy]

τόξον, ου, τό the bow as a weapon Rv 6:2.*

τοπάζιον, ου, τό topaz, a bright yellow precious stone Rv 21:20.*

τόπος, ου, ὁ place, position, region—**1.** lit. Mt 14:35; 26:52; Mk 1:35; 15:22; Lk

16:28; J 5:13; 11:48; 20:25 v.l.; Ac 6:13; 12:17; 16:3; 27:2; 1 Cor 1:2; Rv 2:5. Room Lk 2:7; 14:9, 22. Pl. regions, districts Mt 12:43; Mk 13:8; Ac 27:2.—**2.** in special meanings—**a.** place, passage in a book Lk 4:17.—**b.** position, office Ac 1:25a.—**c.** possibility, opportunity, chance Ac 25:16; Ro 12:19; 15:23; Eph 4:27; Hb 12:17.—**d.** ἐν τῷ τόπῳ οὗ ἐρρέθη αὐτοῖς instead of their being told Ro 9:26. [topic]

τοσοῦτος, αὕτη, οὗτον and οὗτο so great, so large, so far, so much, so strong, etc.—**1.** used with a noun Mt 8:10; J 14:9; Hb 12:1; Rv 18:7, 17. Pl. so many Mt 15:33; Lk 15:29; J 12:37; 1 Cor 14:10.—**2.** without a noun—**a.** pl. τοσοῦτοι so many people J 6:9. Cf. Gal 3:4.—**b.** sing. τοσούτου for so much Ac 5:8. Correlative τοσούτῳ . . . ὅσῳ (by) so much (greater, more, etc.) . . . than or as Hb 1:4; 10:25. Cf. 7:20–22.

τότε adv.—**1.** then, at that time Mt 2:17; 13:43; 27:9, 16; 1 Cor 13:12; 2 Cor 12:10; Gal 4:8, 29; 2 Pt 3:6.—**2.** then, thereupon, thereafter Mt 2:7; 4:1; 12:22; 13:26; 21:1; 26:65; Mk 13:14; Lk 24:45; J 11:6, 14; Ac 1:12; 17:14.

τοὐναντίον = τὸ ἐναντίον.

τοὔνομα = τὸ ὄνομα.

τοὐπίσω = τὸ ὀπίσω. S. ὀπίσω 1.

τουτέστιν = τοῦτό ἐστιν.

τράγος, ου, ὁ he-goat Hb 9:12f, 19; 10:4.*

τράπεζα, ης, ἡ table—**1.** lit. Mk 7:28; Lk 22:21, 30; 1 Cor 10:21; Hb 9:2. Specifically for money changers Mt 21:12; J 2:15; bank Lk 19:23.—**2.** fig. a meal, food Ac 6:2; 16:34. [trapeze]

τραπεζίτης, ου, ὁ money changer, banker Mt 25:27.*

τραῦμα, ατος, τό a wound Lk 10:34.* [trauma, traumatic]

τραυματίζω to wound Lk 20:12; Ac 19:16.* [traumatism]

τραχηλίζω pass. be laid bare Hb 4:13.*

τράχηλος, ου, ὁ neck, throat Mt 18:6; ·Mk 9:42; Lk 15:20; 17:2; Ac 15:10; 20:37; Ro 16:4.*

τραχύς, εῖα, ύ rough, uneven Lk 3:5; Ac 27:29.* [trachea; trachyte, volcanic rock]

Τραχωνῖτις, ιδος, ή, ή Τραχωνῖτις χώρα the region of Trachonitis, a district south of Damascus Lk 3:1.*

τρεῖς, τρία three Mt 12:40; Lk 1:56; J 2:19; 1 Cor 13:13; 1 J 5:7. [*tri-*, combining form]

Τρεῖς ταβέρναι see ταβέρναι.

τρέμω be afraid, fear Mk 5:33; Lk 8:47; Ac 9:6 v.l.; 2 Pt 2:10.*

τρέφω—1. feed, nourish, support, provide with food Mt 6:26; 25:37; Lk 12:24; 23:29; Ac 12:20; Js 5:5; Rv 12:6, 14.— **2.** rear, bring up, train, pass. grow up Lk 4:16.*

τρέχω run—**1.** lit. Mt 27:48; Mk 5:6; Lk 15:20; J 20:2, 4; 1 Cor 9:24a, b.—**2.** fig. strive to advance, make progress Ro 9:16; 1 Cor 9:24c, 26; Gal 2:2; 5:7; Phil 2:16; Hb 12:1. Spread rapidly 2 Th 3:1.

τρῆμα, ατος, τό hole, eye of a needle Mt 19:24 v.l.; Lk 18:25.*

τριάκοντα indecl. thirty Mt 13:8; Mk 4:8; Lk 3:23.

τριακόσιοι, αι, α three hundred Mk 14:5; J 12:5.*

τρίβολος, ου, ὁ thistle Mt 7:16; Hb 6:8.*

τρίβος, ου, ή path Mt 3:3; Mk 1:3; Lk 3:4.*

τριετία, ας, ή (a period of) three years Ac 20:18 v.l., 31.*

τρίζω gnash, grind Mk 9:18.*

τρίμηνος, ον of three months subst. τὸ τρίμηνον (a period of) three months Hb 11:23.*

τρίς adv. three times Mt 26:34, 75; Mk 14:30, 72; Lk 22:34, 61; J 13:38; 2 Cor 11:25; 12:8. ἐπὶ τρίς three times or (yet) a third time Ac 10:16; 11:10.* [*Trisagion*, τρίς + ἅγιον]

τρισίν dat. pl. of τρεῖς Mt 27:40; Lk 12:52; Hb 10:28.

τρίστεγον, ου, τό the third story of a building Ac 20:9.*

τρισχίλιοι, αι, α three thousand Ac 2:41.*

τρίτος, η, ον third—**1.** as adj. Mt 16:21; 27:64; Mk 12:21; Lk 18:33; Ac 27:19; 2 Cor 12:2; Rv 4:7.—**2.** as a subst. τὸ τρίτον the third part, one-third Rv 8:7–12; 9:15, 18; 12:4.—**3.** adv. (τὸ) τρίτον for the third time Mk 14:41; Lk 23:22;

J 21:17; in the third place 1 Cor 12:28. τρίτον τοῦτο this is the third time J 21:14. ἐκ τρίτου for the third time Mt 26:44.

τρίχες, τριχός nom. pl. and gen. sing. of θρίξ.

τρίχινος, η, ον made of hair Rv 6:12.* [*trichinosis*]

τριῶν gen. pl. of τρεῖς Mt 18:16; Lk 10:36; Rv 8:13.

τρόμος, ου, ὁ trembling Mk 16:8; 1 Cor 2:3; 2 Cor 7:15; Eph 6:5; Phil 2:12.*

τροπή, ῆς, ή turn(ing), variation, change τροπῆς ἀποσκίασμα Js 1:17 may be shadow of variation or darkening, which has its basis in change.* [Cf. trope.]

τρόπος, ου, ὁ—1. manner, way, kind Ac 15:11; 27:25; Ro 3:2; Phil 1:18; 2 Th 2:3; 3:16; Jd 7. ὃν τρόπον in the manner in which = (just) as Mt 23:37; Lk 13:34; Ac 1:11; 7:28; 2 Ti 3:8.—**2.** way of life, conduct, character Hb 13:5.* [*tropology*, figurative mode of speech or writing]

τροποφορέω bear or put up with Ac 13:18.*

τροφή, ῆς, ή nourishment, food—**1.** lit. Mt 3:4; Lk 12:23; J 4:8; Ac 9:19; Js 2:15.—**2.** fig., of spiritual nourishment Hb 5:12, 14. [*trophic*, pertaining to nutrition]

Τρόφιμος, ου, ὁ Trophimus of Ephesus, a friend of Paul Ac 20:4; 21:29; 2 Ti 4:20.*

τροφός, οῦ, ή nurse, possibly mother 1 Th 2:7.*

τροφοφορέω care for (as a nurse) Ac 13:18 v.l.*

τροχιά, ᾶς, ή wheel track, course, way fig. Hb 12:13.*

τροχός, οῦ, ὁ wheel Js 3:6.* [*trochoid*]

τρύβλιον, ου, τό bowl, dish Mt 26:23; Mk 14:20.*

τρυγάω pick or gather (grapes) Lk 6:44; Rv 14:18; gather the fruit of 14:19.*

τρυγών, όνος, ή turtledove Lk 2:24.*

τρυμαλιά, ᾶς, ή hole, eye of a needle Mk 10:25; Mt 19:24 v.l.; Lk 18:25 v.l.*

τρύπημα, ατος, τό eye of a needle Mt 19:24.*

Τρύφαινα, ης, ή Tryphaena Ro 16:12.*

τρυφάω lead a life of self-indulgence, revel, carouse Js 5:5.*

τρυφή, ῆς, ή indulgence, reveling 2 Pt 2:13. Luxury, splendor Lk 7:25.*

Τρυφῶσα, ης, ή Tryphosa Ro 16:12.*

Τρῳάς, άδος, ή Troas, a city and region in the northwest corner of Asia Minor Ac 16:8, 11; 20:5f; 2 Cor 2:12; 2 Ti 4:13.*

Τρωγύλλιον, ου, τό Trogyllium, a town south of Ephesus Ac 20:15 v.l.*

τρώγω eat Mt 24:38; J 6:54, 56–58; 13:18.*

τυγχάνω—1. meet, attain, gain, find, experience Lk 20:35; Ac 24:2; 26:22; 27:3; 2 Ti 2:10; Hb 8:6; 11:35.—**2.** intr. happen, turn out—**a.** happen to be, find oneself Lk 10:30 v.l.—**b.** εἰ τύχοι if it should turn out that way, perhaps, probably 1 Cor 14:10; 15:37.—**c.** τυχόν (acc. absolute, aor. ptc.) if it turns out that way, perhaps, if possible 1 Cor 16:6; Lk 20:13 v.l.; Ac 12:15 v.l.—**d.** οὐχ ὁ τυχών not the common or ordinary (one), i.e., extraordinary Ac 19:11; 28:2.*

τυμπανίζω torment, torture pass. Hb 11:35.*

τυπικῶς adv. typologically, as an example or warning 1 Cor 10:11.*

τύπος, ου, ὁ—1. mark J 20:25.—**2.** image, statue Ac 7:43.—**3.** form, figure, pattern, mold Ro 6:17; perh. content Ac 23:25.—**4.** (arche)type, pattern, model, design—**a.** technically Ac 7:44; Hb 8:5.—**b.** in the moral life example, pattern Phil 3:17; 1 Th 1:7; 2 Th 3:9; 1 Ti 4:12; Tit 2:7; 1 Pt 5:3.—**5.** the types given by God as an indication of the future Ro 5:14; 1 Cor 10:6, 11 v.l.* [-type, combining form, as in antitype, electrotype, prototype]

τύπτω strike, beat—**1.** lit. Mt 24:49; Mk 15:19; Lk 6:29; 18:13; Ac 21:32; 23:2.—**2.** fig. Ac 23:3a; 1 Cor 8:12. [Cf. tympanum.]

τύραννος, ου, ὁ despotic ruler, tyrant Ac 5:39 v.l.

Τύραννος, ου, ὁ Tyrannus, an Ephesian Ac 19:9.*

τυρβάζω mid. or pass. trouble oneself, be troubled Lk 10:41 v.l.*

Τύριος, ου, ὁ the Tyrian Ac 12:20, 22 v.l.*

Τύρος, ου, ἡ Tyre, an important seaport in Phoenicia Mt 11:21f; 15:21; Mk 7:24, 31; Ac 21:3, 7.

τυφλός, ή, όν blind, adj. and subst.—**1.** lit. Mt 20:30; Mk 8:22f; Lk 6:39; J 9:1, 18, 24; 10:21.—**2.** fig. Mt 23:16f, 19, 24, 26; J 9:40f; Ro 2:19; Rv 3:17. [typhlosis, typhlitis]

τυφλόω to blind, deprive of sight J 12:40; 2 Cor 4:4; 1 J 2:11.*

τυφόομαι be puffed up, conceited 1 Ti 3:6; 6:4; 2 Ti 3:4. But τ. in 1 Ti 6:4 can also mean be blinded, be foolish or stupid.*

τύφω pass. smoke, smolder, glimmer Mt 12:20.* [typhus]

τυφωνικός, ή, όν like a whirlwind ἄνεμος τυφωνικός a typhoon, hurricane Ac 27:14.*

τυχεῖν, τύχοι, τυχόν 2 aor. act. inf., 2 aor. opt. 3 sing., and 2 aor. act. ptc. of τυγχάνω.

Τυχικός, οῦ, ὁ Tychicus, a friend and companion of Paul Ac 20:4; Eph 6:21; Col 4:7; 2 Ti 4:12; Tit 3:12; Eph subscr.; Col subscr.*

τυχόν 2 aor. act. ptc., neut. acc. sing., of τυγχάνω.

Y

ὑακίνθινος, ίνη, ινον hyacinth-colored, i.e. dark blue (dark red?) Rv 9:17.*

ὑάκινθος, ου, ὁ the jacinth or hyacinth, a precious stone, perhaps blue in color Rv 21:20.*

ὑάλινος, η, ον of glass, transparent as glass Rv 4:6; 15:2.*

ὕαλος, ου, ἡ or ὁ glass, crystal Rv 21:18, 21.*

ὑβρίζω treat in an arrogant or spiteful manner, mistreat, scoff at, insult Mt 22:6; Lk 11:45; 18:32; Ac 14:5; 1 Th 2:2.*

ὕβρις, εως, ἡ—1. shame, insult, mistreatment 2 Cor 12:10.—2. disaster, damage Ac 27:10, 21.* [hybris]

ὑβριστής, οῦ, ὁ a violent, insolent man Ro 1:30; 1 Ti 1:13.*

ὑγιαίνω be in good health, be healthy or sound—1. lit. Mt 8:13 v.l.; Lk 5:31; 7:10; 15:27; 3 J 2.—2. fig. be sound or correct 1 Ti 1:10; 6:3; 2 Ti 1:13; 4:3; Tit 1:9, 13; 2:1f.* [hygiene]

ὑγιής, ές acc. ὑγιῆ healthy, sound—1. lit. Mt 12:13; 15:31; Mk 5:34; J 5:4, 6, 9, 11, 14f; 7:23; Ac 4:10.—2. fig. Tit 2:8.

ὑγρός, ά, όν moist, pliant, green Lk 23:31.* [hygrometer]

ὑδρία, ας, ἡ water jar J 2:6f; 4:28.*

ὑδροποτέω drink (only) water 1 Ti 5:23.*

ὑδρωπικός, ή, όν suffering from dropsy Lk 14:2.*

ὕδωρ, ατος, τό water—1. lit. Mt 3:11; Mk 9:41; 14:13; J 5:3f v.l., 7; Hb 10:22; 2 Pt 3:5; Rv 1:15.—2. fig. J 4:10f, 14; 7:38; Rv 7:17; 21:6; 22:1, 17. [hydrant]

ὑετός, οῦ, ὁ rain Ac 14:17; 28:2; Hb 6:7; Js 5:7 v.l., 18; Rv 11:6.* [hyeto-, a combining form, as in hyetograph, a chart showing average annual rainfall]

υἱοθεσία, ας, ἡ adoption (of children), only in a transferred sense Ro 8:15; Gal

4:5; Eph 1:5. In Ro 8:23; 9:4 the emphasis is on the full enjoyment of the privileges of legal heirs.*

υἱός, οῦ, ὁ son—1. in the usual sense—a. lit. Mt 1:21; Mk 6:3; Lk 15:11; Ac 13:21; Gal 4:30. Offspring Mt 21:5.—b. more generally descendant Mt 1:20; Ac 5:21; 10:36; 2 Cor 3:7, 13; Hb 11:22. Of one who is accepted or adopted as a son J 19:26; Ac 7:21.—c. fig.—α. of a pupil, follower, etc. Lk 11:19; Hb 12:5; 1 Pt 5:13.—β. of the members of a large group Mk 3:28; Ac 13:26; Eph 3:5.—γ. of those who are bound to a person by close ties Mt 5:45; 23:31; Ro 8:14, 19; Gal 3:7, 26; Hb 2:10.—δ. υἱός with gen. of the thing, to denote one who shares in this thing Mt 8:12; 9:15; Mk 3:17; Lk 16:8; J 17:12; Ac 4:36; Eph 2:2; 2 Th 2:3.—2. in various combinations as a designation of the Messiah and a self-designation of Jesus—a. Son of David Mt 9:27; 21:9, 15; Mk 10:47f; 12:35, 37; Lk 18:38f.—b. (the) Son of God Mt 2:15; 3:17; 27:43, 54; 28:19; Mk 3:11; 9:7; Lk 1:35; 10:22; J 1:49; 3:16-18, 35f; Ac 13:33; Ro 1:3, 4, 9; Hb 5:5.—c. ὁ υἱὸς τοῦ ἀνθρώπου the Son of Man, the Son of Humanity, the Human Being, always as a self-designation of Jesus to express his identification with the lot of humanity or his ultimate triumph Mt 8:20; 9:6; Mk 8:31, 38; 14:21; Lk 9:22, 26, 44, 58; J 1:51; 6:27, 53, 62; Ac 7:56; Rv 1:13; 14:14.

ὕλη, ης, ἡ wood Js 3:5.* [hylic]

ὑμεῖς nom. pl. of σύ.

Ὑμέναιος, ου, ὁ Hymenaeus 1 Ti 1:20; 2 Ti 2:17.*

ὑμέτερος, α, ον your—1. belonging to or incumbent upon you Lk 6:20; J 7:6; 8:17; 15:20; Ac 27:34; 2 Cor 8:8; Gal 6:13; subst. Lk 16:12.—2. for the objective gen. τῷ ὑμετέρῳ ἐλέει by the mercy shown to you Ro 11:31. νὴ τὴν ὑμετέραν καύχησιν ἣν ἔχω by the pride that I have in you 1 Cor 15:31. τὸ ὑ. ὑστέρημα that which is lacking in you 16:17.*

ὑμνέω—1. trans. sing the praise of Ac 16:25; Hb 2:12.—2. intrans. sing a hymn Mt 26:30; Mk 14:26.*

ὕμνος, ου, ὁ hymn or song of praise Eph 5:19; Col 3:16.*

ὑπάγω—1. go away Mt 4:10; Mk 5:34; 8:33; J 6:67; 18:8; Js 2:16. Go home Mt 8:13; 20:14; Mk 10:52.—2. go Mt 9:6; 18:15; 26:18; Mk 1:44; 14:13; Lk 10:3; J 7:3; 9:11; 21:3; Rv 13:10; 14:4.—Especially of Christ's going to the Father J 7:33; 8:14; 14:28; 16:5a, 10, 17.

ὑπακοή, ῆς, ἡ obedience Ro 1:5; 6:16; 16:19, 26; 2 Cor 10:5f; Hb 5:8; 1 Pt 1:2, 22.

ὑπακούω listen to—1. obey, follow, be subject to w. dat. Mk 1:27; 4:41; Ro 10:16; Eph 6:1, 5; Phil 2:12; 2 Th 3:14; 1 Pt 3:6.—2. open or answer (the door) Ac 12:13.

ὕπανδρος, ον under the power of a man ἡ ὕπανδρος γυνή the married woman Ro 7:2.*

ὑπαντάω (come or go to) meet w. dat. Mt 8:28; 28:9; Mk 5:2; Lk 8:27; J 4:51; 11:20, 30; 12:18; Ac 16:16.—Oppose Lk 14:31.

ὑπάντησις, εως, ἡ coming to meet εἰς ὑπάντησιν to meet w. dat. or gen. Mt 8:34; 25:1; J 12:13.*

ὕπαρξις, εως, ἡ that which one has, property, possession Ac 2:45; Hb 10:34.*

ὑπάρχω—1. (really) exist, be present, be at one's disposal Ac 3:6; 4:34; 19:40; 28:7, 18; 1 Cor 11:18. τὰ ὑπάρχοντα property, possessions Mt 19:21; Lk 8:3; 11:21; 19:8; 1 Cor 13:3.—2. to be, as a substitute for εἶναι Lk 8:41; 9:48; 16:14; Ac 7:55; 21:20; 22:3; Ro 4:19; 1 Cor 7:26; Gal 1:14; Phil 2:6; Js 2:15.

ὑπέβαλον 2 aor. act. ind. of ὑπολαμβάνω.

ὑπέδειξα 1 aor. act. ind. of ὑποδείκνυμι.

ὑπέθηκα 1 aor. act. ind. of ὑποτίθημι.

ὑπείκω yield, give way, submit Hb 13:17.*

ὑπέλαβον 2 aor. act. ind. of ὑπολαμβάνω.

ὑπελείφθην 1 aor. pass. ind. of ὑπολείπω.

ὑπέμεινα 1 aor. act. ind. of ὑπομένω.

ὑπεμνήσθην 1 aor. pass. ind. of ὑπομιμνήσκω.

ὑπεναντίος, α, ον opposed, in Col 2:14 against. οἱ ὑπεναντίοι the adversaries Hb 10:27.*

ὑπενεγκεῖν 2 aor. act. inf. of ὑποφέρω.

ὑπέπλευσα 1 aor. act. ind. of ὑποπλέω.

ὑπέρ prep. w. gen. and acc.—1. w. gen.— a. for, in behalf of, for the sake of Mt 5:44; Mk 9:40; J 11:50–52; Ac 21:26; Ro 5:6–8; 8:31; 16:4; Col 1:7, 9; Phil 1:7; Hb 2:9.—b. w. gen. of the thing in behalf of, but variously translated: with ἁμαρτιῶν in order to remove the sins Gal 1:4; Hb 7:27; 10:12; with ζωῆς to bring life J 6:51; with δόξης to reveal the glory 11:4; with ὀνόματος to spread the name Ro 1:5.—c. in place of, instead of, in the name of 2 Cor 5:14f, 21; Phlm 13.—d. because of, for the sake of, for Ac 5:41; 21:13; Ro 15:9; 2 Cor 12:10; Eph 5:20; Phil 1:29.—e. above and beyond may be the meaning in Phil 2:13; in is also possible.—f. about, concerning J 1:30; Ro 9:27; 2 Cor 1:7f; 12:5.—2. w. acc. over and above, beyond, more than 1 Cor 4:6; 2 Cor 1:8; Eph 1:22; Phlm 16, 21. Superior to Mt 10:24; Lk 6:40; Phil 2:9. Than 2 Cor 12:13; Hb 4:12. More than Mt 10:37; Gal 1:14.—3. ὑπέρ as adv. even more 2 Cor 11:23. [hyper-, combining form, as in hyperbole, hypertrophy]

ὑπεραίρομαι rise up, exalt oneself, be elated 2 Cor 12:7; 2 Th 2:4.*

ὑπέρακμος, ον past one's prime, past the bloom of youth if it refers to the woman; with strong passions if it refers to the man 1 Cor 7:36.* [Cf. acme (ἀκμή).]

ὑπεράνω adv. (high) above, functions as prep. w. gen. Eph 1:21; 4:10; Hb 9:5.*

ὑπερασπίζω shield, protect Js 1:27 v.l.*

ὑπεραυξάνω grow wonderfully, increase abundantly 2 Th 1:3.*

ὑπερβαίνω transgress, sin 1 Th 4:6.*

ὑπερβαλλόντως surpassingly, to a much greater degree 2 Cor 11:23.*

ὑπερβάλλω go beyond, surpass; the participle ὑπερβάλλων, ουσα, ον surpassing; extraordinary, outstanding 2 Cor 3:10; 9:14; Eph 1:19; 2:7; 3:19.*

ὑπερβολή, ῆς, ἡ excess, extraordinary quality or character 2 Cor 4:7; 12:7. καθ' ὑπερβολήν to an extraordinary degree, beyond measure, utterly Ro 7:13; 2 Cor 1:8; Gal 1:13. καθ' ὑπ. ὁδόν a far better way 1 Cor 12:31. καθ' ὑπ. εἰς ὑπ. beyond all measure and proportion 2 Cor 4:17.* [hyperbole]

ὑπερεγώ for ὑπὲρ ἐγώ 2 Cor 11:23; see ὑπέρ 3.

ὑπερέκεινα adv. beyond w. gen. 2 Cor 10:16.*

ὑπερεκπερισσοῦ adv. quite beyond all measure, as earnestly as possible 1 Th 3:10; 5:13. W. gen. infinitely more than Eph 3:20.*

ὑπερεκπερισσῶς adv. beyond all measure, most highly 1 Th 5:13 v.1.; Mk 7:37 v.1.*

ὑπερεκτείνω stretch out beyond, overextend 2 Cor 10:14.*

ὑπερεκχύν(ν)ω pour out over, pass. overflow Lk 6:38.*

ὑπερεντυγχάνω plead, intercede Ro 8:26.*

ὑπερέχω—1. have power over, be in authority (over), be highly placed of authorities in the state Ro 13:1; 1 Pt 2:13.—2. be better than, surpass, excel w. gen. Phil 2:3; w. acc. 4:7.—3. τὸ ὑπερέχον the surpassing greatness Phil 3:8.*

ὑπερηφανία, ας, ἡ arrogance, haughtiness, pride Mk 7:22.*

ὑπερήφανος, ον arrogant, haughty, proud Lk 1:51; Ro 1:30; 2 Ti 3:2; Js 4:6; 1 Pt 5:5.*

ὑπεριδών 2 aor. act. ptc. of ὑπεροράω.

ὑπερλίαν adv. exceedingly, beyond measure as adj. οἱ ὑπερλίαν ἀπόστολοι the superapostles 2 Cor 11:5; 12:11.*

ὑπερνικάω win a most glorious victory Ro 8:37.*

ὑπέρογκος, ον excessive size, haughty, bombastic 2 Pt 2:18; Jd 16.*

ὑπεροράω overlook, disregard Ac 17:30.*

ὑπεροχή, ῆς, ἡ—1. superiority καθ' ὑπεροχήν as a superior person 1 Cor 2:1.—2. a position of authority 1 Ti 2:2.*

ὑπερπερισσεύω—1. intrans. be present in (greater) abundance Ro 5:20.—2. trans. cause to overflow pass. overflow 2 Cor 7:4.*

ὑπερπερισσῶς adv. beyond all measure Mk 7:37.*

ὑπερπλεονάζω be present in great abundance 1 Ti 1:14.*

ὑπερυψόω raise to the loftiest height Phil 2:9.*

ὑπερφρονέω think too highly of oneself, be haughty Ro 12:3.*

ὑπερῷον, ου, τό upper story, room upstairs Ac 1:13; 9:37, 39; 20:8.*

ὑπεστειλάμην 1 aor. mid. ind. of ὑποστέλλω.

ὑπετάγην 2 aor. pass. ind. of ὑποτάσσω.

ὑπέταξα 1 aor. act. ind. of ὑποτάσσω.

ὑπέχω undergo Jd 7.*

ὑπήκοος, ον obedient Ac 7:39; 2 Cor 2:9; Phil 2:8.*

ὑπήνεγκα aor. act. ind. of ὑποφέρω.

ὑπηρετέω serve, render service, be helpful w. dat. Ac 13:36; 20:34; 24:23.*

ὑπηρέτης, ου, ὁ servant, helper, assistant Mt 5:25; Mk 14:54, 65; Lk 4:20; J 7:32, 45f; 18:18, 36; Ac 13:5; 26:16; 1 Cor 4:1.

ὕπνος, ου, ὁ sleep lit. Mt 1:24; Lk 9:32; J 11:13; Ac 20:9; fig Ro 13:11.* [hypnotic]

ὑπό prep. w. gen. and acc.—1. w. gen. by, denoting the agent or cause Mt 1:22; 8:24; J 14:21; Gal 1:11; 1 Cor 10:29; Rv 6:13; at the hands of Mk 5:26; 2 Cor 2:6.—2. w. acc. under, below Mt 8:8f; Ac 4:12; Ro 6:14f; 16:20; 1 Cor 9:20; 15:25, 27; Col 1:23; (below) at Js 2:3; about Ac 5:21. [hypo-, combining form in numerous words] ὑποβάλλω instigate (secretly), suborn Ac 6:11.*

ὑπογραμμός, οῦ, ὁ model, example 1 Pt 2:21.*

ὑπόδειγμα, ατος, τό—1. example, model, pattern J 13:15; Hb 4:11; Js 5:10; 2 Pt 2:6.—2. copy, imitation Hb 8:5; 9:23.*

ὑποδείκνυμι or ὑποδεικνύω show, prove, set forth Lk 6:47; 12:5; Ac 9:16; 20:35. Warn Mt 3:7; Lk 3:7.* ὑποδείξω fut. act. ind. of ὑποδείκνυμι.

ὑποδέχομαι receive, welcome, entertain as a guest Lk 10:38; 19:6; Ac 17:7; Js 2:25.*

ὑποδέω mid. tie or bind beneath, put on (footwear) Mk 6:9; Ac 12:8; Eph 6:15.*

ὑπόδημα, ατος, τό sandal, footwear Mt 10:10; Mk 1:7; Lk 15:22; 22:35; Ac 7:33. ὑπόδησαι 1 aor. mid. impv. of ὑποδέω.

ὑπόδικος, ον answerable, accountable Ro 3:19.*

ὑποδραμών 2 aor. act. ptc. of ὑποτρέχω.

ὑποζύγιον, ου, τό donkey, ass Mt 21:5; 2 Pt 2:16.*

ὑποζώννυμι undergird, brace with cables around the hull Ac 27:17.*

ὑποκάτω adv., functions as prep. w. gen. under, below, down at Mt 22:44; Mk 6:11; J 1:50; Rv 5:3, 13.

ὑπόκειμαι be found, lit. 'lie below' Lk 6:42 v.l.*

ὑποκρίνομαι pretend, make believe Lk 20:20.*

ὑπόκρισις, εως, ἡ hypocrisy, pretense, outward show Mt 23:28; Mk 12:15; Lk 12:1; Gal 2:13; Js 5:12 v.l.; 1 Ti 4:2; 1 Pt 2:1.*

ὑποκριτής, οῦ, ὁ hypocrite, pretender, dissembler, lit. 'playactor' Mt 6:2, 5, 16; 7:5; 23:13–15; Mk 7:6; Lk 6:42; 12:56; 13:15.

ὑπολαβών 2 aor. act. ptc. of ὑπολαμβάνω.

ὑπολαμβάνω—1. take up Ac 1:9.—2. receive as a guest 3 J 8.—3. reply Lk 10:30.—4. assume, think, believe Lk 7:43; Ac 2:15.*

ὑπολαμπάς, άδος, ἡ probably window Ac 20:8 v.l.*

ὑπόλειμμα, ατος, τό remnant Ro 9:27.*

ὑπολείπω leave remaining pass. be left (remaining) Ro 11:3.*

ὑπολήνιον, ου, τό vat placed beneath a winepress Mk 12:1.*

ὑπόλιμμα a different spelling for ὑπόλειμμα.

ὑπολιμπάνω leave (behind) 1 Pt 2:21.* ὑπομείνας 1 aor. act. ptc. of ὑπομένω. ὑπομεμενηκώς pf. act. ptc. of ὑπομένω.

ὑπομένω remain, stay (behind) Lk 2:43; Ac 17:14.—Remain, stand one's ground, hold out, endure Mk 13:13; Ro 12:12; 1 Cor 13:7; Hb 12:2, 7; Js 5:11; 1 Pt 2:20.

ὑπομιμνῄσκω—1. act. remind J 14:26; Tit 3:1; 2 Pt 1:12; Jd 5. Call to mind, bring up 2 Ti 2:14; 3 J 10.—2. pass. remember, think of w. gen. Lk 22:61.*

ὑπομνῆσαι, ὑπομνήσω 1 aor. act. inf. and fut. act. ind. of ὑπομιμνῄσκω.

ὑπόμνησις, εως, ἡ remembering ἐν ὑπ. by a reminder, i.e. as I remind you 2 Pt 1:13; 3:1. Remembrance ὑπόμνησιν λαμβάνειν receive a remembrance = remember 2 Ti 1:5.*

ὑπομονή, ῆς, ἡ—1. patience, endurance, fortitude, steadfastness, perseverance Lk 21:19; Ro 2:7; 5:3f; 8:25; 2 Cor 12:12; 2 Th 3:5; Js 1:3f; 5:11; Rv 2:2f; 13:10.—2. (patient) expectation Rv 1:9.

ὑπονοέω suspect, suppose Ac 13:25; 25:18; 27:27.*

ὑπόνοια, ας, ἡ suspicion, conjecture 1 Ti 6:4.*

ὑποπιάζω a variant spelling of ὑπωπιάζω.

ὑποπλέω sail under the lee of an island Ac 27:4, 7.*

ὑποπνεύσας 1 aor. act. ptc. of ὑποπνέω.

ὑποπνέω blow gently Ac 27:13.*

ὑποπόδιον, ου, τό footstool Mt 22:44 v.l.; Lk 20:43; Ac 2:35; Hb 1:13.

ὑπόστασις, εως, ἡ—1. substantial nature, essence, actual being, reality Hb

1:3; 11:1.—**2.** *undertaking, project* 2 Cor 9:4; 11:17; Hb 3:14.* [*hypostasis*]

ὑποστέλλω—1. act. *draw back, withdraw* Gal 2:12.—**2.** mid. *draw back in fear* Hb 10:38. *Shrink from, avoid* Ac 20:27. *Keep silent about* 20:20.*

ὑποστολή, ῆς, ἡ *shrinking, timidity* Hb 10:39.*

ὑποστρέφω *turn back, return* Lk 1:56; 4:14; Ac 8:25, 28; 12:25; Gal 1:17; Hb 7:1; *turn away* 2 Pt 2:21.

ὑποστρωννύω *spread out underneath* Lk 19:36.*

ὑποταγή, ῆς, ἡ *subjection, subordination, obedience, submission* 2 Cor 9:13; Gal 2:5; 1 Ti 2:11; 3:4.* [Cf. *hypotaxis*.]

ὑποταγήσομαι 2 fut. pass. ind. of ὑποτάσσω.

ὑποτάσσω *subject, subordinate*—**1.** act. 1 Cor 15:27a, c, 28c; Eph 1:22; Hb 2:5, 8a.—**2.** pass. *become subject* Ro 8:20a; 1 Cor 15:27b, 28a; Hb 2:8c. *Subject oneself, be subjected* or *subordinated, obey* Lk 2:51; 10:17, 20; 1 Cor 14:34; 15:28b; 16:16.

ὑποτέτακται pf. pass. ind. 3 sing. (1 Cor 15:27) of ὑποτάσσω.

ὑποτίθημι act. *lay down, risk* Ro 16:4; mid. *suggest,* or *order,* or *teach* 1 Ti 4:6.* [*hypothesis*]

ὑποτρέχω *run* or *sail under the lee of* Ac 27:16.*

ὑποτύπωσις, εως, ἡ *model, example, prototype* 1 Ti 1:16; *standard, outline* 2 Ti 1:13.*

ὑποφέρω *bear (up under), submit to, endure* 1 Cor 10:13; 2 Ti 3:11; 1 Pt 2:19.*

ὑποχωρέω *retreat, withdraw, retire* Lk 5:16; 9:10; 20:20 v.l.*

ὑπωπιάζω *strike under the eye*—**1.** lit., in a weakened sense *annoy greatly, wear out, browbeat* Lk 18:5.—**2.** fig. *treat roughly, torment, maltreat* 1 Cor 9:27.*

ὗς, ὑός, ἡ *the female of the swine, sow* 2 Pt 2:22.*

ὑσσός, οῦ, ὁ *javelin* J 19:29 v.l.*

ὕσσωπος, ου, ἡ and ὁ also **ὕσσωπον, τό** *the hyssop* (Heb. loanword), a small bush with highly aromatic leaves, used

in purification J 19:29; Hb 9:19.* See ὑσσός.

ὑστερέω—1. act.—**a.** *come too late, miss, be excluded* Hb 4:1; 12:15.—**b.** *be in need of, lack* Lk 22:35.—**c.** *be less than, be inferior to* w. gen. of comparison 2 Cor 11:5; 12:11. *Be inferior, lack* Mt 19:20; 1 Cor 12:24.—**d.** *fail, give out, lack* J 2:3. ἕν σε ὑστερεῖ *you lack one thing* Mk 10:21.—**2.** pass. *lack, be lacking, go without* Lk 15:14; Ro 3:23; 1 Cor 1:7; 8:8; 12:24; 2 Cor 11:9; Phil 4:12; Hb 11:37.*

ὑστέρημα, ατος, τό—1. *need, want, deficiency* Lk 21:4; 2 Cor 8:14; 9:12; 11:9; Col 1:24. *Absence* 1 Cor 16:17; Phil 2:30.—**2.** *shortcoming* 1 Th 3:10.*

ὑστέρησις, εως, ἡ *need, lack, poverty* Mk 12:44; Phil 4:11.*

ὕστερος, α, ον used as a comparative and superlative—**1.** as adj., comp. *latter, second* Mt 21:31 v.l. Superl. *last* Ti 4:1, though *later* is also possible.—**2.** neut. ὕστερον as adv., comp. *in the second place, later, then, thereafter* Mt 21:29, 32; Mk 16:14; J 13:36; Hb 12:11. Superl. *finally* Mt 21:37; 26:60; Lk 20:32; *last* Mt 22:27. [Cf. *hysteron proteron*.]

ὑφαίνω *weave* Lk 12:27 v.l.*

ὑφαντός, ή, όν *woven* J 19:23.*

ὑψηλός, ή, όν *high*—**1.** lit. Mt 4:8; Rv 21:10, 12; *uplifted* Ac 13:17. Comparative ὑψηλότερος Hb 7:26.—**2.** fig. *exalted, proud, haughty* Lk 16:15; Ro 11:20; 12:16.

ὑψηλοφρονέω *be proud, haughty* 1 Ti 6:17; Ro 11:20 v.l.*

ὕψιστος, η, ον *highest, most exalted*—**1.** in a spatial sense Mt 21:9; Mk 11:10; Lk 2:14; 19:38.—**2.** *the Most High,* i.e. God Mk 5:7; Lk 1:32, 35, 76; 6:35; 8:28; Ac 7:48; 16:17; Hb 7:1.*

ὕψος, ους, τό *height*—**1.** lit. Eph 3:18; Rv 21:16. *High place, heaven* Lk 1:78; 24:49; Eph 4:8.—**2.** *of rank high position* Js 1:9.* [*hypsophobia*] ὑψόω *lift up, raise high*—**1**. lit. Lk 10:15; J 3:14; Ac 2:33.—**2**. fig. *exalt* Mt 23:12; Lk 1:52; Ac 5:31; 2 Cor 11:7; Js 4:10; *make great* Ac 13:17.

ὕψωμα, ατος, τό *height, exaltation* Ro 8:39. *That which rises up, pride* 2 Cor 10:5.*

Φ

φαγεῖν, φάγομαι 2 aor. act. inf. and fut. mid. ind. of ἐσθίω.

φάγος, ου, ὁ *glutton* Mt 11:19; Lk 7:34.* [*sarcophagus*, σάρξ + φαγεῖν]

φαιλόνης, ου, ὁ *cloak* 2 Ti 4:13.*

φαίνω—**1**. act. intrans. *shine, give light, be bright* J 1:5; 5:35; 2 Pt 1:19; Rv 1:16; 8:12; 18:23; 21:23.—**2**. φαίνομαι—**a**. *shine, flash* Mt 24:27; Phil 2:15.—**b**. *appear, be* or *become visible, be revealed* Mt 9:33; 24:30; Hb 11:3; Js 4:14; 1 Pt 4:18.—**c**. *appear, make one's appearance, show oneself* Mt 1:20; 6:5, 16, 18; Mk 16:9; Lk 9:8.—**d**. *appear as something, appear to be something* Mt 23:27f; Lk 24:11; 2 Cor 13:7. *Be recognized* Ro 7:13.—**e**. *have the appearance, seem* Mk 14:64. [*phenomenon*]

Φάλεκ, ὁ indecl. *Peleg* Lk 3:35.*

φανεῖται fut. mid. ind. 3 sing. of φαίνω.

φανερός, ά, όν—**1**. adj. *visible, clear, plainly to be seen, plain, known* Mt 12:16; Mk 6:14; Ac 4:16; Ro 1:19; 1 Cor 3:13; Gal 5:19; Phil 1:13; 1 J 3:10.—**2**. τὸ φανερόν subst. *public notice, the open* Mk 4:22; Mt 6:4 v.l., 6 v.l. ἐν τῷ φ. *outwardly* Ro 2:28. [*phanerogam*, φανερός + γάμος, a flowering plant]

φανερόω *reveal, make known, show* Mk 4:22; J 7:4; 17:6; 21:14; Ro 1:19; 3:21; 2 Cor 2:14; 5:10f; Eph 5:13f; 1 Ti 3:16; Tit 1:3; Hb 9:8, 26; 1 J 1:2; 2:28.

φανερῶς adv. *openly, publicly* Mk 1:45; J 7:10; Ac 10:3.*

φανέρωσις, εως, ἡ *disclosure, announcement* 1 Cor 12:7; 2 Cor 4:2.*

φάνῃ, φανήσομαι 1 aor. act. subj. 3 sing. (Rv 8:12; 18:23) and 2 fut. pass. ind. of φαίνω.

φανός, οῦ, ὁ *lantern* J 18:3.*

Φανουήλ, ὁ indecl. *Phanuel* Lk 2:36.*

φαντάζω *make visible*, pass. *become visible, appear* τὸ φανταζόμενον *sight, spectacle* Hb 12:21.*

φαντασία, ας, ἡ *pomp, pageantry* Ac 25:23.* [*fantasy*]

φάντασμα, ατος, τό *apparition, ghost* Mt 14:26; Mk 6:49; Lk 24:37 v.l.* [*phantom*]

φανῶ 2 aor. pass. subj. of φαίνω.

φάραγξ, αγγος, ἡ *ravine, valley* Lk 3:5.*

Φαραώ, ὁ indecl. *Pharaoh*, title of the Egyptian kings, then a proper name Ac 7:10, 13, 21; Ro 9:17; Hb 11:24.*

Φαρές, ὁ indecl. *Perez* Mt 1:3; Lk 3:33.*

Φαρισαῖος, ου, ὁ *Pharisee*, lit. 'separatist,' member of a Jewish sect that held in great respect the Torah and the tradition of its interpretation. The more liberalizing approach of Jesus and especially of St. Paul evoked resistance from some members of the sect Mt 3:7; 5:20; 9:11, 34; 23:26; Mk 2:16; 3:6; Lk 7:36f, 39; Ac 23:6–9; 26:5; Phil 3:5.

φαρμακεία, ας, ἡ *sorcery, magic* Gal 5:20; Rv 9:21 v.l.; 18:23.* [*pharmacy*]

φαρμακεύς, έως, ὁ *mixer of poisons, magician* Rv 21:8 v.l.* [*pharmaceutical*]

φάρμακον, ου, τό *magic potion, charm* Rv 9:21.*

φάρμακος, ου, ὁ *magician* Rv 21:8; 22:15.*

φασίν pres. act. ind. 3 pl. of **φημί**.

φάσις, εως, ἡ *report, news* Ac 21:31.* [Cf. **φημί**.]

φάσκω *say, assert, claim* Ac 24:9; 25:19; Ro 1:22; Rv 2:2 v.l.*

φάτνη, ης, ἡ *manger, stall* Lk 2:7, 12, 16; 13:15.*

φαῦλος, η, ον *worthless, bad, evil, base* J 3:20; 5:29; Ro 9:11; 2 Cor 5:10; Tit 2:8; Js 3:16.*

φέγγος, ους, τό *light, radiance* Mt 24:29; Mk 13:24; Lk 11:33 v.l.*

φείδομαι—1. *spare* w. gen. Ac 20:29; Ro 8:32; 11:21; 1 Cor 7:28; 2 Cor 1:23; 13:2; 2 Pt 2:4f.—2. *refrain* from 2 Cor 12:6.*

φειδομένως adv. *sparingly* 2 Cor 9:6.*

φελόνης an alternative spelling for **φαιλόνης**.

φέρω—1. *bear, carry*—a. lit. and fig. Lk 23:26; Hb 1:3.—b. *bear patiently, endure, put up with* Ro 9:22; Hb 12:20; 13:13.—c. *bring with one, bring along* Lk 24:1; J 19:39.—2. *bear, produce* Mt 7:18 v.l.; J 12:24; 15:2, 4f.—3. *move out of position, drive* lit. Ac 27:15, 17; *rush* 2:2. Fig. *be moved* 2 Pt 1:21b; *move on* Hb 6:1.—4. *bring (on), produce*—a. *bring (to), fetch* Mt 14:11, 18; Mk 6:27f; 11:2, 7; J 4:33; Ac 4:34, 37; 14:13; Rv 21:24, 26.—b. *bring, utter, make* J 18:29; 2 Pt 1:17f; 2:11; 2 J 10; *be established* Hb 9:16. *Reach out* J 20:27.—c. *bring* or *lead* Mk 1:32; 7:32; 15:22; Lk 5:18; J 21:18; Ac 5:16.—d. *of a gate, lead* somewhere Ac 12:10. [*metaphor*, μετά + φέρειν]

φεύγω—1. lit. *flee, seek safety in flight* Mt 8:33; Mk 14:50; 16:8; Lk 21:21; J 10:5, 12; Ac 27:30; Js 4:7; Rv 9:6.—2. *escape* Mt 23:33; Lk 3:7; Hb 11:34; 12:25 v.l.—3. *flee from, avoid, shun* 1 Cor 6:18; 10:14; 1 Ti 6:11; 2 Ti 2:22.—4. *vanish, disappear* Rv 16:20; 20:11. [*fugitive*, via Latin]

Φῆλιξ, ικος, ὁ Antonius *Felix*, a freedman prominent in the reign of the Emperor Claudius; he was the husband of Drusilla and procurator of Palestine

about 52–60 A.D. Ac 23:24, 26; 24:3, 22, 24f, 27; 25:14.*

φήμη, ης, ἡ *report, news* Mt 9:26; Lk 4:14.* [*fame*, via Latin]

φημί—1. *say, affirm* Mt 8:8; 13:29; Mk 9:12; Lk 7:44; J 9:38; Ac 8:36; 25:5, 22; 1 Cor 6:16; 2 Cor 10:10; Hb 8:5.—2. *mean* by one's statement Ro 3:8; 1 Cor 7:29; 10:15, 19; 15:50.

φημίζω *spread* (a report) *by word of mouth* Mt 28:15 v.l.; Ac 13:43 v.l.*

φησίν pres. act. ind. 3 sing. of **φημί**.

Φῆστος, ου, ὁ Porcius *Festus*, successor to Felix (see **Φῆλιξ**) as procurator of Palestine; the date of his death was probably in the early 60s. Ac 24:27; ch. 25 passim; 26:24f, 32.*

φθάνω—1. *come before, precede* 1 Th 4:15.—2. *arrive, come, overtake* Mt 12:28; Lk 11:20; Ro 9:31; 2 Cor 10:14; Phil 3:16; 1 Th 2:16.*

φθαρῇ 2 aor. pass. subj. 3 sing. of **φθείρω**.

φθαρήσομαι 2 fut. pass. ind. of **φθείρω**.

φθαρτός, ή, όν *perishable* 1 Cor 9:25; 15:53f; 1 Pt 1:18, 23; *mortal* Ro 1:23.*

φθέγγομαι *speak, utter, proclaim* Ac 4:18; 2 Pt 2:16, 18.*

φθείρω *ruin, corrupt, spoil* 1 Cor 3:17a; 15:33; 2 Cor 7:2; Eph 4:22; 2 Pt 2:12; Jd 10; Rv 19:2; pass. *be led astray* 2 Cor 11:3.—*Destroy* 1 Cor 3:17b.*

φθερεῖ fut. act. ind. 3 sing. of **φθείρω**.

φθινοπωρινός, ή, όν *belonging to late autumn* Jd 12.*

φθόγγος, ου, ὁ *sound, tone* Ro 10:18; 1 Cor 14:7.* [*diphthong*, δίς + φθόγγος]

φθονέω *envy, be jealous of* w. dat. Gal 5:26; cf. Js 4:2 v.l.*

φθόνος, ου, ὁ *envy, jealousy* Mt 27:18; Ro 1:29; Gal 5:21; 1 Ti 6:4; Tit 3:3; Js 4:5.

φθορά, ᾶς, ἡ *ruin, destruction, dissolution, corruption* Ro 8:21; 1 Cor 15:42, 50; Gal 6:8; Col 2:22; 2 Pt 2:12; *depravity* 2 Pt 1:4; 2:19.*

φιάλη, ης, ἡ *bowl* used for offerings Rv 5:8; 16:1–4, 8, 10, 12, 17. [*phial, vial*]

φιλάγαθος, ον *loving what is good* Tit 1:8.*

Φιλαδέλφεια, ας, ἡ Philadelphia, a city in west central Asia Minor Rv 1:11; 3:7.*

φιλαδελφία, ας, ἡ brotherly-sisterly love in an extended sense Ro 12:10; 1 Th 4:9; Hb 13:1; 1 Pt 1:22; 2 Pt 1:7.*

φιλάδελφος, ον loving one's brother or sister 1 Pt 3:8.*

φίλανδρος, ον loving her husband Tit 2:4.* [philander]

φιλανθρωπία, ας, ἡ love for humanity, kindness, generosity Tit 3:4; hospitality Ac 28:2.* [philanthropy]

φιλανθρώπως adv. benevolently, kindly Ac 27:3.*

φιλαργυρία, ας, ἡ love of money, avarice 1 Ti 6:10.*

φιλάργυρος, ον fond of money, avaricious Lk 16:14; 2 Ti 3:2.*

φίλαυτος, ον loving oneself, selfish 2 Ti 3:2.*

φιλέω—1. love, have affection for, like Mt 6:5; 10:37; 23:6; Lk 20:46; J 5:20; 11:3, 36; 12:25; 15:19; 16:27; 20:2; 21:15–17 (see ἀγαπάω 1); 1 Cor 16:22; Tit 3:15; Rv 3:19; 22:15.—2. kiss Mt 26:48; Mk 14:44; Lk 22:47.* [S. φίλος.]

φίλη, ης, ἡ see φίλος 2.

φιλήδονος, ον loving pleasure 2 Ti 3:4.*

φίλημα, ατος, τό a kiss Lk 7:45; 22:48; Ro 16:16; 1 Cor 16:20; 2 Cor 13:12; 1 Th 5:26; 1 Pt 5:14.*

Φιλήμων, ονος, ὁ Philemon, a Christian who probably lived at Colossae; owner of the slave Onesimus Phlm 1; subscr. and title.*

Φίλητος, ου, ὁ Philetus 2 Ti 2:17.*

φιλία, ας, ἡ friendship, love Js 4:4.*

Φιλιππήσιος, ου, ὁ the man from Philippi, the Philippian Phil 4:15; title.*

Φίλιπποι, ων, οἱ Philippi, a city in Macedonia, location of the first Christian church founded in Europe Ac 16:12; 20:6; Phil 1:1; 1 Th 2:2; 1 and 2 Cor subscr.*

Φίλιππος, ου, ὁ Philip—1. son of Herod I and Cleopatra, of Jerusalem; he was tetrarch of several districts northeast of Palestine; died 33/34 A.D. Mt 16:13; Mk 8:27.—2. the first husband of Herodias Mt 14:3; Mk 6:17.—

3. one of the twelve apostles Mt 10:3; Mk 3:18; Lk 6:14; J 1:43–46, 48; 6:5, 7; 12:21f; 14:8f; Ac 1:13.—4. one of the seven 'helpers' in Jerusalem Ac 6:5; 8:5–13, 26–40; also an evangelist 21:8f.

φιλόθεος, ον loving God 2 Ti 3:4.*

Φιλόλογος, ου, ὁ Philologus Ro 16:15.*

φιλον(ε)ικία, ας, ἡ dispute, strife Lk 22:24.*

φιλόν(ε)ικος, ον quarrelsome, contentious 1 Cor 11:16.*

φιλοξενία, ας, ἡ hospitality Ro 12:13; Hb 13:2.*

φιλόξενος, ον hospitable 1 Ti 3:2; Tit 1:8; 1 Pt 4:9.*

φιλοπρωτεύω wish to be first, like to be leader 3 J 9.*

φίλος, η, ον—1. adj. kindly disposed, devoted Ac 19:31.—2. subst.—a. ὁ φίλος the friend Mt 11:19; Lk 7:6; 11:6, 8; 16:9; 21:16; 23:12; J 15:13–15; Ac 10:24; 27:3; Js 2:23; 4:4; 3 J 15.—b. ἡ φίλη the (woman) friend Lk 15:9. [phil-, philo-, combining forms, as in philharmonic, philology]

φιλοσοφία, ας, ἡ sophistry Col 2:8.*

φιλόσοφος, ου, ὁ philosopher Ac 17:18.*

φιλόστοργος, ον loving dearly, devoted Ro 12:10.*

φιλότεκνος, ον loving one's children Tit 2:4.*

φιλοτιμέομαι have as one's ambition, consider it an honor, aspire Ro 15:20; 2 Cor 5:9; 1 Th 4:11.*

φιλοφρόνως adv. in a friendly manner, hospitably Ac 28:7.*

φιλόφρων, ον, gen. ονος well disposed, friendly, kind 1 Pt 3:8 v.l.*

φιμόω muzzle—1. lit. 1 Ti 5:18; 1 Cor 9:9 v.l.—2. fig. (put to) silence Mt 22:34; 1 Pt 2:15. Pass. be silenced, be silent Mt 22:12; Mk 1:25; 4:39; Lk 4:35.*

φιμώθητι 1 aor. pass. impv. of φιμόω.

φλαγελλόω = φραγελλόω Mk 15:15 v.l.*

Φλέγων Phlegon Ro 16:14.*

φλογίζω set on fire Js 3:6.* [phlogiston, theory of combustion]

φλόξ, φλογός flame Lk 16:24; 2 Th 1:8; Rv 1:14. [phlox, a flower] φλυαρέω *talk nonsense about, bring unjustified charges against* 3 J 10.*

φλύαρος, ον *gossipy, foolish* 1 Ti 5:13.*

φοβερός, ά, όν *fearful, terrible, frightful* Hb 10:27, 31; 12:21.*

φοβέω *only pass.* φοβέομαι—**1.** *be afraid,* aor. *often become frightened*—**a.** *intrans.* Mt 1:20; 9:8; 17:6f; Mk 5:36; 16:8; Lk 2:9f; 12:4, 7; Ac 16:38; 23:10; Gal 4:11.—**b.** trans. *fear something or someone* Mt 10:26; Mk 6:20; 11:32; Lk 12:5; 22:2; J 9:22; Ac 5:26; Ro 13:3; Gal 2:12; Hb 11:23, 27.—**2.** *fear in the sense reverence, respect* Lk 1:50; 18:2, 4; Ac 10:2, 22, 35; 13:16, 26; Col 3:22; 1 Pt 2:17; Rv 11:18; 14:7; 19:5.

φόβητρον *and* φόβηθρον, ου, τό *terrible sight or event, horror* Lk 21:11.*

φόβος, ου, ὁ—**1.** *the causing of fear, that which arouses fear, a terror* Ro 13:3; 1 Pt 3:14; perh. 2 Cor 5:11 (see below).—**2.** *in a passive sense*—**a.** *fear, alarm, fright* Mt 28:4, 8; Lk 1:12, 65; J 7:13; Ac 5:5, 11; 2 Cor 7:5, 11, 15; 1 Ti 5:20; Hb 2:15; 1 Pt 1:17.—*Slavish fear* Ro 8:15; 1 J 4:18.—**b.** *reverence, respect* Ac 9:31; Ro 3:18; 13:7; 2 Cor 7:1, perh. 5:11; Eph 5:21; 6:5; Phil 2:12; 1 Pt 2:18; 3:2, 16. [*phobia; -phobia,* a combining form, as in *hydrophobia*]

Φοίβη, ης, ἡ *Phoebe* Ro 16:1.*

Φοινίκη, ης, ἡ *Phoenicia,* the seacoast of central Syria; Tyre and Sidon were its most important cities. Ac 11:19; 15:3; 21:2.*

Φοινίκισσα *see* Συροφοινίκισσα.

I. φοῖνιξ *or* φοίνιξ, ικος, ὁ *the palm tree, the date palm*—**1.** *the tree as such* J 12:13.—**2.** *palm branch, palm leaf* Rv 7:9.*

II. Φοῖνιξ, ικος, ὁ *Phoenix,* a seaport city on the south coast of Crete Ac 27:12.*

φονεύς, έως, ὁ *murderer* Mt 22:7; Ac 3:14; 7:52; 28:4; 1 Pt 4:15; Rv 21:8; 22:15.*

φονεύω *(commit) murder, kill* Mt 5:21; Mk 10:19; Lk 18:20; Ro 13:9; Js 4:2; 5:6.

φόνος, ου, ὁ *murder, killing* Mk 7:21; 15:7; Lk 23:19; Ac 9:1; Ro 1:29.

φορέω *bear (regularly), wear*—**1.** lit. Mt 11:8; J 19:5; Ro 13:4; Js 2:3.—**2.** fig. 1 Cor 15:49.*

φόρον, ου, τό *see* Ἀππίου φόρον.

φόρος, ου, ὁ *tribute, tax* Lk 20:22; 23:2; Ro 13:6f.*

φορτίζω *load, burden,* with double acc. *cause someone to carry something* Lk 11:46. Pf. pass. ptc. πεφορτισμένοι *those who are burdened* Mt 11:28.*

φορτίον, ου, τό *burden, load*—**1.** lit. *cargo* Ac 27:10.—**2.** fig. Mt 11:30; 23:4; Lk 11:46; Gal 6:5.*

φόρτος, ου, ὁ *cargo* Ac 27:10 v.l.*

Φορτουνᾶτος, ου, ὁ (Latin name) *Fortunatus,* a Christian of Corinth 1 Cor 16:15 v.l., 17; subscr.*

φραγέλλιον, ου, τό (Latin loanword: flagellum) *whip, lash* J 2:15.*

φραγελλόω (via Latin flagellum) *flog, scourge* Mt 27:26; Mk 15:15.*

φραγῇ, φραγήσομαι 2 aor. pass. subj. 3 sing. and 2 fut. pass. ind. of φράσσω.

φραγμός, οῦ, ὁ *fence, wall, hedge*—**1.** lit. Mt 21:33; Mk 12:1; Lk 14:23.—**2.** fig. *barrier* Eph 2:14.*

φράζω *explain, interpret* Mt 13:36 v.l.; 15:15.* [*phrase*]

φράσον 1 aor. act. impv. of φράζω.

φράσσω *shut, close, stop*—**1.** lit. Hb 11:33.—**2.** fig. *silence* Ro 3:19; 2 Cor 11:10.*

φρέαρ, ατος, τό *a well* Lk 14:5; J 4:11f. *Pit, shaft* Rv 9:1f.*

φρεναπατάω *deceive* Gal 6:3.*

φρεναπάτης, ου, ὁ *deceiver, misleader* Tit 1:10.*

φρήν, φρενός, ἡ pl. *thinking, understanding* 1 Cor 14:20.* [*frenzy; phrenology; schizophrenia,* σχίζω + φρήν]

φρίσσω *shudder from fear* Js 2:19.*

φρονέω—**1.** *think, hold or form an opinion, judge* Ac 28:22; Ro 11:20; 12:3a, 16a; 15:5; 1 Cor 13:11; 2 Cor 13:11; Gal 5:10; Phil 1:7; 2:2; 3:15; 4:2, 10.—**2.** *set one's mind on, be intent on, espouse someone's cause* (φρ. τά τινος) Mt 16:23; Mk 8:33; Ro 8:5; 12:3b, 16b; Phil 3:19; Col 3:2; *observe* Ro 14:6.—

3. *have thoughts* or *attitudes, be minded* or *disposed* Phil 2:5.

φρόνημα, ατος, τό *aim, aspiration, striving* Ro 8:6f, 27.*

φρόνησις, εως, ἡ—1. *way of thinking, (frame of) mind* Lk 1:17.—2. *understanding, insight, intelligence* Eph 1:8.*

φρόνιμος, ον *sensible, thoughtful, prudent, wise* Mt 7:24; 10:16; 24:45; 25:2, 4, 8f; Lk 12:42; Ro 11:25; 12:16; 1 Cor 4:10; 10:15; 2 Cor 11:19. Comp. φρονιμώτερος *shrewder* Lk 16:8.*

φρονίμως adv. *wisely, shrewdly* Lk 16:8.*

φροντίζω *be careful* or *concerned* Tit 3:8.*

φρουρέω—1. *guard* 2 Cor 11:32.—2. *hold in custody, confine* Gal 3:23.—3. *guard, protect, keep* Phil 4:7; 1 Pt 1:5.*

φρυάσσω *be arrogant, haughty, insolent* Ac 4:25.*

φρύγανον, ου, τό *thin, dry wood; brushwood* Ac 28:3.*

Φρυγία, ας, ἡ *Phrygia,* a large district in central Asia Minor Ac 2:10; 16:6; 18:23; 1 Ti subscr.*

φυγαδεύω—1. trans. *cause to become a fugitive, banish from the country* Ac 7:29 v.l. (ms. E).—2. intrans. *be a fugitive, live in exile* Ac 7:29 v.l. (ms. D).*

φυγεῖν 2 aor. act. inf. of φεύγω.

Φύγελος or **Φύγελλος, ου, ὁ** *Phygelus* 2 Ti 1:15.*

φυγή, ῆς, ἡ *flight* Mt 24:20; Mk 13:18 v.l.* [*fugitive*]

φυείς 2 aor. pass. ptc. of φύω.

φυλακή, ῆς, ἡ *a watch, guard*—1. *guarding, watch* as an action Lk 2:8.—2. *guard, sentinel* as a person Ac 12:10.—3. *prison,* the place of guarding Mt 5:25; 25:36, 39, 43f; Mk 6:17; Lk 12:58; 22:33; J 3:24; Ac 5:19, 22; 12:4, 6, 17; 22:4; Hb 11:36; 1 Pt 3:19. *Haunt* Rv 18:2.—4. *a watch (of the night);* the time between 6 P.M. and 6 A.M. was divided into four *watches* of three hours each Mt 14:25; 24:43; Mk 6:48; Lk 12:38 (the watches are named in Mk 13:35).

φυλακίζω *imprison* Ac 22:19.*

φυλακτήριον, ου, τό *phylactery,* a small box containing scripture verses, bound on forehead and arm by Jews during prayer (see Deut 6:8) Mt 23:5.*

φύλαξ, ακος, ὁ *guard, sentinel* Mt 27:65 v.l.; Ac 5:23; 12:6, 19.*

φυλάσσω—1. act. *watch, guard, defend*—a. φυλάσσειν φυλακάς *keep watch* Lk 2:8.—b. *guard* someone to prevent him from escaping Lk 8:29; Ac 12:4; 23:35; 28:16.—c. *guard, protect, keep* Lk 11:21; J 12:25; Ac 22:20; 2 Ti 1:12, 14; 2 Pt 2:5; Jd 24.—d. *keep, observe, follow* a law, etc. Mt 19:20; Lk 18:21; J 12:47; Ac 7:53; Ro 2:26; Gal 6:13; 1 Ti 5:21.—2. mid.—a. *(be on one's) guard against, look out for, avoid* Lk 12:15; Ac 21:25; 2 Ti 4:15; 2 Pt 3:17.—b. *keep, observe, follow* as the act. in 1d above Mt 19:20 v.l.; Mk 10:20; Lk 18:21 v.l. [*prophylactic,* πρό + φυλάσσειν]

φυλή, ῆς, ἡ—1. *tribe* Lk 2:36; 22:30; Phil 3:5; Hb 7:13f; Js 1:1; Rv 7:4–8.—2. *nation, people* Mt 24:30; Rv 5:9; 11:9; 14:6. [*phyletic, phylum*]

φύλλον, ου, τό *leaf* Mt 24:32; Mk 11:13; Rv 22:2. [-*phyll,* combining form, as in *chlorophyll*]

φύραμα, ατος, τό *that which is mixed* or *kneaded, (a lump* or *batch of) dough* Ro 11:16; 1 Cor 5:6f; Gal 5:9. *Lump of clay* Ro 9:21.*

φυσικός, ή, όν *belonging to nature*—1. *natural, in accordance with nature* Ro 1:26f.—2. φυσικά *creatures of instinct* 2 Pt 2:12.* [*physical*]

φυσικῶς adv. *naturally, by instinct* Jd 10.*

φυσιόω *blow up, puff up, inflate* fig. 1 Cor 8:1. Pass. *become puffed up* or *conceited, put on airs* 1 Cor 4:6, 18f; 5:2; 13:4; Col 2:18.*

φύσις, εως, ἡ *nature*—1. *natural endowment* or *condition* Ro 2:27; 11:21, 24; Gal 2:15; Eph 2:3.—2. *natural characteristics* or *disposition* Gal 4:8; 2 Pt 1:4; perh. Js 3:7b (see 4 below).—3. *nature* as *the regular natural order* Ro 1:26; 2:14; 1 Cor 11:14.—4. *(natural) being, creature, species, kind* Js 3:7a; probably 3:7b (see 2 above).*

[*physi-, physio-*, combining forms in a number of words]

φυσίωσις, εως, ἡ being puffed up, pride, conceit 2 Cor 12:20.*

φυτεία, ᾶς, ἡ a plant Mt 15:13.*

φυτεύω to plant Mt 15:13; 21:33; Mk 12:1; Lk 13:6; 17:6, 28; 20:9; 1 Cor 3:6–8; 9:7.*

φύω grow (up), come up Lk 8:6, 8; Hb 12:15.*

φωλεός, οῦ, ὁ den, lair, hole Mt 8:20; Lk 9:58.*

φωνέω—1. produce a sound—**a.** crow Mt 26:34, 74f; Mk 14:30, 68, 72; Lk 22:34, 60f; J 13:38; 18:27.—**b.** call or cry out, speak loudly, say with emphasis Mk 1:26; Lk 8:8, 54; 23:46; Rv 14:18.—**2.** call someone—**a.** in the sense address as J 13:13.—**b.** call to oneself, summon Mt 20:32; Mk 9:35; 10:49; Lk 19:15; J 1:48; 2:9; 9:18, 24; 10:3; Ac 9:41.—Invite Lk 14:12.

φωνή, ῆς, ἡ—1. sound, tone, noise Mt 2:18; Lk 1:44; J 3:8; 1 Cor 14:7f; Rv 4:5; 6:1; 8:13b; 9:9; 10:7; 19:6b.—**2.** voice—**a.** generally Mt 27:46, 50; Lk 17:13, 15; 19:37; J 5:25, 28; Ac 7:57; 12:14; Hb 3:7, 15; Rv 5:2. Tone Gal 4:20.—**b.** call, cry, outcry, loud or solemn declaration Mk 15:37; Lk 23:23; Ac 12:22; 13:27; 19:34; 2 Pt 1:17f.—**c.** a voice speaks from heaven Mt 3:17; Mk 1:11; J 12:28; Ac 7:31; 22:7, 9; Rv 14:13; 19:5.—**d.** special cases: ἐπέστρεψα βλέπειν τὴν φωνὴν ἥτις ἐλάλει μετ' ἐμοῦ I turned around to see (to whom) the voice that was speaking to

me (belonged) Rv 1:12. φωνὴ βοῶντος ἐν τῇ ἐρήμῳ (listen!) someone is calling in the desert Mt 3:3; Mk 1:3; Lk 3:4. John the Baptist applies these words to himself the voice of one calling in the desert J 1:23.—**3.** language 1 Cor 14:10f; 2 Pt 2:16. [phonetic]

φῶς, φωτός, τό light—**1.** lit.—**a.** generally Mt 17:2; Lk 8:16; J 11:10; Ac 12:7; 2 Cor 4:6; 6:14; Rv 18:23.—**b.** that which gives light, light(-bearer) Mt 6:23; Lk 11:35; J 11:9; Ac 16:29; Js 1:17. Fire Mk 14:54; Lk 22:56.—**2.** light as the element and sphere of the Divine J 1:4, 7–9; 9:5; 12:35f, 46; 1 Ti 6:16; 1 J 1:5, 7b.—**3.** fig. Mt 4:16; 5:14; Lk 16:8; J 8:12; Ac 13:47; 26:18; Ro 2:19; 13:12; Eph 5:13; Col 1:12; 1 J 2:8–10. [phospho-, phosph-, photo-, combining forms in a number of words]

φωστήρ, ῆρος, ὁ star Phil 2:15. Splendor, radiance Rv 21:11.*

φωσφόρος, ον bearing or giving light subst. ὁ φ. the morning star, Venus, fig. 2 Pt 1:19.* [phosphorus]

φωτεινός, ή, όν shining, bright, radiant Mt 17:5. Full of light, illuminated 6:22; Lk 11:34, 36.*

φωτίζω—1. intrans. shine Rv 22:5.—**2.** trans.—**a.** lit. give light to, light (up), illuminate Lk 11:36; Rv 18:1; 21:23; 22:5 v.l.—**b.** fig. enlighten, shed light upon J 1:9; Eph 1:18; 3:9; Hb 6:4; 10:32.—**c.** bring to light, reveal 1 Cor 4:5; Eph 3:9 v.l.; 2 Ti 1:10.*

φωτισμός, οῦ, ὁ illumination, enlightenment, light 2 Cor 4:4; bringing to light, revealing 4:6.*

Χ

χαίρω—1. rejoice, be glad Mt 2:10; 5:12; Mk 14:11; Lk 15:32; 22:5; J 3:29; 16:20, 22; Ac 5:41; Ro 16:19; 2 Cor 7:9, 16; Phil 1:18; 3:1; Col 1:24.—**2.** as a for-

mula of greeting—**a.** as a form of address χαῖρε, χαίρετε welcome, good day, hail (to you), I am glad to see you Mt 26:49; 27:29; Mk 15:18; Lk 1:28; J

19:3; 2 J 10f; *good morning* Mt 28:9 and possibly others.—**b.** elliptically at the beginning of a letter χαίρειν *greetings* Ac 15:23; 23:26; Js 1:1.

χάλαζα, ης, ἡ *hail* Rv 8:7; 11:19; 16:21.*

χαλάω *let down* Mk 2:4; Lk 5:4f;ʹ Ac 9:25; 27:17, 30; 2 Cor 11:33.*

Χαλδαῖος, ου, ὁ *Chaldaean,* an inhabitant of Chaldaea in Mesopotamia Ac 7:4.*

χαλεπός, ή, όν *hard, difficult* 2 Ti 3:1; *hard to deal with, violent, dangerous* Mt 8:28.*

χαλιναγωγέω *guide with a bit and bridle* fig. *bridle, hold in check* Js 1:26; 3:2.*

χαλινός, οῦ, ὁ *bit, bridle* Js 3:3; Rv 14:20.*

χαλινόω *bridle, hold in check* Js 1:26 v.l.*

χαλκεύς, έως, ὁ *coppersmith, blacksmith, metal worker* 2 Ti 4:14.*

χαλκηδών, όνος, ὁ *chalcedony,* a precious stone, the exact nature of which is uncertain Rv 21:19.*

χαλκίον, ου, τό *(copper) vessel, kettle* Mk 7:4.*

χαλκολίβανον, ου, τό or **χαλκολίβανος, ου, ὁ** perh. *gold ore, fine brass* or *bronze;* its exact nature is unknown Rv 1:15; 2:18.*

χαλκός, οῦ, ὁ *copper, brass, bronze:* the metal itself Rv 18:12, or anything made of it: *a (brass) gong* 1 Cor 13:1; *copper coin,* or simply *money* Mt 10:9; Mk 6:8; 12:41.* [*chalcography,* χαλκός + γράφειν, art of engraving on copper]

χαλκοῦς, ῆ, οῦν *made of copper, brass,* or *bronze* τὰ χαλκᾶ acc. neut. pl. Rv 9:20.*

χαμαί adv. *to* or *on the ground* J 9:6; 18:6.*

Χανάαν, ἡ indecl. *Canaan,* the land west of the Jordan in the time of the patriarchs Ac 7:11; 13:19.*

Χαναναῖος, α, ον *Canaanite* (see the previous entry) Mt 15:22.*

χαρά, ᾶς, ἡ *joy*—**1.** lit. Mt 28:8; Lk 24:41; J 16:20–22; Ac 8:8; Ro 14:17; 2 Cor 7:4; 8:2; Gal 5:22; Phil 1:4, 25; Phlm 7; Hb 12:11; Js 1:2; 1 Pt 1:8.—**2.** fig.—**a.** the

person or *thing that causes joy, (the object of) joy* Lk 2:10; Phil 4:1; 1 Th 2:19f.—**b.** *a state of joyfulness* Mt 25:21, 23; Hb 12:2.

χάραγμα, ατος, τό—**1.** *a mark* or *stamp* Rv 13:16f; 14:9, 11; 15:2 v.l.; 16:2; 19:20; 20:4.—**2.** *a thing formed, an image* Ac 17:29.*

χαρακτήρ, ῆρος, ὁ *reproduction, (exact) representation* Hb 1:3.* [*character*]

χάραξ, ακος, ὁ *palisade* Lk 19:43.*

χαρῆναι, χαρήσομαι 2 aor. pass. inf. and 2 fut. pass. ind. of χαίρω.

χαρίζομαι—**1.** *give* or *grant freely as a favor* Lk 7:21; Ac 3:14; 25:11, 16; 27:24; Ro 8:32; 1 Cor 2:12; Phil 1:29; 2:9; Phlm 22: perh. Gal 3:18 (see 3 below). *Dispense with, cancel* Lk 7:42f.—**2.** *remit, forgive, pardon* 2 Cor 2:7, 10; 12:13; Eph 4:32; Col 2:13; 3:13.—**3.** *show oneself to be gracious* Gal 3:18 (see 1 above).*

χάριν acc. of χάρις, used as a prep. w. gen., usually coming after the word it governs; *for the sake of, on behalf of, on account of*—**1.** indicating the goal Gal 3:19; 1 Ti 5:14; Tit 1:5, 11; Jd 16.—**2.** indicating the reason χάριν τίνος; *for what reason? why?* 1 J 3:12. Cf. Lk 7:47. Eph 3:1, 14 may be classed under 1 or 2.*

χάρις, ιτος, ἡ—**1.** *graciousness, attractiveness* Lk 4:22; Col 4:6.—**2.** *favor, grace, gracious care* or *help, goodwill* Lk 1:30; 2:40, 52; Ac 2:47; 7:10; 14:26; Ro 3:24; 4:4; 5:20f; 11:5f; Gal 1:15; Eph 2:5, 7f. *Credit* Lk 6:32–34. *That which brings* (God's) *favor* 1 Pt 2:19f.—(Divine) *grace* or *favor* in fixed formulas at the beginning and end of Christian letters, e.g. Ro 1:7; 16:20; 2 Cor 1:2; 13:13; 1 Th 1:1; 5:28; Hb 13:25; 1 Pt 1:2; Rv 1:4.—**3.** *practical application of goodwill, a (sign of) favor, gracious deed* or *gift, benefaction* J 1:14, 16f; Ac 13:43; 24:27; 25:3, 9; Ro 5:2; 6:14f; 1 Cor 16:3; 2 Cor 1:15; Eph 4:29; Hb 10:29; Js 4:6; 1 Pt 5:10.—**4.** of exceptional effects produced by divine grace Ro 1:5; 12:6; 1 Cor 15:10a, b; 2 Cor 8:1; 9:8, 14; 1 Pt 4:10. Hardly to be differentiated from *power, knowledge,* glory Ac 6:8; 1 Cor 15:10c; 2 Cor 1:12; 2 Pt 3:18.—**5.** *thanks, gratitude* χάριν ἔχειν *be grateful* 1 Ti 1:12; 2 Ti 1:3; Hb 12:28. In other expressions Ro 6:17; 7:25; 1 Cor 10:30; 15:57; 2 Cor 9:15; Col 3:16. [*Charissa*]

χάρισμα, ατος, τό *a gift (freely and graciously given), a favor bestowed*—**1.** generally Ro 1:11; 5:15f; 6:23; 11:29; 1 Cor 1:7; 2 Cor 1:11.—**2.** of special gifts bestowed on individual Christians 1 Cor 7:7; 1 Ti 4:14; 2 Ti 1:6; 1 Pt 4:10. Of *spiritual gifts* in a special sense Ro 12:6; 1 Cor 12:4, 9, 28, 30f.*

χαριτόω *bestow favor on, favor highly, bless* Eph 1:6. κεχαριτωμένη *one favored* (by God) Lk 1:28.*

Χαρράν, ἡ indecl. *Haran,* a place in Mesopotamia Ac 7:2, 4.*

χάρτης, ου, ὁ *a sheet of paper,* i.e. *papyrus* 2 J 12.* [*chart*]

χάσμα, ατος, τό *chasm* Lk 16:26.*

χεῖλος, ους, τό *lip*—**1.** pl. *the lips* Mt 15:8; Mk 7:6; Ro 3:13; 1 Cor 14:21; Hb 13:15; 1 Pt 3:10.—**2.** *shore* of the sea Hb 11:12.*

χειμάζω *expose to bad weather, toss in a storm* Ac 27:18.*

χείμαρρος or **χειμάρρους, ου, ὁ** *winter torrent, ravine, wadi* J 18:1.*

χειμών, ῶνος, ὁ—**1.** *rainy and stormy weather* Mt 16:3; Ac 27:20.—**2.** *winter* Mt 24:20; Mk 13:18; J 10:22; 2 Ti 4:21.*

χείρ, χειρός, ἡ *hand*—**1.** lit. Mt 22:13; Mk 3:1; Lk 24:39; J 20:25; Ac 19:26; 21:11; 1 Cor 4:12; Rv 9:20; 20:1. *Handwriting* 1 Cor 16:21; Gal 6:11; Col 4:18; 2 Th 3:17; Phlm 19. Equivalent to *activity* Mk 6:2; Ac 2:23; 19:11; Gal 3:19. *Finger* Lk 15:22. Perh. *arm* Mt 4:6; Lk 4:11.—**2.** fig.—**a.** the *hand* of God, Christ, or an angel Lk 1:66; J 3:35; 10:28f; 13:3; Ac 7:35, 50; 13:11; Hb 1:10; 10:31.—**b.** *hostile power* Mt 17:22; 26:45; Lk 24:7; J 10:39; Ac 12:11; 21:11b; 2 Cor 11:33. [*chiropractic*]

χειραγωγέω *take* or *lead by the hand* Ac 9:8; 22:11.*

χειραγωγός, οῦ, ὁ *one who leads another by the hand, leader* Ac 13:11.*

χειρόγραφον, ου, τό *certificate of indebtedness, bond* Col 2:14.*

χειροποίητος, ον *made by human hands* Mk 14:58; Ac 7:48; 17:24; Eph 2:11; Hb 9:11, 24.*

χειροτονέω *choose* or *elect (by raising hands)* 2 Cor 8:19. *Appoint, install* Ac 14:23.*

χείρων, ον, gen. **ονος** comparative of κακός, *worse, more severe* Mt 27:64; Mk 2:21; 5:26; Lk 11:26; J 5:14; 1 Ti 5:8; 2 Ti 3:13; Hb 10:29; 2 Pt 2:20.

Χερούβ, τό indecl., but pl. **Χερουβίν** *cherub,* one of the two winged figures over the ark of the covenant Hb 9:5.*

χήρα, ας, ἡ fem. of χῆρος = *bereft* (of one's spouse)—**1.** generally γυνὴ χήρα *a widow* Lk 4:26. Subst. (ἡ) χήρα *(the) widow* Mk 12:40, 42f; Lk 2:37; 4:25f; 20:47; Ac 6:1; 1 Cor 7:8; 1 Ti 5:3b, 4, 5, 11, 16; Js 1:27.—**2.** of a special class in the Christian communities 1 Ti 5:3, 9.

χθές adv., v.l. for ἐχθές *yesterday* in J 4:52; Ac 7:28; Hb 13:8.*

χιϛ´ see χξϛ´.

χιλίαρχος, ου, ὁ *military tribune,* commander of a cohort, about 600 men, roughly equivalent to major or colonel Mk 6:21; J 18:12; Ac 21:31–33, 37; 23:17–19; 25:23; Rv 6:15; 19:18. [*chiliarch*]

χιλιάς, άδος, ἡ (a group of) *a thousand* Lk 14:31; Ac 4:4; Rv 5:11; 7:4–8; 11:13; 14:1, 3. [*chiliad*]

χίλιοι, αι, α *a thousand* 2 Pt 3:8; Rv 11:3; 12:6; 14:20; the millennium 20:2–7.*

Χίος, ου, ἡ *Chios,* an island (with a city by the same name) off the west coast of Asia Minor Ac 20:15.*

χιτών, ῶνος, ὁ *tunic, shirt* a garment worn next to the skin, and by both sexes Mt 5:40; 10:10; Mk 6:9; Lk 3:11; 6:29; 9:3; J 19:23; Ac 9:39; Jd 23. Pl. *clothes* Mk 14:63.* [*chiton*]

χιών, όνος, ἡ *snow* Mt 28:3; Mk 9:3 v.l.; Rv 1:14.*

χλαμύς, ύδος, ἡ *cloak* used by travelers and soldiers Mt 27:28, 31.* [*chlamys*]

χλευάζω *mock, sneer, scoff* Ac 2:13 v.l.; 17:32.*

χλιαρός, ά, όν *lukewarm* Rv 3:16.*

Χλόη, ης, ή *Chloe,* an otherwise unknown woman. οἱ Χλόης *Chloe's people* (slaves or freedmen) 1 Cor 1:11.*

χλωρός, ά, όν—**1.** *yellowish green, (light) green* Mk 6:39; Rv 8:7; 9:4.—**2.** *pale,* as of a person in sickness Rv 6:8.* [*chlorophyll,* χλωρός + φύλλον]

χ ξ ϛ ´ *six hundred sixty-six* (χ´ = 600, ξ´ = 60, ϛ´ = 6) the reading of the 'Received Text.' The v.l. χιϛ´ = 616. Rv 13:18.*

χοϊκός, ή, όν *made of dust* or *earth, earthy* 1 Cor 15:47–49.*

χοῖνιξ, ικος, ή *choenix* a dry measure, almost = a liter Rv 6:6.*

χοῖρος, ου, ὁ *pig, swine* Mt 7:6; Mk 5:11–13, 16; Lk 15:15f.

χολάω *be angry* J 7:23.*

χολή, ῆς, ή *gall, bile*—**1.** lit., of a bitter substance Mt 27:34.—**2.** fig. χολὴ πικρίας *bitter gall* Ac 8:23.*

Χοραζίν, ή indecl. *Chorazin,* a place in Galilee Mt 11:21; Lk 10:13.*

χορηγέω *provide, supply (in abundance)* 2 Cor 9:10; 1 Pt 4:11.* [*choric*]

χορός, οῦ, ὁ *(choral) dance, dancing* Lk 15:25.* [*chorus*]

χορτάζω *feed, fill, satisfy;* pass. *eat one's fill, be satisfied* lit. Mt 14:20; 15:33; Mk 8:4, 8; Lk 6:21; J 6:26; Phil 4:12; Js 2:16; Rv 19:21. Fig. *be satisfied* Mt 5:6.

χόρτασμα, ατος, τό *food* Ac 7:11.*

χόρτος, ου, ὁ *grass* Mt 6:30; 14:19; Mk 6:39; J 6:10; Js 1:10f; 1 Pt 1:24; Rv 9:4. *Blade, stalk* of grain Mk 4:28. *Hay* 1 Cor 3:12.

Χουζᾶς, ᾶ, ὁ *Chuza* Lk 8:3.*

χοῦς, χοός, acc. χοῦν, ὁ *dust* Mk 6:11; Rv 18:19.*

χράομαι *use*—**1.** *make use of, employ*—**a.** w. dat. Ac 27:17; 1 Cor 9:12, 15; 1 Ti 5:23; *make the most of, take advantage* (supply either τῇ δουλείᾳ or τῇ ἐλευθερίᾳ) 1 Cor 7:21.—**b.** w. acc. 1 Cor 7:31.—**2.** *act, proceed* 2 Cor 1:17; 13:10.—**3.** w. dat. of the person and an adv. *treat a person in a certain way* Ac 27:3.

χράω another form for κίχρημι.

χρεία, ας, ή—**1.** *need, necessity* Lk 10:42; Hb 7:11. χρείαν ἔχειν *have need* Mt 3:14; 6:8; Mk 11:3; Lk 19:31, 34; 1 Cor 12:21, 24; Hb 5:12; 10:36.—**2.** *need, lack, want, difficulty* χρείαν ἔχειν be *in need, lack something* Mk 2:25; Ac 2:45; 4:35; Eph 4:28; Rv 3:17.—In other expressions Ac 20:34; Ro 12:13; Phil 4:16, 19.—**3.** *the thing that is necessary* Eph 4:29.—**4.** *office, duty, service* Ac 6:3.

χρεοφειλέτης and χρεωφειλέτης, ου, ὁ *debtor* Lk 7:41; 16:5.*

χρή *it is necessary, it ought* Js 3:10.*

χρῄζω *(have) need (of)* Mt 6:32; Lk 11:8; 12:30; Ro 16:2; 2 Cor 3:1.*

χρῆμα, ατος, τό—**1.** pl. *property, wealth, means* Mk 10:23, 24 v.l.; Lk 18:24.—**2.** *money,* mostly pl. Ac 8:18, 20; 24:26; rarely sing. 4:37.*

χρηματίζω—**1.** of God *impart a revelation* or *injunction* or *warning* Mt 2:12, 22; Lk 2:26 and 26 v.l.; Ac 10:22; Hb 8:5; 11:7; 12:25.—**2.** *bear a name, be called* or *named* Ac 11:26; Ro 7:3.*

χρηματισμός, οῦ, ὁ *a divine statement* or *answer* Ro 11:4.*

χρῆσαι 1 aor. mid. impv. of χράομαι.

χρήσιμος, η, ον *useful, beneficial, advantageous* 2 Ti 2:14; Mt 20:28 v.l.*

χρῆσις, εως, ή *relations, function* Ro 1:26f.*

χρῆσον 1 aor. act. impv. of κίχρημι.

χρηστεύομαι *be kind, loving, merciful* 1 Cor 13:4.*

χρηστολογία, ας, ή *smooth, plausible speech* Ro 16:18.*

χρηστός, ή, όν *useful, worthy, good*—**1.** adj.—**a.** of things *good, pleasant, easy* Lk 5:39; Mt 11:30; *(morally) good, reputable* 1 Cor 15:33.—**b.** of persons *kind, loving, benevolent* Lk 6:35; Eph 4:32; 1 Pt 2:3.—**2.** subst. τὸ χρηστόν *kindness* Ro 2:4.* [*chrestomathy,* χρηστός + μάθη, a selection of passages]

χρηστότης, ητος, ή—**1.** *goodness, uprightness* ποιεῖν χρηστότητα *do what is right* Ro 3:12.—**2.** *goodness, kindness, generosity* Ro 2:4; 9:23 v.l.; 11:22;

218   χρῖσμα–χωρίς

2 Cor 6:6; Gal 5:22; Eph 2:7; Col 3:12; Tit 3:4.*

χρῖσμα, ατος, τό anointing 1 J 2:20, 27.* [chrism]

Χριστιανός, οῦ, ὁ the Christian Ac 11:26; 26:28; 1 Pt 4:16.*

Χριστός, οῦ, ὁ—1. as a title the Anointed One, the Messiah, the Christ Mt 2:4; 16:16; Mk 8:29; Lk 2:26; 4:41; J 1:41; 4:25; Ac 3:18; 5:42; Ro 9:5; Rv 11:15.— 2. as a proper name Christ Mk 1:1; 9:41; Ac 24:24; Ro 1:4, 6, 8; Hb 3:6; 1 Pt 1:1–3.

χρίω anoint fig. Lk 4:18; Ac 4:27; 10:38; 2 Cor 1:21; Hb 1:9.*

χρονίζω—1. take time, linger, fail to come (or stay away) for a long time Mt 24:48; 25:5; Hb 10:37.—2. w. inf. following delay, take a long time in doing something Mt 24:48 v.l.; Lk 12:45.—3. stay (somewhere) for a long time Lk 1:21.*

χρόνος, ου, ὁ time Mt 25:19; Lk 8:27; J 7:33; Ac 1:7; 14:3, 28; 17:30; Ro 16:25; 1 Cor 16:7; Gal 4:4; Hb 5:12; Rv 6:11.— Delay, respite Rv 2:21; 10:6. [chronology]

χρονοτριβέω spend time, lose or waste time Ac 20:16.*

χρύσεος uncontracted form of χρυσοῦς.

χρυσίον, ου, τό gold 1 Cor 3:12 v.l.; Hb 9:4; 1 Pt 1:7; Rv 3:18; 21:18, 21.—Gold ornaments, jewelry 1 Ti 2:9; 1 Pt 3:3; Rv 17:4; 18:16.—Coined gold Ac 3:6; 20:33; 1 Pt 1:18.*

χρυσοδακτύλιος, ον with a gold ring (or rings) on one's finger(s) Js 2:2.*

χρυσόλιθος, ου, ὁ chrysolite, the yellow topaz Rv 21:20.*

χρυσόπρασος, ου, ὁ chrysoprase, an apple-green quartz Rv 21:21.*

χρυσός, οῦ, ὁ gold Mt 2:11; 10:9; 23:16f; Ac 17:29; 1 Cor 3:12; Rv 9:7; 18:12. [chrysanthemum, χρυσός + ἄνθεμον; Chrysostom]

χρυσοῦς, ῆ, οῦν golden, made of or adorned with gold 2 Ti 2:20; Hb 9:4; Rv 1:12f, 20; 9:13, 20; 21:15.

χρυσόω gild, adorn with gold Rv 17:4; 18:16.*

χρῶ pres. mid. impv. 2 sing. (1 Ti 5:23) of χράομαι.

χρώς, χρωτός, ὁ skin, surface of the body Ac 19:12.*

χωλός, ή, όν lame, crippled Mt 11:5; 15:30f; Mk 9:45; Lk 14:13, 21; J 5:3; Ac 3:2; 14:8. τὸ χωλόν the lame leg(s) Hb 12:13.

χώρα, ας, ἡ country, land—1. district, region, place Mt 8:28; Mk 6:55; Lk 15:13–15; Ac 10:39; 13:49; 16:6; 26:20.—2. the (open) country in contrast to the city J 11:55; Ac 8:1.—3. (dry) land in contrast to the sea Ac 27:27.—4. field, cultivated land pl. Lk 21:21; J 4:35; Js 5:4. Sing. land, farm Lk 12:16.—5. ἐν χώρᾳ καὶ σκιᾷ θανάτου in the land of the shadow of death Mt 4:16. [chorography, χώρα + γραφή]

Χωραζίν see Χοραζίν.

χωρέω make room, give way—1. go, go out or away lit. Mt 15:17; 20:28 v.l. Fig. come 2 Pt 3:9.—2. go forward, make progress J 8:37, though find place is also probable.—3. have room for, hold, contain—a. lit. J 2:6; 21:25. μηκέτι χωρεῖν there was no longer any room Mk 2:2.—b. fig. χωρήσατε ἡμᾶς make room for us 2 Cor 7:2.—Grasp, understand, comprehend, accept Mt 19:11f.*

χωρίζω—1. act. divide, separate Mt 19:6; Mk 10:9; Ro 8:35, 39.—2. pass. separate (oneself), be separated of divorce 1 Cor 7:10f, 15.—Be taken away, take one's departure, go away Ac 1:4; 18:1f; Phlm 15.—In Hb 7:26 κεχωρισμένος means not only that Christ is separated from sinful people but that he is also different from them.*

χωρίον, ου, τό place, piece of land, field Mt 26:36; Mk 14:32; J 4:5; Ac 1:18f; 4:34, 37 v.l.; 5:3, 8; 28:7.*

χωρίς adv.—1. used as an adv. separately, apart, by itself J 20:7.—2. functions as prep. w. gen. without, apart from—a. w. gen. of the person apart from someone, far from someone, without someone J 1:3; 15:5; Ro 10:14; 1 Cor 4:8; 11:11; Eph 2:12.—Besides, in addition to Mt 14:21; 15:38.—b. w. gen. of the thing outside (of) something 2 Cor 12:3.—Without, apart from Mt

13:34; Lk 6:49; Ro 3:28; 7:8; Phil 2:14; Phlm 14; Hb 4:15; 9:28; 10:28; Js 2:20.— *Besides, in addition to* 2 Cor 11:28.

χωρισμός, οῦ, ὁ *division* Ac 4:32 v.l.*

χῶρος, ου, ὁ *the northwest* Ac 27:12.*

Ψ

ψάλλω *sing, sing praise* Ro 15:9; 1 Cor 14:15; Eph 5:19; Js 5:13.*

ψαλμός, οῦ, ὁ *song of praise, psalm* Lk 20:42; 24:44; Ac 1:20; 13:33; 1 Cor 14:26; Eph 5:19; Col 3:16.*

ψευδάδελφος, ου, ὁ *false brother, untrue friend* 2 Cor 11:26; Gal 2:4.*

ψευδαπόστολος, ου, ὁ *false* or *bogus apostle* 2 Cor 11:13.*

ψευδής, ές *false, lying* Ac 6:13; Rv 2:2. Subst. *the liar* 21:8.*

ψευδοδιδάσκαλος, ου, ὁ *false teacher* 2 Pt 2:1.*

ψευδολόγος, ον *speaking falsely, lying* subst. *liar* 1 Ti 4:2.*

ψεύδομαι—1. *lie, tell a falsehood* Mt 5:11; Ac 5:4; 14:19 v.l.; Ro 9:1; 2 Cor 11:31; Gal 1:20; Col 3:9; 1 Ti 2:7; Hb 6:18; Js 3:14; 1 J 1:6; Rv 3:9.—**2.** *(try to) deceive by lying, tell lies to, impose upon* Ac 5:3.*

ψευδομαρτυρέω *bear false witness, give false testimony* Mt 19:18; Mk 10:19; 14:56f; Lk 18:20; Ro 13:9 v.l.*

ψευδομαρτυρία, ας, ἡ *false witness* Mt 15:19; 26:59.*

ψευδόμαρτυς, υρος, ὁ (also accented ψευδομάρτυς) *one who gives false testimony, a false witness* Mt 26:60; 1 Cor 15:15.*

ψευδοπροφήτης, ου, ὁ *false prophet* Mt 7:15; Mk 13:22; Ac 13:6; 1 J 4:1; Rv 16:13.

ψεῦδος, ους, τό *lie, falsehood, lying* J 8:44; Ro 1:25; Eph 4:25; 2 Th 2:9, 11; 1 J 2:21, 27; Rv 14:5; 21:27; 22:15.*

ψευδόχριστος, ου, ὁ *a false Christ, bogus Messiah* Mt 24:24; Mk 13:22.*

ψευδώνυμος, ον *falsely called* 1 Ti 6:20.* [*pseudonymous*]

ψεῦσμα, ατος, τό *lying, untruthfulness, undependability* Ro 3:7.*

ψεύστης, ου, ὁ *liar* J 8:44, 55; Ro 3:4; 1 Ti 1:10; Tit 1:9 v.l., 12; 1 J 1:10; 2:4, 22; 4:20; 5:10.*

ψηλαφάω *feel (about for), touch, handle, grope after* Lk 24:39; Ac 17:27 (ψηλαφήσειαν 1 aor. act. opt. 3 pl.); Hb 12:18; 1 J 1:1.*

ψηφίζω *count (up), calculate* Lk 14:28; Rv 13:18.*

ψῆφος, ου, ἡ *pebble, vote* Ac 26:10; used as an amulet Rv 2:17.* [*psephite, psephology*]

ψιθυρισμός, οῦ, ὁ *whispering, gossip, talebearing* 2 Cor 12:20.*

ψιθυριστής, οῦ, ὁ *whisperer, talebearer* Ro 1:29.*

ψίξ, χός, ἡ *bit, crumb* Mt 15:27 v.l.; Lk 16:21 v.l.*

ψιχίον, ου, τό *a very little bit, crumb* Mt 15:27; Mk 7:28; Lk 16:21 v.l.*

ψυγήσεται 2 fut. pass. ind. 3 sing. of ψύχω.

ψυχή, ῆς, ἡ *soul, life;* it is often impossible to draw hard and fast lines between the meanings of this many-sided word.—**1.** lit.—**a.** of life in its physical aspects—α. *(breath of) life, life-principle, soul* Lk 12:20; Ac 2:27; Rv 6:9.—β. *earthly life* itself Mt 2:20; 20:28; Mk 10:45; Lk 12:22f; J 10:11; Ac 15:26; Phil 2:30; 1 J 3:16; Rv 12:11.—**b.** *the* soul as seat and center of the inner life of a person in its many and varied aspects, desires, feelings, emotions Mk 14:34; Lk 1:46; 12:19; J 12:27; 1 Th 2:8; Hb 12:3; Rv 18:14; *heart* Eph 6:6; Col 3:23; *mind* Phil 1:27.—c. the soul as seat and center of life that transcends the earthly Mt 10:28, 39; 11:29; 16:26; Mk 8:35–37; 2 Cor 12:15; Hb 6:19; Js 1:21; 1 Pt 1:9; 2:11.—d. ψυχή sometimes expresses a reflexive relationship and may be translated *self* Mt 26:38; Mk 10:45; J 10:24; 2 Cor 1:23; Rv 18:14.—2. by metonymy *that which possesses life* or *a soul, creature, person* Ac 2:41, 43; 3:23; 27:37; Ro 2:9; 1 Cor 15:45; 1 Pt 3:20; Rv 16:3. [*psyche*]

ψυχικός, ή, όν *pertaining to life,* in this case the life of the physical world rather than of the Spirit.—1. adj. *unspiritual* 1 Cor 2:14; Js 3:15; *physical* 1 Cor 15:44.—2. subst. τὸ ψυχικόν *the physical* 1 Cor 15:46. ψυχικοί *worldly people* Jd 19.* [*psychic*]

ψῦχος, ους, τό *cold* J 18:18; Ac 28:2; 2 Cor 11:27.*

ψυχρός, ά, όν *cold*—1. lit. Mt 10:42 v.l. τὸ ψυχρόν *cold water* 10:42.—2. fig. *cool, cold* Rv 3:15f.*

ψύχω pass. *grow cold, be extinguished* Mt 24:12.*

ψωμίζω *feed* Ro 12:20. In 1 Cor 13:3 the meaning is either *dole out* or *fritter away.**

ψωμίον, ου, τό *(small) piece* or *bit of bread* J 13:26f, 30.*

ψώχω *rub* Lk 6:1.*

Ω

Ω, ὦ *omega,* last letter of the Greek alphabet Rv 1:8, 11 v.l.; 21:6; 22:13.* [*omega,* the 'great o']

ὦ interjection *O!* Mt 15:28; Mk 9:19; Ac 1:1; Ro 2:1, 3; 11:33.

Ὠβήδ v.l. for Ἰωβήδ.

ὧδε adv.—1. *here* in the sense *to this place, hither* Mt 8:29; 22:12; Mk 11:33; Lk 19:27; J 6:25; Rv 11:12.—2. *here* in the sense *in this place* Mt 12:6, 41f; Mk 14:32; Lk 4:23; 15:17; Ac 9:14; Col 4:9; Hb 13:14.—With the local meaning weakened *in this case, on this occasion, under these circumstances* 1 Cor 4:2; Rv 13:10, 18; 14:12; 17:9. ὧδε . . . ἐκεῖ *in one case . . . in the other* Hb 7:8.

ᾠδή, ῆς, ἡ *song* Eph 5:19; Col 3:16; Rv 5:9; 14:3; 15:3.*

ὠδίν, ῖνος, ἡ *birth pain(s)*—1. lit. 1 Th 5:3.—2. symbolically Mt 24:8; Mk 13:8; Ac 2:24.*

ὠδίνω *suffer birth pangs, bear amid throes* Gal 4:19 (fig.), 27; Rv 12:2.*

ὦμος, ου, ὁ *shoulder* Mt 23:4; Lk 15:5.*

ὤμοσα, 1 aor. act. ind. of ὀμνύω.

ὠνέομαι *buy* Ac 7:16.*

ᾠόν, οῦ, τό *egg* Lk 11:12.*

ὥρα, ας, ἡ—1. *time of day, hour* Mt 14:15; 24:36, 50; Mk 6:35; 11:11; Lk 12:39f, 46; Rv 3:3.—2. *hour*—a. as a (short) space of time Mt 20:12; 26:40; Lk 22:59; J 5:35; 11:9; Ac 5:7; 2 Cor 7:8; Gal 2:5; Phlm 15; Rv 9:15; 18:10, 17, 19.—b. as a moment of time named from the hour that has just passed. The period of daylight was divided into twelve 'hours' (more than 60 minutes each in summer, less than 60 minutes in the winter); the 'first hour' was approximately 6 A.M., the second was 7 A.M., and so on. Mt 20:5, 9; Mk 15:25; Lk 23:44; J 1:39; 4:6; Ac 3:1; 10:30; 22:13; 23:23; 1 Cor 4:11.—3. *the time* of an occurrence Mt 8:13; 18:1; Mk 13:11; Lk 1:10; 10:21; J 2:4; 7:30; 12:23; 16:21; 19:27; Ac 16:33; Rv 11:13; 14:7, 15. [*horologe, ὥρα + λόγος*]

ὡραῖος, α, ον—1. *happening* or *coming at the right time* Ro 10:15.—**2.** *beautiful, fair, lovely* Mt 23:27; Ac 3:2, 10.*

ὤρυξα 1 aor. act. ind. of ὀρύσσω.

ὠρύομαι *roar* 1 Pt 5:8.*

ὡς adv.—**I.** *as a comparative particle as, like* Mt 26:39; 27:65; Mk 10:15; 1 Cor 3:15; 7:17; 13:11; Eph 5:28, 33; Col 3:18; 1 Th 5:2; Hb 11:29. *How* Lk 24:35; Ro 11:2; 2 Cor 7:15.—**II.** *as a conjunction denoting comparison, as* Mt 6:10; 13:43; 22:30; Mk 4:36; Lk 3:23; 12:27; 15:19; J 7:46 v.l.; Ac 23:11; 25:10; 1 Pt 3:6. ὡς θάλασσα *something like a sea* Rv 4:6. ἤκουσα ὡς φωνήν *I heard what sounded like a shout* Rv 19:1, 6. ἀρνίον ὡς ἐσφαγμένον *a lamb that appeared to have been slaughtered* 5:6.—**III.** ὡς introduces the characteristic quality of a person, thing, action, etc., *as* Lk 16:1; 23:14; J 1:14; Ro 1:21; 3:7; 9:32; 1 Cor 3:10; 4:7; Col 3:23; 2 Th 2:2.—*As one who, because* Ac 28:19; 2 Pt 1:3.—**IV.** Other uses of ὡς—**1.** as a temporal conjunction—**a.** *when, after* Lk 1:23, 41, 44; J 2:9; 4:1; Ac 5:24; 10:7, 25.—**b.** *while, when, as long as* Lk 12:58; 24:32; J 12:35f; 20:11; Ac 1:10; 8:36; 21:27.— *Since* Mk 9:21.—**c.** ὡς ἄν *when, as soon as* Ro 15:24; 1 Cor 11:34; Phil 2:23.— **2.** as a conj. denoting result *so that* Hb 3:11; 4:3.—**3.** as a particle denoting purpose *in order that* Ac 20:24; Hb 7:9.—**4.** *that,* after verbs of knowing, saying, etc. Lk 6:4; 24:6; Ac 10:28; Ro 1:9; Phil 1:8; 1 Th 2:11a.—**5.** with numerals *about, approximately, nearly* Mk 5:13; Lk 1:56; J 6:10, 19; Ac 13:18, 20; Rv 8:1.—**6.** in exclamations *how!* Ro 10:15; 11:33.—**7.** with the superlative ὡς τάχιστα *as quickly as possible* Ac 17:15.

ὡς ἄν (also written ὡσάν) *as if, as it were, so to speak* 2 Cor 10:9.*

ὡσαννά indecl. *hosanna* (Heb. or Aram. 'help' or 'save, I pray') Mt 21:9, 15; Mk 11:9f; J 12:13.*

ὡσαύτως adv. *(in) the same (way), similarly, likewise* Mt 20:5; Mk 12:21; Ro 8:26; 1 Cor 11:25; 1 Ti 2:9; 3:8, 11.

ὡσεί—1. *particle denoting comparison as, like, something like* Mt 3:16; 9:36; Mk 9:26; Lk 22:44; Ac 2:3; 6:15; Ro 6:13.—**2.** *with numbers and measures about* Mt 14:21; Lk 3:23; 9:14; 23:44; Ac 1:15; 19:7.

'Ωσηέ or **'Ωσῆε, ὁ** indecl. *Hosea;* metonymically of his book Ro 9:25.*

ὡσί dat. pl. of οὖς.

ὥσπερ *(just) as* Mt 6:2, 7; 18:17; 24:27, 37; J 5:21, 26; Ac 2:2; Ro 5:19; 2 Cor 8:7; Hb 9:25; Js 2:26.

ὡσπερεί *like, as though, as it were* 1 Cor 4:13 v.l.; 15:8.*

ὥστε—1. introducing an independent clause *for this reason, therefore, so* Mt 12:12; Mk 2:28; Ro 7:4, 12; 1 Cor 3:7; 5:8; 15:58; 2 Cor 5:16f; Gal 3:9, 24; Phil 2:12; 1 Th 4:18.—**2.** introducing a dependent clause—**a.** indicating the actual result *so that* Mt 8:24; 27:14; Mk 1:45; 2:12; J 3:16; Ac 1:19; 2 Cor 1:8; Gal 2:13.—**b.** indicating the intended result *for the purpose of, with a view to, in order that* Mt 10:1; 27:1; Lk 4:29; 9:52 v.l.; 20:20.

ὦτα nom. and acc. pl. of οὖς.

ὠτάριον, ου, τό *ear* Mk 14:47; J 18:10.*

ὠτίον, ου, τό *ear* Mt 26:51; Mk 14:47 v.l.; Lk 22:51; J 18:10 v.l., 26.*

ὠφέλεια, ας, ἡ *use, gain, advantage* Ro 3:1; Jd 16.*

ὠφελέω *help, aid, benefit, be of use (to)* Mt 16:26; Mk 7:11; 8:36; 1 Cor 13:3; 14:6; Gal 5:2; Hb 4:2. *Accomplish* Mt 27:24; J 12:19. *Be of value* J 6:63; Ro 2:25.

ὠφέλιμος, ον *useful, beneficial, advantageous* 1 Ti 4:8; 2 Ti 3:16; Tit 3:8.*

ὤφθην 1 aor. pass. ind. of ὁράω.